Anglo-Saxon England 17

Her mon mæg giet gesion hiora swæð

ANGLO-SAXON ENGLAND

17

Edited by

PETER CLEMOES
University of Cambridge

SIMON KEYNES
University of Cambridge

MICHAEL LAPIDGE
University of Cambridge

PETER BAKER
Emory University

MARTIN BIDDLE
University of Oxford

DANIEL CALDER
University of California, Los Angeles

ROBERT DESHMAN
University of Toronto

KLAUS DIETZ
Freie Universität Berlin

ROBERTA FRANK
University of Toronto

HELMUT GNEUSS
Universität München

MALCOLM GODDEN
University of Oxford

FRED ROBINSON
Yale University

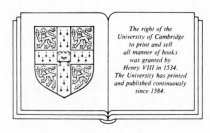

The right of the University of Cambridge to print and sell all manner of books was granted by Henry VIII in 1534. The University has printed and published continuously since 1584.

CAMBRIDGE UNIVERSITY PRESS

Cambridge

New York   Port Chester   Melbourne   Sydney

Published by the Press Syndicate of the University of Cambridge
The Pitt Building, Trumpington Street, Cambridge CB2 1RP
32 East 57th Street, New York, NY 10022, USA
10 Stamford Road, Oakleigh, Melbourne 3166, Australia

Typeset by
Servis Filmsetting Ltd
Manchester

Printed in Great Britain by
The Camelot Press
Southampton

ISBN 0 521 36571 6
ISBN 0263-6751

Contents

Versions of the four items immediately following the record of the third conference of the International Society of Anglo-Saxonists were read at that conference. Professor Bately read a version of her item to the Society in 1985 and Professor Bodden a version of hers in 1983

Abbreviations listed before the bibliography (pp. 283–5) are used throughout the volume without other explanation

Illustrations

ACKNOWLEDGEMENTS

By permission of the Trustees of the British Museum the design on the cover is taken from the obverse of a silver penny issued to celebrate King Alfred's occupation and fortification of London in 886

Permission to publish a photograph or photographs has been granted by: the Trustees of the British Museum (pls. I and II); the Bibliothèque Nationale, Paris (pl. V); the Beinecke Library, Yale University (pl. VI); the Ellis Library, University of Missouri, Columbia (pls. VII and VIII)

Material should be submitted to the editor most convenient regionally, with these exceptions: an article should be sent to Martin Biddle if concerned with archaeology, to Robert Deshman if concerned with art history, to Simon Keynes if concerned with history, numismatics or onomastics, and to Michael Lapidge if concerned with Anglo-Latin or palaeography. Whenever a contribution is sent from abroad it should be accompanied by international coupons to cover the cost of return postage. A potential contributor is asked to get in touch with the editor concerned as early as possible to obtain a copy of the style sheet and to have any necessary discussion. Articles must be in English.

The editors' addresses are:

Professor P. S. Baker, Department of English, Emory University, Atlanta, Georgia 30322 (USA)

Mr M. Biddle, Christ Church, Oxford OX1 1DP (England)

Professor D. G. Calder, Department of English, University of California Los Angeles, Los Angeles, California 90024 (USA)

Professor P. A. M. Clemoes, Emmanuel College, Cambridge CB2 3AP (England)

Professor R. Deshman, Graduate Department of History of Art, University of Toronto, Toronto, Ontario M5S 1A1 (Canada)

Professor K. Dietz, Institut für Englische Philologie, Freie Universität Berlin, Gosslerstrasse 2–4, 1000 Berlin 33 (Germany)

Professor R. Frank, Centre for Medieval Studies, University of Toronto, Toronto, Ontario M5S 1A1 (Canada)

Professor H. Gneuss, Institut für Englische Philologie, Universität München, 8000 München 40, Schellingstrasse 3 (Germany)

Dr M. R. Godden, Exeter College, Oxford OX1 3DP (England)

Dr S. D. Keynes, Trinity College, Cambridge CB2 1TQ (England)

Dr M. Lapidge, Department of Anglo-Saxon, Norse and Celtic, Faculty of English, University of Cambridge, 9 West Rd, Cambridge CB3 9DP (England)

Professor F. C. Robinson, Department of English, Yale University, New Haven, Connecticut 06520 (USA)

Record of the third conference of the International Society of Anglo-Saxonists, at Toronto, 20–3 April 1987

I The following papers were presented, many of which pertained to the general theme of the conference, word studies and lexicography.

Alfred Bammesberger, 'Etymological Analysis and Old English Grammar'
Rolf H. Bremmer, Jr, 'The Old Frisian Component in Holthausen's *Altenglisches etymologisches Wörterbuch*'
Joyce Hill, 'Ælfric's Use of Etymologies'
E.G. Stanley, 'No Joy in Old English *wenn*'
R.I. Page, 'Hard Words in Old English'
Rosemary Cramp, 'On Reconstructing the Word and Image'
James A. Graham-Campbell, 'The Archaeology of Anglo-Saxon Secular Drinking Vessels'
Robert D. Stevick, 'The Rationalities of Cross Page Designs in the Lindisfarne, Echternach and Schloss Harburg Gospels'
Maria Amalia D'Aronco, 'The Botanical Lexicon of the Old English *Herbarium*: A Typological Analysis'
Nancy Porter, 'The Still Hand and the Silent Voice: Language and Sign-Language in the Corpus of Old English'
René Derolez, 'A Report on the Anglo-Saxon Glossography Conference (Brussels 8–9 September 1986)'
Matti Rissanen, 'The Helsinki Corpus of English Texts: Diachronic and Dialectal'
Jane Roberts, 'The Old English Materials for the Glasgow Historical Thesaurus'
Victor Strite, 'A Survey of Old English Semantic Field Studies'
Michael Lapidge, 'Frithegod of Canterbury: The Problems of Lexicography and Textual Criticism'
Christine Fell, 'Mild and Bitter: A Problem of Semantics'
George H. Brown, 'Bede and the Monastic Virtue of *discretio*'
Brian Green, '*Lof*: Interlocking Denotations in *Beowulf*'
M. Jane Toswell, 'The Effect of Alliteration on Meaning and Usage in the *Paris Psalter*, metrical version'
David N. Dumville, 'The Anglo-Saxon Charters of Worcester Cathedral: Diplomatic and History'
Russell Poole, 'Cnut's Conquest of England: An Overlooked Source'
Milton McC. Gatch, 'The Blickling Homilies: Post-Prandial Divagations'
Carl Berkhout, 'In Search of Laurence Nowell'

T.F. Hoad, 'Indirect Evidence and the Lexicographer: Recording the Unattested Vocabulary of Old English'

Fred C. Robinson, 'The Latest Old English Literature'

II General Business Meeting, held in Room 140, University College, University of Toronto, on 23 April 1987, at 12.00 noon, President Roberta Frank presiding.

A The Record of the General Business meeting held in the University of Cambridge on 22 August 1985, as published in *ASE* 15 (1986), 1–4, was approved by the Assembly as the minutes of that meeting. A copy of this record, signed by the President, was placed in the files as the official minutes.

B Election of Officers. Professor Frank recalled the terms and duties of the officers of the Society according to its Constitution. Rosemary Cramp thus automatically becomes the new President as of 1 January 1988, to serve until 31 December 1989, and will host the fourth conference (see below). On the nomination of the Executive Committee, the Assembly elected for the same term of office Paul Szarmach as First Vice-President and Patrizia Lendinara as Second Vice-President. Mary P. Richards was elected Executive Director by the Executive Committee for the period 1 July 1987 to 31 December 1993, and this election was reported to the conference.

C The President reported, on behalf of the Executive Committee:

1 Membership. As of the date of the Toronto meeting, the Society had 330 members. Dues are to remain the same, namely $10 per year, from 1 July 1987 until 30 June the following year.

2 Membership of the Advisory Board. The following have been appointed as members of the Advisory Board from 1 January 1988 to 31 December 1991: Alfred Bammesberger, Andreas Fischer, Allen Frantzen, David Rollason and Leslie Webster. Continuing on the Board until 31 December 1989 are Janet Bately, Helmut Gneuss, Michael Lapidge and Gillian Fellows Jensen.

3 Honorary Membership of the Society. The following have been appointed as Honorary Members of the Society: Peter Clemoes and Stanley B. Greenfield.

4 In recognition of their distinguished service to the Society, Daniel Calder and Stanley Greenfield were presented *in absentia* with the St George Award.

5 Next conference. The fourth conference of the Society will be hosted by the University of Durham in the second week of August 1989.

D Professor Clemoes reminded those who had read papers that they were invited to submit their papers, in fully publishable form and following the style sheet, to the editors of *Anglo-Saxon England* up to 31 October 1987 for consideration for the next volume of the journal. Up to half that volume's space was being reserved for this purpose.

E   The meeting closed with a warm round of applause for Professor Frank and her colleagues at the University of Toronto for hosting so enjoyable a conference.

III   Exhibitions in Toronto included a display in the Thomas Fisher Rare Book Library of medieval manuscripts and early printed books from private and institutional collections in Toronto; an exhibition entitled 'Canada Collects the Middle Ages' at the George R. Gardiner Museum; and, in the Rotunda, University College, a collection of documents illustrating the history of Anglo-Saxon studies. Receptions during the conference were hosted by the *Dictionary of Old English*, the University of Toronto Press, the Lieutenant Governor of Ontario, and the Premier of Ontario. A dinner was held in the Great Hall, Hart House, at which the speaker was M. McC. Gatch (see above, I).

Registration forms for the ISAS conference to be held in Durham in August 1989 and full information about the meeting will be sent to all paid-up members of the Society. Cheques for $10, drawn on a branch of an American bank and made payable to the International Society of Anglo-Saxonists, should be sent to Professor Mary P. Richards, Dean of Liberal Arts, 2046 Haley Center, Auburn University, Alabama, 36849-5223, USA. For those members outside the US the equivalent of $ in sterling may be sent to the ISAS account, Midland Bank, 32 Market Hill, Cambridge, CB2 3NU; bank code 401608, account no, 21241605.[1]

---

[1] The record of ISAS meetings is normally kept by the Second Vice-President. The Second Vice-President at the time of the Toronto meeting was Stanley Greenfield, whom illness prevented from attending the meeting. He died, on 30 July 1987, to the great regret of all Anglo-Saxonists. The present record was compiled by Michael Lapidge and Roberta Frank who, in the circumstances, apologize for any inadvertent omissions or inaccuracies.

The Old Frisian component in Holthausen's *Altenglisches etymologisches Wörterbuch*

ROLF H. BREMMER, JR

The publication of the first fascicule of the Toronto *Dictionary of Old English*[1] bears witness to the fulfilment of many vows made at symposia in the past. One of these was to abandon the practice of Bosworth–Toller[2] of providing entries with etymological information. To meet the objections raised against this policy at the second *DOE* conference in 1970, Christopher Ball assured the audience that entries would contain etymological information only if it would be impossible to establish the meaning of a word otherwise. 'Frivolous' etymology, as Ball termed it, such as linking OE *fōt* to Latin *pedem*, would be omitted.[3] The editors of *DOE* will have been confirmed in their attitude by the fact that in those years Dr Alfred Bammesberger announced a plan for a new etymological dictionary for Old English.[4] Since then, besides numerous articles, he has published a volume of *Beiträge zu einem etymologischen Wörterbuch des Altenglischen*.[5] In the preface to this book, Bammesberger stresses that the preparation of such a new dictionary is a project which will not be completed in the immediate future.[6] So, for the time being, the comparist will have to make do with *BT* and Ferdinand Holthausen's etymological dictionary of Old English.[7] This seems an appropriate time, therefore, to focus our attention on that component of Holthausen's dictionary which concerns the closest relative of English, (Old) Frisian: not least because Holthausen himself devoted so much attention to it.

---

[1] *The Dictionary of Old English: D*, ed. A. Cameron *et al.* (Toronto, 1986).

[2] J. Bosworth and T.N. Toller, *An Anglo-Saxon Dictionary* (Oxford, 1898); T.N. Toller, *Supplement* (Oxford, 1921) (henceforth *BT*). A. Campbell's *Enlarged Addenda and Corrigenda* (Oxford, 1972) discontinued *BT*'s practice in this respect.

[3] R. Frank, 'The Dictionary of Old English Conference', *A Plan for the Dictionary of Old English*, ed. R. Frank and A. Cameron (Toronto, 1973), p. 7.

[4] *Ibid.* p. 7, n. 5.

[5] Anglistische Forschungen 139 (Heidelberg, 1979).

[6] *Beiträge*, p. v: 'Mit einem Abschluss dieses langwierigen Unternehmens ist in absehbare Zeit noch nicht zu rechnen.'

[7] *Altenglisches etymologisches Wörterbuch*, 2nd edn (Heidelberg, 1963) (henceforth *AeW*).

When Ferdinand Holthausen wrote the preface to his *AeW* in 1933, he had reached the advanced age of seventy-three.[8] It had taken him some forty years to reach this point – one of the highlights in his academic career – and in the preface he enumerated some of the reasons which had caused the delay in the publication of this dictionary. Thus he had decided, for example, to await the completion of Walde-Pokorny's *Vergleichendes Wörterbuch der indogermanischen Sprachen*, of which the first instalment appeared in 1927.[9] Holthausen saw other advantages in the delayed publication. It had enabled him to extend his knowledge in various relevant fields, notably that of Frisian.[10] In fact, by way of prelude to his *AeW*, he had compiled a dictionary of Old Frisian which was published in 1925.[11]

The origin of this dictionary, or, as he called it in his own words, *kurzgefasstes Glossar* ('concise glossary'), was occasioned by a growing discontent with the shortcomings and inadequacies of the state of Old Frisian lexicography. For its time, the *Afr.Wb.* meant a considerable improvement on dictionaries published until then. Holthausen estimated the increase of entries, as compared to Karl Freiherr von Richthofen's *Altfriesisches Wörterbuch* of 1840, to be about 1800.[12] The eighteen pages of *Berichtigungen, Nachträge* and *Addenda* are an indication that the work most likely was neither complete nor perfect. Unfortunately, two years after the publication of Holthausen's dictionary, a series was founded in Friesland (the Netherlands) which planned to re-edit all published editions of Old Frisian texts and to edit those that had remained unedited. In a way, the *Oudfries[ch]e Taal- en Rechtsbronnen* had a function similar to that of the EETS, in that it aimed to provide the materials for a new dictionary of Old Frisian, an ambitious project which – largely due to lack of manpower and money, one presumes – is still awaiting completion.[13] It

[8] On F. Holthausen (1860–1956), particularly with respect to Frisian studies, see H. T. J. Miedema, *Paedwizers fan de Fryske Filology* (Leeuwarden, 1961), pp. 241–5.

[9] *AeW*, p. vii.   [10] *Ibid.*

[11] *Altfriesisches Wörterbuch* (Heidelberg, 1925) (henceforth *Afr.Wb.*), p. v.

[12] *Afr.Wb.*, p. viii.

[13] Originally, the compilation of this dictionary was begun in Germany; see *De Eerste Emsinger Codex*, ed. P. Sipma, Oudfries(ch)e Taal- en Rechtsbronnen (henceforth OTR) 4 ('s-Gravenhage, 1943), viii. However, after the Second World War the project was started afresh in Groningen; see B. Sjölin, 'Het Grote Oudfriese Woordenboek: terugblik, balans, problematiek', *Us Wurk* 21–22 (1972–3), 193–206, at 193. For a detailed account of the history of Old Frisian lexicography until 1925, see D. Hofmann, 'Die Erschliessung des altfriesischen Wortschatzes', *Philologia Frisica Anno 1969* (Grins/Groningen, 1970), pp. 100–14, at 101–4. For a general bibliography of Frisian lexicography, including that of Old Frisian, see F. Claes *et al.*, 'A Bibliography of Frisian Dictionaries', *Us Wurk* 33 (1984), 1–24, and R. H. Bremmer, Jr, 'Additions and Corrections to F. Claes' *Bibliography*', *ibid.* 100–2.

is now estimated on the basis of sample studies that the number of entries in Holthausen's concise dictionary can be increased by about a quarter to a third.[14] At present Professor Dietrich Hofmann of Kiel is completely rewriting it, and in a span of over twenty years he has reached the letter K. By way of an interim solution, he has recently published a corrected edition of Holthausen's *Afr.Wb.*, corrected to the extent that it is solely limited to the material contained therein, so it does not constitute a supplement.[15] The number of corrections is considerable, varying from the signalling of ghost-words to correcting erroneous interpretations.

If the Old Frisian lexicographical works are to be updated, it goes without saying that this will have repercussions for the Frisian material cited in *AeW*. Holthausen allotted an important place to Frisian in *AeW*: the list of related Germanic words, if available, always begins with the Frisian cognate. In his preface Holthausen does not make clear whether this procedure is based on the assumption of a special Anglo-Frisian sub-group within West Germanic, or not. Bammesberger is slightly more informative on this matter. He intends to stick to the same order of West Germanic dialects, and adds that one 'might assume a specific Ingvaeonic as precursor of Old English and Old Frisian and certain strata of Old Saxon'.[16]

Now the close links between English and Frisian are well known and have been the subject of continuous study and speculation ever since the early sixteenth century. Recently, Hans Frede Nielsen, in what is probably the most detailed monograph on this matter, has established once more that of all the Germanic languages Old English shares most phonological and morphological features with Old Frisian.[17] Less well known are the efforts that have been undertaken to discover whether Old English also shares a striking number of lexical parallels with Old Frisian. On the whole, such word-geographical studies indicate that this is indeed the case. The most extensive study in this field is that by the Swede Ernst Löfstedt, who published a series of articles

---

[14] L.-E. Ahlsson, *Die altfriesische Abstraktbildungen* (Uppsala, 1960), for example, contains a third more abstract nouns than *Afr.Wb.*; cf. Hofmann, 'Erschliessung', p. 113, and G. Köbler, *Altfriesisch-neuhochdeutsches und neuhochdeutsches-altfriesisches Wörterbuch*, Arbeiten zur Rechts- und Sprachwissenschaft 22 (Giessen, 1983), v.

[15] (Heidelberg, 1985). For an evaluation of the present state of Old Frisian lexicography, see my 'De wyn en de sekken: resint wurk op it mêd fan de Aldfryske leksikografy', *Tydskrift foar Fryske Taalkunde* 3 (1987), 60–8.

[16] *Beiträge*, p. 4.

[17] *Old English and the Continental Germanic Languages. A Survey of Morphological and Phonological Interrelations*, Innsbrucker Beiträge zur Sprachwissenschaft 33, 2nd edn (Innsbruck, 1985), 257; for the *Forschungsgeschichte* concerning Anglo-Frisian, see pp. 40–7 and R. H. Bremmer, Jr, 'Old English – Old Frisian: the Relationship Reviewed', *Philologia Frisica Anno 1981* (Leeuwarden, 1982), pp. 79–90, at 79–81.

from 1963 to 1969.[18] According to his findings, English and Frisian share three times as many unique parallels as Frisian does with Scandinavian. The same ratio of three to one holds for unique parallels of alliterative phrases, like *clippan and cyssan* ('to embrace and kiss') and OFris *kissa and kleppa*, or OE *synn and sacu* and OFris *seka ni sinna* ('enmity and strife').[19]

For a number of years I have been noting various sorts of mistakes in the Frisian material in *AeW*, at first incidentally, but later on more systematically, by collating glossaries of modern editions of Old Frisian texts with the contents of *AeW*. There is hardly a page in my copy of it which does not now carry some sort of correction. These corrections to the Frisian component entail the following requirements: (1) printing errors must be corrected; (2) ghost-words must be eliminated; (3) erroneously adduced cognates must be deleted; (4) new cognates must be added; (5) new etymologies must be provided; and (6) Löfstedt's list of Anglo-Frisian isoglosses must be tidied up. I shall briefly exemplify these six points, beginning with the printing errors.

(1) Although it is evident that in a work of such a size printing errors are bound to occur, it is hard for me to join the opinion of one of the reviewers of the book who said he could compile a 'horrifying list' of printing errors.[20] Here are some: s.v. *āðexe* 'Eidechse', for nl. *haagdis* read *hagedis*; s.v. *æcern* 'Nuss, Mast, Eichel, Ecker', for nl. *acker* read *aker*; s.v. *swēor* 'father-in-law', for afr. *swiaring* read *swiāring*; s.v. *dāman* 'richten, urteilen, etc.', for nfr, *dǣma* read afr., and so on. Since this category is not very spectacular I shall not further discuss it here.

(2) Ghost-words must be eliminated. Deleting an Old Frisian ghost-word from a series of well-established Germanic cognates does not invalidate the etymology. But the situation is more serious if the removal of a ghost-word leaves an Old English word without any Germanic cognates. Still, this does not leave the word without an etymology. Thus, Hofmann's convincing rejection of an OFris *flēma* 'to carry away' in favour of OFris *flei(n)a* 'to remove',[21] leaves OE *flīeman* 'to put to flight' isolated. Yet, the derivation of the latter from Gmc *flaum-jan-* remains valid.

---

18 'Beiträge zur nordseegermanischen und nordseegermanischen-nordischen Lexicographie', *Niederdeutsche Mitteilungen* 19–21 (1963–5), 281–345; 22 (1966), 39–65; 23 (1967), 11–61; and 25 (1969), 25–39. See also, e.g., G. Lerchner, *Studien zum nordwestgermanischen Wortschatz* (Halle am Saale, 1965) and H.H. Munske, *Der germanische Rechtswortschatz im Bereich der Missetaten; Philologische und sprachgeographische Untersuchungen I: Die Terminologie der älteren westgermanischen Rechtsquellen* (Berlin and New York, 1973).

19 Bremmer, 'Old English – Old Frisian', pp. 83–5.

20 W. Wokatsch, *Archiv* 168 (1935), 103–5, at 105.

21 D. Hofmann, 'Das altfriesische Wortpaar *flēta* und *fleia/fleina* "wegschaffen, beiseite schaffen"', *Miscellanea Frisica. A New Collection of Frisian Studies*, ed. N. Århammar *et al.* (Assen, 1984), pp. 79–87.

OFris *fereth* ('life') has likewise been shown not to exist; it rests solely on misreadings of *ferech* in the manuscripts. But removal of this form leaves OE *ferhð* ('life, soul') without any cognate. Holthausen is clearly correct in linking it with OE *feorh* (the direct cognate of OFris *ferech*), though it is difficult to explain exactly what the relationship is.[22]

Sometimes a whole entry in *AeW* is based on ghost-words. Thus, for OE *geloda* ('brother'), Holthausen only adduces OFris *ilodskipi* ('guild, brotherhood'). This Old Frisian word, however, is a curiously metathesized form of *ioldskipi*, *jold(e)* being the Old Frisian for 'guild'.[23] Having thus deprived OE *geloda* of its only cognate, it appeared to me that Clark Hall[24] does not list the word at all (although the *Microfiche Concordance* does, s.v. *gelodan*: AntGl 6 (Kindschi) 209 [Fratres] gebroþru uel siblingas).[25] In Toller's *Supplement*, the entry *geloda* has a reference to *gelanda*, and there it becomes clear that the manuscript form *geloda* lacks a nasal stroke, and should be read as *gelonda* ('compatriot, kinsman'). It is puzzling that Holthausen should have listed this word, despite the information available to him through Toller, and despite the fact that he based his dictionary on Clark Hall. Presumably he included it on the basis of the Old Frisian ghost-word.

(3) Erroneously adduced cognates must be deleted. This category will turn out to be relatively small, particularly where Anglo-Frisian parallels are concerned. Some well-documented West Germanic cognates must lose their Frisian cognate. For example, OFris *bōg* 'Zweig, Bug' must be deleted s.v. *bōg* 'Arm, Schulter'.[26] Sometimes I have been unable to trace a Frisian cognate adduced by Holthausen, the existence of which becomes very questionable, therefore. In the *Nachträge und Berichtigungen*, Holthausen (s.v. *bruneða* 'Brennen, Jucken') mentions an OFris *brund*, which I have not found so far. Likewise, I have in vain tried to substantiate OFris *gāk*, listed under OE *gēac* 'Gauch, Kuckuck'. Neither word occurs in his *Afr.Wb.*

Erroneously listed under *cāg(e)* 'Schlüssel, Lösung' is mnd. *keie*. Although Middle Low German dictionaries do list such a word, the meaning they

---

[22] R.H. Bremmer, Jr, 'Old English *feoh and feorh*, Old Norse *fé ok fjǫr*, ergo: Old Frisian *fiā and ferech* "money and life"', *Us Wurk* 32 (1983), 55–62.

[23] *De Eerste Riustringer Codex*, ed. W.J. Buma, OTR 11 ('s-Gravenhage, 1961), 204 (s.v. *joldfretho* and *joldskipi*).

[24] J.R. Clark Hall, *A Concise Anglo-Saxon Dictionary*, 4th edn with supplement by H.D. Meritt (Cambridge, 1960). Meritt's supplement is the only difference between the third and the fourth editions.

[25] R.L. Venezky and A. diPaolo Healey, *A Microfiche Concordance to Old English* (Toronto, 1980).

[26] *Die 'Fivelgoer' Handschrift, I: Einleitung und Text*, ed. B. Sjölin, OTR 12 ('s-Gravenhage, 1970), 182–3.

provide it with is different from Holthausen's,[27] and the word is not a cognate, leaving OFris *kaie, keie* 'key' as the only cognate of the English word.

Under *tela, tila* ('well, fitly, very'), Holthausen adduces OFris *tela* as its only Germanic cognate. The word is not entered in his *Afr.Wb.* and must in all probability be deleted, bringing the number of parallels down by one.

(4) New cognates must be added. This category will prove to be the largest. Entries where an Old Frisian cognate, or sometimes a Modern Frisian one, must be added, run into hundreds. The main reason for this lies partly in the fact that Holthausen did not consult his Frisian dictionaries properly, and partly in the fact that the state of Frisian lexicography has improved so much since 1925. The necessary additions usually confirm Holthausen's etymology, but should certainly not be omitted for that reason.[28]

For OE *līra* (< **ligiza-*) 'muscle, calf of the leg', Holthausen adduces no exact cognates, but compares it to ON *lær* 'thigh' (< **lahaz-*). Actually, OE *līra* has its counterparts in MDu *liere* 'calf of the leg', recorded only twice from a Flemish medical treatise, and in ModFris *ljirre* 'smoked beef', recorded from *c.* 1600 onwards.[29] The word apparently is North Sea Germanic, and will owe its survival in ModFris to its specialized meaning.

OE *grindan* 'to grind', according to Holthausen, has no cognates within Germanic. In this opinion he is followed by Onions, and most recently by Hoad.[30] However, the verb is also recorded in the modern North and East Frisian dialects: note, for example, ModNFris *grinj* (Island of Sylt) and ModEFris *griene* (Saterland).[31]

27 K. Schiller and A. Lübben, *Mittelniederdeutsches Wörterbuch* II (Bremen, 1876), s.v. *Keye, keyge* 'Wurfspiess oder Speer'; G. Cordes, *Mittelniederdeutsches Handwörterbuch* II (Neumünster, 1965), s.v. *keye (keyge)* 'Kieselstein'. Both dictionaries give the same illustration, of which Cordes's translation is to be preferred. On this Anglo-Frisian isogloss, see also Löfstedt, 'Beiträge', p. 316, and T.L. Markey, 'NFris *Kūch*, English "key", and the Unshifted Consonant Question', *Zeitschrift für Dialektologie und Linguistik* 46 (1979), 41–55.

28 It should also be noted that Holthausen treated the Latin loans in a cavalier fashion. As often as not, he provided such words with other Germanic cognates, which has resulted in an obliteration of the relative chronology of the Latin loans in Old English. Some examples where Frisian has similarly borrowed from Latin, but which Holthausen failed to record, are: OE *force*, OFris *forke* 'fork'; OE *līne*, OFris *līne* 'line, rope'; OE *æle*, OFris *ele* 'oil'; OE *pāl*, OFris *pāl* 'pole'; and OE *ungel*, OFris *ungel* 'fat, tallow'.

29 W.J. Buma, 'Wurdsneuperijen 8. *ljirre*', *Us Wurk* 7 (1958), 23–4; see also R.B. ten Cate-Silfwerband, *Vlees, Bloed en Been. Synoniemvergelijkend onderzoek van drie Germaanse woordformaties* (Assen, 1958), pp. 120 and 124. She is unaware, however, of the Frisian and Dutch cognates of OE *līra*.

30 See C.T. Onions, *The Oxford Dictionary of English Etymology* (Oxford, 1966); and T.F. Hoad, *The Concise Oxford Dictionary of English Etymology* (Oxford, 1986). E. Seebold, *Vergleichendes und etymologisches Wörterbuch der germanischen starke Verben* (The Hague and Paris, 1970), p. 240, is also unaware of the parallel.

31 G.B. Droege, 'OE *grindan* – OFris **grinda* 'to grind': an English–Frisian Isogloss within Germanic', *Us Wurk* 24 (1975), 12–18.

OE *wann* 'dark, dusky' is another word with a Frisian cognate that has been overlooked by Holthausen. Onions and Hoad have no cognates at all. According to Onions it is 'of unknown origin and having no certain cognates'. Holthausen tentatively compares it to OIr *fann*, Welsh *gwan* 'weak' (so too the OED). He obviously forgot to check his own *Afr.Wb.*, for there he lists *wann* 'dark', and for its etymology compares it to OE *wann*. Actually, the adjective *per se* is not recorded for Old Frisian, as Holthausen suggests. It only occurs in the compounds *wanfelle*, *wanfellich* 'with bruised skin, black and blue', and in the de-adjectival noun *wonnelsa* 'bruise'.[32] The relation between the Old English and the Old Frisian word was already hinted at by von Richthofen in 1840.[33] Similarly, OE *dwǣscan* 'to extinguish', for which Holthausen gives no cognates, is paralleled by ModWFris *dwest(g)je* and ModNFris *däski*.[34] OE *bōian* 'to boast', for which Holthausen provides no Germanic cognates, is related to OFris *bāgia*, MDu *boghen*, meaning the same.[35] OE *bōnian* 'to ornament' is cognate with MLG *bonen*, ModDu *boenen* 'to polish', and can also be posited for Old Frisian (*bēna*, with i-mutation) on the basis of OFris *bĕnwisp* 'broom' (literally 'polish-wisp').[36] Examples like these could easily be multiplied.

(5) New etymologies must be provided. This is not as spectacular a category as the preceding one, and a few examples will suffice to characterize it. In his *Beiträge* Bammesberger remarks of the verb *tōgelan* 'to diffuse' that it owes its existence to the once recorded pp. *togolen* which occurs in a doublet *togolen 7 togoten* in the Oxford manuscript of Wærferth's translation of Gregory's *Dialogi*. According to Bammesberger, a strong verb *gelan* is otherwise unknown and does not admit of an etymological allocation.[37] However, he does not bother to reject Holthausen's queried suggestion that the verb *tōgelan* may be related to OE *gielm(a)* 'handful, sheaf'. Indeed, under *gielm(a)* the reverse is suggested, 'zu *gelan*?'. The references are circular, and apparently Holthausen knew of no cognates. *Gielm(a)*, however, can satisfactorily be traced to an IE root *ghel* 'to cut' and a suffix *-mo(n)*. Moreover, it has a cognate in a dialect of Modern West Frisian, namely in that of the island of Schiermonnikoog, *galm* 'armful, e.g. of hay'.[38] Now that OE *gielm(a)* can be separated from *tōgelan*, this

---

[32] Löfstedt ('Beiträge', p. 60) also points out a possible Scandinavian cognate.

[33] K. von Richthofen, *Altfriesisches Wörterbuch* (Göttingen, 1840), p. 1138, s.v. *wonfelle*.

[34] W. J. Buma, 'Noardfrysk *deaski* "dwêste"', *Us Wurk* 7 (1958), 72. A. Bammesberger (*Deverbative jan- Verba des Altenglischen* (Munich, 1965), pp. 62–3), doubts whether OE *dwǣscan* should be linked to OE *dwīnan*, as is suggested by Holthausen.

[35] See e.g. J. de Vries, *Nederlands Etymologisch Woordenboek* (Leiden, 1971), s.v. *bogen*.

[36] De Vries, *Woordenboek*, s.v. *boenen*; for the Frisian word, see C. Stapelkamp, 'Wurdboekstúdzjes 2. *benwispen*', *Us Wurk* 2 (1953), 41–2.

[37] *Beiträge*, p. 63. Seebold, *Wörterbuch*, does not mention the verb.

[38] W. J. Buma, 'Wurdsneuperijen 23. Skierm. *galm*', *Us Wurk* 11 (1962), 5–8; see also A. Spenter, *Der Vokalismus der akzentuierten Silben in den Schiermonnikooger Mundart. Eine geschichtliche Studie*

hapax is even more isolated etymologically. Yet again, Old Frisian could provide a cognate in the noun *blōdjelene* 'bruise'. In 1925 Holthausen had entered the word in his *Afr.Wb.*, without being able to provide it with a meaning, just as von Richthofen had done before him. For all I know, the Old Frisian word, like OE *tōgolen*, is a hapax, too, and occurs in a context where related texts have the word *blōdresene* 'bruise'.[39] Some scholars have argued, therefore, that the manuscript form *bloedielene* is a scribal error for the more common *blōdresene*,[40] whereas the most recent editors of the manuscript in which it occurs allow the manuscript reading to stand, with an appeal to OE *tōgelan*.[41] The situation here is similar to that sketched above for OE *geloda* – OFris *ilodskipi*. There are two ghost-words, perpetuating each other's existence. Accordingly, either the Frisian word must be dismissed as an error, or it must be allowed to stand with OE *tōgelan*, with the addition: 'of unknown origin'. I see no possibility of linking these two words to OE *wīd-gil(l)* 'broad, spacious, extensive', and Holthausen has no solution either.[42]

For the etymology of OE *lorg* 'pole, distaff, weaver's beam', Holthausen adduces OIr *lorg*, with a reference to Walde-Pokorny. Bammesberger has shown that the word cannot be cognate with OIr *lorg*, and could at most be (based on) a loan. He also points out that Max Förster does not mention the word in his studies on Celtic loans into Old English.[43] Actually, a Germanic cognate survives in ModNFris *lurreg* (f.) 'thigh, loin'. NFris *lurreg* corresponds to OE *lorg* as NFris *surreg* (f.) 'sorrow' corresponds to OE *sorg*.[44] There seem to be no cognates outside Germanic for this word.

Etymologists must be prepared to change their minds, as Holthausen certainly was. In 1925 in his *Afr.Wb.* he entered an *ond-reda* stv. 'fürchten' and

---

des autochthonen westfriesischen Inseldialekts (Copenhagen, 1968), p. 70, n. 320, who demonstrates that the *a* in *galm* reflects a regular feature in the Schiermonnikoog dialect, the lowering of *e* to *a* before *l*. Buma had argued that OE *gielm* descended from IE *ghel-, and Fris *galm* from IE *ghol-.

[39] See Munske, *Der germanische Rechtswortschatz*, § 208.

[40] R. His, *Das Strafrecht der Friesen im Mittelalter* (Leipzig, 1901), p. 319, n. 7: 'Die Form *blodielene* . . . ist blosser Schreibfehler (frdl. Mitteil. von Prof. [Th.] Siebs).' Hofmann, in his revision of Holthausen's *Afr.Wb.*, is of the same opinion (see p. 154).

[41] *Jus Municipale Frisonum*, ed. W. J. Buma and W. Ebel, Altfriesische Rechtsquellen 6.2 (Göttingen, 1977), no. XXIII.6; the reference to OE *tōgelan* is to be found in Buma's unpublished glossary to *Jus*, p. 90. Regrettably, this voluminous glossary of over 700 pages had a very limited imprint and circulation, and is not for sale. It can be consulted at the Frisian Institute of the University of Groningen.

[42] Holthausen's reference to OHG *gellōn (AeW*, p. 421) is out of place here. OHG *gellōn*, w.vb. 2 'mucken, in winselndem Tone vortragen' (see T. Starck and J.C. Wells, *Althochdeutsches Glossenwörterbuch* (Heidelberg, 1975), p. 196) is cognate to OE *giellan*, st. vb. 3; see Seebold, *Wörterbuch*, pp. 222–3. [43] *Beiträge*, p. 93.

[44] As pointed out by Löfstedt, 'Beiträge', p. 33.

supplied OE *ond-rǣdan* and OIcel *hrǣðoa* as cognate forms. In *AeW*, however, he listed the Old English verb as *on-drǣdan*, without referring to the Old Frisian verb. In 1977 Bammesberger pleaded for a return to Jacob Grimm's suggestion of seeing the verb as a compound of *ond-* (< *and-*) + *rǣdan*. He further underpins what has been set forth by Pogatscher in 1903 who, unlike Bammesberger, also drew attention to the Old Frisian noun *drēde* 'fear'.[45] The existence of the above-mentioned verb *ond-rēda* is now queried by Hofmann,[46] but it must of necessity be posited to explain the well-attested form *drēde*. This occurrence of metanalysis in cognate words is a feature shared by English and Frisian, and should be added to the list of phonological and morphological parallels compiled by Nielsen.[47]

(6) Löfstedt's list of unique Anglo-Frisian cognates must be tidied up. Although Löfstedt himself did much to bring together disparate material and in many cases pointed out the uniqueness of certain parallels, it will be clear that his list cannot be definitive. Compared with the phonological and morphological material, the lexical evidence is much harder to assemble. One of the reasons why Löfstedt's list is provisional – and he himself must have been aware of it – is the fact that a considerable part of the Old Frisian vocabulary has not been recorded in dictionaries or glossaries or is not readily available to the international scholarly community. The same applies to the Frisian written in the Low Countries from 1600 to 1800, which undoubtedly will contain much archaic material.

The publication of the *Dictionary of Old English*, which intends comprehensive coverage of the Old English word-hoard, will take care of one aspect of the subject. About the Frisian end of the subject I am slightly pessimistic. For the time being, the material for the dictionaries of Old Frisian (up to *c.* 1500) and Middle Frisian (up to *c.* 1800) held on fiche at the Frisian Institute of the University of Groningen, Netherlands, must function as a substitute. Nonetheless, before Professor Bammesberger has finished his etymological dictionary of Old English, I hope to have published my findings. That a critical re-examination of the Old Frisian component in Holthausen's *AeW* is both necessary and rewarding may have become clear from this initial report.[48]

---

[45] A. Bammesberger, 'Zur Herkunft von ae. *ondrǣdan* und *andrysne*', *BDGSL* 99 (1977), 206–12; see also his *Beiträge*, p. 38, and A. Pogatscher, 'Etymologisches', *Beiblatt zur Anglia* 14 (1903), 181–5, at 182–5.   [46] *Afr.Wb.*, p. 17.

[47] *Old English*, ch. 3. The contents of this chapter have been conveniently summarized by the same author, 'Old Frisian and the Old English Dialects', *Us Wurk* 30 (1981), 49–66.

[48] I should like to thank Patrick Styles for his valuable comments on a draft of this paper, David Pelteret and Henk and Christine van Halen for hospitality, and especially my brother Marius, *sinces brytta*.

The botanical lexicon of the Old English *Herbarium*

MARIA AMALIA D'ARONCO

Recent research has established beyond question that, in the study of medicine at least, Anglo-Saxon England was far from being 'a backwater in which superstition flourished until the mainstream of more rational and advanced Salernitan practices flowed into the country in late medieval times'.[1] On the contrary, Anglo-Saxon medicine was at least at the same level as that of contemporary European schools. In ninth-century England the medical works inherited by 'post-classical Latin medical literature (which included translations and epitomes of Greek and Byzantine medical authorities)' were not only well known,[2] but served as the basis for original reworking and compilation, as the example of the *Læceboc* shows.[3] More important, it was in pre-Conquest England that, for the first time in Europe, medical treatises were either compiled in or translated into a vernacular language rather than being composed in Latin or Greek. Ancient medicine made substantial use of drugs obtained from plants; and therefore, since the sources of Anglo-Saxon medical lore were in Latin (or in Greek: but invariably known through the medium of Latin), it is not surprising that most medicinal herbs used in the preparation of Old English prescriptions were not indigenous to England or even to conti-

---

[1] M. L. Cameron, 'The Sources of Medical Knowledge in Anglo-Saxon England', *ASE* 11 (1983), 135–55, at 135.

[2] M. L. Cameron, 'Bald's *Leechbook*: its Sources and their Use in its Compilation', *ASE* 12 (1983), 153–82, at 177. On the conditions of medical knowledge in Anglo-Saxon England see the recent and excellent studies by C. H. Talbot, 'Some Notes on Anglo-Saxon Medicine', *Medical Hist.* 9 (1965), 156–69; L. E. Voigts, 'Anglo-Saxon Plant Remedies and the Anglo-Saxons', *Isis* 70 (1979), 250–68; Cameron, 'The Sources of Medical Knowledge'; and A. L. Meaney, 'Variant Versions of Old English Medical Remedies and the Compilation of Bald's *Leechbook*', *ASE* 13 (1984), 235–68.

[3] As Talbot and Cameron have shown, among the classical and post-classical sources used by the compiler of the *Læceboc* are two treatises, the *Passionarius Galeni* and the *Practica Petrocelli Salernitani*, both traditionally attributed to Salernitan physicians of the eleventh century, Gariopontus and Petrocellus respectively. But since copies of the second work are known to have existed already in the ninth century, the traditional attribution is evidently to be disregarded; cf. Talbot, 'Some Notes', p. 168, and Cameron, 'The Sources of Medical Knowledge', p. 143 and 'Bald's *Leechbook*', pp. 162–4. The latter suggests the possibility of an English origin for the *Petrocellus*: 'The more I use the *Petrocellus* and *Leechbook*, the more I am struck by their similar forms, suggesting a common tradition in the making of medical books, and a possible English origin for the *Petrocellus*' ('Bald's *Leechbook*', p. 164).

15

nental Germany. And since such medicinal herbs were not indigenous to northern Europe, it is evident that, in using them, speakers of vernacular languages were obliged to create a vocabulary appropriate to denote them. In the present paper I propose to analyse the Old English botanical terminology which was created in order to render the various Latin terms for medicinal herbs.

Our knowledge of the Old English botanical lexicon is based mainly on treatises such as the *Læceboc*,[4] *Lacnunga*,[5] *Peri Didaxeon*,[6] Old English *Herbarium*,[7] a number of glossaries, interlinear and individual glosses, and scattered prescriptions.[8] In this study, however, I shall limit my analysis to the Old English *Herbarium* for various reasons: firstly, because it is the one treatise which deals specifically with *herbae* and thus provides the greatest scope for identifying the plants; secondly, because, being a translation, it permits a direct comparison between the Latin source and the Old English rendering. The other treatises (*Læceboc*, *Lacnunga* and *Peri Didaxeon*) are compilations which go back to different, not always reconstructable, sources; furthermore, in these treatises, the plants are simply named in the various prescriptions with no qualification, so that sometimes it is immensely difficult to identify them. On the other hand, the approach of the translator of the Old English *Herbarium* was completely different: his aim was to provide all kinds of information useful for the recognition of herbs, by means of listing their characteristics as well as their virtues. Pre-eminent among the former is the name itself. In fact, in pre-Linnean times, knowledge of the exact name was of great importance in

---

4 Ptd *Leechdoms, Wortcunning and Starcraft of Early England*, ed. O. Cockayne, 3 vols. (London, 1864–6) II, 2–299; *Kleinere angelsächsischen Denkmäler, I. 1. Das Læceboc. 2. Die Lacnunga. 3. Der Lorica-Hymnus. 4. Das Lorica-Gebet*, ed. G. Leonhardi, Bibliothek der angelsächsischen Prosa 6 (Hamburg, 1905), 1–109. For the identification of the plants see P. Bierbaumer, *Der botanische Wortschatz des Altenglischen: I. Das Læceboc*, Grazer Beiträge zur englischen Philologie 1 (Bern and Frankfurt-am-Main, 1975) (hereafter referred to as BW1).

5 Ptd *Leechdoms*, ed. Cockayne, III, 1–80; *Kleinere angelsächsischen Denkmäler*, ed. Leonhardi, pp. 121–55; J.H.G. Grattan and C. Singer, *Anglo-Saxon Magic and Medicine. Illustrated Specially from the Semi-Pagan Text 'Lacnunga'* (London, 1952), pp. 96–205. For analysis of the botanical lexicon of this text, see P. Bierbaumer, *Der botanische Wortschatz des Altenglischen: II. Lacnunga, Herbarium Apuleii, Peri Didaxeon*, Grazer Beiträge zur englischen Philologie 2 (Bern, Frankfurt-am-Main and Munich, 1976) (hereafter referred to as BW2).

6 Ptd *Leechdoms*, ed. Cockayne, III, 82–145; *Peri Didaxeon*, ed. M. Löweneck, Erlangen Beiträge 12 (Erlangen, 1896). Analysis of the botanical terminology is found in BW2.

7 Ptd *Leechdoms*, ed. Cockayne, I, 1–325; *The Old English Herbarium and Medicina de quadrupedibus*, ed. H. J. De Vriend, EETS os 286 (London, 1984). For analysis of its botanical lexicon, see BW2.

8 The botanical lexicon of these texts has been analyzed by P. Bierbaumer, *Der botanische Wortschatz des Altenglischen: III. Der botanische Wortschatz in altenglischen Glossen*, Grazer Beiträge zur englischen Philologie 3 (Frankfurt-am-Main, Bern and Las Vegas, 1979) (hereafter referred to as BW3).

the identification of herbs; accordingly the plants in the Old English *Herbarium* were provided both with the Latin name, often with its Greek synonym, and the Old English equivalent, sometimes followed by a synonym. Consider the following two entries:

ch. v: (Henbane) ðeos wyrt þe man symphoniacam nemneð 7 oðrum naman belone 7 eac sume men hennebelle hataþ . . .[9]

ch. xxxv: (Earthgall) . . . genim þas wyrte þe grecas centauria maior and angle curmelle seo mare nemnað and eac sume men eorðgeallan hatað.[10]

This procedure is not original in any way but conforms to the tradition of antique herbals, a tradition which goes back to Pedanius Dioscorides of Anazarb, who described every plant by giving the details of its vegetal parts – trunk, leaves, flowers, fruits and roots – by mentioning its origin and habitat and its medicinal properties and dosages, and, last but not least, by giving a list of synonyms in Greek and sometimes even in Latin.[11] Let us now look more closely at the Old English *Herbarium*.

THE OLD ENGLISH *HERBARIUM*

The Old English *Herbarium* is a translation of originally separate Latin treatises that at a very early date became part of the textual tradition of one of them, the *Herbarium Pseudo-Apulei*,[12] which in turn is a compilation from many sources (including particularly Pliny's *Naturalis Historia*)[13] and which enjoyed an enormous popularity throughout the Middle Ages, as is indicated by the number of its surviving manuscripts.[14] The pseudo-Apuleius *Herbarium* is a product of late antiquity in the main line of Greek herbal tradition which

---

[9] *Old English Herbarium*, ed. De Vriend, p. 48: 'The herb that is called *symphoniacam* and with another name *belone*, and also some people call it henbane.'

[10] *Ibid.*, p. 80: 'Take that herb that is called *centauria maior* in Greek, *curmelle* in English and which, by some people, is also called earthgall.'

[11] *Pedanii Dioscoridis Anazarbei De materia medica libri quinque*, ed. C. Sprengel, Medicorum Graecorum Opera quae extant 25 (Leipzig, 1829); *Pedanii Dioscuridis Anazarbei De materia medica libri V*, ed. M. Wellmann, 3 vols. (Berlin, 1906–14).

[12] *Antonii Musae De herba vettonica liber, Pseudo-Apulei Herbarius, Anonymi De taxone liber, Sexti Placiti Liber medicinae ex animalibus, etc.*, ed. E. Howald and H. E. Sigerist, Corpus Medicorum Latinorum 4 (Leipzig, 1927), 13–225.

[13] See *Pseudo-Apulei Herbarius*, ed. Howald and Sigerist, p. xix.

[14] For discussion of the manuscripts, see *ibid.* pp. v–xiv, and the subsequent articles by H. E. Sigerist, 'Zum Herbarius Pseudo-Apulei', *Archiv für Geschichte der Medizin* 23 (1930), 197–204; 'The Medical Literature of the Early Middle Ages', *Bull. Hist. Medicine* 2 (1934), 26–52; 'Materia Medica in the Middle Ages', *Bull. Hist. Medicine* 7 (1939), 417–23. Howald and Sigerist list some forty-seven manuscripts and fragments, while Beccaria lists twenty-five manuscripts earlier than the twelfth century; see A. Beccaria, *I codici di medicina del periodo presalernitano*, Edizione di storia e letteratura 53 (Rome, 1956).

ultimately goes back to the fourth century BC;[15] it was composed, very probably in Latin,[16] in the fourth century AD[17] in North Africa or in Sicily.[18] It has traditionally been attributed to the Platonic philosopher Apuleius of Madaura (born *c.* AD 125), since his name appears in the incipits and/or the ornamental rubrics of most manuscripts.[19] Although it is not possible to know the identity of the author, it is quite certain that the attribution to the second-century philosopher is fictitious; accordingly the author is usually referred to as Apuleius Barbarus or pseudo-Apuleius.[20]

The *Herbarium*, which in its original form consisted of 130 chapters to which another one on the powers of mandrake (ch. cxxxi: *Effectus herbae mandragorae*) had already been added at an early date,[21] soon became associated in manuscripts with other treatises: *De herba vettonica liber* falsely attributed to Antonius Musa, physician to the Emperor Augustus; and the anonymous *De taxone liber* and the *Liber medicinae ex animalibus, pecoribus 'et bestiis uel auibus* of Sextus

15 C. Singer, 'The Herbal in Antiquity and its Transmission to Later Ages', *Jnl of Hellenic Stud.* 47 (1927), 1–52.
16 According to Singer ('The Herbal in Antiquity', p. 37) it was composed in Greek; however there is no linguistic evidence to support his opinion. For a complete bibliography on this question, see L. E. Voigts, 'The Significance of the Name "Apuleius" to the *Herbarium Apulei*', *Bull. Hist. Medicine* 52 (1978), 215–27, at 215, n. 8.
17 *Pseudo-Apulei Herbarius*, ed. Howald and Sigerist, p. xx.
18 Cf. R. Simonini, *Medicinae varia in un codice dell'viii secolo conservato nell'archivio capitolare della Metropolitana di Modena, Apulei Liber* (Modena 1929), pp. 24–6; C. H. Talbot, 'Medico-Historical Introduction', *Medicina Antiqua. Facsimile Vol. XXVII: Codex Vindobonensis 93 der österreichischen Nationalbibliothek* (Graz, 1972), *Kommentarband*, p. 30. According to Hunger (*The Herbal of Pseudo-Apuleius from the Ninth Century MS. in the Abbey of Monte Cassino – Codex Casinensis 97 – Together with the first printed Edition of Joh. Phil. de Lignamine – Editio princeps Romae 1481 – both in Facsimile*, ed. F. W. T. Hunger (Leiden, 1935), p. xviii), the nature of the author's Latin, some plant names and the descriptions of two identifiable reptiles point to an African origin for the author.
19 'HERBARIUS APULEI PLATONICI quem accepit a Cirone centauro, magistro Achillis, et ab Aesculapio', (*Pseudo-Apulei Herbarius*, ed. Howald and Sigerist, p. 15). In the eleventh-century illustrated manuscript containing the Old English translation of the pseudo-Apuleius herbal (London, British Library, Cotton Vitellius C. iii), the rubric runs as follows: '(H)ERBARIU(M) APUL(EI P)LAT(ONIC)I QUOD AC(CE)PIT AB ESCOLAPIO ET (A) CH(I)RONE CENTAURO MAGISRO ACHILLIS' (19v); see *Old English Herbarium*, ed. De Vriend, p. xiii.
20 Among the different opinions as to why the name of Apuleius came to be associated with this work, the most plausible one seems to be that suggested by L. E. Voigts who, assuming from the evidence of Apuleius's works that he 'associated himself with the god of medicine', suggests that 'it may well be this association with Aesculapius which links the Madauran to the *Herbarium*' ('The Significance of the Name "Apuleius"', p. 223). She concludes: 'It is plausible then that a factor or perhaps *the* factor in the decision of the fourth-century herbalist to appropriate the name of Apuleius of Madaura was the wish to declare that the ultimate source of the *Herbarium* was the god of medicine' (*ibid.* p. 227).
21 See *Pseudo-Apulei Herbarius*, ed. Howald and Sigerist, p. xvii.

Placitus Papiriensis.[22] In some manuscripts two other treatises are sometimes added to these, a work known as *Liber medicinae ex herbis femininis*, wrongly attributed to Dioscorides,[23] and an anonymous treatise on the healing powers of the mulberry.[24]

We do not know with any certainty how long the Latin *Herbarium* had been known in Anglo-Saxon England, but there is the possibility that it might have been known already in the ninth century. In fact, as M. L. Cameron has recently observed,[25] there existed in the Gräflich Nesselrode'sche Bibliothek at Herrnstein über Siegberg, before the 1939–45 war destroyed it, a manuscript, then Herten, Westfalia, 192 whose first part (fols. 1–20), datable to the ninth century and thought to be of English origin, contained an illustrated version of the pseudo-Apuleius *Herbarium*.[26] In any case, towards the end of the tenth century the *Herbarium*-complex was translated into Old English[27] and the four surviving manuscripts[28] testify to the popularity of this remedy book, the use of which was not limited to the specialist. In fact, thanks to the peculiar

---

[22] *Ibid.* pp. xxi–xxii. These treatises are printed at pp. 1–11, 227–32 and 233–86 respectively. It has not been possible to identify Sextus Placitus. Perhaps it is best to accept the opinion of Cockayne (*Leechdoms*, p. lxxxix), according to whom Sextus Placitus is a 'nominis umbra' – just like 'that other creature of imagination, Idpartus in the *Liber de taxone*' (De Vriend, *Old English Herbarium*, pp. lxvi–lxvii). The text of the *Liber medicinae ex animalibus* is found in two different versions, a short one (the A-version, also called α-version), and a long one or B-version (β-version). These recensions are so different that Howald and Sigerist print them (pp. 227–32) in two parallel columns; cf. also *Old English Herbarium*, ed. De Vriend, pp. lxiv–lxvi.

[23] Ptd H. F. Kästner, 'Pseudo-Dioscoridis de herbis femininis', *Hermes* 31 (1896), 578–636; 32 (1897), 160. Cf. also *Pseudo-Apulei Herbarius*, ed. Howald and Sigerist, p. xvii, and J. M. Riddle, 'Pseudo-Dioscorides' *Ex herbis femininis* and Early Medieval Medical Botany', *Jnl of the Hist. of Biology* 14 (1981), 43–81; and 'Dioscorides', *Catalogus Translationum et Commentariorum*, ed. F. E. Cranz and P. O. Kristeller, 4 vols. (Washington DC, 1980) IV, 1–143.

[24] The earliest codex which contains this text is Lucca, Biblioteca Governativa, 296 (northern Italy, s. viii/ix: see *Old English Herbarium*, ed. De Vriend, p. xlvii); the treatise on the mulberry is at 18r–v, and precedes the A-version of Sextus Placitus, *Liber medicinae ex animalibus* (18v–26v) and the pseudo-Dioscorides, *Liber medicinae ex herbis femininis* (26v–45v). There are strong affinities between this manuscript and a later illustrated codex, London, Wellcome Historical Medical Library, 573 (s.xiii² or xiii^med?); cf. *Old English Herbarium*, ed. De Vriend, p. xlix.

[25] See Cameron, 'The Sources of Medical Knowledge', p. 149 and n. 47.

[26] For the description and illustration of the manuscript cf. Beccaria, *Codici*, pp. 208–13 (no. 55), and K. Sudhoff, 'Codex Medicus Hertensis (nr. 192)', *Archiv für Geschichte der Medizin* 10 (1917), 265–313.

[27] Cf. *Old English Herbarium*, ed. De Vriend, p. xlii.

[28] The manuscripts are: London, BL, Cotton Vitellius C. iii (s. xi); Harley 585 (s. x/xi); Harley 6258B (s. xii²); Oxford, Bodleian Library, Hatton 76 (s. xi). Cotton Vitellius C. iii is illustrated throughout with coloured drawings of plants and animals. In Harley 6258B, the plants from

arrangement of the text, where each chapter deals with a single plant, describing its features (and sometimes even giving an illustration), the places where it
can be found and the diseases which it cures, anyone who could read the
vernacular could easily learn how to preserve his health and to cure the
common ailments – not an easy task at any time and particularly difficult in that
age of perennial pestilence and plague, aggravated by a dismal state of public
and private hygiene and a scarcity of doctors.[29]

When compared to its Latin source, the Old English translation of the
Herbarium shows some noteworthy differences. First of all, the three treatises
(*Pseudo-Apulei Herbarius, De herba vettonica liber* and *Liber medicinae ex herbis
femininis*) do not appear as separate texts, each with its *incipit* and *explicit*, but
are merged into one so that the *De herba vettonica* forms the first chapter and the
Liber medicinae ex herbis femininis, chs. cxxxiii–clxxxv.[30] The translator omitted
some parts of the *De herba vettonica*, such as the greetings of Antonius Musa to
M. Agrippa and the celebration of the 'virtues' of the betony and the final
prayer to the plant, while retaining all useful information regarding its use, the
places where it could be found and the instructions for the appropriate time to
gather it. Similarly, the chapters that contain the pseudo-Dioscorides material
show striking differences from the *Liber medicinae ex herbis femininis*. In
particular, the Old English *Herbarium* treats only fifty-three plants, while the
Liber medicinae ex herbis femininis treats seventy-one;[31] there is no agreement in
the order in which the plants are treated;[32] there are changes in the medical uses
of the herbs; and some of the plants that appear in the Old English *Herbarium*

the original three texts are arranged in alphabetical order according to their Latin names (*a*-
order). Because of its late date, this manuscript was not included by Wanley, Beccaria and Ker
in their catalogues. Nevertheless there is abundant evidence that its language is late Old
English and not Middle English. For descriptions of the manuscripts, lists of their contents,
their interrelationships and their relationship to the Latin source, see *Old English Herbarium*,
ed. De Vriend, pp. xi–lv.

29 Cf. Cameron, 'The Sources of Medical Knowledge', pp. 175–7.

30 The same treatment of the *Herbarium*-complex translation is found for the three other
treatises which belong to the textual tradition of the pseudo-Apuleius *Herbarium*. They too
are merged into a continuous text known (since Cockayne used the term in 1864) as *Medicina
de quadrupedibus* (cf. *Old English Herbarium*, ed. De Vriend, p. lxii), where *De taxone liber* comes
first and is followed by the treatise on the healing properties of the mulberry and, finally, by
the short (or A-) version of the *Liber medicinae ex animalibus*.

31 Montecassino, Archivio della Badia, v. 97, contains (at pp. 476a–476b and 523a–532b) forty-
three chapters; Lucca, Biblioteca Governativa, 296, 26v–45v, contains forty-two chapters;
see *Old English Herbarium*, ed. De Vriend, pp. xlv and xlvii–xlviii. Cameron ('The Sources of
Medical Knowledge', p. 149) suggests that the source of this section of the Old English
Herbarium could be another treatise, also attributed to Dioscorides, namely the *Curae
herbarum*.

32 Cf. *Old English Herbarium*, ed. De Vriend, pp. 174–233.

derive directly from Dioscorides, *De materia medica*,[33] while for others there seems to be no direct Latin source.[34]

Another peculiar characteristic of the Old English *Herbarium* is the presence of a table of contents where the names of the herbs are given in Latin and Old English and those of the cures in Old English. Although two Latin recensions of the *Herbarium* contain an index of *tituli morborum*, this differs from that in the Old English translation. In fact while in the Latin manuscripts the ailments are listed according to the traditional head-to-foot order, from *a capitis fractura* to *ad tisicos*, and under each entry is listed the number of the chapter where the remedy can be found,[35] the index of the Old English translation provides the names of the plants with the numbers of the relevant chapters followed by a list of ailments or symptoms for which the plant supplies remedies, as in the following entry for ch. xxxi:

Herba lactuca siluatica þæt is wudulectric
1. Wiþ eagena sare.
2. Eft wiþ eagene dymnysse.[36]

As Linda Voigts points out, the Old English contents list, although not so sophisticated as the *tituli morborum*, nevertheless bears witness that the medieval herbals, far from reflecting the mindless copying of sterile formulae as Charles Singer maintained, were meant for practical usage in the cure of the sick.[37]

THE BOTANICAL LEXICON

Up to ten years ago, when Peter Bierbaumer began the publication of what may be considered the first true dictionary of botanical terms in Old English, *Der botanische Wortschatz des altenglischen*,[38] no other field of English lexicography had been more neglected than botanical terminology. As early as 1889, in

---

[33] Cf. chs. cli, clviii, clxiii and clxiv.
[34] Cf. W. Hofstetter, 'Zur lateinischen Quelle des altenglischen pseudo-Dioskurides', *Anglia* 101 (1983), 315–60.
[35] *Pseudo-Apulei Herbarius*, ed. Howald and Sigerist, pp. 16–20.
[36] *Læceboc*, ed. Leonhardi, I, xix: 'The herb lactuca silvatica, that is, wood lettuce. 1. For soreness of the eyes. 2. Again, for dimness of eyes.'
[37] Voigts, 'Anglo-Saxon Plant Remedies', pp. 255–9. According to B. Lawn, although early medieval medicine was pragmatic and empirical, it had a theoretical base; it did not inquire into the causes of diseases but concentrated on the observation of the symptoms and therapeutics: *The Salernitan Questions* (Oxford, 1963), pp. 1–15 and 20–1. See also C. H. Talbot, *Medicine in Medieval England* (London, 1967), pp. 18–20, and G. Majno, *The Healing Hand: Man and Wound in the Ancient World* (Cambridge, Mass., 1975); for the study of the efficacy of various treatments used by Greek and Roman medicine, see pp. 313–422.
[38] As cited above, nn. 4, 5 and 8.

the preface to his thesis on Old English plant names,[39] Johannes Hoops had announced his intention to publish a dictionary of plant names in Old English. Unfortunately, his intention was doomed to remain at the planning stage, and even the material which he had collected seems to have been irreparably lost.[40] Since that time, in spite of an abundance of critical editions of Old English medical and botanical treatises, the publication of Latin–Old English glossaries and glosses and of prescriptions scattered in various manuscripts,[41] all of which accompanied, completed, improved upon and enlarged the three volumes of Oswald Cockayne's *Leechdoms, Wortcunning and Starcraft of Early England* (published between 1864 and 1866), only Bierbaumer's work has provided a thorough treatment of this important field of English lexicogra-

---

[39] J. Hoops, *Über die altenglischen Pflanzennamen* (Freiburg im Breisgau, 1889).

[40] BW1, p. v.

[41] Besides the editions already mentioned (for which see above, nn. 4, 5 and 7), there is the recent discovery of a fragment containing some recipes (Louvain-la-Neuve, Centre Général de Documentation, Fragments H. Omont 3, s. ix[med]), ptd B. Schaumann and A. Cameron, 'A Newly-Found Leaf of Old English from Louvain', *Anglia* 95 (1977), 289–312; described by N. R. Ker, 'A Supplement to *Catalogue of Manuscripts Containing Anglo-Saxon*', *ASE* 5 (1976), 121–31, at 128 (no. 417). The main Latin–Old English glossaries are: Epinal–Erfurt glossary (Epinal, Bibliothèque Municipale, 72 (s. viii[in]) and Erfurt, Wissenschaftliche Allgemeinbibliothek, Amplonianus f. 42 (s. ix[1]), ptd *Old English Glosses in the Epinal–Erfurt Glossary*, ed. J.D. Pheifer (Oxford, 1974); Corpus Glossary (Cambridge, Corpus Christi College 144 (s. viii/ix)), ptd *An Eighth-Century Latin–Anglo-Saxon Glossary*, ed. J.H. Hessels (Cambridge, 1890), and *The Corpus Glossary*, ed. W.M. Lindsay (Cambridge, 1921); the Cleopatra Glossaries (London, British Library, Cotton Cleopatra, A. iii (s. x[med])), ptd T. Wright and R.P. Wülcker, *Anglo-Saxon and Old English Vocabularies*, 2 vols. (London, 1884), (hereafter referred to as WW), nos. 11, 8, and 12; W.G. Stryker, 'The Latin–Old English Glossary in Ms Cotton Cleopatra A. iii' (unpubl. Ph.D. dissertation, Stanford Univ., 1952), and J.J. Quinn, 'The Minor Latin–Old English Glossaries in Ms Cotton Cleopatra A. iii' (unpubl. Ph.D. dissertation, Stanford Univ., 1956); the Antwerp Glossary (Antwerp, Plantin-Moretus Museum, 47 + London, British Library, Add. 32246 (s. xi[1])), ptd M. Förster, 'Die altenglische Glossenhandschrift Plantinus 32 (Antwerpen) und Additional 32246 (London)', *Anglia* 41 (1917), 94–161, and L. Kindschi, 'The Latin–Old English Glossaries in Plantin-Moretus MS 32 and British Museum MS Additional 32246' (unpubl. Ph.D. dissertation, Stanford Univ., 1955); the Brussels Glossary (Brussels, Bibliothèque Royale, 1828–30 (s. xi[in])), ptd WW no. 9, with corrections by H. Logeman, 'Zu Wright-Wülker 1, 204–303', *Anglia* 85 (1890), 316–18; the Harley Glossary (London, BL, Harley 3376 (s. x/xi)), ptd WW, no. 6, and R.T. Oliphant, *The Harley Latin–Old English Glossary*, Janua Linguarum, Series Practica, 20 (The Hague, 1966); the Durham Glossary (Durham, Cathedral Library, Hunter 100, s. xii[in]), ptd *Das Durhamer Pflanzenglossar, Lateinisch und Altenglisch*, ed. B. von Lindheim, Beiträge zur englische Philologie 35 (Bochum-Langendreer, 1941); the Laud Glossary (Oxford, Bodleian Library, Laud Misc. 567 (s. xii)), ptd *The Laud Herbal Glossary*, ed. by J.R. Stracke (Amsterdam, 1974). For Ælfric's Glossary the standard edition is *Ælfrics Grammatik und Glossar*, ed. J. Zupitza, Sammlung englischer Denkmäler 1 (Berlin, 1880; reptd with introduction by H. Gneuss, Berlin, Zürich and Dublin, 1966). For information on scattered botanical glosses, see BW3, pp. viii–xli.

phy. Thanks to this and the invaluable *Microfiche Concordance to Old English*,[42] it is now possible to undertake a thorough analysis of the botanical terminology used in Anglo-Saxon England, and to see how the Anglo-Saxons were able to create a vocabulary to describe medicinal herbs.

In its 185 chapters the Old English *Herbarium* contains some 159 vernacular terms denoting plants and herbs,[43] and thirty-eight terms for their parts, fruits, seeds and derivatives, as well as five terms referring to their cultivation or the place where they grow.[44] In order to determine the influence of Latin sources on the botanical lexicon of Old English, I have analysed this material under several headings. First, terms that belong to the indigenous Germanic heritage have been isolated; thereafter, the different types of linguistic borrowing, whether direct (loan words) or indirect (including semantic loans, i.e. words having meanings adopted from foreign words, and loan formations, i.e. neologisms formed with elements of the native language in order to translate a foreign word),[45] have been examined and classified according to the criterion of their greater or lesser dependence in rendering the source.

The Germanic heritage

When examining the botanical lexicon from the point of view of its relationship with Latin, we are faced with many difficulties. To begin with, although many plants were unquestionably foreign to northern Europe and therefore required to have their names borrowed either directly or indirectly, there are others which are indigenous to northern Europe or to England but whose names, although made up of native elements, do not belong to the oldest

[42] A. diPaolo Healey and R. Venezky, *A Microfiche Concordance to Old English* (Toronto, 1980).
[43] Not all Latin plant names have a corresponding vernacular name; cf., for example, ch. xliv: 'Ðeos wyrt ðe Grecas cotiledon 7 Romane umbilicum ueneris nemnað,' and ch. lviii: 'Ðeos wyrt þe man polion 7 oðrum naman [. . .] nemneð' (*Old English Herbarium*, ed. De Vriend, at pp. 90 and 102 respectively).
[44] Among the botanical terms Bierbaumer lists also the following words: *cyn*, 'kind', 'species'; *stenc*, 'smell' and *swæcc*, 'taste', 'flavour' (BW2, pp. 31, 110 and 115).
[45] The terminology I use for the categories of lexical interference in language is that suggested by H. Gneuss, 'Linguistic Borrowing and Old English Lexicography: Old English Terms for the Books of Liturgy', *Problems of Old English Lexicography. Studies in Memory of Angus Cameron*, ed. A. Bammesberger (Regensburg, 1985), pp. 107–29. Accordingly, a 'loan-formation' is 'a word consisting wholly or partly of native elements and newly formed in order to translate a foreign word' (p. 117). In this category there are three sub-categories: loan translations ('each element of the model must be reproduced by a semantically correspondent element in the borrowing language'), loan renditions (not all their elements correspond to the foreign model, 'but at least one semantically equivalent element is required in them') and loan creations ('none of the elements of a newly formed word corresponds to those of the word translated': *ibid*. p. 119). Gneuss's terminology is substantially based on that of Werner Betz and the English designations suggested by Einar Haugen and Uriel Weinreich, for which see

23

stratum of the original Germanic heritage,[46] implying that the Anglo-Saxons had begun to employ them only after the spread of medical practice based on the knowledge of Latin (and Greek) treatises. One example is *ribbe* (*Plantago lanceolata* Linn., 'ribwort', 'narrow-leaved plantain'), a weak feminine derived from OE *ribb*, 'rib'. The name is determined by the characteristic aspect of the leaves, which are marked by prominent parallel veins. Since the same characteristic determined many of the plant's Latin denominations – *septeneuria*, *eptapleuron*,[47] *quinqueneruia*, *nerualis*, *neruata*, *neruosa*[48] – there seems to be no reason to doubt that the Old English word is a loan-rendition where *ribb* corresponds to Latin *neruus*. In any case, only a few plant names belong to the original Germanic heritage. These are as follows: *bere*, 'barley' (*Hordeum vulgare* Linn.);[49] *bræmbel*, 'bramble' (*Rubus fructicosus* Linn.); *clæfre*, 'clover' (*Trifolium pratense* Linn.); *ellen*, 'elder' (*Sambucus nigra* Linn.); *fearn*, 'fern' (*Filix* Linn.); and *gorst*, 'gorse' (*Ulex europaeus* Linn.). By the same token, all the terms which denote the plant's component parts, fruits and seeds are of Germanic origin, for example: *æppel*, 'apple'; *bean*, 'bean'; *berge*, 'berry'; *blotsma*, 'blossom'; *leaf*, 'leaf' and others. There are two exceptions, namely the loanword *pil* ('prickle') from the Latin *pilum*, 'spear',[50] and the compound *hnescnyss* which translates Latin *mollities*, with the meaning of 'soft or inner part of the fruit'.[51] This term, a loan-translation with adjectival basis according to the correspondence Latin *mollis*/OE *hnesce*, 'nesh', 'soft', 'delicate', 'tender'[52] is rather interesting. In fact, in most of the recorded instances the word appears with a moral connotation; where *hnescness* denotes 'softness', 'delicacy', 'gentleness', 'weakness', 'want of vigour'. Its use to denote the inner part of a fruit is limited to the Old English

H. Schottmann, 'Die Beschreibung der Interferenz', *Sprachliche Interferenz. Festschrift für Werner Betz zum 65. Geburtstag*, ed. H. Kolb and H. Lauffer (Tübingen, 1977), pp. 13–55; D. Duckworth, 'Zur terminologischen und systematischen Grundlage der Forschung auf dem Gebiet der englisch-deutschen Interferenz', *ibid.* pp. 36–56; K. Toth, *Der Lehnwortschatz der althochdeutschen Tatian-Übersetzung* (Würzburg, 1980), ch. 1; R. Gusmani, *Saggi sull' interferenza linguistica*, 2 vols. (Florence, 1981–3).

46 There is little information on plants known in ancient times by the Germanic populations. Fundamental in this field are the following: J. Hoops, *Waldbäume und Kulturpflanzen* (Strassburg, 1905); H. Marzell, *Wörterbuch der deutschen Pflanzennamen*, 5 vols. (Leipzig, 1943); and E. Björkman, 'Die Pflanzennamen der althochdeutschen Glossen', *Zeitschrift für deutsche Wortforschung* 2 (1901), 202–33, 3 (1902), 263–307 and 6 (1904–5), 174–98.

47 *Pseudo-Apulei Herbarius*, ed. Howald and Sigerist, p. 25 (ch. i).

48 Cf. L. André, *Lexique des termes de botanique en latin* (Paris, 1956), p. 254 (*plantago*).

49 Cf. Hoops, *Waldbäume und Kulturpflanzen*, pp. 591–5.   50 Cf. BW 2, p. 92.

51 Cf. *Old English Herbarium*, ed. De Vriend, p. 232 (ch. clxxxv): 'Wið innodes astrynge genim þyses wæstmes hnescnysse innewearde butan þam cyrnlun' ('For motion of the bowels, take the soft part of the interior of this fruit without the kernel') and the corresponding Latin passage: 'Huius intestina mollities a semine separata . . .'

52 Cf. J. Bosworth and T. N. Toller, *An Anglo-Saxon Dictionary* (Oxford, 1898) and *Supplement*, by T. N. Toller (Oxford, 1921), ss. vv.

Herbarium and due perhaps to an extension of meaning favoured by the weak verb *hnescian*, 'become or make soft' and the adjective *hnesc*, 'soft', 'tender', which are commonly used in the Old English *Herbarium*.[53]

Loan words

On the other hand, foreign influence is very apparent in the botanical lexicon, with loan words being the most numerous class, representing almost twice the number of other types of formation. Loan words are generally integrated both phonemically and morphologically and treated as weak feminine nouns in -*e*:[54] *bete*, 'beet' (*Beta vulgaris* Linn.);[55] *coliandre*, 'coriander', 'coliander' (*Coriandrum sativum* Linn.); *petersilie*, 'parsley' (*Petroselinum hortense* Hoff.);[56] *pyse*, 'pea' (*Pisum sativum* Linn.); *rose*, 'rose' (*Rosa* Linn.),[57] and so on. There are, however, nouns which have been taken into other classes as well, such as *cawel*, 'colewort', 'cabbage' (*Brassica* Linn.), *cystel*, 'chestnut' (*Castanea sativa* Miller) and *finol*, 'fennel' (*Foeniculum vulgare* Miller).[58] Other loan words are *win*, 'wine', which appears also as first member in the compounds *wingeard*, 'vine' (*Vitis vinifera* Linn.) and *winberge*, 'grape';[59] and *ele* 'olive oil'[60] unless otherwise specified (cf. *amigdales ele*, 'almond oil', and *rosenan ele*, 'oil of roses').

If the integrated loans are the majority, there are, however, names which retain a Latin aspect but have Old English inflexional endings, such as *saluia* or *amidgal*: note 'genim þas wyrte ðe man saluian nemneð . . . genim þas ylcan wyrte salfian' (ch. ciii);[61] and 'gewyll hy wel mid amigdales ele' (ch. xiii).[62] There are others whose aspect is thoroughly Latin, although they are recorded in a purely Old English context, such as, for instance, *berbena* and its synonym *columbina*, or *lacterida*: 'Ðeos wyrt þe man peristereon 7 oðrum naman

---

53 For the verb see *Old English Herbarium*, ch. ii: 'hnescaþ hyt sona' ('it softens it soon'); ch. iv: 'lege to þære wunde swa oþþæt ða corn þurh þone wætan gehnehsode syn 7 swa toðundene' ('place it on the wound until the humour softens and swells the grains'); for the adjective, see ch. ii: 'Wring on hnesce wulle' ('wring up in soft wool'); ch. vi: 'Heo bið hnesceum leafum' ('it has soft leaves'); and ch. xv: 'Heo ys hnesce on æthrine' ('it is soft to touch').

54 Cf. A. Campbell, *Old English Grammar* (Oxford, 1959), pp. 218–19.

55 Cf. Hoops, *Waldbäume*, p. 601.   56 Cf. *ibid.* pp. 602–3.   57 Cf. *ibid.* p. 615.

58 Cf. Campbell, *Old English Grammar*, pp. 218–19.

59 The Latin term *vinum* passed into all Germanic languages. In English the loan *win* appears in approximately fifty compounds; see C. E. Fell, 'Old English *Beor*', *Leeds Stud. in English* ns 8 (1975), 76–95. For a list of medieval English vineyards, see W. Younger, *Men and Wine* (London, 1966), pp. 466–8.

60 For a history of cultivation of olive trees, see J. Hoops, *Geschichte des Ölbaums* (Heidelberg, 1944).

61 *Old English Herbarium*, ed. De Vriend, p. 148: 'Take the plant that is called sage . . . Take the same plant sage.'

62 *Ibid.* p. 58: 'Boil them well in almond oil.' *Amigdal* is recorded only twice in the Old English *Herbarium* and once in *Peri Didaxeon*; cf. BW2, p. 2.

berbenam nemneð, heo ys culfron swiðe hiwcuð, þanun hy eac sum þeodscipe columbinam hateð (ch. lxvii),[63] or 'Ðeos wyrt þe man titymallos calatites 7 oþrum naman lacteridam nemneþ' (ch. cx).[64] Were we to adopt Funke's system of classification, the former should be listed among 'learned loan words', the latter under the heading 'foreign words'.[65] Nevertheless, as Fred Robinson has warned, we ought to be very cautious about recognizing Latin words as borrowed elements in Old English, given the Anglo-Saxon habit of using Latin forms for the corresponding Old English words,[66] a habit which is also witnessed in the translator of the Old English *Herbarium*. Thus, for example, after giving the vernacular synonym of the plant he is describing in the first lines of the chapter, in the discussion of its virtues which follows he prefers the Latin name to the Old English one:

Ðeos wyrt þe man pollegium 7 oþrum naman dweorgedwosle nemneþ . . . Wiþ ðæs innoþes sare genim þas ylcan wyrte pollegium . . . Eft wið þæs magan sare genim þas sylfan wyrte pollegium (ch. xciv).[67]

There are, however, cases in which the Latin name seems to be used in order to denote a precise plant in opposition to other similar species; accordingly, as Helmut Gneuss has argued, it is difficult to consider such names as purely Latin and not, according to Funke's terminology, a 'foreign word'.[68] Such is the case of *lactuca*, 'lettuce', which is described as follows: 'þeos wyrt þe man

---

63 *Old English Herbarium*, ed. De Vriend, p. 110: 'The herb that is called *peristereon* and, by another name, *berbenam*. It is so familiar to pigeons, that some people call it *columbinam*.'

64 *Ibid.* p. 152: 'The herb that is called *titymallos calatites* and, by another name, *lacteridam*.' Bierbaumer reads *lacteridan* instead of *lacteridam*: BW2, p. 74.

65 O. Funke, *Die gelehrten lateinischen Lehn- und Fremdwörter in der altenglischen Literatur* (Halle, 1914). Funke's system is based on the knowledge of the inflexional paradigm of the loanword. Accordingly a 'learned loan word' appears with flexional Old English suffixes, while a 'foreign word' keeps its original Latin suffix. A third category, according to Funke, includes those loanwords which in the nominative singular keep the Latin ending, while in the oblique cases take Old English endings (*ibid*. p. 42). H. Gneuss stresses instead the importance of the speaker's usage in the classification of loan words (*Lehnbildungen und Lehnbedeutungen im Altenglischen* (Berlin, 1955), p. 19). There are in fact differences between 'a borrowed word that had become current in everyday English, or in some particular level or register of speech, and an apparent borrowing which turns out to be a scholar's whim or a translator's unsuccessful attempt at introducing a new term' (H. Gneuss, 'Some Problems and Principles of the Lexicography of Old English', *Festschrift für Karl Schneider*, ed. E. S. Dick and K. R. Jankowsky (Amsterdam and Philadelphia, 1982), pp. 152–68, at 154).

66 See in particular F. Robinson, 'Latin for Old English in Anglo-Saxon Manuscripts', *Language Form and Linguistic Variation. Papers Dedicated to Angus McIntosh*, ed. J. Anderson (Amsterdam, 1982), pp. 395–400.

67 *Old English Herbarium*, ed. De Vriend, pp. 136 and 138: 'The herb called *pollegium* and, by another name, pennyroyal . . . For abdominal pain take the same wort *pollegium* . . . Afterwards, for pain in the stomach, take the same wort *pollegium*.'

68 Gneuss, 'Linguistic Borrowing', p. 118.

lactucam leporinam 7 oþrum naman þam gelice lactucam nemneþ' (ch. cxiv).[69] *Lactucam* here is clearly a Latin form. Nevertheless, Bierbaumer proposes to consider it an error for *lactucan* because in the Old English *Herbarium*, one usually finds the Old English form in this position,[70] as in this example: 'Genim ðysse wyrte seaw þe man mentam 7 þam gelice oþrum naman mintan nemneð' (ch. cxxii).[71] As a matter of fact, there is in Old English a loan word *lactuca* not integrated in the phonological system of the language,[72] and recorded in the *Læceboc*[73] and in Ælfric's homilies,[74] side by side with *leahtric*, an older loan, perfectly integrated both morphologically and phonologically, and already attested in the first Cleopatra Glossary[75] and in the *Læceboc*.[76] The proof that the translator of the Old English *Herbarium* knew this form lies in the fact that, when he had to translate *lactuca siluatica*, he used the compound *wudulectric*,[77] a loan translation in which *wudu* corresponds to Latin *siluaticus*. We may therefore assume that he knew the difference between *lactuca siluatica* (*Lactuca scariola* Linn.) and *lactuca leporina* (*Lactuca virosa* Linn.), and used the name *lactuca* for the latter because it was already an accepted term to denote some kind of lettuce.[78].

One of the most difficult problems in the study of plant names is the identification of the plant itself, which the very name often helps to obscure. Excellent work has been done by Peter Bierbaumer in this field, too. However, there are cases which present almost insuperable difficulties of identification, and the Old English name of the plant is accordingly difficult or impossible to explain. Consider, for example, the term *galluc* or *galloc*, which in the Old English *Herbarium* designates *herba confirma* ('comfrey', *Symphytum officinale*

---

[69] *Old English Herbarium*, ed. De Vriend, p. 156: 'The herb called *lactucam leporinam* and, by another name, similarly, *lactucam*.'

[70] BW2, p. 75.

[71] *Old English Herbarium*, ed. De Vriend, p. 162: 'Take the juice of the herb that people call *mentam* or, with the same name, mint.'

[72] Cf. Funke, *Die gelehrten lateinischen Lehn- und Fremdwörter*, pp. 66–7, 109, 116, 140, 159 and 169.

[73] 'Lactucas, þæt is leahtric'; 'him is to sellanne lactucas . . .' and 'mid lactucan' (*Læceboc*, ed. Leonhardi, I, xvi; xxiii and xxxvi).

[74] 'Mid feldlicere lactucan'; 'mid . . . feldlicum lactucum'; and 'lactuca hatte seo wyrt þe hi etan sceoldon' (*The Homilies of the Anglo-Saxon Church. The First Part, Containing the Sermones Catholici, or Homilies of Ælfric*, ed. B. Thorpe, 2 vols. (London, 1843–6) II, 264 and 278). According to Funke (*Die gelehrten lateinischen Lehn- und Fremdwörter*, p. 67) the source is the Vulgate Exodus XII.9: 'cum lactucis agrestibus'.

[75] Stryker, 'The Latin–Old English Glossary in Ms Cotton Cloepatra A. iii', L 70; WW I, 432,7.

[76] For the occurrences, see BW1, p. 95.

[77] 'Ðeos wyrt þe man lactucan silfaticam 7 oðrum naman wudulectric nemneð' (*Old English Herbarium*, ch. xxxi, ed. De Vriend, p. 76: 'The herb called *lactucan silfaticam* or, by another name, wood lettuce').

[78] For similar cases, in another semantic field, cf. Gneuss, 'Linguistic Borrowing', p. 118.

Linn.),[79] whereas in the Epinal–Erfurt Glossary and in the Corpus Glossary it translates the Latin headword *galla*, 'gall-nut'.[80] In this second case *galluc* is apparently a loan word from the Latin *galla*, a loan word integrated morphologically by the substitution of the original Latin suffix with the native suffix *-uc, -oc* (a suffix which is used in Old English, Old Low German and Old Dutch in the formation of plant and animal names).[81] As for the translation of *confirma* or its synonym *symphytum*,[82] on the other hand, Förster and Holthausen[83] consider *galloc* to be a neologism based on another loan word, *gealla* ('gall', a blister or painful swelling especially on horses), according to a normal process in the formation of plant names in which the plant is designated by one of its characteristic features. As a matter of fact, in popular medicine comfrey was renowned for its 'virtue' of mending broken bones and healing wounds, whence its Greek and Latin names, *symphytum* from the verb *symphuo* 'I reunite' and *confirma*, *consol(i)da* 'the plant that heals, that reunites'.[84] The same process, according to these scholars, lies behind the neologism *galloc*, that is, 'the plant that cures galls'. However, comfrey is never used in prescriptions for horse galls.[85] Yet if the synonyms given in the Latin text of pseudo-Apuleius (in the chapter dedicated to the *herba confirma*) are taken into consideration, it is clear that, in addition to *sinfitum*, *confirma*, *conserua* and *pecte*, the plant is also

---

79 'Ðeos wyrt þe man confirmam 7 oðrum naman galluc nemneð' (*Old English Herbarium*, ch. lx, ed. De Vriend, p. 102: 'The herb called *confirmam* or, by another name, comfrey').

80 'Galla: *galluc*' (*Old English Glosses in the Epinal–Erfurt Glossary*, ed. Pheifer, line 466); 'galla: *galluc*' (*The Corpus Glossary*. ed. Lindsay, line 969 (G 7)).

81 Cf. H. Krahe and W. Meid, *Germanische Sprachwissenschaft*, 3 vols. (Berlin, 1967) III, 211–12. On morphological integration of loan words, see Gusmani, *Saggi sull'interferenza linguistica* I, 29–71.

82 'Sinfitum: *gallac*' (Brussells Glossary: WW I, 299, 20); 'confirma: *galloc*' and 'sumphitum: *galluc*' (Durham Glossary: *Das Durhamer Pflanzenglossar*, ed. von Lindheim, nn. 129 and 313, respectively); 'adriaca .i. confirma uel *galloc*' and 'confirma: *galluc*' (Laud Glossary: *The Laud Herbal Glossary*, ed. Stracke, nn. 162 and 345 respectively); 'confirie .i. *galluc*' (Dresden, Sächsische Landesbibliothek, Dc. 187 + 160 + 186 + 185, ptd H.D. Meritt, 'Old English Glosses, Mostly Dry Point', *JEGP* 60 (1961), 441–50, at p. 73a,4: 'cumfiria .i. *galloc*'); see also WW I, 555, 4.

83 Cf. Förster, 'Die altenglische Glossenhandschrift Plantinus 32 (Antwerpen) und Additional 32246 (London)', p. 126 (n. 176); F. Holthausen, *Altenglisches etymologisches Wörterbuch* (Heidelberg, 1934), p. 125 (s. v. *gealloc*).

84 André, *Lexique des termes de botanique en latin*, p. 99 (s. vv. *conserua*, *confirma* and *consol(i)da*).

85 Cf. *Læceboc* I, lxxxviii: 'Gif hors geallede sie, nim æþelferdingwyrt 7 gotwoþan 7 mageþan, gecnua wel, do buteran to, wring wætende þurh clað, do hwit sealt on, hrer swiþe, lacna þone geallan mid. Wiþ horses geallan nim æscþrotan 7 gotwoþan uferwearde 7 bogen eac swa, cnua tosomne, wyl on rysle 7 on buteran, aseoh þurh clað, swire mid' (*Læceboc*, ed. Leonhardi, p. 47: 'If a horse be galled, take *æþelferdingwyrt* and *gotwope* and camomile, pound well, add butter, when still wet wring it through a cloth, add white salt, shake thoroughly, cure the gall with it. For horse galls. Take *æscþrotan* and the upper part of *gotwope* and rosemary in equal quantities, pound together, boil in fat and in butter, strain through a cloth, anoint with it').

designated by *alum Gallicum*, often corrupted to *anagallicum*, *algallicum* or *anugallicum*.[86] *Galloc*, therefore, with the meaning of 'comfrey', might be another loan word, more recent in its introduction than *galloc* from Latin *galla*, which is attested earlier. The existence of *galloc* with a different referent did not necessarily hinder the reintroduction of the loan word with a new meaning, therefore. It is not rare for the same name to be used to designate different plants. Moreover, the relative similarity in form of the Latin models *galla* and *anagallum*, or *alum Gallicum*, may have encouraged the re-use of *galloc*, perhaps already familiar as a plant name.[87]

Loan formation

If it is difficult to identify direct borrowings, it is even more problematic to distinguish other types of loans because, in this case, as Gneuss observes, 'there are very few absolutely safe criteria for the identification of . . . indirect loans'.[88] Nevertheless almost all categories of loan formations are represented in the Old English botanical lexicon, although semantic loans seem to be very rare and limited to words referring to parts of the plants, such as *meolc*, 'milk', to denote the milky sap of some plants, or *codd*, usually 'bag' or 'sack', which in the Old English *Herbarium* translates Latin *folliculus*, 'husk', 'pod'.[89] However, on occasions when the Latin plant name was found to be analysable at both the semantic and the formal level, the Old English translator preferred a loan translation. Examples of loan translations are the following: *fifleave*, from 'quinquefolium' (*Potentilla reptans* Linn., 'cinquefoil'); *hundes heafod*, from 'canis caput' (*Antirrhinum orontium* Linn., 'small snap-dragon', 'calf-snout'); *hundes tunge*, from 'cynoglossum' (*Cynoglossum off.* Linn., 'hound's tongue', 'dog's tongue'); *seofonleafe*, from 'eptafillon', 'septifolium' (*Potentilla erecta* Räuschel, 'common tormentil'); or *eorþifig*, from 'hedera terrestris' (*Glechoma hederaceum* Linn., 'ground-ivy', 'ale-hoof'). There are even loan translations on loan words, such as *wudulectric*, from 'lactuca siluatica' (*Lactuca* Linn., 'prickly lettuce'); *brocminte*, from 'mentha aquatica' (*Mentha aquatica* Linn., 'water-mint', 'brook-mint'); *leonfot*, from 'pes leonis' (*Alchemilla vulgaris* Linn., 'lady's mantle'). Loan renditions include, for example, the following words: *attorlaþe*, from 'venenifuga' (*Panicum crus galli* Linn., 'cockspur-grass'), cf. *attor*, 'poi-

---

[86] 'A Graecis dicitur sinfitum, alii confirma, alii conserua, alii pecte, alii alum Gallicum' (*Pseudo-Apulei Herbarius*, ed. Howald and Sigerist, p. 113); see also André, *Lexique*, p. 25 (s. v. *alum*).

[87] For a full discussion see M. A. D'Aronco, 'Inglese antico *galluc*', *AIUON* 28–9 (1985–6), 83–100 and, for another plant name, *elehtre*, 'Divergenze e convergenze lessicali in inglese antico: il caso di *elehtre*', *Romanobarbarica* 10 (1987–8), forthcoming.

[88] Gneuss, 'Some Problems and Principles of the Lexicography of Old English', p. 155.

[89] *Codd* survives in modern English in the dialectal word *peascod*, 'pea-shell'.

son'; *beowyrt*, from 'apiastrum, apiago' (*Melissa off.* Linn., 'sweet balm'), based on the correspondence of Latin *apis* and OE *beo*, 'bee'; *hreodbedd*, 'reed-bed', from 'arundinetum' (cf. *hreod* 'reed', and Latin *arundo*).

Alongside these, however, are names for which precise models in Greek and Latin are not identifiable. Within this category it is necessary to distinguish between the terms for which Latin or Greek models provided the motivation (even if they do not display any precise formal or semantic relation with that model) and those neologisms which seem to be entirely autonomous creations in Old English.

Among the innovations which were stimulated, even if indirectly, by the knowledge of Greek and Latin medicine and botany, one may note the compound *wedeberge* which translates the Latin *elleborum album* (*Veratrum album* Linn., 'white hellebore'). The Old English compound does not correspond either formally or semantically to its Latin model. Nevertheless its first element *wede*, 'lunatic', 'crazy' (cf. OE *wod*, 'madness') finds some justification in the belief which in classical antiquity associated *elleborum* with madness.[90]

For many plant names, however, no foreign model has been found. These are generally nouns which describe their respective referent. The plants were therefore denoted by means of various striking features. Those which describe the plant's appearance include: *brunwyrt*, 'splenion' (*Asplenium ceterach* Linn. or *Phyllitis scolopendrium* Newman, 'finger-fern', 'spleenwort' or 'hart's-tongue'), so named because of the greenish-brown colour of its flowers; *feltwyrt*, 'verbascum' (*Verbascum thapsus* Linn., 'great mullein'): the plant has felt-like leaves, thick and covered with a sort of white down; *hræfnes fot*, 'chamaedafne' (*Ranunculus ficaria* Linn., 'lesser celandine', 'figwort', 'pilewort'), so named because of the shape of its palmate or webbed leaf, which looks like crow or raven claws. Nouns which describe the plant's properties include: *clufþung*, 'scelerata' (*Ranunculus sceleratus* Linn., 'celery-leaved crowfoot'), a kind of clove which is very poisonous; *clufwyrt*, 'batracion' (*Ranunculus acer* Linn. or R. *bulbosus* Linn., 'tall crowfoot' or 'bulbous buttercup'). Sometimes the name denotes the place where they grow or the animals associated with them, as, for example, the following: *mucgwyrt*, 'artemisia' (*Artemisia vulgaris* Linn., 'mugwort'): the plant attracts midges; *eoforfearn*, 'radiola' (*Polypodium vulgare* Linn.), a fern to which wild boar are attracted by the sweetish flavour of its rhizome; *wegbræde*, 'arniglosa' (*Plantago major* Linn., 'waybread', 'great plantago'): the plant grows on the border of the roads and has wide leaves; and *wæterwyrt*, 'gallitricus' (*Callitriche verna* Linn., 'water starwort' or *Asplenium trichomanes* Linn., 'common maidenhair'): the plant grows near the water. Or

---

[90] Cf. E. von Erhardt-Siebold, 'The Hellebore in Anglo-Saxon Pharmacy', *Englische Studien* 71 (1936–7), 161–70.

the name may denote other characteristics of the plant, such as flavour, oiliness, and so on: thus *smeorowyrt*, 'aristolochia' (*Aristolochia rotunda* Linn., 'heartwort', 'birthwort'), a plant widely used in the preparation of ointments.

This type of terminology clearly implies the Anglo-Saxons' direct knowledge of the plants. Contrary to the opinion of Charles Singer, who described the entire corpus of Anglo-Saxon medical texts as 'the darkest and deliquescent stage of a [*sic*] outdated culture',[91] recent studies have demonstrated not only the Anglo-Saxons' extensive knowledge of medicine but also their ability to recognize and use the herbs of Mediterranean and Middle Eastern origin mentioned in herbals and medical treatises.[92] These herbs arrived in England both 'in not-for-profit exchange and by way of commercial trade',[93] or were grown there in the most sheltered parts of monastic herb gardens, like the one in Ely, known from the seventh century on, or like that at Thorney, not far from Ely.[94] Perhaps it should be remembered that these two monasteries are not distant from Bury St Edmunds, where the famous Latin manuscript of the pseudo-Apuleius herbal (now Oxford, Bodleian Library, Bodley 130) was copied and illuminated.[95]

CONCLUSIONS

From the comparison of the Latin text of the *Herbarium Pseudo-Apulei* with its Old English translation, the autonomy of the Anglo-Saxon translator *vis-à-vis* his model becomes apparent, not only because he condensed three separate treatises into a single text, following a uniform pattern and omitting all inessential information, but also because of the way he translated the individual names of the plants. This is particularly evident when the Latin and Old

---

[91] C. Singer, 'Introduction' to the reprint of Cockayne's *Leechdoms, Wortcunning and Starcraft of Early England* (London, 1961) I, i–xlvii, at xlvii.

[92] See above, nn. 1, 2 and 37. [93] Voigts, 'Anglo-Saxon Plant Remedies', p. 259.

[94] Although we do not have records of the herb-gardens of English monasteries, the so-called St Gallen plan can by analogy give some idea of monastic organization for the cure of the sick. As it appears in the plan, the medical garden (*herbularius*) lies in the north-east corner of the monastic site, and is adjacent to the *domus medicorum*, the house of the physicians. It is a small garden, surrounded by a wall or fence, divided into sixteen plots, each distinguished by the name of a medical plant: see W. Horn and C. W. Jones, *The Plan of St. Gall*, 3 vols. (Berkeley and London, 1979) II, 175–84. On the plan of St Gall which, according to B. Bischoff (*Mittelalterlichen Studien*, 3 vols. (Stuttgart, 1966–81) I, 41–9) was copied at Reichenau, see also W. Horn, 'On the Origins of the Medieval Cloister', *Gesta* 12 (1973), 13–53; P. Jung, 'Das Infirmarium im Bauriss des Klosters von St. Gallen vom Jahre 820', *Gesnerus* 6 (1949), 1–8, figs. 1–2; G. Noll, 'The Origin of the so-called Plan of St. Gall', *JMH* 8 (1982), 191–240.

[95] Described by N. R. Ker, *Catalogue of Manuscripts Containing Anglo-Saxon* (Oxford, 1957), no. 302. For the facsimile, see *The Herbal of Apuleius Barbarus from the Early Twelfth-Century Manuscript formerly in the Abbey of Bury St. Edmunds (MS. Bodley 130)*, ed. R. T. Gunther, Roxburghe Club Publ. 182 (London, 1925).

English terms are analysable at both the semantic and the formal level: for instance, *hundes tunge*, 'dog's tongue' (a loan translation whose model is Latin *lingua canis, cynoglossum*),[96] which instead translates Latin *lingua bubula*, 'ox-tongue': 'Ðeos wyrt þe Grecas buglossam 7 Romane lingua bubula nemnað 7 eac Engle glofwyrt 7 oðrum naman hundes tunge hатað' (ch. xlii).[97] It is obvious that the translator – unlike Æthelwold, when he tackled the translation of the *Regula S. Benedicti*[98] – was not called upon to create a new terminology but already knew the native equivalents of names which appear in his source. In effect, already by the eighth century glosses from the *Hermeneumata medico-botanica* had been taken over into the Latin–Old English glossaries.[99] The number of such glosses was destined to increase in later glossaries, and it is worth noting that in the *Læceboc*, compiled towards the end of the ninth century, a large number of the names of the herbs of the Old English *Herbarium* are already attested.[100]

The most relevant fact to emerge from this analysis is that the botanical terminology of the Old English *Herbarium*, as regards the names of plants, consists largely of loan words, loan translations and loan renditions, while the terminology related to the parts of plants, the fruits and seeds, is mostly Germanic. This situation is understandable, given that a large number of the plants described in the herbals are of Mediterranean or eastern origin. Nevertheless, as has been seen, numerous plant names remain which designate both native and foreign plants and which are analysable as autonomous creations in Old English. These are compounds created according to a pattern based on taxonomic categories; in effect, they provide a summary description of the plant by reference to what are considered its salient features. These categories are relatively uniform, as may be seen from the adoption of certain terms, such as, for the first element, *wudu-* to designate a woodland or wild species (*wudulectric* to translate 'lactuca siluatica', 'prickly lettuce'; *wudupistel* for 'cardus siluaticus', 'sow-thistle'); or *cluf(u)-*, which indicates a species with serrated leaves (*clufþunge* or *clufþung*, *Ranunculus sceleratus* Linn., 'celery-leaved crowfoot'; *clufwyrt*, *Ranunculus acer* Linn., 'buttercup');[101] or, as second ele-

---

96 Cf. André, *Lexique*, pp. 112 (s.v. *cynoglossum*) and 188 (s.v. *lingua canis*).

97 *Old English Herbarium*, ed. De Vriend, p. 88: 'The herb that the Greeks call *buglossam*, the Romans *lingua bubula*, and the English call *glofwyrt* or, by another name, dog's tongue.'

98 Cf. H. Gneuss, 'The Origin of Standard Old English and Æthelwold's School at Winchester', *ASE* 1 (1972), 63–83, esp. 74–9; M. Gretsch, 'Æthelwold's Translation of the *Regula Sancti Benedicti* and Its Latin Exemplar', *ASE* 3 (1974), 125–51, and *Die 'Regula Sancti Benedicti' in England und ihre altenglische Übersetzung* (Munich, 1973), pp. 235–306, for a discussion of Æthelwold's technique of translation.

99 Cf. *Old English Glosses in the Epinal–Erfurt Glossary*, ed. Pheifer, pp. xliv–xlv.

100 Cf. BW2.

101 The same name could also denote *Ranunculus bulbosus* Linn., 'bulbous buttercup', cf. BW2, p. 25.

ment, *-corn* to indicate seeds (*gipcorn, Daphne laureola* Linn., 'spurge laurel'; *piporcorn*, 'peppercorn'; *sundcorn, Saxifraga granulata* Linn., 'saxifrage'); *-berge* for berry-like fruits (*streawberge, Fragaria vesca* Linn., 'wild strawberry'; *winberie*, 'grape'); or *-wyrt* to denote a herbaceous species, stressing the positive qualities of the plant, whereas *-þung* is used to designate a poisonous herb (besides *clufwyrt* and *clufþung*, there are, for instance, *banwyrt, Viola tricolor* Linn., 'heartsease' or 'wild pansy', which was used for healing wounds and bones; *ellenwyrt, Sambucus ebulus* Linn., 'dwarf elder', an herbaceous plant, in opposition to *ellen, Sambucus nigra* L., 'elder', which is a bush).

The abilty to create compounds to express new objects or concepts is one of the most characteristic features of the Germanic languages. Nevertheless, the structural homogeneity of these new formations, which are mostly descriptive and whose model is to be found in the Greek treatises, leads one to suppose that even these creations were stimulated by the knowledge which the Anglo-Saxons possessed of Greek and Latin botanical terminology, which they had learned in turn through the study of Latin herbals and medical treatises.[102]

[102] This research was made possible by grants from the Ministero Pubblica Istruzione, Italy. I should like to express my gratitude to Michael Lapidge who kindly helped me far beyond his editorial duties.

Ælfric's use of etymologies

JOYCE HILL

Augustine, Jerome, Bede, Gregory, Smaragdus and Haymo, the exegetical authorities acknowledged by Ælfric in the Latin preface to the *Catholic Homilies*,[1] frequently used etymologies as one of their techniques for penetrating the words of the biblical text in order to arrive at their spiritual essence. To the modern student of language their interpretations often seem arbitrary, even bizarre, but the idea that there was an intimate connection between the signifying name and the person, place or thing signified was well established within the scriptural canon and was extended and confirmed by the cumulative authority of the exegetes themselves. It was Isidore of Seville, in his *Etymologies*, who provided the most systematic definition of this tradition of etymologizing.[2] As he explained it, it was a method for determining the true essence of the thing designated by the process of penetrating its appellation, since all things and all activities which were named 'secundum naturam' (as opposed to those arbitrarily named 'secundum placitum') were designated by those words which had etymologies enshrining the very quality or idea so designated. Given this definition, with its underlying philosophical and linguistic assumptions, it is easy to understand why etymologies were exploited in Christian exegesis and teaching. It was accepted that biblical names were in the category 'secundum naturam' since they were God-given or at least divinely sanctioned, and the rationale and method of their penetration had the advantage of harmonizing closely with the general interpretative process that was employed.

Ælfric stood firmly within this tradition and made frequent use of etymologies in his exegetical homilies. Time and again, in his orthodox interpretation of the lection, he simply repeated the etymologies of the bible, where names were often interpreted, or the etymologies of his source text. Inevitably, and indeed properly from Ælfric's point of view, his etymologies were derivative,

---

[1] *The Homilies of the Anglo-Saxon Church: the First Part containing the Sermones Catholici or Homilies of Ælfric*, 2 vols., ed. B. Thorpe (London, 1844–6) I, I.

[2] *Isidori Hispalensis Episcopi Etymologiarum sive originum libri XX*, ed. W. M. Lindsay, 2 vols. (Oxford, 1911) I.xxix. For discussion of Isidore's definitions, see J. Engels, 'La Portée de l'étymologique isidorienne', *SM* 3rd ser. 3 (1962), 99–128, and G. de Poerck, 'Etymologia et origo à travers la tradition latine', *ANAMNHCIC: Gedenkboek Prof. Dr. E. A. Leemans* (Bruges, 1970), pp. 191–228, esp. 212–19.

as we can see from the studies by Hanspeter Schelp and Fred C. Robinson.[3] But it is precisely our awareness of Ælfric's careful reliance on Latin authorities and our ability to identify his sources that enable us to go further, to determine the nature and extent of his commitment to etymologies as a didactic technique and to assess whether his evident interest in words and their meanings was typical of Anglo-Saxon homilists, or whether it was yet another symptom of Ælfric's personal intellectual position, which set him apart, as he himself recognized, from many other vernacular writers.[4]

In the Palm Sunday homily from the First Series of *Catholic Homilies* (*CH* I xiv) Ælfric offers the standard interpretations of Sion as 'Sceawung-stow' and of Jerusalem as 'Sibbe gesihð'.[5] Two sources have so far been identified for this homily. One was by Bede, which was included in the homiliary of Paulus Diaconus, a collection much used by Ælfric; the other was by Haymo, who apparently used Bede as his own major source, although he included variations which were reflected by Ælfric.[6] There is thus a fair degree of similarity between the two source texts, and for much of Ælfric's homily it is impossible to be sure which he was following. For the etymologies, however, the situation is clear. Bede etymologized Jerusalem, but Haymo did not, and neither provided an etymology for Sion, although both used the name and equated it with Jerusalem. Ælfric at this point chose to follow Bede, where there was an etymology for Jerusalem, and then went beyond both his major sources in adding the etymology of Sion.

The preceding homily, for the Feast of the Annunciation (*CH* I xiii), provides a similar set of examples. Förster and Smetana have identified two

---

[3] H. Schelp, 'Die Deutungstradition in Ælfrics Homiliae Catholicae', *ASNSL* 196 (1959), 273–95, and F. C. Robinson, 'The Significance of Names in Old English Literature', *Anglia* 86 (1968), 14–58, esp. 16–24. The problem with the study by T. M. Pearce ('Name Patterns in Ælfric's *Catholic Homilies*', *Names* 14 (1966), 150–6) is that it shows no awareness of Ælfric's indebtedness to specific sources.

[4] The point is clearly made in the Old English preface to the *Catholic Homilies*, throughout both series of homilies in Ælfric's observations on what he regards as unreliable, sensational or otherwise problematic material, and in the concluding prayer to the Second Series. For the First Series, see *The Homilies of the Anglo-Saxon Church*, ed. Thorpe; for the Second Series, see *Ælfric's Catholic Homilies: the Second Series, Text*, ed. M. Godden, EETS ss 5 (London, 1979). A similar attitude is to be found elsewhere in Ælfric's work.

[5] *The Homilies of the Anglo-Saxon Church*, ed. Thorpe, I, 210.

[6] *Bedae Venerabilis opera. Pars III: Opera homiletica*. ed. D. Hurst, CCSL 122 (Turnhout, 1955), 200–6, first identified by M. Förster, 'Über die Quellen von Ælfrics exegetischen Homiliae Catholicae', *Anglia* 16 (1894), 1–61, at 21–2, and shown by C. L. Smetana to have been known to Ælfric through its inclusion in the homiliary of Paulus Diaconus ('Ælfric and the Early Medieval Homiliary', *Traditio* 15 (1959), 163–204, at 188–9); and Haymo, *Homiliae de Tempore*, PL 118, cols, 353–8, identified by C. L. Smetana, 'Ælfric and the Homiliary of Haymo of Halberstadt', *Traditio* 17 (1961), 457–69, at 459–60, including brief comment on Haymo's dependence on Bede.

Bedan homilies as Ælfric's sources, both of which occurred in the homiliary of Paulus Diaconus, although for the Wednesday and Friday of the Ember Week before Christmas and not for the Annunciation.[7] The first of Bede's homilies gave the etymology of Gabriel ('fortitudo Dei'), the second the etymology of Israel ('uir uidens Deum'); neither etymologized Jacob, although the first homily discussed his typological significance in some detail. Ælfric used both etymologies available to him for Gabriel ('Godes strengð') and Israel ('God geseonde'), drawing one from each major source, and to these he added the etymology of Jacob ('Forscrencend'),[8] meaning 'supplanter', as Robinson has pointed out,[9] and not 'withering' as mistakenly translated by Thorpe.[10] Ælfric's etymology, not surprisingly, was the standard one, listed by Jerome in his *Liber interpretationis hebraicorum nominum*.[11] It was neither idiosyncratic, as Pearce had believed on the basis of Thorpe's confusion of *forscrincend* and *forscrencend*,[12] nor is it attributable to folk etymology, as Schelp had rather desperately suggested.[13]

Another First Series homily which illustrates Ælfric's commitment to etymologies is that for the first Sunday in Lent (*CH* I xi). The major source, identified by Förster, was a Gregorian homily which was used for the same occasion in the homiliary of Paulus Diaconus,[14] but, since it did not include the interpretation of 'Nyðer-hreosende' which Ælfric provided for Satan's name, Förster attributed this etymology to Jerome's commentary on Ephesians.[15] In fact its probable immediate source, as Smetana has since shown, was a homily by Haymo.[16] What this example demonstrates, however, is not simply that Ælfric, as elsewhere, drew upon a minor source to provide an etymology, but that he regarded etymologies as a matter of serious scholarly concern. His homily, in the authoritative manuscript printed by Thorpe (Cambridge,

---

[7] Bede, *Opera homiletica*, ed. Hurst, pp. 14–20 and 21–31, identified by Förster, 'Über de Quellen', p. 20, and shown by Smetana, 'Ælfric and the Early Medieval Homiliary', p. 188, to have been available through the homiliary of Paulus Diaconus (which, however, did not have the Feast of the Annunciation).

[8] *The Homilies of the Anglo-Saxon Church*, ed. Thorpe, I, 196 (Gabriel) and 198 (Israel and Jacob).

[9] 'Names', p. 18, n. 11.

[10] *The Homilies of the Anglo-Saxon Church*, ed. Thorpe, I, 199. The mistranslation is repeated, *ibid.* p. 587.

[11] Ed. P. de Lagarde, CCSL 72 (Turnhout, 1959), 67, 'Iacob subplantator'.

[12] 'Name Patterns', p. 155. Thorpe's second mistranslation (see above, n. 10) evidently prompted Pearce's comment, although no reference is given.

[13] 'Die Deutungstradition', p. 291, n. 46.

[14] Gregory, *XL Homiliarum in evangelia*, PL 76, cols. 1135–8, identified by Förster, 'Über die Quellen', p. 11. Its availability in the homiliary of Paulus Diaconus was pointed out by Smetana, 'Ælfric and the Early Medieval Homiliary', pp. 187–8.

[15] 'Über die Quellen', p. 44.

[16] 'Ælfric and the Homiliary of Haymo of Halberstadt', p. 462. The homily is in PL 118 at cols. 190–203.

University Library, Gg. 3. 28), precedes the vernacular explanation of Satan's name with a short passage in Latin which includes the etymology of Satan ('Deorsum ruens') and a discussion, taken from later in Haymo's homily, of the reliability of the reading 'Uade retro Satanas' as opposed to its variant 'Uade' and of the difference between 'Uade retro' addressed by Christ to Satan and 'Uade retro me' addressed by Christ to Peter.[17] This note, like others in this manuscript, was probably incorporated into the body of the text by a scribe who was copying, either directly or indirectly, a manuscript to which Ælfric had added a number of observations, prompted perhaps by comments and questions from Archbishop Sigeric, to whom the *Catholic Homilies* were dedicated.[18] It is obvious that Ælfric regarded etymologies as didactically useful, but it is equally obvious from this example that he also regarded them as a proper subject for precise and learned consideration.

It is evident, then, that Ælfric used etymologies with some deliberation, not always contenting himself with merely repeating what was in his major source, but sometimes adding standard etymological interpretations, or exercising a preference for the more etymological of two sources. The former practice is well illustrated by the First Series homily for the Feast of St Andrew (*CH* I xxxviii), where Ælfric listed the first four apostles and gave the etymological interpretation for each independently of his exegetical source.[19] The latter practice is exemplified by the Second Series homily for the Second Sunday after Epiphany (*CH* II iv), in which Ælfric included etymologies for Cana, Galilee, Babylon and Jerusalem, following his supplementary source, Haymo, rather than his main one, Bede, who interpreted only the first three.[20]

---

17 *The Homilies of the Anglo-Saxon Church*, ed. Thorpe, I, 172. Ælfric brings together material from PL 118, cols. 198 and 201–2.

18 For a list of the Latin notes in this manuscript, see N.R. Ker, *Catalogue of Manuscripts Containing Anglo-Saxon* (Oxford, 1957), p. 13. Their origin is discussed by Godden, *Ælfric's Catholic Homilies*, p. lxxxiii.

19 The source of Ælfric's exegesis of the calling of Andrew has been identified by C.R. Davis, 'Two New Sources for Ælfric's *Catholic Homilies*', *JEGP* 41 (1942), 510–13, as a homily by Gregory, but it has no etymologies. Ælfric's comments on the apostles' names stand as a postscript, introduced with the words, 'We habbað nu ðyses godspelles traht be dæle oferurnen, nu wylle we eow secgan ða getacnunge ðæra feowera apostola namena, þe Crist æt fruman geceas' (*The Homilies of the Anglo-Saxon Church*, ed. Thorpe, I, 586). The etymologies of Andrew ('ðegenlic') and John ('Godes gifu') were standard. The etymologies of the other three names are not as strange as they at first appear: for Jacob/James ('forscrencend'), see above, p. 37 and nn. 8–13, and for Simon ('gehyrsum') and Peter ('oncnawende'), see Robinson, 'Names', pp. 23–4 and 17–18.

20 *Ælfric's Catholic Homilies*, ed. Godden, pp. 30 (Cana and Galilee) and 37 (Babylon and Jerusalem). The Bedan source, identified by Förster, 'Über die Quellen', p. 22, is in *Opera homiletica*, ed. Hurst, at pp. 95–104. As Smetana noted ('Ælfric and the Early Medieval Homiliary', p. 196), it was available in the homiliary of Paulus Diaconus. The homily by

The careful rhetorical emphasis that Ælfric often gave to an etymology, sometimes following the suggestion of his source, sometimes acting independently of it, is a further sign of his interest and commitment. An example of rhetorical elaboration in imitation of the source text is in the Easter Sunday homily from the First Series of *Catholic Homilies* (*CH* I xv), where the standard etymology of Galilee, 'Ofer-færeld', was taken from the Gregorian source and was then woven into the text in a variety of nominal and verbal forms ('wæs afaren', 'farað', 'færelde'), just as Gregory had woven into his homily forms of 'transmigratio' and 'transmigrare'.[21] In the homily on St Stephen in the First Series (*CH* I iii) we have, by contrast, a text in which Ælfric went beyond his source, sharpening the etymological focus and elaborating the rhetoric. The homily of Fulgentius, which Smetana identified as Ælfric's source, via the homiliary of Paulus Diaconus,[22] alluded to the appropriateness of Stephen's name, but did not articulate the observation as an etymology. Ælfric, however, made an explicit etymological point, which he went on to develop didactically: 'Stephanus is Grecisc nama, þæt is on Læden, Coronatus, þæt we cweðað on Englisc, Gewuldorbeagod; forðan ðe he hæfð þone ecan wuldorbeah, swa swa his nama him forwitegode.'[23] Then, at the end of the homily, having once more named the saint as 'Stephanus', he elaborated rhetorically on the etymology of the name, as Fulgentius had not, emphasizing the glory of Stephen's martyrdom by juxtaposing 'gewuldorbeagod', 'wuldor' and 'wuldrað'.

Striking as such instances are, it is the treatment of the image of 'Christus medicus' and the use and interpretation of 'Hælend' that most clearly illustrates Ælfric's awareness of the rhetorical and didactic value of etymologies. The image of Christ the physician, the saviour who brings spiritual health to those wounded by sin, is well established in Christian teaching and was common in the Latin source texts available to Anglo-Saxon writers. Frequently, as in the second of Pope's *Homilies of Ælfric*, where Ælfric's source for

---

Haymo, identified by Smetana, 'Ælfric and the Homiliary of Haymo of Halberstadt', pp. 463–4, is in PL 118 at cols. 126–37.

[21] *The Homilies of the Anglo-Saxon Church*, ed. Thorpe, I, 224. The source, identified by Förster, 'Über die Quellen', p. 2, and shown by Smetana, 'Ælfric and the Early Medieval Homiliary', p. 189, to have been available via the homiliary of Paulus Diaconus, is in PL 76, at cols. 1169–74.

[22] *Sancti Fulgentii Episcopi Rupensis opera*, ed. J. Fraipont, CCSL 91A (Turnhout, 1968), 905–9, identified by Smetana, 'Ælfric and the Early Medieval Homiliary', pp. 183–4. For further comment on the sources of this homily, see J. E. Cross, 'Ælfric and the Medieval Homiliary – Objection and Contribution', *Scripta minora Regiae Societatis Litterarum Lundensis* 4 (1961–2), 18–20.

[23] *The Homilies of the Anglo-Saxon Church*, ed. Thorpe, I, 50. 'Stephanus is a Greek name, which is Coronatus [Crowned] in Latin, which we called Gewuldorbeagod [Crowned in Glory] in English, because he has the eternal crown of glory, just as his name predicted for him.'

lines 98–114 was Augustine, the image was rhetorically developed by an interplay betewen 'Salvator', used for Christ, and the range of sickness and healing vocabulary used in the development of the image.[24] The etymology of 'Salvator' which is implied by the rhetorical context is in fact invalid, but it was generally accepted and often exploited by patristic writers, no doubt because of the aural similarity with *salus* and its adjective *salvus*. Following Augustine, Ælfric produced an equivalent rhetorical etymology by reiterating 'hælan' in a variety of forms alongside 'Hælend' for 'Salvator'. But whilst Ælfric was often close to his source, he frequently clarified the etymological point and gave it greater emphasis. In this same homily, when retelling the story of the miracle of healing by the pool of Bethesda, from John v, Ælfric called Jesus 'Hælend' in order to draw attention, aurally, to his activity as the one who healed: the verb used is 'hælan'.[25] The biblical account used 'Iesus' and 'Dominus', but Ælfric substituted 'Hælend' in preparation for his rhetorically and didactically effective statement in the exegesis of the miracle that: '(Hys) nama is Hælend, for þan þe he gehælþ (his folc, swa swa se eng)el cwæþ be him, ær þan þe he acenned (wære: He gehælþ hys fol)c fram heora synnum.'[26] It is true that Ælfric's major sources for this homily, Alcuin, Bede and Augustine, treated the miracle in terms of the image of 'Christus medicus', but there was no equivalent in them for Ælfric's explanation of the saviour's name, an etymological statement for which he had carefully prepared by his independent use of 'Hælend' in the retelling of the biblical narrative.

The etymology of Jesus's name as 'ipse . . . salvum faciet populum suum a peccatis eorum' is given in Matthew 1.21 and was taken up by Ælfric's sources for homily VIII in Pope's collection.[27] Gregory and Haymo both made the rhetorical connection between 'salus' and 'Salvator', and Ælfric, in explaining that Jesus means 'Hælend' (which he substituted for 'Salvator'), paralleled his sources' rhetoric by associating 'Hælend' with 'hælu'. But, although in this instance Ælfric did no more than his sources, there were other occasions, as

---

[24] *The Homilies of Ælfric: a Supplementary Collection*, 2 vols., ed. J.C. Pope, EETS os 259–60 (London, 1967–8), 234. For the frequency of this image in the writings of Augustine and its relationship to the broader Christian tradition, see R. Arbesmann, 'The Concept of "Christus Medicus" in St Augustine', *Traditio* 10 (1954), 1–28. It is striking how many of the instances cited by Arbesmann are in Augustine's sermons, which indicate that he regarded it as a useful image for teaching the people. Christine Mohrmann ('Das Wortspiel in den Augustinischen Sermones', *Mnemosyne* 3rd ser. 3 (1935–6), 33–61) has analysed Augustine's rhetorical devices in his sermons (which differ from those in such works as *De civitate dei*) and noted the extent to which a reader would be made aware of words as such. One of the devices she has discussed is the drawing together of words which have an apparently similar root.

[25] *The Homilies of Ælfric*, ed. Pope, pp. 230–2.

[26] *Ibid.* p. 234, lines 95–7. 'His name is Hælend [Healer, Saviour] because he heals his people, just as the angel said of him before he was born, "He will heal his people from their sins."'

[27] *Ibid.* p. 359, with reference to lines 59–62.

with Pope's homily II discussed above, where he was more deliberate than his source in highlighting the etymology by rhetorical association. Examples from Pope's collection, which can easily be checked against the sources so conveniently provided, are to be found at homily V, line 194, homily VII, lines 189–94, and homily XV, lines 188–90. In the homily for the Feast of the Annunciation in the First Series of *Catholic Homilies* (*CH* I XIII) Ælfric interpreted Jesus as 'Hælend' and explained that the name is appropriate 'forðan ðe he gehælð ealle ða þe on hine rihtlice gelyfað',[28] but the explanation was Ælfric's own: the Bedan source simply interpreted Jesus as 'Salvator', without further elaboration.[29] Similarly in *CH* II XII, where he spelled out the equivalence between 'Iesus', 'Saluator' and 'Hælend', the comment that 'he gehælð his folc fram heora synnum' was independent of the sources so far identified.[30] A much fuller gloss on the etymology was provided in the Second Series homily for the Feast of St Matthew (*CH* II XXXII), prompted by Christ's own reference to spiritual healing in his words to the pharisees and scribes, Matthew IX.12:

Drihten him cwæð to. ne behofiað ða halan nanes læces. ac ða untruman; He is hælend gehaten. for ðan ðe he hælð ægðer ge manna lichaman ge heora sawle. and for ði he come to mancynne þæt he wolde ða synfullan gerihtlæcan. and heora sawla gehælan; Se ðe wenð þæt he hal sy. se is unhal; Þæt is. se ðe truwað on his agenre rihtwisnysse. ne hogað he be ðam heofenlican læcedome;[31]

The healing imagery was present in the Bedan homily which was Ælfric's source, but 'Saluator' was not drawn into the image by rhetorical association with 'salus' (which was not used), and there was no discussion of the etymolgy of 'Saluator' as a name.[32]

In all these instances Ælfric showed an awareness of etymology and a willingness to exploit it as a teaching technique which set him apart from most other vernacular homilists. The imagery of Christ as healer of the wounds of

---

[28] *The Homilies of the Anglo-Saxon Church*, ed. Thorpe, I, 198.

[29] For details of the source, see above, pp. 36–7 and n. 7. Bede's reference to Jesus's name ('Nam manifestissime dominum Iesum, id est saluatorem nostrum') is in the first of the two homilies at *Opera homiletica*, ed. Hurst, p. 16.

[30] *Ælfric's Catholic Homilies*, ed. Godden, p. 122. Possible sources for parts of the homily were proposed by Förster, 'Über die Quellen', pp. 46–7, but further source identification is clearly needed.

[31] *Ælfric's Catholic Homilies*, ed. Godden, pp. 273–4. 'The Lord said to them, "It is not the healthy who need a physician, but the sick." He is called Hæland [Healer, Saviour] because he heals both the bodies of men and their souls. And thus he came to mankind because he wanted to direct the sinful and to heal their souls. He who thinks he is healthy is sick. That is, he who trusts in his own righteousness does not care about heavenly healing.'

[32] Bede, *Opera homiletica*, ed. Hurst, pp. 148–55 (p. 152 for the passage under discussion), identified as the source by C.R. Davis, 'Two New Sources', pp. 510–13.

sin is common enough in Old English homilies, as in the Christian tradition generally, but there are no other homilists who fix it in our minds by the exploitation of 'Hælend', either by rhetorical juxtaposition with 'hælan', 'hælu' and 'hal' or by explicit etymologizing of the kind that Ælfric used. Indeed, other homilists made very little use of etymologies of any sort. In part this was because they were writing not exegetical homilies, which demanded a systematic interpretation of word and phrase, but moral homilies which appealed primarily to the emotions, so that etymologies were not particularly appropriate. But it is significant that even the non-Ælfrician homilists who did produce biblical exegesis gave etymologies only occasionally and rarely exploited them in ways comparable to Ælfric.[33] The contrast can be illustrated most clearly by reference to Vercelli v, for Christmas Day, which used the same source as that employed for Ælfric's Christmas Day homily in the First Series of *Catholic Homilies* (*CH* I II), and to Blickling homily II, for Quinquagesima Sunday, the source for which was also used by Ælfric for his First Series Quinquagesima Sunday homily (*CH* I x).

The pericope for Vercelli v[34] was Luke II.1–14 and the source, given by Gatch following Willard, was a homily by Gregory.[35] The Vercelli homilist's exegesis of the gospel narrative included the etymology of Bethlehem, 'domus panis, hlafes hus', following Gregory, but that was the only etymology provided both in the Old English text and in the Latin source. By contrast, Ælfric etymologized Bethlehem ('Hlaf-hus'), Augustus ('geycende his rice')

33 The best non-Ælfrician use of etymologies that I have found is Vercelli xvII, an exegetical homily structured in the same way as Ælfric's, where Jerusalem is etymologized as 'sybbe gesyhðe' and where 'sybbe' is then reiterated in the following sentences: *Vercelli Homilies ix–xxiii*, ed. P. Szarmach (Toronto, 1981), p. 52. No specific source has yet been identified. Blickling vi also gives the standard etymology for Jerusalem (*The Blickling Homilies*, ed. R. Morris, EETS os 58, 63 and 73 (London, 1874–80), 81), but no rhetorical or didactic use was made of it; it is, in any case, a muddled and unfocussed homily, as will be shown in a forthcoming article in *Leeds Studies in English* by C. A. Lees ('The Blickling Palm Sunday Homily and its Revised Version'). There is an unsatisfactory attempt at etymologizing in Blickling xii (ed. Morris, p. 135), where interpretations of Paraclete are offered without the name itself being present in the text (cf., e.g., Ælfric's retention of 'Paraclitus' in *The Homilies of the Anglo-Saxon Church*, ed. Thorpe, I, 322). In view of what we have seen of Ælfric's practices, it is interesting to note that neither Blickling xiv, on the birth and naming of John the Baptist, nor Vercelli xxiii, on St Guthlac, takes the obvious opportunities to provide etymolgies.
34 *Die Vercelli-Homilien: I.–VIII. Homilie*, ed. M. Förster, Bibliothek der angelsächsischen Prosa 12 (Hamburg, 1932), 107–31. The etymology of Bethlehem is on p. 121.
35 M. McC. Gatch, 'Eschatology in the Anonymous Old English Homilies', *Traditio* 21 (1965), 117–65, at 139. The Gregorian source (PL 76, cols, 1103–5) was first identified by R. Willard, 'The Vercelli Homilies, an Edition of Homilies I, IV, V, VII, VIII, XI, and XII' (unpubl. PhD dissertation, Univ, of Chicago, 1934), p. 160. Gatch notes that it was a source 'only in a general way', but, if something more precise is found, the contrast with Ælfric will remain.

and Cyrenius ('Yrfenuma'), and adopted his common practice of weaving the intepretations into the exegesis.[36] Ælfric's homily in fact had a longer pericope than Vercelli v, continuing as far as Luke 11.20, but for the exegesis of the first part (which included the proper names), one of his major sources was the same Gregorian homily.[37] Gregory, however, as noted in connection with Vercelli v, gave an etymology only for Bethlehem. Förster suggested that Ælfric also drew upon Bede's commentary on Luke,[38] but there too only Bethlehem was given an etymology. Smetana, in demonstrating Ælfric's use of the homiliary of Paulus Diaconus (which included the Gregorian source), showed that Ælfric certainly made use of one Bedan homily from the homiliary in addition, and perhaps even two,[39] but again neither provided an etymology for Augustus or Cyrenius, although both interpreted Bethlehem. The additional etymologies given by Ælfric were orthodox, being the same as those in Jerome's *Liber interpretationis hebraicorum nominum*.[40] It may be that he took them from another homiletic source as yet unidentified, but their inclusion marks a significant contrast between Ælfric and the Vercelli homilist. Ælfric here, as elsewhere, made in his one homily more use of etymologies than did any one of his source texts; the Vercelli homilist simply repeated what his major source provided.

The other contrastive example, Blickling 11,[41] an exegesis of the healing of the blind man on the way to Jericho (Luke XVIII.31–43), used the same Gregorian source as Ælfric for the same occasion,[42] but whereas Ælfric, in making a point about the transience of human life, related it etymologically to the biblical text by giving the meaning of Jericho as 'mona', symbolic of mortality, following Gregory, and then underlined the point by repeatedly

---

[36] *The Homilies of the Anglo-Saxon Church*, ed. Thorpe, I, 32–4.

[37] See above, n. 35. The homily was first identified as one of Ælfric's sources by Förster, 'Über die Quellen', p. 13; its availability in the homiliary of Paulus Diaconus was pointed out by Smetana, 'Ælfric and the Early Medieval Homiliary', p. 182.

[38] 'Über die Quellen', p. 13. Smetana, 'Ælfric and the Early Medieval Homiliary', p. 182, in referring to Förster's identification, cited it as 'Smaragdus (PL 102, cols. 24–5)', with the obvious implication that he considered Ælfric to have known this material as transmitted verbatim by Smaragdus. For Förster's general comments on Ælfric's use of the Smaragdus material in PL 102, see 'Über die Quellen', p. 39.

[39] 'Ælfric and the Early Medieval Homiliary', p. 182. The Bedan homily certainly used is an *Opera homiletica*, ed. Hurst, at pp. 37–45; the other is at pp. 46–51.

[40] *Liber interpretationis*, ed. de Lagarde, p. 139.

[41] *The Blickling Homilies*, ed. Morris, pp. 15–25, esp. 17.

[42] The common source (PL 76, cols, 1081–6) was identified for Blickling 11 by Gatch, 'Eschatology', p. 120, and for Ælfric, *CH* Ix, by Förster, 'Über die Quellen', p. 2. As Smetana has pointed out, ('Ælfric and the Early Medieval Homiliary', p. 187), it was also used for Quinquagesima Sunday in the homiliary of Paulus Diaconus.

referring to the moon in his explanation (as Gregory had not),[43] the Blickling homilist failed to give the etymology and so introduced the subject of transience and its symbolic representation as a moon in an arbitrary way. Since the etymological connection was not made, there was no obvious reason why the story should generate a remark about transience, or why the homilist should feel it necessary to allude to the symbol of the moon.

The unsatisfactory nature of the Blickling homily at this point indicates a possible reason why Ælfric was drawn to etymologies: they justified and articulated stages in the orthodox exegesis of a biblical text, and the preacher and teacher, by providing them, maintained a logical progression which might have helped at least some in his audience to remember *what* the text meant because they remembered *why* it was so. It is, of course, a sound pedagogical technique: arbitrary information, or information that seems arbitrary, is harder to recall than information that is, or seems to be, rational and logical. Evidence of Ælfric's awareness of this fact, as a good teacher, is found throughout his *Grammar*, where the terminology was translated and explained using quasi-etymological techniques and techniques of rhetorical repetition that were akin to those used in the exegetical homilies. Other reasons for his use of etymologies must have been his familiarity with patristic tradition, his commitment to exegetical orthodoxy and his thorough knowledge of Latin grammar, which included etymology.[44] Ælfric's definition of 'ethimologia', near the end of his Latin *Grammar*, is 'namena ordfruma and gescead, hwi hi swa gehatene sind'.[45] The examples that follow, '*rex* cyning is gecweden A REGENDO, þæt is fram recendome ...' and '*homo* mann is gecweden fram HUMO, þæt is fram moldan ...', are those used by Isidore,[46] and they identify the tradition within which Ælfric stood. His definition and practical application of what he understood to be etymology would not satisfy the modern lexicographer or philologist, but it is nevertheless appropriate for us to attempt to understand the interest that words could have for an Anglo-Saxon writer and above all to realize the extent to which this interest was one of the aspects of Ælfric's approach to certain kinds of teaching which set him apart from most other vernacular homilists.

43 *The Homilies of the Anglo-Saxon Church*, ed. Thorpe, I, 154. The corresponding passage in Gregory is PL 76, col. 1082. For another use by Ælfric of the 'moon' etymology, see *Ælfric's Catholic Homilies*, ed. Godden, p. 122. For comment on the sources of this homily, see above, n. 30.
44 For comments on the relationship between etymology and grammar, see de Poerck, 'Etymologia et origo'.
45 *Ælfrics Grammatik und Glossar*, ed. J. Zupitza (Berlin, 1880), p. 293.
46 *Etymologiarum sive originum libri XX*, ed. Lindsay, I.xxix.3.

A Frankish scholar in tenth-century England: Frithegod of Canterbury/Fredegaud of Brioude

MICHAEL LAPIDGE

In 948 King Eadred of Wessex conducted a military campaign in Northumbria against Eric Blood-Axe.[1] During the course of this campaign the minster church at Ripon – which had been founded by St Wilfrid and which housed his remains – was burnt down.[2] This unfortunate incident was used as the pretext for a notorious *furta sacra*: the relics of St Wilfrid were seized and were duly conveyed to Archbishop Oda of Canterbury.[3] In order to celebrate the acquisition of these distinguished relics, Oda built a new altar in honour of St Wilfrid[4] and commissioned a member of his Canterbury household, one

---

[1] *Two of the Saxon Chronicles Parallel*, ed. C. Plummer, 2 vols. (Oxford, 1892–9) I, 112: 'Her Eadred cyning oferhergode eall Norðhymbra land, for þæm þe hi hæfdon genumen him Yryc to cyninge.'

[2] *Ibid.*: '⁊ þa on þære hergunge wæs þæt mære mynster forbærnd æt Rypon, þæt sancte Wilferð getimbrede.'

[3] The evidence is Oda's own statement in his prefatory *epistola* to Frithegod's poem, where he says that when 'certain men carried off the venerable relics of Wilfrid . . . I reverently received them' (*Breuiloquium*, ed. Campbell (as cited below, n. 7), p. 2: 'cum . . . quidam transtulissent, reuerenter excepi'). In the twelfth century both William of Malmesbury (*Gesta pontificum*, ed. N.E.S.A. Hamilton, RS (London, 1870), p. 22) and Eadmer (*Historians of the Church of York*, ed. J. Raine, 3 vols., RS (London, 1879–94) I, 224) state that Oda accompanied King Eadred on this northern expedition and thus was (presumably) present at the burning of the church and the theft of Wilfrid's relics, though Oda's own words contain no indication of his complicity. It is also curious that Byrhtferth, in his *Vita S. Oswaldi* (v.9), tells an entirely different story according to which Archbishop Oswald, while touring his diocese, came upon the ruined minster of Ripon and discovered there the remains of Wilfrid, which he duly honoured by constructing a magnificent reliquary (*Historians*, ed. Raine, p. 462). Oswald was Oda's nephew, and may have been with him on the Northumbrian expedition while still a young man. It is possible that Byrhtferth misunderstood the context of an anecdote told to him by Oswald many years after the event.

[4] According to his prefatory *epistola* once again, Oda 'thought it worthwhile . . . to glorify them with a more imposing shrine' (*Breuiloquium*, ed. Campbell (as cited below, n. 7), p. 3: 'editiore eas entheca decusare'). Eadmer gives details about the appearance and location of this shrine: 'in "editiore entheca" (ut ipsemet scribit), hoc est in maiori altari, quod in orientali praesbiterii parte, parieti contiguum, de impolitis lapidibus et cemento extructum erat' (A. Wilmart, 'Edmeri Cantuariensis Cantoris noua opuscula de sanctorum ueneratione et obsecratione', *Revue des sciences religieuses* 15 (1935), 184–219 and 354–79, at 365); see also N. Brooks, *The Early History of the Church of Canterbury* (Leicester, 1984), pp. 53–4.

Frithegod, to compose a poem in honour of St Wilfrid. Frithegod responded by producing the *Breuiloquium uitae Wilfridi*,[5] a poem of some 1,400 Latin hexameters which is closely based on the early eighth-century prose *Vita S. Wilfridi* by *Stephanus* or Stephen of Ripon. Since the poem bears in its closing lines a dedication to Archbishop Oda,[6] it must have been finished before the archbishop's death on 2 June 958; in other words, it was written between 948 and 958. Frithegod's poem is one of the most brilliantly ingenious – but also damnably difficult – Latin products of Anglo-Saxon England. Although it has been edited on three occasions,[7] it remains to be properly understood, and virtually nothing is known of its author.[8] In what follows I shall attempt to glean what can be known of the author from the text of his poem and from the manuscripts in which it is transmitted.

THE LIFE AND WRITINGS OF FRITHEGOD

We know little of Frithegod beside his name, and even the name is problematical. The conventional form of his name – *Frithegod* – is that given to him by twelfth-century English historians. On the face of it, given this spelling, the name might seem to be English, composed of the themes *frithu-* and *-god* ('good').[9] But the name is exceedingly rare in Anglo-Saxon sources, there being only one attested occurrence earlier than the twelfth century.[10] This is found in an original single-sheet document which records the will of one Æthelweard concerning the rents of a Canterbury estate at Ickham (Kent) and which was witnessed by Archbishop Oda (hence before 958) and his house-

5 Listed by D. Schaller and E. Könsgen, *Initia Carminum Latinorum saeculo undecimo Antiquiorum* (Göttingen, 1977), nos. 8137 and 922 respectively; and in the Bollandists' *Bibliotheca Hagiographica Latina*, 2 vols. (Brussels, 1898–1901), no. 8892.
6 Line 1393: 'Nunc oleate mihi faueas, industrio Odo.'
7 First by J. Mabillon, *Acta Sanctorum Ordinis S. Benedicti*, 9 vols. (Paris, 1668–1701), Saeculum III, pars prima (1672), pp. 171–96 (from L), to be supplemented by Saeculum IV, pars prima (1677), pp. 722–6 (the deficiency of L made good by a transcript of lines 1219–1396 made for Mabillon by Thomas Gale; Mabillon's combined edition is rptd PL 133, 981–1012); secondly by Raine, *Historians*, I, 105–59 (from C, but reporting variants from L and P); and lastly by A. Campbell, *Frithegodi monachi Breuiloquium Vitae Beati Wilfredi et Wulfstani Cantoris Narratio Metrica de Sancto Swithuno* (Zürich, 1950), pp. 1–62 (from L, but reporting variants from C and P).
8 See J. Bale, *Scriptorum Illustrium Maioris Brytanniae quam nunc Angliam & Scotiam uocant Catalogus*, 2 vols. (Basel, 1557–9) I, 136–7, whose account is repeated by J. Pits, *Relation[es] Historic[ae] de rebus Anglicis* (Paris, 1619), pp. 174–5; P. Leyser, *Historia poetarum et poematum medii aevi* (Halle, 1721), pp. 280–1; T. Wright, *Biographia Britannica Literaria*, 2 vols. (London, 1842–6) I, 433–4; and M. Manitius, *Geschichte der lateinischen Literatur des Mittelalters*, 3 vols. (Munich, 1911–31) II, 497–501.
9 This suggestion was made by R. E. Zachrisson, 'Notes on Early English Names in *-god, -got*', *Englische Studien* 50 (1917), 341–58, at 347; but cf. below, n. 12.
10 W. G. Searle, *Onomasticon Anglo-Saxonicum* (Cambridge, 1897), p. 248.

hold.[11] Among Oda's household as recorded in this authentic document is one *Freðegod diaconus*, who is almost certainly identical with our poet. The spelling of the first theme of the name, *Freðe-*, brings to mind numerous Frankish names which have a first theme *Frede-*, such as Fredebald, Fredebert or Fredegar. Moreover, it has been demonstrated conclusively that Anglo-Saxon names with the second theme *-god* derive almost invariably from continental Germanic names in *-gaut* ('Goth').[12] In the present case, the termination *-god* suggests an antecedent West Frankish name in *-gaud* rather than an equivalent Old High German form.[13] It is very likely, therefore, that the spelling *Freðegod* represents an anglicisation of the Frankish name Fredegaud,[14] but the likelihood needs still to be tested against evidence of other sorts.

Later sources add a few sparse details to our knowledge of the poet. The twelfth-century Ramsey Chronicle, for example, provides the information that Frithegod served as tutor to Oda's nephew Oswald, the future archbishop of Worcester and York; this same source remarks that Frithegod was reckoned by his contemporaries to be the most learned man of his time, in both secular and divine learning.[15] But beyond these notices, and the fact that he composed the *Breuiloquium uitae Wilfridi* at Archbishop Oda's request, we know nothing of Frithegod.

---

[11] Listed P. H. Sawyer, *Anglo-Saxon Charters: An Annotated List and Bibliography* (London, 1968), no. 1506, and ptd W. deG. Birch, *Cartularium Saxonicum*, 3 vols. (London, 1885–93), no. 1010, as well as by A. J. Robertson, *Anglo-Saxon Charters* (Cambridge, 1939), pp. 58–61 (no. 32); see discussion by Brooks, *The Early History*, pp. 236–7.

[12] See T. Forssner, *Continental-Germanic Personal Names in England* (Uppsala, 1916), p. 94; E. Björkman, 'Ältere englische Personennamen mid *-god*, *-got* im zweiten Gliede', *Englische Studien* 51 (1917), 161–79, esp. 172. In face of the evidence adduced by Forssner and Björkman, Zachrisson withdrew his earlier arguments (above, n. 9), and conceded that English names in *-got* and *-god* are to be derived from continental Germanic names: see *Englische Studien* 52 (1918), 194–203.

[13] In OHG final /t/ was shifted to become the affricate /z/ (see W. Braune, *Althochdeutsche Grammatik*, 13th edn, rev. H. Eggers (Tübingen, 1975), pp. 152–3), thereby producing forms in *-goz*, such as *Fridegoz*: see E. Förstemann, *Altdeutsches Namenbuch I. Personennamen*, 2nd edn (Bonn, 1900), cols. 607–10, and R. Schützeichel, *Die Grundlagen des westlichen Mitteldeutschen* (Tübingen, 1961), pp. 259–64. This sound shift rules out the possibility, mooted by various scholars, that Frithegod was German: see P. Chaplais, 'The Anglo-Saxon Chancery: From the Diploma to the Writ', in *Prisca Munimenta*, ed. F. Ranger (London, 1973), pp. 43–62, at 46, and Brooks, *The Early History*, p. 229.

[14] For attestations of this name in West Frankish sources, see Förstemann, *Altdeutsches Namenbuch*, col. 533, and M.-T. Morlet, *Les Noms de personne sur le territoire de l'ancienne Gaule du VIe au XIIe siècle I: Les noms issus du germanique continental* (Paris, 1968), p. 93.

[15] *Chronicon Abbatiae Rameseiensis*, ed. W. D. Macray, RS (London, 1886), p. 21; the same information is given by Eadmer (*Historians of the Church of York*, ed. Raine, II, 5). It is not clear where and when the tutelage took place: presumably before Oswald's elevation to the bishopric of Worcester in 961, but before his trip to Fleury in the 950s? In any event it is curious that in his *Vita S. Oswaldi* Byrhtferth makes no mention of Frithegod.

Concerning Frithegod's writings (again excepting the *Breuiloquium*) we know nothing from contemporary sources. However, the sixteenth-century antiquary John Bale (1495–1563) twice had occasion to list the writings of Frithegod known to him, and it is evident from his lists that he had access to various manuscripts of Frithegod which have subsequently been lost.[16] Bale's report is thus a precious testimony to Frithegod's literary output. In his *Catalogus* he lists six works, all said to be written in hexameters ('Fridegodus uero a patrono suo Odone praedicto rogatus carminibus heroicis scripsit'):[17]

Vuilfridi Riponensis uitam, Lib. i.
Andoeni monachi uitam, Lib. i.
De peccatrice in Euangelio, Lib. i. Dum pietate multimoda Deus.
De Hierusalem supera, Lib. i. Ciues coelestis patriae, regi.
De uisione beatorum, Lib. i.
Contemplationes uarias. Lib. i. Et alia quaedam.

Of these six items, the first is evidently the *Breuiloquium uitae Wilfridi*.[18] The second, a hexametrical *vita* of St Ouen (Audoenus), has not survived or has not yet been identified; however, given that Oda acquired for Canterbury the relics of St Ouen, it is very possible that Frithegod was asked to commemorate the acquisition in verse, just as he had done for St Wilfrid.[19] The third work, *De*

---

[16] *Scriptorum Illustrium . . . Catalogus* I, 137, and *Index Britanniae Scriptorum: John Bale's Index of British and Other Writers*, ed. R. L. Poole and M. Bateson (Oxford, 1902), pp. 72–3 and 483. In the latter work, which was begun *c.* 1550 and finished after 1557, Bale is careful to specify sources of his information pertaining to all British authors. For Frithegod he cites three: William of Malmesbury, *Gesta pontificum* (see below, n. 26), the *Venationes Nicolai Brigam.* (that is, the lost treatise *De venantionibus rerum memorabilium* by the antiquary Nicholas Brigham (*ob.* 1558), which was evidently a record of Brigham's antiquarian searches for manuscripts); and two manuscripts *ex officina Ioannis Cocke.* I have been unable to trace either John Cocke or his two Frithegod manuscripts.

[17] *Scriptorum Illustrium . . . Catalogus* I, 137.

[18] In his *Index* (ed. Poole and Bateson), Bale claims knowledge of the *Breuiloquium* from three sources: *ex uenantionibus Nicolai Brigan.* (p. 72), *ex Guil. Malmesbury de Pont.* (p. 73) and *ex officina Ioannis Cocke* (p. 483); see above, n. 16.

[19] According to a report by Eadmer, four clerics came to King Edgar, announcing that they possessed relics of St Ouen. Edgar sent for Oda, who in turn sent for a leper, so that the authenticity of the relics could be tested. When Oda made the sign of the cross over the leper with one of the relics, he was duly cured. Edgar then entrusted the relics to Oda for keeping at Christ Church, Canterbury, where the clerics subsequently became monks (see Wilmart, 'Edmeri Cantuariensis Cantoris noua opuscula', p. 364). On Eadmer's evidence the incident took place between Edgar's accession (957) and Oda's death (12 June 958). There are several surviving prose *vitae* of St Ouen (see *Bibliotheca Hagiographica Latina*, nos. 750–62), of which one has often been attributed to Frithegod (ptd *Acta Sanctorum*, August. IV, 810–19); but if Bale's report is accurate, Frithegod's work was in hexameters, and the various surviving prose *vitae* do not come into question.

peccatrice in Euangelio beginning 'Dum pietate multimoda Deus', has not survived or has not yet been identified. From the notice in Bale's *Index*, it is clear that this work concerned Mary Magdalene,[20] but nothing further is known of it. It is also clear from Bale's *Index* that the next two works (*De Hierusalem supera* and *De uisione beatorum*) are one and the same.[21] It is possible to identify this work from the incipit which Bale gave, namely 'Ciues coelestis patriae / Regi'. A poem with this incipit,[22] consisting of sixteen six-line stanzas of octosyllables and treating the twelve jewels of Revelation on the basis of Bede's *Explanatio Apocalypsis*, survives in a number of manuscripts, among which one of the earliest and best is a manuscript written at St Augustine's, Canterbury, in the mid-eleventh century (Cambridge, University Library, Gg. 5. 35, 362r–v).[23] There are persuasive reasons why 'Ciues celestis patrie', which is transmitted anonymous in manuscript, might be attributed to Frithegod: like the *Breuiloquium* its diction contains many grecisms and archaisms; the earliest attested use of the poem is a lemma in an early eleventh-century English glossary; and CUL Gg. 5. 35 is from Canterbury.[24] However, there are problems with its transmissional history which require explanation: one of the earliest surviving copies of 'Ciues celestis patrie' is found in an early eleventh-century hymnal from Moissac in the Auvergne (the so-called 'Hymnarium Moissacense'),[25] and the hypothesis of Frithegod's authorship of the poem would need to account for its transmission to the Auvergne by the early eleventh century. I shall return to this question later; for now we must direct our attention to the one poem which can be securely attributed to Frithegod, namely the *Breuiloquium uitae Wilfridi*.

---

[20] *Index*, ed. Poole and Bateson, p. 73, where the work is described as being *de muliere illa que lauit pedes Domini* (a reference to John xii. 1–8), and its incipit is given more fully as 'Dum pietate multimoda deus omnia gubernans'. These words do not constitute a hexameter (perhaps read 'Multimoda pietate deus dum cuncta gubernans'? – but no such incipit is recorded in Schaller and Könsgen, *Initia Carminum*). Bale claims knowledge of this work *ex officina Ioannis Cocke*; see above, n. 16.

[21] *Ibid.*: 'De Hierusalem supera seu de uisione bonorum, li. .i., "Ciues celestis patrie, regi regum".'   [22] Schaller and Könsgen, *Initia Carminum*, no. 2326.

[23] The poem has been printed many times, most recently by P. Dronke, 'Tradition and Innovation in Medieval Western Colour Imagery', *Eranos Jahrbuch* 41 (1972), 51–106, at 78–9 (rptd in his *The Medieval Poet and his World* (Rome, 1984), pp. 78–80), from CUL Gg. 5. 35; and P. Kitson, 'Lapidary Traditions in Anglo-Saxon England: Part ii, Bede's *Explanatio Apocalypsis* and Related Works', *ASE* 12 (1983), 73–123, at 109–23, from some sixteen manuscripts.   [24] See Kitson, *ibid.* p. 122 (reporting my views).

[25] See K. Gamber, *Codices Liturgici Latini Antiquiores* (Fribourg, 1963), no. 1672, and P. Salmon, *Les Manuscrits liturgiques latins de la Bibliothèque Vaticane* i (Vatican City, 1968), 52, where the manuscript (Vatican City, Biblioteca Apostolica Vaticana, Rossianus lat. 205) is dated respectively s. x/xi and s. x^ex.

THE STYLE AND DICTION OF THE *BREVILOQVIVM VITAE WILFRIDI*

We have seen that Frithegod was regarded by the twelfth-century Ramsey chronicler as the most learned man of his time. The nature of his learning is adumbrated by William of Malmesbury who, after mentioning Oda's acquisition of Wilfrid's relics and his commissioning of Frithegod's poem, remarks that 'the work was carried out by a certain Frithegod in verses which would not be so reprehensible were it not that the author, scorning Latin, had embraced Greek and used a large number of Greek words, so that one might rightly apply that verse of Plautus: "Except for the Sibyl herself, no one can understand them".'[26] We can quickly form an appreciation of William's judgement by looking at a few lines of the poem. I have selected (more or less at random) a passage describing how Wilfrid, having been expelled from his Northumbrian see, set off for Rome in order to obtain papal support for his restitution. But as he set off, his enemies in England attempted to abort this plan:

> Tunc inimica seges – igni tradenda perenni! –
> non contenta sue uirus fudisse kakie
> legatos regi Francorum dirigit atque
> oechonomum Domini predari impune petiuit.
> Sed superi pietate ducis conamina falsa:
> machario nullas quibant inferre ruinas.
> Loetiferas uero scrobibus uersute latentes
> decipulas sensit Winfridus presul eisdem
> perditus insidiis, tantum monogrammate lusus.
> Preterea flabris aliorsum prospere uersis
> Freisonum laetis portum percepit in oris.
> Gentiles stupuere nimis; sed summa mekotes
> regem cum ducibus placatos reddidit omnes.
> Cathegorans ergo diuinum sperma popello
> aptauit dulces in salsis rupibus amnes . . . (648–62)[27]

The point of William of Malmesbury's remark will be clear from the use in this passage of seven Greek words: *kakie* (from κακία, 'wickedness'), *oechonomum (from οἰκονόμος,* 'steward'), *machario* (from μακάριος, 'blessed'), *monogrammate*

---

26 *Gesta pontificum*, ed. Hamilton, p. 22. The quotation is not taken direct from Plautus (*Pseudolus* 1.i.23) but indirectly from Jerome, *Aduersus Iouinianum*: see R. [M.] Thomson, *William of Malmesbury* (Woodbridge, 1987), p. 49, n. 70.

27 'Then that hostile faction – fit to be cast into eternal flame! – not content to have poured out the venom of its *own* wickedness (*kakie*), sent messengers on to the king of the Franks and sought to rob God's steward (*oechonomum*) with impunity. But, through the mercy of our heavenly Lord, these undertakings (proved to be) in vain: they were unable to inflict any disaster on the blessed man (*machario*). However, Bishop Winfrid was caught in the very same

(from μονογράμματος, 'consisting of one letter'), *mekotes* (from μηκότης, 'greatness'), *cathegorans* (from κατηγορέω, 'to indicate', 'to affirm') and *sperma* (from σπέρμα, 'seed'). Note that the gender of each of the Greek nouns is correctly given (thus *sperma* is rightly treated as neuter, not – as a Greekless reader might suppose from its -*a* ending – feminine). More important is the fact that at least two of these words are excessively rare even in the Greek lexicon (*monogrammatos* and *mekotes*): neither is found in a Greek–Latin glossary of the tenth century or earlier, and *mekotes* is apparently attested only once in Greek.[28] That is to say, these Greek words may not have been derived from a glossary but from genuine contact (whether written or oral) with the language.[29] In any event, knowledge of Greek is a crucial factor in the attempt to elucidate the seemingly impenetrable diction of Frithegod's poem. But other factors are equally important, and I shall begin with one which has not hitherto been explored, namely the palaeography of the manuscripts in which the poem is transmitted.

THE MANUSCRIPTS OF THE *BREVILOQVIVM VITAE WILFRIDI*

The *Breuiloquium uitae Wilfridi* is preserved in three manuscripts.

Description of the manuscripts

London, British Library, Cotton Claudius A. i, fols. 5–36 (= C)

These folios constitute a single manuscript (consisting of four quires of eight).[30] The main text is written throughout by a single scribe in continental Caroline minuscule, probably of mid-tenth-century date (see pl. I). The manuscript is of a respectable size (228 × 175 mm); the text of the poem is written with some concern for calligraphy, and includes rubrics in uncial script and red ink. The recognizable features of the main hand are: **g** with a circular,

---

ambush (and) experienced the deadly snares lurking deceptively in the (roadside) ditches – having been betrayed by a single letter (*monogrammate*) in his name. Thereafter Wilfrid, with winds having fortunately changed direction, reached port on the pleasant shores of the Frisians. These pagans are astonished at his arrival; but the Highest Majesty (*mekotes*) rendered everyone – the king and his leaders – peaceable. Wilfrid, therefore, preaching (*cathegorans*) the Divine Word (*sperma*) to the people, infiltrated his sweet streams into the salty rocks . . .'

28 In Galen: see E. A. Sophocles, *Greek Lexicon of the Roman and Byzantine Periods* (New York, 1900), s.v.

29 Cf., however, the valuable caveat of A. C. Dionisotti, 'Greek Grammars and Dictionaries in Carolingian Europe', *The Sacred Nectar of the Greeks: The Study of Greek in the West in the Early Middle Ages*, ed. M. Herren (London, 1988), pp. 1–56, who stresses that our knowledge of what Greek–Latin glossaries were available in the tenth century is far from complete.

30 See N. R. Ker, *Catalogue of Manuscripts containing Anglo-Saxon* (Oxford, 1957), pp. 176–7 (no. 140).

back-hitched bowl; two forms of **x**, one of which is nearly square in shape, sits on the line and has arms of approximately equal length, the other of which has a looping downward stroke; and an **rt** ligature the second stroke of which begins with a mannered hook. At some point after he had copied the poem the principal scribe added Oda's prefatory prose *epistola* (a text in Oda's name, but, to judge from its language, almost certainly composed by Frithegod) on two leaves which he had originally left blank (5v–6r). It is not possible to say precisely how much time elapsed between the copying of the poem and the adding of the prefatory *epistola*, but it is apparent that the poem remained without the *epistola* at least until the time that L was copied from C, since the *epistola* is lacking in L (see below).

The text (both *epistola* and poem) was subsequently glossed by four English scribes writing Anglo-Caroline minuscule with various Square minuscule letter forms, the presence of which implies a date no later than *c.* 1000 (see pls. I and II).[31] The contributions of these four glossators may be distinguished as follows (the sequence of numbers indicates the probable sequence of their contributions); the two principal glossators are C[1] and C[2].

C[1]: the writing is often squarish in aspect (note especially the flat-topped, Square minuscule **a**); it is carefully proportioned, and makes use of horizontal serifs on minims and frequently adds horizontal serifs to the top of ascenders; the **g** is usually 8-shaped (see pl. II, the gloss *ornamenta regalia uel signa plagarum* on *stigmata*, or *scriptura non recipienda* on *apocripha*). This glossator adds three glosses in Old English.[32]

C[2]: unlike C[1], C[2] avoids foot-serifs and does not add serifs to ascenders; the script has a more spindly appearance than that of C[1]; C[2] characteristically uses an open, 3-shaped **g**. The difference between the two scripts may be seen on pl. II, where in the gloss to *agalma*, C[1] has written *.i. forma*, to which C[2] has added *uel statua uel imago*.

C[3]: adds a very few isolated glosses at various points (e.g. 7v, 9r); the script is featureless (the OE gloss *fornesta* over *epimenia* on 11r (pl. I) was probably added by C[3]).

C[4]: writes the long gloss on *industrius Odo* on 36v in a very pointed and slightly mannered Anglo-Caroline minuscule; the same scribe copied the Alcuin poem ('Lux est orbis honor')[33] on to 5r, an originally blank page at the beginning of the manuscript.

The quality of the glossing varies: sometimes a gloss will reveal an impressive knowledge of Greek, whereas at other times the explanation of a Greek word

---

[31] See now D. N. Dumville, 'English Square Minuscule Script: the Background and Earliest Phases', *ASE* 16 (1987), 147–79, at 149–50.

[32] *Old English Glosses, Chiefly Unpublished*, ed. A. S. Napier (Oxford, 1900), no. 38.

[33] Listed Schaller and Könsgen, *Initia Carminum*, no. 9116; ptd MGH, PLAC 1, 347.

will be simple nonsense. In these circumstances it is impossible to determine whether an individual gloss derives ultimately from Frithegod himself, or simply represents an inspired (or uninspired) guess by a later reader.

However, the most interesting feature of C is the fact that the principal scribe worked conscientiously through the text of the entire poem, making some eighty alterations (usually over erasures) to what he had originally written. These alterations are the fulcrum on which any interpretation of the poem and its transmission must turn, and I shall come back to them shortly.

Concerning the origin of C nothing certain can be said. Various considerations indicate that it was written in England by a continental scribe, since it is unlikely that a poem written 948 × 958 could have been transmitted to the continent, copied there, and then carried back to England in order to be glossed by several English scribes before *c.* 1000. The manuscript itself contains no clue as to where in England it was written, nor is anything certain known of its later medieval provenance.[34]

Leningrad, Public Library, O. v. XIV. 1 (= L)

L is very different in appearance from C: it is of slightly smaller format (212 × 112 mm) and is written in an uncalligraphic variety of Caroline minuscule (see pls. III and IV).[35] It lacks the rubrics found in C as well as the prefatory prose *epistola* in Oda's name. It also lacks the final 177 lines (lines 1219–1396), but this lack is due simply to physical loss. As presently constituted, L consists of three irregular quires, the first consisting of eight folios (fols. 99–106), the second of ten (fols. 107–16) and the third of four (fols. 117–20); a fourth quire, also (presumably) of four folios and containing the final 177 lines, has been lost from the end of the manuscript. The manuscript was written by five collaborating scribes who divided the work up among themselves such that Scribes I and II copied the first quire, Scribe III the second, and

---

[34] A thirteenth-century scribe added on 5r the title *Vita sancti Wilfridi metrice*, and this wording corresponds precisely to that in the 1247/8 Glastonbury catalogue (see below, n. 56), which may suggest that the manuscript was at Glastonbury at that time; it was subsequently seen there by the antiquary John Leland. It was also possibly seen by the antiquary Nicholas Brigham, who, on the evidence of Bale, recorded the identical title in his lost *Venantiones*. It subsequently came into the possession of John Joscelyn (Matthew Parker's Latin secretary) who added a note on 1r to the effect that the work was written by Frithegod at Oda's command ('conscripta per Fridegodum ad hoc rogatum a patrone suo Odone archiepiscopo Cantuariensi. Joannis Josselyn'). There is an unprinted list of *libri saxonica lingua conscripti* in Joscelyn's handwriting in BL, Cotton Nero C. iii, 208r, which includes the entry 'Vita Wilfridi episcopi per Fridegodum', no doubt a reference to Claudius A. i: see C. E. Wright, 'The Dispersal of the Monastic Libraries and the Beginnings of Anglo-Saxon Studies', *Trans. of the Cambridge Bibliographical Soc.* 1 (1949–53), 208–37, at 218.

[35] See A. Staerk, *Les Manuscrits latins du Ve au XIIIe siècle conservés à la Bibliothèque Impériale de Saint Petersbourg*, 2 vols. (Leningrad, 1910) I, 222.

Scribes IV and V the third. Their scribal stints are as follows: I (99v–100v6; illustrated in pl. III); II (100v7–106v); III (107r–116v);[36] IV (117r–118r3 and 119v7–120v; illustrated in pl. IV); and V (118r4–119v6). The script of all these scribes is highly compressed (they vary between 21 and 41 lines per page), and the compression in effect rules out the possibility of adding interlinear glosses (there are only eleven glosses in L, nine of them by Scribe II).[37] The fact that the Caroline script of two of the scribes (my Scribes I and V) includes various Anglo-Saxon Square minuscule letter-forms suggests that L was copied in England before *c.* 1000,[38] a dating which is apparently confirmed by the fact that the poem begins with a chrismon (see pl. III) which has its closest parallel in a charter of King Æthelred.[39] This dating of L has implications for the dating of C, for one of the scribes of L – my Scribe IV – is none other than the principal scribe of C. L and C were evidently produced in the same scriptorium, therefore, and in fact it can be demonstrated that L was copied from C before the principal scribe of C had made the eighty-odd alterations and had added the prefatory *epistola*, and hence before the various glossators had worked over the altered text in C. At some point in its later history (we cannot say when) L was taken to the continent, for it was at Corbie in the seventeenth century, when it was used by Mabillon for the *editio princeps* of the poem.[40] At some later point in its history, too, it was combined (probably at Corbie) with several other manuscripts to make up a composite volume consisting of the following parts (note that the last quire containing lines 1219–1396 had been lost by then):[41]

I. fols. 1–98: Paris, Bibliothèque Nationale, lat. 14088, fols. 1–98 (*Ars Donati*, various works of Bede, including *De schematibus et tropis*, *De natura rerum*, *De temporibus*, *De arte metrica* and *De temporum ratione*).[42] Corbie, s. ix[1].

II. fols. 99–120: Leningrad O. v. XIV. 1 (Frithegod; my L).

---

[36] The script of Scribe III is illustrated *ibid.* II, pl. lxx.

[37] L shares one gloss with P (*cosmica: mundana* in line 126), and a partial gloss with C (to *Thetis* in line 124 C[3] adds the gloss *.i. maris*; L has the gloss *dea maris*). No link between the glossing in L and that in the other manuscripts can be established on the basis of this evidence.

[38] See above, n. 31.

[39] Chrismons in Anglo-Saxon charters are mainly a feature of the second half of the tenth century (from 956 onwards). The closest parallel to the chrismon in L is found in a cartulary copy of a charter dated 984 (Sawyer, *Anglo-Saxon Charters*, no. 583), where the cartulist was imitating the appearance of a (now lost) charter of King Æthelred. I am grateful to Simon Keynes for advice on this matter.   [40] See above, n. 7.

[41] See L. Delisle, *Inventaire des manuscrits de Saint-Germain-des-Prés conservés à la Bibliothèque Impériale* (Paris, 1868), p. 127, and C. Jeudy, 'Nouveau complément à un catalogue récent des manuscrits de Priscien', *Scriptorium* 38 (1984), 140–50, at 148.

[42] See L. Holtz, *Donat et la tradition de l'enseignement grammatical* (Paris, 1981), pp. 378 and 493–7.

F oedere consosti seruabant · scitaque uulgi
A rdenter animis subdi celestibus orgiis ;
N ec potuit latebris abdifax missa nefandis ;
M oxproceres inter rumusculus egit aulę
S cilicet aduentasse uirum uistu te serenū
O ptima clauigeris qui satur dogmata celi ;
R egalis sane subito proscenia fundi ;
P axdomui tunc infit huic; carptimque loquelas
T ractat euuangelicas quas indice discere xpō
P romerunt late penetrans ydraulia rome
Q ueque subargutis congesserat optima gallis;
A ttonitus stupidis princeps sermonibus: ultro
N onpuduit glauco telluri sternier ostro ·
O repetens agni confestim te benedicis;
T xpleunt; cum rege manens sat multa benigno
I ptinuit merito pecuaria predia censu:
A tque monasterium uulgari nomine hripis;
G uinon gratas instabat condere gazas
O apsilis ast cunctis dedans epimenia uitę ·
P auperibus largas prebebat sedulus escas:
E xemplo pandens pariat quid spiritus ardens;
M guXLiTCON GECRATUS PRESBT FACTE
M ateriem fandi dabit amodo gratia tanti ;
I mmea bo regprę sul defessur abortis

(marginal glosses right: orgis · proscenia · ydraulia · epimenia)

I London, British Library, Cotton Claudius A. i, 11r

Crepuit magno manet incombustus abigne
Ut petrus xpi fichio uestigia petri
Per colit equoreis numquam time factus inundis
O egeneres populi quid prodest uelle beari
Virtus siqua placet patris pepulistis aboris
Enucatum liquido summe instituis agalma
Smorata que sanxere nonhaec oblitteret usquam
A ut regalis apex aut ecclesiasticus ordo
Nobiscum sapiat quixpi stigmata gestat

Neferale chaos euitandam queme phitim
Senascat rigidi retrusus inima barathri
Quicquid neutericis confinxit apocripha biblis
Assecui priscis legatio censeo dictis
Quisduo quidecies denos pariter quoque quinos

Elogio archontes queat infamare maligno
His coram fidei uir hic confessus honorem
Extunc uitali merito craxatus inalbo
Cestus expectat celestia dona diebus
Ut reperciriat quod spe patienter et optat

Huic quidis sentit nimis inquam prorsus ineptit
Haec eadem sacris usserunt indere libris

More cleantheo solitus bullata sigillis
Regibus & clero matteres atque popello

Inscius egregios egrui conatibus actus ;
Ordior en multalum quo (est) fiducia sensum ;
Ausibus insidiis uiderit sed calculus igni
Forcipe uaticum sola uis purgare labellum ;
Tunc apotens opifex anchara pandulus in deb
Spiritus intemnis animans dulcoribus an ora
Cordis amara mei ne quid displodat inepti
Lingua tenax iussi quo non potente repe nas
Efficeret haud phoebus redas ... cinthia par cas
Secla priora quidem lubrico ... mato lusa
Et coluere suos uano terrore tiran nos
At postqua summi uoluit regnator oliphi
Uirginis intacte thalamos inuisere generans
Dissepsit uarios eliso principe lurcos
Per que crucis lignum legis soluit maledictu
Asperquas ubi glorificus pecucurrit adar cos
Presens ipse suis iugiter cultoribus almu
Nubibus erum mis directo splendide flauum
Is que quater uernos ignita luce clientes
Imburo & dignis numerum successibus auctio
huius linet hausie (per) dulcia pocula ue no
Sancte uult fridus fama super ardua notus
Est uotum nobis sisuppetat auctor herilis
Nomen & laetus cuius de pmere palmas
hucados ofor mose di per climata tetris
Nam que pates bon emmtua me pellet to honeras ;
Scilicet indulcanda modis odisque canorus
Celo urea micans terris oratio prestans
Ergoage deciduas precibus suppleo loquelas
Affer presidium ne sit subpscependum ;
Tellus equo peus circum gyratur abundis
Oula petat olim scelerum culteris que deoru
Anglicus et truso colit hanc unhleta brito uino
huius inoeciduis conuen papabus anbis
Nature solitum uultu fridus per cultos oram
Anbia dum genitrix parte hanc contra subumbris
Flami uemit lampas radius presaga futuri
Celicer enturo uicinia pmus omnis
Pre pete concupiit nuauta pertone gressu
Ignis eclat soer rubeat ne culmina tecti
heruit mmeu nondum miracula (christi)

Indulsit facinus sicut praecepit ihs
Ergo uado stratu poscunt miseramina xpi
Inq́ uicē culpis p̄fecto corde remissis
Gaudebant lacrimis sobria defronte p̄fusis
k Iam fasces regni iam publica sceptra p̄empti
Sumserat aldfridus mox pastor scripsit eous
Sedib; abreptas reddi debere beatu
Xp̄i machicen post tanta pericula sen nem
Necontangat huic moriens quod p̄tulit ekfrid
Q inuoluit dm̄ primus spoliare patronum
hoc & idem cunctas statim designat amicis
Aelfledę que uirgineo succincta pudore
Pascebat nitidas ihū pudenter ouillas
Tuque clientelę princeps memores tocupri͡e
Scripsit edilredo cognato morte sapito
Q uistuduit toto uuilfridū pellere mundo
Nunc age communi s uuuas optime uoto
Sepemeis fateor parebas phronime dictis
Iam quoq; pastoris extremos crede rogatus
Ut tua praecluibus gliscens euprępia sceptris
Ardua romulei seruet precepta uigoris
Q uiestatuere patres petri uectigal alentes
Agatho precipuus benedictus sergius atq́;

Cathegorans ergo diuinum sperma popello·

Aprauit dulces falsis inrupibus amnes·

Tum pecudu foetura habilis· tu semen inarmis

Creuit et exultant sollempniter opiliones·

Post modicu multis tribuit baptisma salutis·

Et fundauit eas uiullibrordus quas habet arces·

Aequiperans tantu fidei feruore magistrum·

Quomodo insidias francorum euasit·

Hec tutela ducem· quem multe copia gaze

Francoru rupto· furis accendit acerbis·

Singraphide sculpsit· munus uenale notauit

Qui ret adalgisum collatis subdole regem

Implanare opibus· effluuius philocompos·

Legati properant· parafrastica iussa reuelant·   Parafrastica

Rex uero fronimus scindens ferale uolumen   F· sapiens ronimus

Aspinatus eos flammis piecit maltus·

Impcor eterno pereat sic caumate quisquis

Compacte querit fidei dissoluere nodos·

Infit· et infestos iussit remeare latrones·

Haud dubium quin lustratus fulgore supno·

Adcunas agi quondam qui luxit abalto·

QUALITER REGINA RESIPUERIT·

Imprudens mulier· iustum furialibus armis

Cur stimulas· facerat patria expunxisse beatum·

Quid mare sollicitas· qd casses abde caribdi·

Num tibi quadripatens famulatur machinaru·

Tene iubente poli rutilabit dextimus axis·

Siste capesse fidem· dinami capieris eadem   ·Dinamis + naturalis potentia·

paraphrastes dr malus interpres·

V   Paris, Bibliothèque Nationale, lat. 8431, 35r

VI New Haven, Beinecke Library, Beinecke 578, endleaf verso

VII   Columbia, Missouri, University of Missouri, Fragmenta Manuscripta 1, recto

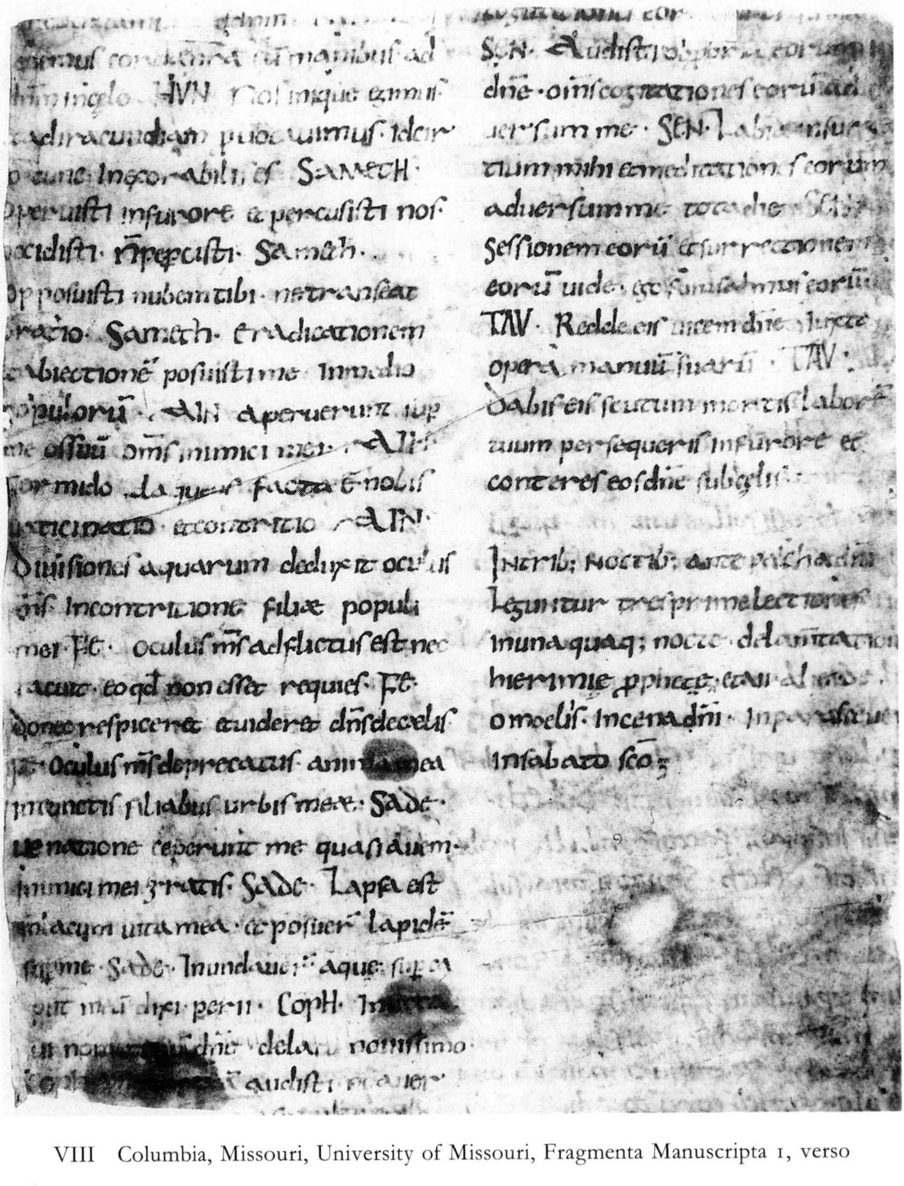

VIII Columbia, Missouri, University of Missouri, Fragmenta Manuscripta 1, verso

III.fols. 121–36: Leningrad O. v. XVI. 1 (Priscian, *Ars de nomine*).[43] English, s. x[1].

IV.fols. 137–57: Paris, BN lat. 14088, fols. 99–119 (*olim* 137–57) (collection of episcopal *ordines*; computistica).[44] French (?Corbie), s. ix[1].

The manuscript was broken up again before 1805, when pts II and III were acquired by Peter Dubrovsky and taken to Leningrad; pts I and IV were then recombined and refoliated such that IV followed consecutively on from I.

Paris, Bibliothèque Nationale, lat. 8431 (= P)

In its present form the manuscript is composite and consists of two parts, of which we are concerned solely with the second (fols. 21–48; size: 214 × 177 mm).[45] The first folio of this second part is a sort of flyleaf; Frithegod's *Breuiloquium* is contained on 22r–48v. The text of Frithegod's poem in P is complete, and includes the various rubrics found in C as well as the prefatory *epistola* in Oda's name. The text was written throughout by one scribe in a form of Caroline minuscule which is exceedingly difficult to date and localize (see pl. V). The scribe of P also added a substantial number of glosses and scholia to the text. In many (but not all) cases these glosses and scholia correctly explain difficult lemmata in Frithegod, and they frequently reveal a sound knowledge of Greek.[46] The text in P was evidently copied from that in C in its present form, that is, after it had been altered by the principal scribe of C.[47] A different situation may obtain with respect to the glosses and scholia, however, for it would seem that the glosses in C were copied from those in P, not vice versa. This relationship is seen in two examples. To the word *uestibulo* in line 1158, P has the following gloss (44r):

uestibulum est arcus qui ingressu templi ante accessum ianue edificatur uel porticus, et dicitur eo quod regias templi uestiat.

---

[43] See N. R. Ker, 'A Supplement to *Catalogue of Manuscripts containing Anglo-Saxon*', *ASE* 5 (1976), 121–31, at 127.

[44] The various *ordines* are described by M. Andrieu, *Les Ordines Romani de haut moyen âge*, 5 vols. (Louvain, 1931–61) I, 276–9.

[45] See the Bollandists' *Catalogus codicum hagiographicorum latinorum . . . in Bibliotheca Nationali Parisiensi*, 4 vols. (Brussels, 1889–93) II, 557. In the description of P which follows I owe much to the kind advice of Jean Vezin.

[46] For example, to *spermologus* in 269: 'sperma grece, sementum latine; logos. sermo uel ratio; inde spermalogus dicitur diuini sermonis seminator' (27v); to *monarchos* in 618: 'monarchus dicitur singularis princeps uel rex; monos grece unus, archos princeps' (34r); and to *eutices* in 619: 'eutices dicitur bene fortunatus uel felix; eu grece bonum uel bene; tichos fortuna' (34r); and so on.

[47] C could not have been copied from P, because P contains a number of errors not found in C, such as 458 *theosopho* C, *theodopho* P, or 1204 *agalma* C, *agalalma* P. None of the frequent erroneous readings in P are recorded by Campbell in the apparatus criticus to his edition (cited above, n. 7).

The gloss in C (copied on 31v by my scribe C[1]) would appear to be an abbreviation of that in P: 'uestibulum est arcus qui in ingressu est ostii uel ante ianue accessum spatium'. Similarly, to the word *offex* in line 1321 P has the following gloss (47r):

offex .i. impeditor. officere enim dicimus obstare nocere uel impedire.

Again, C[1] has copied what appears to be an abbreviation of this gloss into C (35r): 'impeditor, officere obstare nocere impedire'. If some of the glosses in C were copied from P (the evidence is suggestive but not decisive, I think), the implication is that P with its glosses was written before *c.* 1000, for (as we have seen) the Anglo-Saxon Square minuscule letter-forms in the glosses in C preclude a date much later than the turn of the tenth century. Furthermore, it would imply that P was written in the same scriptorium as that which produced C and L.

That this scriptorium was located in England is also suggested by the script of P. Even though its Caroline script is not immediately recognizable as English, certain of its letter-forms (particularly its form of **g** and its abbreviation of *qui*) are more recognizably English than French.[48] It is also worth noting that an inscription on the flyleaf (21v) is in a more recognizable English hand. This inscription reads: '.Lan. Perigesis Prisciani cum uita sancti Vuilfridi'. (The text of Priscian's *Periegesis* has been lost, by the way.) What the letters .Lan. mean is not clear, but they are found in other English manuscripts, and it has been suggested that they are an eleventh-century Canterbury shelfmark.[49] If so, given the Canterbury connections of the other Frithegod manuscripts, it is possible that P too was written in Canterbury. The later provenance of P, however, is continental, for in the seventeenth century it was seen by the historian Philippe Labbé in the library of the Carmelites in Clermont-Ferrand.[50] How the manuscript made its way from England to the Auvergne is a question which will occupy us presently.

The origin of the manuscripts

The (rather complex) palaeographical evidence brings a new perspective to the genesis and transmission of the poem. It establishes, for example, that all three

---

[48] Jean Vezin has written to me as follows (4.7.1987): 'A première vue, on serait tenté de penser que le scribe était anglais; mais il ne s'agit que d'une impression. Seule, la lettre **g** ressemble bien à ce qu'on observe dans les manuscrits anglais contemporains . . . Toutefois, je ne pense pas que ce scribe soit français . . . Le scribe abrège pratiquement toujours *qui* de la façon suivante: q; ce n'est pas un usage français.'

[49] I owe this information to Patricia Stirneman, who observes that .*Lan.* is also found in Paris, BN lat. 6401, a manuscript unquestionably of English (and probably Christ Church) origin.

[50] P. Labbé, *Nova Bibliotheca MSS. Librorum* (Paris, 1653), p. 207, who describes it as follows: 'Vita sanctae Benedictae Martyris metro scripta [= fols. 1–20]. Item B. Wlfridi metro scripta ab Odone [= fols. 21–48].'

manuscripts are the product of one scriptorium. Taken together, they reveal a communal and concerted effort by a number of scholars to correct and interpret this difficult poem. Where the scriptorium was located is not clear from the manuscripts themselves, but various converging evidence points to Canterbury in general and to Christ Church in particular. First, the poem was evidently composed at Canterbury; second, the text presented by the surviving manuscripts is not far removed (if at all) from that of the author; third, one of the manuscripts bears an eleventh-century inscription which may be a Canterbury shelfmark. If we recall that the household of Archbishop Oda will have been housed at Christ Church, and that a copy of the *Breuiloquium* was certainly available at Christ Church for the use of Eadmer in the early twelfth century,[51] then it is to Christ Church that we ought to look for the location of the scriptorium which produced the three manuscripts of Frithegod's poem. Other evidence corroborates the supposition of a Christ Church origin for the manuscripts of the poem: as we shall see, there is a copy of the dedicatory *epistola* to Oda in Boulogne, Bibliothèque municipale 189,[52] a manuscript written at Christ Church *c.* 1000, and a Christ Church catalogue of the late twelfth century lists a 'Vita Sancti Wilfridi . . . uersifice' which is almost certainly a reference to a copy of Frithegod's poem.[53] Certainty, however, is unobtainable, for the poem was probably known at Winchester in the late tenth century,[54] was certainly known to William of Malmesbury (who may, of course, have seen it at Canterbury) in the early twelfth,[55] and again at Glastonbury in the mid-thirteenth.[56] A late fifteenth-century catalogue of St Augustine's, Canterbury, also lists a 'vita sancti Wilfridi metrice'.[57] So although the three surviving manuscripts may arguably have originated at Christ Church, the wider diffusion of the poem in post-Conquest times should incline us to caution.

---

[51] In his *Vita S. Wilfridi* (*Historians of the Church of York*, ed. Raine, i, 161–226), Eadmer quotes some fifty lines of the *Breuiloquium*. Unfortunately none of the quoted lines contain a significant variant, so it is not possible to tell which manuscript Eadmer was using.

[52] See below, p. 62.

[53] M. R. James, *The Ancient Libraries of Canterbury and Dover* (Cambridge, 1903), p. 11 (no. 187).

[54] An unsusual metrical cadence probably coined by Frithegod (*caelica Tempe*: line 980) is used by Lantfred and in two poems composed at Winchester during Æthelwold's bishopric, perhaps by Lantfred himself: see M. Lapidge, 'Three Latin Poems from Æthelwold's School at Winchester', *ASE* 1 (1972), 85–137, at 89.   [55] See above, n. 26.

[56] See T. W. Williams, *Somerset Medieval Libraries* (Bristol, 1897), p. 76: 'Vita sancti Wilfridi metrice'. Note that this title agrees precisely with that added by a thirteenth-century scribe to Claudius A. i (5r). The same Glastonbury manuscript was subsequently seen by the antiquary John Leland: see J. P. Carley, 'John Leland and the Contents of English Pre-Dissolution Libraries: Glastonbury Abbey', *Scriptorium* 40 (1986), 107–20, at 115 (no. 17).

[57] James, *The Ancient Libraries*, p. 239. This St Augustine's manuscript is described as follows: 'Beda de metrica arte et in eodem libro vita sancti Wilfridi metrice et Avianus'. This description does not correspond to any surviving Frithegod manuscript.

THE RELATIONSHIP OF THE MANUSCRIPTS

Let us now turn from the manuscripts to the text which they purvey, and attempt to clarify the relationship between them. In the first place, L was evidently copied from C before C had received the prefatory *epistola* and before its scribe had systematically altered the text at some eighty-odd places (this much can be confirmed by ultraviolet light, for it is often possible to establish that a reading lying under an erasure in C corresponds to the reading in L). Conversely, the text of P was evidently copied from that of C in its present form, that is, after it had been altered by the scribe of C. This gives the following picture of intensive scribal activity: one scribe produced C but left space for the prefatory *epistola* to be added later; he then collaborated with four other scribes to produce L; later still he returned to C, added the prefatory *epistola* and altered the text in eighty-odd places; the scribe of P then produced a copy of this altered form of C, adding at the same time a number of glosses and scholia; finally, various glossators copied some of the glosses in P into the text of C, while simultaneously adding glosses of their own devising. All this scribal activity took place, probably in Canterbury, after the poem was composed (948 × 958) but before *c.* 1000.

Now the nub of the question is this: what is the status or merit of the scribal alterations in C?[58] Are they revisions which have the authority of the poet himself? Or are they merely the product of a wilful scribe, tampering illegitimately with the poet's hallowed text? Alistair Campbell, who produced the only critical edition of the poem, took the latter view: in his opinion, the scribe of C made the corrections in order to show how clever he was (*ad se acerrimo uirum ingenio comprobandum*).[59] But in this attempt the scribe was undone by his own stupidity, for the alterations he made, so Campbell argued, merely revealed him as *omnium mortalium stultissimus*. Campbell cited three instances where the scribe's stupidity was most clearly in evidence,[60] and we may best begin by looking at them.

The first instance occurs in line 226. The context is Stephen of Ripon's description (*Vita S. Wilfridi*, ch. 8) of Wilfrid's generosity to the poor and the weak once he had been made abbot of Ripon. Frithegod rendered Stephen's passage as follows: 'Wilfrid did not set about accumulating bronze treasures; rather, he was bountiful to everyone, giving out the [*ermenia* (L) or *epimenia* (CP)] of life; he conscientiously provided abundant food for the poor':

---

58 This question was treated brilliantly by D. C. C. Young, 'Author's Variants and Interpretations in Frithegod', *Archivum Latinitatis Medii Aevi* 25 (1955), 71–98, who demonstrated that many of the eighty-odd alterations are to be understood as corrections made *metri gratia*. Several alterations, including the three treated below, defeated him, however.

59 *Frithegodi monachi Breuiloquium*, ed. Campbell, p. viii.   60 *Ibid.* p. ix, n. 7.

L: dapsilis ast cunctis, dedans *ermenia* uitae,
pauperibus largas praebebat sedulus escas . . .

C,P: dapsilis ast cunctis, dedans *epimenia* uitae,
pauperibus largas praebebat sedulus escas . . .

The reading in L derives from the Greek word ἑρμηνεία, meaning 'interpretation' or 'explanation'. There are problems with its usage here: it is fem. sg., and the accusative form required after *dedo*, namely *(h)ermeneian*, would be metrically unacceptable in that position; but the nominative form is equally unacceptable. In any event it is unclear why Wilfrid should have wished to feed the starving masses with 'interpretations of life', when what they most urgently required was food. *Epimenia*, the altered reading of C and P, gives them their food, and in a grammatically and metrically acceptable way, for *epimenia* (from Greek ἐπιμήνια, n. pl.) means 'monthly rations', 'provisions'. *Epimenia* is a well attested word in Greek, and one which had been naturalized in Latin in Juvenal and Gildas.[61] In this first instance, therefore, the altered reading in C gives perfectly satisfactory sense and metre, whereas that in L gives neither.

Campbell's second instance (line 217) is more problematical. It concerns the return of Wilfrid to Northumbria after having spent time studying in Rome, and his conversations with King Alhfrith on matters such as ecclesiastical discipline, all of which Frithegod renders as follows: '(Wilfrid) explains individually the words of the gospel, which he had been worthy enough to learn through Christ's guidance when enrolling in the [*gimnasia* (L) or *ydraulia* (CP)] of widespreading Rome.'

L: carptimque loquelas
tractat euangelicas, quas indice discere Christo
promeruit, latae penetrans *gimnasia* Romae.

C,P: carptimque loquelas
tractat euangelicas, quas indice discere Christo
promeruit, latae penetrans *ydraulia* Romae.

The word *gimnasia* here is perfectly acceptable: *gymnasium*, originally from Greek γυμνάσιον, was well acclimatised in Latin with the meaning 'school' or 'college'. On the face of it, the reading *ydraulia* in CP is incomprehensible at best, nonsensical at worst. A glossator in C (my C²) explained *ydraulia* as *orgnana cum aqua canentia* (see pl. I), apparently understanding that Wilfrid spent his

---

[61] Juvenal, *Sat.* VII.120; Gildas, *De excidio Britanniae*, ch. 23. It is perhaps worth noting that one of the few surviving manuscripts of Gildas was perhaps at St Augustine's, Canterbury, in the tenth century: London, BL, Cotton Vitellius A. vi.

time in Rome frequenting water organs. If this is indeed what the alteration in C intends, then the scribe may justly be described as *stultissimus*. However, elsewhere in the *Breuiloquium* we find a compound word with the second element *-aulia*: *cliaulia* in line 138, referring to the church of St Andrew in Rome. The word *cliaulia* is explained, correctly I think, by a glossator of C (again, my C²) as *famosum atrium*, implying that the word is a neologism made up of two Greek elements: *cli-* (from Greek κλέος, 'fame', the glossator's *famosum*) and *-aulia* (from Greek αὐλή, 'hall', the glossator's *atrium*). Let us assume that *ydraulia* represents a similar neologism, with *-aulia* as its second element. What, in this case, of the first element *ydr-*? The spelling with *y-* suggests Greek ὕδωρ ('water'), and that is how the glossator in C took it. However, in medieval manuscripts *y* and *i* are completely interchangeable in the orthography of Greek words. Accordingly, if *ydr-* is an orthographic variant of *idr-*, an interesting possibility arises, namely that *idr-* is from the uncommon but attested Greek noun ἰδρεία, 'knowledge' (or its corresponding adjectival form ἴδρις, 'knowledgeable'). On this hypothesis *idraulia* is a neologism meaning 'halls of knowledge', a poetic circumlocution of 'schools' – and it is these, not water organs, which Wilfrid was frequenting in Rome. In other words, the alteration of *gimnasia* to *ydraulia* in C was the work of someone thoroughly familiar with Greek: a stroke of ingenuity, not of stupidity.

Campbell's third instance (line 332) presents even more formidable problems at first glance. The discussion concerns Wilfrid's election to the episcopacy: Stephen tells us that kings and all the more humble populace agreed to Wilfrid's election (ch. 11: 'tunc quoque consenserunt reges et omnis populus huic electioni'). Frithegod recasts Stephen's statement so as to read: 'the noblemen conceded, as did the magnates, as well as the [*calones* (L) or *meandri* (CP)].

> L: indulgent proceres, magnates necne *calones*.
> C,P: indulgent proceres, magnates necne *meandri*.

The word *calo* (plural *calones*) in L is an unusual Latin word meaning 'servant' or 'drudge', and gives satisfactory sense here as a poetic equivalent of Stephen's term *omnis populus* (note only that the quantity is false: the first syllable of *calo* is naturally long). The alteration in C – *meandri* – is apparently less satisfactory, for what are *meandri*? The scribe of P, followed by a glossator in C (my C²), thought of 'meanderings', after the winding river Maiandros in Phrygia, whence their gloss *meandri: flexurae* ('bends': in fact the ModE word 'meander' does derive, via French, from this same river Maiandros). But this reading makes little sense in context: 'the noblemen conceded, as did the meanderings'. Let us assume, as we did in the case of *ydraulia*, that *meandri* is a Greek neologism made up of two elements: *me-* and *-andri*. Beginning with

-andri: the Greek word for 'man' was ἀνήρ, plural ἄνδρες. This plural form would be latinised as *-andri*, 'men'. What then of *me-*? The Greek word for 'small' (μικρός) had as its (irregular) comparative the form μείων, 'lesser'; declined in the nom. masc. pl. it would be μείους, the first syllable of which would be latinised as *me-*. In other words, the form *meandri* can be satisfactorily explained as a neologism, formed from two Greek elements, meaning 'lesser men' – precisely the sense required in the context where, following Stephen's account, the noblemen assented as did the lesser men. Once again the scribe's alteration is a stroke of ingenuity, not of stupidity.

In each of the three instances just mentioned, an apparently incomprehensible alteration in C can be satisfactorily explained as an ingenious employment of Greek vocabulary, some of it far from usual, even within the Greek lexicon. We have seen that Frithegod possessed some knowledge of Greek, and it requires no stretch of credulity to think that the alterations in C derive from Frithegod himself. The manuscript evidence even compels us to go one step further and to argue that the alterations in C were actually made by Frithegod: in other words, that C is an autograph of Frithegod. Such a supposition would be supported by the nature of the great majority of the eighty-odd corrections in C, whose principal rationale is the removal of minor peccadilloes of scansion and rhythm.[62]

EVIDENCE FOR THE LATER CAREER OF FRITHEGOD

The appearance in tenth-century England of a scholar learned in Greek is a singular occurrence – I can think of no English parallel since the days of Archbishop Theodore – and inevitably raises questions about where and how Frithegod acquired his Greek learning. Once again the manuscript transmission of the *Breuiloquium* can offer some suggestive clues. If C is an autograph manuscript, then we will be obliged to conclude that Frithegod was not English, for the Caroline script of C is certainly continental, probably Frankish. Such a conclusion is supported by internal evidence in the *Breuiloquium*, such as the spelling of English names and a contemptuous reference to the English language.[63] And if he was Frankish, we have good reason to suppose that his name – Frithegod or, more correctly, Freðegod – is

---

[62] Cf. Young, 'Author's Variants', p. 84: 'One has the impression in these corrections, not of a mere copyist's caprice, but of a renewed attempt, by the original mind creating the whole poem, to express some difficult material found in his source'; and p. 89: '. . . one must conclude that, of some eighty changes, half are metrical corrections and the other half are amendments of sense or grammar consistent with the personality of Frithegod and attributable to his own revision.'

[63] In line 1393 Frithegod spells his patron's name in the continental form (*Odo*) rather than the English (*Oda*), and in line 96 refers contemptuously to the English language as *barbaries inculta*.

simply an anglicization of the Frankish name Fredegaud, which is moderately well attested in tenth-century Frankish sources.[64] On the hypothesis of a Frankish Fredegaud, we might further speculate that Oda had met this Fredegaud on the occasion of his continental journey in 936, when he was in France conducting negotiations with Duke Hugh for the safe return to France of Louis d'Outremer, then living in England;[65] and having met Fredegaud on this occasion, Oda will subsequently have invited him to join his household following his elevation to the archbishopric in 941.

Assuming that Fredegaud came to England in the personal patronage of Oda, and there executed commissions for the archbishop – including the *Breuiloquium uitae Wilfridi* and a lost poem on St Ouen, occasioned by the archbishop's acquisition of relics of that saint – the death of the archbishop in 958 will have left Fredegaud without an English patron. There is some manuscript evidence to suggest that Fredegaud returned to France after the death of his patron. In Boulogne, Bibl. mun. 189, a manuscript written *c.* 1000 at Christ Church, Canterbury, and whose principal contents are the poems of Prudentius, there is a hitherto unnoticed (on 2r–v) copy of the prefatory prose *epistola* to the *Breuiloquium*.[66] Immediately following this copy of the *epistola* is an anonymous collection of commemorative drinking-verses (usually known as *caritas-lieder*)[67] for various ecclesiastical feasts (2v–3r): Nativity of the Virgin, St Michael, Assumption of the Virgin, Feast of the Innocents, Easter, and so on.[68] The fifty-six lines of verse in this manuscript contain no indication of authorship or place of origin, nor is there any obvious reason why they should be there. Their presence in Boulogne 189, immediately following the prose preface of the *Breuiloquium*, would therefore seem to demand some explanation. There is only one other known copy of these verses, in Vatican City, Biblioteca Apostolica Vaticana, Reg. lat. 321, the principal contents of

---

64 See above, n. 14.

65 Oda's embassy to the continent is described by Richer of Rheims in his *Historia Francorum*, ed. R. Latouche, *Richer: Histoire de France 888–995*, 2 vols., Les classiques de l'histoire de France au moyen âge 12 and 17 (Paris, 1930–7) I, 130.

66 See Ker, *Catalogue*, p. 5 (no. 7), and H. D. Meritt, *The Old English Prudentius Glosses at Boulogne-sur-Mer* (New York, 1967). The *epistola* is ptd from this manuscript by A. Holder, 'Die Bouloneser angelsächsischen Glossen zu Prudentius', *Germania* 11 (1878), 385–403, at 386–7. Collation indicates that the *epistola* in Boulogne 189 was copied from that in C. The Boulogne manuscript was unknown to Campbell; I owe my knowledge of it to David Dumville.

67 See B. Bischoff, 'Caritas-Lieder', in his *Mittelalterliche Studien*, 3 vols. (Stuttgart, 1966–81) II, 56–77, at 60.

68 The poem is listed by Schaller and Könsgen, *Initia Carminum*, no. 4819; it is ptd E. Dümmler, 'Lateinische Gedichte des neunten bis elften Jahrhunderts', *Neues Archiv* 10 (1885), 333–57, at 347–51; and by P. von Winterfeld, MGH, PLAC IV, 350–3. Both editions are based solely on the Vatican manuscript (see below); neither editor was aware of the Boulogne manuscript.

which are, like Boulogne 189, the poems of Prudentius.[69] The Prudentius poems are written by one French scribe of the late ninth century; however, the *caritas-lieder* (on 64v–65r) are an addition to the manuscript, probably of tenth-century date. Furthermore, the Vatican manuscript preserves a fuller version of the verses than that in the manuscript written at Christ Church: it has five additional poems (forty-four verses) added at the end of those in the Boulogne manuscript. From various shared and independent errors it is clear that the Boulogne and Vatican manuscripts were not copied one from the other, but that both derive from a common exemplar. Now it is immediately striking that the *caritas-lieder* in the Boulogne and Vatican manuscripts share many stylistic features with Frithegod's poetry, particularly the use of Greek words, as an example will make clear. The poem for Michaelmas on 29 September begins as follows:

> Quod Michahel idicos merito celebratur in aruis,
> Insinuat Danihel apocalipsisque Iohannis.
> Utimur et stathmo terris taumasticos acto,
> Quod talem cultum sibimet sacrauerit ipse.   (9–12)[70]

As in the case of Frithegod, the Greek words in these poems seem to imply first-hand knowledge of Greek: in fact two lines in the *caritas-lieder* are composed entirely in Greek.[71] Some of the unusual grecisms and neologisms in these commemorative verses are also found in Frithegod's *Breuiloquium*.[72] In other words, a strong case can be made on stylistic grounds that the commemorative verses were composed by Frithegod himself,[73] and the situation of

---

[69] See A. Wilmart, *Codices Reginenses Latini*, 2 vols. (Vatican City, 1937–45) II, 219–21. It would be interesting to collate the texts of Prudentius in this manuscript with those in Boulogne 189.

[70] MGH, PLAC IV, 350-1: 'The Book of Daniel (x.13) and the Apocalypse of John (XII.7) indicates that St Michael rightly is especially ($\epsilon\grave{\iota}\delta\iota\kappa\hat{\omega}\varsigma$) celebrated on earth. And we benefit from his authority ($\sigma\tau\alpha\vartheta\mu\hat{\omega}$) wondrously ($\vartheta\alpha\upsilon\mu\alpha\sigma\tau\iota\kappa\hat{\omega}\varsigma$) enacted on earth, that he himself should have devoted such veneration to himself.'

[71] *Ibid.* p. 353 (lines 97–8): 'Theotocos kai partonos, cosmi basilissa, / ypsyleon arkos, si sit katfige per eon.' These lines may be rendered in Greek as follows:
$\vartheta\epsilon o\tau \acute{o}\kappa o\varsigma$ $\kappa\alpha\grave{\iota}$ $\pi\alpha\rho\vartheta\acute{\epsilon}\nu o\varsigma$, $\kappa\acute{o}\sigma\mu o\upsilon$ $\beta\alpha\sigma\acute{\iota}\lambda\iota\sigma\sigma\alpha$,
$\grave{\upsilon}\psi\eta\lambda\hat{\omega}\nu$ $\grave{\alpha}\rho\chi\grave{o}\varsigma$, $\sigma o\acute{\iota}$ sit $\kappa\alpha\tau\alpha$ $\phi\upsilon\gamma\acute{\eta}$ per $\alpha\grave{\iota}\grave{\omega}\nu[\alpha]$.

[72] With *theosebia* in line 50 compare *pseudotheosebia* in the *Breuiloquium* (line 630), and with *summipotens* in line 93 compare *summipotentis* in the revised text of the *Breuiloquium* (line 161 CP).

[73] I am cautioned by Neil Wright that the commemorative verses contain a number of serious metrical faults, worse probably than any in the *Breuiloquium* (e.g. *în arce* in line 73, *pectŏribus* in line 75, *gēnere* in line 99), which in his view makes Frithegod's authorship of the verses unlikely. However, it is important to recall that Frithegod worked systematically through his *Breuiloquium* with the express purpose of removing metrical errors; he may have intended to do likewise with the commemorative verses.

the poems in the Boulogne manuscripts (adjacent to the prefatory letter to the *Breuiloquium*) also points in the direction of Frithegod's authorship.

If Frithegod was their author, then these verses throw fresh light on his subsequent career. Among the additional verses found in the Vatican manuscript is a poem in honour of St Cerneuf (*Syreneus*), a third-century Greek martyr whose relics were preserved and culted at Billom in the Auvergne, about twenty km east of Clermont-Ferrand.[74] Another additional poem commemorates St Julian, in whose patronage the land of Aquitaine is said to rejoice (line 82: 'auxilio cuius gaudet Aquitanica tellus'). The reference to Aquitaine establishes that the saint in question is not the better known Julian of Le Mans, but the Julian who was the patron saint of the canonry of Brioude in the Auvergne, some forty km south of Clermont-Ferrand.[75] From the late ninth century onwards the canonry of Brioude was under the patronage of the duke of Aquitaine, who acted as its lay-abbot.[76] It is significant in this connection, therefore, that the final poem among the commemorative verses is in honour of Duke William of Aquitaine. Given the date of the manuscripts, the Duke William here in question is almost certainly William IV (963–95).[77] The conjunction in these verses of St Julian with Duke William of Aquitaine is most easily explained on the assumption that their author was attached to the canonry of Brioude. And if Frithegod is indeed the author of the verses, we should be obliged to assume that, after the death of his patron Oda in 958, he returned to his native France, to Brioude in the Auvergne. Once again, such a hypothesis would help to explain many peculiarities of the manuscript transmission of Frithegod's writings. On leaving England, for example, he will have taken copies of his writings with him: recall that P (BN lat. 8431) has every appearance of being a fair copy of C, and that, by the seventeenth century at the latest, it was in the possession of the Carmelites of Clermont-Ferrand, in the heart of the Auvergne. Similarly, one of the earliest surviving manuscripts of 'Ciues celestis patrie' is from Moissac in the Auvergne. Some explanation is required to account for how these separate works of Frithegod – the

---

74 See *Acta Sanctorum*, Febr. III, 364–6.

75 See the *Dictionnaire d'archéologie chrétienne et de liturgie* VIII, 407–12, s.v. 'Julien', and H. Delehaye, *Les Origines du culte des martyrs* (Brussels, 1933), pp. 343–4.

76 See A. Chassaing, *Spicilegium Brivatense* (Paris, 1886); A.-M. and M. Baudot, *Grand Cartulaire du chapitre Saint-Julien de Brioude. Essai de restitution* (Clermont-Ferrand, 1935), p. 157, s.v. 'Guillemus dux et abbas', and the charters there cited; L. Auzias, *L'Aquitaine carolingienne (778–987)* (Toulouse and Paris, 1937), pp. 453 and 459; and C. Lauranson-Rosaz, *L'Auvergne et ses marges (Velay, Gévaudan) du VIIIe au XI siècle* (Le Puy, 1987), pp. 252–9, 356–64 and passim.

77 S. Baluze, *Histoire généalogique de la maison d'Auvergne*, 2 vols. (Paris, 1708) I, 27–8, and Auzias, *L'Aquitaine*, pp. 508–18. Note that I dissent from the opinion of von Winterfeld, and agree with that of Dümmler (above, n. 68) concerning the identity of the Duke William addressed in these verses.

Breuiloquium, the hymn 'Ciues celestis patrie' and the commemorative drinking verses – were transmitted at such an early date to the Auvergne. The most economical explanation is probably that the poet himself took copies of them with him when he returned to his native land and to the patronage of Duke William at Brioude in the Auvergne.[78]

Let me sum up these various speculations. Towards the middle of the tenth century a Frankish scholar named Fredegaud came to England on the personal invitation of Oda, archbishop of Canterbury. While at Canterbury as a member of Oda's household Fredegaud (now known by an anglicized form of his name as Freðegod) executed several commissions for Oda, including the *Breuiloquium uitae Wilfridi*, probably the most difficult Latin poem ever composed in pre-Conquest England, and a hexameter poem now lost on St Ouen; while there he also composed the octosyllabic hymn 'Ciues celestis patrie'. Fredegaud himself worked continuously on the text of his *Breuiloquium*, altering and correcting its metre and diction and incorporating a number of ingeniously constructed Greek neologisms into the body of the poem; his persistent attention to the poem explains the separate stages of redaction represented by the surviving manuscripts. While in England Fredegaud also began work on a series of commemorative verses for various saints' days but, on the death of Oda his patron in 958, decided to return to France. He found a home at the canonry of Brioude in the Auvergne, under the patronage of Brioude's lay-abbot, Duke William of Aquitaine, and in his new patron's honour he completed his series of commemorative verses, ending the series with a prayer for Duke William himself. I should end by stressing how much of this reconstructed career is based on hypothesis; yet it will be clear that it is only through study of the manuscripts and transmission of Frithegod's writings that we can gain any knowledge whatsoever of the origins and career of this extraordinary scholar who was regarded by his contemporaries as the most learned man of his time.

---

[78] It is also worth recording that the famous Franks Casket was at Brioude no later than the French Revolution. No satisfactory explanation has ever been given of how it got there, for Brioude is not on any pilgrimage route. Could it have been carried there by Frithegod himself? I am grateful to Ian Wood for this tantalizing (but as yet unprovable) suggestion.

The Yale fragments of the West Saxon gospels

ROY MICHAEL LIUZZA

The manuscripts which contain the Old English translation of the gospels have been little studied since Skeat's compendious editions of the last century,[1] yet the interest and importance of these codices, no less than that of the texts they preserve, should not be underestimated. The vernacular translation of a biblical text stands as a monument to the confidence and competence of Anglo-Saxon monastic culture; the evidence of the surviving manuscripts can offer insights into the development and dissemination of this text. The following study examines two fragments from an otherwise lost manuscript of the West Saxon gospels, which are preserved as an endleaf and parchment reinforcements in the binding of a fourteenth-century Latin psalter now in the Beinecke Library at Yale University, Beinecke 578. I shall first discuss the psalter and its accompanying texts in the attempt to localize the manuscript and its binding. I shall then turn to the West Saxon gospel fragments; after presenting a description and, for the first time, a complete transcription, I shall attempt to locate this text in the context of other Anglo-Saxon gospel manuscripts.

DESCRIPTION AND HISTORY OF BEINECKE 578

The collation of Beinecke 578 is as follows:

Fols. 186 + i; foliated 1–186; endleaf not foliated. 148 × 102 mm. Collation: 1^6, $2–11^{12}$, 13^{12} (plus one (fol. 145) added after 6), $14–16^{12}$. Quires 1–11 have parchment strips as binding stays on the outside of each quire. Medieval binding of wooden boards covered in leather.

The main text is a psalter, litany and hymnal in a small textura hand of s. xiv. The text consists of 180 parchment folios; to this is added, at the beginning of the manuscript, a calendar (fols. 1–6). Fol. 145, in a different hand on rougher

---

[1] W. W. Skeat, *The Holy Gospels in Anglo-Saxon, Northumbrian, and Old Mercian Versions*, 4 vols. (Cambridge, 1871–87); the four separate volumes appeared as follows: *Mark* (1871), *Luke* (1874), *John* (1878) and *Matthew* (1887), and were subsequently collected into one volume. The edition of J. W. Bright for the Belles-Lettres series (4 vols., Boston, 1904–6), though later than Skeat, is generally neglected today. The edition of M. Grünberg, *The West-Saxon Gospels: A Study of the Gospel of St Matthew with Text of the Four Gospels* (Amsterdam, 1967), is complete only for Matthew.

parchment, has been added to an otherwise normal quire of twelve leaves; it contains prayers, and some obliterated lines on the verso. Part of the binding is an endleaf and pastedown, taken from an earlier manuscript in Anglo-Saxon minuscule, which contains text from the Old English translation of the gospels. The parchment binding stays are also taken from the same (now dismembered) Old English manuscript.

Beinecke 578 contains the following names, added in margins, which may represent early owners or users of the manuscript: Wyllyam Medlycott (6r), Wyllyam Emey (55v), Wyllyam Hendeley (89v), all in s. xvi hands; in a hand of s. xvii, Johannes Browne (104r); in a still later hand, probably s. xviii, James King, on endleaf. In the twentieth century the manuscript was owned by Sir Sydney Cockerell and C. H. St John Hornby; it was in the collection of Major J. R. Abbey, Storrington, Sussex, where it was catalogued as JA 3242. At this time it was listed as the first item in Ker's *Catalogue*.[2] It was sold by Sotheby's on 24 March 1975 (lot 2955) and acquired by the Beinecke Library, through the Beinecke Fund, from H. P. Kraus on 19 June 1975.[3]

The psalter and litany (7r–130v)

The psalms appear in the traditional order with no interpolated matter and no indication of antiphons; each begins with an initial of two lines. Larger initials, occupying five or six lines with a decorated border around the page, appear at the following points: ps. I (*Beatus vir*), XXVI (*Dominus illuminatio mea*), XXXVIII (*Dixi custodiam*), LI (*Quid gloriaris*), LII (*Dixit insipiens*), LXVIII (*Salvum fac*), LXXX (*Exultate Deo*), XCVIII (*Cantate Domino*), CI (*Domine exaudi*), CIX (*Dixit Dominus domino*) and CXXXVII (*Confitebor tibi Domine*). Emphasis by larger initial is also given to ps. XX (*Domine in virtute tua*: 4 lines, no border), LXXIX (*Qui regis Israel*: 3 lines, half border) and XCVII (*Cantate Domino*: 3 lines, half border).[4]

The litany (127v–130v) contains regional saints whose veneration was peculiar to Wales and the south-west: Wulmarus, Wulfrannus, Corentinus, Hiltutus, Winwaloe, Petroc, Cadoc, David, Furseus, Sativola and Jutwara. Many of these local saints are not found in the calendar.

---

[2] N. R. Ker, *Catalogue of Manuscripts containing Anglo-Saxon* (Oxford, 1957).

[3] The endleaf and manuscript have been described in the following catalogues: Ker, *Catalogue*, p. 1; R. L. Collins, *Anglo-Saxon Vernacular Manuscripts in America* (New York, 1976), pp. 36–7 (a plate of the verso of the endleaf is included); and 'Medieval and Renaissance Manuscripts at Yale', *Yale Univ. Lib. Gazette* 52 (1978), 182.

[4] For the most part, these large initials conform to the normal tenfold division of the later medieval psalter. Ps. XCVIII is emphasized instead of ps. XCVII, which receives only minor decoration here; this may be no more than an error, as both ps. XCVII and XCVIII begin with the words *Cantate Domino canticum novum*. Ps. CXIX (*Ad Dominum cum tribularer*), the beginning of the gradual psalms (CXIX–CXXXIII), is emphasized with a five-line initial without border; such emphasis is not uncommon in some other, earlier English psalters: see A. Hughes, *Medieval Manuscripts for Mass and Office: a Guide to their Organization and Terminology* (Toronto, 1982), p. 228 and also p. 374, n. 17.

The calendar (1r–6v)

Because the hand and page size are slightly different from that of the psalter text, the calendar may have a different origin; the script of the calendar, however, is contemporary with that of the main text (s. xiv). The calendar is without illumination and entirely free of astronomical or computistical lore. Several universal commemorations are absent; notable omissions include Agatha (5 February), Mark and Marcellinus (18 June), Christopher (25 July), Rufus (27 August), and, most surprisingly, Luke the Evangelist (18 October). The dates on which these feasts occur are not taken by other, more local saints, which suggests that scribal oversight might be blamed for their absence here.

Like the litany, the calendar of Beinecke 578 contains saints whose veneration was most common in the south-west of England. The calendar generally follows the Use of Sarum, which was adopted in the diocese of Worcester after 1240,[5] and many of its exceptions and additions are found in the calendars of other medieval manuscripts from this diocese.[6] Some of the less common feasts in the calendar of Beinecke 578 also occur in the twelfth-century calendars of St Peter's Abbey[7] and Winchcombe Abbey, both in Gloucestershire: Mary of Egypt (1 April), Leo (11 April), Marcellus (26 April), Conception of John (24 September) and Columbanus (21 November). The feasts of St Cyneburga (of Gloucester, 25 June, added to Beinecke 578 in a later hand) and Piran (5 March) are also found in the Gloucester calendar, as additions made probably in Hereford.[8]

Several other feasts in the calendar of Beinecke 578, most notably Genovefa (3 January), Germanus (29 April), Evortius (7 September), Ignatius (17 December), and the earlier feast for Leo (11 April, in addition to the later commemoration on 28 June) are found in Anglo-Saxon and twelfth-century observance[9] but are not, as a rule, in the later English monastic calendar. Their

---

[5] See *The Victoria History of the County of Gloucester* (hereafter *VCH*), ed. W. Page, 2 vols. (London, 1907) II, 11.

[6] See F. Wormald, *English Benedictine Kalendars After A.D. 1100*, 2 vols., HBS 77 and 81 (London, 1939–46) and *English Kalendars Before A.D. 1100*, HBS 72 (London, 1934). The calendar of Evesham Abbey, Worcester, is ed. in the former work (II, 21–38), and some Anglo-Saxon calendars from Worcester are found in the latter (pp. 197–209, 211–223 and 225–237). See also B. D. H. Miller, 'The Early History of Bodleian MS Digby 86', *Annuale Medievale* 4 (1963), 23–56, where other Worcester calendars are discussed.

[7] Oxford, Jesus College 10 (ptd Wormald, *Kalendars after 1100* II, 39–55, and dated there 'before 1170'). The calendar of Winchcombe is found in London, British Library, Cotton Tiberius E. iv (Winchcombe, s. xii).

[8] These are identified as having been made in Hereford by Wormald, *Kalendars after 1100* II, 39–43.

[9] Germanus is found, e.g., in the calendars ptd Wormald, *Kalendars after 1100* II, nos. 4 (Glastonbury), 5 (St Augustine's, Canterbury), 6 ('West Country'), and 7 (Exeter); Evortius is found in Wormald, *Kalendars before 1100*, nos. 7 and 8 (Wells, Somerset), as well as in the twelfth-century calendar from Winchcombe, Gloucestershire, cited above, n. 7.

presence in Beinecke 578 may be the result of an archaic exemplar, but more probably represent evidence of the survival of these observances in parts of Gloucestershire.

Ker connects the calendar of Beinecke 578 with Tewkesbury, because of an obit added in s. xv against 20 June for John Abingdon, abbot;[10] on 4 May appears the addition (also in a hand of s. xv) *obiit Edwardus princeps* which commemorates, rather quietly, the battle of Tewkesbury in 1471. In addition, many of the other feasts in Beinecke 578 are found in the thirteenth-century Tewkesbury calendars preserved in London, British Library, Royal 8. C. VII and Cambridge, University Library, Gg. 3. 21.[11] Beinecke 578 follows these Tewkesbury calendars in commemorating both the deposition and translation of Wulfstan (19 January and 7 June, respectively), but only the deposition of Oswald (28 February) and the translation of Ecgwine (10 September), not the translation of the former (8 October) or the deposition of the latter (30 December). In calendars from Worcester itself all six feasts are normally present.[12] The translation of Ecgwine, however, which receives no special grading in Beinecke 578, is graded *in albis* in other Tewkesbury calendars. A *festum reliquiorum* appears on 2 July, as in CUL Gg. 3. 21; this is the date on which the feast occurred in Tewkesbury Abbey.[13] Beinecke 578, however, lacks the dedication of the church of Tewkesbury (18 June) and its octave, whereas this feast is present in other surviving Tewkesbury calendars. Clearly the calendar of Beinecke 578 is based on that of Tewkesbury, but it does not follow it in every detail.

Several unusual commemorations suggest a continental, probably French, influence: the translation of James (30 December),[14] Clodouualdus (i.e., St Cloud, 6 September), Dionysius (of Alexandria, 3 October),[15] Aurea (4

---

10 Ker, *Catalogue*, p. lxiv (*corrigendum* to no. 1).

11 Some of these feasts, it should be noted, are also found elsewhere: Paul the Hermit (10 January), Ignatius (1 February), Octave of BVM (9 February, though graded more highly in Tewkesbury calendars), Teilo (9 February), Æthelwold (added to Beinecke 578 in a later hand, 1 August), Cuthburg (31 August, with the same unusual grading of twelve lessons in Beinecke 578 and CUL Gg. 3. 21), and Ordination of Ambrose (7 December). The grading of twelve lessons given in Beinecke 578 to Kenelm (17 July) is also found in these other Tewkesbury calendars.

12 Miller, 'The Early History', pp. 47–8.   13 *VCH* (Gloucester) II, 62.

14 This is a Visigothic feast, according to F. G. Holweck, *A Biographical Dictionary of the Saints* (London, 1924), p. 518; its presence in Beinecke 578 has yet to be explained, unless it may be ascribed to the fact that the priory of St James, Bristol, since its foundation in 1137, was a dependency of Tewkesbury Abbey. But the feast is not in the Tewkesbury calendars in BL Royal 8. C. VII or CUL Gg. 3. 21; its presence in Beinecke 578 may represent nothing more than memorabilia of a journey to Compostella.

15 The saint is also found in the calendar of the Douce Psalter (Oxford, Bodleian Library, Douce 293), a northern English manuscript; see E. Temple, 'The Calendar of the Douce Psalter',

October) and Maglorius (St Magloire, 24 October). The psalter, particularly a small and plain copy such as Beinecke 578, was more often a personal than an institutional book; these uncommon French saints may suggest that the owner was for a time in Paris, or had some other personal reason for venerating continental saints alongside the more local English saints of Tewkesbury. This assortment of saints not found in other medieval calendars from the region, and the absence of church dedications, suggest that Beinecke 578 may have been in private hands from its creation.

Binding

The psalter and calendar were bound in their present form, at some point after the production of the texts, in the fourteenth century;[16] during the binding process, scraps of an Anglo-Saxon manuscript of the West Saxon gospels were used as an endleaf and pastedown and binding stays.[17] The binding is of the early fourteenth century, and apparently somewhat archaic or provincial at that; but its construction nevertheless presents several points of interest. The quires of the psalter were first sewn into three split leather thongs with what appears to be a standard kettle stitch; the thongs were then passed along parallel grooves on the outside of the boards, through holes in the boards, and then along grooves in the inside cover to be secured with a peg. On the inside of the back cover, however, the grooves all meet at the centre of the board; the three split leather bands are twisted and drawn to a single peg, making a figure like a large capital V with a vertical bar through it. The head- and tailbands are secured at the end of smaller diagonal grooves which run from the inner corners of the board. The joining of two bands by one peg is a fourteenth-century innovation;[18] this triple-band pattern may be characteristic of a particular bindery, but no other examples of triple-band pegging in a small book are known to the present author, and the binding of Beinecke 578 may simply be the chance survival of an uncharacteristic expedient used only on one manuscript.

Bodl. Lib. Record 12 (1985), 13–38. The abbey of Deerhurst near Tewkesbury was an alien priory of Saint-Denis in the thirteenth and fourteenth centuries; the proximity of the two houses may account for some of the French saints in Beinecke 578.

16 My description of the binding of Beinecke 578 is indebted to G. Pollard, 'Describing Medieval Bookbindings', *Medieval Learning and Literature: Essays presented to R. W. Hunt*, ed. J. J. G. Alexander and M. T. Gibson (Oxford, 1976), pp. 50–65.

17 It need hardly be said that the process by which a Kentish manuscript in Old English, later used as binding, got to Tewkesbury or its environs must remain a mystery. Speculation might centre on Abbot Alan of Tewkesbury (1186–1202), a former prior of Christ Church, Canterbury, whose literary interests are mentioned in *VCH* (Gloucester) II, 62 and who might have been responsible for the transfer of manuscripts from one house to the other.

18 See G. Pollard, 'The Construction of English Twelfth-Century Bindings', *The Library* 5th ser. 17 (1962), 1–22, esp. 10.

The front cover of Beinecke 578 differs considerably from the back cover; a corresponding centre hole has been cut for a peg, as if for the triple-band joining, but no grooves have been cut to the hole: instead the bands, not split at this point, join two to one peg, one to another. Again the head- and tailbands are led through diagonal grooves from the corners of the board. The leather bands are no longer split before they enter the outside grooves of the front cover. The binder may have been led to change his pattern midway through his design by the fact that he had underestimated the length of strap he would have left over; the remaining length of the bands may simply have been insufficient for the triple-band pattern.

The wooden boards are cut in what Pollard calls a 'bevel' pattern,[19] though the gradual slope of the corner makes it akin to a 'cushioned bevel'. The boards are covered with leather, once probably whittawed; the remains of a leather strap, contemporary with the binding, can still be seen on the centre inside edge of the front cover. In the centre of the outside back cover is a hole, apparently for a pin to which one might secure the strap; this sort of clasp seems to have fallen out of fashion by the fourteenth century, though it cannot be dated precisely.[20] Its use here, not unlike the preservation of archaic saints in the calendar, may be due to the provincial origin of the manuscript rather than a supposed early date.

THE GOSPEL FRAGMENTS

Binding strips

Quires 1–11 have thin strips of parchment glued around the outside of each gathering as reinforcement for the stitching. Most of these parchment strips are blank; it has not been hitherto noticed, however, that those around quires 6 (fols. 55–66) and 7 (fols. 67–78) have Old English text from the same manuscript as the endleaf.[21] The text on these reinforcing strips is Matthew XXVIII.17–19, apparently representing the last folio from a manuscript copy of the gospel of Matthew; the reverse, facing outward from the quires, is blank. It is possible that the first line of the surviving text was the top line of the page in the Old English manuscript; there is enough room on the top part of the binding strip around quire 6 (opposite 66v) for another line of script, but none is visible. The strips have been cut to 142 × 18–20 mm. The leaf from which these strips were taken was cut in the middle of the second line of text; thus the strip opposite 55r has the top half of the line, and the strip opposite 67r has the

---

[19] *Ibid.* p. 9.   [20] *Ibid.* p. 17.

[21] I am grateful to Professor Linda E. Voigts, of the University of Missouri at Kansas City, for pointing out the additional text on these strips, and for her interest and advice during my early examination of Beinecke 578.

bottom half. About three letters have been cut away from the left edge of each strip.[22]

The presence of this text on the binding strips, from another part of the same manuscript as the endleaf, is good evidence that the binder of Beinecke 578 had access to a fairly substantial part of the Old English manuscript.

Endleaf

The gospel fragment, a single leaf turned sideways and folded to form an endleaf and pastedown over the back cover, was originally trimmed to about 184 × 145 mm. The upper half of the leaf, of which about 43 mm remains, has come free from the board to which it was pasted and is mostly in tatters, though parts of six lines are visible; on the lower half (about 90–6 mm vertically) nine lines remain. The pricking has been trimmed from the leaf, but ruling in drypoint is still visible on the recto, which is the hair-side. Several illegible scribbles and blottings, in much later hands, are faintly visible on the verso.

Hand

Ker describes the hand of the endleaf, which he dates 's. xi', as 'angular, rather sprawling'.[23] Both Latin and Old English are written in insular script.[24] The letter **a** in the digraph **æ** is often flat-topped, with a projecting horn to the left side, whereas **a** elsewhere is rounded; **c** and **e** are 'horned' with a heavy first stroke; the back of **d** is horizontal and does not project above the top of the minim height; **e** is low, but the projecting tongue combines with following letters whenever possible, even the back of **d** (see pl. VI *[ge]bygedum*: verso, line 10). **g** is made like an angular figure 3; **o** is sometimes round, sometimes rather square, with a heavy initial stroke and a slightly projecting horn on the left. Capital **S** is partly below the line. In this small sample of the main hand **ð** is not used; **y** is dotted, and made much like **s** with the left-hand stroke nearly vertical (in *cnyowum*, line 10 on the verso, the right-hand stroke is the longer: see pl. VI).

Descenders, including that of the Tironian **et** sign, are straight. Downstrokes and minims begin with an upward tick to the right similar to the projecting 'horn' on the letters **a**, **c**, **e** and **o**; on ascenders and the letter **i** the top of the stroke is then finished with a thin line projecting either vertically or slightly to the right. This gives ascenders the appearance of being slightly 'split'; their manner of writing, however, differs from the common split ascenders in other English manuscripts of the eleventh century, where the

---

[22] The OE text, transcribed from the endleaf and binding strips, is presented in the Appendix, below, pp. 80–2.   [23] Ker, *Catalogue*, p. 1; see pl. VI.

[24] See *ibid.* p. xxvii, for other Anglo-Saxon manuscripts in which this distinction is not observed.

downstroke begins at the right and is then tagged to the left. Rather, its right-hand tag appears to be identical to the manner of forming wedge-shaped finials in English manuscripts of the tenth century; when the letters were made hurriedly the two strokes may have separated to create the fork at the top of the ascender. The hand thus represents either a transitional period between the older wedge-shaped finials and later forked ascenders or an idiosyncratic attempt to imitate a newer style using an older technique. In Beinecke 578 the effect appears to be deliberate, but the appearance of 'split' ascenders in this fragment may be deceptive; in a hand of such apparent fluency and speed, a small sample of text may preserve anomalies not characteristic of the script as a general rule.

The Old English rubric, written with a metallic red ink that has so badly oxidized that it is now barely legible, is in another and much smaller hand; the rubricator uses **ð**, a more rounded **g**, long **s**, and a slanted **y** in which the right limb is the longer. The paragraph on the verso begins with an initial **7** in metallic red that has oxidized differently from the red of the rubric; on the recto, initial **H** is green.[25] On the recto the Latin text is the same size as the Old English, on a regular line of the folio; on the verso it is somewhat smaller, though in the same hand, and placed between two lines. Punctuation is by a simple dot placed midway above the line for medial pauses; the *punctus versus* for final pauses is used on the binding strip 1 and recto 13, in the latter case where it is followed by a capital letter. There are no accents or marks of abbreviation in the Old English portion of the text. A *punctus* appears to be used to indicate a word divided at the end of a line, like a modern hyphen, in *hripi.*/*[g]ende* in lines 13–14 of the recto; there is room for a letter at the end of line 13 but only the *punctus* is visible, and one letter, which must have been **g**, is lost at the beginning of line 14.

The hand of Beinecke 578 displays a collection of features found only sporadically in manuscripts after the early part of the eleventh century: the preference for a projecting 'horn' on the lefthand downstroke of **a, c, e** and **o**, the misuse of **e** ligatures, the horizontal back of the letter **d**, the making of 'split' ascenders in a manner identical to the making of older wedged ascenders, and the use of insular script for Latin headings. Appearing together in the hand of the endleaf they suggest a date in the early part of the eleventh century, although the apparent idiosyncrasy of the hand makes any determination of date tentative at best. If this collection of 'early' features in the hand does indeed justify a date of s. xi[1], then the endleaf and binding strips of Beinecke 578 are contemporary with the earliest surviving copies of the West Saxon gospels.

---

[25] Ker (*ibid*. p. 1) states that both initials are in red, but this is in error.

Language and orthography

The endleaf and binding fragments provide too short a textual sample to undertake a full analysis of their orthography; nevertheless, some features should be noted. The most striking characteristic of the orthography of the fragments is the consistent appearance of *yo* for WS /eo/. Both the long and short diphthongs are spelled *yo*; there is no evidence in the surviving text to suggest that a differentiation is made between /e:o/, written *io* or *yo*, and /eo/, written *eo*. The consistency with which /eo/ appears as *yo* suggests that *y* does not represent merely a Kentish back-spelling for /e/, but a genuinely raised first element of the diphthong. The following forms appear in the text (the abbreviations r[ecto], v[erso], and b[inding], are used): for WS /eo/, *(he)twyox* (r6), *dyofel* (v7), *hyofenan* (b4), *hyora* (r11, v6); for WS /e:o/, *byo* (v13), *cnyowum* (v10), *hryofla* (v9), *syocnesse* (v7), *syo* (v14), *twyonedan* (b2).

The use of *yo* or *io* for WS /eo/ is universally regarded as a feature of Kentish orthography.[26] Another indication of Kentish origin is the use of *-an* and *-ad* in verbal conjugation.[27] *a* is regularly used in the preterite plural: *coma[n]* (r11), *geeapmeddan* (b1), *gesawan* (b1), *sædan* (r14), *twyonedan* (b2), *[wæ]ran* (v2), and in the preterite and past participle of second-class weak verbs: *geclænsad* (v14), *gemilt[s]ade* (v12); an exception is *wundredo[n]* (r5). Thus the fragments in the binding of a fourteenth-century psalter from Gloucestershire were taken from a manuscript that was apparently written in the south-east.

castum appears for *gastum* in r8, probably a dittography caused by the preceding word *unclænum* and not arising from the occasional equivalence of *c* and *g* finally or medially in some Kentish manuscripts, for example, in the writing of *-unc* for *-ung* in the *Kentish Glosses* (London, British Library, Cotton Vespasian D. vi).[28] In one word, *anwalde* (r7), the spelling indicates Anglian retraction of /æ/ rather than breaking to /ea/, but the form is *anweald* in b4; the occasional appearance of *a* for *ea* before /l + cons./ in southern texts of the eleventh century is probably without significance.[29]

THE TEXTUAL RELATIONS OF THE FRAGMENTS

The Old English translation of the gospels survives in six complete manuscripts and two fragments. These may be divided into three groups or textual traditions, differing in details of text, paragraphing, marginal additions and orthography. The first tradition is represented by Cambridge, University

[26] A. Campbell, *Old English Grammar* (Oxford, 1959), §§288–98.
[27] *Ibid.* §757.   [28] *Ibid.* §450.
[29] Campbell (*ibid.* §143) stresses the regularity of *ea* spellings in eleventh-century WS manuscripts, but this is an optimistic overstatement, especially with regard to the surviving copies of the West Saxon gospels.

Library, Ii. 2. 11 (= A: Ker, *Catalogue*, no. 20),[30] written in an Exeter script of the eleventh century and given to Exeter by Bishop Leofric before 1072. The fragment in Beinecke 578 agrees with A against all other manuscripts in omitting the Tironian abbreviation 7 before *þus cwæþ* in Mark 1.41 (v14); this is, however, a common enough omission in the work of any scribe. Moreover, the conjunction is not present in the Latin text[31] *et tangens eum, ait illi,* and may have been omitted independently by two different scribes conscientiously trying to bring the translation closer to the Latin of its original.[32]

Also suggestive of a connection with A is the presence of the Old English rubric 'þis godspel gebyrað on wodnesdæg on þære fifteoðan wucan ofer pe[ntecosten]' before Mark 1.40 on the verso. Only A had these vernacular directions in its original state (they were, however, copied from A into B during the sixteenth century). The purpose of these Old English rubrics is not clear; despite Grünberg's confident assertion that the rubrics indicate that the West Saxon gospels were read in Mass,[33] one might as easily assume that the translation served as 'crib' for the less learned clergy, with the rubrics as a sort of index system, or for private devotional reading keyed to the liturgical year, and was not intended for public use. Certainly the general plainness of the surviving manuscripts, their small size and lack of ornamentation, suggests that they were not part of the ecclesiastical furniture of a church.

The rubric in the Yale Fragments is written in a different hand, inserted between two regular lines of text, after the main text was produced. In A the rubrics are all part of the text; although not all rubrics are present, space was invariably left for them before each paragraph. They are written in A in the same hand and script as the translation, and appear on regular lines of each

---

[30] The manuscript sigla used by Skeat and others, and reference numbers in Ker, *Catalogue*, are given in parentheses.

[31] The conjunction appears in some, but not the most prominent, of the manuscripts of the Vetus Latina; see the edition of Mark by A. Jülicher (Berlin, 1940). For speculation on the nature of the Latin text from which the Old English translation was made, see H. Glunz, *Die lateinische Vorlage der westsächsischen Evangelienversion* (Leipzig, 1928); it should be noted that a later text which may have been used to 'correct' or modify the translation may have been of a different sort altogether.

[32] Many of the alterations shared by two twelfth-century texts (London, BL Royal I. A. xiv and Oxford, Bodleian Library, Hatton 38) seem to have arisen from a desire to have the translation conform more precisely to the syntax of the Latin Bible, rather than a simple need to clarify the language, by then archaic, of the original translation.

[33] Grünberg, *West-Saxon Gospels*, p. 369. This assumption has been accepted without question in most casual descriptions of the West-Saxon Gospels, but ought to be considered more closely. There is little evidence, beyond the rubrics in CUL Ii. 2. 11 themselves, of any Anglo-Saxon liturgy conducted either wholly or partly in English.

page. The wording of the rubric in the Yale Fragments, *Þis godspel gebyrað* and so on, differs from that of A, 56v6: 'Ðys sceal on wodnesdæg on þare fifteoðan wucan ofer pent[ecosten].' If there is a direct connection between A and the Yale Fragments, the latter may be thought to precede the more formal and integrated arrangement of A; more cautiously one can suggest that the Fragments share a common origin with A, or that the rubric was later borrowed from a manuscript similar to A into the Fragments, or that the rubrics arose independently in the two texts from the same need to relate the translation to the order of the liturgical year. In itself the rubric does not prove a relation between A and the Fragments.

The second group of manuscripts consists of three nearly contemporary eleventh-century manuscripts remarkable for their close textual homogeneity; Skeat, with slight exaggeration, noted that these 'scarcely differ in a single letter'.[34] These are as follows:

Cambridge, Corpus Christi College 140 (Cp: Ker, *Catalogue*, no. 35). The hand is from the early part of the eleventh century. A colophon at the end of Matthew (45v) records that the scribe Ælfric wrote the book in Bath and presented it to the prior Brihtwold; later additions to originally blank spaces in the manuscript also associate it with Bath.[35]

London, British Library, Cotton Otho C. i. (C: Ker, *Catalogue*, no. 181). This manuscript, damaged in the Cottonian fire of 1731, received an addition to fols. 68–9 some time in the middle of the eleventh century; this addition concerns Malmesbury and suggests that the manuscript was there at that time and may have been produced there.

Oxford, Bodleian Library, Bodley 441 (B: Ker, *Catalogue*, no. 312), of the eleventh century. The manuscript has not been localized. Some leaves, all titles and chapter numbers, some initials, most hyphens, and Old English rubrics (copied from A) were added in the sixteenth century, apparently while the manuscript was in the possession of Archbishop Parker;[36] the sixteenth-century leaves supply losses to the beginning of Mark, the middle of Luke xvi, and the ends of Mark, Luke, and John. Some of these leaves were lost by the twelfth century; lacunae in the text of Luke in the twelfth-century manuscripts (see below) correspond exactly to the missing leaf in B, and new translations for the ends of three gospels in these later texts begin at exactly the points at which B has missing text. Thus the surviving twelfth-century copies are derived from B either directly or indirectly.

The third group of the West Saxon gospel manuscripts is distinguished by its numerous textual variants from both A and CpBC; the number and

---

[34] Skeat, *Luke*, p. xi.   [35] Ker, *Catalogue*, pp. 47–8.   [36] *Ibid.* p. 376.

apparent deliberateness of these variations are evidence of a second recension of the translation made at some time after B was produced. This second recension survives in two twelfth-century manuscripts:

London, BL, Royal 1. A. xiv (R: Ker, *Catalogue*, no. 245). A rough undisciplined hand of s. xii²; two additions which Ker dates s. xii/xiii, a title at the beginning of Mark (3r) and a note at the beginning of Matthew (33r) which gives the names of the evangelists in the order Mark, Matthew, Luke, John, the same as their order in the binding today, suggest that the four gospels were bound in their present order early in their history. The upper margin of 3r contains the following note: *D[istinctio] xvi* (the number has been altered) *Gra[dus] IIII*, a medieval pressmark from Canterbury; this copy of the gospels is probably to be identified with the *textus iv euangeliorum anglice* in the fourteenth-century catalogue of Christ Church.[37]

Oxford, Bodleian Library, Hatton 38 (H: Ker, *Catalogue*, no. 325). The hand and decorations are of s. xii/xiii; in this copy, more than in R, linguistic forms are south-eastern.

It has been asserted, however, that the large number of surviving manuscripts does not imply that the text had a wide distribution; the close similarities between Cp, B and C led Skeat to suggest that they were copied from the same exemplar,[38] and he further argued that B, R and H form an uninterrupted series of exemplars and copies.[39] The unusually close textual relations between the surviving manuscripts led Skeat to suggest that copies of the Old English translation of the gospels may never have been widespread, and that the manuscripts and fragments now extant may represent the bulk of the copies produced. His rigorously simple stemma[40] reflects this view of the limited production and distribution of copies of the text.

Skeat's view has been challenged in recent years by Madeleine Grünberg, who concludes her study of Matthew by remarking that the relation between any two surviving copies is 'indirect'.[41] Her stemmatic reconstruction of the descent of the West Saxon gospels is a complex web of dotted lines representing lost exemplars that were brought in to correct the existing manuscripts. An example of Grünberg's reasoning may be found in her explanation of the doublets which appear only in the twelfth-century copies R and H, such as *swa micel 7 swa mihtig* where other manuscripts have only *swa mihtig* (Matt. iii.9). She states that these must have been added to the text of the common exemplar of RH in a conflation made 'with the help of an earlier exemplar',[42] the archetype of which she places near the origin of the translation and calls 'z'. As

---

[37] See M. R. James, *Medieval Libraries of Canterbury and Dover* (Cambridge, 1903), p. 51 (no. 314).
[38] Skeat, *Mark*, p. vii. [39] Skeat, *Luke*, p. viii, and *John* p. vii. [40] Skeat, *Luke*, p. x.
[41] Grünberg, *West-Saxon Gospels*, p. 364. [42] *Ibid.*

these doublets are found in none of the other copies of the gospel text, she must then postulate that from her 'z' to a hypothetical 'y' all these expressions were eliminated, to reappear only in the two latest texts. Her reasons for assuming this remain obscure; conceivably she trusted that no twelfth-century scribe would have had the ingenuity or the audacity to alter his text.

Yet however questionable such assumptions may be, Grünberg is right to abandon the simplicity of Skeat's stemmatic reconstruction. It cannot be denied that the texts of the West Saxon gospels are remarkably consistent, and one must suppose a fairly close relation between the surviving manuscripts; nevertheless, the patterns of error, omission and variation that do exist among the surviving witnesses suggest that these relations are not, in fact, direct. Another fragment of the West Saxon gospels is preserved in Oxford, Bodleian Library. Eng. Bib. C. 2, four leaves known as the 'Lakelands Fragment' (Ker, *Catalogue*, no. 322) from an unlocalized eleventh-century manuscript; this contains passages from John (II.6–III.34 and VI.19–VII.11) which share some readings with A, and others with CBCp.[43] From this fragment one must infer that a 'mixed' version of the text existed which contained some of the readings of each surviving branch of the stemma. Such a 'mixed' text cannot be made to fit Skeat's stemma, except as the original translation, and this is unlikely.

Another clue to the dissemination of the text lies in the *mise-en-page* used by the scribes. Bodley 441 has occasional Latin headings, in a different hand, added in the margins; these are absent in C and Cp, and are in the text of A, like the OE rubrics, in the main hand. In the later copies derived from B, the Latin headings are also incorporated into the text in the body of the page by the main scribe. In the Yale Fragments, the Latin text for Mark 1.29, 'et protinus egredientes de sinagoga uenerunt in d[omum symonis et andreae]', appears on a separate line, suggesting that it was present in the exemplar from which the manuscript was produced. This heading is found in A, R and H (but not in B) and follows the wording of A. The text for Mark 1.40, however, 'et uenit ad eum leprosus deprecans eum et gen[u flexo dixit. domine, si uis potes me mundare]', is written somewhat smaller, though in the same hand, between two lines, as if the scribe had not provided for it in the course of his copying – and as if it were not in his exemplar or in the original design of his layout. In both these Latin headings the text, unless it had been uncharacteristically abbreviated from that found in corresponding copies, apparently ran well into the margins, for much of it was trimmed away when the leaf was made into binding. But in both cases the scribe, as he produced his text, made some effort to incorporate the Latin text into the body of the page, rather than leave it entirely in the margins as in a copy like B.

---

[43] A. S. Napier, 'Bruchstücke einer ae. Evangelienhandschrift', *ASNSL* 87 (1891), 255–61.

The fragment, then, may illustrate a middle point in the transmissional history of the West Saxon gospels, between the marginal annotations – borrowings or afterthought – of a copy like B, and a later generation of copies represented by A, R and H where such annotations were placed inside the body of the page. The evidence of B, R and H suggests that at least one other manuscript, a copy of B, must have been produced to serve as the exemplar of the later texts; R and H have far more Latin headings than B, all incorporated into their pages and thus all apparently in their exemplars. The manuscript from which the Yale Fragments were taken demonstrates the process by which this occurred; Latin texts in the exemplar were written as text; more texts were drawn from the Latin bible as the scribe wrote, or furnished shortly thereafter, and these were made to fit into the page *ad hoc*. From one copy to the next the system of Latin headings would gradually become more complete, and more integrated into the page design.

Yet if at least four textual traditions must be postulated to account for the surviving manuscripts of the West Saxon gospels, one branch surviving in CpBC, another in A and possibly the Yale Fragments, a later recension (based on B) in RH, and a 'mixed' text such as the Lakelands Fragment, and this textual dissemination was broad enough to encompass an uncharacteristically early dialectal copy such as the Yale Fragments and deep enough to reveal at least three stages in the process of scribal incorporation of marginal additions, then the textual history of the West Saxon gospels is more complex than Skeat assumed, and the Old English translation may have been far more widely available than has been previously supposed. These points bear further investigation, both into the possible influence of the translation or other Old English prose writings and into the manuscript tradition of the gospels in the full texts that survive. In any case the surviving lines on the binder's waste of Beinecke 578 offer a glimpse of what may have been lost.[44]

[44] I am grateful to Professor Fred Robinson of Yale University and Dr Malcolm Parkes of Keble College, Oxford, for their suggestions during the writing and revising of this essay.

APPENDIX

TRANSCRIPTION OF THE FRAGMENTS

In the transcription of the parchment binding strips, missing letters at the beginning of each line have been supplied in parentheses. In the transcription of the endleaf, damaged letters are restored and enclosed in square brackets; missing letters are indicated by points unless, as in the first three lines of each side, much has been torn away. For the sake of clarity, a simple *punctus* in the manuscript – a dot slightly raised above the line – has been indicated by a comma, a *punctus versus* by a modern semicolon. In the restored text, partially visible letters have been treated as completely visible, and textual lacunae have been supplied, enclosed in parentheses, from Cambridge, University Library, Ii. 2. 11. Throughout, OE *wynn* is transcribed as *w* and insular *ʒ* as *g*. Manuscript abbreviations in the Latin have been expanded silently.

BINDING STRIPS

opposite
folio

55r (7 hi)ne þær gesawan 7 hi to him geeaþmeddan; witod

67r (lic)e sume hi twyonedan , þa genealæhte se hælend ,
     (7 s)præc to him þas þing 7 þus cwæþ , me is geseald
78v (æl)c anweald on hyofenan 7 on eorþan , faraþ wi

Endleaf: recto

1 h
2 Ic wat [þ]
3 him 7 cwæþ ,
4 [c]læna gast [h].[n].....[t].........mic[e]
5 .....de him of eode , þa wundredo..
6 ....twyox him cwæd....hwæt i...
7 ....niw....[r]..þæt he on anwalde....lænu.
8 castum bebyt , 7 hi hyrsumiaþ him , 7 sona fer
9 de his hlisa to galilea rice :
10   et protinus egredientes de sinagoga uenerunt in d.
11 [H]rædlice of hyora ge samnunge hi coma.
12   on si[m]ones , 7 a[n].reas hus , mid iacobe 7 [i].
13 hanne; Soþlice þa sæt simones sweger hriþi ,
14 .ende 7 hi him be hire sædan , 7 ge nealæcende h.
15 hi up ahof hire handa ge gripenre , 7 hrædlice

Endleaf: verso

1   .d
2   [r]an, 7 þ
3   [e]al þis folc
4   [þ] he , [f]....[e]....e.ende tun....
5   .....r [b]odie , witodlice [to þ]...
6   .....bodie.de on hyora ge........
7 gum , 7 ealle galilea 7 dyofel syocnessa....
   Þis godspel gebyrað on wodnesdæg on þære fifteoðan wucan ofer þe
8 adrifende et uenit ad eum leprosus deprecans eum et gen
9 7 to him com sum hryofla hine biddende , [7]..

10 bygedum cnyowum him to cwæþ , drihte[n]
11 gif þu wilt þu miht ge clænsian me , Soþ...
12 [s]e hælend him ge milt.ade , 7 hi[s] hand aþe....
13 hine æthrinende þus cwæp , Ic wille , byo þu
14 [g]e clænsad , 7 þa he þus cwæp , sona syo hr...
15 [n]es him fram gewat , 7 he wæs ge clænsa[d]

RESTORED TEXT OF THE ENDLEAF

Recto (Mark 1.24–31)

(7 se un)clæna gast h(i)n(e sly)t(ende 7) mice(lre stefne clypien) de him of eode . þa wundredo(n hig ealle swa þæt hig be)twyox him cwæd(on .) hwæt i(s þis . hwæt is þeos) niw(e la)r(e .) þæt he on anwalde (unc)lænu(m) castum bebyt . 7 hi hyrsumiaþ him . 7 sona ferde his hlisa to galilea rice:

et protinus egredientes de sinagoga uenerunt in d(omum symonis et andreae)

Hrædlice of hyora gesamnunge hi coma(n) on simones . 7 an(d)reas hus . mid iacobe 7 (io)hanne ; Soþlice þa sæt simones sweger hriþigende 7 hi him be hire sædan . 7 genealæcende h(e) hi up ahof hire hands gegripenre . 7 hrædlice (se fefer hig forlet. 7 heo þenode him;)

Verso (Mark 1.35–42)

(. . . on weste stowe 7 hyne þar gebæ)d (7 hine fyligde simon. 7 þa þe myd hym wæ)ran . 7 þ(a he hyne gemetton hig sædon him) eal þis folc (þe secþ; þa cwæ)þ he . f(are w)e (on g)e(h)ende tun(as 7 ceastra. þæt ic þæ)r bodie . witodlice to þ(am ic com 7 he wæs) bodie(n)de on hyora ge(somnun)gum . 7 ealle galilea 7 dyofel syocnessa (ut) adrifende.

þis godspel gebyrað on wodnesdæg on þære fifteoðan wucan ofer pe(ntecosten:) Et uenit ad eum leprosus deprecans eum et gen(u flexo dixit domine si uis potes me mundare)

7 to him com sum hryofla hine biddende. (7 ge)bygedum cnyowum him to cwæþ. drihte(n) gif þu wilt þu miht geclænsian me. Soþ(lice) se hælend him ge milt(s)ade. 7 his hand aþe(node 7) hine æthrinende þus cwæþ. Ic wille. byo þu geclænsad. 7 þa he þus cwæþ. sona syo hr(eof)nes him fram gewat. 7 he wæs geclænsad

A fragment of an Anglo-Saxon liturgical manuscript at the University of Missouri

LINDA EHRSAM VOIGTS

A single leaf may be a valuable witness to an early manuscript that does not otherwise survive, even when it raises as many questions as it answers.[1] Such is the case of the first fragment in a collection of some 217 leaves and fragments of medieval manuscripts owned by the University of Missouri and housed in the Rare Books Department of the Ellis Library on the Columbia, Missouri, campus. This collection, titled *Fragmenta Manuscripta*, derives largely from that assembled in the late seventeenth or early eighteenth century by John Bagford (d. 1716), an eccentric shoemaker-turned-bookseller.[2] Bagford was, however, not responsible for the first two leaves in the collection. They were added to the collection by the trustees of Archbishop Tenison's School in preparation for sale on 3 June 1861.[3] The first fragment and the second, an Insular leaf of not later than tenth-century date containing grammatical excerpts,[4] had both been removed from the binding of another volume owned by the Tenison Library. That manuscript, now London, British Library, Add. 24193, a continental codex containing the poems of Venantius Fortunatus with replacement quires supplied in two tenth-century English Caroline minuscule hands, has attracted the attention of Anglo-Saxon scholarship,[5] but the early Insular binding fragments removed from it have remained largely unknown.

[1] See, for example, M.B. Parkes, 'A Fragment of an Early-Tenth-Century Anglo-Saxon Manuscript and its Significance', *ASE* 12 (1983), 129–40. I am deeply grateful to three scholars who have been particularly generous of their time and advice during the preparation of this study: Dr M.B. Parkes on matters of paleography and codicology; Professor H. Gneuss on Anglo-Saxon service books; and Mr P. Meyvaert on the Vulgate text oi Lamentations. I am also grateful for the comments and suggestions of Mrs L. Brownrigg, Dean M. McC. Gatch, Dr M.T. Gibson, Professor K.D. Hartzell, Dr M. Lapidge, Professor R.W. Pfaff and Dr N. Webb.

[2] On John Bagford, see two articles by M. McC. Gatch: 'John Bagford as a Collector and Disseminator of Manuscript Fragments', *The Library* 6th ser. 7 (1985), 95–114; and 'John Bagford, Bookseller and Antiquary', *Brit. Lib. Jnl* 12 (1986), 150–71.

[3] A full account of the collection will be published by Gatch in his historical introduction to a catalogue of *Fragmenta Manuscripta* prepared by K. Gould and L. Voigts. Dean Gatch kindly provided this information in advance of his publication of the history of the collection.

[4] *Fragmenta Manuscripta* 2 has been the subject of detailed study by N.H. Webb, 'Early Medieval Welsh Book-Production' (unpubl. Ph.D. dissertation, London Univ., forthcoming).

[5] R.W. Hunt, 'Manuscript Evidence for Knowledge of the Poems of Venantius Fortunatus in

DESCRIPTION OF *FRAGMENTA MANUSCRIPTA* I

The single leaf is thick but supple parchment, both recto and verso now having a 'suede' finish. The leaf has been irregularly cropped so that the present dimensions are 245/254 × 210/213; up to three letter-spaces have been cropped from the left of the recto, five from the right. There is no discernible ruling for the twenty-nine intact text lines, but three vertical drypoint lines are clearly visible between the columns, approximately 8 mm apart. Cropping of the text at top and bottom makes it difficult to estimate original dimensions, but because approximately forty-three words are missing between the end of col. a and the beginning of col. b, the leaf probably did not exceed by much the usual maximum dimensions of 300 × 200 noted by Bishop for English Caroline manuscripts.[6] All writing, including the rubric on the verso, is in a dark brown ink.

The display script, used for the Hebrew letters at the beginning of each verse, is eclectic, appropriating letter-forms from a number of scripts (see pls. VII and VIII), including square capital (**H** and **M**), uncial (**A**, **G** and **L**) and minuscule (**E** and **T**). Letters are crudely formed but serifs have been elaborated into split wedge-shaped finials on letters like **H**, **L** and **T**. Forms of uncial **G** and **T** – as in 'Gemel' (recto, col. a, line 17) and 'Teth' (recto, col. b, line 14) – are reminiscent of those found in earlier English specimens of imitation Roman uncial such as the Codex Amiatinus and related manuscripts from Wearmouth–Jarrow, and London, BL Cotton Vespasian A. i from Canterbury.[7] The haphazard appearance of the display script is not necessarily indicative of an early date; contrast the careless display script – particularly when compared to the careful text hand – of p. 100 of Cambridge, Corpus Christi College 191, an Exeter manuscript from the third quarter of the eleventh century containing Chrodegang's *Regula canonicorum*.[8]

The text hand is Caroline with Insular forms: **e** is tall in ligature, especially with the Insular **g** (recto, col. a, line 16; verso, col. b, line 8), and the Insular form for **f** was used (verso, col. a, line 17). There is the Insular form of **g** alongside a '3'-shaped Caroline form; both occur on line 6 of recto, col. a. Descenders can be found occasionally on **s** (recto, col. b, line 11 and verso, col. a, lines 19 and 24). The shoulder stroke of the short **r** was formed with a broad double curve, often terminating in a prominent upward curl when in final position or when not joined to a following letter. The Insular dotted **y** can be

late Anglo-Saxon England', *ASE* 8 (1979), 279–87; with 'Appendix: Knowledge of the Poems in the Earlier Period' by M. Lapidge, pp. 287–95.

6 T. A. M. Bishop, *English Caroline Minuscule* (Oxford, 1971), p. xii.

7 M. B. Parkes, *The Scriptorium of Wearmouth–Jarrow*, Jarrow Lecture (Jarrow, 1982).

8 See Bishop, *English Caroline Minuscule*, p. 24 and pl. XXIV.

seen on recto, col. a, line 12. The most idiosyncratic letter-form is **x** (see recto, col. a, line 7 and col. b, line 9), but unclosed **p** may be idiosyncratic too (recto, col. b, line 6). The handwriting has a pronounced slope to the right. It bears a general resemblance to the script of the mid-tenth century Smaragdus, Cambridge, University Library, Ee. 2. 4.[9]

Abbreviations were used only sparingly; there are, for example, no ampersands. In addition to its use for *nomina sacra*, the common mark of abbreviation occurs primarily for medial vowels (verso, col. a, line 20) and for final **m** or **n** (verso, col. a, lines 10 and 11). *Est* was written as **e** with the common mark of abbreviation, both with and without surrounding *punctus* (recto, col. a, line 22 and col. b, line 8). In the rubric the sign resembling a modern semicolon has been used for **-us** and **-ue** (verso, col. b, lines 15 and 17) and the **e** with 'cedilla' for **-ae** (verso, col. b, line 18).

Punctuation is limited to the raised *punctus* for both medial and final pauses and – at the end of the rubric – the *positura* (verso, col. b, line 20).[10] Word separation is poor. In addition to the instances of the common confusion between free and bound morphemes (in, for example, prepositions and prefixes), there are instances of words grouped with scarcely any space between them (recto, col. a, line 26). This pattern of word separation, or 'word linking', could reflect the nature of the exemplar, perhaps a ninth-century continental codex.[11]

The fragment displays evidence of its use in binding. On the recto, in the space between columns from line 9 to 12, a twelfth-century *probatio pennae* can be seen. A later scribe has written, lengthwise in the intercolumnar space, the abbreviations for *quoniam non* and *Dominus dixit*. Although one would expect no connection between this pen-testing and the original text on the leaf, it should be noted that col. b, line 9 also contains the words *Dominus dixit*. It seems less likely, however, that these notes are any sort of gloss on the Lamentations text than that there is some connection between them and the twelfth-century pen trials found on 1r of the Tenison Fortunatus.[12] If there is such a connection, then it appears that *Fragmenta Manuscripta* 1 has been a discrete leaf, serving as flyleaf or pastedown to what is now London, BL Add. 24193, since the twelfth century. A second feature of the fragment that

---

[9] *Ibid*. p. 2 and pl. II; see also below, pp. 91–2.

[10] On the *positura*, see M. B. Parkes, 'The Contribution of Insular Scribes of the Seventh and Eighth Centuries to the "Grammar of Legibility"', *Grafia e interpunzione del latino nel medioevo*, ed. A. Maierù (Rome, 1987), pp. 15–30.

[11] On word separation, see *ibid*. pp. 24–6; see also H. Gneuss, 'Guide to the Editing and Preparation of Texts for the Dictionary of Old English', *A Plan for the Dictionary of Old English*, ed. R. Frank and A. Cameron (Toronto, 1973), pp. 11–23, esp. p. 18.

[12] Hunt, 'Manuscript Evidence', p. 280, provides a transcription of the pen trials in Add. 24193.

probably derives from its use as binder's waste is the sequence of twenty small vertical slits each *c*. 2 mm high and 2 mm apart that can be seen in line 27 of col. b of the recto and col. a of the verso. Although these may appear to be neumes in a photograph, that is not the case.

TEXT

Fragmenta Manuscripta 1 contains a biblical text, intended, as the rubric on the verso indicates, for reading at monastic offices. The text, from Lamentations II and III, is fragmentary because of the cropping of the leaf but now contains the following verses or portions of verses: Lam. II.22- III.14; Lam III.19–35; Lam. III.40–56; and Lam. III.60–6. The text falls within the Vulgate tradition. Of the thirty-one variants from the Rome edition of 1972, twenty-two can be found in manuscripts used in that edition.[13] Although there is insufficient text from which to draw any firm conclusions, it should be noted that of the four manuscripts with six or more variant readings corresponding to the *Fragmenta Manuscripta* 1 text, three fall in a single group: Cava, Archivio della Badia 1 (14) (Spain, s. ix²); León, Archivo catedralicio 6 (A.D. 920); and León, S. Isidoro (A.D. 960). Six variants also correspond to the text in Autun, Bibl. mun. 2 (S. I) (s. viii^ex).

Although the text can be placed in the early medieval Vulgate tradition, *Fragmenta Manuscripta* 1 is not a leaf from a bible, for at the end of the last verse of Lam. III is a short space after which the scribe has supplied the following rubric:

In tribus noctibus ante pascha Domini leguntur tres prime lectiones in una quaque nocte de lamentatione Hierimie prophete et .vi. alie de omoeliis in cena Domini in parasceue [et] in sabato sancto.

These instructions can be placed in a well-documented tradition of monastic readings for the three night Offices (Nocturns) during the last three days in Holy Week, the *triduum*.[14] Particularly important for Anglo-Saxon monastic use was a Roman *ordo* from the second half of the eighth century, *Ordo* XIIIA as edited by Andrieu.[15] The sections in that *ordo* relevant to the rubric in the Missouri fragment include separate instructions for Nocturns for each day of the *triduum*:

---

[13] 'Liber Hieremiae et Lamentationes', *Biblia sacra iuxta latinam vulgatam versionem ad codicum fidem iussu Pauli PP. VI* (Rome, 1972), pp. 295–301.

[14] A. Hughes, *Medieval Manuscripts for Mass and Office* (Toronto, 1982), pp. 60–3, and S. J. P. van Dijk, 'The Bible in Liturgical Use', *Cambridge History of the Bible*, ed. P. R. Ackroyd *et al.*, 3 vols. (Cambridge, 1963–70) II, 220–52. Also very helpful, although it concentrates on the Office after the 970s, is M. McC. Gatch, 'The Office in late Anglo-Saxon Monasticism', *Learning and Literature in Anglo-Saxon England*, ed. M. Lapidge and H. Gneuss (Cambridge, 1985), pp. 341–62.

[15] M. Andrieu, *Les ordines Romani du haut moyen âge*, 5 vols. (Louvain, 1931–61) II, 469–88.

Caena Domini

3. Feria .v. in caena Domini legunt lectiones tres de lamentatione Hieremiae et tres de tractatu Augustini in psalmo *Exaudi Deus*... tres de apostolo ubi ait ad Corinthios...

4. In parasceven similiter tres lectiones de lamentatione Hieremiae prophetae, tres de tractatu Sancti Augustini de psalmo LXVIIII, tres de apostolo ubi ait ad Hebreos....

5. In sabbato sancto in psalmis, in lectionibus, in responsoriis similiter omnia complenda sunt, sicut superius diximus et, si fuerint sermones de proprie, legantur.[16]

Although the rubric is much less specific regarding the readings that follow Lamentations, the instruction that the first three lessons for each of the three days come from Lamentations is similar.

There is certainly no doubt about the monastic tradition for these office readings, but the question of what kind of service book is evidenced by this fragment – proto-breviary, homiliary, or lectionary of biblical lessons – is much more complex and is probably unresolvable on the basis of a single leaf.[17] One possibility is that the leaf derives from what Helmut Gneuss calls a 'primitive' breviary, a forerunner of the breviary known in England from the twelfth century onwards which 'combines all the texts sung or read in the Office – psalms, antiphons, lessons, responsories, chapters, collects etc. – in the order in which they actually occur in the services'.[18] Gneuss cites a continental breviary from the first half of the ninth century and a number of eleventh-century English manuscripts which represent 'various stages of development of the full breviary'.[19]

---

[16] *Ibid.* pp. 482–3.

[17] H. Gneuss, 'Liturgical Books in Anglo-Saxon England and their Old English Terminology', *Learning and Literature in Anglo-Saxon England*, ed. Lapidge and Gneuss, pp. 91–141.

[18] *Ibid.* p. 110; see also p. 120, and J.B.L. Tolhurst, 'Introduction to the English Monastic Breviaries', *The Monastic Breviary of Hyde Abbey, Winchester*, 6 vols., HBS 69, 70, 71, 76, 78 and 80 (London, 1932–42), VI.

[19] Gneuss, 'Liturgical Books', p. 111. I have undertaken the following comparison of readings from Lamentations at Nocturns during the *triduum*:

BREVIARIES CONTAINING LESSONS FOR THE FIRST NOCTURN

	feria .v. in cena Domini	*feria .vi. in parasceve*	*in sabbato sancto*
Hereford (ptd ed. of 1505; HBS 26)	Lam. I.1–6	Lam. I.10–15	Lam. II.1–6
Ely (CUL Ii. 4. 20)	Lam. I.1–6	Lam. II.1–6	Lam. III.1–14
Hyde Abbey (HBS 69)	Lam. I.1–5	Lam. III.1–9	Lam. IV.1–4
Coldingham (BL Harley 4664)	Lam. I.1–6	Lam. III.1–3	Lam. IV.1–6
Muchelney (BL Add. 43405)	Lam. I.1–6	Lam. II.1–6	Lam. IV.1–8
Hereford (s. xiii; HBS 26)	Lam. I.1–9	Lam. III.1–21	Lam. IV.1–10
St Albans (BL Royal 2. A. x)	not relevant		

Although these breviaries are all later than the Anglo-Saxon period, they may shed some light on the Missouri lectionary leaf. Note that manuscripts three to six include readings from

A second possibility is that the leaf derives from a homiliary, for early manuscripts of the influential homiliary of Paul the Deacon[20] include texts from Lamentations with the Holy Week homilies. London, British Library, Royal 2. C. III (? Rochester, s. xi^ex) includes Lam. I.1–17 on 34r (*cena Domini*), Lam. II.1–14 on 38v (*parasceve*), and Lam. III.1–36 on 43r (*sabbato sancto*). Cambridge, University Library, Kk. 4. 13 (Norwich, s. xi/xii) contains identical readings for the three days on 27r, 31v, and 36r.[21] On the evidence of these two manuscripts, the primary arguments against *Fragmenta Manuscripta* I deriving from a homiliary seem to be threefold: the fragment contained apparently all, not part, of Lamentations III, unlike the homiliaries; a space, rather than another reading, follows the rubric on the verso; and, most important, Lamentations III follows immediately after Lamentations II on the fragment, with nothing intervening as in the cases of the homily codices. The latter two arguments could also be raised against the leaf as a folio from a breviary, at least from a breviary as we know it from the twelfth century, even if not against its derivation from a 'primitive' breviary of unknown nature.

The third possibility is that the fragment is a leaf from a kind of Anglo-Saxon codex that does not otherwise survive, a volume containing all the biblical readings necessary for Nocturns. Gneuss does not know of such a book, nor of a bible that might have been used at Nocturns, but he suggests that booklists 'would appear to show that both types of book must have been used'.[22] With a single leaf, however, we cannot know if this fragment was from either type of manuscript. We can only infer from the rubric, and from the space following it, that the codex contained Lamentations I–III for the purpose of reading at the night Offices of the *triduum*. Happily, a number of descriptive terms survive from Anglo-Saxon England that are sufficiently imprecise for us to use them to describe the codex from which *Fragmenta Manuscripta* survives.[23] There are the Old English terms *rædingboc* and *redeboc* and the temporally more precise *winterrædingboc* to indicate a lectionary with readings up to the Easter service which would mark the beginning of the

---

Lamentations IV, a situation apparently different from that of the Missouri leaf, which seems to have given inclusive readings for Lamentations I–III, but not IV.

[20] On the homiliary of Paul the Deacon, see Gneuss, 'Liturgical Books', pp. 122–3.

[21] I am grateful for the advice of Helmut Gneuss regarding this comparison, as well as that of breviaries described in n. 19. It should be noted that two other codices containing homiliary material from Paul the Deacon, London, BL, Harley 652, and CUL Ii. 2. 19, are not relevant here because they are instances of the *sumerrædingboc*, providing readings from Easter vigil to the fourth Sunday after Epiphany and fifth Sunday after Christmas respectively.

[22] Gneuss, 'Liturgical Books', p. 122; see also pp. 120–1, and Gatch, 'The Office', p. 346.

[23] Gneuss points out that imprecise terminology may reflect the varying contents of manuscripts, for example, a homiliary-cum-legendary that survives in fragmentary form from the eleventh century (*ibid.* p. 120).

sumerrædingboc.[24] Ambiguous Latin terminology from surviving Anglo-Saxon booklists includes *lectionarius*[25] and 'libri in quibus ad matutinas legitur'.[26] Although it is not possible to say precisely that the leaf bears witness to a proto-breviary, a biblical lectionary, or – least likely – a homiliary, we are fortunate to have a number of terms in both Latin and the vernacular of Anglo-Saxon England that are appropriate for the original manuscript containing the leaf under discussion.

DATE AND ORIGIN

To turn finally to the question of date and place of origin of *Fragmenta Manuscripta* 1 is to acknowledge that these issues may be as unresolvable as is the matter of precisely what kind of *rædingboc* the medieval codex must have been. Nonetheless, these questions must be addressed, for inherent in them is the issue of a merger of traditions – the continental as represented by the Caroline minuscule that the scribe who wrote the fragment was attempting to employ, however ineptly, and the Insular as revealed by the vestiges of the Insular minuscule script in which the scribe was almost certainly experienced. As was pointed out earlier (p. 84), the scribe used throughout his text hand some Insular features such as high **e** in ligature, and other Insular forms such as **s** with descender appear occasionally, perhaps when the scribe lapsed into a familiar and comfortable penstroke.

One possible explanation for this mixture of scripts is that *Fragmenta Manuscripta* 1 was written by a scribe trained in the minuscule hand of Anglo-Saxon England who encountered the unfamiliar Caroline hand on the continent and attempted to master it.[27] We have recently been told by Simon Keynes of 'the personal links between the West Saxon royal family and different ruling families on the continent' in the first half of the tenth century, complemented by 'more informal relations between the West Saxon kings and religious houses outside their realms, by visits of foreigners to England, and by the travels of Englishmen abroad'.[28] Relevant here is Keynes's discussion of the confraternity book of Reichenau (Zürich, Zentralbibliothek, Rh. hist. 27)

---

[24] On the Old English nomenclature, see Gneuss, 'Liturgical Books', p. 121, and 'Linguistic Borrowing and Old English Lexicography: Old English Terms for the Books of the Liturgy', *Problems of Old English Lexicography: Studies in Memory of Angus Cameron*, ed. A. Bammesberger, Eichstätter Beiträge 15 (Regensburg, 1985), 107–29, esp. 112, 119 and 122.

[25] See, for example, M. Lapidge, 'Surviving Booklists from Anglo-Saxon England', *Learning and Literature in Anglo-Saxon England*, ed. Lapidge and Gneuss, pp. 33–89, esp. pp. 78 and 81, n. 44.   [26] Gneuss, 'Liturgical Books', p. 120.

[27] It is difficult to assess precisely when Caroline manuscripts began to influence Anglo-Saxon book production; see below, nn. 31 and 32.

[28] S. Keynes, 'King Athelstan's Books', *Learning and Literature in Anglo-Saxon England*, ed. Lapidge and Gneuss, pp. 143–201, esp. 197.

containing an entry that apparently refers to an English visit to German monasteries in 929; Keynes concludes that this entry was not written by the Englishman Wigheard named in it because of the German spelling of his name and the Caroline hand in which it was written.[29] Although the addition is too brief for detailed comparison with the hand of *Fragmenta Manuscripta* 1, two striking similarities between the two hands should be pointed out. The Reichenau addition contains an Insular **f** that contrasts with the Caroline form on the rest of the page but is quite similar to the letter-form found on lines 16 and 17 of col. a of the verso of the Missouri fragment. Likewise one finds in the Reichenau addition **x** written in the same way as the unusual form found on the recto, col. a, line 7 and col. b, line 9, of *Fragmenta Manuscripta* 1.

The early tenth century is, of course, not the only period when one might expect to find an English monk on the continent attempting the script of his hosts.[30] Yet the argument that can be raised against the copying out of a lectionary by an Anglo-Saxon scribe on the continent attempting to employ the local script is that of the difference between a brief entry in a confraternity book and a large service book. It is less difficult to explain a brief addition to a manuscript than to posit an entire large service book copied on the continent by an Anglo-Saxon scribe, employing a script he had not entirely mastered, in the company of expert practitioners of that script. It is then more probable that the lectionary was written by an Anglo-Saxon scribe in his native land than that it was executed on the continent, and the fact that the fragment survived in a volume, the Tenison Fortunatus, part of which was written in Anglo-Saxon England, along with another fragment, *Fragmenta Manuscripta* 2, at least part of which was written in England, would also suggest that the original lectionary was more likely to have been written in England than on the continent.

The earliest efforts to employ the new script in the writing of English manuscripts may well not survive; Bishop found no evidence from before the mid-tenth century,[31] although others have argued that Caroline scripts known to have been in early tenth-century England must have had some impact on English book production.[32] Still, those surviving attempts to produce the new script in England – even if they are partial, unrepresentative, and do not testify to the earliest stages[33] – should be compared to the hand of *Fragmenta*

---

[29] *Ibid.* p. 200; see also pl. xv (p. LXX of the Zürich manuscript).

[30] Michael Lapidge has suggested to me that this could have happened in the eleventh century as well, although presumably my reservations about the copying out of a lectionary would be applicable late as well as early.   [31] *English Caroline Minuscule*, pp. xiv and xix.

[32] See, for example, K. D. Hartzell, 'The Early Provenance of the Harkness Gospels', *Bull. of Research in the Humanities* 84 (1981), 85–97, esp. 93.

[33] Bishop, *English Caroline Minuscule*, p. xv, cautions that more than half of the surviving instances of the script derive from seven scriptoria.

Manuscripta 1, and such a comparison reveals that three of the surviving mid-tenth-century English manuscripts in the new Caroline minuscule illustrate similar, if by no means identical, features of hand to those found in the Missouri fragment. All three of them have been associated, on the basis of arguments that vary in their merits,[34] with the Glastonbury circle of Dunstan.

To look first at Dunstan's text hand in the famous classbook apparently written at Glastonbury, presumably before his exile to Ghent in 956 (Oxford, Bodleian Library, Auct. F. 4. 32, fols. 20 (partial), 36 (partial) and 47r) is to find that it bears some similarity in letter-forms to the hand of the Missouri fragment, but it is more carefully written.[35] Comparable letter-forms are **a**, **e** and high **e** in ligature, Insular **f**, **r** with double curve and upward curl, **s** with descender and dotted **y**. Both **g** and **x** differ, however. Punctuation and word separation are similar, but abbreviations differ.

Dunstan's glossing hand, identified by Malcolm Parkes in Vatican City, Biblioteca Apostolica Vaticana, lat. 3363, is similar to his text hand but less formal and – perhaps because of that – bears more similarity to *Fragmenta Manuscripta* 1.[36] Again there is similarity in the letter-forms for **a**, **e** (two forms), **f**, **r**, **s**, and dotted **y**. However, **d**, **g**, and **h** differ, and the angle of intersection of **x** is somewhat different. Word separation and abbreviations are generally similar to the fragment. Difference in abbreviation forms between the classbook and the Boethius gloss may suggest that Dunstan copied the abbreviations of his exemplar. Another, probably contemporary, glossing hand in the Vatican Boethius bears even more resemblance to the hand seen on the Missouri fragment. That hand employs all the similar letter-forms found in the Dunstan glossing hand in addition to **d**, **g**, and **h**. Word separation is similar, but there is no basis for comparison of abbreviations.

The text hand, as opposed to glossing hand, most similar to the Missouri fragment is that found in the copy of Smaragdus's *Expositio in Regulam S. Benedicti* in Cambridge, University Library, Ee. 2. 4 + Oxford, Bodleian Library, lat. theol. c. 3, fols. 1, 1* and 2, a codex described by Bishop as mid-tenth-century, possibly written at Glastonbury.[37] Letter forms for **a**, **d**, **e** (two

---

[34] It should be acknowledged that N. R. Ker accepted only three tenth- and eleventh-century attributions to Glastonbury, and of those three only Oxford, Bodleian Library, Auct. F. 4. 32, is considered here; see *Medieval Libraries of Great Britain: A List of Surviving Books*, 2nd ed. (London, 1964), pp. 90–1.

[35] For the facsimile, see R. W. Hunt, *Saint Dunstan's Classbook from Glastonbury: Codex Biblioth. Bodl. Oxon. Auct. F. 4.32*, Umbrae codicum occidentalium 4 (Amsterdam, 1961). See also Bishop, *English Caroline Minuscule*, p. 1, pl. 1.

[36] M. B. Parkes, 'A Note on MS Vatican, Bibl. Apost., lat. 3363', *Boethius, His Life, Thought and Influence*, ed. M. T. Gibson (Oxford, 1981), pp. 425–7. I am particularly grateful to Dr Parkes for providing me with photocopies of many leaves from this codex.

[37] *English Caroline Minuscule*, p. 2, pl. II, and Bishop, 'An Early Example of Insular-Caroline', *Trans. of the Cambridge Bibliographical Soc.* 4 (1964–8), 396–400.

forms), **f, r** and **s** bear comparison to the Missouri fragment, but there are some differences between the fragment and the Smaragdus codex in the letter-forms for **g, h, x** and dotted **y**. Punctuation and abbreviations are generally similar, although the Smaragdus scribe used the ampersands eschewed by the lectionary scribe. 'Word linking' is less common in the Smaragdus than the fragment, but it can be found.

The similarity, if not the identity, of the hand of *Fragmenta Manuscripta* 1 with two text hands and two glossing hands in three manuscripts associated with Glastonbury in the mid-tenth century may take on additional significance from the fact that the Tenison Fortunatus, with which the lectionary leaf seems to have been bound from at least the twelfth century, has been suggested as a Glastonbury manuscript.[38] However, it must be emphasized that – given the erratic patterns of survival of tenth-century English manuscripts and the absence of compelling evidence to afford identification of the lectionary scribe with the four hands most closely resembling his – the mid-tenth-century Glastonbury connection must remain only a hypothesis, albeit the most attractive of the possibilities.

[38] Hunt, 'Manuscript Evidence', p. 286. This codex must have been, however, only one of a number of Fortunatus manuscripts in Anglo-Saxon England; see, in addition to Hunt, Lapidge, 'Appendix: Knowledge of the Poems', and 'Surviving Booklists', pp. 46–8.

Old English prose before and during the reign of Alfred

JANET M. BATELY

Old English poetry had its origins in the pagan continental past of the Anglo-Saxons. The development of an Old English literary prose is generally supposed to have taken place many centuries later in Christian England. According to a recent work by Michael Alexander, for instance.

Old English prose . . . was called into being by a decision of Alfred, king of Wessex from 871 to 899. The worthy citizen in Molière's play Le Bourgeois Gentilhomme was astonished to discover that he had been speaking prose all his life. But though the Angles and Saxons had been speaking Old English for centuries, there is little evidence that this speech was cultivated for compositions of an unmetrical form, unlike Old Irish for instance, whose heroic saga is always in prose. . . . Writing was then a clerical monopoly, and its language was Latin.[1]

And again: 'Apart from a small amount of legal writing, and the exceptional mini-saga of Cynewulf and Cyneheard . . . the only English from before Alfred appears in the glosses inserted between the lines of the Latin texts of the Psalms and Canticles; this does not amount to prose.'[2] And finally, 'Alfred wrote in an England where clerics could not read Latin, laymen could not read, and English had not previously been written.'[3] In the words of C. L. Wrenn, 'Old English literary prose begins with King Alfred, since all that went before was non-literary.'[4]

---

[1] M. Alexander, Old English Literature (London, 1983), p. 132.

[2] Ibid., p. 133. There is in fact no evidence at all to support the theory that the Cynewulf and Cyneheard annal is a faithful representation of prose from the period 'before Alfred', rather than a slightly clumsy paraphrase of a 'lay' (transmitted either orally or in written form), which a late-ninth-century chronicler interpolated in a series of annals dealing with the second half of the eighth century. See C. L. Wrenn, A Study of Old English Literature (London, 1967), pp. 53 and 202–5, and J. Bately, 'The Compilation of the Anglo-Saxon Chronicle 60 B.C. to A.D. 890: Vocabulary as Evidence', PBA 64 (1980 for 1978), 93–129; see further, below, n. 215.

[3] Alexander, Old English Literature, p. 150. For a warning against taking literally claims made in the prefatory letter to the Pastoral Care concerning the lack of literacy in England, see, e.g., J. Morrish, 'King Alfred's Letter as a Source on Learning in England in the Ninth Century', Studies in Earlier Old English Prose, ed. P. E. Szarmach (Albany, NY, 1986), pp. 87–107; see also C. P. Wormald, 'The Uses of Literacy in Anglo-Saxon England and its Neighbours', TRHS 5th ser. 27 (1977), 95–114.

[4] Wrenn, A Study, ch. 12; esp. p. 205. Cf. 'Alfred's purposes in starting up the process which eventually came to be known as English literature were, in the proper sense of the word, political, and practical rather than artistic' (Alexander, Old English Literature, p. 133).

However, although the theory of a relatively late development for vernacular prose is generally accepted, the part played by King Alfred in its establishment as a literary medium is still very much a matter of dispute. As long ago as 1953, Vleeskruyer argued against the view that the history of English prose should be held to begin with the early West Saxon revival of learning in Wessex, concluding that, 'for all Alfred's great achievement as a scholar and educator, such a generalization as this cannot be sustained in the face of the accumulating evidence that a vigorous tradition of Mercian vernacular writing preceded his work and, to a large extent, rendered it possible'.[5] And in 1986, Greenfield and Calder, while conceding to Alfred the central rôle in creating a national prose literature,[6] not only accepted Vleeskruyer's view that there was a group of Mercian prose texts already in existence before Alfred began to translate, composed in 'a style that was to find its most refined use in the works of Ælfric and Wulfstan', but also saw a 'tradition of native composition . . . deeply imbedded in English culture from the seventh to the eleventh centuries'.[7] However, their conclusion is that 'we need not posit a whole Mercian school of translation such as Alfred later created'.[8] My purpose in this paper is to reconsider these conflicting views.[9]

THE CORPUS OF SURVIVING WORKS WHICH ARE TO BE DATED BEFORE 900

Any discussion of the development of Old English prose has to begin with an attempt to establish the corpus of works surviving from the period ending with the death of Alfred in 899. If we were to confine ourselves to palaeographical evidence as a criterion, the corpus would be very small indeed. On the one hand, we would have a few legal documents – charters, wills, ownership inscriptions and the like[10] – a brief annal-type account of the arrival

---

[5] *The Life of St Chad*, ed. R. Vleeskruyer (Amsterdam, 1953), p. 41.

[6] S. B. Greenfield and D. G. Calder, *A New Critical History of Old English Literature* (New York, 1986), pp. 38–9.

[7] *Ibid.* pp. 63 and 38; see also 'There were, of course, translations into English before Alfred's time', *ibid.* p. 63.   [8] *Ibid.*

[9] The first version of this paper, entitled 'On the Development of Vernacular Written Prose in the Early Old English Period', was given at the ISAS conference of 1985 and was dedicated to the memory of Professor Rowland Collins, 'who contributed in so many ways to our understanding and our appreciation of a much neglected and undervalued corpus of early literature'.

[10] E.g., Stockholm Kungliga Biblioteket. A. 135 (the Codex Aureus), dated 's. ix med.' by N. R. Ker, *Catalogue of Manuscripts containing Anglo-Saxon* (Oxford, 1957), no. 385, and ptd *The Oldest English Texts*, ed. H. Sweet, EETS os 83 (1885), 174–5; also London, British Library, Cotton Augustus II. 19 (P. H. Sawyer, *Anglo-Saxon Charters. An Annotated List and Bibliography* (London, 1968), no. 1200), and BL Stowe Charter 8 (Sawyer no. 1500). I exclude runic inscriptions and non-continuous glosses from the corpus.

of Cerdic in Britain and the succession of West Saxon kings to Alfred,[11] and probably also continuous psalter glosses[12] and a prayer commonly known as the Lorica Prayer.[13] On the other hand, we would have three 'major' pieces of literary prose, one seemingly Mercian and two West Saxon in origin: the anonymous Old English Martyrology,[14] King Alfred's *Pastoral Care*,[15] and the *Anglo-Saxon Chronicle* to 890,[16] a work which survives in a manuscript of s. ix/x and which was used by Alfred's biographer, Asser, in 893.[17] However, these

---

[11] BL Add. 23211, 1v (Ker, *Catalogue*, no. 127 ('s. ix ex.')). Although this text is generally described as a regnal list, it is written in continuous prose. The fact that it ends with King Alfred appears to indicate a date of composition (though not necessarily of copying) before 900. For the most recent edition, see D. Dumville, 'The West Saxon Genealogical Regnal List', *Anglia* 104 (1986), 1–32.

[12] BL Cotton Vespasian A. i and *The Oldest English Texts*, ed. Sweet, pp. 183–420; Ker, *Catalogue*, no. 203, dates the hand of the Vespasian Psalter gloss as 'probably of s. ix med.' However, cf. K. Sisam, 'Canterbury, Lichfield, and the Vespasian Psalter', *RES* ns 7 (1956), 1–10 and 113–31, at 120 and 128, where a possible link with Plegmund and the late ninth century is suggested, but a tenth-century date for the gloss is not ruled out.

[13] Cambridge, University Library, Ll. 1. 10, ptd *The Oldest English Texts*, ed. Sweet, p. 174; see Ker, *Catalogue*, no. 27, art, a, 's. ix–x'.

[14] See BL Add. 23211, fol. 2, and above, n. 11. Since the Martyrology scribe seems also to have written the text of the West Saxon regnal list ending with Alfred in the same manuscript, he must have been working after 871. For another early fragmentary copy, see BL Add. 40165 A, fols 6–7, dated 's. ix/x' by Ker, *Catalogue*, no. 132. For the Mercian characteristics of the Martyrology text of Add. 23211 and its West Saxon veneer, see C. Sisam, 'An Early Fragment of the Old English *Martyrology*', *RES* ns 4 (1953), 209–20, and for the language of the Martyrology as a whole, see *Das altenglische Martyrologium*, ed. G. Kotzor, Bayerische Akademie der Wissenschaften, Phil.-Hist. Klasse, Neue Forschung 88 (Munich, 1981), an important edition which supersedes *An Old English Martyrology*, ed. G. Herzfeld, EETS os 116 (1900).

[15] The two oldest surviving manuscripts of this work date from the time of 'publication'. These are Oxford, Bodleian Library, Hatton 20, and the badly fire-damaged BL Cotton Tiberius B. xi + Kassel, Landesbibliothek, Anhang 19, both dated 890–7 by Ker, *Catalogue*, nos. 324 and 195. See further, K. Sisam, *Studies in the History of Old English Literature* (Oxford, 1953, repr. 1967), pp. 140–7, and *King Alfred's West-Saxon Version of Gregory's Pastoral Care*, ed. H. Sweet, EETS os 45 and 50 (Oxford, 1871), hereafter referred to as *Pastoral Care*. For the Latin text, see *Liber regulae pastoralis*, PL 77 (Paris, 1862), 13–128, hereafter referred to as *Cura pastoralis*.

[16] See *The Anglo-Saxon Chronicle: a Collaborative Edition*, ed. D. Dumville and S. Keynes, in progress: vol. 3, *MS A*, ed. J.M. Bately (Cambridge, 1986), and vol. 4, *MS B*, ed. S. Taylor (Cambridge, 1983).

[17] See *Asser's Life of King Alfred*, ed. W.H. Stevenson (Oxford, 1904, repr. with an article by D. Whitelock, Oxford, 1959) and *Alfred the Great: Asser's Life of King Alfred and other Contemporary Sources*, ed. and trans, S. Keynes and M. Lapidge (Harmondsworth, 1983). For the dating of the first hand of MS A (Cambridge, Corpus Christi College 173) to 's. ix/x', see *The Anglo-Saxon Chronicle, MS A*, ed. Bately, pp. xxi–xxv. A late-ninth-century date can thus be established for the *Pastoral Care* and *Chronicle* and, even allowing for a margin of error in dating by handwriting, a similar date appears likely for the Martyrology; see further, below, p. 103, and K. Sisam, 'Canterbury, Lichfield, and the Vespasian Psalter', pp. 113–14.

texts are certainly not the only early prose works to have come down to us.[18] A further body of charters and other legal documents, composed before 900 and including King Alfred's will, has survived in copies made after that date,[19] as have the laws of the Kentish kings from Æthelberht to Wihtred, and the West Saxon kings Ine and Alfred.[20] Some of these documents may be translations from Latin, made long after the original date of issue.[21] However, in the light of Bede's statement that the legal codes of Æthelberht were 'conscripta Anglorum sermone',[22] it seems reasonable to suppose that even the earliest of the laws were composed in the vernacular – though transmission for a time by word of mouth[23] can never be ruled out, and some updating of language has clearly taken place between the time of composition and the making of surviving copies. As Dorothy Whitelock has said in the context of certain later codes, 'it is easy to conceive that when a text is being copied, not out of antiquarian interest, but with the intention of incorporating it in new legislation, absolute fidelity to the ancient wording is not felt necessary'.[24]

'Literary' texts in prose to be assigned with certainty to the period before 900 and to the West Saxon area, but, unlike the *Pastoral Care*, preserved only in later copies, are the Old English versions of Boethius's *De consolatione philosophiae*[25] and Augustine's *Soliloquia*[26] and the preface to the laws of

---

[18] Early texs which have not survived and which were arguably in prose include the translations of parts of the Gospel of St John and Isidore, *De natura rerum* by the Northumbrian scholar, Bede (see *Venerabilis Baedae Opera historica*, ed. C. Plummer (Oxford, 1896, repr. 1975), pp. lxxv–lxxvi and clxii). The Council of Clofesho (746/7) allowed translations not only of the Creed and Lord's Prayer, but also of the offices of Mass and Baptism; see Wormald, 'Literacy', pp. 103–4. Other lost works that may have been partly or wholly in vernacular prose are the laws of Offa and Mercia, King Alfred's handbook and (perhaps) a version of Hrabanus Maurus; see D. Whitelock, *Alfred the Great* (forthcoming).

[19] E.g., *Anglo-Saxon Charters*, ed. A. J. Robertson (Cambridge, 1939), nos. VII, XI, XII and XIV, and *Select English Historical Documents of the Ninth and Tenth Centuries*, ed. F. E. Harmer (Cambridge, 1914), nos. VIII and XI–XVII.

[20] *The Laws of the Earliest English Kings*, ed. F. L. Attenborough (Cambridge, 1922).

[21] E.g., *Anglo-Saxon Charters*, ed. Robertson, nos. I and II; see *ibid*. pp. 259–60, where it is suggested (not implausibly) that these translations could have been made in the time of Werferth.

[22] *Bede's Ecclesiastical History of the English People*, ed. B. Colgrave and R. A. B. Mynors (Oxford, 1969) II.5. This text is hereafter referred to as *Historia ecclesiastica*.

[23] See, e.g., H. Vollrath, 'Gesetzgebung und Schriftlichkeit. Das Beispiel der Angelsächsischen Gesetze', *Historisches Jahrbuch* 99 (1979), 28–54, and Wormald, 'Literacy', pp. 111–12.

[24] *English Historical Documents* c. 500–1042, ed. D. Whitelock (2nd edn, London, 1979), p. 358.

[25] *King Alfred's Old English Version of Boethius De Consolatione Philosophiae*, ed. W. J. Sedgefield (Oxford, 1899), hereafter referred to as *Alfred's Boethius*. For the Latin text, see *Anicii Manlii Severini Boethii Philosophiae consolatio*, ed. L. Bieler, CCSL 94 (Turnholt, 1957), hereafter referred to as *De consolatione*.

[26] *King Alfred's Version of St Augustine's 'Soliloquies'*, ed. T. A. Carnicelli (Cambridge, Mass.,

Alfred,[27] all three works containing material attributing their authorship to King Alfred. The only Mercian text that can be securely assigned to the late ninth century is the translation of Gregory's *Dialogi*.[28] This not only has a preface by King Alfred, stating that he had commissioned it from his friends, but is also referred to by Asser in his life of King Alfred, where it is attributed to Werferth, bishop of Worcester.[29] Other works for which there are strong claims for a pre-tenth-century origin are the prose psalms of the Paris Psalter,[30] the Old English Orosius[31] and the first continuation of the *Anglo-Saxon Chronicle* to 896, pt 1, each with features linking them either to King Alfred or to late-ninth-century Wessex: the prose psalms have been identified with the translation attributed to King Alfred by William of Malmesbury;[32] the Orosius is a West Saxon work which was apparently composed after 889 and was possibly used by Alfred in his Boethius,[33] while the first continuation of the *Anglo-Saxon Chronicle*, likewise written in a West Saxon dialect, gives what

---

1969), hereafter referred to as *Alfred's Soliloquies*. The attribution to Alfred in this text could be a later scribal addition; see, however, *idem*, pp. 38–40, and J. M. Bately, 'King Alfred and the Translation of the Old English Orosius', *Anglia* 88 (1970), 433–60.

27 *Die Gesetze der Ags. I Text und Übersetzung*, ed. F. Liebermann (Halle, 1903), 16–88. For 'Alfredian' vocabulary in this text, see Bately, 'King Alfred and the Translation of the Old English Orosius', pp. 452–3. I exclude the body of the laws from this part of the discussion.

28 *Bischof Wærferths von Worcester Übersetzung der Dialoge Gregors des Grossen*, ed. H. Hecht (Leipzig, 1900–7, repr. Darmstadt, 1965), hereafter referred to as *Dialogues*. For the Latin text, see *Gregoire le Grand, Dialogues*, ed. A. de Vogüé, with translation by P. Antin, *Sources Chrétiennes*, 260 and 265 (Paris, 1979 and 1980), hereafter referred to as *Dialogi*.

29 *Asser's Life of King Alfred*, ed. Stevenson, ch. 77.

30 *Liber Psalmorum. The West-Saxon Psalms*, ed. J. W. Bright and R. L. Ramsey (Boston and London, 1907). Alfred was using a version of the Roman psalter.

31 *The Old English Orosius*, ed. J. Bately, EETS, ss 6 (Oxford, 1980), hereafter referred to as *Old English Orosius*. For the Latin text, see *Pauli Orosii Historiarum adversus paganos libri VII*, ed. C. Zangemeister, CSEL 5 (Vienna, 1882), hereafter referred to as *Historiarum libri septem*. William of Malmesbury's attribution of this work to King Alfred has now been discredited; see J. Raith, *Untersuchungen zum englischen Aspekt, I. Grundsätzliches Altenglisch* (Munich, 1951), pp. 54–61; E. M. Liggins, 'The Authorship of the Old English Orosius', *Anglia* 88 (1970), 289–322; and Bately, 'King Alfred and the Old English Translation of Orosius', pp. 433–60. Although Alexander (*Old English Literature*, pp. 144–5) claims that 'even sceptics . . . credit [Alfred] with the addition of a few pages on northern geography to the text of Orosius', I for one have been strenuously denying this in print since 1970.

32 *Willelmi Malmesbiriensis Monachi De gestis regum anglorum libri quinque*, ed. W. Stubbs, RS (London, 1887–9) I, 132. A. J. Frantzen, *King Alfred* (Boston, 1986), p. 91, describes Alfred's authorship as 'established beyond reasonable doubt'. For nineteenth- and twentieth-century attributions of the translation to Alfred and for an assessment of the evidence, see J. M. Bately, 'Lexical Evidence for the Authorship of the Prose Psalms in the Paris Psalter', *ASE* 10 (1982), 69–95.

33 See *Old English Orosius*, pp. lxxxvi–xciii, and J. M. Bately, 'Those Books that are Most Necessary for All Men to Know: the Classics and Ninth Century England, a Reappraisal', *The Classics in the Middle Ages*, ed. A. S. Bernardo and S. Levin (forthcoming).

seems to be a contemporary account of the last wars of Alfred.[34] Also traditionally associated with King Alfred is the Old English Bede.[35] However, in spite of attributions of the work to Alfred by Ælfric and William of Malmesbury,[36] attempts by Sherman Kuhn to explain away Mercianisms as due to the use of a Mercian gloss by the king,[37] and Michael Alexander's belief that it is a West Saxon work, undertaken at Alfred's request after the translation of Gregory's *Dialogi* and *Cura pastoralis*,[38] the consensus today is against a West Saxon author, be it Alfred or another, and in favour of a Mercian one.[39] If Alfred's authorship of the Bede is rejected, as it must surely be, the only *terminus post quem non* that we have for this work is the date of the oldest surviving manuscript fragment, i.e. 's. x in.',[40] and the translation can no longer be placed in the ninth century without fresh argument.

On this showing, then, there is a not inconsiderable body of ninth-century, or possibly ninth-century, prose texts surviving to the present day, most of them associated with King Alfred, and almost all of them in what we call West Saxon, apparently justifying the claims of supporters of the theory of Alfred's predominant rôle in the development of early Old English literary prose. Over recent years, however, scholars have sought to extend further the list of early works of Mercian, or less specifically Anglian, origin,[41] building up an impressive library of texts preserved in late-tenth-, or eleventh- or even

---

34 See T.A. Shippey, 'A Missing Army: some Doubts about the Alfredian *Chronicle*', *In Geardagum* 4 (1982), 41–55; R. Waterhouse, 'The Hæsten Episode in 894 *Anglo-Saxon Chronicle*', *SN* 46 (1974), 136–41; and J. Bately, 'The Compilation of the *Anglo-Saxon Chronicle* Once More', *Leeds Stud. in Eng.* ns 16 (1985), 7–36.

35 *The Old English Version of Bede's Ecclesiastical History of the English People*, ed. T. Miller, EETS os 95, 96, 110 and 111 (Oxford, 1890–8, repr. 1959), hereafter referred to as *Old English Bede*.

36 *Ælfric's Catholic Homilies: the Second Series*, ed. M. Godden, EETS ss 5 (Oxford, 1979), 72, and *De gestis regum*, ed. Stubbs I, 132. The Latin couplet in MS Ca of the Bede, attributing the work to King Alfred, is in a hand of the sixteenth century.

37 S.M. Kuhn, 'Synonyms in the Old English Bede', *JEGP* 46 (1947), 168–76, following a suggestion by J. Schipper, *Die Geschichte und der gegenwärtige Stand der Forschung über König Alfreds Übersetzung von Bedas Kirchengeschichte* (Vienna, 1898), p. 8; also Kuhn, 'The Authorship of the OE Bede Revisited;, *NM* 73 (1972), 172–80.

38 'His hand is not obvious in the West Saxon version of Bede', but he had it translated (*Old English Literature*, pp. 144–5).

39 See *Old English Bede*, Introduction; also Liggins, 'The Authorship', and G.G. Waite, 'The Vocabulary of the Old English Version of Bede's Historia ecclesiastica' (unpbl. Ph.D. dissertation, Toronto Univ., 1984). Did Ælfric read this work in a late manuscript with its most prominent Anglian features removed, or did he simply not associate with a specific geographical area what we today take to be distinctive Anglian features?

40 BL Cotton Domitian ix, fol. 11; see Ker, *Catalogue*, no. 151, art. 1. A second early manuscript is Oxford, Bodleian Library, Tanner 10; see Ker, *Catalogue*, no. 351 ('s. x¹').

41 For the terms 'Anglian' and 'Mercian', see, e.g., A. Campbell, *Old English Grammar* (Oxford, 1959, repr. 1974), §§6–8 and 19. A West Saxon text controversially attributed to the ninth century, this time on linguistic grounds, is the translation of the gospels, which Grünberg

twelfth-century copies, with a West Saxon veneer but, in their view, originally composed in an Anglian dialect before 900 and in some cases 'before Alfred'. These are:

(*i*) the 'Mercian' *Apocalypse of Thomas*,[42] *Epistola Alexandri ad Aristotelem*,[43] *St Chad*,[44] *St Guthlac*,[45] *The Wonders of the East*[46] and, more controversially, the Christopher homily;[47]

suggests was made in the ninth century by a West Saxon using a Mercian gloss. See *The West Saxon Gospels: a Study of the Gospel of St Matthew with Text of the Four Gospels*, ed. M. Grünberg (Amsterdam, 1967). However, Grünberg's arguments have not found acceptance and will not be considered here.

[42] M. Förster, 'A New Version of the Apocalypse of Thomas in Old English', *Anglia* 73 (1955), 6–36; see also F. Wenisch, *Spezifisch anglisches Wortgut in den nordhumbrischen Interlinearglossierungen des Lukasevangeliums* (Heidelberg, 1979), p. 72, where it is dated 'spätestens 1.H. des 9. Jhs.'

[43] *Three Old English Prose Texts in MS Cotton Vitellius A xv*, ed. S. Rypins, EETS os 161 (Oxford, 1924, repr. 1971), 1–50. Wenisch, *Spezifisch anglisches Wortgut*, p. 19, dates this text '2.H. des 9. Jhs'. For Sisam (*Studies*, p. 85), 'a certain uncouthness in the translation . . . points to an early date', insufficiency in Latin becoming less likely as the tenth century advances, while (*ibid.* p. 88) 'the spirit of the translation, like its style, accords well with the period of King Alfred's wars'.

[44] Vleeskruyer puts the translation 'at some time between, roughly, 850 and 900', but is inclined to favour the earlier date and to suggest that composition was not later than the third quarter of the ninth century (*St Chad*, p. 70); H. Schabram, *Superbia: Studien zum altenglischen Wortschatz, Teil I: Die dialektale und zeitliche Verbreitung des Wortguts* (Munich, 1965), p. 35, includes this work with the Martyrology and *Epistola Alexandri* among *Voralfredische Denkmäler*; and Greenfield and Calder, *A New Critical History*, p. 62, give the date of composition as *c.* 850.

[45] *Das angelsächsische Prosa-Leben des hl. Guthlac*, ed. P. Gonser (Heidelberg, 1909, repr. Amsterdam, 1966). Wenisch, *Spezifisch anglisches Wortgut*, p. 42, dates the work 'spätestens 1.H. des 10. Jhs.', and L.-G. Hallander, *Old English Verbs in '-sian', a Semantic and Derivational Study*, Acta Universitatis Stockholmiensis, Stockholm Stud. in Eng. 15 (Stockholm, 1966), 2.6.5, ninth-century. For J. Crawford (now J. Roberts), 'although it was possible that the original translation of the *Vita sancti Guthlaci* was made within the ninth century, . . . little if any specific evidence can be advanced to prove that it was made before the tenth century' ('*Guthlac*: an edition of the Prose Life' (unpubl. Ph.D dissertation, Oxford Univ., 1967), p. 230). See further, below, n. 122.

[46] *Three Old English Prose Texts*, ed. Rypins, pp. 51–67; also '*Wonders of the East*: a Synoptic Edition of the Letter of Pharasmanes and the Old English and Old Picard Translations', ed. A. Knock (unpubl. Ph.D dissertation, London Univ., 1982), with an important discussion of texts and source materials. Vleeskruyer (*St Chad*, p. 50, n. 1) assigns this text to the ninth century; see also Wenisch, *Spezifisch anglisches Wortgut*, p. 79.

[47] *Three Old English Prose Texts*, ed. Rypins, pp. 68–76. Sisam (*Studies*, pp. 68–9 and 62) argues that the Anglo-Saxon version, which is 'in good average Late West Saxon', was 'probably made about or soon after the middle of the tenth century'. However, Vleeskruyer (*St Chad*, p. 56) believes that 'archaic traits' might point to a considerably earlier period, while for Wenisch (who, following Vleeskruyer and Schabram, sees the text as 'Ws. Kopie eines merz. Originals'), the original is 'Wahrscheinlich 10., möglicherweise auch 9. Jh.' (*Spezifisch anglisches Wortgut*, p. 72).

Janet M. Bately

(*ii*) the 'Anglian, possibly Mercian' *Lacnunga*;[48]

(*iii*) the 'Anglian, probably Mercian' Bald's *Leechbook*;[49]

(*iv*) the 'Anglian' *Medicina de quadrupedibus*,[50] the Omont medical fragment[51] and possibly also the *Herbarium Apuleii*.[52]

A group of homilies generally taken to be Mercian in origin and composed between 875 and 950 includes the Blickling collection[53] and certain items in the Vercelli Book,[54] as well as a number of separate items, such as Napier XL and the *Vita Malchi* in Assmann XVIII.[55]

48 *Anglo-Saxon Magic and Medicine: Illustrated Specially from the Semi-Pagan Text Lacnunga*, ed. J. H. G. Grattan and C. Singer (London, 1952), pp. 96–227. See Wenisch, *Spezifisch anglisches Wortgut*, pp. 54–5 ('Ws. Kopie eines angl. wahrscheinlich merz. Originals. 9 Jh.').

49 *Leechdoms, Wordcunning, and Star-Craft of Early England*, ed. O. Cockayne (London, 1864–6) II, and G. Leonhardi, *Kleinere angelsächsische Denkmäler* I (Hamburg, 1905). Randolph Quirk (*Bald's Leechbook*, ed. C. E. Wright, EEMF 5 (Copenhagen, 1955), 32) sees certain spellings in the Leechbook as 'possibly suggesting an archetype of perhaps fifty years earlier', i.e. *c*. 900. However, Wenisch (*Spezifisch anglisches Wortgut*, p. 54) describes it as 'Ws. Kopien eines angl., vermutlich merz. Originals . . . Wahrscheinlich vor 900'. A. L. Meaney ('Variant Versions of Old English Medical Remedies and the Compilation of Bald's *Leechbook*', ASE 13 (1984), 235–68, at 251) suggests that the compiler of the 'original version' of Bald's *Lechbook* 'was arguably working in Winchester in or just before King Alfred's time'.

50 *The Old English Herbarium and Medicina de quadrupedibus*, ed. H. J. de Vriend, EETS os 286 (Oxford, 1984).

51 B. Schauman and A. Cameron, 'A Newly-Found Leaf of Old English from Louvain', *Anglia* 95 (1977), 289–312. For medical material in Nowell's transcript of BL Cotton Otho B. xi, possibly also ultimately derived from a ninth-century compilation, see R. Torkar, 'Zu den ae. Medizinaltexten in Otho B. xi und Royal 12. D. xvii', *Anglia* 94 (1976), 319–38. For the dates assigned to these texts, see below, nn. 62–4.

52 *The Old English Herbarium*, ed. De Vriend, pp. 234–73.

53 Princeton University Library, W. H. Scheide Collection 71; Ker, *Catalogue*, no. 382, 's. x/xi'. See *The Blickling Homilies*, ed. R. Morris, EETS os 58, 63 and 73 (Oxford, 1874–80, repr. as one volume, 1967). Wenisch (*Spezifisch anglisches Wortgut*, p. 30) dates the collection between 875 and 950; Vleeskruyer puts it before 900 (see below, n. 123).

54 *Die Vercelli-Homilien. I–VIII. Homilie*, ed. M. Förster (Hamburg, 1932, repr. Darmstadt, 1964) and *Vercelli Homilies IX–XXIII*, ed. P. E. Szarmach (Toronto, 1981). Wenisch (*Spezifisch anglisches Wortgut*, pp. 72–8), reporting Schabram's dating of between 875 and 925 for the bulk of these, isolates Vercelli II–VI, X, XIII–XVI, XVIII and XXI as first-half-tenth-century at the latest. Szarmach, ('The Earlier Homily: *De Parasceve*', *Studies*, ed. Szarmach, p. 382), quotes D. G. Scragg, *The Language of the Vercelli Homilies* (unpubl. Ph.D dissertation, Manchester Univ., 1970), pp. 378–9, as suggesting that the composition of Vercelli I may be as early as the ninth century. See, now, however, D. G. Scragg, 'The Corpus of Vernacular Homilies and Prose Saints' Lives before Ælfric', *ASE* 8 (1979), 223–77, at 223: 'Although there have been attempts to show that individual pieces were composed in the ninth century, we still have no sure means of distinguishing between homilies of the tenth century and any that are earlier.' For a Mercian origin for a number of the Vercelli Homilies, see D. G. Scragg, 'The Compilation of the Vercelli Book', *ASE* 2 (1973), 189–207.

55 *Wulfstan, Sammlung der ihm zugeschriebenen Homilien nebst Untersuchungen über ihre Echtheit I Text und Varianten*, ed. A. S. Napier (Berlin, 1883), and *Angelsächsische Homilien und Heiligenleben*, ed. B. Assmann (Kassel, 1889, repr. Darmstadt, 1964), pp. 194–207; see also Wenisch,

A relatively high proportion of the texts named above are medical works and thus do not properly belong to a literary corpus.[56] Nevertheless, since they have been taken to provide support for the theory of the existence of a Mercian prose tradition before the tenth century, it is necessary to investigate their claims to early composition. Writers on the subject have generally favoured the ninth century.[57] An eighth-century date of composition, however, has been proposed for the *Herbarium* and *Medicina de quadrupedibus* by their editor, H. J. de Vriend.[58] The one specific argument for an eighth-century origin for these texts put forward by de Vriend is the weight-value of the *pening*:

It is remarkable that the ratios 1 *pening*: 1 *dragma* and 1 *pening*: ⅓ *dragma* occur in *MdQ* only. This may be seen as an indication that the text of *MdQ* is directly descended from an earlier Anglian version. In the earlier Anglo-Saxon period the *pening* was probably still often equated with the Roman *dragma* . . . Zupko . . . mentions the establishment by King Offa of Mercia (757–96) of a silver penny weighing 1·46 g.[59]

Professor Philip Grierson, however, kindly confirms my opinion that the material cited by de Vriend is not capable of bearing such an interpretation:

I equally doubt if any conclusion can be drawn from the different reckonings in question. For one thing, I do not believe that Anglo-Saxon weights and measures descended from those of Rome, as is implied in the passage on p. lxxxii: 'In the earlier Anglo-Saxon period the *pening* was often equated with the Roman *dragma*.' They were rather adopted through the church and other continental contacts, and these, of course, provided most of the terminology. Translations were very hit and miss, as usually happens when one has to deal with foreign measures, or those of the bible. I would interpret the variations set out on p. lxxxii as implying that the translators had no clear idea of the capacity of Roman units, and to pick out one particular equivalence as being of special significance seems to me without justification.[60]

Spezifisch anglisches Wortgut, pp. 45 and 49. Although Vleeskruyer (*St Chad*, pp. 59–60 and n. 6) describes *Vita Malchi* as displaying 'all the characteristics of the ninth-century Mercian translations', Wenisch, following Sisam, *Studies*, pp. 210–11, suggests that it was probably not composed before the second half of the tenth century.

[56] Greenfield and Calder (*A New Critical History*, p. 117) describe the *Leechbook* as 'a plain but elegant remnant of Anglo-Saxon culture'.

[57] See above, nn. 48–9, and below, nn. 61–2 and 64. For the complicated relationships between the various medical texts and the possible derivation of a number of them from a single large compilation, see Meaney, 'Variant Versions'.

[58] *The Herbarium*, pp. xliii and xlii. De Vriend concludes that both these texts were 'translated into OE during an early period, probably the eighth century', that is, 'in the period of Northumbrian cultural ascendancy. . . . The extant text of *OEH* is either directly descended from [the] early version . . . or it is a new translation direct from Latin, which was subsequently supplemented by a pre-existing Anglian-coloured *MdQ*. The extant text of *MdQ* is closely connected with the early Anglian version.' [59] *Ibid.* p. lxxxii.

[60] Private communication. Grierson goes on to suggest that 'there is one feature which might suggest an early date – no mancus (ninth century onwards) and no ora or mark (tenth/eleventh century)', but he says that this could be because these were thought of as being specific to precious metals.

That the 'Anglian' translations of the *Herbarium* and *Medicina* were made in the eighth century is therefore no more than a theory.[61]

Arguments for a ninth-century date for a second group of medical texts are based partly on the presence of a handful of archaic spellings and letter forms in the early-tenth-century Omont fragment,[62] the mid-tenth-century manuscript of the *Leechbook* and Nowell's transcript of medical material from the fire-damaged Cotton manuscript, Otho B. xi,[63] and partly on what are taken to be early Anglican linguistic features in these texts and in *Lacnunga*.[64] The orthographical evidence certainly appears to indicate an early, and possibly even a pre-tenth-century, date of composition[65] for at least some of the

---

61 But not a wholly implausible one. For what appears to be 'an imperfectly achieved translation into Old High German' of an Old English medical recipe, preserved in an eighth-century continental manuscript, see Basle, Universitätsbibliothek, F. III. 15ᵃ, fol. 17, and Ker, *Catalogue*. App. 3.

62 I follow here the dating of N. R. Ker ('A Supplement to *Catalogue of Manuscripts containing Anglo-Saxon*', *ASE* 5 (1976), 128) rather than that of Schauman, who believes that the leaf 'probably predates the manuscripts associated with the reign of King Alfred' and suggests a date of *c.* 850, and Cameron, who puts it between 850 and 900 ('A Newly-Found Leaf', esp. pp. 290, 301, 302 and 312). I do not find any of Schauman's palaeographical arguments for her early date convincing, while, as Cameron himself observes (*ibid.* p. 312), many features of the orthography are shared with manuscripts of not only the late ninth but also the early tenth century.

63 See esp. Nowell transcript *eburfean* for *eaforfearn*, and *Leechbook earban* for *earfan* and *innel/begnid* for *innelfe gnid*; see also Torkar, 'Zu den ae. Medizinaltexten', pp. 325–6, and above, n. 51. The fact that the *Leechbook* contains prescriptions allegedly sent to King Alfred by Elias, patriarch of Jerusalem, *c.* 879–907, does not necessarily require us to suppose a close connection between the work and the prose of Alfred's reign, though it obviously gives a *terminus ante quem non* of *c.* 880 for one part of the *Leechbook*. We may compare the reference to an interview betwen Alfred and Ohthere in the Old English Orosius; see my edition, esp. pp. 194–5, and below, n. 143.

64 See, e.g., *St Chad*, ed. Vleekruyer, p. 33, n. 2, and Meaney ('Variant Versions', pp. 247 and 251), following Torkar, 'Zu den ae. Medizinaltexten', pp. 331–8, where it is suggested that the remedies transcribed from BL Cotton Otho B. xi are ultimately derived from a text which belongs 'at latest to the very beginning of Alfred's reign', and (more tentatively) that the scribe of Otho B. xi was copying from the last few surviving sheets of the 'massive compilation' of which Bald's *Leechbook* forms a part.

65 But not necessarily pre-890. The spellings cited by Schauman and Cameron ('A Newly-found Leaf; pp. 305–6) and Torkar ('Zu den ae. Medizinaltexten', pp. 325–7) are certainly typical of very early texts; however, *b* for *f* and *uu* or *u* (post-consonantal) for *w* occur occasionally in the *Pastoral Care*, in word such as *næbre, febranne, diobul* and *cuom*; the spelling *ę* is frequent in hand 1 of the *Anglo-Saxon Chronicle*, MS A and still found on three occasions in the work of hands 2c,, 2d and 3 (annal for 937); a Worcester charter of 904 (*Anglo-Saxon Charters*, ed. Robertson, no. XVIII) has *ae* and *uu*, and a charter of 969 (*ibid.* no. XLVI) has *twuam*, while the late-tenth-century Durham Ritual and Lindisfarne Gospels glosses have spellings such as *diobul* and *diubol* alongside *diofles, diowlas* etc., *esuica, uutedlice, cuedo, drygi* and *giseni*. Doubling of vowels is sporadic throughout Old English. With spellings such as *eolectran* cf. the Durham Ritual gloss *elechtre* and Latin *electrum*. As for *wælcalo*, is this an error for *wælscalo*?

remedies. However, any attempt to use other types of linguistic evidence, particularly that of vocabulary, to determine the date – and indeed the dialect – of the medical material is necessarily bound up with a consideration of the date of the other allegedly 'Mercian' or 'Anglian' texts.

Of these other, 'literary', texts, as we have seen, only two, the *Dialogues* and the Martyrology, can be assigned to the ninth century with any degree of confidence. The former must have been written by 893 at the latest, since it is referred to by Asser, and it could well also predate the circular letter prefixed to the *Pastoral Care* (*c.* 890–7);[66] it need not, however, post-date Alfred's invitation to Werferth and other scholars from Mercia in (perhaps) the late 880s.[67] As for the Martyrology, the palaeographical and source evidence seems to point to a date of completion between *c.* 850[68] and the very end of the ninth century, when the oldest surviving manuscript appears to have been written, and Archbishop Plegmund has been suggested as a possible author for it.[69] When the Old English Bede was produced must remain a matter of conjecture. The consensus of opinion today appears to be that a link with Alfred's plan for a revival of learning is quite likely, and that its author was 'perhaps connected with the Mercian group of scholars Alfred gathered at his court'.[70] However, on the one hand, the fact that Bede's *Historia ecclesiastica* is a text whose

---

[66] *Asser's Life of King Alfred*, ed. Stevenson, ch. 77. For the dating of the prefatory letter, see above, n. 15. Alfred's preface to the *Dialogues* implies that this translation was intended primarily for his own private use, not commissioned as part of a grand plan for the revival of learning. However, the very existence of the preface shows that he subsequently circulated copies of it.

[67] Since Asser implies that the Mercian helpers came before Asser (885?) and Grimbald (886?), Keynes and Lapidge (*Alfred the Great*, p. 26) suggest that they most likely arrived in the early 880s. So Mercian translations inspired by King Alfred could date from a period before 885. For Werwulf as a possible collaborator with Werferth, see D. Whitelock, 'The Prose of Alfred's Reign', *Continuations and Beginnings, Studies in Old English Literature*, ed. E. G. Stanley (London, 1966), pp. 67–8, and *Alfred the Great*, ed. Keynes and Lapidge, p. 293.

[68] See, e.g., C. Sisam, 'An Early Fragment', pp. 209–20, and J. E. Cross, '*Legimus in ecclesiasticis historiis*: a Sermon for All Saints and its Use in Old English Prose', *Traditio* 33 (1977), 101–35; also *Das altenglische Martyrologium*, ed. Kotzor. pp. 443–54.

[69] See above, n. 14, and C. Sisam, 'An Early Fragment', p. 217. A date of composition shortly after 899 cannot, however, be ruled out; see K. Sisam, 'Canterbury, Lichfield and the Vespasian Psalter', pp. 113–14, for warnings about firm datings based on palaeographical evidence.

[70] M. Swanton (*Anglo-Saxon Prose* (London, 1975), p. xvii) is one of many to suggest that the Bede was the work of one or other of Alfred's four known Mercian helpers, Werferth, Plegmund, Athelstan and Werwulf. Vleeskruyer (*St Chad*, pp. 61–2) tentatively names Plegmund, Æthelbald (*sic*) and Werwulf. However, if the *Dialogues* adequately reflects Werferth's usage, he cannot also have been the author of the Bede, while Plegmund seems an unlikely candidate, given the reference to the monastery of St Peter and St Paul (i.e. St Augustine's, Canterbury) as the burial place of archbishops of Canterbury. See D. Whitelock, 'The Old English Bede', *PBA* 48 (1962), 58, 67 and 70.

translation might well have been desired by Alfred is not proof that the surviving translation was made at the king's request, and thus a 'pre-Alfredian' date cannot be ruled out.[71] On the other hand, the fact that the oldest surviving manuscript copy – consisting of extracts – appears to have been written very early in the tenth century means that composition shortly after 900 cannot be ruled out either.[72] Notwithstanding, Vleeskruyer was confident enough of a late-ninth-century date for the Bede to use this work, along with the Martyrology and *Dialogues*, to set up a relative chronology of Mercian texts. *St Chad* and the Martyrology, for instance, are taken to be more 'archaic' than the Bede and *Dialogues*,[73] but they are also said to belong to an already well-established and 'vigorous tradition of Mercian vernacular writing' which preceded Alfred's work and 'to a large extent, rendered it possible'.[74] Vleeskruyer makes a detailed case for the existence of such a tradition, and his conclusions seem to have been accepted with very little query by scholars concerned with linguistic and textual chronology.[75] His 'evidence' takes two forms. First of all, there is what he sees as the accumulating linguistic and stylistic evidence for the existence of a Mercian tradition of vernacular prose literature older even than his 'oldest' surviving Mercian texts.[76] Second, there is what he sees as evidence that these texts themselves actually predated Alfred's prefatory letter to the *Pastoral Care* and Alfred's first translation.[77]

Some of the arguments Vleeskruyer puts forward depend on unsubstantiated assumptions and need not engage us for long here – for instance, that 'the existence of Mercian glossaries of before A.D. 800' points in the direction of the existence of a Mercian literary dialect in the early ninth

---

[71] See *ibid.* esp. pp. 61 and 77. Cf. Waite, 'The Vocabulary', pp. 57–8, where the postulation of a date for the composition of the Bede earlier than Alfred's reign is said to be 'dependent upon more positive proof of a Mercian tradition of vernacular writing in the ninth century'. Wenisch (*Spezifisch anglisches Wortgut*, p. 47), following Schabram (*Superbia*, pp. 45–6), assigns the Bede to the second half of the ninth century or earlier.

[72] See above, p. 98. For Ker's practice of dating at quarter-century intervals, see *Catalogue*, p. xx. Waite ('The Vocabulary', p. 57) is wrong in claiming that 'we know for certain that the OE Bede does not postdate Alfred's reign'. Not only does the date of the manuscript not preclude a date of composition after 900, but, even if Alfred commissioned the Bede, it need not have been completed until after his death.

[73] *St Chad*, pp. 19–20 and 69. Vleeskruyer claims that the 'singularly archaic quality' of *St Chad* 'suggests strongly that its archetype was composed before the educational reform of the later ninth century'; he dates the Bede 'late ninth century' (*St Chad*, p. 53).   [74] *Ibid.* p. 41.

[75] They are, for instance, generally adopted in the important word studies of Schabram and Wenisch. See, however, the review of Vleeskruyer's edition by C. Sisam, *RES*, ns 6 (1955), 302, where it is pointed out that 'his arguments, both linguistic and paleographical, are not decisive', and that 'it may be doubted whether the words he cites, such as . . . *þreat* and *onseon* would have seemed archaic or poetic to Mercians in the late ninth or early tenth century, or whether alliteration in prose is a mark of earliness'.

[76] *St Chad*, Introduction, *passim*.   [77] *Ibid.* p. 69.

century and before;[78] that the words 'an ærendgewrit of Lædene on Englisc
areccean' 'definitely' imply that translating was one of the accomplishments of
pre-Alfredian scholarship;[79] and that one of the many indications of the
vigorous tradition of vernacular writing in Mercia is the 'significantly large
proportion of Mercians amongst those who aided Alfred in his efforts to
reanimate culture'.[80] Potentially of greater significance are Vleeskruyer's
linguistic arguments for a 'pre-Alfredian' date, 'not later than the third quarter
of the ninth century', i.e., before 875, for *St Chad*. These arguments are based
on a number of features, of which the most noteworthy are:

(*i*) misreadings which could be due to the use of certain archaic letter forms in an
exemplar;
(*ii*) the distribution of *þ* and *ð* in the surviving (twelfth-century) manuscript ('there is
. . . a distinct possibility that the original contained *ð* exclusively, or almost so');
(*iii*) use of archaic or non-standard spellings, such as *cwic-* and the *u* of the suffixes *-ul*
and *-ur*;
(*iv*) syncope of medial vowels;
(*v*) frequent use of the instrumental case;
(*vi*) peculiarities of style and syntax, including the use of constructions combining
possessive and demonstrative and of inflected participles in *-u*;
(*vii*) use of words which apparently became obsolete in West Saxon during the later
Old English period, especially *tylig*, 'rather', 'on the contrary'.[81]

Some of these and other linguistic features to which Vleeskruyer draws
attention could certainly indicate an early date of composition – if by early we

[78] *Ibid.* p. 46, referring apparently to both prose and verse in this medium. Even if we accept that
the existence of glossaries indicates the existence of a literary dialect – and I know of no good
reason why this should be so – the origin of these is far from certain. See, e.g. *Old English
Glosses in the Épinal-Erfurt Glossary*, ed. J.D. Pheifer (Oxford, 1974), p. lvii: 'Bradley's
suggestion that "the archetype of Épinal and Erfurt was compiled in the school of Aldhelm at
Malmesbury . . ." is an attractive possibility which is not at variance with the linguistic
evidence.'
[79] *St Chad*, p. 40, n. 4. The ability to translate Latin documents does not necessarily imply the
existence of a tradition of written prose; moreover, although Alfred's claim (*Pastoral Care*, ed.
Sweet, p. 5, lines 18–21) that translation had not been attempted by the scholars of the past
may be exaggeration, it is made in a letter which must surely have been read and checked by
some of his Mercian advisers. Alfred obviously finds it necessary to make a case for the
desirability of translation, even if what he says may be 'persuasive rather than factual' (see
Morrish, 'King Alfred's Letter', p. 90).
[80] *St Chad*, p. 42. Alfred's helpers were certainly scholars and they may well have constructed
homilies out of a variety of Latin sources (as the author of the Martyrology seems to have
done with hagiographical material); however, that does not necessarily mean that they were
also already producers of written translations for circulation.
[81] *Ibid.* Introduction, esp. sections III, IV and V. For a discussion of Vleeskruyer's claims
concerning style, see below, pp. 132–8.

mean 'before the late tenth century'. However, none of them actually requires us to suppose a 'pre-Alfredian' or even a pre-tenth-century origin for *St Chad*. For instance, (*i*) the scribal error *hi* for *in* cited by Vleeskruyer from line 151 of his text may well have arisen as a result of the misreading of a 'long' *i + n* in the scribe's exemplar, but 'long' *i* is still to be found in early-tenth-century annals relating to the years 914 to 920 and entered into the Parker manuscript of the *Chronicle* in the 920s or 930s,[82] while, even if we agree that emendation of *weccenum* in *St Chad* 127 is indeed necessary, the *cc*-type *a*, which Vleeskruyer sees as lying behind it, is still to be found in works composed in the second half of the tenth century.[83] (*ii*) The proportions of *þ* to *ð* and the distribution patterns of these letters, far from indicating a ninth-century origin, correspond very closely indeed to the usage of tenth-century manuscripts and texts composed after 900. For instance, Hand 2b of MS A of the *Chronicle* has *þ* as its norm in initial position, where it occurs 230 times, beside forty-five instances of *ð* and one of *Ð*; medially *ð* is preferred (61:13), while only *ð* is found in final position. Tenth-century annals entered in this hand have initial *þ* 72 ×, *ð* 17 ×; with *ð* medially 31 ×, *þ* 4 ×.[84] In *St Chad* Vleeskruyer reports that *þ* is likewise normal in initial position, with *ð* 10 × (including *forðon*, but not counting the capital form *Ð*); that the proportion of medial *þ:ð* is 'about 1:6'; and that final *þ* occurs only twice. (*iii*) Spellings such as *-ul*, *-ur* are found in charters as late as the 960s,[85] while 'archaic' *cwic-* occurs in copies of tenth-century legal codes

---

82 See, e.g., *The Parker Chronicle and Laws (Corpus Christi College, Cambridge, MS. 173). A Facsimile*, ed. R. Flower and H. Smith (London, 1941), 21v21, *innan* (annal for 914), and cf. *St Chad*, ed. Vleeskruyer, p. 69 and line 151, beside Ker, *Catalogue*, p. xxx, 'old forms occur occasionally still in manuscripts of s. x.'.

83 For the form *weccenum*, see, e.g., Campbell, *Grammar*, §193c, and also Wenisch, *Spezifisch anglisches Wortgut*, p. 306, n. 192. In his comments on a *cc*-type *a* (*St Chad*, p. 69 and n. to line 127), Vleeskruyer is following W. Keller, *Angelsächsische Palaeographie*, Palaestra 43 (Berlin, 1906), as also on p. 44, where he takes the letter forms *g* and *t* in the ninth-century manuscripts of the *Pastoral Care* to show unmistakable signs of Mercian influence; however, Keller's identification has not found general acceptance. For the *cc*-type *a*, see Ker, *Catalogue*, p. xxviii. Its last appearance in a dated manuscript known to Ker is in a charter of 969 from Worcester: 'probably it survived as a genuine element of the script longer in the west and north . . . but its actual last appearance, except as a copyist's archaism . . . seems to be in an ill-written addition to the annal for 1001 in the Parker Chronicle'.

84 See *The Anglo-Saxon Chronicle, MS A*, ed. Bately, pp. xxix–xxx and cxxx. We may compare the Hatton manuscript of the *Pastoral Care*, with *þ* hardly used at all by the main hand, the Worcester charter of 904 (see above, n. 64) with only two examples of *þ*, and the Omont fragment with *ð* only. For Vleeskruyer's comments on the distribution of the two letters, see *St Chad*, pp. 7 and 69–70.

85 See, e.g., the Mercian charter of 969 (*Anglo-Saxon Charters*, ed. Robertson, no. xlvi), Ru¹ (for which, see below, n. 94) *elcur, deoful, degul* etc.; and the *Anglo-Saxon Chronicle*, MS A, annal 914 *pearruc*.

and in the writings of Ælfric.[86] (*iv*) Syncope of medial vowels does not prove ninth-century dating: the examples cited again have plenty of parallels in works of Ælfric.[87] (*v*) The instrumental is used in the *Chronicle* MS A up to annal 975.[88] (*vi*) A predilection for predicative participles with inflectional -*u* is not necessarily an early or an archaic feature; nor is the use of constructions combining possessive and demonstrative.[89] As for other orthographical features – and I will include here the presence of 'early West Saxon' *ie* spellings in Mercian prose texts other than *St Chad*, seen by Vleeskruyer as strongly suggesting a date before 900[90] and used by Förster as an argument for early-ninth-century composition of the *Apocalypse of Thomas*[91] – all of these are still

---

[86] See *A Microfiche Concordance to Old English*, ed. R. L. Venezky, A. diPaolo Healey *et al.* (Toronto, 1980).

[87] See *ibid.*, the entries for *halga*, *micle* etc. See further, Campbell, *Grammar*, §388, and also A. C. Amos, *Linguistic Means of Determining the Dates of Old English Literary Texts* (Cambridge, Mass., 1980), p. 28.

[88] See further, *ibid.* pp. 125–8, and also B. Mitchell, *Old English Syntax*, 2 vols. (Oxford, 1985) I, 566: 'Neither a preference for nor the avoidance of the instrumental case provides sufficient grounds for dating a text.'

[89] See *ibid.* I, 17, n. 7, and also *St Chad*, ed. Vleeskruyer, p. 68: 'inflexional -*u* is most probably a peculiarity of ninth-century Mercian prose under Latin influence; but it is not an archaism in the sense apparently intended by Napier'. For the construction combining possessive and demonstrative, see Mitchell, *Old English Syntax* I, 51–6, esp. 55: 'It is hard to see in what sense [these patterns] can be "archaic".'

[90] *St Chad*, p. 56; see also *ibid.* p. 45, n. 2: 'That Mercian prose translations were also actively copied during the EWS. period is proved by the appearance of the characteristic EWS. diphthong *ie*.' We have to be wary of generalizations based on the presence of Mercian spellings in early West Saxon texts and vice versa. Alfred himself acknowledges the help of Mercian scholars; Mercian-trained scribes could have been employed in West Saxon scriptoria, while the possibility of Mercian copies of West Saxon texts cannot be ruled out. Moreover, as C. L. Wrenn points out ('Standard Old English', *TPS* (1933), 73) 'there are reasons for expecting considerable variety in the language of the Wessex of Alfred's time', with little unifying force to be set against strong centrifugal tendencies. For the use of more than one scriptorium, see the metrical preface to the *Pastoral Care* (ed. Sweet, p. 9, lines 12–15), and Sisam, *Studies*, pp. 140–7. Typical West Saxon spellings were in use long before Alfred's reign: see, e.g., the Æthelwulf charter of 847 (*The Oldest English Texts*, ed. Sweet, p. 433), with *æwielme*, *fordealf*, *wealdenes* etc. besides 'non-West Saxon' spellings such as *wælles* and *Alhstan*.

[91] 'A New Version', p. 35: 'it seems . . . safe to assume that the form of the text as we have it in the Exeter MS. has been copied from an Old West Saxon text of the first half of the ninth century – and that this Old West Saxon form had been transcribed from an Old Mercian form of the text. At least this would cover all the phonological data before us.' See also Wenisch, *Spezifisch anglisches Wortgut*, p. 72. However, I wonder whether Förster's reference to the ninth century is not in fact an error in translation. The forms he notes (occasional *ie* spellings, *o* + nasal, primary and secondary *io*, and uncontracted verb forms) are all still to be found in tenth-century texts. Ker, *Catalogue*, no. 32, art. 12, describes the only surviving manuscript copy (Cambridge, Corpus Christi College 41) as 's. xi¹'.

to be found in texts·of the early tenth century, the diagraph *ie*, for instance, being a regular feature of the *Anglo-Saxon Chronicle*, MS A, up to the annal for 920 and occurring sporadically in charters of both West Saxon and Mercian origin up to at least the mid-tenth century.[92]

The significance of lexical items is another matter. Vleeskruyer's discussion of the vocabulary of *St Chad* is an important and detailed one and has had a considerable influence on both literary and linguistic studies. The conclusions he draws, however, are, in my view, frequently unsafe, and his distinctions are sometimes blurred or even unsound. For instance, he often does not make it clear whether he is classifying a given word as 'archaic', or 'dialectal', or typical of an individual author, or indeed 'poetic' (he seems to equate 'poetic' with 'early'). Moreover, the terms 'archaic', 'Anglian', 'obsolescent' and 'obsolete in Old English' are apparently sometimes treated as virtually interchangeable terms and used to identify texts of ninth-century Mercian origin.[93] Yet, thanks to the anonymity of much Old English prose and the virtual non-existence of texts – other than a few charters, laws and chronicle entries[94] – to which a date

---

92 See further, J. Bately, 'Linguistic Evidence as a Guide to the Authorship of Old English Verse: a Reappraisal with Special Reference to *Beowulf*', *Learning and Literature in Anglo-Saxon England*, ed. M. Lapidge and H. Gneuss (Cambridge, 1985), pp. 411–13; and see, e.g., the forms *anliesnesse* and *hiered* in King Eadred's will (*c.* 951–5; *Select English Historical Documents*, ed. Harmer, no. XXI) and the Worcester charter of 969 (see above, n. 65).

93 See *St Chad*, Introduction, *passim*. I find very revealing Vleeskruyer's comment, concerning the occurrence of words that he believes became obsolete during the later West Saxon period (*ibid.* p. 68), '*St Chad* is most definitely not more modern than *Orosius* or the *Pastoral Care*.'

94 In addition to those already mentioned, texts with a *terminus apud quem non* of 's. x. med.' provided by Ker's dating of the manuscripts in which they have been preserved include the prose *Solomon and Saturn* of Cambridge, Corpus Christi College 422, the collection of remedies that follows Bald's *Leechbook* in BL Royal 12. D. XVII, and a confessional prayer in BL Cotton Vespasian D. XX. Some glosses also survive in tenth-century manuscripts of 's. x¹' and 's. x. med.' The most important of these is the interlinear gloss to the Lindisfarne Gospels (BL Cotton Nero D. iv; Ker, *Catalogue*, no. 165), usually dated to the period 950–70. Literary texts preserved in manuscripts of the second half of the tenth century or later for which an earlier date of composition has been conjectured include the Macarius Homily of the eleventh-century Cambridge, Corpus Christi College 201 (*Theodulfi Capitula in England*, ed. H. Sauer (Munich, 1978), pp. 411–16, and composed perhaps as early as the first half of the tenth century according to Sauer, *ibid.* p. 512). Texts from the period *c.* 950–80 include the 'Anglian' Durham Ritual and Rushworth glosses. The Durham Ritual glosses, in Durham Cathedral Library, A. IV. 19 (Ker, *Catalogue*, no. 106), were probably written *c.* 970. The Rushworth glosses, in Oxford, Bodleian Library, Auct. D. 2. 19 (Ker, *Catalogue*, no. 292, 's. x²'), fall into two groups. The first group (Ru¹) consists of glosses in a Mercian dialect to Matthew, Mark 1–II.15 and John XVIII.1–3; the second group (Ru²) consists of Northumbrian glosses to the remaining gospel texts. In view of the apparent dependence of Ru² on the Lindisfarne glosses, the possibility that others of the glosses are also copies of earlier texts cannot be ruled out. A translation of part of Genesis already existed when Ælfric translated the rest of the book; see *The Old English Version of the Heptateuch*, ed. S. J. Crawford, EETS os 160 (1922 for 1921, repr. 1969), 76, lines 4–6.

of composition in the period *c.* 900 to *c.* 970 can be securely assigned, 'not late' means little more than 'composed before the time of Æthelwold and Ælfric'. In any case, the lifespan of the one identifiable Mercian translator of Alfred's reign, Werferth, extended to 915, while Alfred himself died in 899 at the relatively early age of fifty, so that a contemporary with similar linguistic habits could have been writing well into the tenth century.

What is more, in spite of the reservations he expresses about the term '(West) Mercian', Vleeskruyer uses it to define the language of a group of writers of Mercian origin,[95] and to justify his theory that the history of English prose does not begin with Alfred's initiatives in Wessex. Yet, given the small amount of early material that has come down to us and the manner of its transmission, the terms 'early Mercian' in the context of vocabulary virtually means 'not found in the Orosius or the works of Alfred, but used in surviving manuscript copies of the Martyrology, Bede and *Dialogues*'. I am not convinced that all the so-called Mercian words must originally have been peculiar to the territory called Mercia, or even to territory controlled by Mercians. They could have been current also in a large area of Wessex and used by writers of West Saxon origin.[96] We simply do not know, any more than we can determine the extent to which scribes of works preserved only in post-ninth-century copies have removed archaic or dialectal terminology which they found in their exemplars.[97] At the same time, absence could on occasion be due to lack of opportunity, the non-occurrence of certain concepts in a particular author's works. Thus the terms 'oratory' and 'apostolic' are never used by Alfred or the author of the Orosius, nor is the collocation 'band of angels', and so the absence of *gebedhus, apostolic* and *þreat* from early West Saxon texts and their presence in *St Chad* and compositions of Mercian origin is not in dialect terms significant.[98] 'Absence from late West Saxon' similarly means little more than

---

[95] *St Chad*, pp. 24–5, 49–50 and 61–2. Vleeskruyer (p. 62) is wrong in seeing the vocabulary of the early Middle English Katherine Group as 'that of the LWS. homilies', see J. M. Bately, 'On Some Aspects of the Vocabulary of the West Midlands in the Early Middle Ages: the Language of the Katherine Group', *Medieval English Studies presented to George Kane*, ed. D. Kennedy, R. Waldron and J. Wittig (Cambridge, 1988), pp. 55–77.

[96] See further, J. Bately, 'Some Words for Time in Old English Literature', *Problems of Old English Lexicography*, ed. A. Bammesberger (Regensburg, 1985), pp. 47–64.

[97] For linguistic heterogeneity in early Old English, see above, n. 90; for Anglian words surviving into Middle English, see Bately, 'Some Aspects'; for scribal 'updating' of lexical items, see, e.g., Amos, *Linguistic Means*, pp. 141–56; and for an example of such 'updating', see D. Yerkes, *The Two Versions of Wærferth's Translation of Gregory's Dialogues: an Old English Thesaurus* (Toronto, 1979). Yerkes's lists of items of vocabulary removed from the version of the *Dialogues* in MS H include a number of the words discussed below; however, others remain unchanged.

[98] For *gebedhus* and *þreat*, see *St Chad*, ed. Vleeskruyer, pp. 21–2 and 28. Vleeskruyer's information is sometimes inaccurate, with a number of words enjoying a wider currency than

absence from the works of three or four authors – perhaps even 'not approved by the school of Æthelwold'.[99]

But to return to specific detail: Vleeskruyer lists a number of words occurring in *St Chad* as 'archaic' or 'archaic Mercian' or 'obsolescent'. However, a close examination of the distribution patterns of these words shows that their presence in a work does not prove a ninth-century date of composition. Many of them are found in texts known to have been composed in the tenth century or even later. For instance, *carcern*, 'prison', is still being used in the laws of Athelstan (924–40).[100] *Herenes*, 'praise', occurs in the Lindisfarne, Rushworth (Ru¹) and Durham Ritual glosses,[101] while *stræl*, 'arrow', survived into the Middle English period and beyond.[102] Indeed, an exhaustive comparison[103] of the vocabulary of *St Chad* with that of Ælfric yields very few words that are to be found in the first and not in the second, and the majority of these, like the forms mentioned above, either are represented in the tenth-century Mercian and Northumbrian interlinear glosses[104] or are found in late West Saxon texts other than the works of Ælfric,[105] or are recorded in Middle English texts from the Midlands.[106] A few words do appear at first sight to link

---

he supposed. See, e.g., *bled*, described as 'apparently not found in WS.' (*ibid.* p. 26), but in fact used by Ælfric in the very collocation named by Vleeskruyer, 'windes blæd'.

99 See H. Gneuss, 'The Origin of Standard Old English and Æthelwold's School at Winchester', *ASE* 1 (1972), 63–83.

100 Vleeskruyer describes *carcern* as 'obsolete in LWS' (*St Chad*, p. 26). For its distribution in Old English texts, including *Theodulfi Capitula*, the so-called Laws of Edward and Guthrum, commonly attributed to Wulfstan, and the Lindisfarne and Rushworth glosses, see Wenisch, *Spezifisch anglisches Wortgut*, pp. 114–120, and the *Microfiche Concordance*. Other words in Vleeskruyer's list which are recorded in tenth-century laws include *lar(e)dom* (also in the Durham Ritual gloss), *medmicel* (also in Ru¹) and *monung* (also in Ru¹); for *medmicel*, see also *Theodulfi Capitula*, ed. p. Sauer, p. 251.

101 *Herenes*, described by Vleeskruyer variously as a 'Mercian archaism' and 'an archaic formation' (*St Chad*, pp. 55 and 58, n. 2), is found also in the late-tenth-century Northumbrian Durham Ritual and Lindisfarne glosses and both parts of the Rushworth glosses and is used, alongside *hering*, in early West Saxon texts.

102 Vleeskruyer (*St Chad*, p. 55) lists the word amongst 'Mercian archaisms'; see, however, Bately, 'Some Aspects', p. 61, and Oxford English Dictionary *streale*, and cf. *St Chad*, p. 33, with its reference to the views of Jordan.

103 I am deeply indebted to the authors of the *Microfiche Concordance*, whose work made this exhaustive study possible.

104 See, e.g., the entries for *byrgan*, *ymbsellan*, *dwolian* and variants in the *Microfiche Concordance*.

105 See, e.g., the entries for *agangan*, *spyrian*, *getimbre*, *tocerran*, *þunorrad* and variants in the *Microfiche Concordance*. For a rebuttal of the claim that *tid* is 'more or less archaic' in the sense of time' (*St Chad*, p. 33), see, e.g., M. Gretsch, *Die Regula Sancti Benedicti in England und ihre altenglische Übersetzung* (Munich, 1973), pp. 355–6, and also *Theodulfi Capitula*, ed. Sauer, pp. 261–3.

106 E.g., *beotian*, *bold*, *forhwon*, *higian*, *hrinan*, *miþan*, *nænig*, *swæp*, *þreat*, *stræl*, *wigbed*, *winnan* ('strive'), and *(ge)eadmodian*; see further, Bately, 'Some Aspects', pp. 59–64.

St Chad specifically with the Bede and *Dialogues*, or with early Old English prose in general, namely *forewesan*, 'preside', 'be in charge',[107] *leofwynde*, 'kind', 'benevolent',[108] *slaulice*, 'sluggishly, reluctantly',[109] *tylig*, 'rather', 'on the contrary',[110] and *pearfednes*, 'poverty',[111] while a handful of others, including *rihtgeleafful*, 'orthodox',[112] are confined to a combination of texts known to have been written before the late tenth century and texts for which the date of composition is uncertain.[113] *Tylig* (along with its superlative *tylgest*) is described by Vleeskruyer as a 'Mercian archaism, perhaps the most noteworthy lexical element in the text', which 'goes far to prove, even without the support of other evidence, that the homily is a ninth-century production'.[114] However, it is so rare of occurrence[115] that it is unsafe to use it as firm evidence. The other words are all compounds, made up of commonplace elements, and in none of these cases is early date the only possible explanation for the distribution

---

[107] Translating *praeesse* and found also in the Bede; see below, n. 116.

[108] Apart from *St Chad*, where it translates *amabilis*, *leofwynde* is recorded only in verse, Boethius and the mid-tenth-century glossaries of BL Cotton Cleopatra A. iii, which Joan Turville-Petre (unpublished monograph, lodged in the Anglo-Saxon Archive of King's College, London) has shown to incorporate much older glossary material; cf. the similarly formed but commonplace compound *halwende*. For *amabilis* the Bede has *lufiendlic* and *leof*, both words still in use in late West Saxon texts.

[109] Recorded from *St Chad* and *Pastoral Care* only. However, the word is not uncommon in Middle English; cf. modern English 'slowly'.

[110] Translating Latin *potius*, *maxime*. Forms of this word are found also in the Corpus and Épinal-Erfurt glossaries, in one manuscript of the *Dialogues* and in the *Leechbook*. The example in the *Dialogues* is at p. 277, line 25, MS O *tilg7 swyðor*, for which the printed text (MS C) reads only *swypur*. Other instances may have been similarly removed by later scribes.

[111] Translating Latin *paupertas* and recorded also in *Dialogues*, Bede, the Vespasian Psalter gloss and some related psalter glosses, with *pearfness* in the psalter gloss of Oxford, Bodleian Library, Junius 27 (apparently a copy of the Vespasian Psalter gloss) and the Benedictine Rule gloss of BL Cotton Tiberius A. iii; cf. the rendering *wædl* for *paupertas* in *Epistola Alexandri*. I exclude the form *penede*, otherwise found only in the Vespasian Psalter, but occurring in the form *gepenede* in the later Mercian texts.

[112] Translating Latin *catholicus* and recorded also from the Bede, *Dialogues*, Boethius, the glossaries of BL Cotton Cleopatra A. iii and an anonymous life of St Mary of Egypt (*Ælfric's Lives of Saints*, ed. W. W. Skeat, EETS os 94 and 114 (Oxford, 1890–1900) II, 2–52); cf. the common form *geleafful*, beside *rihtgelyfed* and *ryhtgelyfende*.

[113] Words found only in a combination of early and undatable texts include *arful*, *gecignes*, *forplutan* (see also *leat forp*), *onlysan* and *unepnes*. However, the Durham Ritual has *onlesend* and a charter of Edward the Confessor *uneapnes*, while the Lindisfarne Gospels have *epnisse*. Cf. *orleahtor*, confined to a handful of texts whose date of composition is uncertain, including *Beowulf*. [114] *St Chad*, pp. 33 and 68.

[115] For the dangers of dating texts according to the proportions of hapax legomena see Amos, *The Linguistic Means*, pp. 146–7. Similar caution needs to be exercised in drawing conclusions from the presence in a text of words of limited distribution. See, e.g., *mipan*, recorded from a combination of early and undatable texts only, but also found in early Middle English, and cf. the entries relating to the Bede and Ælfric in Waite's list of words in the Bede found otherwise only in one other Old English text or author ('The Vocabulary', pp. 264–7).

patterns.[116] Moreover, unless one supposes a sudden and dramatic and simultaneous change of usage over a large area around the year 900, the most that could be argued about any of these words is that they might indicate a date of composition prior to the last thirty years or so of the tenth century. There is no evidence at all to support Vleeskruyer's claim that the 'West Mercian translating activity came to a standstill after its tradition had been grafted on the new EWS. literature by its last bearers', whatever that means.[117] And, no less significantly, there is no evidence to support the claim that *St Chad* is actually older than the Martyrology, Bede and *Dialogues* or predates the literary activities promoted by King Alfred.

The same objections apply to the case that has been made on the grounds of lexis for a ninth-century origin for *St Christopher*, the *Life of Guthlac*, *Epistola Alexandri* and other purportedly early Mercian or (less specifically) Anglian texts, including homilies and medical treatises. Indeed, Vleeskruyer's arguments in respect to these texts depend on his dating of *St Chad*. He compares the usage of *St Chad* with that of the other texts, and if they are found to be in agreement with it, they too are deemed to be early. He considers 'Mercian archaisms' in the *St Christopher*, for instance, to be 'numerous',[118] yet there is only one word in Vleeskruyer's list that is not recorded from texts datable to the late tenth century,[119] and that is the rare compound *abregan*, whose simplex is found in a range of texts from Alfred's *Pastoral Care* to Ælfric's *Catholic Homilies*.[120] The *Epistola Alexandri*, in contrast, certainly contains a number

---

[116] E.g., none of the Latin words *amabilis, catholicus, paupertas, praeesse* and *segniter* is used in the gospels, so that we have no knowledge of what their equivalents in the dialect of the authors of Ru[1] and the Lindisfarne glosses might have been. However, these have *ðorfendlic* and *ðarfe* for *pauperculus* and *pauper*, and *geleaffull* for *fidelis*, and use the suffix -*wende* in *halwoende*. *Forewesan* is recorded by Waite ('The Vocabulary', p. 265) as found only in the Bede and *St Chad*; however, the two elements are also recorded separately, as in Ælfric's *Grammar*, where *prae-esse* is translated 'fore wesan' and *praesum* as 'fore eom'.

[117] *St Chad*, p. 50, n. 1. Indeed Vleeskruyer himself seems to imply that the activity could have continued into the tenth century by referring to the possible hastening of the displacement of Mercian as the official language at Worcester by the cessation of Werferth's influence with his death in 915.

[118] See *St Chad*, p. 55. For Sisam's opinion that *St Christopher* is a mid-tenth-century text, see above, no. 47.

[119] For *herenis, medmicel, stræl* and *tid*, see above. *Broga, gefea* and *sigor* are all used by Ælfric.

[120] The verbal prefix *a*- is a very common one in Old English; see, however, Waite's comment ('The Vocabulary', p. 268), 'It will be seen that many cOE verbs are found prefixed by *ā*- only or predominantly in Anglian and poetic texts.' *Abregan*, 'terrify', is otherwise recorded only from a handful of texts, including the *Dialogues, Leechbook* and Blickling Homilies; *bregan* is found in a wide range of texts including the works of Alfred, Ælfric and Wulfstan. We may compare the Lindisfarne glosses where *terrere* is renderd by *afyrhtigan, forhtigan* and *gefyrhtigan* and *terror* by *fyrhtnesse*. See also *gebrosnodlic*, found otherwise only in Blickling Homily x and Napier XLIX; cf. the entries *brosnendlic, brosniendlic* and *brosnodlic* in the *Microfiche Concordance*. Apart from a handful of hapax legomena and words of very rare occurrence, I have found no other items of special interest in the *St Christopher*.

of 'dialectal' and unusual words, some apparently otherwise confined to 'early' or undatable texts, giving it a stronger case than most for 'early' composition, but of these 'early words' the most that can be said is that they are not recorded from texts known to have been written after about 970, while other rare words in this work are found otherwise only in demonstrably late texts.[121] As for the making of the original translation of the *Life of Guthlac*, even if a date during Alfred's reign may be 'the most attractive of the various possibilities open',[122] this cannot be confirmed from the evidence of vocabulary or indeed of any other linguistic feature.[123] Finally, although Vleeskruyer, Schabram and Wenisch see the Bede as composed in the second half of the ninth century or even earlier, and the palaeographical evidence suggests that it was written

[121] I am tempted by the high proportion of hapax legomena and of words typical of the Bede and *Dialogues* to favour a ninth- or early-tenth-century date for the *Epistola Alexandri*. Hapax legomena include *anæglede* (cOE *nægled*), *fromnes*, *gryto*, *unretu* and *gimmisc*. Words confined to *Epistola Alexandri* and texts known to have been composed before *c.* 950 include *godsprecum* (Be *godgespræce*), *gelise* (Be *geles*), *fromscipe*, *fremsumlice* and *hreaðemus*. However, the need for great caution in interpreting these forms can be illustrated from the words *wreþian* (in Old English apparently confined to verse and to 'early' texts – Bede, Cleopatra Glosses and *Epistola Alexandri* – but recorded also from Middle English and beyond) and *pullian* (*Epistola Alexandri*, beside *apullian* in *Medicina de quadrupedibus*); see also *epistol* (Bede, *Pastoral Care*, Orosius, *Dialogues* and *Epistola Alexandri* only, with the word replaced by *ærendgewrit* in MS H of the *Dialogues*). In view of the significantly large number of Latin loan words in the *Epistola Alexandri*, and since *epistol* could have been borrowed or reborrowed at any time in Old English, this distribution need not be significant. Also a feature of *Epistola Alexandri* is a fondness for compounding of a type typical of poetry; see, e.g., *byrnwiga*, *cynegierela*, *leodþeaw*, *hronfisc*, *oferhleoþrian* (found otherwise only in poetry) and the hapax legomena *stanhol*, *longscaft* and *godmægen*.

[122] J. Roberts, 'The Old English Prose Translation of Felix's *Vita Sancti Guthlaci*', *Studies*, ed. Szarmach, pp. 363–79, at 367. Dr Roberts concludes (*ibid.* pp. 368–9) that 'few indeed if any of the words cited are diagnostic of ninth-century dating. However, together they suggest that the original prose Guthlac was a non-West-Saxon translation made at a time not late in the tenth century.' For a detailed examination of the evidence for Anglian origin for the vocabulary of Guthlac, and the relationship of the Vita to Vercelli Homily xxiii, see J. Crawford (Roberts), 'Guthlac', cited above, n. 45.

[123] E.g., the list of 'words often presented as evidence for the early composition of prose texts' (Roberts, 'The Old English Prose Translation', p. 368) contains six still in use in both late Old English and Middle English (*bearn*, *geara*, *nænig*, *rec*, *stræl* and *tid* in the sense 'time'), nine words and groups still used by Ælfric (*broga*, *bregean*, *campian*, *eac swylce*, *forþfor*, *gefea*, *neowolnes*, *semninga* and *smyltnes*), and six words not in the works of Ælfric but used in the Lindisfarne and Rushworth glosses or in the Durham Ritual (*ac* interrogative, *cigan* ('cry', 'summon'), *gefeon*, *iumanna*, *medmycclan* and *ymbsellan*). *Gæstliþnesse* is indeed limited otherwise to verse, known early texts and the Blickling Homilies, with *gæstliþende* in the *Wonders of the East*, but the word *hospitalitas* is not used in the gospels , while Ælfric has the related adjective *gistliþe*. Of the items in the list of words 'which, because they tend to disappear from successive psalter glosses, are also often presented as evidence for the early composition of prose texts' eleven are still used by Ælfric (*adreogan*, *andlyfen*, *æfter þon*, *bysmr*- forms, *clypung*, *ehtnes*, *geondstregde*, *goma*, *intinga*, *geunrotsod* and *þeaw*), while the Durham Ritual has *æfæstnes* and *tælnysse*. *Gefeannesse*, *leasliccetung*, *ungeþeawe* and *witedomlic* are apparently hapax legomena

before the end of the first quarter of the tenth century at the latest, Waite's detailed analysis of the vocabulary yields no material that might suggest that its author used an older form of Old English than did Werferth, who, as we have seen, died in 915.[124]

From the evidence hitherto provided, then, there is no good reason why any of the so-called early literary Mercian texts other than the *Dialogues* and probably also the Martyrology should be dated late-ninth-century rather than early-tenth-century. There is no reason at all to require us to assume a 'pre-Alfredian' dating for these texts, whatever hypotheses might appear attractive to us.

However, there is one detail which appears not to have been noted by Vleeskruyer or Wenisch or any other writer on early or dialect vocabulary and which might help in the difficult task of dating. That is the use of *Scotta ealond* for 'Ireland' in *St Chad*[125] and in material relating to the Irishman Niall, common to Napier homilies XLIII and XLIV.[126] The Latin words for 'Ireland' used in Bede's *Historia ecclesiastica* are *Hibernia* and *Scottia*, with the people of the country referred to as *Scotti*. The earliest datable English documents either employ the Latin term *(H)ibernia*, though very often adding a rider such as that in the Martyrology, 'in Hibernia mægðe, þæt is on Scotta lande',[127] or else they replace it by the name of the people. Thus, in annual 565 of the *Anglo-Saxon Chronicle* we find the entry, 'Her Columba mæssepreost of Scottum com

---

(for a full list of these from the Life and the related Guthlac homily in the Vercelli Book, see Crawford, 'Guthlac', pp. 215–17). Found only in texts of uncertain date are *æfþancas* and *orleahtor*. Found only in early texts and in texts of uncertain date are *beotung*, *onbærnan*, *wolberende* and *ondrysenlic* (cf. the laws of Athelstan I, *c.* 927–30, *ondryslic*. Similarly non-proven is Vleeskruyer's claim about the Blickling Homilies (*St Chad*, p. 56), 'the archaic vocabulary shared by all the homilies suggests strongly that none of them can have been composed even in the early tenth century', and about *Vita Malchi* (*ibid.* pp. 59–60, n. 6), '*Malchus* . . . in general shows all the characteristics of the ninth-century Mercian transla-tions'; see further, above, n. 55. The *Apocalypse of Thomas* has three words from Vleeskruyer's lists, *nænig*, *gefea* and *scyldig*, none of them indicative of an exclusively early date (see above, p. 110). I have found no other items to support the theory of composition before 950.

124 See esp. Waite, 'The Vocabulary', Appendices 1, 2 and 3, and above, n. 71. I am preparing a detailed study of early Old English vocabulary with the aid of Dr Jane Roberts's materials for a thesaurus of Old English.

125 Ed. Vleeskruyer, line 187, rendering Latin 'in Hibernia'.

126 *Wulfstan*, ed. Napier, pp. 205, lines 5–17, and 215, lines 15–22. Wenisch (*Spezifisch anglisches Wortgut*, p. 49) describes the date and dialect of these homilies as *unbekannt*. For Niall, a *diacon*, living 'on Scotta ealonde' (var. *Sceotland*), who prophesied that fire would consume first *Scotta land*, then *Brytwealas*, then *Angelcynn*, see D. Whitelock, 'Bishop Ecgred, Pehtred and Niall', *Ireland in Early Mediaeval Europe*, ed. D. Whitelock, R. McKitterick and D. Dumville (Cambridge, 1982), pp. 47–68. Niall's death is reported in the Annals of Ulster, *s.a.* 860, so that a late-ninth-century date for the material shared by these passages is a possibility.

127 Entry for 16 January, St Fursey.

in Brettas to lærenne Peohtas 7 in Hi þam ealonde mynster worhte',[128] with *of Scottum* rendering the *de Scottia* of its source, the chronological summary at the end of Bede's *Historia ecclesiastica*. In the annal for 902, the Irish abbot Virgilius is described as 'abbud of Scottum'. We may compare the practice in the rewritten opening of the *Anglo-Saxon Chronicle*, MSS D and E, commonly known as the 'northern recension', which on textual grounds has been tentatively assigned to the late ninth century.[129] This begins with a reference to Gaels (*Scottas*) living in Ireland, and then explains how some of them migrated to Britain: 'Scotta sumdæl gewat of Ybernian on Brittene 7 þes landes sumdæl geeodon.'[130] That the author of this section equated *Scottas* with the inhabitants of *Hibernia* is proved by the statement that Julius Caesar left his army 'mid Scottum' – a statement founded on an attested incorrect manuscript reading, *Hibernia* for *hiberna*, in the *Historia ecclesiastica*.[131]

Those sections of the Orosius which directly translate the Latin retain the term *Ibernia* for 'Ireland'; however, they also give *Scotland* as the native equivalent. Thus, in the geographical first chapter we find *Ibærnia*, *Ibernia* and 'Igbernia, þæt we Scotland hatað', translating the *Hibernia* of Orosius's Latin, and we find *Scotland* on its own on two occasions where the Old English author is rewriting or expanding the Latin of his source.[132] We may compare this usage with that of the Bede, which normally renders *Hibernia* and *Scotti* by 'Hibernia, Scotta ealond' and *Scottas*, but on a couple of occasions uses the noun *Scotland* – at least in the surviving manuscript versions.[133]

However, in vernacular texts that can be securely dated to the tenth century, the terms *Scotland* came to be used of the northern part of Britain and *Scottas* of

---

[128] 'Here the priest Columba came from Ireland to Britain to teach the Picts and built a monastery in the island of Iona.' Restoration of erased entry in the Parker Manuscript; see *The Anglo-Saxon Chronicle, MS A*, ed. Bately, p. 23.

[129] For the 'northern recension' and the text of MS E, see *Two of the Saxon Chronicles Parallel*, ed. C. Plummer on the basis of an edition by J. Earle (Oxford, 1899, repr, 1965); *English Historical Documents*, ed. Whitelock, p. 113; and J. M. Bately, 'Manuscript Layout and the Anglo-Saxon Chronicle', *John Rylands Bull.* 70 (1988), 21–43, at 23.

[130] 'A proportion of the Gaels departed from Hibernia into Britain and settled part of that land.' Reading from MS E.

[131] 'Regressus in Galliam legiones in hiberna (*var.* hibernia) dimisit' (*HE* I.2) and 'þa he forlet his here abidan mid Scottum 7 gewat into Galwulum' (*Anglo-Saxon Chronicle* entry for 60 BC (MS E)).

[132] *Old English Orosius*, p. 19, lines 14, 18 and 15, besides pp. 9, line 10, and 19, line 5; see also 'wið Peohtas 7 wið Scottas' (p. 142, line 12).

[133] See, e.g., *Old English Bede*, 'Hibernia, Scotta ealonde' (p. 270, line 12), beside *Scotland* (pp. 22, line 28, and 28, line 9), for Latin *Hibernia*, and see further, below, n. 136. Is it coincidence that of the instances of *Scotland* in this text, one is in the list of chapter headings? For problems posed by the chapter headings, see D. Whitelock, 'The List of Chapter-Headings in the Old English Bede', *Old English Studies in Honour of J. C. Pope*, ed. R. B. Burlin and E. B. Irving (Toronto, 1974), pp. 263–84.

the Scots, with *Irland* or *Iraland* ('land of the Irish') for Ireland. So we find *Irland* in annals 914 and 941D of the *Anglo-Saxon Chronicle* and *Iraland* in annal 937,[134] beside *Scotland* (for 'Scotland') in annal 933A and *Scottas* (for the inhabitants of Scotland) in annals 920, 926D, 937, 945 and 946B. MSS D and E continue with this terminology right up to the end of the Old English period and in post-Conquest entries. *Iraland* for *Hibernia* and *Scotland* for north Britain is also the regular usage in works by Ælfric, though on one occasion Fursey is sent on an unhistorical journey to Scotland as well as to his native Ireland[135] – a detail which may have had its origin in an error of the type found in the reading, 'Ibernia, Scotland 7 Breotone' for 'Ibernia, Scotta ealond 7 Breotone' in the Tanner manuscript of the Bede.[136] We may compare also the reading *Sceotlande* of Napier homily XLIII for the *Scotta ealonde* of Napier XLIV and the reference to *Scotl[ande]* in the late West Saxon text known as the *Life of Machutus*, seemingly also for 'Ireland'.[137] However, given the (apparent) belief of at least one *Chronicle* scribe that Columbanus was abbot of Iona, the author of the *Machutus* may have taken the term *Scotti* of his source to refer to the Scots.[138]

---

134 For the variant *hira land* in MS A, see *The Anglo-Saxon Chronicle, MS A*, ed. Bately, p. cxxxi.

135 'He ferde ða geond eal ýrrland. and scótland. bodiende ða ðing þe he geseah. and gehyrde' (*Ælfric's Catholic Homilies*, ed. Godden, p. 197, lines 252–3). MSS D, G and P omit the words *and Scotland*. Godden (*ibid.* p. 366) notes that 'Ælfric's main source, the *Vita Fursei*, does not mention Scotland but refers at this point to Hibernia and its inhabitants the *Scotti*. Bede (not definitely consulted for this homily by Ælfric, but certainly available to him) says that Fursey was in *Scotia*, clearly meaning Ireland. Ælfric's error in placing Fursey in Scotland as well could have been induced by either the *Vita* or Bede (Scotia could apparently mean modern Scotland by the end of the tenth century). The omission of *and Scotland* by D, G, and P presumably reflects Ælfric's correction of the error, unless we assume that one of his scribes coincidentally dropped the phrase by accident. *Yrum and scottum* is allowed to stand at 258 in all manuscripts; perhaps Ælfric missed this phrase, or perhaps he felt that, with *and scotland* deleted, the reference to *scottum* could be allowed to stand, for the sake of the rhythm, as a term for the inhabitants of Ireland.'

136 'Meuanias Brettonum insulas, quae inter Hiberniam et Brittaniam sitae sunt, Anglorum subiecit imperio' (*HE* II.5); at *Old English Bede*, pp. 108, line 32–110, line 2. MS T here reads 'Swelce he eac mónige Bretta ealond, þa seondon geseted betweoh Ibernia, Scotland (MSS O and Ca *Scotlande*) 7 Breotone, Ongolcynnes rice underþeodde', and MS B (Cambridge, Corpus Christi College 41) '. . . betwyh Hibernia Scotta iglande 7 Brytene'. Miller, giving *monige* a capital M, translates, 'He also brought under the authority of the English Man, islands of the Britons lying between Ireland, Scotland and Britain.' The Mevanian islands are Anglesey and Man.

137 *The Old English Life of Machutus*, ed. D. Yerkes (Toronto, 1984), p. 29, line 21. The corresponding passage in the Latin (*ibid.* p. 29, line 15) reads 'Scottorum partibus ueniens'. As Yerkes observes (*ibid.* p. xxxvi), the vocabulary of *Machutus* is very close to that of the late West Saxon 'Winchester group'. However, rewriting of the type found in the revision of the *Dialogues* cannot be ruled out.

138 *The Anglo-Saxon Chronicle, MS A*, ed. Bately, annal 565, *Columban*, recte *Columba*.

The only instances of the later form *Iraland* in a text for which there is good evidence of composition before 914 occur in the Orosius. In the section of the work containing a report of Ohthere's journey from *Sciringesheal* to Hedeby, there are two references to *Iraland* as a place lying on the Norwegian seafarer's starboard as he travelled south down the Norwegian coast.[139] However, as we have seen, the normal rendering of *Hibernia* in the Orosius is *Scotland*. There are several possible explanations for this striking anomaly. First of all, Ohthere's report contains a number of linguistic features uncharacteristic of the usage of the body of the work,[140] while the usual Norse name for Ireland is *Írland*.[141] So the term *Iraland* could have been introduced by an interpreter or by Ohthere himself. At the same time, there is a body of opinion which finds the reference to Ireland as west of Scandinavia unacceptable and would emend *Iraland* to *Island*,[142] while the untypically abrupt way in which the reports of both Ohthere and another seafarer, Wulfstan, are inserted into a chapter which otherwise demonstrates very careful rewriting and restructuring of its Latin source could be due to interpolation not by the late-ninth-century translator but, at a later date, by someone for whom such an 'emendation' would have been natural.[143] The occurrence of *Iraland* in the Orosius, then, does not prevent us from distinguishing between a group of early West Saxon texts using the terms *Scotta ealond* and *Scotland* for *Hibernia* and a later group (from at least 914) with the terms *Iraland* and *Irland*. The terminology of the Bede suggests for late-ninth- or early-tenth-century Mercia a usage similar to that of

---

[139] *Old English Orosius*, p. 16, lines 6 and 7.   [140] See *ibid.* p. lxxii.

[141] However, see the comment in *An Icelandic–English Dictionary*, ed. R. Cleasby and rev. G. Vigfusson, 2nd edn with a Supplement by Sir William Craigie (Oxford, 1957), under *Skotar*, that in some passages of the *Landnamabok* the terms *Skotar* and *Skotland* seem to be used of the Irish and Ireland.

[142] See. e.g., W. A. Craigie, '"Iraland" in King Alfred's "Orosius"', *MLR* 12 (1917), 200–1; see also Christine Fell's comment (*Two Voyagers at the Court of King Alfred*, ed. N. Lund, translated by C. E. Fell, with contributory essays by O. Crumlin-Pedersen, P. H. Sawyer and C. E. Fell (York, 1984), p. 63): 'It seems to me highly likely that Ohthere spoke of *Ísland*, and not at all improbable that a West-Saxon scribe should have got it wrong. It may indicate one of the times when communication between Ohthere and his interrogator remained unsuccessful.'

[143] All the signs are that the passages were added after the translation and rewriting of Orosius, *Historiarum libri septem* i.ii was completed and that the *terminus ad quem* is the date of the Lauderdale manuscript (BL Add. 47967), which is in a hand very close to that of the scribe of *Anglo-Saxon Chronicle*, MS A; see *The Anglo-Saxon Chronicle, MS A*, ed. Bately, p. xxxii. There is no attempt to link the last words of the account of northern Europe and the statement (*Old English Orosius*, p. 13, lines 29–30) 'Ohthere sæde his hlaforde, Ælfrede cyninge, þæt he ealra Norðmonna norþmest bude', though the insertion at this point has clearly been prompted by the reference to *Norþmenn* as living west of the Swedes in the passage immediately preceding. There is similarly no transition between the account of Ohthere's voyage and that of Wulfstan.

Wessex. The terminology of *St Chad* and the Niall material common to Napier homilies XLIII and XLIV may thus be interpreted as indicating either that in the dialect of their authors the use of *Scotland* for *Hibernia* persisted longer than in that of the author(s) of the annals for the last years of Edward and Elder, 912–20, or that these works were composed before the second quarter of the tenth century.[144]

The corpus of vernacular prose literature that can be safely attributed to the period before 900, therefore, consists of two or three Mercian texts (the *Dialogues* and possibly the Martyrology and Bede) and seven West Saxon ones, comprising five by Alfred (the *Pastoral Care*, the Boethius, the *Soliloquies*, the prose psalms of the Paris Psalter and the introduction to the laws), the Orosius and the opening sections of the *Chronicle*, to 896. Almost all of these texts seem to have been composed during the last thirty years of the ninth century.[145] Homilies and saints' lives may also have been composed in this period,[146] and these could have included *St Chad*, the common source of the Niall passages in Napier homilies XLIII and XLIV,[147] and perhaps also the *Epistola Alexandri*. However, there is no evidence at all to allow us to attribute any of the surviving texts in this group to the ninth century with any certainty.

THE VARIETIES OF LITERARY PROSE IN USE BEFORE 900

The stylistic achievement of the works that form the corpus of texts composed, or probably composed, before 900 varies considerably, as does the nature of the prose which they contain. On the one hand, we have the very plain prose of the first part of the *Anglo-Saxon Chronicle* and the only slightly less plain styles of the Martyrology and the account of the voyages of Ohthere and Wulfstan in the Orosius. On the other hand, we have the Latinate prose and 'highly literary style'[148] of the *Dialogues* and the Bede, translations which are occasionally so faithful to their originals that the result is unidiomatic.[149] In between the two

---

144 The period when scribe 2c of the *Chronicle*, MS A, whose last entry is for 920, appears to have been writing; see *The Anglo-Saxon Chronicle, MS A*, ed. Bately, pp. xxv–xxxiv.

145 See above, pp. 96–8.

146 Cf. Alexander, *Old English Literature*, p. 132, 'Thousands of sermons, for example, must have been preached in Old English in the seventh century and some may have reached written form.' However, see the important assessment of preaching and preaching materials in Anglo-Saxon England by M. McC. Gatch, *Preaching and Theology in Anglo-Saxon England: Ælfric and Wulfstan* (Toronto, 1977), esp. chs. 4 and 5.

147 See above, p. 114. This source has a number of features which link it with texts of 'Mercian' or potentially early origin; e.g., use of words such as *arlic* and *nænig*, forms such as *cymeþ*, word pairs and occasionally constructions combining possessive and demonstrative.

148 Waite, 'The Vocabulary', p. 148.

149 For convenience I am assuming that the Martyrology and Bede are ninth-century texts (though this is not proven) and that the Ohthere and Wulfstan passages of the Orosius are based on notes made in the late ninth century.

extremes, we have the prose of Alfred's works and the Orosius, where close translation is less frequent than free paraphrase, and where the authors frequently introduce lengthy and syntactically complex passages of their own composition, without the aids or constraints of a Latin original.

Some parts of the texts in the plain style might appear, at first sight, to justify Michael Alexander's description of the prose of Alfred's reign as 'rude and rudimentary',[150] Here parataxis predominates, with temporal subordination (and correlation) as the major variation on a string of coordinate clauses, and, in the case of the *Chronicle*, with the repetition of formulaic expressions such as 'ahton wælstowe gewald' and 'sige nam', as the most obvious mannerism. However, in the case of the voyages of Ohthere and Wulfstan what we have is virtually a record in note form of the replies given by the two visitors to Alfred's court to a series of unreported questions,[151] while the simplicity of the *Chronicle* entries is the result of a combination of the general unavailability of detailed information to the late-ninth-century compiler(s)[152] and the deliberate adoption of an annalistic style.[153] As for the Martyrology, this text certainly shows a marked preference for coordination, and, in spite of its dependence on Latin source material, its style is not much more sophisticated than that of the earlier entries in the *Anglo-Saxon Chronicle* or the laws of Ine. We may compare annal 837 of the *Chronicle*, 'Her Wulfheard aldormon gefeaht æt Hamtune wiþ .xxxiii. sciphlæsta 7 þær micel wel geslog 7 sige nom, 7 þy geare forþferde Wulfheard, 7 þy ilcan geare gefeaht Eþelhelm dux wiþ deniscne here on Port mid Dornsætum 7 gode hwile þone here gefliemde, 7 þa Deniscan ahton welstowe gewald 7 þone aldormon ofslogon',[154] which is made up of a string of

---

150 *Old English Literature*, p. 133.

151 See *Old English Orosius*, esp. notes to pp. 13, lines 29–30, 14, line 11, 15, line 6, and 16, lines 7–8. For instance, the problems inherent in p. 15, lines 2–6, vanish if we suppose that Ohthere had been asked (*i*) how big the 'horse-whales' were; (*ii*) where the best whale-hunting was; (*iii*) how big the largest whales were in his own country; and (*iv*) what was the biggest catch of whales that he had ever made.

152 See C. Clark, 'The Narrative Mode of *The Anglo-Saxon Chronicle* before the Conquest', *England before the Conquest*, ed. P. Clemoes and K. Hughes (Cambridge, 1971), pp. 215–35.

153 See, e.g., annal 592, 'Her micel wælfill wæs æt Woddesbeorge, 7 Ceawlin wæs ut adrifen', and annal 409, 'Her Gotan abræcon Romeburg, 7 næfre siþan Romane ne ricsodon on Bretone', which is a translation of *Historia ecclesiastica* v.24, 'Anno CCCCVIIII Roma a Gothis fracta, ex quo tempore Romani in Brittania regnare cessarunt.' The statement by C. Sprockel, *The Language of the Parker Chronicle* (The Hague, 1965–73) II, 73: 'As for the frequent use of *and* in A to string sentences together instead of conjunctions or adverbs that express the logical relation, this is generally regarded as characteristic of a primitive style', must be read in the context of Amos's warning (*The Linguistic Means*, p. 161), against using degrees of hypotaxis and parataxis as indicators of date.

154 'Here ealdorman Wulfheard fought at Hamton against thirty three ship loads and there inflicted great slaughter and took victory; and in this year Wulfheard died. and in this same year dux Æthelhelm fought against a Danish force at Port with the men of Dorset and for a

coordinate clauses linked by 'and', with the opening paragraph of the Martyrology, which is likewise composed almost entirely of coordinate clauses:

On þone forman dæig on geare, þæt is on þone ærestan Geoheldæig, eall Cristen folc worþiað Cristes acennednesse. Sancte Maria hine acende on þære nihte on anum holum stanscræfe beforan Bethlehem ðære ceastre 7 sona ða he acenned wæs, heofanlic leoht scean ofer eall þæt land, 7 Godes engel ætiwde sceaphirdon on anre mile beeastan þære cestre 7 him sæde þæt eallra folca Hælend wære acenned, 7 ða hirdas gehirdon micelne engla sang on eorðan.[155]

However, both syntax and style adequately serve the author's purpose and the result is clarity.

A very different kind of prose is to be found in the *Dialogues*. Werferth, bishop of Worcester, was, according to Asser, the first to translate Gregory's *Dialogi* into the English language, 'sometimes rendering sense for sense, translating intelligently and in a very polished style'.[156] We cannot, of course, do more than guess at the features of his translation that Asser was apparently admiring, although they probably included what appear to us today to be its most marked mannerisms. In spite of Asser's statement concerning rendering 'sense of sense', the translation keeps very close to its original. To paraphrase Simeon Potter, we may say that Werferth endeavoured to follow the Latin text slavishly, but, thanks to the easy and unaffected language of Gregory, he could afford to be literal: it was even possible for him to retain the original sentence structure.[157] His style is relatively sophisticated, and he employs a wide variety of clause types, largely because the Latin he is translating also has complex sentence structure, Moreover, some of the constructions he uses deliberately mimic those of Latin, with, for instance, almost half of the ablative absolutes of

good length of time put the enemy force to flight, and the Danes had control of the battle field and slew the ealdorman' (reading from MS A).

[155] Entry for 25 December: 'On the first day of the year, that is on the first Yule-day, all Christian folk celebrate Christ's birth. St Mary gave birth to him on that night in a hollow cave outside the town of Bethlehem, and immediately when he was born, a heavenly light shone all over the land, and God's angel appeared to shepherds a mile to the east of the town, and told them that the Saviour of all peoples had been born; and the shepherds heard a great song of angels on earth.'

[156] *Asser's Life of King Alfred*, ed. Stevenson, ch. 77: 'Werfrithum . . . qui, imperio regis, libros Dialogorum Gregorii papae et Petri sui discipuli de Latinitate primus in Saxonicam linguam, aliquando sensum ex sensu ponens, elucabratim et elegantissime interpretatus est'. It should be noted that Asser does not claim that Werferth was the first person ever to translate into Old English.

[157] S. Potter, *On the Relation of the Old English Bede to Werferth's Gregory and to Alfred's Translations* (Prague, 1931), pp. 2 and 4.

the Latin represented by dative absolutes.[158] However, Werferth does make some important concessions to English idiom and he takes some deliberate stylistic decisions of his own. The most marked mannerisms, apart from the use of dative absolute constructions, are a fondness for constructions combining possessive and demonstrative,[159] and a tendency to render one Latin word by two English ones, not infrequently alliterating with one another.[160] However, there are other, subtler, modifications of the Latin original, including a certain amount of syntactical resolution and expansion. For instance, subordinate constructions are sometimes turned into coordinate ones;[161] phrases are turned into clauses;[162] active constructions are substituted for passive ones and vice versa;[163] and a number of words, phrases and clauses are added for clarification or for purely stylistic reasons,[164] while alliteration is used to link widely separated elements in the sentence.

An example of Werferth's general practice, selected at random, is *Dialogues*, pp. 322, line 25–323, line 3,

forþon full manige men syndon, þa þe eallinga wyrcað fela godra weorca, ac swa þeah þonne gyt beoð gehrinene mid lichamlicum uncystum on þære lustfulnesse heora geþohtes, þæt is swyðe rihtlic, þæt þa þær ymbsitte se mist þære fulnesse, þa ðe her þonne gyt blissað 7 gelustfullaþ se lust þæs lichaman. be þon se eadiga Iob cwæð, þa þa he geseah þa ylcan lustfullnesse þæs lichaman, þæt heo wæs in þære fylnesse, he spræc þa þysne cwyde be þam wrænan 7 slidenan men: 'eall seo lustfulness 7 swetnes þæs lichaman weorðeþ to wyrma geride',[165]

rendering *Dialogi* iv.xxxviii. 4,

---

[158] Potter, *ibid.* p. 22, gives the figures as 123 in the Old English for 265 in the Latin. The late-tenth-century reviser adds more instances than he removes; see D. Yerkes, *Syntax and Style in Old English* (Binghampton, NY, 1982). For the dative absolute in Old English, see Mitchell, *Old English Syntax* II, §§3804–31.

[159] See, e.g., *Dialogues*, p. 261, line 3, 'urum þam ærestan mæge Adame', and p. 35, line 21, 'se his wisdom'.

[160] See, e.g., *ibid.* p. 11, line 5, 'fæsten 7 forhæfdnesse' for *abstentia*, and p. 221, line 13, 'wregend 7 wrohtbora' for *accusator*. For a detailed list, see *ibid.* II, 87–96.

[161] Or less commonly vice versa; cf. Potter, *The Relation*, p. 4, 'Again and again it was sufficient for the translator to make subordinate clauses – especially adverb clauses of cause, purpose and result – non-dependent, and to insert co-ordinating conjunctions.' For a detailed discussion of the manner of the translation, see the second part of Hecht's edition.

[162] See, e.g., *Dialogues*, p. 71, lines 6–7, 'þæt he þa unclænan gastas of mannum aflyman mihte', for *Dialogi* i.x, 'in exfugandis spiritibus'. [163] See, e.g., *Dialogues* II, 78.

[164] See, e.g., the added reference to a monastery, *Dialogues*, p. 5, lines 23–4, quoted below, p. 122, and see also *ibid.* II, pp. 38–53.

[165] 'Because there are very many men, who completely do many good works but nevertheless are yet touched with carnal vices in the delight of their thought, that is very just that the mist of that foulness beset there those whom the pleasure of the flesh still delights and pleases

quia sunt plerique qui multa bona opera faciunt, sed tamen adhuc carnalibus uitiis in cogitationis delectatione tanguntur, et iustum ualde est ut illic nebula foetoris obsideat, quos hic adhuc carnalis [var. carnis] foetor delectat. Vnde et eandem delectationem carnis esse beatus Iob in foetore conspiciens, de luxurioso ac lubrico sententiam protulit, dicens: *Dulcedo illius uermis*.[166]

Werferth and his collaborator(s) have here made some minor additions and expansions: an adverbial clause replaces the phrase introduced by the present participle *conspiciens*, the verbless quotation is expanded into a clause and two sets of word pairs are added to the single pair in the source. The Old English version also makes clever use of alliteration and of parallelism, but otherwise renders the Latin fairly closely.

Large-scale expansions are very few, the most worthy of note being *Dialogues*, p. 5, lines 13–30,

Geseoh, nu, Petrus, þæt me is gelicost þam, þe on lefan scipe byð, þæt byð geswenced mid þam yþum mycclan sæs: swa ic eom nu onstyred mid þam gedrefednyssum þissere worulde, 7 ic eom gecynssed mid þam stormum þære strangan hreohnesse in þam scipe mines modes. 7 þonne ic gemune mines þæs ærran lifes, þe ic on mynstre ær on wunode, þonne asworette ic 7 geomrige gelice þam, þe on lefan scipe neah lande gelætað, 7 hit þonne se þoden 7 se storm on sæ adrifeð swa feorr, swa he æt nyhstan nænig land geseon ne mæg,[167]

developing the seafaring metaphor[168] of *Dialogi* i.Prol.5,

here. About which the blessed Job pronounced when he saw the same delight of the body that it was in that foulness, he spoke then this speech about the wanton and slidden [for *slidoran* 'slippery'?] man: "all the delight and sweetness of the body will become as food(?) for worms".' In this and subsequent translations I have attempted to follow the original as closely as possible, in order to demonstrate similarities and differences between the Latin and Old English versions.

166 'Because there are a considerable number who do many good works, but nevertheless are yet touched with carnal vices in the delight of thought, and it is extremely just that a cloud of foulness beset there those whom the carnal foulness [var. foulness of the flesh] still delights here. Whence the blessed Job, seeing that same delight of the flesh to be in foulness, offered this observation on the wanton and slippery man, "The sweetness of that man [is that] of a worm".' For a polished translation into French see *Dialogi*, ed. de Vogüé.

167 'See, now, Peter, that I am most like the person who is on a frail ship, that is hard-pressed by the waves of a great sea: so I am now stirred up by the tribulations of this world, and I am struck with the storms of the strong tempest in the ship of my mind. and when I recall that my previous life which I spent previously in a monastery, then I sigh and murmur, like the person who approaches land in a frail ship and the whirlwind and storm then drive(s) it so far on the sea that he finally can see no land.'

168 Cf. the frequently cited fondness for images concerning water and boats in Alfred's translations.

Ecce etenim nunc magni maris fluctibus quatior atque in naui mentis tempestatis ualidae procellis inlidor, et cum prioris uitae recolo, quasi post tergum ductis oculis uiso litore suspiro.[169]

Here four clauses have been expanded to thirteen, with stylistic embellishments including tautological word pairs, alliteration and the construction possessive plus demonstrative. Gregory's balanced clauses, ending with *quatior* and *inlidor* are reflected by the no less balanced 'ic eom nu onstyred mid . . . 7 ic eom gecnyssed mid . . .', while, somewhat surprisingly in view of Old English poetic practice, Gregory's metaphor has been replaced by two similes.

The Old English author whose approach is closest to that of Werferth and his collaborators is the translator of the *Historia ecclesiastica*. Word pairs, both tautological and non-tautological,[170] are especially in evidence in this text, with sometimes as many as four sets in a short sentence, as, for instance, *Old English Bede*, pp. 50, line 29–52, line 2, '7 him Bryttas *sealdan 7 geafan* eardungstowe betwih him þæt hi for *sibbe 7 hælo* heora eðles *campodon 7 wunnon* wið heora feondum, 7 hi him *andlyfne 7 are* forgeafen for heora gewinne',[171] translating *Historia ecclesiastica* 1.15, 'Susceperunt ergo qui aduenerant, donatibus Britannis, locum habitationis inter eos, ea condicione ut hi pro patriae *pace et salute* contra aduersarios militarent, illi militantibus debita stipendia conferrent.'[172] In this passage the translator has not only added three tautological word pairs to the single non-tautological pair of the Latin, he has also made a number of other alterations to his exemplar. So, for instance, he has removed the ablative absolute, turning *Britannis* into the subject of the sentence, and he has also replaced the phrase 'locum habitationis' by a compound noun *eardungstow*. The use of a compound to replace two words in

---

[169] 'Behold now indeed I am battered by the waves of a great sea and struck in the ship of my mind by the storms of a powerful tempest, and when I recall my previous life, as though with eyes turned behind me, with the shore having been seen, I sigh.'

[170] For a list of word pairs translating a single Latin word, or added to the Latin, see Waite, 'The Vocabulary', pp. 205–30, and also *ibid.* pp. 30–47, and for partial lists, see A. Schmidt, *Untersuchungen über König Ælfreds Bedaübersetzung* (Berlin, 1889), pp. 36–9, and Potter, *The Relation*, pp. 23–6.

[171] 'And the Britons gave and granted them a dwelling-place among them, on condition that they fought and battled against their enemies for the peace and safety of their country, and that they granted them wages and property in return for their warfare.' For a polished translation, see *Old English Bede*.

[172] 'Those who had arrived, therefore, received (with the Britons giving) a place of dwelling among them, on that condition that these should fight against the foes for the peace and safety of the country, [and that] those should grant to the people fighting the payment owed.' For a polished translation, see *Historia ecclesiastica*.

the Latin is a relatively common feature of the Bede,[173] as is the use of alliteration, perhaps under the influence of poetry.[174] Like Werferth and his collaborator(s), however, this author normally follows the syntactical structures of his source closely, often translating a sentence segment by segment. It is therefore not surprising to find a fairly high proportion of ablative absolutes rendered by dative constructions[175] and a number of unidiomatic expressions. For instance, we may compare *Old English Bede*, p. 46, lines 15–17, 'Wið þyssum stod on þam fæstene ufanweardum se earga feða Brytta 7 þær forhtigendre heortan wunode dæges 7 nihtes',[176] with *Historia ecclesiastica* I.12, 'Statuitur ad haec in aedito arcis acies segnis, ubi trementi corde stupida die noctuque marcebat',[177] and *Old English Bede*, pp. 48, line 29–50, line 2, '7 nalæs þæt an þæt ðas þing dyden weoruldmen, ac eac swylce þæt Drihtnes eowde, 7 his hyrdas. 7 hi druncennesse 7 oferhydo 7 geciide 7 geflite 7 æfeste 7 oðrum man(n)um þysses gemetes wæron heora swiran underþeoddende, on weg aworpenum Cristes geoce þam leohtan 7 þam swetan',[178] with *Historia ecclesiastica* I.14, 'Et non solum haec saeculares uiri sed etiam ipse grex Domini eiusque pastores egerunt, ebrietati animositati litigio contentioni inuidiae ceterisque huiusmodi facinoribus sua colla, abiecto leui iugo Christi, subdentes.'[179] However, as in the *Dialogues*, there is not infrequent syntactical resolution: hypotactic Latin constructions are rearranged into their paratactic Old English equivalents (as in the first quotation) and participial or absolute constructions are reformed

---

173 See Whitelock, 'The Old English Bede', pp. 76–7, and Waite, 'The Vocabulary', pp. 25–6 and ch. 2.

174 See, e.g., *Old English Bede*, p. 54, line 4, 'sume ofer sæ sarigende gewiton', and also F. Klaeber, 'Zur ae Bedaübersetzung', *Anglia* 25 (1902), 257–315, and 27 (1904), 243–82 and 399–435, at 25, 291; for a list of poetic words, see Waite, 'The Vocabulary', pp. 291–2. *Eardungstow* is, however, also used in a range of prose texts.

175 Potter's figures ('The Relation', p. 22) are *Historia ecclesiastica* 558 ablative absolutes, *Old English Bede* 100 dative absolutes. For examples, see also Schmidt, *Untersuchungen*, pp. 53–4.

176 'In addition to this the cowardly band of Britons stood on the top of the fortification and there remained day and night with trembling hearts.'

177 'In addition to this the slothful army was stationed along the top of the defence, where day and night, they drooped with trembling and benumbed hearts.'

178 'And not only did laymen do these things, but also the Lord's flock and His shepherds. And they were subjecting their necks to drunkenness and pride and strife and dispute and envy and other sins of this kind, with Christ's light and sweet yoke having been cast away.' For the compound *weoruldmen*, replacing 'viri saeculares', see above, p. 123, and n. 173. Note also the word pair 'þam leohte 7 þam swete' for Latin *leui*.

179 'And not only did secular men do these things, but also the Lord's flock itself and His shepherds, subjecting their necks to drunkenness, enmity, quarrelling, strife, and envy and other crimes of this kind, with Christ's light yoke having been cast off.' *Animositas* in ecclesiastical Latin has the meaning 'wrath, enmity'; in post-classical texts, however, it can be translated 'courage, spirit, impetuosity'.

into coordinate clauses.[180] In brief, one finds in the Bede 'a curious mix of the pedantic and the poetic, of literal exactitude alongside rhetorical embellishment', with the variation between literal and free translation running throughout the work.[181]

Since Alfred had a number of scholars from Mercia, including Werferth, to help him with his translations,[182] as well, presumably, as the *Dialogues* to serve as a model,[183] it is not surprising that some of the features mentioned above occur also in the first work he undertook, namely the *Pastoral Care*.[184] So, for instance, word pairs are frequently employed. We may compare *Cura pastoralis* III.ii, 'Paupercula tempestate convulsa', with *Pastoral Care*, p. 181, lines 11–12, 'Ðu earma, ðu ðe eart mid ðy storme 7 mid ðære yste onwend 7 oferworpen',[185] where three words are rendered by fifteen, including two sets of wordpairs, and *Pastoral Care*, p. 25, lines 11–13, 'From ðære dura selfre ðisse bec, ðæt is from onginne ðisse spræce, sint adrifene 7 getælde ða unwaran, ðe him agniat ðone cræft ðæs lareowdomes ðe hi na ne geleornodon',[186] with *Cura pastoralis* I.Prol., 'ab ipso libri hujus reprehendantur exordio; ut quia indocti ac præcipites doctrinæ arcem tenere appetunt, a præcipitationis suæ ausibus in ipsa locutionis nostræ janua repellantur'.[187] The word pairs in these examples

---

[180] For a study of the Old English translator's technique, see D. K. Fry, 'Bede Fortunate in his Translator: the Barking Nuns', *Studies*, ed. Szarmach, pp. 345–62, and also R. W. Clement, 'An Analysis of Non-Finite Verb Forms as an Indication of the Style of Translation in Bede's *Ecclesiastical History*', *Jnl of Eng. Ling.* 12 (1978), 19–28.

[181] Waite, 'The Vocabulary', pp. 29–30, and Whitelock, 'The Old English Bede', p. 76.

[182] *Asser's Life of King Alfred*, ed. Stevenson, ch. 77.

[183] Since Asser does not mention Alfred's translations, it is generally assumed that they all postdated the translation of the *Dialogi*. It should be noted, however, that Asser's reference to Alfred as not yet having begun to read anything, in the same paragraph as the reference to Werferth's translation, is in no way a confirmation of this chronology. The reference to the translation occurs in a general description of Werferth, which accompanies a reference to that bishop's arrival at Alfred's court.

[184] The priority of the *Pastoral Care* is a reasonable assumption; however, it has not always been maintained; see e.g., *King Alfred's Anglo-Saxon Version of the Compendious History of the World by Orosius*, ed. J. Bosworth (London, 1859), pp. viii–x, where the order Boethius, Bede, Orosius and *Pastoral Care* is suggested.

[185] *Cura pastoralis*, 'You poor little one, overthrown with a tempest'; *Pastoral Care*, 'You poor man, who are overturned and thrown over with the storm and with the tempest.' For other instances of 'doublets' in the *Pastoral Care*, see W. H. Brown, 'Method and Style in the Old English *Pastoral Care*', *JEGP* 68 (1969), 666–84, at 669–74. For a polished translation of these passages, see Henry Davis, *Ancient Christian Writers* XI (1950).

[186] 'From the very door of this book, that is, from the beginning of this discourse, the unwary are driven away and reproved, who appropriate to themselves the art of that mastership which they never learned.'

[187] 'Let them be reproved from the very beginning of this book, that since unlearned and hasty they desire to hold the citadel of teaching, they may be driven back from the attempts of their

arise from the substitution of two words for one in the Latin. However, elsewhere they result from a deliberate rearrangement of existing items in the Latin. We may compare, for instance, *Cura pastoralis* i.iv, 'Nonne hæc est Babylon magna, quam ego ædificavi in domum regni, et in robore fortitudinis meæ et in gloria decoris mei',[188] with *Pastoral Care*, p. 39, lines 16–18, 'Hu ne is ðis sio micle Babilon ðe ic self atimbrede to kynestole 7 to ðrymme, me selfum to wlite 7 wuldre, mid mine agne mægene 7 strengo?'[189]

However, as Potter has pointed out, for 100 ablative absolutes in the *Cura pastoralis* there is only one dative absolute in the Old English translation.[190] Moreover, although word for word and unit for unit translation does occasionally occur, Alfred's technique is better described as translation sentence by sentence, with syntactical resolution employed far more frequently than in the *Dialogues* or the Bede, with balance and verbal parallelism (often reinforced by alliteration) as the most marked stylistic features, rather than Latinisms, and with a subtle and sophisticated use of word pairs, not just an automatic rendering of one word in the Latin by two in the Old English.[191] For instance, *Pastoral Care*, p. 23, lines 9–11, 'þu leofusta broður, suiðe freondlice 7 suiðe fremsumlice ðu me tældesð, 7 mid eaðmode ingeðonce ðu me ciddesð, forðon ic min mað, 7 wolde fleon ða byrðenne ðære hirdelecan giemenne',[192] is a deliberate rearrangement of *Cura pastoralis* i.Prol., 'Pastoralis curæ me pondera

---

hastiness at the very door of our discourse.' Did the manuscript used by Alfred read *artem* for *arcem*?

[188] 'Is not this great Babylon which I have built as the house of the kingdom, in the power of my strength and in the glory of my honour?' *Decus* and *gloria*, like *wlite* and *wuldor* in the Old English version, can both have the meaning 'glory'.

[189] 'How, is not this the great Babylon which I myself built as a royal throne and for magnificence, as an adornment and glory for myself, with my own power and strength?' For Ælfric's use of this sentence, see M. Godden, 'Ælfric and the Vernacular Prose Tradition', *The Old English Homily and its Backgrounds*, ed. P. E. Szarmach and B. F. Huppé (Albany, NY, 1978), pp. 99–117, at 103–4.   [190] *The Relation*, p. 22.

[191] For a detailed survey, see W. H. Brown, *A Syntax of King Alfred's Pastoral Care* (The Hague, Paris, 1970); see also *idem*, 'Method and Style'. Brown (*ibid.* p. 678) describes Alfred's purpose as utilitarian: 'he translates literally when he can conveniently do so, when he can take the Latin over with no substantial change in diction or syntax and still write understandable English'. I disagree with Brown's conclusion that the result is 'unadorned and, as a rule, undistinguished'. For a different picture of the achievement of Alfred and his helpers, see Potter, *The Relation*, p. 48, where it is said that the knowledge of Latin of the translator of *Cura pastoralis* is superior to that of the authors of the Old English Bede and the *Dialogues*: 'This is proved beyond dispute by his accurate and skilful renderings of very intricate passages.' For Alfred's stylistic achievement in the letter prefixed to the *Pastoral Care*, see, e.g., B. F. Huppé, 'Alfred and Ælfric: a Study of Two Prefaces', *The Old English Homily*, ed. Szarmach and Huppé, pp. 119–37.

[192] 'Dearest brother, very friendlily and very kindly you reproved me, and with humble intent you chid me, because I hid myself and wished to flee the burden of pastoral care.'

fugere delitescendo voluisse, benigna, frater carissime, atque humili intentione reprehendis',[193] replacing the first of Gregory's pair of adjectives (*benigna*) with a pair of adverbial phrases and creating a similarly matched pair of clauses from Gregory's single clause.[194]

In addition, unlike Werferth and the author of the Bede, Alfred amplifies and enlarges freely. For instance, Gregory's simile of a boat is expanded from twenty-eight words in four clauses to fifty-six words in nine clauses, with *Cura Pastoralis* III.xxxiv, 'In hoc quippe mundo humana anima quasi more navis est contra ictum fluminis conscendentis: uno in loco nequaquam stare permittitur, quia ad ima relabitur, nisi ad summa conetur',[195] rendered in *Pastoral Care*, p. 445, lines 9–14, as 'Ac ælces mannes mod on ðys middangearde hæfð scipes ðeaw. Ðæt scip wile hwilum stigan ongean ðone stream, ac hit ne mæg, buton ða rowend hit teon, ac hit sceal fleotan mid ðy streame: ne mæg hit no stille gestondan, buton hit ankor gehæbbe, oððe mon mid roðrum ongean tio; elles hit gelent mid ðy streame.'[196]

Moreover, there are a number of changes of detail within sentences and paragraphs. For instance, *Cura pastoralis*, I.Prol., 'Quadripartita vero disputatione liber iste distinguitur, ut ad lectoris sui animum ordinatis allegationibus quasi quibusdam passibus gradiatur',[197] becomes *Pastoral Care*, p. 23, lines 16–19, 'Nu ic wilnige ðætte ðeos spræc stigge on ðæt ingeðonc ðæs leorneres, suæ suæ on sume hlædre, stæpmælum near 7 near, oððæt hio fæstlice gestonde on ðæm solore ðæs modes ðe hi leornige; 7 forðy ic hi todæle on feower',[198] with the order of the sentence reversed, Gregory's simile foregrounded, and effective use of alliteration.

The other West Saxon translations are generally even less close verbally to their Latin sources than is the *Pastoral Care*. There is once again little or no evidence of Latinate constructions, and only five dative absolutes are reported

---

[193] 'You reprove me, dearest brother, with kind and humble intent for having wished to flee the burdens of pastoral care by hiding myself.'

[194] Note also the alliteration on *f*, reflecting alliteration on *p* and *f* in the Latin.

[195] 'For in this world the human soul is, as it were, in the manner of a ship ascending against the current of a river: it is never suffered to stay in one place, for it floats back again to the lowest parts, unless it strives to reach the highest parts.'

[196] 'Every man's mind in this world has the manner of a ship. The ship sometimes wishes to ascend against the current, but it cannot, unless the rowers impel it, but must float with the current; it cannot remain still, unless an anchor hold it or it be impelled forward by oars; otherwise it goes with the current.'

[197] 'Now this book is divided into quadripartite debate, that it may enter into the mind of its reader by orderly propositions, as if by certain steps.'

[198] 'Now I wish that this discourse should rise into the mind of the learner as on a ladder, step by step, nearer and nearer, until it firmly stands in the upper chamber of the mind which learns it; and therefore I divide it into four.' Sweet here weakens and distorts Alfred's metaphor by translating *solore* as 'floor'.

by Potter from the Orosius, none at all from the Boethius.[199] Parallelism, balance and alliteration are important stylistic features, and there are word pairs in plenty – though the latter do not obtrude, as they do in the Bede and to a lesser extent in the *Dialogues*, and they are not infrequently separated by other pieces of material.[200] Significantly, those passages that are totally independent of the Latin are no less complex stylistically than those that have sophisticated Latin models. So, for instance, we may compare *Old English Orosius*, pp. 82, line 32–83, line 6,

Ðyllicne gebroðorscipe, cwæð Orosius, hie heoldon him betweonum þe an anum hierede wæron afedde 7 getyde, þætte hit is us nu swiþor bismre gelic þæt we þæt besprecað, 7 þæt þæt we gewinn nu hatað, þonne us fremde 7 ellþeodge an becumaþ 7 lytles hwæt on us bereafiað 7 us eft hrædlice forlætað, 7 nyllað geþencan hwelc hit þa wæs þa nan mon ne mehte æt oþrum his feorh gebycggan, ne furþon þætte þa wolden gefriend beon þe wæron gebroðor of fæder 7 of meder,[201]

a passage corresponding to *Historiarum libri septem* iii.xxiii.65–7,

Haec sunt inter parentes filios fratres ac socios consanguinitatis societatisque commercia. tanti apud illos diuina atque humana religio pendebatur. erubescant sane de recordatione praeteritorum, qui nunc interuentu solius fidei Christianae ac medio tantum iurationis sacramento uiuere se cum hostibus nec pati hostilia sciunt; quibus indubitatissime probatur, quia . . . nunc inter barbaros ac Romanos . . . tantam fidem adhibita in sacramentum seruant euangelia, quantam tunc nec inter parentes ac filios potuit seruare natura,[202]

with *Old English Orosius*, pp. 102, line 34–103, line 7,

---

[199] Potter, *The Relations*, p. 22.

[200] For recent discussions of aspects of the style of these works, see J. S. Wittig, 'King Alfred's Boethius and its Latin Sources: a Reconsideration', *ASE* 11 (1983), 157–98; *Old English Orosius*, pp. c–cv; and E. M. Liggins, 'Syntax and Style in the Old English *Orosius*', *Studies*, ed. Szarmach, pp. 245–73. For pairings and parallel constructions in the *Soliloquies*, see *Alfred's Soliloquies*, p. 25–6.

[201] 'Such brothership, said Orosius, they held among themselves, who were nurtured and instructed in one family, that it is now to us much more like a mockery that we complain about that, and that we now call that war, when strangers and foreigners come upon us and plunder us of some little and again quickly leave us and will not think how it then was, when no man could buy his life of another, nor even that those then would be friends who were brothers by father and by mother.'

[202] 'Such are the ties of blood and fellowship between parents, sons, brothers, and friends. Such is the importance they attach to heavenly and earthly bonds. Let the people of this generation blush with shame over the recollection of these past events, who now realize that it is only by the intervention of the Christian faith and by means of the sworn oath that they live at all with their enemies and suffer no injury. This proves beyond question that now barbarians and Romans . . . assure one another such loyalty by the oath taken on the Gospels, as nature was unable in those days to ensure even between fathers and sons.' Translation from *Seven Books of History against the Pagans*, trans. I. W. Raymond (New York, 1936).

Hu magon nu Romane, cwæð Orosius, to soþe gesecgean þæt hie þa hæfden beteran tida þonne hie nu hæbben, þa hie swa monega gewin hæfdon emdenes underfongen? i wæs on Ispania, ii on Mæcedonia, iii on Capadotia, iiii æt ham wið Hannibal, 7 hie eac oftost gefliemde wurdon 7 gebismrade. Ac þæt wæs swiðe sweotol þæt hie wæron beteran þegnas þonne hie nu sien, þæt hie þeh þæs gewinnes geswican noldon, ac hie oft gebidon on lytlum staþole 7 on unwenlicum, þæt hie þa æt nihstan hæfdon ealra þara anwald þe ær neh heora hæfdon,[203]

which corresponds to a lengthy passage in the *Historiarum libri septem* iv.xvi, beginning 'Pudet recordationis. quid enim dicam improbitatem magis an miseriam Romanorum?' and ending 'et tamen fortis an alterutrum desperatio in meliora profecit, nam in his omnibus desperando pugnarunt, pugnando uicerunt. ex quo euidenter ostenditur non tempora tunc fuisse tranquilliora otiis, sed homines miseriis fortiores'.[204]

In the Boethius we may compare the passage *Alfred's Boethius*, p. 11, lines 2–9,

Sona swa ic þe ærest on þisse unrotnesse geseah þus murciende ic ongeat þæt þu wære ut afaren of þines fæder eðele, þæt is for minum larum. Þær ðu him fore of þa þu þine fæstrædnesse forlete, 7 wendest þæt seo weord [wyrd J] þas woruld wende heora agenes ðonces buton Godes geþeahte 7 his þafunge 7 monna gewyrhtum. Ic wiste þæt þu afaren wære, ac ic nysste hu feor, ær ðu þe self hit me gerehtest mid þinum sarcwidum,[205]

which has lexical variation and alliteration on *f*, *w* and *þ*, and both opens and closes with temporal clauses, and which renders *De consolatione* i, pr. v, 2, 'Cum

---

[203] 'How can the Romans, said Orosius, now say with truth, that they had better times then than they now have, when they had undertaken so many wars at the same time? One was in Spain, a second in Macedonia, a third in Cappadocia, a fourth at home against Hannibal; and they were, moreover, most often put to flight and disgraced. But that was very obvious that they were better soldiers then than they now are; that they, nevertheless, would not cease from the fight; (but they often remained in a little and hopeless position), so that at last they had control over all those who before nearly had [control] over them.'

[204] See esp. 18–25, 'And who would believe that at this time when, as we have said, they could not wage even one war at home, they undertook three more wars across the seas: one in Macedonia against Philip . . . another in Spain . . . a third in Sardinia . . . a fourth against Hannibal, who was pressing them hard in Italy. And yet a display of courage, bred of desperation, led to better fortune in every case; for in all these wars it was desperation that made them fight, and fighting that made them victorious. From this it is clearly evident that the times were not then more peaceful for the pursuits of leisure than they are at present, but that the men were braver as a result of their miseries.' For the Old English translator's handling of his sources, see *Old English Orosius*, pp. xciii–xcvi.

[205] 'As soon as I first saw you lamenting thus in this sadness, I perceived that you had departed from your father's land – that is, in spite of my teachings. You there departed from it when you forsook your steadfastness and believed that Fate directed this world at her own pleasure, regardless of God's purpose and consent and of the deeds of men. I knew that you had departed, but I did not know how far, before you yourself explained it to me with your plaints.'

te, inquit, maestum lacrimantemque uidissem, ilico miserum exsulemque cognoui; sed quam id longinquum esset exsilium, nisi tua prodidisset oratio, nesciebam,'[206] with such passages as *Alfred's Boethius*, p. 100, lines 4–6, 'Me þincð þæt ðu me dwelle 7 dydre, swa mon cild deð. lædst me hidres 7 ðidres on swa þicne wudu ðæt ic ne mæg ut aredian,'[207] which combines a metaphor with a simile and replaces a very different metaphor in the Latin, III, pr. xii, 30, 'Ludisne, inquam, me inextricabilem labyrinthum rationibus texens, quae nunc quidem qua egrediaris introeas, nunc uero qua introieris egrediare,'[208] and *Alfred's Boethius*, p. 40, lines 6–14,

Eala, Gesceadwisnes, hwæt, þu wast þæt me næfre seo gitsung 7 seo gemægð þisses eorðlican anwealdes forwel ne licode, ne ic ealles forswiðe ne girnde þisses eorðlican rices, buton tola ic wilnode þeah 7 andweorces to þam weorce þe me beboden was to wyrcanne; þæt was þæt ic unfracodlice 7 gerisenlice mihte steoran 7 reccan þone anweald þe me befæst wæs. Hwæt, þu wast þæt nan mon ne mæg nænne cræft cyþan ne nænne anweald reccan ne stioran butan tolum 7 andweorce,[209]

a passage which is independent of the Latin but no less syntactically complex than those passages which are based on the Latin.

As for the other works which are attributable to Alfred in whole or in part, these vary from very free renderings and independent prose (in the *Soliloquies*) to fairly close translation (in the prose psalms of the Paris Psalter), with the introduction to the laws combining the two in the form of Old and New Testament translation and Alfred's own statements.[210] In those works too the style is controlled and accomplished and those mannerisms that Alfred adopts are unobtrusive. So, for instance, we may compare Paris Psalter, VII.23–13,

Drihten þe is rihtwis dema 7 strang 7 geþyldig, hwæðer he yrsige ælce dæge? Bute ge to him gecyrren, se deofol cwecð his sweord to eow. 7 he bende his bogan, se is nu gearo

---

[206] 'When I saw you sad and weeping, I immediately knew you to be wretched and an exile; but I would not have known how far that banishment was, if your speech had not reported it.'

[207] 'It seems to me that you are misleading and baffling me, as one does a child; you lead me hither and thither into a wood so thick that I cannot get out.' See further, Bately, 'Those Books' (forthcoming).

[208] 'Are you not playing with me, I said, by weaving an inextricable labyrinth of arguments? now indeed you enter where you will come out, now you come out where you went in.'

[209] 'O Philosophy, lo, you know that covetousness and greed for worldly dominion never greatly delighted me, nor did I all too greatly desire this earthly rule, but yet I desired tools and material for the work that I was charged to perform; that was that I should worthily and fittingly steer and rule the dominion entrusted to me. Now you know that no man can reveal any talent or rule and steer any dominion without tools and material.' (Translation based on Whitelock, *English Historical Documents*, p. 919.) One of the mannerisms of this passage is the use of the collocation 'steoran 7 reccan'; cf. *Old English Bede* 'heold 7 rehte' etc., and Waite, 'The Vocabulary', pp. 217–18.

[210] For a valuable discussion of the laws, see Frantzen, *King Alfred*, ch. 2.

to sceotanne; he teohað þæt he scyle sceotan þæt deaðes fæt, þæt synt þa unrihtwisan; he gedeð his flan fyrena þæt he mæge mid sceotan, 7 bærnan þa þe her byrnað on wrænnesse 7 on unðeawum,[211]

with Paris Psalter XVII.12–14, '7 þa urnan swa swa ligetu beforan his ansyne; 7 he gemengde hagol 7 fyres gleda. 7 worhte þunorrada on heofonum; 7 se hyhsta sealde his stemne. He sende his strælas 7 hi tostencte, 7 gemanigfealdode his ligeta 7 gedrefde hig mid þy', [212] the first using *flan* and the second *strælas* for 'arrows, darts' for the sake of alliteration and variation. And we may compare the second passage with the partial rendering of the same verses in the Bede, at p. 268, lines 27–9, 'Drihten hleoðrað of heofonum 7 se hehsta seleð his stefne; he sendeð his stræle 7 heo toweorpeð; legetas gemonigfealdað 7 heo gedrefeð',[213] and in *St Chad*, at lines 168–70, 'drihten leoðrað of heofone 7 se hehsta seleð his stefne. he sendeð his strelas 7 he hio tostenceð. he gemonigfaldað legeto 7 he heo gedrefeð',[214] corresponding to the Latin of the Vespasian Psalter, 'Praefulgure in conspectu eius nubes transierunt grando et carbones ignis. Et intonuit de caelo dominus. et altissimus dedit uocem suam. Misit sagittas suas et dissipauit eos fulgura multiplicauit et conturbauit eos.'[215] The simple but balanced sentence structure of the three renderings comes straight from the Latin; what significant variation and initiative there is occurs not in the Mercian *St Chad* or Bede but in Alfred's West Saxon version. There is nothing rude or rudimentary here.

---

[211] 'The Lord who is a just ruler and strong and patient, will he be angry every day? Unless you turn to him, the devil will brandish his sword at you, and he will bend his bow, which is now ready to shoot; he intends that he should shoot the vessel of death, that is the unrighteous [ones]; he makes his arrows fiery, that he may shoot with and burn those who here burn in licentiousness and vices'; cf. Vespasian Psalter VII.12–13, 'Deus iudex iustus fortis et longanimis numquid irascitur per singulos dies. nisi conuertamini gladium suum uibra[u]it. Arcum suum tetendit et parauit illum. et in ipso parauit uasa mortis sagittas suas ardentibus effecit', and 1611 Bible, 'God judgeth the righteous, and God is angry with the wicked every day. If he turn not, he will whet his sword; he hath bent his bow and made it ready. He hath also prepared for him the instruments of death; he ordaineth his arrows against the persecutors making his arrows fiery shafts.'

[212] 'And then there ran as it were flashes of lightning before his countenance; and he mixed hail and coals of fire and made thunderclaps in the heavens, and the highest gave his voice. He sent his arrows and scattered them and multiplied his lightnings and violently moved them with that.'

[213] 'The Lord resounds from heaven and the highest gives his voice. He sends his arrows and disperses them; he multiplies lightnings and violently moves them.'

[214] 'The Lord resounds from heaven and the highest gives his voice. He sends his arrows and he scatters them, he multiplies lightnings and he violently moves them.'

[215] 1611 Bible. 'At the brightness that was before him his thick clouds passed hailstones and coals of fire. The Lord also thundered in the heavens, and the Highest gave his voice; hail stones and coals of fire. Yea, he sent out his arrows and scattered them; and he shot out lightnings and discomfited them'.

How are we to explain this flowering of vernacular prose in the late ninth century? Is it a new development, initiated by King Alfred, as Alexander would have it, with earlier prose confined to brief non-literary texts? Do we have innovation by Werferth or the author of the Bede, who then provided models both for King Alfred and for the writers of the tenth century? Or was there already a well-established tradition of vernacular prose, such as that suggested for Mercian by Vleeskruyer, going back perhaps to the eighth century, as de Vriend seems to imply, and giving Asser a yardstick against which to measure Werferth's stylistic achievement? What were the models of the late-ninth-century prose writers?[216]

Alexander and Vleeskruyer, as we have seen, suppose Old English prose to have had vernacular poetry as its prime model:[217] indeed it is the 'rather less conspicuous degree of . . . poetic influence concomitantly with greater translating proficiency and command of syntax', as well as the proportions of what Vleeskruyer takes to be archaisms, that leads him to date the Bede and *Dialogues* later than *St Chad* and the Martyrology.[218] Yet poetic influence, stimulating the use of alliteration, word pairs and rhythmical units, could have exerted itself on any prose writer at any time in the Old English period, while, even if we ignore the possibility of a native tradition of oral prose,[219] there was another, and most prestigious, prose model available in Latin. Anyone with a reasonable training in Latin would also have acquired a training in the ordering of ideas and in the constructing of complex sentences; he would have learned to use rhetorical figures (including alliteration[220] and word pairs) and to think in the abstract. The bulk of the Old English texts that have come down to us – whether in prose or in verse – are essentially Latin-based. And in the case of the translations, the most important decisions that normally face an author had

---

[216] Unfortunately, because of the problems involved in dating the Martyrology, it is not possible to determine whether it was early enough to be a possible model for these writers.

[217] See, e.g., *St Chad*, ed. Vleeskruyer, p. 22, where poetic technique is said to constitute the 'only autochthonous model by virtue of which a prose style could be created'.

[218] *Ibid.* pp. 19–20.

[219] The story of Cynewulf and Cyneheard in annal 755 of the *Chronicle* is often cited as evidence of such a tradition, and prose must surely have regularly been used for oral narrative. However, the hypothetical lay underlying annal 755 could have been in verse, while the 'ambiguous' use of pronouns, so often taken to be a sign of oral origin, might equally well represent Latin *hi, illi*. See further, above, n. 2.

[220] There is not infrequent alliteration in the Latin texts translated by Alfred and his contemporaries; see, e.g., *Dialogi* 1.i.4, 'ut nunc usque montem cernentibus casura pendere uideatur', translated, also with alliteration, as *Dialogues* p. 12, lines 19–20, 'ac gyt nu todæg he hangaþ swa hreosende, swylce he feallan wylle, 7 þæt magon geseon þa þe þone munt sceawiað', and also *De consolatione* I, pr. v, 'Sed tu quam procul a patria non quidem pulsus es, sed aberrasti; ac si te pulsum existimari mauis, te potius ipse pepulisti.'

already been made.[221] The main problems remaining for the Anglo-Saxon writers were ones of vocabulary, style and cultural difference, the same problems that were to face vernacular prose writers many centuries later. The solutions could, of course, be personal ones,[222] but some at least may have been adopted collectively. Waite indeed sees the Bede as a transitional work from an evolutionary point of view, 'being an outgrowth of the early vernacular writing of the glossators and glossary writers, and a precursor of the more mature vernacular traditions . . . initiated by Alfred on the one hand and the monastic reformers of Edgar's reign on the other'.[223] And Vleeskruyer agrees with Potter in supposing that agreements between the *Dialogues* and the Bede (and to a lesser extent also the Vespasian Psalter gloss) in the selection of identical words to render specific Latin terms and in translating practice, including the use of dative absolutes and word pairs, could have been inspired in the first instance by similar techniques in the interlinear glosses to Latin texts or could be due to the existence of a school of translation.[224]

What evidence is there, then, for an established 'Mercian' prose style in existence before Alfred and his collaborators began their work? The most pronounced stylistic features of the *Dialogues* and the Bede are, as we have seen, the adoption of a 'Latinate' prose, the frequent use of dative absolutes, tautological word pairs and alliteration, and the employment of constructions combining possessive and demonstrative. The proponents of the theory of a 'vigorous tradition' of Mercian prose might appear to find support from the

---

[221] See W. Wetherbee, 'Some Implications of Bede's Latin Style', *Bede and Anglo-Saxon England*, ed. R. T. Farrell, BAR 46 (Oxford, 1978), and also J. M. Hart, 'Rhetoric in the Translation of Bede', *An English Miscellany presented to Dr Furnivall* (Oxford, 1901), pp. 150–4.

[222] See, e.g., the variety of renderings for 'consul' and 'philosopher' in the Orosius, Bede and Boethius. It should be remembered that access to Old English prose works may have been strictly limited. However, Vleeskruyer's comment, (*St Chad*, p. 45) that it is 'a legitimate supposition that in the latter half of the ninth century no fixed literary terminology existed in the South-West, and that the hapax legomena of the *Pastoral Care* are the result of an attempt to supply this need', has to be read in the light of the fact that Mercian scholars participated in the translation of that work.

[223] 'The Vocabulary', p. 2. He continues, 'The contribution of the glossators in establishing the foundations of an English literature has to a large extent been obscured by our preoccupation with Anglo-Saxon poetry as the early manifestation of vernacular literature.'

[224] *St Chad*, p. 24. See also Whitelock, 'The Old English Bede', pp. 75–6, 'The author was the product of a school of translating similar to that which trained Bishop Werferth . . . They both often translate over-literally, retaining Latinate constructions and using a word-order unnatural to English, to an extent which suggests that they were influenced by the practice of interlinear glossing of a text.' For Waite ('The Vocabulary', pp. 32–3), 'It remains a moot point whether doubling is to be associated in particular with translation or whether it is passed over from a school of original prose writing.'

presence of these mannerisms in Worcester charters of the last quarter of the ninth century. Thus, for instance, the English section of a charter of 883 between Æthelred of Mercia and Berkeley Abbey begins with a dative absolute, word pairs and alliteration: 'For þære wisan, ic Æðelræd ealdorman, inbryrdendre Godes gefe gewelegod 7 gewlenced mid sume dæle Mercna rices, for Godes lufan 7 for alesnessa minra gylta 7 synna 7 for benum abbodes 7 þære heorædene æt Berclea 7 eac for ealre Merce – ic heo gefreoge ecelice þæs gafoles þe hio nu get to cyninges handa ageofan sceolan.'[225]

It was an appearance of some of the same stylistic mannerisms, along with certain lexical agreements, in 'Mercian' literary texts, such as the *Epistola Alexandri*, the Lives of Guthlac and Chad and the Blickling and Vercelli homilies, that led Vleeskruyer and others to postulate a ninth-century origin for these works too, and even to attempt to date some or all of them before the Bede and *Dialogues*.[226] So, for instance, the *Epistola Alexandri* not infrequently uses word pairs and constructions combining possessive and demonstrative, and so does the Life of Guthlac, though only the Guthlac has dative constructions rendering ablative absolutes. An examination of texts written after *c.* 900, however, reveals that the tradition persisted into the tenth century and beyond. Thus the Worcester charter of 904, like that of 883, opens with a dative absolute construction and a word pair as well as some alliteration:

Rixiendum on ecnisse ussum drihtne hælende Criste, seðe all ðing gemetegað ge on heofenum ge on eorðan, þæs inflæscnisse ðy gere þe agen wæs DCCCC wintra 7 IIII winter 7 ðy VII gebongere, ic Uuerfrid biscop mid mines arweorðan heorodes geðafuncga 7 leafe in Weogernaceastre, sylle Wulfsige minum gerefan wið his holdum mægene 7 eadmodre hernesse anes hides lond on Easttune.[227]

---

[225] *Select English Historical Documents*, ed. Harmer, no. XII, 'For this cause, I Earl Aethelred, by God's inspiring grace made wealthy and enriched with a portion of the realm of the Mercians, for the love of God and for the remission of my sins and offences, and because of the entreaties of the abbot and the community at Berkeley, and also on behalf of the whole of Mercia – I grant them remission for ever of the tribute which they are still obliged to give to the king'; see also *Anglo-Saxon Charters*, ed. Robertson, nos. I and II.

[226] See above, pp. 99–100, and cf. *St Chad*, ed. Vleeskruyer, pp. 55 and 58–61. Vleeskruyer claims (p. 59) that Napier homily XL retains 'occasional traces of an early archetype, such as the possessive with demonstrative, *leornjað* "read", and more generally, in its markedly poetic style'. In this context it should be noted that *St Chad* has virtually no word pairs that are not straight translations of the Latin and at least two of these, 'underþeode 7 cyðde' (120) and 'secað 7 tocumað' (216), are non-tautological expansions.

[227] *Anglo-Saxon Charters*, ed. Robertson, no. XVIII. 'With our Lord the Saviour Christ reigning in eternity, who governs all things both in the heavens and on earth, in the year of the incarnation when nine hundred years and four years have passed and in the seventh Indiction; I bishop Werfrith, with the permission and leave of my honourable community in

Since both these charters are in the name of Werferth, it is not surprising that they should have some of the same stylistic features as the *Dialogues*. However, word pairs and alliteration are mannerisms also of texts from the late tenth century,[228] the opening absolute construction of the 904 charter is still being used in charters of Edward the Confessor, and constructions combining possessive and demonstrative continue to appear, with users including Ælfric and the author of Worcester charter of 1042.[229] At the same time, this was not the only prose style demonstrably in use by Mercians in the ninth century: the Martyrology – a text apparently composed between *c.*850 and 900 and depending on Latin sources – is virtually free of these mannerisms. Phrases and clauses such as 'þenode 7 þeowode', or 'þonne ablacode he eall 7 abifode' and 'se micla 7 se mæra dæg' and constructions of the type 'his þæt beorhte leoht' and 'seo his swaðu'[230] are very much the exception and not the rule, and dative absolutes are never found. The most prominent stylistic features of the work are the use of alliteration and correlation and of constructions consisting of adjective, noun and adjective, as, for instance, 'mid irenum gyrdum tyndehtum' and 'oðer rice man hæþen',[231] while what might otherwise be too plain a prose is heightened by the use of similes and verbal and syntactical parallels. Thus, for instance, we may compare 23 September, St Thecla, in which syntactical parallelism is exploited,

On ðone ilcan dæg bið sancte Teclan tid þære halgan fæmnan, seo wæs in ðære ceastre Ioconio, 7 heo wæs þær beweddedo æðelum brydguman. Ða gehyrde heo Paules lare ðæs apostoles; ða gelyfde heo Gode 7 awunode in hyre mægðhade, 7 forðon heo arefnde monegu witu. Hy mon wearp in byrnende fyr, 7 [þæt] hio nolde byrnan, 7 hy mon sende in wildra deora menigo, in leona 7 in berena, 7 ða hie noldon slitan. Hy mon wearp in sædeora seað, 7 þa hyre ne sceðedon. Hy mon band on wilde fearras, 7 ða hyre ne geegledon. 7 þa ætneahstan heo scear hyre feax swa swa weras 7 gegyrede hy mid

---

Worcester, grant to Wulfsige my reeve for his loyal efficiency and humble obedience, one hide of land [*lit.* land of one hide] at Aston.'

228 See Otto Funke, 'Studien zur Alliterienden und Rhythmisierendan Prosa in der älteran altenglischen Homiletic', *Anglia* 80 (1962), 9–36. For similar features in Middle English, see the texts of the Katherine Group.

229 *Anglo-Saxon Charters*, ed. Robertson, no. cxx. For this construction in texts by Alfred, see Bately, 'Lexical Evidence', p. 94.

230 Martyrology entries for 26 December, St Eugenia ('served and ministered'), 16 January, St Fursey ('then he grew pale and trembled'), 6 January, the Epiphany ('the great and famous day'), 26 March, Christ's Decent into Hell ('his bright light') and 5 May, the Ascension ('that his footprint'); for a list of word pairs, see *Das altenglische Martyrologium*, ed. Kotzor, pp. 421–5.

231 9 August, St Romanus, 'with red-hot iron rods', and 4 March, St Adrianus, 'another powerful heathen man'.

weres hrægle 7 ferde mid Paulum þam Godes ærendracan. Tecle wæs swa myhtigu fæmne þæt heo geðingode to Gode sumre hæðenre fæmnan gæste hwylcehwegu ræste in ðære ecan worulde,[232]

with the slightly more complex and alliterative, '7 se gerefa þe hi cwellan het, se wæs sona mid swa miclum sare gewitnad þæt he nolde læng libban; ac he het his agene men hine sændan on ðone sæ, 7 þa sædeor hine sona forswulgon þæt his ne com þy furðor an ban to eorðan.'[233] If there was an established Mercian prose tradition of the type reflected in the *Dialogues* and Bede, then, either the author did not know of it, or he had the self-confidence and assurance to choose not to follow it.[234]

Moreover, King Alfred did not need to learn from Werferth or his Mercian colleagues such mannerisms as he adopts. They were already available to him in documents with West Saxon connections,[235] where they give the impression of having become part of the legal register.[236] For instance, a grant by Alfred's elder brother Æthelberht to Sherborne, dated 864, uses a construction combining demonstrative and possessive, 'ðam ure hefenlican 7 þæm unasecgendlican rice', and a number of word pairs, both tautological and non-tautological: 'eadinysse 7 gesælinysse', 'ic þence 7 me on gemynde is', 'mid geðeahte 7 mid geðafonge', etc.[237] Certainly the tradition appears to go back to

---

[232] 'On that same day is the festival of saint Tecle the holy maiden, who was in the city of Iconium and she was there wedded to a noble bridegroom. Then she heard the teaching of Paul the apostle, then she believed in God and remained in her virginity, and therefore she suffered many tortures: she was cast into burning fire and that would not burn her, and she was sent into a multitude of wild animals, into [a multitude] of lions and of bears, and those would not tear her; she was cast into a pit of sea-beasts, and those did not harm her; she was bound to wild bulls, and those did not injure her; and then finally she cut off her hair just like men and dressed herself with a man's garment and went with Paul the messenger of God. Tecle was so mighty a maiden that she procured from God some rest in the eternal world for the spirit of a certain heathen maiden.'

[233] 19 January, St Ananias: 'and the reeve who ordered them to be killed was immediately tormented with such great pain, that he would not live longer, but he ordered his own men to send him into the sea, and the sea-beasts immediately swallowed him, so that not even one bone of his came to the land again'.

[234] We may compare the late-ninth-century *Chronicle* entries which must have been written at about the same time that Alfred's translations were being produced, or shortly after, but which share few of their stylistic features; see Bately, 'The Compilation of the *Anglo-Saxon Chronicle* Once More'.

[235] That is not to say, of course, that the West Saxon documents themselves could not have been influenced by Mercian traditions.

[236] Cf., e.g., 'gefæstnode 7 getrymede' (laws of Ine, cited below, n. 238), 'trymme 7 faestna' (*Select English Historical Documents*, ed. Harmer, no. III, dated to 844–5) and variants such as 'festnie 7 write' and 'gesette 7 gefestnie' (*ibid.* no. IV, dated to 843–62) and 'write 7 geðeafie' (*ibid.* no. II, dated to 833–9). Nos. IV and II both have 'bidde 7 bebeode', while no. IV has 'soecende 7 smeagende'. See also *ibid.* no. XII.

[237] *Anglo-Saxon Charters*, ed. Robertson, no. XI. This charter begins like the Worcester charter

the end of the seventh century. The laws of Ine, as recorded by Alfred, are characterized by balance, assonance and alliteration. Thus, for instance, the preface consists of a single sentence, with a number of pairings and the demonstrative with possessive construction:

Ic Ine, mid Godes gife Wesseaxna kyning, mid geðeahte ond mid lare Cenredes mines fæder 7 Heddes mines biscepes 7 Eorcenwoldes mines biscepes, mid eallum minum ealdormonnum 7 þæm ieldstan witum minre ðeode 7 eac micelre gesomnunge Godes ðeowa, wæs smeagende be ðære hælo urra sawla, 7 be ðam staþole ures rices, þætte ryht æw 7 ryhte cynedomas ðurh ure folc gefæstnode 7 getrymede wæron, þætte nænig ealdormonna ne us undergeðeodedra æfter þam wære awendende ðas ure domas.[238]

The laws themselves are less elaborate, though they are not without adornment, as, for example, clause LXIV: 'Gif feorcund mon oððe fremde butan wege geond wudu gonge, 7 ne hrieme ne horn blawe, for ðeof he bið to profianne oððe to sleanne oððe to aliesanne.'[239] As for those few early entries in the *Anglo-Saxon Chronicle* that may be based on, and preserve the stylistic characteristics of, contemporary materials, these contain a handful of sentences with alliteration or marked rhythm,[240] as, for instance, 473 'Her Hengest 7 Æsc gefuhton wiþ Walas 7 genamon unarimedlico herereaf, 7 þa Walas flugon þa Englan swa þær fyr',[241] and 491 'Her Ælle 7 Cissa ymbsæton Andredescester 7 ofslogon alle þe þe þærinne eardedon; ne wearþ þær forþon an Bret to lafe',[242] recalling the syntax and style of the Martyrology, while the

---

of 904 with a dative absolute, 'Ricsiendum urum dryhtne hælendun Criste in ecnisse', rendering Latin 'Regnante in perpetuum domino nostro Iesu Christo'. The sentence structure of the earliest wills and charters has obviously been influenced by the conventions of their Latin predecessors.

[238] *Sweet's Anglo-Saxon Reader*, ed. D. Whitelock (London, 1967, repr. 1983) item XI: 'I, Ine, by the grace of God, king of the West Saxons, with the advice and with the instruction of my father Cenred, and my bishop Hædde, and my bishop Eorcenwold, with all my ealdormen and the chief councillors of my people, and also a great assembly of the servants of God, have been inquiring about the salvation of our souls and about the security of our kingdom, that the true law and true statutes might be established and strengthened throughout our people, so that none of the ealdormen or of those subjected to us might afterwards change these our decrees.'

[239] *Ibid.* p. 53: 'If a man from a distance or a foreigner goes through the wood off the track, and does not shout nor blow a horn, he is to be assumed to be a thief, to be either killed or redeemed.' For the style of the laws and for Sievers's theory of Sagvers, see D. Bethurum, 'Stylistic Features of the Old English Laws', *MLR* 27 (1932), 263–79.

[240] Henry Sweet, 'Some of the Sources of the *Anglo-Saxon Chronicle*', *ES* 2 (1879), 310–12. Sweet cites annal 491 ('with alliteration and poetical diction') and annal 501, which he says 'looks like an attempt to eke out a few poetical epithets into an historical statement'.

[241] 'Here Hengest and Æsc fought against the Britons and captured countless spoils, and the Britons fled from the English as from fire.'

[242] 'Here Ælle and Cissa besieged *Andredesceaster* and killed all who dwelt inside, and there was not even a single Briton left.'

annal for 597, which is surely non-contemporary but composed before 890, has a word pair more typical of the Bede, 'feaht 7 won'.[243]

Asser relates that Alfred had as his most peculiar and characteristic habit either to read books aloud himself or to listen to others doing so, by day and night,[244] and it may be for this reason that he was able to write more simply, more clearly and more fluently than some of his contemporaries. On the other hand, it could merely be that his intentions, like those of the author of the Orosius, were different: perhaps the author of the Bede aimed above all at providing a teaching text for people who were attempting to learn Latin, while the West Saxon texts and the Martyrology were intended for people with no Latin background at all.[245]

So, yes there was already by the 890s a tradition of prose writing with well-developed mannerisms, co-existing with the plainer and more workmanlike style of the *Chronicle* and laws, and possibly also the Martyrology, and no, it was not the exclusive property of Mercia, any more than the plain style appears to have been restricted to works of West Saxon origin.[246] The achievement of Alfred and the author of Orosius was to break loose from the more rigid constraints of that tradition as practised by at least one of Alfred's teachers and mentors, and to produce a new version that combined the very best of that tradition and of the plainer but none the less assured prose found on a small scale in the *Chronicle* and laws. As Bruce Mitchell[247] has said, the prose of Alfred's reign is sometimes stiff and unwieldy but often very powerful. The prose of Ælfric and Wulfstan and the later *Chronicle* may be more flexible, more controlled, more varied, but rarely (if ever) does it reach such heights as those attained on occasion by the Orosius author and by Alfred himself.

---

[243] 'Fought and battled'. This collocation is found four times in the Bede.

[244] *Asser's Life of King Alfred*, ed. Stevenson, ch. 81; see also chs. 76 and 77.

[245] It is sometimes suggested that the *Dialogues* was also a teaching text; however, its preface describes it as composed for leisure reading by Alfred.

[246] We have no knowledge of Northumbrian literary prose of the early Old English period; see above, n. 18.   [247] *Old English Syntax* II, 985.

Winchester and the standardization of Old English vocabulary

WALTER HOFSTETTER

Over a century ago Eduard Dietrich noted that Ælfric, pupil of Bishop Æthelwold and educated at Winchester, consistently used certain words (e.g. *ælfremed*, *(ge)gearcian*,[1] *(ge)fredan*) in preference to synonyms (e.g. *fremde*, *(ge)gearwian*, *(ge)felan*) commonly found in other writers.[2] The small number of words given by Dietrich as characteristic of Ælfric's usage has been increased as a result of some lexical studies of more recent date. Karl Jost, for example, notes, among several other peculiarities of his vocabulary, Ælfric's exclusive use of *behreowsian* and *behreowsung* instead of their synonyms *hreowsian* and *hreowsung*.[3] Hans Schabram's study of the Old English terminology for *superbia* shows that Ælfric's language displays a remarkable uniformity in the almost exclusive choice of *modig* and its derivatives.[4] One of the results of Elmar Seebold's work on the Old English equivalents for *sapiens* and *prudens* is to show that Ælfric always employed *snotor* and *snotornes* to express the concepts '*prudens*' and '*prudentia*'.[5] Furthermore, in his study of the Old English vocabulary for *corona*, Josef Kirschner argues that Ælfric's almost exclusive use of *wuldorbeag* for *corona* in a figurative-religious sense (e.g. 'corona vitae aeternae', 'corona martyrii') suggests a deliberate attempt to standardize

---

[1] The enclosure of *ge-* within round brackets indicates that a given word occurs both with and without this prefix.

[2] E. Dietrich, 'Abt Aelfrik. Zur Literatur-Geschichte der angelsächsischen Kirche', *Zeitschrift für historische Theologie* 25 (1855), 487–594 (I) and 26 (1856), 163–256 (II); the reference to Ælfric's usage is at I, 544–5, n. 140.

[3] K. Jost, *Wulfstanstudien*, Schweizer Anglistische Arbeiten 23 (Bern, 1950), 176. For Ælfric's consistent use of *behreowsian* and *behreowsung*, see also L. G. Hallander, *Old English Verbs in '-sian': a Semantic and Derivational Study*, Acta Universitatis Stockholmiensis, Stockholm Stud. in Eng. 15 (Stockholm, 1966), 372. For the use of Dietrich's and Jost's findings as evidence of Ælfric's authorship, see *Homilies of Ælfric: a Supplementary Collection*, ed. J.C. Pope, 2 vols., EETS 259–60 (London, 1967–8), 99–103; Pope here adds a few peculiarities of Ælfric's usage which have emerged from his own study of the texts.

[4] H. Schabram, *Superbia: Studien zum altenglischen Wortschatz*, I: *Die dialektale und zeitliche Verbreitung des Wortguts* (Munich, 1965), pp. 92–3, and 'Das altenglische *superbia*-Wortgut: eine Nachlese', *Festschrift Prof. Herbert Koziol zum siebzigsten Geburtstag*, ed. G. Bauer *et al.*, Wiener Beiträge zur Englischen Philologie 75 (Vienna, 1973), 272–9, at 276.

[5] E. Seebold, 'Die ae. Entsprechungen von lat. *sapiens* und *prudens*: eine Untersuchung über die mundartliche Gliederung der ae. Literatur', *Anglia* 92 (1974), 291–333, at 311–13.

vocabulary.[6] However, as Connie Eble has demonstrated in her study of noun inflection in the text of Ælfric's First Series of *Catholic Homilies* in London, British Library, Royal 7. C. XII,[7] Ælfric, besides applying consistency in his use of certain words, also made a conscious effort to regularize the morphology of his language. The text in BL Royal 7. C. XII, which represents the earliest extant stage of the *Catholic Homilies*, was probably written and corrected under Ælfric's supervision and, indeed, some entries are in his own hand.[8] The noun inflections are extremely regular and, in summarizing her results, Eble comes to the conclusion that her study 'supports the view that Ælfric was a meticulous grammarian intentionally striving to establish or maintain a set of norms for writing the English language'.[9]

Apart from Ælfric's obvious striving for linguistic uniformity,[10] scholars have also observed that there are certain correspondences between his vocabulary and that found in a number of òther texts. Uno Lindelöf notes some remarkable points of lexical agreement between the works of Ælfric, the Old English interlinear versions of the psalter in London, Lambeth Palace Library, 427 (the Lambeth Psalter) and BL Stowe 2 (the Stowe Psalter) and the late Old English revision of Bishop Werferth's translation of Gregory's *Dialogi* preserved in Oxford, Bodleian Library, Hatton 76.[11] The striking correspondences between the Lambeth Psalter and the Stowe Psalter in their rendering of certain Latin lemmata made Celia and Kenneth Sisam think 'of some influential monastic school in which these standard equivalents were taught'.[12] Similarly, after observing close connections in the choice of words between the Lambeth Psalter and the interlinear gloss to the *Expositio hymnorum* preserved in BL Cotton Julius A. vi and Vespasian D. xii, Helmut Gneuss was led to draw the tentative conclusion that the works of Ælfric, the Lambeth Psalter, certain glosses in the Stowe Psalter and the interlinear gloss to the *Expositio hymnorum* represent a group of texts whose vocabulary suggests the

---

[6] J. Kirschner, *Die Bezeichnungen für Kranz und Krone im Altenglischen* (Munich, 1975); for Ælfric, see esp. the summary of Kirschner's survey of Ælfric's *corona* vocabulary at pp. 215–16.

[7] C.C. Eble, 'Noun Inflection in Royal 7 C. xii, Ælfric's First Series of Catholic Homilies' (unpubl. Ph.D dissertation, Univ. of North Carolina at Chapel Hill, 1970).

[8] Cf. *ibid.* p. 2.

[9] *Ibid.* p. 86. For Ælfric's efforts to regularize his language, see also K. Sisam, *Studies in the History of Old English Literature* (Oxford, 1953), pp. 183–5, and P. Clemoes, *Ælfric's First Series of Catholic Homilies: BM Royal 7 C. xii*, ed. N. Eliason and P. Clemoes, EEMF 13 (Copenhagen, 1966), 33.

[10] For certain changes which Ælfric's vocabulary underwent in the course of his literary career, see M.R. Godden, 'Ælfric's Changing Vocabulary', *ES* 61 (1980), 206–23.

[11] *Der Lambeth-Psalter*, ed. U. Lindelöf, Acta Societatis Scientiarum Fennicae 35, no. 1, and 43, no. 3 (Helsingfors, 1909–14) II, 41–3 and 55–6.

[12] *The Salisbury Psalter*, ed. C. and K. Sisam, EETS 242 (London, 1959), 74.

activity of a particular school.[13] As far as the locality of this school is concerned, Gneuss argued that there were clear pointers to Winchester: Ælfric was educated 'in scola Aðelwoldi'[14] and it is very probable that both the Stowe Psalter and the original version of the gloss to the *Expositio hymnorum* were produced at Winchester.[15] Before Gneuss the importance of the monastic school at Winchester had already been pointed out by Hans Hecht, who assumed that the reviser of Werferth's translation of Gregory's *Dialogi* was a member of Æthelwold's school.[16]

More detailed evidence to show that Æthelwold's school at Winchester was indeed the key factor underlying the above-mentioned lexical correspondences was presented by Gneuss in a study of the origin of Standard Old English.[17] A group of texts which date from the end of the tenth or the first half of the eleventh century, and are directly or indirectly related to Winchester and therefore called the 'Winchester group' (the works of Ælfric, the Lambeth Psalter, the gloss to the *Expositio hymnorum* and the Old English translation of the Rule for Canons by Chrodegang bishop of Metz), display a remarkable degree of uniformity in the choice of vocabulary in a number of semantic fields. It is true to say that this uniformity is not equally pronounced in all the semantic fields in question; nevertheless, it cannot have been the result of mere coincidence, but must, as Gneuss convincingly argues, have been due to the deliberate attempt of some cultural centre to standardize vocabulary, and the only possible centre is the school of the Old Minster in Winchester. The vocabulary given by Gneuss[18] as characteristic of the 'Winchester group' includes such words ('Winchester words') as *ælfremed* 'foreign', *(ge)dyrstlæcan* 'to dare', *gelaðung* 'the whole/a local Christian community', *modig* 'proud' and *wuldorbeag* 'crown' in a figurative-religious sense; these words were preferred to synonyms such as *fremde*, *(ge)ðristlæcan*, *cirice*, *ofermod* and *cynehelm*, which were commonly used in contemporary West Saxon texts with the meanings given for their Winchester equivalents.

Gneuss also points out that there are obvious links in usage between the 'Winchester group' and Æthelwold's translation of the Benedictine Rule, the Old English interlinear gloss to the psalter in BL Royal 2. B. v (the Regius Psalter) and the revision of Werferth's translation of Gregory's *Dialogi* in

---

[13] H. Gneuss, *Hymnar und Hymnen im englischen Mittelalter*, Buchreihe der Anglia 12 (Tübingen, 1968), 186–7.

[14] *Ælfrics Grammatik und Glossar*, ed. J. Zupitza, 2nd edn. with contr. by H. Gneuss (Berlin, 1966), p. 1.   [15] *Hymnar und Hymnen*, pp. 187–8.

[16] *Bischof Wærferths von Worcester Übersetzung der Dialoge Gregors des Grossen*, ed. H. Hecht, Bibliothek der angelsächsischen Prosa 5 (Leipzig and Hamburg, 1900–7) II, 131.

[17] 'The Origin of Standard Old English and Æthelwold's School at Winchester', *ASE* 1 (1972), 63–83, at 75–83.   [18] *Ibid.* pp. 76–7.

Hatton 76.[19] The Old English Benedictine Rule, translated from the Latin by Æthelwold in about 970,[20] represents an intermediate stage between an earlier usage and that of the 'Winchester group', the latter probably evolving only gradually within Æthelwold's school. The Regius Psalter, written about the middle of the tenth century, 'shows some striking correspondences with the "modern" vocabulary of the Old English Benedictine Rule and with the Winchester group',[21] and the reviser of Werferth's translation of Gregory's *Dialogi* has, with the lack of consistency typical of this kind of work,[22] modernized the older text in a number of places by means of 'Winchester words'.

The correspondences established by Gneuss between the members of the 'Winchester group' and some related texts have a striking parallel in the results of Seebold's study of the Old English equivalents for *sapiens* and *prudens*. On the basis of the vocabulary used in the semantic fields '*superbia*' and '*prudentia*', the corpus of Old English texts of southern provenance can be arranged in four groups;[23] despite some divergences, the first of these groups, referred to by Seebold as the 'Benediktiner-Gruppe',[24] clearly corresponds to the group of texts shown by Gneuss to be linked with each other by the use of 'Winchester words'.[25] Gneuss and Seebold suggest different, though not mutually exclusive, explanations for the existence of the distinctive choice of vocabulary of the 'Winchester group' and the 'Benediktiner-Gruppe' respectively. Whereas Gneuss thinks that the specific vocabulary of the 'Winchester group' is due mainly to stylistic considerations and an attempt at standardization,[26] Seebold argues that there must be a difference of subdialect behind the divergences between the 'Benediktiner-Gruppe' and the three other groups of texts of southern origin.[27]

Further evidence that Gneuss's 'Winchester group' and Seebold's

---

[19] *Ibid.* pp. 78–81.

[20] For a discussion of Æthelwold's authorship and the date of the translation, see M. Gretsch, *Die Regula Sancti Benedicti in England und ihre altenglische Übersetzung*, Texte und Untersuchungen zur Englischen Philologie 2 (Munich, 1973), 9–11.

[21] Gneuss, 'The Origin of Standard Old English', p. 79.

[22] For inconsistency in revisions of Old English texts, see Schabram, *Superbia*, pp. 44 and 47–8, and Gneuss, *ibid.* p. 66, n. 2.

[23] Seebold, 'Die ae. Entsprechungen von lat. *sapiens* und *prudens*', pp. 323–30. The four groups are: 'Benediktiner-Gruppe', 'Gruppe Alfred und Wulfstan', 'Gruppe der Bibelübersetzungen' and 'Orosius'. [24] *Ibid.* pp. 324 and 327.

[25] *Ibid.* pp. 324 (n. 64) and 331. The 'Benediktiner-Gruppe' favours *modig* and *snotor* with their derivatives within the semantic fields '*superbia*' and '*prudentia*' respectively.

[26] 'The Origin of Standard Old English', pp. 76 and 78.

[27] 'Die ae. Entsprechungen von lat. *sapiens* und *prudens*', pp. 330–1. Seebold argues that in the 'Benediktiner-Gruppe' a particular South English subdialect was used to a large extent and perhaps even raised to the status of a written standard.

'Benediktiner-Gruppe' represent the same usage has recently been presented by Shigeru Ono in an analysis of the distribution of the Old English synonyms *ongietan, undergietan* and *understandan*.[28] Out of these, *undergietan*, which is never found in the works of Wulfstan,[29] occurs only in a relatively limited group of texts and is especially favoured by members of the 'Winchester group' and the 'Benediktiner-Gruppe'. Sixty-eight per cent of the total incidence is concentrated in these two groups,[30] and the revision of Werferth's translation of Gregory's *Dialogi* in the Hatton manuscript, the close links of which with the 'Winchester group' have been pointed out by Gneuss, also contains two instances of the 'Winchester word' *undergietan*.[31]

The present article sets out to show the most important results of a study which follows on from the work of Gneuss and Seebold in further investigating the efforts of Winchester to achieve linguistic standardization. My procedure was to analyse the distribution throughout the corpus of published Old English texts of a substantial number of words characteristic of the 'Winchester group' and related texts, together with certain of their synonyms.[32]

THE WORD GROUPS

The words whose distribution has been investigated in this study form thirteen groups, each of which represents a semantic field. The members of a particular word group are, of course, not total but only partial synonyms, i.e. words which can, in certain contexts, fulfil the same semantic function; Gneuss defines them as 'words of which it can be proved from similar contexts in other contemporary texts . . . that they could have been replaced by synonyms'.[33] The word *terrores*, for instance, in Luke XXI.11 'et fames, terroresque de caelo, et signa magna erunt' is rendered by *ogan* in the Second Series of Ælfric's *Catholic Homilies*,[34] by *eg(e)san* in the West Saxon gospels,[35] and by *fyrhtnisso* in

---

[28] Sh. Ono, '*Undergytan* as a "Winchester" word', *Linguistics across Historical and Geographical Boundaries: in Honour of Jacek Fisiak on the Occasion of His Fiftieth Birthday*, ed. D. Kastovsky and A. Szwedek, Trends in Ling., Stud. and Monographs 32, 2 vols. (Berlin, 1986) I, 569–77.

[29] For a doubtful case, see *ibid.* I, 571 and 574.   [30] *Ibid.* I, 572.   [31] *Ibid.* I, 572–3.

[32] W. Hofstetter, *Winchester und der spätaltenglische Sprachgebrauch: Untersuchungen zur geographischen und zeitlichen Verbreitung altenglischer Synonyme*, Texte und Untersuchungen zur Englischen Philologie 14 (Munich, 1987).

[33] 'The Origin of Standard Old English', p. 76. Cf. also J.M. Bately, 'The Compilation of the Anglo-Saxon Chronicle 60 B.C. to A.D. 890: Vocabulary as Evidence', *PBA* 64 (1980 for 1978), 93–129, at 95: 'In the majority of cases the presence of a certain word in a given text is of potential significance only if it can be shown to have been used at the expense of another word, or to be restricted to one of several possible contexts or groups of contexts.'

[34] *Ælfric's Catholic Homilies: the Second Series*, ed. M. Godden, EETS ss 5 (London, 1979), no. xxxvii, line 47.

[35] *The Gospel according to Saint Luke in Anglo-Saxon and Northumbrian Versions*, ed. W.W. Skeat (Cambridge, 1874), p. 200 (XXI.11).

the Old English gloss to the Lindisfarne Gospels;[36] in the given context, the words *oga*, *eg(e)sa* and *fyrhtnes* mean 'terror', 'something terrible' and may therefore be regarded as lexical alternatives or synonyms. Apart from the common denotative meaning, which is the essential basis for a vocabulary study with the above-mentioned aim, there may, of course, have existed differences in connotation and stylistic value between the individual members of a group of synonyms. The noun *oga*, for instance, which is attested only in late Old English texts, is listed by Eric Stanley[37] as being among the 'words common in prose but not used, or only rarely used, in "strict" verse',[38] whereas the synonymous noun *eg(e)sa* is a word commonly used in poetry.[39]

I have divided the words in each of the thirteen semantic fields in question into three sections according to their distribution. These sections are referred to below by the letters A, B and C.

Section A comprises those words which I regard as characteristic of a usage that evolved in Winchester as a result of Æthelwold's activity as a teacher in the school of the Old Minster. This view is based on the predominance of these words in texts which are linked to Winchester by authorship, palaeography, content or liturgical usage.[40] Members of section A of a semantic field will be called 'A words', and the terms 'Winchester word', 'Winchester vocabulary' and 'Winchester usage' will henceforth be employed only with reference to the 'A words' in the thirteen semantic fields discussed.

Section B comprises those words whose distribution is not distinctive since they occur both in texts which use Winchester vocabulary (in such texts 'B words' are often found side by side with 'A words') and in texts whose vocabulary does not conform to that of the Winchester usage.

Section C comprises those words which are normally avoided in the Winchester usage. 'C words' may be common Old English words (e.g. *fremde*) or may represent features of Anglian or West Saxon dialect vocabulary such as *oferhygd* and *ofermod* respectively.

'B words', which have been considered only in the case of eight of the thirteen semantic fields, are, of course, of limited relevance in the present study; nevertheless, as the following example shows, establishing their presence or absence in a given text may provide valuable evidence. To express the concept 'virtue' in the religious or moral sense, Æthelwold employed only the common Old English 'B word' *mægen* while in the works of his pupil Ælfric, the 'A word' *miht* 'virtue' (thirty-eight instances) represents a new usage and is already on a par with the 'B word' *mægen* (forty instances). The interlinear gloss

---

[36] *Ibid.* p. 201 (XXI.11).
[37] 'Studies in the Prosaic Vocabulary of Old English Verse', *NM* 72 (1971), 385–418, at 397.
[38] *Ibid.* p. 392.   [39] Cf. Hallander, *Old English Verbs in '-sian'*, pp. 155–6.
[40] See the discussion of texts I.1–13, below, pp. 157–9.

to the *Expositio hymnorum*, which is extant in two mid-eleventh-century manuscripts and may be regarded as a product of Winchester, shows the ultimate triumph of the new usage in the exclusive use of the 'A word' *miht* 'virtue'.[41]

I shall now list the thirteen word groups selected for my study, defining their respective semantic areas and specifying the words which constitute them. The letters A, B and C refer to the three sections I have defined above.

Group 1

Semantic area

The adjectival concept 'foreign' and its verbal and substantival equivalents (Latin: mostly *alienus, extraneus; alienare; alienatio*).

Member words

A *(ge)ælfremed, geælfremod; ælfremedung.*
C *framðe, fremde, fremed, fremðe, uta(n)cund; afremdan, afremdian, fremdian, fremedlæcan; afremdung.*

Group 2

Semantic area

The substantival concepts 'martyr' and 'martyrdom' (Latin: *martyr; martyrium*).

Member words

A *cyðere.*
B *martir, martyre; martirdom;* in compounds: *martircynn, martirracu.*
C *ðrowere, ðrowyestre; martirhad, martirung, ðrowendhad, ðrowerhad, ðrowethad.*

Group 3

Semantic area

The verbal concepts 'to dare', 'to make bold', 'to presume', and their substantival equivalents (Latin: mostly *audere* and *praesumere* with their derivatives).

Member words

A *(ge)dyrstlæcan; gedyrstlæcing.*
B *(ge)dyrstignes, gedyrstnes.*
C *aðristian, gedyrstigian, forneðan, (ge)neðan, geðristian, (ge)ðristlæcan, geðyrstigian; dearfscipe, neðing, noð, geðristlæcing, ðristlæcnes, geðristlæcung, ðristnes, geðyrstignes.*

---

[41] For another interesting example, see the discussion of Ælfric's use of *cyðere* and *martir* in Godden, 'Ælfric's Changing Vocabulary', pp. 208–9, and Hofstetter, *Winchester*, pp. 41–4; in my terminology *cyðere* is an 'A word', *martir* a 'B word'.

Group 4

Semantic area

The verbal concepts 'to prepare', 'to get ready', 'to procure', 'to grant', with their substantival equivalents (Latin: mostly *(prae)parare, praebere, exhibere* and *praestare*, with their derivatives). The semantic range of the member words *(ge)gierwan* and *(ge)gearwian* includes the special meanings 'to clothe' and 'to put on' (Latin: *vestire* and *induere*), which, for the purposes of this article, are subsumed under the concept of 'to get ready'. Consequently their antonyms *ongierwan* and *ungierwan* 'to unclothe', 'to strip' (Latin: *exuere*), both derived from *gierwan*, have also been taken into account in this group.

Member words

A *(ge)gearcian; gearcing, gearcung*; in a compound: *(ge)gearcungdæg.*
C *fore(ge)gearwian, (ge)gearwian, (ge)gierwan, togegearwian, ymbgearwian; foregearwung, gearwing, (ge)gearwung, gegearwungnes, gegierwing, midgearwing*; with a negative prefix: *ongierwan, ungierwan, ungegearwod, ungegierwed*; in compounds: *fullgearwian, fyrgearwung, gearwungdæg.*

Group 5

Semantic area

The following substantival concepts expressed in Latin by the noun *ecclesia*:

(*a*) 'the whole Christian community';
(*b*) 'a local Christian community';
(*c*) 'the Church Triumphant', i.e. the faithful departed already experiencing the vision of God in heaven;
(*d*) in the context of the Old and the New Testaments, 'an assembly', 'a congregation'. Here words have only been counted as belonging to this group if it can be proved that they translate the Latin *ecclesia* used in the sense of 'assembly', 'congregation'.

Member words

A *(ge)ladung.*
B *ecclesia* (as a foreign word), *geferræden.*
C *cirice, gesamning, (ge)samnung, halig samning, halig samnung.*

The word *cirice* is often used to combine sense (*a*) or (*b*) above with meanings such as 'church as a material structure', 'church as a place of worship', 'church as a unit of ecclesiastical administration', 'clergy'. Ambivalent uses of this kind, as well as cases where the meaning of *cirice* is not unquestionably within the semantic area described above, do not qualify for membership of this group.

Group 6

Semantic area

The substantival concept 'virtue' in the religious or moral sense (Latin: *virtus*).[42] The word *mægen*, which is very frequently used in the sense of 'virtue', can also have the special meaning of 'virtuous deed'; *mægen* in this sense is also regarded as belonging to the semantic area of this group.

Member words[43]

A   *miht*[a].
B   *mægen*[a]; in compounds: *heafodmægen*[a], *heahmægen*[a].
C   *cræft*[a], *mægenðrymm*[a], *strengð*[a], *strengu*[a].

Group 7

Semantic area

This group consists of words which translate the Latin noun *virtus* used with any meaning except 'virtue' in the religious or moral sense.[44] The most important of these meanings are:[45]

(*a*)   'power', 'strength', used of God;
(*b*)   'power', 'strength', 'ability', used of human beings;
(*c*)   'power', 'virtue', used of a thing;
(*d*)   'power to work miracles', 'miraculous power';
(*e*)   'mighty work', 'miracle';
(*f*)   'the powers of the heavens' (cf. Matthew xxiv.29);
(*g*)   the angelic order '*virtutes*';
(*h*)   'the heavenly hosts'.

Member words[46]

A   *miht*[b].
C   *anweald*[b], *cræft*[b], *mægen*[b], *mægenðrymm*[b], *gemiht*[b], *strengð*[b], *strengu*[b]; in compounds: *innoðmægen*[b], *leodmægen*[b].

[42] For a study of the Old English vocabulary for this concept, based on a representative selection of texts, see H. Käsmann, '"Tugend" und "Laster" im Alt- und Mittelenglischen: eine bezeichnungsgeschichtliche Untersuchung' (unpubl. Ph.D dissertation, Freie Universität Berlin, 1951).

[43] The members of this group are distinguished from those of group 7 by the superscript letter 'a'.

[44] For words expressing the concept 'virtue' in the religious or moral sense, see group 6.

[45] Käsmann ('"Tugend" und "Laster"') has studied the Old English equivalents for the Latin *virtue* in the semantic area of this group on the basis of a selection of texts. For the meanings listed below, cf. Käsmann, '"Tugend" und "Laster"', pp. 3–4.

[46] The members of this group are distinguished from those of group 6 by the superscript letter 'b'.

Since an item can qualify for this group only if the Old English author or translator can be shown to have used it to translate the noun *virtus* from his Latin source in any meaning other than 'virtue' in the religious or moral sense, this kind of evidence is confined to glosses, translations and texts or passages from texts which are quite evidently based on known Latin sources.

Group 8

Semantic area

The following substantival concepts (Latin: mostly *terror, horror, timor, metus, pavor, formido*):

(a) 'terror', 'dread';
(b) 'fear', 'awe';
(c) 'something inspiring fear, awe or terror'.

Member words[47]

A *oga*.
B *broga, ege, fyrhto*; in compounds: *egewielm, woruldege*.
C *anda, andesn, andesnes, andesnu, angrisla, anoða, egesa, gefyrhtu, gryre*; in compounds: *brogðrea, -broga,*[48] *egesgrima, -egesa,*[49] *gryre-,*[50] *-gryre.*[51]

Group 9

Semantic area

The following verbal concepts and their substantival equivalents, which have the notion of 'straightness', 'correctness' or 'direction (towards an aim)' as a dominant semantic feature:

(a) 'to make straight', 'to straighten', 'to put into proper condition' (Latin: mostly *rectum facere, dirigere; directio*);
(b) 'to correct', 'to rectify', 'to amend' (Latin: mostly *corrigere, emendare; correctio, emendatio*);
(c) 'to direct (towards an aim)' (Latin: mostly *dirigere; directio*).

These concepts are closely related and in a large number of cases it is impossible to assign the meaning of a word to (a) or (b) or (c) alone.

---

47 For *ege* and *egesa* (and their compounds), cf. Hallander, *Old English Verbs in '-sian'*, pp. 143–57. Most of the compounds listed in section C are attested only in the poetry.
48 Compounds with *-broga* as their second element: *brynebroga, gryrebroga, hellebroga, hellewitebroga, herebroga, sæbroga, sperebroga, wæterbroga, witebroga, wiðerbroga*.
49 Compounds with *-egesa* as their second element: *bælegesa, blodegesa, flodegesa, folcegesa, gledegesa, hildegesa, liegegesa, mægðegesa*(?), *nihtegesa, ðeodegesa, wæteregesa*.
50 Compounds with *gryre-* as their first element: *gryrebroga, gryregeatwe, gryregiest, gryrehwil, gryreleoð, gryremiht, gryresið*.
51 Compounds with *-gryre* as their second element: *færgryre, heortgryre, hinsiðgryre*(?), *leodgryre, lustgryre*(?), *wælgryre, westengryre, wiggryre*.

Member words

A *(ge)rihtlæcan; rihtlæcing, rihtlæcung.*
B *(ge)rihtan; rihting, rihtung;* with a negative prefix: *ungeriht;* in a compound: *rihtingðræd.*
C *(ge)reccan, (ge)rehtan; gerecednes, gerec(e)nes, gerehtnes, gerihtnes.*

Group 10

Semantic area

The verbal concepts 'to crush', 'to bruise', 'to grind to pieces', 'to break to pieces', 'to dash', 'to demolish', 'to destroy', and their substantival equivalents; the meaning may also be metaphorical: 'to break in spirit', 'to reduce to contrition' (Latin: frequently *(at)terere, conterere, confringere, allidere, collidere* and *(con)quassare,* with their derivatives).

Member words

A *(ge)cwysan, tobrytan, tocwysan; tobrytendlic;*[52] *tobrytend; tobrytednes, tobryting, tocwysednes.*
C *abreotan, abrytan, breotan, (ge)brytan, gebrytian, forbrytan, forgnidan, forðræstan, (ge)nætan, toðræstan, (ge)ðræstan; abreotnes, bryting, forbrytednes, forbrytnes, forgnidennes, forðræstednes, forðræstnes, geðræstednes.*

Group 11

Semantic area

The following verbal concepts and their substantival equivalents:[53]

(*a*) In a religious sense: 'to repent', 'to do penance' (Latin: mostly *paenitere, paenitentiam agere; paenitentia, paenitudo*).
(*b*) In a secular sense: 'to feel sorrow', 'to grieve', 'to regret' (Latin: e.g. *paenitere, dolere, compati*).

In a number of cases (*a*) and (*b*) are inextricably fused.

Member words

A *behreowsian; behreowsing,*[54] *behreowsung;* in a compound: *behreowsungtid.*
C *hreowan, (ge)hreowian, (ge)hreowsian; (ge)hreow, (ge)hreownes, hreowsung.*

---

[52] This deverbal adjective has also been included in group 10.
[53] For a detailed semantic and syntactic investigation of the vocabulary of this group, see Hallander, *Old English Verbs in '-sian'*, pp. 352–84. For my study I have collected the evidence directly from the Old English texts, adding to Hallander's material mainly by registering occurrences of the words in question in texts that have meanwhile become available in editions.
[54] *Behreowsing* is attested only in a manuscript dating from the twelfth century.

Instances of the use of *(ge)hreowan* are relevant to the present study only if this verb is employed (as are the other verbs in this group) in a syntactic construction where the person feeling penitence or sorrow is the subject of the sentence.[55] However, instances where the person feeling penitence or sorrow is an object (in the dative or accusative) of the verb *(ge)hreowan*[56] have been disregarded because they occur in texts characterized by the Winchester usage as well as elsewhere.

Group 12

Semantic area

The concept 'pride' represented in nouns, adjectives, adverbs and verbs (Latin: mostly *superbia, superbus, superbe, superbire*).[57]

Member words

A *modignes; modig, modiglic; modiglice; (ge)modigian.*

B *oferprydo, prutnes, prutscipe, prutung, prydo, pryte, pryto; oferprut, prud, prut, prutlic; prutlice; prutian*; in compounds: *prutswongor, woruldpryde.*

C nouns: *oferhygd,*[58] *oferhygdig,*[58] *oferhyg(e)dnes, ofermedla, ofermedu, ofermettu, ofermod,*[58] *ofermodgung, ofermodignes, ofermodnes; oferhoga*; adjectives: *oferhygd,*[58] *oferhygdig,*[58] *oferhygdlic, ofermede, ofermod,*[58] *ofermodig, ofermodlic*; adverbs: *oferhygdiglice, oferhygdlice, ofermodiglice, ofermodlice*; verbs: *oferhygdigian, ofermodigian.*

Group 13

Semantic area

The substantival concepts 'crown' and 'wreath', with their verbal equivalents (Latin: mostly *corona; coronare*).[59]

Member words

A *wuldorbeag; (ge)wuldorbeagian.*

B *cynehelm*[a]*, helm, hring, trendel, ymbgang; (ge)cynehelmian*[a]*, (ge)helmian.*

C *beag, corenbeag, corona, cynebænd, cynegold, cynehelm*[b]*, cyninggierela, gyldenbeag, heafodbænd, heafodbeag, heafodgold, hroðgierela, mind, sigebeag, wuldorhelm, wuldres helm;*

---

55 Construction (ββ) in Hallander, *Old English Verbs in '-sian'* (p. 366).

56 For possible constructions, see *ibid.* pp. 365–6.

57 Schabram has made a comprehensive analysis of the Old English vocabulary for 'pride' (see above, n. 4). For my study I have again collected the evidence directly from the texts, adding to Schabram's material by instances of 'pride' words in sources that have been made accessible in editions in the meantime.   58 Used both as noun and as adjective.

59 Kirschner has completed a comprehensive study of the Old English *corona* vocabulary (see above, n. 6). I have again collected the material from the Old English texts, increasing Kirschner's evidence by instances of the words in texts which have become available in editions since he carried out his survey.

(ge)beagian, gecoronian, (ge)sigefæstan, (ge)sigefæstian, (ge)sigefæstnian; with the concept 'crown' as one of the elements of a compound: *beagwise*.

The superscript letters 'a' and 'b' assign the use of *cynehelm* and *(ge)cynehelmian* to two different sections within the semantic area of this group.[60] The 'C word' *cynehelm*[b] stands for 'crown' in a figurative-religious sense, e.g. 'corona vitae aeternae', 'corona gloriae', 'corona martyrii'.[61] The 'B words' *cynehelm*[a] and *(ge)cynehelmian*[a] may have any of the meanings within the semantic scope of the group except those of 'crown' and 'to crown' in a figurative-religious sense.[62] Any instances where it is impossible to decide whether we are dealing with *cynehelm*[a] or *cynehelm*[b] or where the meaning of *cynehelm* is not unquestionably and, indeed, exclusively that of *cynehelm*[b] have been treated as *cynehelm*[a].

THE TEXT GROUPS

I have divided into two groups the texts which use the vocabulary listed above:[63]

I. Those whose vocabulary is strongly marked by the Winchester usage,[64] i.e. those which employ, either exclusively or predominantly, 'A words' and 'B words'.

II. Those which favour vocabulary which does not conform to the Winchester usage, i.e. those which employ, either exclusively or predominantly, 'C words' and 'B words'.

To qualify for membership of group I, a text must fulfil the following three conditions:

(1) The text must contain at least five occurrences of 'A words'.

(2) These 'A words' must be drawn from at least three of the thirteen word groups.

(3) The number of occurrences of 'A words' in the text must amount to at least fifty per cent of the total number of occurrences of 'A words' and 'C words' together.[65]

Conditions (1) and (3) are, however, subject to the following modifications: (*a: condition (1)*) If a text does not contain any 'C words', i.e. if the proportion of 'A words' according to condition (3) is 100 per cent, three occurrences of 'A

---

[60] A semantic differentiation of this kind would be irrelevant for the other members of the group.

[61] For details, see Kirschner, *Kranz und Krone*, pp. 91–7 and 122. In Kirschner's semantic scheme (p. 122), this figurative-religious sense of 'crown' is referred to as 'bildlich'.

[62] *Cynehelm*[a] and *(ge)cynehelmian*[a] are used in senses referred to as 'eigentlich' and 'abstrakt' in Kirschner's semantic scheme (*ibid.*).

[63] Texts using only 'B words' have been disregarded.

[64] For the definition of the term 'Winchester usage', see above, p. 144.

[65] 'B words' are not regarded as criteria in the above-mentioned arrangement of texts.

words' are sufficient. Condition (2) remains unaltered. This modification allows for texts which are short or fragmentary or which, as a result of their subject matter, offer little relevant material.

(*b*: *condition (3)*) If, by comparison with an older version, a text can be established as a later revision in which 'A words' have been substituted for 'C words' to a considerable extent, a proportion of 'A words' amounting to ten per cent of the total number of occurrences of 'A words' and 'C words' is considered sufficient. Conditions (1) and (2) remain unaltered. This modification takes into account the circumstances that the vocabulary of a text has a relatively high degree of resistance to change and that revisers are very inconsistent in replacing words,[66] with the result that an increase of the proportion of 'A words' to ten per cent (or more) of the total number of occurrences of 'A words' and 'C words' is conceivable only if the 'A words' represent a dominant feature of the usage of the reviser or revisers.

The resulting groups are listed below. The titles of the texts are followed by the appropriate reference number(s) in A. Cameron, 'A List of Old English Texts', *A Plan for the Dictionary of Old English*, ed. R. Frank and A. Cameron, Toronto OE Ser. 2 (Toronto, 1973), 25–306. The letters A, B and C preceding the figures refer to the three sections defined above, p. 144. The figures represent the totals of 'A words', 'B words' and 'C words' for the text in question. The percentage following the total of 'A words' in round brackets represents the proportion of 'A words' to 'A' and 'C words' combined (see condition (3) for membership of group I, above, p. 151). An asterisk indicates that modification (*b*) applies (see above, pp. 151–2).

Group I

1 Æthelwold's translation of the Benedictine Rule (B.10.3.1–2)
    A 41 (62·1%)   B 38   C 25
2 Account of King Edgar's establishment of monasteries (B.17.11)
    A 5 (83·3%)   B 3   C 1
3 The works of Ælfric (B.1.1.1–9.10)
    A 967 (98·3%)   B 397   C 17
4 Interlinear gloss to the psalter and canticles in BL Stowe 2 (the Stowe Psalter)[67] (C.7.10, 11.10)
    A 80 (40·8%)*   B 28   C 116
5 Interlinear gloss to the psalter and canticles in BL Cotton Vitellius E. xviii (the Vitellius Psalter)[68] (C.7.8, 11.7)
    A 40 (17·4%)*   B 33   C 190

---

[66] Cf. above, n. 22.

[67] The Stowe Psalter is an extensively modernized gloss of the textual type of the Regius Psalter; for the remarkable increase in the proportion of 'A words', cf. below, text II.20.

[68] The Vitellius Psalter is a partly modernized gloss based on the textual type of the Regius Psalter except for pss. I–XVII.35 and the later additions, which depend on the type of the

6 Interlinear gloss to the psalter and canticles in BL Arundel 60 (the Arundel Psalter)[69] (C.7.5, 11.4)

	A 23 (10·4%)*	B 33	C 198

7 Interlinear gloss to the psalter and canticles in London, Lambeth Palace Library, 427 (the Lambeth Psalter)[70] (C.7.11, 11.11)

	A 166 (66·1%)	B 31	C 85

8 Fragment of a translation of the *Regularis concordia* in Cambridge, Corpus Christi College 201 (B.10.5.1)[71]

	A 3 (100%)	B 1	C 0

9 Translation of the enlarged Rule of Chrodegang (B.10.4.1–3)

	A 35 (54·7%)	B 45	C 29

10 Interlinear gloss to the *Expositio hymnorum* (C.18.3)

	A 80 (100%)	B 5	C 0

11 Interlinear gloss to the 'prose version' of the monastic canticles in BL Cotton Vespasian D. xii (C.12)

	A 15 (100%)	B 4	C 0

12 Interlinear gloss to the metrical hymns in Durham, Cathedral Library, B. III. 32 (the Durham Hymnal)[72] (C.18.2)

	A 67 (77·9%)	B 8	C 19

13 Interlinear gloss to the monastic canticles in Durham, Cathedral Library, B. III. 32 and BL Cotton Julius A. vi (C.12)

	A 12 (100%)	B 4	C 0

14 Interlinear gloss to the Benedictine Rule in BL Cotton Tiberius A. iii (C.4)

	A 83 (96·5%)	B 15	C 3

15 Interlinear gloss to Benedict of Aniane's *Memoriale* (C.5)

	A 5 (100%)	B 0	C 0

Vespasian Psalter. The Vitellius Psalter has been included in this group because comparison with the Vespasian Psalter (cf. below, text II.5) and the Regius Psalter (cf. below, text II.20) shows an increase in the proportion of 'A words' which, in my view, can be convincingly explained only by the assumption that these 'A words' represent a dominant feature in the usage of the reviser(s) (cf. above, pp. 151–2, modification (*b*)).

[69] The Arundel Psalter is a partly modernized gloss which depends on the textual type of the Vespasian Psalter for (approximately) pss. I–LI and LXIII–LXXV and on the type of the Regius Psalter for the rest. Although the proportion of 'A words' amounts to only a little over ten per cent (cf. above, p. 151, condition (3)), I have included the Arundel Psalter in this group because, as in the case of the Stowe Psalter (I.4) and the Vitellius Psalter (I.5), comparison with the Vespasian Psalter (cf. below, text II.5) and the Regius Psalter (cf. below, text II.20) shows an increase in the proportion of 'A words' which, in my opinion, presupposes that the language of the reviser(s) was strongly marked by the Winchester usage (cf. above, pp. 151–2, modification (*b*)).

[70] The Lambeth Psalter is a late Old English compilation with numerous double and multiple glosses drawn from various sources.

[71] The modification of condition (1) (cf. above, pp. 151–2) is applicable to this text.

[72] The glosses to three metrical hymns in BL Cotton Julius A. vi and to some metrical hymns and stanzas in BL Cotton Vespasian D. xii are closely related to those of the Durham Hymnal; they are either derived from the same source as these or copied from them.

16 Anglo-Saxon Chronicle in BL Cotton Domitian viii (B.17.3)

    A 5 (100%)   B 6   C 0

17 Glosses to Aldhelm's *De laudibus virginitatis* (prose) in Brussels, Bibliothèque Royale, 1650 (C.31.1)

    A 26 (70·3%)   B 4   C 11

18 Glosses to Aldhelm's *De laudibus virginitatis* (prose) in Oxford, Bodleian Library, Digby 146 (C.31.13)

    A 23 (76·7%)   B 4   C 7

19 Translations of Latin titles to illustrations of Prudentius's *Psychomachia* in Cambridge, Corpus Christi College 23 (C.26)

    A 15 (100%)   B 0   C 0

20 Legend of St Giles (B.3.3.9)

    A 7 (70%)   B 1   C 3

21 Revision of Werferth's translation of Gregory's *Dialogi* in Oxford, Bodleian Library, Hatton 76 (B.9.5)

    A 23 (32·9%)*   B 25   C 47

22 Homily *De temporibus anticristi*[73] (B.3.4.34)

    A 7 (58·3%)   B 5   C 5

23 Legend of the Seven Sleepers (B.3.3.34)

    A 8 (61·5%)   B 24   C 5

Group II

For reasons of space I am able to give only a small selection from the 244 items comprising this group.

1 Glossary in Cambridge, Corpus Christi College 144 (the Corpus Glossary) (D.4)

    A 0   B 0   C 6

2 Old English Martyrology (B.19)

    A 2 (4·1%)   B 103   C 47

3 Life of St Chad (B.3.3.3)

    A 0   B 6   C 5

4 Werferth's translation of Gregory's *Dialogi* in Cambridge, Corpus Christi College 322 (B.9.5)

    A 5 (2·3%)   B 112   C 212

5 Interlinear gloss to the psalter and canticles in BL Cotton Vespasian A. i (the Vespasian Psalter) (C.7.7, 11.6)

    A 0   B 28   C 223

6 Blickling Homilies (B.3.1.1)

    A 4 (4·2%)   B 29   C 92

7 Vercelli Homilies (B.3.1.2)

    A 3 (2·1%)   B 51   C 138

---

[73] Item XLII in *Wulfstan: Sammlung der ihm zugeschriebenen Homilien*, ed. A. Napier (Berlin, 1883; repr. with a bibliographical supplement by K. Ostheeren, Dublin, 1967).

8 Farman's gloss to the Rushworth Gospels[74] (C.8.2)

     A o   B o   C 52

9 Aldred's gloss to the Durham Ritual (C.13, 18.1, 21)

     A 6 (3·8%)   B 21   C 154

10 King Alfred's translation of Gregory's *Regula pastoralis* (B.9.1)

     A 4 (1·7%)   B 91   C 233

11 King Alfred's translation of the prose parts of Boethius's *De consolatione philosophiae* (B.9.3)

     A 1 (1·3%)   B 15   C 78

12 King Alfred's translation of St Augustine's *Soliloquia* (B.9.4)

     A o   B 1   C 19

13 Translation of Orosius's *Historia adversus paganos* (B.9.2)

     A o   B 27   C 31

14 Old English prose psalms of the Paris Psalter (B.8.2)

     A o   B 16   C 57

15 The works of Wulfstan (B.2.1.1–5.12)[75]

     A 2 (2·6%)   B 75   C 76

16 Anonymous parts of the Old English Hexateuch[76] (B.8.1)

     A 1 (2·6%)   B 10   C 38

17 West Saxon gospels (B.8.4)

     A 16 (17·6%)   B 23   C 75

18 Byrhtferth's *Handbook* (B.20.20.1–2)

     A 1 (25%)   B 6   C 3

19 List of relics given to the monastery at Exeter by King Athelstan (B.16.10.8)[77]

     A 2 (100%)   B 41   C o

20 Interlinear gloss to the psalter and canticles in BL Royal 2. B. v (the Regius Psalter) (C.7.9, 11.9)

     A 7 (3·3%)   B 38   C 204

---

[74] This is the Mercian gloss to Matthew, Mark I–II.15 and John XVIII.1–3 in Oxford, Bodleian Library, Auct. D. 2. 19 ('Rushworth¹').

[75] The texts listed under the Cameron reference numbers B.2.6.1–5 ('Works attributed to Wulfstan') do not contain any relevant material, with the exception of B.2.6.3 *Gerefa*, which has been treated separately. In assembling the evidence for the works of Wulfstan, I have treated as separate texts those of his homilies which represent extensions or revisions of earlier versions or which contain parts of earlier works, i.e. relevant words in parallel passages have been counted as separate occurrences. This also applies to the two versions of the *Institutes of Polity* and the laws written by Wulfstan.

[76] *Genesis* IV–V.31, X, XI and XXIV.15 to the end; *Exodus*; *Leviticus*; *Numbers* I–XII, a few words in XIII.4 and XIII.5–17; *Deuteronomy*; *Joshua* I.1–10 and XII (P. Clemoes, *The Old English Illustrated Hexateuch*, ed. C.R. Dodwell and P. Clemoes, EEMF 18 (Copenhagen, 1974), 48, and A.B. Smith, *The Anonymous Parts of the Old English Hexateuch: a Latin–Old English/Old English–Latin Glossary* (Cambridge, 1985), p. x, n. 11).

[77] This is one of the entries on two preliminary quires of Oxford, Bodleian Library, Auct. D. 2. 16 made at Exeter in the second half of the eleventh century (N.R. Ker, *Catalogue of Manuscripts Containing Anglo-Saxon* (Oxford, 1957), no. 291).

21 Interlinear gloss to the psalter and canticles in Salisbury, Cathedral Library, 150 (the Salisbury Psalter)[78] (C.7.13, 11.12)

    A 12 (6·1%)   B 37   C 185

22 Interlinear gloss to Defensor's *Liber scintillarum* (C.15)

    A 24 (10·3%)   B 143   C 210

23 Interlinear gloss to the *Regularis concordia* (C.27)

    A 1 (3·1%)   B 13   C 31

24 Interlinear gloss to prayers and forms of confession in BL Arundel 155 (C.23.1)

    A 8 (25·8%)   B 4   C 23

25 Glosses to Prudentius in Boulogne-sur-Mer, Bibliothèque Municipale, 189 (C.94.1)

    A 1 (33·3%)   B 0   C 2

26 Interlinear glosses to the *Proverbia Salomonis* and Alcuin's *De virtutibus et vitiis* in BL Cotton Vespasian D. vi ('Kentish Glosses') (C.29, 49)

    A 1 (7·1%)   B 3   C 13

27 The corpus of Old English poetry (A.1–53)

    A 7 (1·4%)   B 62   C 501

DISCUSSION

The distribution of the Winchester vocabulary in the corpus of Old English texts makes the following three points obvious:

(1) The Winchester usage is a South English phenomenon. Irrespective of the time when they originated, all the texts for which Anglian provenance may be assumed show a vocabulary differing radically from that of the Winchester usage.[79] Only Northumbrian texts dating from the second half of the tenth century are exceptional in their use of *miht* (besides *mægen*) to render the Latin *virtus* within the semantic area of word group 7.[80]

(2) The Winchester usage is a late Old English phenomenon. The vocabulary of early West Saxon texts such as the works of King Alfred (II.10–12), the Old English Orosius (II.13) or the Old English prose psalms of the Paris Psalter (II.14)[81] is conspicuously different from that of the Winchester usage[82]

---

[78] The Salisbury Psalter is a late Old English gloss based on the type of the Regius Psalter.

[79] For examples, see texts 11.1–9.

[80] For details concerning this use of *miht* in Northumbrian texts, see Hofstetter, *Winchester*, texts 233, 238 and 264.

[81] For the question of the authorship of the Old English prose psalms in the Paris Psalter, which are very probably attributable to King Alfred, see J. M. Bately, 'Lexical Evidence for the Authorship of the Prose Psalms in the Paris Psalter', *ASE* 10 (1982), 69–95, and Hofstetter, *Winchester*, text 119.

[82] Some of the divergences in question, it is true, may be due also to differences of subdialect: according to Seebold's results, we have to assume that the works of King Alfred, the Old English Orosius and the group of texts representing the Winchester usage (essentially Seebold's 'Benediktiner-Gruppe') belong to three different subdialects (see esp. Seebold, 'Die ae. Entsprechungen von lat. *sapiens* und *prudens*', pp. 323–33).

and the only early Kentish text available for comparison, a charter of Oswulf and Beornthryth to Christ Church, Canterbury,[83] also diverges from the Winchester usage in employing the 'C word' *gegearwian*.[84]

(3) The words characteristic of the Winchester usage make up a 'prosaic' vocabulary (cf. II.27). Certainly this is mainly due to the fact that, with very few exceptions, the Winchester vocabulary came into use in the south of England in the late Old English period, whereas the greatest part of extant Old English poetry was composed at an earlier period and in the Anglian dialect, and poets even later imitated the diction of the older poetry.

Among the authors of the late Old English period, Ælfric (I.3) – in striking contrast to his contemporary Wulfstan (II.15)[85] – used the Winchester vocabulary with a degree of consistency that can be most convincingly explained by the assumption that he acquired this vocabulary as an essential element of the education which he received at the Old Minster at Winchester. With his translation of the Benedictine Rule (I.1) Æthelwold, Ælfric's teacher, created the first Old English text which combined a large proportion of Winchester words with vocabulary of an earlier tradition.[86] We may therefore assume that he was the decisive force behind the development of a new usage which, after an initial or intermediate stage, attained full maturity in the generation of his pupils, and of which the 'A words' discussed in this article are characteristic elements.[87]

Besides the works of Ælfric, Æthelwold's translation of the Benedictine Rule and the account of King Edgar's establishment of monasteries (I.2), now commonly attributed to Æthelwold,[88] a considerable number of texts in group I have direct or indirect links with Winchester and hence support the view that the 'A words' are features of a standard maintained at Winchester itself and most probably also within the sphere of influence of this great religious and cultural centre. The Vitellius Psalter (I.5) and the Arundel Psalter

---

[83] P. H. Sawyer, *Anglo-Saxon Charters: an Annotated List and Bibliography*, R. Hist. Soc. Guides and Handbooks 8 (London, 1968), no. 1188.

[84] See Hofstetter, *Winchester*, text 179.

[85] For evidence of the possibility that certain differences in vocabulary usage between Ælfric and Wulfstan are due to differences of subdialect, see Seebold, 'Die ae. Entsprechungen von lat. *sapiens* und *prudens*', pp. 323–33, esp. 324, 327–8 and 331–3.

[86] The first indications of the Winchester usage are to be found in the Regius Psalter (II.20), which was written about the middle of the tenth century, perhaps at Winchester. This gloss provides the earliest occurrences of the Winchester words *ælfremed, ælfremedung, tobrytan, towcwysan* and *gewuldorbeagian* (for details, see Hofstetter, *Winchester*, text 226).

[87] *Snotor* 'prudent' (cf. above. p. 142 and n. 25) and *undergietan* 'understand, perceive' (cf. above, pp. 142–3) may also be regarded as characteristic elements of this new usage. For the question of how extensive the vocabulary typical of this usage was, see Gneuss, 'The Origin of Standard Old English', pp. 76 and 80; cf. also Hofstetter, *Winchester*, pp. 6–7.

[88] See *ibid.* text 2 and the references there cited.

(I.6) were written at Winchester, and there are a number of indications that the Stowe Psalter (I.4) also comes from Winchester.[89] The origin of the Lambeth Psalter (I.7) is not known, but its striking agreements with Ælfric's usage and its definite links with the Stowe Psalter and the Vitellius Psalter suggest that its glossator(s) had access to one or more manuscripts produced at or connected with Winchester.[90] CCCC 201, pp. 1–178, which contains a fragment of a translation of the *Regularis concordia* (I.8), was in Winchester about the middle of the eleventh century.[91] Further evidence that the translation of the *Regularis concordia* extant in this manuscript is connected with Winchester has been provided by Joyce Hill in her discussion of Ælfric's 'silent days'.[92] She points out that in the whole corpus of Old English literature the words *swig-dæg*, *swig-uhte* and *swige-niht*, monastic technical terms for the last three days of Holy Week, are used only by Ælfric and the translator of the fragment of the *Regularis concordia* in CCCC 201, pp. 1–178, and she is 'tempted to suggest that *swig-dæg*, *swig-uhte* and *swige-niht* were "Winchester words"'.[93]

In a section explaining that canons should address each other by both their names and their ranks, the Old English Rule of Chrodegang (I.9), extant in an Exeter manuscript, has an extension of the Latin original, and in this extension five examples of such forms of address are given by way of illustration. All the names mentioned in this additional passage are to be found in a list of monks of the Old Minster at Winchester written about 1000, and it seems certain that the extant manuscript of the Old English Rule of Chrodegang is derived from one produced at Winchester.[94] The gloss to the *Expositio hymnorum* (I.10) is found in two manuscripts that were probably written at Canterbury, but the Latin text of the *Expositio* belongs to the type of hymnal in use at Winchester and not at Canterbury. The Durham Hymnal (I.12) was almost certainly produced at Christ Church, Canterbury, and its Latin text belongs to the type of hymnal in use at Canterbury, but 'the hymns (and stanzas) peculiar to Canterbury usage

---

89 For details, see *ibid.* texts 4–6.
90 For a detailed account of the points of agreement between the Lambeth Psalter, the Stowe Psalter and the Vitellius Psalter, see *ibid.* texts 4 and 7.
91 T. A. M. Bishop (*English Caroline Minuscule* (Oxford, 1971), p. xv, n. 2) has identified the hand which wrote CCCC 201, pp. 170–6, as that of a New Minster scribe; for the date of this hand, see Ker, *Catalogue*, p. 90 (Part B, hand (3)).
92 J. Hill, 'Ælfric's "Silent Days"', *Sources and Relations: Studies in Honour of J. E. Cross*, ed. M. Collins, J. Price and A. Hamer, Leeds Stud. in Eng. ns 16 (Leeds, 1985), 118–31, esp. 123–5.
93 *Ibid.* p. 125.
94 M. Förster, 'Lokalisierung und Datierung der altenglischen Version der Chrodegang-Regel', *Sitzungsberichte der Bayerischen Akademie der Wissenschaften*, Phil.-hist. Abteilung, Jahrgang 1933, Schlussheft, pp. 7–8, and Ker, *Catalogue*, p. 74. Like Æthelwold's translation of the Benedictine Rule, the Old English Rule of Chrodegang combines a large proportion of Winchester words with vocabulary pointing back to an earlier usage.

are largely unglossed, [which] points to a Winchester origin of either the OE glosses or the hymnal to which these glosses were first applied.'[95] The glosses to the monastic canticles in BL Cotton Vespasian D. xii (I.11) and in Durham, Cathedral Library, B. III. 32 as well as BL Cotton Julius A. vi (I.13) have the same provenance as the glosses to the *Expositio hymnorum* (I.10) and the Durham Hymnal (I.12) respectively.[96] The high percentage of 'A words' in the glosses to Aldhelm's *De laudibus virginitatis* extant in two Abingdon manuscripts (I.17 and 18) may also be regarded as a pointer to Winchester: there were very close relations between the monasteries of Winchester and Abingdon, and it is highly probable that Winchester manuscripts were used or copied at Abingdon and that the usage of the school at Abingdon was influenced by that of Winchester.[97]

Since Winchester was a very influential religious and cultural centre, we may assume that its usage spread, to a certain extent, even beyond its immediate sphere of influence; this would explain the fact that a large number of texts, mostly of uncertain origin, contain a small percentage of Winchester vocabulary.[98] Manuscripts produced by the Winchester scriptoria found their way to various parts of the country, and, for instance, in the case of the interlinear glosses to the Benedictine Rule (I.14) and Benedict of Aniane's *Memoriale* (I.15), both extant in a manuscript which almost certainly comes from Christ Church, Canterbury, we might well have copies derived from Winchester manuscripts. Exeter is known to have had close connections with Winchester in the second half of the eleventh century,[99] and several texts certainly or very probably written at Exeter after the middle of the eleventh century support the conclusion that the Winchester usage influenced the vocabulary in use at Exeter.[100]

The influence of the Winchester usage is particularly obvious in the south-

---

[95] Gneuss, *Hymnar und Hymnen*, p. 445.

[96] For details concerning the glosses to the *Expositio hymnorum*, the Durham Hymnal and the monastic canticles, see Hofstetter, *Winchester*, texts 10–13 and the references there cited.

[97] Further evidence pointing to Winchester is provided by the texts discussed *ibid.* texts 56, 159 and 175. Apart from the vocabulary no relation with Winchester can be established for I.14–16 and 19–23; for a possible connection of I.21 (Revision of Werferth's translation of Gregory's *Dialogi*) with Winchester, see *ibid.* text 21.

[98] It is of course possible that some of the Winchester words were also in use in some parts of the country independently of any Winchester influence. After all, the Winchester usage cannot have been created *ex nihilo*; its initiators certainly chose its vocabulary from language already in existence. The significant point is that, outside Winchester and its sphere of influence, these words were not made elements of a standard usage.

[99] Cf., e.g., M. Clayton, 'Feasts of the Virgin in the Liturgy of the Anglo-Saxon Church', *ASE* 13 (1984), 209–33, at 227–9, and *The Salisbury Psalter*, ed. C. and K. Sisam, p. 5, n. 3.

[100] II.19 and Hofstetter, *Winchester*, texts 36, 44, 53, 102, 190 and 191.

east of England with its closely associated centres of Canterbury and Roches-ter.[101] A considerable number of texts connected with this area use Winchester words, though only to a limited extent and very often inconsistently. Taken together, these texts show a decidedly mixed vocabulary obviously deriving from different traditions, one of which was the Winchester usage.[102] The metropolis of Canterbury in particular must have been a linguistic crossing point; that it underwent considerable influence from Winchester is suggested by the mere fact that, among the archbishops of Canterbury in the late Old English period, there were Æthelgar (988–90), who had been abbot of the New Minster, Ælfheah (1005–12), previously bishop of Winchester, and Stigand, who held the sees of Winchester and Canterbury in plurality 1052–70.[103] Although a deliberate attempt to standardize vocabulary cannot be established in the case of Canterbury, certain special features are identifiable: the words *acofrian, fordimmian, forgyting, fyndel, halbære, oferprut, reafol, stæfwis, twiseht, twisehtan, twisehtnes, ðrinen, ungecoplic, ungecoplice* and *unstæfwis*, which occur only in a number of glosses connected with Christ Church, Canterbury, may well be lexical peculiarities of this great cultural centre.[104]

It is difficult to ascertain exactly how the Winchester usage came into existence. There may have been stylistic reasons prompting the preference of certain words to synonyms otherwise commonly used in late Old English prose texts and glosses.[105] In some cases, the choice of a particular word may have been determined by pastoral considerations: in employing the words *gelaðung* 'church = Christian community' and *cyðere* 'martyr', the reformers probably wanted to express concepts central to the Christian religion more vividly by the use of native terms than could be done with the corresponding loanwords *cirice* and *martir*.[106] The loan translation *wuldorbeag* used in the religious sense of 'crown of glory'[107] is also more expressive and more specific than are the synonyms *beag* and *cynehelm*, for example, these often being used for non-religious concepts of crown and wreath also.[108] *Miht*, as employed in

---

[101] For evidence of the possibility that Winchester vocabulary was used also in the south-eastern Danelaw, see *ibid.* texts 20, 72 and 77.

[102] For examples of texts connected with the south-east of England, see I.16 and II.22–6 and *ibid.* texts 16, 32 ('Zusammenfassung'), 59, 108 (corrections), 123, 131, 145, 176–7, 187, 212–21, 227, 232, 236 and 247.

[103] The fact that Æthelsige, a monk of the Old Minster, Winchester, became abbot of St Augustine's, Canterbury, in 1061, also deserves to be mentioned in this connection.

[104] For details, see *ibid.* p. 109 and texts 212–18.

[105] Cf. Gneuss, 'The Origin of Standard Old English', p. 76.

[106] The Winchester words *gelaðung* and *cyðere* translate the Latin *ecclesia* 'assembly, congregation = church' and *martyr* 'witness = martyr', both of which have been borrowed from the Greek. Besides their use as Winchester words, *gelaðung* and *cyðere* also occur in the non-religious senses of 'invitation, assembly' and 'witness' respectively.

[107] Latin 'corona gloriae'.   [108] Cf. also Kirschner, *Kranz und Krone*, pp. 258–9.

word groups 6 and 7, may have been taught as a standard Old English equivalent for the Latin *virtus* in the school at Winchester, where, as part of their training in Latin, pupils certainly translated Latin texts into Old English.[109] The influence of local or regional peculiarities must also be regarded as an important factor in the development of the Winchester usage: it seems very likely that certain elements of the Winchester vocabulary were derived from the dialect spoken in Winchester and the surrounding area.[110]

Whatever the forces at work in the development of the Winchester usage, the evidence points to the conclusion that it was the result of a deliberate attempt, probably initiated by Æthelwold, to regularize vocabulary. We may assume that this was a standard,[111] inculcated through education and training, which was maintained at Winchester and probably also at some monasteries closely associated with Winchester. In Ælfric, who, despite the changes his vocabulary underwent in the course of his literary career,[112] used the Winchester words with a quite remarkable degree of consistency[113] and was also anxious to regularize the syntax and inflections of his language,[114] Winchester produced the greatest witness to its concern for language. Being a political, religious and cultural centre of unique prestige and influence, Winchester, through the conscious effort of its monastic school to standardize language, must also have become a factor of prime importance in the evolution of the literary standard in use throughout England in the late Old English period.[115]

---

[109] Godden ('Ælfric's Changing Vocabulary', p. 222) suggests that the practice of glossing Latin texts in the school at Winchester may have produced 'as a perhaps unintentional byproduct a Winchester set of Latin–Old English equivalents which influenced the practice of literary writers trained in the school too'.

[110] For the importance of subdialects in the distribution of the Old English vocabulary for *prudentia* and *superbia*, see Seebold, 'Die ae. Entsprechungen von lat. *sapiens* und *prudens*', pp. 322 and 330–1; cf. also above, p. 142.

[111] Further investigation will be necessary to ascertain the extent of the vocabulary characteristic of this standard; cf. also above, n. 87.

[112] Cf. Godden, 'Ælfric's Changing Vocabulary'.

[113] Some of Ælfric's deviations from the Winchester standard are explicable by his concern for style (for details, see Hofstetter, *Winchester*, text 3). In his search for variety in his diction, for example, Ælfric occasionally used a synonymous 'C word' to avoid repetition (for 'elegant variation' between synonyms as a feature of Ælfric's style, see *Homilies of Ælfric*, ed. Pope, p. 123, and Godden, 'Ælfric's Changing Vocabulary', p. 221).

[114] Cf. above, p. 140, and the references cited in n. 9.

[115] I am grateful to Professor Helmut Gneuss for his helpful suggestions in connection with this article.

The Latin textual basis of *Genesis A*

PAUL G. REMLEY

Received scholarly opinion regards *Genesis A* as an Old English versification of the Latin text of Genesis in Jerome's Vulgate revision of the bible.[1] This view has prevailed in modern editions of the poem, which normally print a critical text of the Vulgate Genesis in their apparatus.[2] The textual basis of *Genesis A* is perhaps 'vulgate' in character in so far as the poem renders Genesis readings that were commonly known in Anglo-Saxon England, but the identification of this base text with that of the Hieronymian Vulgate remains an untested hypothesis.[3] Ten years ago A. N. Doane printed a list of readings in the Old English text which show affinity with the ancient versions of Genesis that emerged before the completion of Jerome's translation, readings associated with the *Vetus Latina* or Old Latin bible.[4] Doane did not, however, challenge the long-standing belief that *Genesis A* follows a single, lost exem-

---

[1] An early comparative study by A. Ebert, 'Zur angelsächsischen Genesis', *Anglia* 5 (1882), 124–33, at 124, assumes that the Latin source of *Genesis A* is 'selbstverständlich [die] Vulgata'. This assumption underlies numerous critical summaries of the poem, though in *A New Critical History of Old English Literature* (New York, 1986), at pp. 207–9, S. B. Greenfield and D. G. Calder do not reproduce the reference to 'additions to and changes from the Vulgate text' that appeared in Greenfield's earlier *Critical History* (New York, 1965), at p. 148.

[2] The edition of F. Holthausen, *Die ältere Genesis* (Heidelberg, 1914) supplies a Vulgate text of Genesis at the foot of each page. A. N. Doane, in *Genesis A: a New Edition* (Madison, Wisc., 1978) prints a convenient Latin running text of individual verses from the Vulgate (with an uneven selection of non-Vulgate variants) on pages facing the corresponding lines of Old English. An excerpt of the *Genesis A* account of Abraham and Isaac in *Bright's Old English Grammar and Reader*, ed. F. G. Cassidy and R. N. Ringler, 3rd edn (New York, 1971), at pp. 289–95, includes the Vulgate text of Gen. XXII.

[3] The terms 'textual basis' and 'base text' refer to an archetypal group of readings corresponding in point of detail to those parts of *Genesis A* that derive from a Latin source (in most cases, the text of Gen. I–XXII). The authorship, date and unity of *Genesis A* and the probability that the exemplary series of readings behind it once existed in a single manuscript are peripheral concerns here, but no evidence has been found to contradict Doane's view (*Genesis A*, pp. 36–7 and 61) that the received text of *Genesis A* in Oxford, Bodleian Library, Junius 11 (?Christ Church, Canterbury, s. x/xi) represents a late, defective copy of a unified work by one poet (Doane places his florescence *c.* 650–900) who sought to render faithfully a single Latin text of Genesis in Old English verse. Even if early theories of multiple authorship over many years (*ibid.* pp. 39–40) were vindicated, they would not affect either the textual findings of this study or its conclusion that discernible principles influenced the choices of readings that constitute the base text.

[4] *Genesis A*, p. 60. Doane concedes that his groundbreaking selection of Old Latin parallels is uncritical in so far as readings are taken 'without discrimination as to their origin' (p. 59, n. 51) from *Genesis*, ed. B. Fischer, Vetus Latina 2 (Freiburg, 1951–4).

plar that contained in all essentials the text established by Jerome.[5] The present study attempts to survey, without any preconceptions, all the details in the poem that might derive from Latin sources;[6] its intention is to make a first step towards the recovery of the Latin textual basis of *Genesis A*.

The complex and frequently mysterious origins of the earliest Latin translations of Genesis are bound up with the fortunes of the Hebrew and Greek versions of the Old Testament in the early Christian era.[7] Quotations from the text of Genesis in the Septuagint – a term used generally to refer to the Greek translations of the Hebrew writings of the Old Testament – have been dated before 200 BC, and these form part of a programmatic and stylistically unified translation of the Torah (the Old Law or Pentateuch, comprising the first five books of the Old Testament) which was probably completed during the third century BC.[8] For those without recourse to Hebrew texts, Greek scripture offered an excellent translation of Genesis that had been produced in accordance with consistently applied methodological principles. No comparably sound Latin text appeared until Jerome founded a standard translation of the Pentateuch on Hebrew and Greek scripture before 404.[9] During the six centuries that separated the appearance of the Septuagint and Jerome's new version, Latin translations of varying quality emerged (probably by *c.* 200) which circulated in Africa and parts of Europe. Jerome's efforts were intended

---

5 He concludes (*Genesis A*, p. 59) that the 'biblical text behind *Genesis A* appears to be a Vulgate of a fairly pure Roman or Gregorian type, predominantly Jeromian, with some admixture of Old Latin elements'.

6 Textual questions have been largely ignored in the continuing debate concerning the poet's knowledge and use of non-biblical Latin texts (patristic exegesis, liturgical and homiletic sources) initiated by the study of B. F. Huppé, *Doctrine and Poetry: Augustine's Influence on Old English Poetry* (Albany, NY, 1959), pp. 131–216. Doane doubts many of Huppé's assertions (*Genesis A*, pp. 42–3), but his own commentary draws frequently and perhaps excessively on topics of patristic exegesis. The 'exegetical' approach to the poem has been criticized by N. Boyd, 'Doctrine and Criticism: a Revaluation of *Genesis A*', *NM* 83 (1982), 230–8.

7 For a general introduction to the scriptural resources consulted in the preparation of this article, see the first two volumes of *The Cambridge History of the Bible: From the Beginnings to Jerome*, ed. P. R. Ackroyd and C. F. Evans (Cambridge, 1970), chs. 5–7 and 16–18, and *The West from the Fathers to the Reformation*, ed. G. W. H. Lampe (Cambridge, 1969), chs. 1–5.

8 According to legend this translation was prepared for use in the royal library at Alexandria by seventy Jewish scholars (whence the name Septuagint, or 'seventy') at the command of Ptolemy II. Historically it served the needs of the Jews of Mediterranean regions after the Diaspora and was codified under the authority of the synagogues. Christian commentators championed the scriptural authority of the Septuagint from the first century onwards. For a recent study and additional references, see P. Walters, *The Text of the Septuagint: its Corruptions and their Emendation*, ed. D. W. Gooding (Cambridge, 1973).

9 H. D. F. Sparks, 'Jerome as a Biblical Scholar', *The Cambridge History of the Bible* I, ed. Ackroyd and Evans, 510–41, at 516.

to supersede these earlier, determinedly literalistic renderings from the Greek, but the ancient manuscripts and patristic authors witness the continuing use of an Old Latin bible whose pedigree can still be reconstructed despite the relative obscurity of its sources.[10]

Some scholars believe that a standard Old Latin translation of the bible originated in Africa in the second century, but by the beginning of the Anglo-Saxon period several versions were extant. Bonifatius Fischer, in his monumental edition of the Old Latin Genesis,[11] distinguishes five main types of text that had emerged by the fifth century: an early Old African text, notably the mid-third-century Carthaginian text witnessed by Cyprian (siglum K); a later Old African text to the end of the fourth century, as in Augustine (C);[12] a late African or Spanish text (S); a controversial Italian version witnessed by Ambrose, Jerome and others (I);[13] a common European text (E, including types S and I) and the common form of the *Vetus Latina* (L, including all of the preceding).[14] The possible knowledge and use of some or all of these texts by the Anglo-Saxons is a question that has received scant attention, but passages in the works of such authors as Aldhelm and Bede suggest that Old Latin texts

[10] For discussion of the many problems associated with the Old Latin bible, see A. V. Billen, *The Old Latin Texts of the Heptateuch* (Cambridge, 1927) and the review by F. C. Burkitt, *JTS* 29 (1928), 140–6; H. F. D. Sparks, 'The Latin Bible', *The Bible in its Ancient and English Versions*, ed. H. W. Robinson (Oxford, 1940), pp. 100–27, at 100–10; B. J. Roberts, *The Old Testament Text and Versions* (Cardiff, 1951), pp. 237–46; B. Fischer, 'Bibelausgaben des frühen Mittelalters', *SettSpol* 10 (Spoleto, 1963), 519–600; and E. Würthwein, *Der Text des Alten Testaments*, 4th edn (Stuttgart, 1973), pp. 90–3. See also E. von Dobschütz, 'A Collection of Old Latin Bible Quotations: Somnium Neronis', *JTS* 16 (1915), 1–27, and B. Bischoff, 'Neue Materialien zum Bestand und zur Geschichte der altlateinischen Bibelübersetzungen', *Miscellanea Giovanni Mercati*, 6 vols., Studi e testi 121–6 (Vatican City, 1946) I, 407–36.

[11] *Genesis*, ed. Fischer, is the cornerstone of a continuing project to reconstruct critically the entire text of the Old Latin bible now under the supervision of a team of scholars at the Vetus-Latina-Institut at Beuron. As a rule, the term *Vetus Latina* will refer here to the readings (including interlinear variants) printed in the critical edition while the phrase 'Old Latin (bible)' refers more generally to the lost text which Fischer and his successors seek to recover and its extant primary (manuscript) and secondary (patristic) witnesses.

[12] See W. Süss, *Studien zur lateinischen Bibel, I: Augustin's Locutiones und das Problem der lateinischen Bibelsprache*, Acta et commentationes B29.4 (Tartu, 1932), and F. C. Burkitt, 'St Augustine's Bible and the *Itala*', *JTS* 11 (1910), 258–68.

[13] Since the publication of a partially reconstructed Old Latin biblical text by P. Sabatier, *Bibliorum sacrorum latinae versiones antiquae, seu Vetus Italica*, 3 vols. (Rheims, 1743–9), the term 'Itala' has been frequently if imprecisely used as a synonym for 'Old Latin bible'. See, e.g., the vocabulary study by H. Rönsch, *Itala und Vulgata*, 2nd edn (Marburg, 1875). The assertion of F. C. Burkitt, *The Old Latin and the Itala*, Texts and Stud. 4.3 (Cambridge, 1896), 55–65 (cf. Burkitt, as cited above, n. 12), that the Itala mentioned by Augustine is in fact the Vulgate, typifies the arguments that have exacerbated the terminological confusion surrounding the Italian textual type. [14] *Genesis*, ed. Fischer, pp. 14*–22*.

were available from the earliest period of English Christianity[15] and this view may be confirmed rather strikingly by a close reading of *Genesis A*.

Any attempt to recover a lost Latin text from an ancient vernacular source confronts difficult questions of judgement and interpretation. How reliable are the words of the extant source as witnesses to specific readings in the Latin? Do they allow reasonable conjectures regarding Latin vocabulary, syntax or both? Which words and phrases should be dismissed from consideration as literary inventions added for metrical or narrative effect? In Old English scriptural verse, the formal requirements of alliterative prosody frequently obscure the content of the base text of a poem. Fortunately *Genesis A* is exceptional in that it reproduces faithfully the nuance of many readings that it renders from the Latin Genesis.[16] The probability that a particular word or phrase in the Latin text will find a close equivalent in *Genesis A* is very high.[17] A trial collation of the section of the poem describing the separation of land and water (Gen. 1.9) with Vulgate and Old Latin scripture bears out this impression:[18]

Gen. 1.9	(H)	dixit vero Deus	congregentur aquae
GenA	157b–8	Frea engla heht þurh his *word*	wesan wæter gemæne
	(H)	quae sub caelo	sunt
	159	þa *nu* under roderum	heora *ryne* healdað,
	(H)	in unum locum	et appareat arida;
	160a	stowe *gestefnde*.	(cf. below, 164–5a)
	(H)	factumque est ita.	
		(cf. below, 160b–5a)	
	(E)	et congregata est	aqua quae est sub caelo
	160b–1a	ða stod *hraðe* (+ 162a)	holm under heofonum
	(E)		in congregationes suas
	161b–2a	*swa se halga bebead,*	sid ætsomne
	162b–3a	*ða gesundrod wæs*	*lago wið lande.*

---

15 See below, pp. 180–2.

16 Doane, confirming earlier observations of Grein, Holthausen, Klaeber and others, states that 'the poet has systematically, virtually phrase by phrase, reproduced in traditional poetry the essential meaning of the Latin Genesis which he had before him as he worked. The paraphrase is nearly complete and continuous up to Genesis 22.13' (*Genesis A*, ed. Doane, p. 61).

17 'Overall, the ratio of omitted whole biblical verses to those represented is two to five. In most chapters the actual ratio of omissions is considerably lower . . . [and] almost everything is represented' (*ibid.* p. 63).

18 Citations of the Vulgate (siglum H) follow *Biblia sacra iuxta vulgatam versionem*, ed. R. Weber, 2nd edn, 2 vols, (Stuttgart, 1975). Readings of the Old Latin Genesis normally derive from *Genesis*, ed. Fischer.

(E)	et paruit	arida
163b–4	geseah þa *lifes weard*	drige stowe, *dugoða hyrde,*
165a	*wide* æteowde[19]	

These lines offer an example of the usual method of translation observed in *Genesis A* in response to a specific Latin scriptural locus. Almost every word of the Latin text finds some counterpart in verse and additional material (italicized above) is limited to variations on Latin 'dixit . . . deus' ('frea engla heht', 'se halga bebead'), stock synonyms for the deity ('lifes weard', 'dugoða hyrde'), alliterative diction (*word, ryne, gestefnde, wide*), metrical chevilles (*nu, hraðe*) and a paraphrase of the whole text of Gen. 1.9 ('gesundrod wæs lago wið lande'). None of these changes alters or obscures the basic meaning of the verse, but the redundant phraseology of the rendering ('wæter gemæne' and 'holm . . . sid ætsomne'; 'under roderum' and 'under heofonum' etc.) raises a question whether the poem reproduces here the readings of a similarly repetitive (or glossed) Latin text or expands the literal meaning of a concise text for poetic effect. After several lines (157b–60a) that could reflect the use of either a Vulgate or Old Latin[20] text of the verse, the poem depicts the completion of the divine action in terms that exhibit close lexical and syntactic agreement with the concluding words of an expanded text of Gen. 1.9 typical of European (E) witnesses of the *Vetus Latina*.[21] Remarkably, the whole passage (*GenA* 157b–65a) corresponds more closely to the Greek text of Gen. 1.9 than to the Vulgate text of the verse and many Old Latin witnesses.[22] Apparent

---

[19] *GenA* 157b–65a: 'The lord of angels commanded by his word that the waters which now hold their course beneath the heavens should draw [lit. 'be'] together, he ordained a place [for them]; then the water beneath the heavens immediately stood together as the holy one ordered, when sea was divided from land. Then the guardian of life, protector of hosts, saw the dry region widely revealed.' Quotations of *Genesis A* derive from Doane's edition with occasional addition of punctuation and capitalized letters. Abbreviations used in citations of Old English texts are those set out by B. Mitchell *et al.*, 'Short Titles of Old English Texts', *ASE* 4 (1975), 207–21, with addenda and corrigenda in *ASE* 8 (1979), at 331–3.

[20] For early witnesses to the Old Latin text of Gen. 1.9, see *Genesis*, ed. Fischer, pp. 12–14 and 530. Previously unrecorded Anglo-Latin citations of the first part of the Old Latin text (reading 'Congregetur aqua in congregationem unam . . .') appear in two works by Bede: *In proverbia Salomonis* I.v.14 (CCSL 119B, 50) and *In epistolas septem catholicas* iii.5 (CCSL 121, 277).

[21] In addition to exhibiting congruence of vocabulary, *GenA* 157b–65a may reflect a shift from past to present subjunctive and perfect tense. The expanded text of the verse, which derives from Hebrew scripture, enters western tradition in Old Latin translations of the Septuagint. Both Greek and Latin texts lose the latter part of the verse as a result of scribal influence, i.e. presumed *homoioteleuton*; see J. Skinner, *A Critical and Exegetical Commentary on Genesis*, 2nd edn, International Critical Commentary (Edinburgh, 1930), pp. 22–3, and Roberts, *The Old Testament Text and Versions*, p. 96.

[22] The Greek text reads: Καὶ εἶπεν ὁ θεός Συναχθήτω τὸ ὕδωρ (var. τὰ ὕδατα) τὸ ὑποκάτω τοῦ οὐρανοῦ εἰς συναγωγὴν μίαν, καὶ ὀφθήτω ἡ ξηρά. καὶ ἐγένετο οὕτως. καὶ συνήχθη τὸ ὕδωρ τὸ

points of agreement between *Genesis A* and Greek and, in some cases, Hebrew scripture against the readings of the Vulgate may indicate the use of a Latin exemplar that preserved (or had been revised in the light of) features of the Septuagint. One such insular witness appears among the bilingual (Greek–Latin) lessons from Genesis 1.1–11.3 and XXII.1–19 preserved in the so-called *Liber Commonei*, Oxford, Bodleian Library, Auctarium F. 4. 32 (*S.C.* 2176), 28va18–31vb3 and 34va1–36rb9 (Wales, s. ix; later provenance Glastonbury): 'et dixit de*us* congregetur aqua quae *est* sub cælo in co*n*gregatione una et pareat arida et factum *est* sic; et congregatae su*n*t aqu*ae* quae erant *sub caelo* [inserted above 29ra21] in congregationib*us* suis et paruit arida.'[23] If a similarly expanded text of Gen. 1.9 stands behind the readings of *Genesis A*, what might appear at first glance to be a poetic expansion of Jerome's rendering 'factumque est ita', that is, *Genesis A* 160b–5a, may in fact reflect a continuous translation of an Old Latin exemplar.

A factor which inevitably qualifies any statement regarding what scriptural materials may have influenced the composition of *Genesis A* is the extreme scarcity of sources for the Anglo-Saxon transmission of Genesis. The method of the present study is to record fully the most important verbal parallels between the poem and such Latin monuments as survive, particularly early insular witnesses, and to draw tentative conclusions on the basis of the evidence thus accumulated. Further comparison of *Genesis A* with the Old Latin lessons of Auct. F. 4. 32, for example, affirms that both witnesses share one of the most distinctive readings of the Old Latin Heptateuch, which occurs in the account of Abraham's binding of Isaac (Gen. XXII.1–19).[24] In rendering the decree by which God directs Abraham to the region of Moriah

ὑποκάτω τοῦ οὐρανοῦ εἰς τὰς συναγωγὰς αὐτῶν, καὶ ὤφθη ἡ ξηρά. Citations of Greek scripture are from *Septuaginta*, ed. A. Rahlfs, 7th edn (Stuttgart, 1962), with variant readings supplied from *Genesis*, ed. Fisher.

23 Auct. F. 4. 32, 29ra17–22 (omitting incipit). The diplomatic transcription supplied here (with additions in italics) is based on the unpaginated facsimile edition of the manuscript, *St Dunstan's Classbook from Glastonbury: Cod. Bibl. Bodl. Auct. F. 4. 32*, ed. R. W. Hunt, Umbrae codicum occidentalium 4 (Amsterdam, 1962); see also Hunt's introductory comments at pp. x–xii. For a critical text and discussion, see B. Fischer, 'Die Lesungen der römischen Ostervigil unter Gregor der Grosse', *Colligere fragmenta: Festschrift Alban Dold*, ed. B. Fischer and V. Fiala, Texte und Arbeiten [s.s.] 2 (Beuron, 1952), 144–59. The Welsh scribe of Auct. F. 4. 32 supplies a transliterated Greek text, revised intelligently at several points to reflect Old Latin usage, which accompanies the Latin lessons in adjacent columns (Fischer, 'Die Lesungen', p. 155 with n. 1). See also A. Rahlfs, *Verzeichnis der griechischen Handschriften des Alten Testaments*, Königliche Gesellschaft der Wissenschaften zu Göttingen, philologisch-historische Klasse: Mitteilungen des Septuaginta-Unternehmens 2 (Berlin, 1914), 165, and H. Schneider, *Die altlateinischen biblischen Cantica*, Texte und Arbeiten 1.29–30 (Beuron, 1938), 68–70.

24 See *Genesis A*, ed. Doane, p. 60. On the origins of the binding legend (or *akedah*), see J. van Seters, *Abraham in History and Tradition* (New Haven, 1975), pp. 227–40.

to offer his son for sacrifice (Gen. XXII.2), Old Latin texts (including that of Auct. F. 4. 32) reproduce a mistaken Greek etymology of the name of the site (τὴν γῆν τὴν ὑψηλήν, 'high land'), reading 'terram altam' (K) or 'terram excelsam' (I).[25] *Genesis A* records that God directs Abraham to 'hrincg þæs hean landes',[26] and the phrase 'hean landes' recurs later in the narrative (2899b). The Old English poetic *Exodus* similarly omits any mention of Moriah in its retelling of the episode and identifies the site of Abraham's offering as *heahlond*.[27] This corroboration of the witness of *Genesis A* might suggest that an Old Latin form of Gen. XXII.2 was in common use among Anglo-Saxon biblical poets, possibly to the exclusion of Jerome's preferred mistranslation of the place-name ('terram visionis', following Symmachus).[28] In addition, there are four other points at which the treatment of Gen. XXII in *Genesis A* exhibits lexical concurrence with readings of the Old Latin bible. The most important of these occurs in the climactic description of Abraham's preparation of Isaac for his divinely decreed immolation: 'and gefeterode fet and honda / bearne sinum'.[29] The Hebrew text of Gen. XXII.9 employs a rare term for the binding of the fore and hind legs of an animal,[30] and the Septuagint approximates this reading with a verb meaning 'to bind hand and foot'.[31] The Vulgate records that Abraham bound his son ('conligasset Isaac filium suum') before placing him on the coals of the altar, but there is no explicit statement that he tied his hands and feet. *Genesis A* may attest the standard Old Latin reading 'alligavit pedes Isaac filio suo' (I),[32] whose syntactic alignment with

---

[25] The text in Auct. F. 4. 32 reads: 'et dixit accipe filium tuum dilectum quem diligis isac et uade in terra excelsa et offers illum ibi holochaustum in unum montem quem tibi dixero' (34va5–9). The Old Latin text of Gen. XXII.2 is treated by Billen, *The Old Latin Texts*, p. 195 with pp. 69, 105, 128, 133, 137, 142, 151 and 200.

[26] *GenA* 2855a: 'a ridge of that high land'. See J. Rosier, '*Hrincg* in *Genesis A*', *Anglia* 88 (1970), 334–6, for the translation of *hrincg* as a scribal corruption of *hrycg*. Doane (*Genesis A*, pp. 60 and 322) correctly notes the probable Old Latin origin of the phrase 'hean landes', but argues inconsistently that *hrincg* shows the influence of Vulgate 'terram visionis'.

[27] *Ex* 385b (ASPR 1, 102). This and all subsequent citations of possible reflexes of Old Latin scripture in Old English verse, unless otherwise noted, have not been exhibited previously.

[28] Jerome, *Hebraicae quaestiones in libro Geneseos* xxii.2 (CCSL 72, 26). On the Moriah crux, see further Bede, *De templo* i (CCSL 119A, 159, lines 475–7) and Skinner, *A Critical and Exegetical Commentary*, pp. 328–9.

[29] *GenA* 2903–4a: 'And he shackled the feet and hands of his son.'

[30] Skinner, *A Critical and Exegetical Commentary*, p. 330, and *A Hebrew and English Lexicon of the Old Testament*, ed. F. Brown *et al.*, corrected impression (Oxford, 1959), p. 785, *s.v.* עקד. Citations of the Hebrew Genesis refer to the text prepared by O. Eissfeldt for *Biblia Hebraica Stuttgartensia*, ed. K. Elliger and W. Rudolph, rev. edn (Stuttgart, 1976–7).

[31] See H. G. Liddell and R. Scott, *A Greek–English Lexicon*, new edn by H. S. Jones (Oxford, 1968), *s.v.* συμποδίζω.

[32] Auct. F. 4. 32 reads 'alligauit pedes isac filio suo' (35ra15); cf. *Genesis*, ed. Fischer, pp. 234–5. A similar reading would account for the Old English text as *fet* bears alliteration and 'and

the lines cited above is striking, or an Old Latin variant closer in point of detail to Hebrew usage (and that of the poem) exemplified by Ambrose: 'conligatis manibus et pedibus Isaac filii sui'.[33] The remaining phrases in which the account of Abraham and Isaac in *Genesis A* appears to reflect Old Latin diction are

geseah hlifigan   hea dune

swa him *sægde* ær   swegles aldor

(compare Old Latin *dixerat* against Vulgate *praeceperat* etc.),[34] 'restað incit her' (*sedete* against *expectate*) and 'wadan ofer wealdas' (*pertransibimus* against *properantes*).[35] On the other hand two possible points of agreement with the Vulgate against the *Vetus Latina* should also be noted.[36]

The preliminary findings set out above raise more questions than they resolve. Is it possible to localize or date *Genesis A* by reference to any extant manuscript containing a text of Genesis? Does a stratum of predominantly Old Latin readings underlie the text of the poem and, if so, where did it originate? Though verbal parallels between the poem and the ninth-century copy of insular Genesis lessons in Auct. F. 4. 32 are significant, examination of the other available records argues against drawing conclusions about any single connection between their Old Latin readings. There are, in addition, points of lexical correspondence between *Genesis A* and at least five Old Latin readings of Lyons, Bibliothèque de la Ville, 403 (329),[37] and two readings recoverable

honda' may have been added to fill out the line. The collocation 'fet and honda' does not occur elsewhere in Old English verse; *gefeterian*, moreover, alliterates with *fote* (translating Lat. *pede*) in *PPs* LXV.5. The phrasing of this detail in *Genesis A* thus does not employ standard Old English poetic diction and *fet* quite possibly renders a Latin term.

33 *De Abraham* I.lxxv (CSEL 32.1, 551). Fischer (supplement to *Genesis*, pp. 557–8) supports his inclusion of the variant with two additional passages: Zeno, *Tractatus* I.xliii.2.5 ('alligat manus . . . Pedes quoque constringit . . .') and I.lix.3.6 ('manus . . . pedem . . . destringit'), now ed. CCSL 22, 115 and 135; cf. also a previously unrecorded witness to the Old Latin text of Gen. XXII.9 in Quodvultdeus, *De quattuor virtutibus caritatis* VII.ii.5 (CCSL 60, 372): 'manus filio ligat, imponit eum in ara supra ligna.'

34 *GenA* 2878–9: '[Abraham] saw a high hill towering just as the prince of heaven told (*sægde*) him before.' Forms of *dicere* (reflecting use of εἶπον in the Septuagint rather than the variant δείκνυμι) appear in Auct. F. 4. 32 at 34va9 (Gen XXII.2 *dixero*), 34va17 and 35ra11 (XXII.3 and 9 *dixerat*) where the Vulgate prefers semantically imperative *monstravero*, *praeceperat* and *ostenderat*. Similar readings (e.g. XXII.3 *dixit*) occur in the I text of the *Vetus Latina*.

35 *GenA* 2881b and 2887a, both following Gen. XXII.5 (cf. Auct. F. 4. 32, 34va21–2, and the I text of the *Vetus Latina*).

36 *GenA* 2864a 'nihtreste ofgeaf' and Vulgate 'de nocte consurgens' against Old Latin 'exsurgens . . . mane' (I) in Gen. XXII.3, and 2926b–7a 'bewlat . . . ofer exle' and 'viditque post tergum' against *vidit* (I) in XXII.13 (cf. 2564b 'under bæc beseah' and Vulgate variant 'respiciens . . . postergum' in XIX.26).

37 With readings from Lyons 403 printed in *Pentateuchi versio latina antiquissima e codice Lugdunensi*, ed. U. Robert (Paris, 1881), at pp. 129–31, cf. Old English renderings of Gen. XVII.1 (*GenA* 2308a 'duguðum stepe' and Old Latin 'prospere age' against Vulgate *ambula*), and, in Gen.

from the lower script of the palimpsest Naples, Biblioteca Nazionale, latinus 1.[38] Moreover the extreme paucity of primary witnesses cannot be ignored. Auct. F. 4. 32, Lyons 403 and Naples BN lat. 1 are three of only four extant manuscripts that preserve Old Latin versions of verses translated in *Genesis A*.[39] The possibility of tracing the patterns of transmission of early insular Genesis texts with, say, the relative precision achieved in the analysis of less inadequately represented gospel books and psalters is quite simply ruled out.[40] But this same deficiency points up the singular importance of *Genesis A*, which embodies the only continuous record of a demonstrably mixed, insular text of nearly half of the chapters of Genesis, as a supplement to scarce manuscript materials. The vernacular witness of the poem corroborates and in some cases confirms that offered by nearly all surviving Latin sources (including quotations in Anglo-Latin works) for purposes of determining the range of variation of readings of the Anglo-Saxon Genesis.

The readings in *Genesis A* that show lexical agreement with Old Latin texts outnumber the two dozen or so that link the poem to the Vulgate, but it is impossible to determine whether these Old Latin readings constituted the original stratum of the poem's base text or were later accretions to a fundamentally Vulgate archetype. Indeed, this distinction matters little. Continuing editorial revision and scribal alteration of scripture in the centuries following Jerome's undertaking obviate any modern notion of 'pure' biblical text (Old Latin or Vulgate) in early western Europe. It is sufficient to recognize that the poem was based on a mixed text.[41] Furthermore the heterogeneous character

---

xIX, verses 5 (2460b 'hæman wolden' and 'coitum faciamus' against *cognoscamus*; cf. *Genesis A*, ed. Doane, p. 60), 7 (2471b–2 'fremmen . . . yfel ylda bearnum' and 'malefacere viris' against 'malum hoc facere'), 10 (2488b–9a) 'abrugdon in under edoras' and 'adtraxerunt . . . in domum' against 'introduxerunt') and 23 (2540b–1 'up . . . eode' and 'ortus est' against 'egressus est'). The readings of Lyons 403 are of the Spanish (S) textual type (*Genesis*, ed. Fischer, pp. 5*–7* and 17*–18*).

[38] See Fischer (*Genesis*, pp. 7*–10*). Cf. readings in Gen. XIII.2 (*GenA* 1877b *ceapas* and Old Latin *pecoribus* against Vulgate *possessione*) and XV.7 (2202 'of caldea ceastre' and 2208a *sceatas* and 'de regione Chaldaeorum' against 'de Ur Chaldeorum': cf. also *Genesis A*, ed. Doane, p. 60 for *GenA* 1730b 'ofer caldea folc', possibly following an Old Latin form of Gen. XI.31).

[39] The fragmentary leaf London, British Library, Papyrus 2052 (see *Genesis*, ed. Fischer, pp. 12*–13*) completes the manuscript record for the Old Latin text of Gen. I–XXII. Verbal correspondence between the Adamic and Noachic genealogical material in Pap. 2052 and *Genesis A* is restricted to common readings attested for both the *Vetus Latina* and the Vulgate.

[40] The fundamental research in the area appears in three studies by H. Glunz, *Die lateinische Vorlage der westsächsischen Evangelienversion*, Beiträge zur englischen Philologie 9 (Leipzig, 1928); *Britannien und Bibeltext. Der Vulgatatext der Evangelien in seinem Verhältnis zur irisch-angelsächsischen Kultur des Frühmittelalters*, Kölner anglistische Arbeiten 12 (Leipzig, 1930); and *History of the Vulgate in England from Alcuin to Roger Bacon* (Cambridge, 1933).

[41] On the development of early medieval 'mixed' texts, see S. Berger, *Histoire de la Vulgate pendant les premiers siècles du moyen âge* (Paris, 1893), pp. 1–60, and Sparks, 'The Latin Bible', pp. 106–7; for a discussion of heterogeneous texts of early Irish bibles, see P. Doyle, 'The Latin

of the passages presented above for comparison with Auct. F. 4. 32 does not in itself fully convey the complexity of the poem's exemplar. Another section of *Genesis A*, the treatment of the history of Adam and Eve after the fall, better represents the poem's extraordinarily well mixed selection of peculiarly Old Latin and Vulgate readings while in addition witnessing to the use of distinctive readings common to both versions, a few apparently conflate renderings and several uncanonical additions or glosses associated elsewhere with Latin scriptural tradition.

The received text of *Genesis A* includes many details which cannot, and probably should not, be linked collectively to any extant recension of Genesis, but which corroborate important Latin readings that have been largely ignored in criticism of the poem. For example, in the account of the creation of Eve, the abstract nouns *fultum* and *wraðu* ('help', 'aid') indicate that God creates Eve as a succour to Adam (Gen. 11.18: *adiutorium*, 'assistance', the usual reading of the *Vetus Latina*, extant Anglo-Latin sources and some critical editions of the Vulgate) rather than as his servant or 'helpmeet' (*adiutor*).[42] The diction of the poem here bears on a text-critical debate regarding the position of Eve that has had a continuous history from the earliest commentaries through Milton's *Paradise Lost* to the present.[43] The phrase 'ateah [*sc.* God] rib of sidan'[44] stands closer to, say, 'detraxisse deum costam de latere' (Augustine's paraphrase of the Old Latin Text of Gen. 11.21)[45] than to Vulgate 'sumpsit deus unam de costis eius', and bolsters the impression that Jerome's shorter reading finds no witness in any extant Old English source.[46] The uncanonical detail of the divine inspiration of Eve's soul,

Bible in Ireland: its Origins and Growth', *Biblical Studies: the Medieval Irish Contribution*, ed. M. McNamara, Proc. of the Irish Biblical Assoc. 1 (Dublin, 1976), 30–45.

[42] *GenA* 173b–4; Doane (*Genesis A*, p. 114) erroneously prints *adiutorem*, a reading he found (albeit as a *locus desperandus*) in the Vatican text of the Vulgate Genesis, *Biblia sacra iuxta latinam vulgatam versionem ad codicum fidem* 1: *librum Genesis*, ed. H. Quentin (Rome, 1926), at Gen. 11.18. *Biblica sacra*, ed. Weber, restores *adiutorium*, the reading preferred, e.g., by Bede, *Adnotationes in principium Genesis* I.ii.18 (CCSL 118A, 53); the same reading would account for Old English prose *Gen* 11.18 *fultum*.

[43] On the problem of rendering the reference to Eve in the Hebrew with either an abstract or concrete term, see Skinner, *A Critical and Exegetical Commentary*, p. 67; cf. *A Hebrew and English Lexicon*, ed. Brown *et al.*, p. 740, *s.v.* עֵזֶר.

[44] *GenA* 177b–8a: '[God] extracted a rib from [Adam's] side.'

[45] *De natura et origine animae* I.xviii.29 (CSEL 60, 330). Augustine explicitly adverts to the authority of scripture ('cum scriptum sit'); Fischer (*Genesis*, p. 51) lists other Old Latin citations of the verse with forms of *detrahere* and similar verbs. For the use of forms of OE *ateon* in glosses of verbs in *-trahere*, see, e.g., *OccGl* 49 776 (*detrahere*), *PsGl(DFIJ)* cxviii.131 (*adtrahere*) etc.

[46] The phrase 'genam him an rib of þa sidan' also appears as a caption in Junius 11 (*Scrib* 2.9.1 9.3) and an Old Latin form of the verse (including the phrase *de* [or *ex*] *latere*) would account for the prose translation 'genam he an rib of his sidan' in *Gen* 11.21 and an identical quotation at *ÆCHom* I *Thorpe* 1 14.20–1.

> worhte god
> freolice fæmnan,   feorh in gedyde,
> ece saula,[47]

recalls early textual and exegetical commentary on the omission of any mention of her soul in Gen. II.23 ('os ex ossibus meis et caro de carne mea').[48] The surviving post-lapsarian narrative in *Genesis A*[49] is textually deficient at a number of points, but those parts that remain correspond variously to a mixed selection of Vulgate and non-Vulgate texts. The poem relates that God visits Adam and Eve in the afternoon (*GenA* 853a 'ofer midne dæg'), indicating the use of an exemplar containing the phrase 'post meridiem' (a standard Vulgate and Old Latin variant reading in Gen. III.8) rather than 'ad vesperam', the critical reading of the *Vetus Latina*.[50] When God confronts the guilty couple in the garden (Gen. III.9–13), Adam initially confesses his nakedness in words that provide one of the most difficult passages of *Genesis A*:

> scyldfull mine,   sceaðen is me sare
> frecne on ferhðe,   ne dear nu forðgan
> for ðe andweardne.   ic eom eall eall nacod.[51]

Strained syntax, unusual diction (*mine, sceaðen* etc.) and the dittography 'eall eall' collectively suggest that some deep-seated corruption underlies these lines and that their original meaning may be irrecoverable. Ambrose, however, offers a paraphrase of an Old Latin text of Gen. III.10 which bears close comparison with nearly every word of the Old English: 'et Adam respondit: timens, quia *nudus eram* et tota *mente* confusus, *ante conspectum tuum venire non ausus sum*.'[52] Excepting the possibility of mere concidence of thought and

---

[47] *GenA* 183b–5a: 'God created a noble woman, he put a spirit in [her], an immortal soul'; see *Genesis A*, ed. Doane, pp. 236–7. F. Biggs argues convincingly that a simile in the next half line (*GenA* 185b 'englum gelice') reflects the influence of a Latin phrase 'sicut angeli' (Isidore and pseudo-Bede) or one of several equivalent expressions found elsewhere in patristic exegesis: '"Englum Gelice": *Elene* line 1320 and *Genesis A* line 185', *NM* 86 (1985), 447–52.

[48] See esp. Ambrose, *De paradiso* L (CSEL 32, 307) 'non anima ex anima, sed: os de ossibus ... et caro de carne' and Augustine (as cited above, n. 45), 'quod dicere debuerit Adam: anima ex anima mea, vel, spiritus de spiritu meo'.

[49] Matter corresponding to Gen. II.24–III.7 (include an account of the fall) appears in Junius 11 in the sequence of apocryphal and canonical Genesis material known as *Genesis B*; see *Genesis A*, ed. Doane, pp. 4–11 and 239–40, and Greenfield and Calder, *A New Critical History*, pp. 207 and 209–12.

[50] Doane (*Genesis A*, p. 59) claims the reading exclusively for the Vulgate, but Fischer's inclusion of 'post meridiem' as an interlinear variant shows that it may be regarded as a common reading.

[51] *GenA* 869–71: 'A guilty, injured conscience is grievously dangerous to me in spirit; I do not dare go forth before your presence. I am completely naked', following Doane (*Genesis A*, p. 241).

[52] *Expositio de psalmo CXVIII* I.xv.2 (CSEL 62, 15); italics added. The sole egregious term in the Latin text, *confusus*, may throw some light on the unusual collocation of *mine* ('memory',

diction in the two passages, three conjectures might be put forward to explain these verbal parallels: Ambrose may witness a textual tradition that exerted an independent influence on the scriptural exemplar of *Genesis A*; the poem's exemplar may have been revised at some stage of its transmission by someone familiar with Ambrosian exegesis; or the Anglo-Saxon poet who wrote these lines may have borrowed directly from Ambrose's *expositio* here and apparently nowhere else. If any one of these suppositions is correct, Adam's confession provides further evidence for the heterogeneity of the Latin textual basis of *Genesis A*.

Between the accounts of the fall of Adam and Eve and their ejection from paradise, Gen. III.14–19 records the three curses which God places on the serpent, Eve and Adam. In the account of God's cursing of the serpent, *Genesis A* shows nearly complete conformity to the sense and diction of the Old Latin version, and this correspondence in one instance provides sound justification for emending the received Old English text in Junius 11: '[p. 42, final lines] þu scealt wideferhð werg [**g** written over erasure] þinum breostum bearm (**m** fills out last line] / [p. 43, first line] tredan brade eorðan'. These words (906–7) as they stand do not lend themselves to division into metrically correct lines, and the grammar does not construe.[53] The standard emendation of *werg* ('accursed') to *werig* ('weary') obscures the content of God's malediction, which condemns the serpent to move on the ground (Gen. III.14).[54] The rare Hebrew word used to describe the underside of a reptile was taken by the compilers of the Septuagint to signify either the breast or the belly of the serpent,[55] and this ambiguity leads to its rendering in the Greek text by two separate terms ($\tau\hat{\omega}$ $\sigma\tau\acute{\eta}\vartheta\epsilon\iota$ $\sigma o\upsilon$ $\kappa\alpha\grave{\iota}$ $\tau\hat{\eta}$ $\kappa o\iota\lambda\acute{\iota}\alpha$) which influenced the Old Latin versions (Bede

---

'conscience') and *sceaðen* ('harmed', 'disrupted'), apparently describing Adam's mental turmoil. The previously unremarked phrase 'sceð(ð)eð on mode' occurs as a textual variant in *Bede(OCa)* 86.34 with reference to original sin and diabolical temptation (see below, n. 54).

53 The original manuscript pointing fails, a point added after *þinum* by a corrector lacks authority, and *bearm*, *brade* and *eorðan* all seem to be in the accusative singular. See facsimile in *The Cædmon Manuscript of Anglo-Saxon Biblical Poetry: Junius XI in the Bodleian Library*, ed. I. Gollancz (London, 1927), at pp. 42–3, and discussion with review of earlier scholarship by Doane (*Genesis A*, pp. 243–4).

54 The emendation appears in ASPR1, at 30, line 906b. This solution ignores the scribe's deliberate correction to *werg* ('accursed'). The prose *Bede* three times (86.29, 86.34 and 88.7) employs the phrase 'se weriga gast' ('the accursed spirit') in translating Gregory's remarks (quoted in *Historia ecclesiastica* I.xxvii.9) on the serpent, original sin and the devil ('malignus spiritus'). The alteration in ASPR of *brade* to *bradre* (907b) does create a reading, 'bearm . . . eorðan' (907), which is a plausible systematic variant of 'eorðan bearm' (*GenA* 1488b; cf. *Beo* 1137a 'foldan bearm'), but this is a misleading felicity of diction.

55 See Skinner, *A Critical and Exegetical Commentary*, pp. 78–9, and *A Hebrew and English Lexicon*, ed. Brown *et al.*, p. 161, *s.v.* גָּחוֹן . The word occurs only once elsewhere in the Old Testament, at Lev. XI.42.

records, 'antiqua translatio habet, *Pectore et uentre repes*').[56] King Alfred witnesses the continuing circulation of this verse in his translation of Gregory's *Cura pastoralis*: 'On ðinre wambe 7 on ðinum breostum ðu scealt snican.'[57] A change of *bearm* to *bearme* in the Old English text cited above produces a reading whose agreement with the Old Latin text of the verse, 'super pectus tuum et ventrem tuum ambulabis' (E), is remarkably precise:[58]

> þu scealt wideferhð,   werg þinum breostum,
> bearme, tredan   brade eorðan.[59]

The emendation removes all metrical and grammatical inconsistency from these lines, and requires only an addition of a single letter precisely where it (or a mark of suspension) would be most likely to drop out (at the end of the last word on the page).[60] The phrase 'þu scealt . . . tredan', moreover, suggests *ambulabis* ('you will walk') from the European text of the Vetus Latina rather than Vulgate *gradieris* or Old Latin *repes* ('you will creep') of the earlier, African text (quoted above from Bede).[61] Similarly in the concluding declaration by

---

[56] *Adnotationes in principium Genesis* I.iii.14 (CCSL 118A, 65). An exegetical interpretation of *pectus* and *venter* which stressed the opposition of intellect and libido provided the Old Latin form of this verse with a wide circulation; the quotation from Bede continues, 'Repit autem pectore cum terrenas hominibus, quos sua membra facere desiderat, cogitationes suggerit. Repit et uentre cum eos ingluuie superatos in aestum libidinis excitat.' Bede's synthetic exegesis has affinities with the commentaries of Ambrose, Augustine and Isidore (see notes by C. Jones in the edition cited) but the form in which he cites the African text (K) of Gen. III.14 is not derived directly from these sources and suggests that he knew the Old Latin text at first hand.

[57] *CP(H)* 311.1. The Gregorian original is identical in form to that cited by Bede. For additional evidence for the circulation of the verse in secondary works known in Anglo-Saxon England, see previously unnoticed loci in Wigbod, *Quaestiones super librum Genesis* (PL 96, col. 1163, following Jerome), and Hrabanus Maurus, *In Genesim* I.18 (PL 107, col. 495, following Bede).

[58] The dual terminology of the emended Old English text closely resembles the Greek text in its inclusion of a single possessive (*þinum*, cf. Greek σοῦ) with *breostum* and none with *bearme*; cf. Ambrose, *De fuga saeculi* xlii (CSEL 32.2, 196), for the single possessive in an Old Latin text. The collocation occurs also in a martyrological allusion to John the Evangelist (*Mart* 1 (27 Dec.) *Herz* 8.17–18), who reclines 'on þæs hælendes bearme ond ofer his breost'; cf. Lat. 'super pectus Magistri' (Isidore, *De ortu et obitu patrum* lxxii: PL 83, col. 151) and, for Anglo-Latin use of a lost source of the tradition, see *Aldhelmi opera*, ed. R. Ehwald, MGH Auct. antiq. 15 (Berlin, 1919), 254 and 372 (esp. *Carmen de virginitate* 462: 'Pectore de sacro sorbebat . . .'). The collocation of *wamb* and *breost* (as in Alfred's translation) is found in *PsGl(CGJ)* XXI.10 (translating Latin 'ex utero . . . ab uberibus' in ps. XXI.10).

[59] This emendation and the proposed scheme of line-division find independent support (without recourse to the Latin text) most recently in Doane's commentary (*Genesis A*, pp. 243–4, corroborating the earlier analyses of Kock and others), which translates, 'You must forever, accursed, on your breast, on your belly, tread broad earth.'

[60] For abbreviation of **e** by a supralinear stroke and examples of loss of final **e**, see *The Cædmon Manuscript*, ed. Gollancz, p. xxvii.

[61] For the translation of *ambulare* by *tredan* in Old English verse, see *PPs* CIII.4 (for ps. CIII.3).

God that the enmity he will cause between the serpent and womankind will rebound on the creature's head (Gen. III.15), 'and þin heafod tredeð / fah mid fotum sinum',[62] *tredeð* agrees with common Old Latin *calcabit* ('will tread under foot') against Vulgae *conteret* ('will pulverize').[63] The account of the cursing of Eve in *Genesis A* also may witness the influence of Old Latin diction in its description of the burdens of childbirth (Gen. III.16):

> . . . þurh wop and heaf   on woruld cennan
> þurh sar micel   sunu and dohtor.[64]

The use of the formula 'wop and heaf'[65] to express the vocal and emotional manifestations of childbirth offers a remarkably apt rendering of the normal form of the verse in the *Vetus Latina*, 'multiplicabo tristitias tuas et gemitus tuos' (L: 'I will increase your sorrows and your groans').[66] While in this respect *Genesis A* clearly stands closer to the Old Latin reading than to Jerome's translation, 'multiplicabo aerumnas tuas et conceptus tuos' ('I will increase your travails and pregnancies'), the exclusive use of an Old Latin form of Eve's curse in *Genesis A* is unlikely in light of additional verbal parallels with Vulgate usage.[67]

---

62 *GenA* 912b–13a: 'and [woman] will tread on your accursed head with her feet', taking *wif* (911b) as subject.

63 Contrast, in the Vulgate-based prose *Gen.* III.15, 'heo tobrytt ðin heafod'. For the use of *tredan* in translations of forms of *calcare* (or *conculcare*), see (in verse) *PPs* LV.1 (following ps. LV.2) and (in prose and glosses) *ÆGram* 137.10, *HomS* 28 *DOE* 93, *HlGlOliph* c.46, *LibSc* 121.8, *MonCaKorb(DV)* 13.2, *MtGl(Rui)* v.13 and vii.6 and *PsGl(E)* xc.13.

64 *GenA* 923–4: 'With crying and groaning [and] with much grief [you shall] bring sons and daughters into the world.'

65 For the collocation of *wop* (or *[be]wepan*) and *heaf* (or *heof[i]an*), see (in verse) *GuthA* 615b–16a, *GuthB* 1047b, *JDay II* 90b and *MSol* 467b–8a and (in prose and glosses) *ÆCHom* 1 Thorpe xi 180.15 and II *Godden* xxvii.128, *ÆHomM* 5 *Assm* vi.63–4 and 8 *Assm* iii.546, *ApT* 8.25 and 10.4, *BlHom* 85.28, 115.15 and 219.9, *GD* 216.21, 243.2–3, 246.8, 258.7–8 and 282.25 (and cf. *GD (CO* against *H)* 125.12–14 and 140.20), *HomS* 23.81, *HomU* 12 Först 18.13, 32 183.1–2 and 55 398.36, *LS* 34.66, *OrBately* 89.18, *VercHom* ii.12; *PsGl(I)* xxxiv.14, *PsThorpe* xlvi.1, *MtGl(Rui)* ii.18, *Lk(WSCp)* vii.32 and viii.52, *Jn(WSCp)* xvi.20 and *LibSc* 26.6, 26.16, 29.15 and 171.8.

66 For *wop* as a gloss of *gemitus*, see *PSG(I)* xxxvii.10. The divergent readings emerge as a result of hendiadys in the Hebrew text, where a phrase with a literal meaning 'your pains and your pregnancy' denotes 'the pains that result from your pregnancy'; see *Genesis*, ed. E. A. Speiser, Anchor Bible (Garden City, NY, 1964), p. 24. Previously unrecorded reminiscences of the Old Latin text of Gen. III.16 occur in Petrus Chrysologus, *Sermones* lxiii.iii.77 and lxxxvii.v.66–7 (CCSL 24A, 376 and 538–9), Quodvultdeus, *Sermo de symbolo* iii.i.2 (CCSL 60, 349) and Gregory I, *Epistula* xi.xxxiv.8 (CCSL 140A, 922).

67 'Þu scealt wæpnedmen wesan on geweald' (*GenA* 919b–20a) clearly agrees with Vulgate 'sub viri potestate eris' (Gen. III.16) against Old Latin '(erit) conversio tua ad virum tuum'; see *Genesis A*, ed. Doane, at p. 59, and cf. R. Bergmeier, 'Zur Septuagintaübersetzung von Genesis 3, 16', *Zeitschrift für die Alttestamentliche Wissenschaft* 79 (1967), 77–9. Insular Latin witnesses to mixed texts of the verse occur in *Lebor Gabála Érenn* i.v, ed. R. A. S. Macalister, 5

The several distinct categories of Latin reading that have been suggested above as possible sources for the Adam and Eve story in *Genesis A* typify the range of Latin material underlying the poem as a whole. The most tenuous connections perhaps are those drawn between the phraseology of the Old English and Latin exegetical passages that have limited scriptural authority (such as the Ambrosian paraphrase of Gen. III.10).[68] This may be a profitable area for future research, as it remains to be established to what extent the poem owes a specific debt to Latin exegesis, glosses or marginalia (possibly embodied by an exemplar), liturgical paraphrases and similar non-biblical sources. Another difficult but promising area of inquiry involves uncanonical readings in *Genesis A* that occur at points where a native speaker of Old English has apparently misconstrued the Latin in a passage of Genesis, as in a reference to the birth of Isaac: 'bearn of bryde þone brego engla / . . . Isaac nemde'.[69] This may reflect an Old Latin reading in Gen. xxi.2–3, 'dominus et vocavit nomen filii sui Isaac' (I, E), where *dominus* is in fact the final word (and subject) of Gen. xxi.2 and the proper subject of *vocavit* (i.e. *Abraham*) is not present in the following verse (as in some texts of the Septuagint and their Old Latin derivatives).[70] A third problematic category of evidence deserving further investigation includes readings whose apparent affinity to the Vulgate arises largely by default because of the insufficient number of witnesses that have survived for the Old Latin bible.[71] These include most of the forms of names and chronological references in *Genesis A*, which have been omitted

---

vols., Irish Texts Soc. 34–5, 39, 41 and 44 (Dublin, 1938–56) I, 18, and Sedulius Scottus, *In epistolam I ad Corinthos* xiv (PL 103, col, 157), but neither witness agrees precisely with the passage in *Genesis A*.

[68] The bible, for example, never explicitly states that the forbidden fruit was an apple, that Adam and Eve hid beneath a single tree, or that they were guilty of sin and knew of it themselves, and yet frequent Latin additions such as 'poma', 'sub arbore' and 'cognoverunt peccatum' are found attached to or interpolated in quotations of versions of Gen. III.8–11 among witnesses to the *Vetus Latina*. *GenA* 880a 'æppel', 859a 'under beamsceade' and the apparently Latinate phrase 857a 'wiste forworhte' could reflect either Latin textual influence (the syntax would seem to support this) or witness a more general, devotional familiarity with traditions of the fall.

[69] *GenA* 2765–7: '. . . [Abraham's] son by that woman [Sarah], whom the prince of angels [God] had named Isaac.' Doane (*Genesis A*, p. 214) notes in the same episode the syntactic alignment of *GenA* 2773b–5a 'Abraham hæfde / wintra hunteontig þa him wif sunu . . . gebær' and Old Latin 'Abraham . . . erat annorum centum quando genuit Isaac' (I) in Gen. xxi.5 (the Vulgate text omits the name and recasts the syntax).

[70] The verse division between the unnumbered texts of Gen xxii.2 and 3 in Codex Amiatinus (see below, p. 184, n. 99) is also classified as minor in *Genesis*, ed. Quentin (under verses).

[71] The *Vetus Latina* fails entirely in Gen. vii.19, viii.17, ix.7 and xxi.24. The collocation of *GenA* 1474a 'grene blædæ', 1517a *ælgrene* and 2551a *grenes* recalls Vulgate diction in Gen. viii.11 'virentibus foliis', ix.3 and xix.25 *virentia* against Old Latin *folium*, *pabuli* and 'quae nascebantur' and *GenA* 1864 'wræc witeswingum' suggests Vulgate *flagellavit* (Gen. xii.17). But the Old Latin record is deficient in all these verses.

from the present study as unreliable for stemmatic purposes.[72] Apart from these speculative categories of Latin textual influence, *Genesis A* witnesses a well-defined range of biblical source material: common readings, peculiarly Vulgate readings and Old Latin readings. Common readings in which the *Vetus Latina* and Vulgate do not differ or in which either version could account for the text of *Genesis A* (e.g., such readings as 'ofer midne dæg' from Lat. 'post meridiem', discussed above, which could reflect either standard Vulgate or Old Latin variant terminology) produce by far the largest number of lexical parallels between Latin and Old English, comprising nearly two hundred of the verses translated in whole or in part in the poem.[73] Characteristically Vulgate readings in *Genesis A* occur sporadically, for example in the rendering of Gen. XI.5 (where *GenA* 1682a 'Adames eaforan' and Vulgate 'filii Adam' stand against Old Latin 'filii hominem'), XVI.12 (2289a 'unhyre' and 'ferus' against 'rusticus' or 'agrestis') and XVIII.20 (2412a 'hefige' and 'adgravatum' against 'magna'). There are many points of agreement between the poem and the Vulgate against the Italian text-type of the *Vetus Latina*[74] and a few against the European text-type.[75] Finally, a surprisingly large number of identifiable Old Latin readings seem to have exerted an influence on the text of *Genesis A* both in general patterns of vocabulary[76] and in specific episodes,

---

72 Typically Old Latin forms of names in *Genesis A* include 1066b *Malalehel*, 1551b *Cham*, 1628a †*Nebroðes*† (Junius 11: 'ne breðer'), 1723a *Sarra*, 1736b *Carran* and 1799b *Bethlem*, against Vulgate *Maviahel, Ham, Nemrod, Sarai, Haran* and *Bethel* (in Gen. IV.18, IX.18, X.8, XI.29, XI.31 and XII.8). Onomastic concurrence with the Vulgate against the Italian text-type of the *Vetus Latina* occurs in Gen. IV.18 (*GenA* 1067a *Iarede* against Old Latin *Gaidad*), VIII.4 (1423b *Armenia* against *Ararat*) and XIV.13 (2027a *Aner* against *Aunan*); cf. *Genesis A*, ed. Doane, pp. 59–60. For a recent study of a chronological reference with a mixed Latin background, see F. M. Biggs, 'The Age of Iared: *Genesis A* (lines 1184 and 1192)', *N&Q* ns 30 (1983), 290–1.
73 Cf. Boyd, 'Doctrine and Criticism', p. 233 (on Gen. V.24), and note that *GenA* 1248a 'bearn godes' clearly derives from Vulgate and frequent Old Latin (following Greek and Massoretic scripture) 'filii dei' rather than the critical reading of the *Vetus Latina* (E) 'angeli dei' at Gen. VI.2. (In *Genesis A*, ed. Doane, p. 59, the former reading is incorrectly claimed exclusively for the Vulgate).
74 E.g., in Gen. IV.12 (*GenA* 1015b 'seleð þe wæstmas' and Vulgate 'dabit tibi fructus' against *Vetus Latina* [I] '. . . virtutem suam dare tibi'), IV.16 (1052a *eastlandum* and 'ad orientalem plagam' against 'contra Edem'), VIII.1 (1412b–13a 'ongan lytligan' and 'inminutae sunt' against *cessavit*), IX.24 (1588b 'of slæpe onbrægd' and *evigilans* against 'sobrius factus est'), X.8 (1632b 'mægen and strengo' and 'potens' against 'gigans'), XIV.22 (2141b *agendfrea* and *possessorem* against *deum*), XV.2 (2183a *freobearnum* and *liberis* against *filiis*) and XIX.1 (2428a 'æt burhgeate' and 'in foribus civitatis' against 'ad portam Sodomorum').
75 E.g., in Gen. IV.12 (*GenA* 1019a 'arleas of earde' and 1039a 'freomagum feor' and Vulgate 'vagus et profugus' against *Vetus Latina* [E] 'gemens et tremens'), VII.2 (1337 'þara . . . lifige' and *animantibus* against *pecoribus*), XIX.1 (2432b–2442a 'eode . . . hnah' and 'ivit . . . adoravitque pronus' against 'exsurrexit . . . in faciem'), XIX.11 (2493a *blind* and *caecitate* against *orbitate*) and XIX.12 (2503a 'of þysse leodbyrig' and 'de urbe hac' against 'de hoc loco').
76 Note, e.g., the choices of poetic terms for living things in the rendering of Gen. I.28 (*GenA* 201b *feoh* and Old Latin *pecorum* against Vulgate *animantibus*), VI.7 (1299a *feoh* and *pecus* against

including Cain's slaying of Abel,[77] the tower-building at Babel,[78] and, most remarkably, the accounts of the flood (despite its status as one of the most inadequately attested chapters of the Old Latin Genesis)[79] and God's covenant with Noah.[80]

The foregoing accumulation of textual evidence, provided that it receives the scrutiny and embodies the corrections of other scholars, has the potential to establish a new basis for evaluation of the literary-historical position of *Genesis A* relative to other Anglo-Saxon biblical writings and devotional literature generally. Proper consideration of this body of lexical material, for which the following tentative comments may provide at best a preliminary sort of ground-clearing, demands both a broad survey of known facts regarding the processes that produced heterogeneous scripture in the early Middle Ages and a careful analysis of the sparse evidence of the transmission of the text

animantia) and XIII.2 (1877b *ceapas*; see above, n. 38); but cf. also above, n. 75, and possible mixed readings at 203a *lifigende*, 1297b 'cucra wuhta' and 1311a *cwiclifigendra*.

[77] Doane (*Genesis A*, p. 60) notes, for Gen. IV.2, *GenA* 972 'eorðan . . . tilode' [*sc.* Cain] and Old Latin 'operabatur terram' against Vulgate 'Cain agricola', to which may be added readings in Gen. IV.5 (980a 'hefig æt heortan' and *contristatus* against *iratus* (but cf. 979b *torn* and 982a *yrre*)), IV.11 (1016b 'wældreore swealh' and 'haus[er]it sanguinem' against 'suscepit sanguinem') and IV.15 (1042b 'seofonfeald wracu' and 'septies vindictam' (or 'septem vindictas') against 'septuplum punietur').

[78] E.g., in Gen. XI.8, *GenA* 1699b–701a '. . . bu / stiðlic stantorr and seo steape burh / samod . . .' and *Vetus Latina* (I) 'civitatem et turrem' against Vulgate 'civitatem' (but cf. Gen. XI.5 'civitatem et turrem' in Old Latin and Vulgate).

[79] The description of the closing of the ark (*GenA* 1363–4a: 'Him on hoh beleac heofonrices weard / merehuses muð', i.e. 'the guardian of the heavenly kingdom closed the mouth of the sea-house behind him [*sc.* Noah]') corroborates a very rare variant in the *Vetus Latina* text of Gen. VII.16: 'clausit dominus deus deforis ostium arcae' (attested in Origen, *Homilia in Genesim* ii.1, trans. Rufinus: PG 12, cols. 163–4; cf. Gen. VI.16 'ostium . . . arcae' in both Old Latin and Vulgate). The characteristically Germanic circumlocution 'merehuses muð' in fact provides a remarkably literal translation of the variant Greek reading τὴν θύραν τῆς κιβωτοῦ. Doane (*Genesis A*, p. 60) notes examples of semantic and syntactic agreement in Gen. VI.9 (*GenA* 1285b 'nergende leof' and Old Latin 'placuit Deo' against Vulgate 'cum deo ambulavit'), VI.14 (1304a *reste* and *nidos* against *mansiunculas*), VIII.7 (1436–7 'fandode . . . hwæðer sincende sæflod' and 'videret utrum cessasset aqua' with no Vulgate equivalent), VIII.9 (1456b–7 'no hweðere reste fand . . . fotum' and 'non inveniens . . . requiem pedibus' against 'cum non invenisset ubi requiesceret pes'), to which may be added Gen. VI.7 (see above, n. 76), VI.11 (1293b 'synnum gehladene' and 1294a 'widlum gewemde' and 'repleta est . . . iniquitatibus' against 'repleta est . . . iniquitate'), VIII.4 (1421b *gesæt* and *sedit* against *requievit*) and VIII.11 (1471b 'gewat fleogan eft' and 'reversa est' against *venit*).

[80] In rendering God's commandment to Noah at Gen. IX.4 (GenA 1518–20: 'næfre ge mid blode beodgereordu / unarlice eowre þicgeað, / besmiten mid synne sawldreore') the compound *sawldreore* ('with blood of the soul'; cf. *Beo* 2693a for the compound and *ÆLetFebr* 223.16–20 on the prohibition) corresponds semantically to Old Latin 'in (*var.* cum) sanguine animae' (L); cf. also readings in Gen. IX.2 (1516b 'on geweald geseald' and Old Latin 'dedi . . . sub potestate' against Vulgate 'manui . . . traditi sunt'), IX.6 (1523a 'aldor oðþringeð' (cf. *Fort* 49b 'ealdor oþþringeð' and *Sea* 71b 'feorh oðþringeð') and 'effundetur anima' against 'fundetur sanguis').

of Genesis in Anglo-Saxon England. Mixed Latin texts of Genesis result quite inevitably from the sporadic nature of Jerome's revision, which variously combined wholly new translations from the Greek and Hebrew with recast readings from the Old Latin bible and left other verses essentially as they are found in surviving witnesses to the *Vetus Latina*.[81] Every Latin text of Genesis produced in the Middle Ages thus preserved a stratum of common, originally Old Latin, readings. A scribe who compared, say, two serviceable Genesis manuscripts, one containing the *antiqua translatio* and the other an acephalous Vulgate text, would have found it difficult if not impossible to determine the authority of the text of either from internal evidence alone. Familiarity with the Septuagint or with Greek or Old Latin liturgical lessons would have in many cases caused the scribe to favour the older version. The words and syntax of the Greek translation exerted a continuing influence on service books that Jerome's efforts were slow to erase.[82] The resulting processes of textual interpenetration would have accelerated in a scriptorium equipped with an adequate library. Patristic authors who flourished before the end of the fourth century (and the emergence of the Vulgate canon) drew regularly on their knowledge and memory of Greek and Old Latin scripture. Latin was, for such writers, a third-hand witness to the holy writings of Genesis and its use was often a matter of expedience, yet their words hold authority even today as a source for Latin readings in Genesis. For these reasons and many more the attempts of scholars to separate Old Latin from Vulgate in early medieval codices, now as in the past, are frequently misguided.

There is no reason to doubt that liturgical and exegetical writings circulated in Anglo-Saxon England throughout the period defined by the extreme dates for the composition of *Genesis A* (from the seventh century up to the date of the manuscript, *c.* 1000) that were in themselves sufficient to account for the Old Latin readings in *Genesis A*.[83] The first unambiguous reference to the availabil-

---

81 See F. Reuschenbach, *Hieronymus als Übersetzer der Genesis* (Limburg, 1948), and, on Jerome's use of the Old Latin bible, the second part of Reuschenbach's unpublished dissertation of the same title (Freiburg, 1942); see also F. C. Burkitt, 'Notes on Genesis in the Latin Vulgate', *RB* 39 (1927), 251–61.

82 See the useful summary by Sparks ('The Latin Bible', pp. 115–21).

83 H. Gneuss lists manuscripts of Anglo-Saxon origin or provenance containing relevant Genesis material in 'A Preliminary List of Manuscripts Written or Owned in England up to 1100', *ASE* 9 (1981), 1–60, under nos. 20, 159, 168, 194, 230, 271, 541, 544, 588, 601, 716, 720, 728, 730, 736, 772 and 845. For presumably lost pre-Conquest manuscripts, including a discrete copy of a *Librum heptaticum Moysi* and Isidorian or pseudo-Isidorian commentaries on Genesis and the Old Testament, see M. Lapidge, 'Surviving Booklists from Anglo-Saxon England', *Learning and Literature in Anglo-Saxon England: Studies presented to Peter Clemoes*, ed. M. Lapidge and H. Gneuss, pp. 33–89, at 66, 70 and 77–8 (under nos. x.46, xi.33 and xiii.23, 36 and 46).

ity of variant texts of Genesis verses in Anglo-Saxon England occurs in the writings of Aldhelm, who cites an Old Latin text containing a description of Noah's ark by name: *altera translatio*.[84] Of more than forty citations of Genesis in Aldhelm only three follow the Old Latin, and although these show some slight affinity with the Late African or Spanish text-type (S) this not need imply more than a familiarity with the works of Isidore.[85] Bede, who carried out intensive work on the text of Genesis,[86] cites nineteen different chapters of the Old Latin Genesis in more than fifty separate quotations, but there may yet be some doubt that he possessed a complete copy of the book (which he cites as the *antiqua translatio*) in its older version, as his notes on particular verses often are taken verbatim and *in extenso* from Augustine and other authorities.[87] Alcuin provides three citations of Genesis for the *Vetus Latina*, only one of which originated at other than second hand, but his efforts in establishing a pure text of the Vulgate bible appear to have had limited immediate impact on Carolingian scholars such as Sedulius Scottus (a source for more than a dozen Genesis readings in the *Vetus Latina*) or Hrabanus Maurus, who continued to cite Old Latin texts in his compendious exegetical syntheses.[88] There is no evidence to suggest that his reforms had a greater impact on ninth-century English scriptural transmission. By the end of the ninth century the writings of Alfred and Asser provide uneven witness to the continuing use of Old Latin texts in Anglo-Saxon literary circles,[89] and by the latter half of the tenth century the crucial Welsh manuscript Auct. F. 4. 32, the single most important primary source for the *Vetus Latina* in the readings of Genesis translated in

---

[84] *De metris* ii (*Aldhelmi opera*, ed. Ehwald, p. 63), citing Gen. VI.16.

[85] *Ibid.* (see comments of Ehwald *ad loc.*). The fact that Aldhelm's Old Latin readings otherwise derive largely from Gen. XLIX further indicates the limitations of his knowledge of the Old Latin Genesis.

[86] See C.W. Jones, 'Some Introductory Remarks on Bede's Commentary on Genesis', *Sacris Erudiri* 19 (1969–70), 115–98. Now, nearly twenty years after the appearance of Jones's excellent edition of Bede's *Adnotationes* (CCSL 118A), the work has received an appreciation by J. McClure, 'Bede's *Notes on Genesis* and the Training of the Anglo-Saxon Clergy', *The Bible in the Medieval World: Essays in Memory of Beryl Smalley*, ed. K. Walsh and D. Wood (Oxford, 1985), pp. 17–30.

[87] See *ibid.* pp. 24–5. To the citations of Bede in the *Vetus Latina* add two citations of the Old Latin text of Gen. 1.4 and 1.16 noted in *Venerabilis Bedae opera historica*, ed. C. Plummer, 2 vols. (Oxford, 1896) II, 393, and the quotations of Gen. 1.9 cited above, n. 20. For Bede's secondary knowledge of Old Latin texts, see *Adn. in princ. Gen.* II.iv.7, where he cites both Hebrew text and *antiqua translatio* but borrows the entire discussion from Augustine, and section II.v.5 of the same work, where he cites the Septuagint yet quotes Augustine extensively (CCSL 118A, 75–6 and 94–5).

[88] See B. Fischer, 'Die Alkuin-Bibeln', in his *Lateinische Bibelhandschriften im Frühen Mittelalter*, Aus der Geschichte der lateinische Bibel 11 (Freiburg, 1985), pp. 203–403.

[89] *Alfred the Great: Asser's 'Life of King Alfred' and other Contemporary Sources*, trans. S. Keynes and M. Lapidge (Harmondsworth, 1983), pp. 53, 258 and 273, and cf. above, p. 175.

Genesis A, had come to Anglo-Saxon England from Wales. If the mixed selection of readings that stand behind *Genesis A* came together through the adoption of citations from patristic authorities or enlightened borrowing from liturgical texts, they could have emerged at virtually any point before the turn of the eleventh century.

Previous discussion warned against inferring untenable connections between *Genesis A* and the Old Latin lessons of Auct. F. 4. 32, but some further consideration of the manuscript may point the way to a proper appreciation of the poem's base text in light of the arguably deliberate choices of reading that account for its heterogeneous character.[90] The *Liber Commonei* has been described by the editor of its facsimile as a 'classbook', but the leaves containing Old Latin and Greek excerpts of Genesis clearly served a liturgical purpose. The bilingual lessons were specifically assembled to perform liturgical ceremonies in the early Welsh church, and, though no detailed record of these Celtic rites survives, the readings presumably had a function similar to that which they served elsewhere in the western Churches.[91] Instructions for holy services found in the *Ordines Romani* require certain lessons to be read aloud in both Greek and Latin.[92] Auct. F. 4. 32 contains important Holy Week readings (including those taken from Gen. I and XXII) from an ancient, variable corpus of liturgical readings in Genesis (most commonly excerpted from chapters I–II, II–III, V–VIII and XXII) and other Old Testament books designated for reading during the Easter vigil.[93] The same group of paschal readings has already been claimed as a secondary source for narrative interpo-

---

[90] The following comments depart from the view of Glunz, *History of the Vulgate*, p. 13, who states that mixed insular and Frankish texts emerged as 'mere chance products of the copying of the originals, whether these contained the Vulgate or a pre-Jeromian text . . . [Scribes] simply took over the text from any available source, without ever inquiring to what extent it was correct or corrupt.'

[91] For discussion of similar collections of readings in European liturgical monuments down to the Carolingian period, see Fischer, 'Die Lesungen', pp. 154–9.

[92] *Ordines* xxiii.26–7: 'Et ascendit lector in ambonem et legit lectionem grecam. Sequitur *In principio . . .*' and xxviii(App.), sec. 2 (for the sabbath): 'Subdiaconus vero statim exuit se planeta, ascendens in ammone et legens non dicit: *Lectio libri Genesis*, sed inchoat ita: *In principio fecit Deus caelum et terram*; nam et reliquae omnes sic inchoantur. In primis greca legitur, deinde statim ab alio latina' (note use of the Old Latin text of Gen. 1.1); full texts are printed in *Les 'ordines romani' du haut moyen âge*, ed. M. Andrieu, 5 vols., Spicilegium sacrum lovaniense: études et documents 11, 23–4, 28 and 29 (Louvain, 1931–61) III, 272 and 412. See also *ordo* xxxB.41 (*ibid.* III, 472): 'Deinde secuntur lectiones . . . tam grece quam latine, sicut ordinem habent.'

[93] These are precisely the chapters of Genesis in which the most important Old Latin reminiscences in *Genesis A* have been observed. The comparative research of J. R. Bernal, 'Lecturas y oraciones en la vigilia pascual Hispana', *Hispania Sacra* 17 (1964), 283–347, at 308–18, demonstrates that the only known liturgical rites that prescribe all of these Genesis lessons

lations in the Old English verse *Exodus*,[94] but *Genesis A* may attest an entirely different sort of influence. It is not necessary to assume that, say, the account of the binding of Isaac in *Genesis A* reflects a special interest in the readings of the Easter vigil on the part of a poet. The poem simply may witness the circulation of a series of Genesis readings in Anglo-Saxon England in which certain verses had been revised over time to conform to the regular lectionary practice of the insular churches.[95] The Latin textual basis of *Genesis A* is intelligible without recourse to theories of contamination or haphazard copying. Its apparent preference for prominent Old Latin readings that adhere more closely to the text of the Septuagint than does Jerome's text may ultimately reflect the influence of Greek readings which would be familiar to many participants in the liturgy (regardless of their language training) from the bilingual lessons of Easter vigil. This, in turn, would suggest that conservative ethical considerations played a part in the compilation of the Latin text.[96] It must be stressed, however, that these conjectures concern only the archetypal Latin source from which *Genesis A* derives. The poem itself does not appear to have been written primarily to fulfil a liturgical purpose, though its inclusion in Junius 11 with other Old Testament material commonly excerpted for pericopes (Exodus and

for the Easter vigil are of Spanish origin. Genesis readings of course find many liturgical contexts apart from the Easter vigil. Pentecostal readings in Gen. I and XXII are listed by Fischer, 'Die Lesungen', p. 155. In 'Ambrosian' liturgy a modified form of Gen. III.8–11 (God's confrontation of Adam and Eve) is used as a *psalmellus* and Gen. XXII is excerpted as a lesson for the Quadragesimal; see *Manuale Ambrosianum ex codice saec. XI*, ed. M. Magistretti, 2 vols., Monumenta veteris liturgiae Ambrosianae 2 (Milan, 1904–5) II, 126 and 139.

94 For a sceptical critique of the evidence, see *The Old English Exodus*, ed. E. B. Irving, Jr, Yale Stud. in Eng. 122 (New Haven, 1953), 4–15.

95 It is almost certain that lessons from Gen. I–II and XXII would have appeared in Anglo-Saxon liturgical rites for the Easter vigil (Bernal, 'Lecturas y oraciones', p. 310, finds that these readings so occur in eight distinct eastern and western rites), and to these may perhaps be added, at the very least, the account of the flood. Alcuin specifies Gen. I.1–II.2 (creation), V.31–VIII.21 (flood) and XXII.1–19 (Abraham and Isaac) as lessons for the Easter vigil; see A. Wilmart, 'Le lectionnaire d'Alcuin', *Ephemerides Liturgicae* 51 (1937), 136–97, at 156; for corroborating evidence and discussion, see also Wilmart, 'Le *Comes* de Murbach', *RB* 30 (1913), 25–69, and E. C. Ranke, *Das kirchliche Pericopensystem aus den ältesten Urkunden der römischen Liturgie* (Berlin, 1847), pp. 342 and 360.

96 A continuous text of Genesis I–XXII that had been harmonized with liturgical lessons would be particularly useful for the prescribed reading of sequential excerpts from the whole text of the Heptateuch specified in early medieval liturgy for days in the Temporale with three nocturns until the close of the Easter season; see A. Hughes, *Medieval Manuscripts for Mass and Office: a Guide to their Organization and Terminology* (Toronto, 1982), p. 61; M. McC. Gatch, 'The Office in late Anglo-Saxon Monasticism', *Learning and Literature*, ed. Lapidge and Gneuss, pp. 341–62, at 354–5. Such a compilation would be 'conservative' in the sense that it sought to recover original readings of the early Latin liturgy and of the Septuagint to the exclusion of 'new' readings from Jerome.

Daniel) and the abrupt conclusion of the poem after Gen. xxII.13 might suggest that it eventually came to serve such a purpose.[97]

The immediate implications of the textual findings set out above are clear. The traditional view of the Vulgate Genesis as a template against which to judge the readings of *Genesis A* must be abandoned. A future comprehensive edition of the poem would do well to supply readers with a synoptic apparatus supplying distinctive Old Latin and Vulgate texts of individual verses (as subsequent evaluation of the present suggestions may find appropriate) and both when either version would account for the words of the Old English. Such a text would hold no less interest for scholars of early insular Latin bibles than that of any of the surviving continuous manuscript fragments of the Old Latin Genesis.[98] The mixed readings of *Genesis A* also raise a large number of theoretical considerations that merit further investigation. The course of future speculation in this area will depend largely on judgements regarding the unity of the poem and the base text that underlies it. As stated above, a diverse collection of Genesis readings could have arisen at virtually any time during the Anglo-Saxon period, but it is hard to place a Latin text of Genesis that was apparently continuous (up to Gen. xxII) and markedly heterogeneous in character at any point after the production of the presentation-quality pandects represented by Codex Amiatinus and the textual reforms initiated by Bede and Alcuin.[99] This does not prove that *Genesis A* or its exemplar antedate, say, the

---

[97] Critics have generally assumed that *Genesis A* is incomplete in its present state, but the fact that it renders only Gen. i–xxII, the most commonly cited part of the book in liturgical usage, could equally well support the impression that the first part of Genesis maintained a special status in Anglo-Saxon England. Among the writings of Bede, of a total of sixty-four citations of Genesis in all of the scientific writings, only one is taken from a chapter after Gen. xxv (see index to CCSL 123c at 705–6). Only six of the fifty citations of Bede quoted in the apparatus of the *Vetus Latina* occur after Gen. xxIII. Ælfric translated only the first half of Genesis into Old English prose: 'ic ne þorfte na mare awendan þære bec buton to Isaace, Abrahames suna, for þam þe sum oðer man þe hæfde awend fram Isaace þa boc oþ ende' (*GenPref* 4–6). No such independent witness to the latter half of Genesis has survived; perhaps Ælfric had in fact translated only that part of the book which his correspondent had requested and his disclaimer serves a rhetorical purpose.

[98] For these fragments, see above, pp. 170–1, with nn. 37–9.

[99] Glunz dates the turning point in insular scriptural history to 'shortly after A.D. 800', when 'the new epoch of the Vulgate history so differs from the earlier period that the later medieval text can on no account be compared with the various groups of the text in the earlier centuries' (*History of the Vulgate*, pp. 1–23, at 3 and 23). The transition may be placed more precisely with the completion of three complete Vulgate bibles at Jarrow or Wearmouth during the abbacy of Ceolfrith (689–716), but the quality of the Vulgate text in these books (witnessed now by Florence, Biblioteca Medicea Laurenziana, Amiatino 1 (Codex Amiatinus) and the fragments of London, British Library, Add. 37777 and 45025) varies greatly; see Berger, *Histoire de la Vulgate*, pp. 37–8. Glunz's own research (see below, n. 106) has shown that mixed texts circulated throughout the ninth century and survived the Norman Conquest.

eighth or early ninth century, since mixed texts of Genesis (and all of the books of the bible) presumably continued to circulate for centuries. But the deficiency in the record of surviving primary witnesses points up the importance of the poem as a unique source for the insular text of Genesis.[100]

The suggestion that a stratum of Old Latin readings underlies the text of *Genesis A* raises the possibility that the base text of the poem might be localized more narrowly within the framework of European scriptural history. Nearly all of the Old Latin readings mentioned in the present study are well established in the European text-group, and none can be associated exclusively with the Old African text attested by Cyprian, Augustine and other early authorities.[101] There are many points of agreement between the readings of *Genesis A* and the Italian text-type of the Old Latin bible, but many of these may be badly attested, common European readings.[102] The apparent affinity of several passages of the poem and the unique Spanish readings of Lyons 403 exhibited above might lead scholars to look more closely at the possibility of Hispano-Visigothic influence in the evolution of the base text of the poem.[103] But the most obvious explanation for the circulation of such a text in Anglo-Saxon England, given the known origin of other insular mixed texts, involves the

---

[100] The physical separability of Genesis leaves has badly limited the number of surviving Anglo-Saxon witnesses. The only extant pre-Conquest manuscript other than Amiatino 1 that preserves a nearly complete text of the Old Testament, London, British Library, Royal 1. E. VII and VIII (Christ Church, Canterbury, s. x^ex) lacks the folios containing Gen. I.1–XXIX.35. With the possible exception of the excerpts in Auct. F. 4. 32, there is quite simply no continuous Old Latin or mixed text of Genesis of insular provenance known at present that might be compared with the readings discussed here.

[101] Fidelity to the readings of Greek scripture (presumably a result of intermediary Old Latin influence) is perhaps the most notable quality of the readings witnessed by *Genesis A*. Comparison of the readings listed below (Appendix) with the Septuagint and with patristic citations printed in the apparatus of *Genesis*, ed. Fischer, reveals that about 70 per cent stand closer to the Greek text than to the Vulgate and about 50 per cent receive independent witness among the writings of such early Greek-speaking writers as Tertullian and Rufinus. Among other patristic authors, the readings show the greatest affinity to the Old Latin text quoted by Ambrose (siglum M in the *Vetus Latina*), who cites nearly 60 per cent of them, including several rare or apparently unique readings. Nearly 50 per cent occur in the writings of Augustine, but less than 25 per cent are recorded by Jerome in his pre-Vulgate citations. These preliminary figures, which may change with the rejection of individual cases or the discovery of new examples (though this is unlikely to alter the relative position of the stated categories), take account of all examples cited above (omitting forms of names and chronological references) and possible Old Latin readings listed below (Appendix) at Gen. III.8, IV.25, IX.21, XII.1, XIV.11 (if 1994a *orlegceap* is taken as a kenning, 'battle-beasts', corresponding to Old Latin *equitatum*), XVI.7, XIX.4, XIX.30, XX.14 and XXI.1 (but cf. 2762b *wordbeot* and Vulgate *promiserat*).

[102] See Appendix; there are other points at which *Genesis A* agrees with the Vulgate against the I text of the *Vetus Latina*: see above, pp. 170, n. 36, and 178, n. 74.

[103] See above, pp. 170–1, n. 37, and pp. 182–3, n. 93.

medium of Irish missionary activity.[104] Fifty years ago a continuous insular text of the psalms or gospels that exhibited a selection of readings as diverse as that witnessed by *Genesis A* would have been classified, *de facto*, as a representative of an established body of mixed Irish biblical texts. There is not sufficient evidence, however, to permit the reconstruction of an Old Latin text of Genesis that contributed to a specifically Irish recension of the Pentateuch, though the undocumented existence of such a text is nevertheless very likely.[105] The designation 'Irish' as applied by earlier scholars to mixed gospel and psalter texts of Anglo-Saxon provenance indicates little or nothing about the region of origin or chronology of a particular text.[106] Confident localization or dating of the readings witnessed by *Genesis A* is not possible at present because the evidence that the poem offers for the circulation of the Latin text of Genesis in Anglo-Saxon England far exceeds that which insular Latin biblical scholarship has yet brought to light.

APPENDIX

The following list is intended to provide readers with a key to the arguments developed above and to facilitate the reappraisal of individual verbal parallels. The first column includes references to chapter and verse in Genesis with parenthetical references to corresponding lines in *Genesis A*. Citations of the relevant pages of this article follow with footnote numbers supplied in parentheses. A necessarily incomplete selection of key words from Greek, Latin and Old English sources fills out the

---

104 On the insular 'Irish' text-type, see Glunz, *Die lateinische Vorlage*, pp. 63–90, and *Britannien und Bibeltext*, pp. 53–88. J. Kenney remarks that in genuine Irish biblical texts 'the Old Latin element is abnormally large even among "mixed" texts. It is irregular in its distribution: the readings sometimes succeed each other in quick succession, sometimes are almost entirely absent for many pages' (*The Sources for the Early History of Ireland: an Introduction and Guide* (New York, 1929), p. 626). The received text of *Genesis A* embodies one certain Irish gloss naming Noah's sons' wives (*GenA* 1547–8: 'nemde wæron Percoba Olla Olliua Olliuani'); see *Lebor Gabála Érenn*, ed. Macalister I, 211–13, and recent discussion by A. Bammesberger, 'Hidden Glosses in Manuscripts of Old English Poetry', *ASE* 13 (1984), 43–9, at 44–7.

105 An early survey of evidence for Old Latin scripture in the early Celtic churches, which is badly in need of revision, appears in *Councils and Ecclesiastical Documents relating to Great Britain and Ireland*, ed. A.W. Haddan and W. Stubbs, 3 vols. in 4 (Oxford, 1869–78) I, 170–98.

106 Manuscripts cited by Glunz, *History of the Vulgate*, pp. 63–9, as sources for the 'Irish' text-type include London, British Library, Royal 1. A. xviii (Britanny, s. ix/x; provenance St Augustine's, Canterbury), BL Royal 1. D. iii (Rochester s. xi), BL Add. 9381 (Cornwall, s. ix/x), Hereford, Cathedral Library, P. i. 2 (Wales, s. viii[ex]; provenance Hereford), and Cambridge, Pembroke College 302 (?Canterbury, s. xi[med]; provenance Hereford). It is clear that a corpus of common insular mixed scripture had appeared by the ninth century. The whole question deserves further consideration, especially with respect to books other than the psalms and gospels.

remaining columns. These citations should be used primarily to fix each complete reading (as indicated in the first column) in its proper context by reference to the printed editions. Readers who consult this list with *Genesis*, ed. Fischer, and *Genesis A*, ed. Doane, close to hand will have a nearly complete record of the available scriptural, patristic and vernacular materials that affect each point. Examples have been divided into three main categories: (1) unambiguous Old Latin readings, defined here as words or phrases in *Genesis A* which are not immediately attributable to conventions of Old English verse and which seem to render closely readings of the *Vetus Latina* (including interlinear variants and citations in Fisher's apparatus (respectively abbreviated *var.* and *app.*)) with no close Vulgate equivalent; (2) probable Old Latin readings which may reflect the influence of poetic usage but seem to render specific words in a Latin exemplar; and (3) possible Old Latin readings whose precise status must remain indeterminate for various reasons (lack of contextual support, deficiency in the Old Latin record etc.). The order of categories does not necessarily indicate the relative importance of their readings. An unambiguous Old Latin reading such as 'hean landes' (following Old Latin 'terram altam' in Gen. xxii.2) could arguably show no more than the influence of a common liturgical lection, while a probable reading (e.g., given the context, the dative plural forms *synnum* and *widlum*, perhaps rendering literally Old Latin *iniquitatibus* in Gen. vi.11), if tenable, would provide a forceful indication that a continuous Old Latin text was used in the course of the preparation of *Genesis A*. The listing of Old Latin readings is intended to be complete (though errors of omission and commission undoubtedly remain), but no attempt has been made to give a full account of the names and chronological references (see above, pp. 177–8 with n. 72), very badly attested readings (see above, p. 177, n. 71), uncanonical detail (see above, pp. 172–4, nn. 47–8 and 51–2; and p. 177, n. 68), common Old Latin and Vulgate readings (see above, pp. 172–3, nn. 42–3 and 50; p. 178, n. 73; and pp. 178–9, n. 76), or twenty-four apparent Vulgate readings in Gen. iii.16, iv.12 (twice), iv.16, vii.2, viii.1, viii.11, ix.3, ix.24, x.8, xi.5, xii.17, xiv.22, xv.2, xvi.12, xviii.20, xix.1 (twice), xix.11, xix.12, xix.25, xix.26, xxii.3 and xxii.13 (see above, p. 170, n. 36; and pp. 176–8, nn. 67, 71, 74 and 75).

References	Septuagint	Vetus Latina	Genesis A	Vulgate
		UNAMBIGUOUS OLD LATIN READINGS		
I.9 (160b–1a): 166–8 (18, 23)	συνήχθη...ἡ ξηρά	congregata est...arida (E)	stod...ætsomne...drige stowe	—
II.21 (178a): 172 (42–6)	μίαν τῶν πλευρῶν	costam [d]e latere (var.)	rib of sidan	unam de costis
III.14 (906b–7a): 174–5 (53–60)	τῷ στήθει σου καὶ τῇ κοιλίᾳ	pectus tuum et ventrem (E)	þinum breostum, bearme	pectus tuum
IV.2 (972): 179 (77)	ἦν ἐργαζόμενος τὴν γῆν	operabatur terram (E)	corðan...tilode	agricola
VI.9 (1285b): 179 (79)	τῷ θεῷ εὐηρέστησεν	placuit Deo (E)	nergende leof	cum deo ambulavit
VII.16 (1363–4a): 179 (79)	τὴν θύραν τῆς κιβωτοῦ (var.)	ostium arcae (var.)	merehuses muð	—
VIII.7 (1436–7): 179 (79)	ἰδεῖν εἰ κεκόπακεν τὸ ὕδωρ	videret utrum cessasset aqua (I)	fandode...sincende sæflod	—
IX.2 (1516b): 179 (80)	ὑπὸ χεῖρας...δέδωκα	dedi...sub potestate (E)	on geweald geseald	manui...traditi sunt
IX.4 (1518–20): 179 (80)	ἐν αἵματι ψυχῆς	in sanguine animae (L)	sawldreore	cum sanguine
XI.8 (1699b–7012a): 179 (78)	τὴν πόλιν καὶ τὸν πύργον	civitatem et turrem (I)	stantorr...burh	civitatem
XI.31 (1730b): 171 (cf. 38)	ἐκ τῆς χώρας τῶν Χαλδαίων	de regione Chaldaeorum (E)	ofer caldea folc	de Ur Chaldeorum
XV.7 (2202): 171 (38)	ἐκ χώρας Χαλδαίων	de regione Chaldaeorum (E)	of caldea ceastre	de Ur Chaldeorum
XVII.1 (2308a): 170–1 (37)	εὐαρέστει	prospere age (S)	duguðum stepe	ambula
XVII.4 (2453–7a): 185 (101)	Σοδομῖται περιεκύκλωσαν	Sodomorum circumdederunt (M)	Sodomware...behæfdon	vallaverunt
XIX.7 (2471b–2): 170–1 (37)	πονηρεύσησθε...ἀνθρώπους	malefacere viris (S)	fremmen...yfel ylda bearnum	malum hoc facere
XIX.10 (2488b–9): 170–1 (37)	εἰσεσπάσαντο...εἰς τὸν οἶκον	adtraxerunt...in domum (S)	abrugdon in under edoras	introduxerunt
XIX.5 (2775b–5a): 177 (69)	Ἀβρααμ...ἐγένετο αὐτῷ Ισαακ	Abraham...genuit Isaac (I)	Abraham...wif sunu...geber	natus est Isaac
XXII.2 (2815a): 168–9 (25–8)	τὴν γῆν τὴν ὑψηλήν	terram altam (K; I: excelsam)	hean landes	terram visionis
XXII.9 (2903): 169–70 (29–33)	συμποδίσας	alligavit pedes (I; var.: manus)	gefeterode fet and honda	conligasset
		PROBABLE OLD LATIN READINGS		
I.28 (201b): 178–9 (76)	τῶν κτηνῶν	pecorum (I)	feoh	(cf. animantibus)
III.14 (906–7a): 175 (61)	πορεύσῃ	ambulabis (E)	þu scealt...tredan	gradieris
III.15 (912b): 176 (62–3)	σοῦ τηρήσει κεφαλήν	tuum calcabit caput (L)	þin heafod tredeð	conteret caput tuum
III.16 (923–4): 176 (64–6)	λύπας...καί...στεναγμῶν	tristitias...et gemitus (L)	wop and heaf	aerumnas...et conceptus
VI.7 (1299a): 178–9 (76–9)	κτήνους	pecus (L)	feoh	animantia

VI.11 (1293b–4a): 179 (79)	ἀδικίας	iniquitatibus (I)	synnum . . . widlum	iniquitate
VIII.4 (1421b): 179 (79)	ἐκάθισεν	sedit (I)	gesæt	requievit
VIII.9 (1456b–7): 179 (79)	εὑροῦσα . . . ἀνάπαυσιν . . . ποιῶ	inveniens . . . requiem pedibus (L)	reste fand . . . fotum	invenisset . . . requiesceret pes
VIII.11 (1471b): 179 (79)	ἀνέστρεψεν	reversa est (L)	gewat fleogan eft	venit
IX.6 (1523a): 179 (80)	ἐκχυθήσεται (var:. . . τὸ αἷμα)	effundetur anima (var.)	aldor oðþringeð	fundetur sanguis
XII.1 (1750b): 185 (101)	δεῦρο, πόρευσο (vars.)	vade (L)	gesec	—
XIII.2 (1877b): 171 (38)	κτήνεσιν	pecoribus (E)	ceapas	possessione
XVI.7 (2268a): 185 (101)	τῇ ἐρήμῳ	deserto (E)	westen	solitudine
XIX.5 (2460b): 170–1 (37)	συγγενώμεθα	coitum faciamus (E)	hæman wolden	cognoscamus
XIX.30 (2793a): 179 (79)	κατοικῆσαι	habitare (E)	eardigean	manere
XX.14 (2720): 185 (101)	ἀργυρίου καὶ πρόβατα (var.)	argenti et oves (I)	feoh and . . . sceolfor	oves
XXI.1 (2761b): 185 (101)	καθὰ εἶπεν	sicut dixit (E)	swa he self gecwæð	sicut promiserat
XXII.3 (2879a): 170 (34)	εἶπεν	dixit (I)	sægde	praeceperat
XXII.5 (2881b): 170 (35)	καθίσατε	sedete (I)	restað	expectate
XXII.5 (2887a): 170 (35)	διελευσόμεθα	pertransibimus (I)	wadan ofer	properantes

POSSIBLE OLD LATIN READINGS

II.18 (173b–4): 172 (42–3)	βοηθόν	adiutorium (L)	fultum . . . wraðe	†adiutorem†
II.21 (177b, 182a): 172 (45)	ἔλαβεν	detraxit (var.)	ateah	tulit
III.8 (857a): 177 (68)	—	cognoverunt peccatum (app.)	wiste forworhte	—
III.8 (860a): 185 (101)	ἐκρίβησαν ὅ	absconderunt se (L)	hyddon hie	abscondit se
III.10 (869–71): 173–4 (51–2)	—	mente . . . conspectum (app.)	mine . . . ne dear . . . andweardne	—
IV.5 (980a): 179 (77)	ἐλύπησεν	contristatus (E)	hefig æt heortan	iratus
IV.11 (1016b): 179 (77)	δέξασθαι τὸ αἷμα	haus[er]pit sanguinem (var.)	wældreore swealh	sescepit sanguinem
IV.15 (1042b): 179 (77)	ἑπτὰ ἐκδικούμενα	septies vindictam (var.)	scofonfeald wracu	septuplum punietur
IV.25 (1113b): 185 (101)	ἀντὶ Ἀβελ	[in] loco Abel (var.)	on leofes [sc. Abel's] stæl	pro Abel
VI.14 (1304a): 179 (79)	νοσσιάς	nidos (S)	reste	mansiunculas
IX.21 (1564–70a): 185 (101)	ὕπνωσεν (var.)	obdormivit (var.)	swæf . . . on slæpe	inebriatus est
XIV.11 (1994a): 185 (101)	τὴν ἵππον	equitatum (I)	orlegceap	substantiam
XIX.23 (2540b–1): 170–1 (37)	ἐξῆλθεν	ortus est (L)	up . . . code	egressus est
XXI.2–3 (2765–7): 177 (69–70)	κύριος . . . ἐκάλεσεν (var.)	dominus . . . vocavit (I)	brego engla . . . nemde	vocavit . . . Abraham
XXII.9 (2904b): 169–70 (32)	τὸν υἱὸν αὐτοῦ	filio suo (I)	bearne sinum	filium suum

Anglo-Saxon medicine and magic

M. L. CAMERON

When J. R. R. Tolkein criticized the critics of *Beowulf*, it was because '*Beowulf* has been used as a quarry of fact and fancy far more assiduously than it has been studied as a work of art.'[1] The Old English medical documents have suffered from a similar treament in that critics have rarely dealt with them primarily as medical documents. So far as I know, none of them has been criticized primarily as a medical work, to the extent that its recipes and remedies have been evaluated for their usefulness as medical treatments. But they have been searched, discussed, emended and evaluated as sources for the study of paganism, magic, superstitions, Christianity and the influence of Christian and Latin culture on the primitive beliefs of the Teutonic peoples, and as indicators of the spread of Greek and Latin science among the Northern peoples.[2] Yet they were all originally conceived, used and finally preserved in writing as *medical* documents. They deserve consideration for what they were intended to be.

These medical texts make up an appreciable part of the corpus of surviving writings in Old English. L. E. Voigts has recently described them and their interrelations in some detail, emphasizing that they occupy more than five hundred leaves or one thousand manuscript pages, and that when we consider how great has been the loss of codices since Anglo-Saxon times, medicine must have been of considerable importance to the Anglo-Saxons.[3] And John Riddle was stating the position correctly when he recently wrote: 'For too long we have believed that the past was filled more with superstition and stupidities than with experienced judgments about medicine.'[4] In view of the effects of this unfortunate belief on the study of Anglo-Saxon medicine it is encouraging to see that scholars are now giving more attention to its medical aspects and less to its superstitious content; among these are Riddle himself, Voigts, Rubin[5] and others, the pioneer in this new approach being C. H. Talbot.[6] In this essay I shall try to show that these Old English texts reveal no small medical expertise on the part of their conceivers and compilers.

[1] J. R. R. Tolkein, 'Beowulf: the Monsters and the Critics', *PBA* 22 (1936), 245–95.
[2] E. G. Stanley, *The Search for Anglo-Saxon Paganism* (Cambridge, 1975).
[3] L. E. Voigts, 'Anglo-Saxon Plant Remedies and the Anglo-Saxons', *Isis* 70 (1979), 250–68.
[4] J. R. Riddle, 'Ancient and Medieval Chemotherapy for Cancer', *Isis* 76 (1985), 319–30.
[5] S. Rubin, *Medieval English Medicine* (London, 1974), pp. 45–69.
[6] 'Some Notes on Anglo-Saxon Medicine', *Medical Hist.* 9 (1965), 156–69, and *Medicine in Medieval England* (London, 1967).

M.L. Cameron

There was some reason in the past for the neglect of the medical aspects of Anglo-Saxon medicine. The early Anglo-Saxonists of Tudor times were more interested in attempts to discover in Old English literature evidence of the position of the early English church with regard to Rome, hoping to show that from its inception the English church had been relatively free from Vatican control. Later, in the eighteenth and nineteenth centuries, the growing cult of Teutonic (and Germanic) superiority led its proponents to search in Old English literature for survivals of Teutonic paganism before it had become tainted and suppressed by Christianity.[7] A chief literary source of supposed pagan Teutonic beliefs was to be found in charms, and as most of the surviving charms are in medical texts, these texts were searched for them to the neglect of their other elements. Then, in the early twentieth century the revolution which had taken place in medicine following the work of Pasteur and Lister in bacteriology and antisepsis, and the development of new drugs (many of them of chemical origin), brought about a rejection of the old herbal cures. The application to medical studies of the scientific method of controlled experiments prompted its practitioners to suppose that no experimental or observational discoveries of medical value could have been made prior to the use of their method. Thus we find Charles Singer (a medical doctor and historian of science) writing:[8] 'Surveying the mass of folly and credulity that makes up A. S. leechdoms, it may be asked, "Is there any rational element here? Is the material based on anything that we may describe as experience?" The answer must be "Very little".' He also wrote: 'A.S. medicine . . . is the last stage of a process that has left no legitimate successor, a final pathological disintegration of the great system of Greek medical thought.'[9] In another context, under the heading *The Leechdoms and Rational Medicine*, he wrote: 'To estimate the therapeutic armory of the leech it would be necessary to enumerate all the plant-names in all the texts. The result of so tiresome a task would not repay the effort.'[10] This attitude also made it possible for Wilfrid Bonser (a pupil of Singer) to write a 440-page book on *The Medical Background of Anglo-Saxon England* without analysing a single surviving remedy for its rational content, but instead devoting more than half of the work to the magical and superstitious elements which he found in Anglo-Saxon medicine. Indeed, he wrote: 'One must not necessarily look in a prescription for any physiological effect which the ingredients might have had on a patient.'[11] And again: 'Sterile

[7] See especially Stanley, *Anglo-Saxon Paganism, passim.*
[8] In J. H. G. Grattan and C. Singer, *Anglo-Saxon Magic and Medicine Illustrated Specially from the Semi-Pagan Text 'Lacnunga'* (Oxford, 1952), p. 92.   [9] *Ibid.* p. 94.
[10] *Leechdoms, Wortcunning and Starcraft of Early England*, ed. O. Cockayne, with a new introduction by C. Singer (London, 1961), p. xlv.
[11] W. Bonser, *The Medical Background of Anglo-Saxon England* (London, 1963), p. 8.

formulas, which could be applied *without any exercise of reasoning* [italics mine], alone survived for use during the Dark Ages. It is these, therefore, with very few exceptions, which appear in Anglo-Saxon medical practice.'[12]

Such a condescending and dismissive attitude to Anglo-Saxon medicine is the more interesting and extraordinary in view of the fact that in the Fitz-Patrick Lectures for 1903 Joseph Payne had drawn attention to its wrongness.[13] He wrote: 'Too often, those few persons who have interested themselves in these monuments of ancient science have treated them in one of two ways. Either they have picked out something especially unlike the ways of modern thought, and held it up to scorn as showing the folly of our ancestors, or else in kinder mood they have condescended to be amused, and calling anything old and unfamiliar "quaint", dismissed it with a smile.' Payne's sensible advice was disregarded: 'The only way to understand these old writers is to try to put ourselves as far as possible in their place, and conceive how nature and science presented themselves to the eyes of the early teacher and learner in the tenth and eleventh centuries.' He also wrote: 'That they tried to understand them at all is a proof of their wisdom, not of their folly.'

The turning point in a reaction to so negative an approach to the medical value of the texts was the demonstration in 1965 by Talbot that much of the surviving Old English medical literature derived from Greek and Roman sources, often intelligently rewritten and selected with obvious attention to the local needs of the compiler's society.[14] Later research of the same kind has only confirmed Talbot's findings.[15] But already before this time, there had been published two important and influential works on Anglo-Saxon magic. Drawing heavily on medical texts for their examples, Grendon in 1909[16] and Storms in 1940[17] had assessed virtually all the surviving charms and magical remedies to be found in Old English or in Latin in Anglo-Saxon manuscripts. Both scholars tried to arrange their material in logical groupings; both tried to relate Old English charm practices to those of other cultures, and both tacitly accepted the thesis that Anglo-Saxon medicine was largely magical and that the *leech* and *medicine-man* were frequently the same individual. Both also tried to trace the development of pagan charms into Christianized forms on the assumption that in a new form they would be more acceptable to the Christian church. Storms wrote: 'This method [his arrangement of the materials] . . .

[12] *Ibid.* p. 35.
[13] J. F. Payne, *English Medicine in the Anglo-Saxon Times* (Oxford, 1904). For the three quotations which follow, see pp. 38–9.   [14] Talbot, 'Some Notes'.
[15] See, for example, M. L. Cameron, 'Bald's *Leechbook*: its Sources and their Use in its Compilation', *ASE* 12 (1983), 155–82.
[16] F. Grendon, 'The Anglo-Saxon Charms', *Jnl of American Folk-Lore* 22 (1909), 105–237.
[17] G. Storms, *Anglo-Saxon Magic* (The Hague, 1948).

enables us to trace the gradual change that came over Anglo-Saxon magic on account of the new religion embraced by the Anglo-Saxons and the growing intensity of their contact with other peoples. At the same time we can see that magic did not lose its influence and its field of operation; it did not die out when Woden and his Valhalla vanished into the dusk, it merely changed its outward appearance and lived on as before.'[18]

It is true that Anglo-Saxon medicine, like that in all ancient and medieval societies, had a large component of magic. It is noteworthy that magical remedies are most common for diseases which were intractable to rational treatments, as many of the same diseases are today. But it is not at all certain that magic (or irrationality) played as large a part in Anglo-Saxon medicine as is implied in much of the commentary on it. I shall try to show that many remedies and practices usually labelled as magical by most editors and critics can be equally well explained as rational remedies. By so doing I hope to show that so-called 'Dark Age' medical practice was frequently based on sound observational and experiential backgrounds and that the physician was using methods which were perhaps as good as any devised before the discovery of the involvement of bacteria and viruses in human illnesses and the development of modern antibiotic therapies and the rise of modern chemotherapeutic treatments. Because Storms has given particularly full analyses of the charms he has discussed and has carefully adduced reasons for classifying remedies as magical, I shall take my examples largely from his *Anglo-Saxon Magic*. That I shall not be able to agree with him in many of his conclusions does not mean that I do not value his work, but it does mean that with a different outlook one may come to conclusions different from his. If one looks for rationality it may be found more often in Anglo-Saxon medicine than would once have been admitted.

A discussion of magical versus non-magical elements in Anglo-Saxon medicine requires that one have a working definition of magic. Magic is a notoriously difficult concept to define strictly, but a strict definition is probably not necessary here. Useful in our context is the statement by W. Nöth: 'The magician's semiotic fallacy is based on his neglecting the principle of independence between the sign and the "thing" referred to. For him, there is a homology or even identity between the sign and the "thing" referred to. The sign and the "thing" referred to are not considered as independent entities but as something forming an undifferentiated unity. In magic, this confusion of the dimensions of "object" and "sign" is accompanied by an additional assumption; it is expected that a manipulation of the sign (more exactly a signifier) causes a simultaneous transformation of the "thing".'[19]

---

[18] *Ibid.* p. 129.
[19] W. Nöth, 'Semiotics of the Old English Charm', *Semiotica* 19 (1977), 59–83, at 66.

In the medical records of the Anglo-Saxons there are, as Nöth has also pointed out, three types of remedies: (1) those containing a magic act and a magic formula; (2) those containing a magic act but no magic formula; and (3) those having no magic features.[20] There is little difficulty in recognizing a remedy of type (1); to it belong the famous charms. But to distinguish between remedies of types (2) and (3) may be very difficult indeed, our classification depending to a great extent on whether we believe that a remedy was used because of its supposedly magical powers or because experience had shown that it contained ingredients found to be effective against specific ailments. Distinction of types may also be influenced by the fact that a magical remedy may benefit the patient and a rationally conceived one may fail. At any rate, just because we may find it possible to give a magical interpretation to a remedy, we need not assume that it was magical to its medieval user. Although editors and commentators have been prone to assume the non-rationality of any remedy for which they could adduce a magical feature, on the premise that Anglo-Saxon medicine was primarily non-rational, it is equally permissible to assume that medieval physicians observed and interpreted intelligently the effects of their treatments, and prescribed medicine on the basis of what they had learned by experience to be useful for various ailments, sometimes using rational treatments, sometimes magical ones. It is permissible for us to suppose that a treatment was a rational one to its prescriber if we find in it elements which to us have a rational basis, especially if we have independent evidence that some of the surviving medical texts were compiled by apparently competent individuals. Even a casual comparison of *Bald's Leechbook*[21] with *Lacnunga*[22] will show that one was compiled by an expert physician (or under his supervision) and that the other was put together by someone with no obvious knowledge either of medicine or of order.

That there is more than one way to look at an Old English recipe may be illustrated by this one from *Lacnunga*:[23] 'Wið geswel genim lilian moran 7

---

[20] *Ibid.* p. 62.

[21] References to *Bald's Leechbook* will be to *Leechdoms, Wortcunning and Starcraft of Early England*, ed. O. Cockayne, 3 vols., Rolls Ser. (London, 1864–6) II, 1–299. Of this *Leechbook* Payne (*English Medicine*, p. 34) wrote: 'There is one book, a sort of manual for a doctor's use, of which I shall speak presently, the only surviving work of its class, which seems to imply the existence of others of the same kind. Had the single MS. which remains of this work been destroyed, we should not know what an Anglo-Saxon professional manual was like.'

[22] References to *Lacnunga* will be to Grattan and Singer, *Anglo-Saxon Magic*, pp. 96–205. Talbot (*Medicine*, p. 23) described *Lacnunga* thus: 'The *Lacnunga* is a rambling collection of about two hundred prescriptions, remedies, and charms derived from many sources, Greek, Roman, Byzantine, Celtic and Teutonic . . . The *Lacnunga* may show "the final physiological disintegration of Greek medical thought", but it does not show that Anglo-Saxon scholars were involved in it.' Yet this was the work on which Singer chose to base his opinions of Anglo-Saxon medicine, some of which have been quoted above.

[23] Grattan and Singer, *Anglo-Saxon Magic*, p. 106.

ellenes spryttinge 7 porleaces leaf 7 scearfa swiðe smale 7 cnuca swiðe 7 do on
ðicne clað 7 bind on' ('For a swelling, take root of lily and shoot of elder and
"porleek" leaf and shred very small and pound thoroughly and put on a thick
cloth and bind on'). Storms called it a charm and added: 'Just as the swellings
of these plants are cut up and pounded, so the swelling of the patient is made to
disappear.'[24] In another context he wrote: 'The three ingredients of which the
paste consists show some thickening or swelling, and just as these swellings
disappear by cutting them up and pounding them, so the swelling of the
patient will disappear . . . This principle of sympathy and antipathy is an
integral part of magic . . .'[25]

Let us see what another authority has to say about these ingredients. Mrs
Grieve writes of the lily (*Lilium candidum*):[26] 'Owing to their highly
mucilaginous properties, the bulbs are chiefly employed externally, boiled in
milk or water, as emollient cataplasms for tumours, ulcers and external
inflammations and have been much used for this purpose in popular practice.
*The fresh bulb, bruised and applied to hard tumours, softens and ripens them sooner than
any other application*' [italics mine]. Of the dwarf elder she writes:[27] 'The leaves,
bruised and laid on boils and scalds, have a healing effect.' The identity of
porleac is too doubtful to attempt to find it in a modern herbal. That the other
two plants are known today to be effective against tumours, used in the same
way as recommended in the Old English recipe, is a strong argument in favour
of our asserting that they were used rationally and not magically by the Anglo-
Saxons.

Storms makes much of the difficulty experienced by the magician or
medicine man in maintaining secrecy in the preparation of his medicines,
especially when trees or parts of trees are used, and quotes this recipe for
earache as an exceptional application of the magician's efforts to that end:[28]
'Genim grenne æscenne stæf lege on fyr genim þonne þæt seaw þe him of gæp
do on þa ilcan wulle wring on eare 7 mid þære ilcan wulle forstoppa þæt eare'
('Take a green ash twig and lay it in the fire, then take the juice which comes
out of it, put on wool, wring into the ear and with the same wool stop up the
ear').[29] It is difficult to see where there is magic or secrecy in this procedure,
which appears only to be an ingenious way to get fresh sap from a hard twig. At
any rate, the remedy is not Anglo-Saxon, for it is found in much the same form
in Marcellus: 'Fraxini recentem surculum, id est umore proprio adhuc
madentem, ex una parte in foco pones. Cum per aliam partem sucus ebulliet,

---

[24] Storms, *Anglo-Saxon Magic*, p. 57.   [25] *Ibid.* p. 29.
[26] M. Grieve, *A Modern Herbal* (Darien, Conn., 1970), p. 483.
[27] *Ibid.* p. 277.   [28] Storms, *Anglo-Saxon Magic*, pp. 83–5.
[29] *Leechdoms*, ed. Cockayne, II, 42.

suspicies eum diligenter et oleo addito tepefactum auribus instillabis.'[30]

Let us now examine a remedy which Storms classed as magical[31] and which Nöth assigned to his type (2):[32] 'Wið heafod ece hundes heafod gebærn to ahsan 7 snið þæt heafod lege on' ('For headache, hound's head, burn to ashes and shave the head, lay on').[33] Storms's comment on this remedy was: 'In pronouncing a comparison the magician supposes the two elements to be similar in hopes to make them similar. The idea that two objects are connected with each other may be based on similarity in sound, meaning, form, colour and so on.'[34] Nöth, using it as an example of his type (2), wrote 'The text reports a magic act since the effectiveness of the remedy is evidently believed to rely on the relationship of similarity between the therapeutic act on the one hand and the process of recovery on the other: just as the dog's head burns to ashes, the headache is believed to vanish.'[35] These commentators agree that there is a relationship of contiguity between the hound's head and the human head, and a relationship of similarity between the destruction of the hound's head and the disappearance of the headache. These are indeed magical concepts, and if they apply to this remedy, then it is a magical one.

It is useful when considering a recipe to compare it with similar ones found in other contexts and cultures. Marcellus gave two recipes in which *canis caput* ('hound's head') reduced to ashes was an ingredient. One was a remedy for anal fissures and the other for moist ulcers of the genitals.[36] For one of these treatments, Marcellus wrote that these ashes of hound's head were more effective than spodium (zinc oxide), which is a desiccant and still an ingredient of the zinc ointments prescribed for skin eruptions. There is a possibility that the hound's head in these recipes of Marcellus was magical in intent, the effectiveness depending on a relationship of negative contiguity (head *vs.* perineum). But the comparison of the ashes with spodium makes it doubtful; it appears that the ashes were prescribed simply because they were known to dry up wet ulcers better than another well-known desiccant.

The *Leechbook* recipe and those of Marcellus are very brief. They give no supplementary information to aid us in choosing one translation of *canis caput* or *hundes heafod* over another. In fact, ch. 88 of the *Herbarium of Pseudo-Apuleius* deals with a plant called in the Latin version *canis caput* and in the Old English version *hundes heafod*.[37] Only one treatment is given, for epifora (excessive

---

[30] *Marcelli De Medicamentis Liber*, ed. M. Niedermann, rev. R. Liechtenhan, 2 vols., Corpus Medicorum Latinorum 5 (Berlin, 1968), 170.

[31] Storms, *Anglo-Saxon Magic*, p. 56.   [32] Nöth, 'Semiotics', pp. 63–4.

[33] *Leechdoms*, ed. Cockayne, II, 20.   [34] Storms, *Anglo-Saxon Magic*, p. 56.

[35] Nöth, 'Semiotics', p. 64.   [36] *Marcelli de medicamentis*, ed. Niedermann, pp. 548 and 566.

[37] *The Old English Herbarium and Medicina de quadrupedibus*, ed. H. J. De Vriend, EETS os 286 (London, 1984), 126.

watering of the eyes) which it was said to relieve quickly. It should be noticed that this ailment presumably required a desiccating agent. Now, this *canis caput* is a species of snapdragon, *Antirrhinum orontium*, which together with related species of the same genus and with toadflax (*Linaria vulgaris*) of a closely related genus is still prescribed in herbal medicine to treat ulcers, skin eruptions and haemorrhoids.[38] On the other hand, three remedies in the *Medicina de quadrupedibus* call for the ashes of burned dog's head, for a cancerous wound, for a hangnail and for bite of a mad dog.[39] These are quite different from the uses assigned to *hound's head* by Marcellus and the *Leechbook*. There is a good possibility that the *canis caput* of Marcellus and the *hundes heafod* of the *Leechbook* was a plant, and if it was a plant then the arguments for contiguity and similarity brought forward by Storms and Nöth do not apply. At this late time we do not have the information to decide between plant and animal origin for the ashes, but while there is any doubt at all we are not in a position to assert that the recipe was magical to its medieval users.

Two other remedies for headache in the same chapter of the *Leechbook* have ashes as an ingredient.[40] Storms has not commented on the one of them which calls for ashes of willow and oil made up to a paste with three other crushed herbs. The other calls for ashes of hart's horn mixed with vinegar and juice of roses. Storms[41] used the same arguments of similarity and contiguity as he used for *hundes heafod* to give it a magical significance. But ashes of hart's horn (calcined hart's horn) was a common source of ammonium salts in ancient and medieval times, and with vinegar formed 'smelling salts', giving off the vapour of ammonia. The recipe of the *Leechbook* is very old, and was given earlier by Pliny,[42] Pliny the Younger[43] and Marcellus[44] as a treatment for headache. As a remedy it is completely rational, and there is no need to ascribe magical properties to it.

Another remedy to which Storms attributed the magical concept of similarity is this one: 'Wiþ magan wærce . . . gnid on eced 7 on wæter polleian sele drincan sona þæt sar toglit' ('For distress of the stomach . . . rub pennyroyal in vinegar and water, give to drink, the pain [or sickness] goes away at once').[45] Storms translated *magan wærce* by *heartburn* and commented:[46] 'There is the notion of similarity: the sharp sour taste of vinegar is employed against the

---

[38] Grieve, *Herbal*, p. 746 (who does not mention haemorrhoids).

[39] *Old English Herbarium*, ed. De Vriend, p. 270.

[40] *Leechdoms*, ed. Cockayne, II, 18 and 20.   [41] Storms, *Anglo-Saxon Magic*, p. 57.

[42] *C. Plinii Secundi naturalis historiae libri XXXVII*, ed. K. Mayhoff and L. Jan, 5 vols. (Leipzig, 1875–1906) V, 301.

[43] *Plinii Secundi Iunioris qui feruntur de medicina libri tres*, ed. A. Önnerfors, Corpus Medicorum Latinorum 3 (Berlin 1946), 8.

[44] *Marcelli de medicamentis*, ed. Niedermann, p. 72.

[45] *Leechdoms*, ed. Cockayne, II, 356.   [46] Storms, *Anglo-Saxon Magic*, p. 70.

sharp sour taste produced by heartburn.' The *Leechbook* remedy seems to be a direct descendant of one given by Marcellus:[47] 'puleium tritum uel in aqua maceratum adiecto aceti paululo et potum nauseam stomachi sedat.' It had already been given by Dioscorides:[48] '[pennyroyal] drunk with sour wine soothes nausea and gnawings of the stomach.' It is found in the *Herbarium of Pseudo-Apuleius* and in its Old English translation where *nauseam* is translated by *wlættan*.[49] As the Latin originals do not refer to heartburn (*cardiaglia, cardiacus morbus*), it is doubtful that the English translation equated *wærc* or *wlætta* with it either, so that Storms's translation is at best misleading. Moreover, pennyroyal (*Mentha pulegium*), like most species of the genus *Mentha*, is carminative and still has a place in medicine for its ability to relieve a distressed stomach.[50] It was formerly used as a seasoning for sausages, but that use has been largely abandoned because its peculiar, strong taste is not to our liking today. However, garden mint is still prepared with vinegar as a sauce to accompany meats, especially lamb and mutton, where it serves to counteract the effects of the fattiness of the meat. If the complaint for which the remedy was prescribed was not heartburn, then the similarity between vinegar and acid eructation is lost. That pennyroyal is an effective carminative indicates that the remedy is almost certainly rational and not magical. It seems to me certain that it was a rational remedy with no magical connotations for its medieval prescriber.

Whenever possible, remedies should be considered in context with reference to their origins when these can be determined. Storms found magical elements in the first of the two remedies which follow: 'Wiþ ealdum heafod ece genim dweorge dwostlan wyl on ele oððe on butran smire þe þunwongan 7 bufan þam eagum on ufan þæt heafod þeah him sie gemynd oncyrred he biþ hal. Wiþ swiþe ealdum heafod ece nim sealt 7 rudan 7 ifig crop cnua ealle to somne do on hunig 7 smire mid þa þunwangan 7 þone hnifel 7 ufan þæt heafod' ('For old headache, take pennyroyal, boil in oil or in butter, anoint the temples and above the eyes on top of the head; even if his mind is turned he will be well. For very old headache, take salt and rue and ivy cluster, pound all together, add honey and with it anoint the temples and the forehead and the top of the head').[51]

Marcellus gave three recipes which among them contain the features of these two Old English remedies: 'Expertum est mihi puleium in oleo coquere eoque frontem et tempora et cerebrum perungere';[52] '[ad capitis dolorem . . .]

[47] *Marcelli de medicamentis*, ed. Niedermann, p. 334.
[48] *Pedanii Dioscuridis Anazarbei de materia medica libri V*, ed. M. Wellmann, 3 vols. (Berlin, 1906–14) II, 41: Ναυσίας τε καὶ δηγμοὺς στομάχου μετ' ὀξυκράτου ποθεῖσα παραμυθεῖται.
[49] *Old English Herbarium*, ed. De Vriend, pp. 138–9.   [50] Grieve, *Herbal*, pp. 624–6.
[51] *Leechdoms*, ed. Cockayne, II, 304–6.   [52] *Marcelli de medicamentis*, ed. Niedermann, p. 70.

item prodest eodem modo ruta per se uel cum hederae baci decocta et capiti tepide infusa';[53] and 'Sal cum ruta tritum adiecto melli fronti inlitum certissimum remedium est.'[54]

Storms translated the first of the two Old English recipes thus:[55] 'Against an old headache. Take pennyroyal, boil in oil or in butter, rub the temples with it and above the eyes, moving on to them from the head. Though his mind be turned he is hale.' He subjected the remedy to a long analysis, finding in it only one rational procedure, the sedative effect of rubbing the head. For the rest, he found magical significance, because an old, persistent headache must have had an abnormal cause in the opinion of the Anglo-Saxons; because the Old English name of pennyroyal is *dweorge dwostle* and *dweorg* meaning 'dwarf' had magical connotations to the Anglo-Saxons; because the direction for anointing the head required it to be done in a certain way; because the magical number *three* was associated with the anointing (on the temples, the forehead, above the eyes); because *oncyrran* may bear the magical meaning of 'turned', 'perverted by magic' and because the final words *he biþ hal* are typical of magic and of medicine.

Let us examine these arguments in turn. In the first place, we really have no knowledge of how an Anglo-Saxon perceived a chronic headache, so there is no basis to assume that it 'must have had an abnormal cause', except in so far as all departures from health may be said to be abnormal. It is only in his translation that Storms found evidence for certain directions in the anointing of the head, and it is very doubtful that this translation is valid. The remedy does seem to be derived from Marcellus, and it is easy to see the Old English words as a rendering of 'eoque frontem et tempora et cerebrum perungere'.[56] The reference to pennyroyal (*puleium*) being *dweorge dwostle* in Old English is irrelevant in this context. The remedy originated in Latin or Greek where there is no association of *pennyroyal* with *dwarf*, so that it cannot have been conceived with dwarf magic in mind. The number *three* frequently has magical associations; that they applied here is extremely unlikely. It seems to me that the head was to be anointed on those parts most likely to benefit from the application of the medicine. It is true that *oncyrran* can mean 'turned or perverted by magic'; but it can also mean simply 'turned'. Anyone suffering from a headache of long standing undoubtedly also suffered from a more deep-seated cause, such as malarial infection, high blood pressure, infected sinuses, constipation, and so on, any of which might contribute to depression, i.e., turning of the mind. That the phrase *he biþ hal* is found in magical formulas is no more significant than that it is found in non-magical ones. Indeed, it may simply correspond to the Latin phrase *certissimum remedium est*.[57] Finally, this

---

[53] *Ibid.* p. 54.   [54] *Ibid.* p. 68.   [55] Storms, *Anglo-Saxon Magic*, pp. 39–40.
[56] *Marcelli de medicamentis*, ed. Niedermann, p. 70.   [57] *Ibid.* p. 68.

supposedly magical remedy is found together with another for 'very old headache', also derived from Latin sources. Storms has not attributed any magical connotations to it, although it contains three ingredients and is to be applied to three parts of the head. It seems to me that this analysis of Storms's analysis demonstrates the thesis that if one is determined enough one can find magic in almost any Anglo-Saxon medical remedy, especially if one is willing to believe that Anglo-Saxons could not think and act rationally in medical matters.

Examination of the simple recipes just discussed may have shown that they were not necessarily of magical intent, but does not present convincing evidence that the Anglo-Saxons used remedies which were developed on rational grounds to treat specific ailments. The question before us here is: did ancient and medieval physicians use ingredients and methods which were likely to have had beneficial physiological and pharmaceutical effects on the ailments for which they were prescribed? My answer is: Yes. To justify this answer, I shall choose first a remedy quoted by Storms. He discussed it in a section of his introduction entitled 'Mystification', which opens with these words:[58]

The magical atmosphere relies to a great extent on the sentiments of wonder and awe it excites in the specatator, on the feeling of smallness and impotence in the heart of the outsider. The magician is looked up to because he knows how to deal with extraordinary incidents, preternatural phenomena. Only an insider knows all the facts of the magic performance, and in order to keep his advantage all sorts of trivial details are added that derive their significance exclusively from being part of a rite. The origin and explanation of such details is difficult to trace. Even if they had some original significance, the meaning may have got lost in the course of the years, and we may be sure that in many cases details were only added to bewilder the on-looker.

I have no quarrel with this description of a magician's procedure but I do not think that it applies to the remedy quoted by Storms.

The remedy reads: 'Wyrc eagsealfe wiþ wænne genim cropleac 7 garleac begea emfela gecnuwa wel tosomne genim win 7 fearres geallan begea emfela gemeng wiþ þy leace do þonne on arfæt læt standan nigon niht on þæm arfæt awring þurh claþ 7 gehlyttre wel do on horn 7 ymb niht do mid feþere on eage se betsta læcedom' ('Make an eyeslave for a wen: take cropleek and garlic equal amounts of both, pound well together, take wine and bull's gall equal amounts of both, mix with the "leeks", then put in a brass vessel, let stand for nine nights in the brass vessel, wring out through a cloth and clear well, put in a horn and about night time put on the eye with a feather. The best remedy').[59]

---

[58] Storms, *Anglo-Saxon Magic*, p. 65.
[59] *Leechdoms*, ed. Cockayne, II, 34.

According to Storms, the main feature of mystification in the remedy was the use of a brass vessel.[60]

The ailment (a stye on the eyelid) would most likely have been a staphylo-coccal infection of a hair folicle. The ingredients of the salve were onion, garlic, bull's gall, wine and copper salts (these last produced in the brass vessel). Onion and garlic are antibiotics. Garlic juice in particular, even at high dilution, inhibits the growth of species of *staphylococcus* and of several other kinds of bacteria.[61] Bull's gall, still in the pharmacopoeia as oxgall, has detergent properties which make it an effective agent against many bacteria, especially Gram-positive ones such as the *staphylococci*.[62] Wine, freshly applied to a wound or sore, is also an antibiotic, but its active component, a polyphenol, is quickly inactivated by proteins.[63] In this salve it would have no antibiotic effect after having been in contact with plant proteins for nine days. But wine contains tartarates, and the methods of manufacture and storage of wine in medieval times were almost certain to produce a sour wine containing also a generous amount of acetic acid. Copper reacts with acids to form copper salts and also combines with tartarates. The chief value of the wine in the recipe would be to react with the copper of the brass vessel to form copper acetates and copper tartarates. The acids of the plant juices would also form copper salts. These salts are all cytotoxic, destroying human cells as well as bacteria.[64] The loss of a few tissue cells would be a small price to pay for the destruction of many bacteria and the clearing up of the infection. It is significant that the preparation was to be kept in the brass vessel for only nine days (during which the copper salts would form) after which it was to be stored in a non-reactive horn container until needed.

The remedy, then, contained four antibiotic agents, two of them (onion and garlic) especially active against staphylococci, bull's gall destructive of bacteria generally and the fourth (copper salts) toxic to all cells. The active principles of the plants would be mostly dissolved in the oily components of the plant juices and the bull's gall, in addition to its antibacterial properties, would serve to keep them in solution and to promote their penetration through any oily layer on the surface of the eyelid. Applied to a stye, this medicine should have helped to destroy bacteria at the site of the infection and to have prevented the spread of infection to other sites. It was right to call it *se betsta lǽcedom*.

---

[60] Storms, *Anglo-Saxon Magic*, pp. 71–2.
[61] E. Block, 'The Chemistry of Garlic and Onions', *Scientific American* 252 (no. 3) (1985), 114–19.
[62] Dr R. Brown, personal communication.
[63] G. Majno, *The Healing Hand: Man and Wound in the Ancient World* (Cambridge, Mass., 1975), pp. 186–8.
[64] *Ibid.* pp. 111–15.

The use of copper salts for prophylactic and remedial treatment of the eyes is very old. Anyone who has seen the Tutankhamen treasure must have noticed the green pigment depicted around the eyes of the mask and the painted head. It represents the eye paint much used by the Egyptians for cosmetic and medical purposes. Eye-paints were made by grinding the copper ores malachite and chrysocolla.[65] Where these were not readily available, as in Greece and Asia Minor, copper acetate was made by putting vinegar in a pot, covering the pot with a brass or copper lid and leaving it for a few days, or by hanging a brass or copper sheet above vinegar in a closed vessel.[66] Modern eye-shadow and mascara are lineal descendants of these ancient prophylactics. One must admire the long line of observant practitioners who developed the recipe. They not only made up an antibiotic treatment but included in it ingredients highly specific against the kinds of bacteria causing the infection, and did this with no knowledge of bacteria. To call them mystifying 'medicine-men' is to insult their observational and experiential pragmatism.

It appears, then, that there was no mystification in the use of a brass vessel. Indeed, a little thought should have shown that this treatment could not have been mystifying to a patient even without showing that the remedy was rationally conceived. Suppose such a patient called on the 'medicine-man' who recognized the ailment as a stye on the eyelid, and that the medicine-man said: 'I can cure your sore eye. I mix these ingredients and I put them in this rare and wonderful brass pot. Come back in nine days and I will put the medicine on your eye.' One can imagine the sufferer going instead to a 'leech' who said: 'Ah, yes, my lad. I see you have a nasty stye there; it must be pretty painful. I have here a hornful of just the thing to handle it. I'll put a bit on your eyelid now and give you some more to put on when you go to bed tonight. Here is a feather you may use to apply it. Take care not to get any of it into your eye.' No one with a stye on the eye is going to wait around for more than a week before being treated, no matter how mystified he may be by brass pots.

Storms referred also to other remedies in the same chapter of the *Leechbook* which called for brass or copper vessels to contain medicines for the eyes, and implied that the vessels contributed to the rigmarole of ritualistic and mystifying procedures.[67] It is significant that in all these recipes there is at least one ingredient with which copper would react to form copper salts. That the physician recognized the value of these salts is made clear in the last prescription of the chapter, in which curds (containing lactic acid) are to be added to the dregs in the copper vessel from which the medicine had been drained. The last injunction to the user is: 'Screp þonne of þæm fæte þæt biþ swiðe god sealf

---

[65] *Ibid.*   [66] *Dioscuridis libri V*, ed. Wellmann, III, 49.
[67] Storms, *Anglo-Saxon Magic*, p. 72.

þam men þe hæfð þicca bræwes' ('Then scrape off the vessel, that will be a very good salve for one who has thick eyelids').[68]

When the sense of a remedy is clear or when a remedy can be compared with analogous ones from other sources, it becomes easier to decide whether it has magical features or not. Let us examine one for the eyes which is found in the *Leechbook* in two slightly different forms, one of which reads: 'Læcedomas wiþ eagna miste genim celþenian seaw oþþe blostman gemeng wið dorena hunig gedo on ærenfæt wlece listum on wearmum gledum oþþæt hit gesoden sie þis bið god læcedom wiþ eagna dimnesse' ('Remedies for mistiness of the eyes; take celandine juice or blossoms, mix with bumble-bee honey, put in a brass vessel, warm cunningly on warm coals until it is cooked. This is a good remedy for dimness of the eyes').[69] Storms's comment on it was: 'The use of bumble-bee honey, of a brass vessel, and the heating over glowing coals instead of over an ordinary fire, together with the adverb *listum*, "skilfully, cunningly" belong to the sphere of magic.'[70]

If we trace the remedy back through time to its earliest recorded appearance, we get a picture different from that envisaged by Storms. A very close relative of the *Leechbook* version is found in the *Herbarium of Pseudo-Apuleius*: 'Ad caliginem oculorum. Herbae celidoniae sucus vel flos eius expressus et mixtus cum melle attico in vase aereo, leniter cineri [ferventi] commixtus decoctusque singulare remedium contra caliginem oculorum.'[71] Pliny, writing on *chelidonia*, gave a form of the recipe which is almost certainly the source of the one in the *Herbarium*. 'Sucus florentibus exprimitur et in aereo vase cum melle attico leniter cinere ferventi decoquitur singulari remedio contra caligines oculorum.'[72] Dioscorides put it more simply: 'Its juice being mixed with honey and cooked in a brass vessel over coals is good for sharpening the sight.'[73] Elsewhere he began a chapter on honey with the words, 'Attic honey is best.'[74] Attic honey, originally honey from Attica, became honey of wild bees through a series of misunderstandings and errors of translation. In the Septuagint and Vulgate versions of the Old Testament among foods forbidden to the Hebrews is mentioned *attacus*, an insect, apparently some kind of locust. At some time, this *attacus* became confused with *atticus* and both came to be used to describe a wild bee.[75] In Old English *mel atticum* was consistently translated as

[68] *Leechdoms*, ed. Cockayne, II, 38.   [69] *Ibid.* p. 26.

[70] Storms, *Anglo-Saxon Magic*, pp. 133–4.

[71] *Old English Herbarium*, ed. De Vriend, p. 117.

[72] C. *Plinii Secundi Naturalis Historiae Libri XXXVII*, ed. Mayhoff and Jan, IV, 146.

[73] *Dioscuridis Libri V*, ed. Wellman, I, 251: Ταύτης ὁ χυλὸς μιγεὶς μίλιτι καὶ ἑψηθεὶς ἐν χαλκῷ <ἀγγείῳ> ἐπ' ἄνθρακος ἁρμόζει πρὸς ὀξυωπίαν.

[74] *Ibid.* I, 165: Μέλι πρωτεύει τὸ Ἀττικόν.

[75] *Old English Herbarium*, ed. De Vriend, p. 332, n. 13.

if it meant honey of wild bees. As the bumble bee is the only wild bee in Britain which stores enough honey to make it worthwhile to rob its nests, the *atticus* there came to mean *dora*, the bumble bee.

We are now in a position to analyse the recipe. The greater celandine (*Chelidonium majus*) exudes a bright orange juice or latex from all injured parts. This juice in the fresh state is powerfully irritant, yet it has been used successfully (after drying or heating, which weaken or destroy the irritant properties) to remove films or spots from the cornea of the eye.[76] We have already seen that copper salts were used to destroy bacteria, because of their cytotoxic property. Honey also is bactericidal.[77] So the remedy should have done some good for a bacterial infection of the surface of the eye complicated by spotting or filming of the cornea. Both the juice and the honey are rather thick liquids and therefore easily burned when heated. This explains the directions calling for the use of a gentle fire and for skilful or cunning attention to the process of cooking. On the whole, the Old English recipe stresses just those procedures of preparation which could be problems for an inexperienced operator. Thus we see, when we have looked into the matter, that the supposedly mystifying elements of the recipe are in fact just the opposite; they are there to clarify difficult aspects of the preparation of a demanding recipe. This would not have been clear without the background supplied by the older forms of the recipe, and warns us not to jump to unwarranted conclusions because our information may be incomplete.

By far the majority of Anglo-Saxon remedies used plant materials. Even today, more than half of the drugs used in medicine are of natural origin, at least one quarter of them coming from flowering plants. Many of the plants supplying drugs today were in use in ancient times as well. This implies that some ancient remedies must have had beneficial effects. We have already analysed recipes where this seems to have been true and it shows that Singer's evaluation of the ancient herbals cannot be accepted without qualification: 'Most herbals are quite devoid of any rational basis. It may be taken for granted that the writer of a herbal is unable to treat evidence on a scientific basis.'[78]

Much evaluation is now in progress in pharmaceutical laboratories to test the medicinal value of many of the plants recommended in the old herbals. The results are often of much interest, as a few examples will show. Plantain (*Plantago*) species were frequently prescribed for a number of ailments, both in Anglo-Saxon medicine and in earlier times. They entered commonly into wound applications, and a number of remedies in the *Leechbook* and *Lacnunga*

---

[76] Grieve, *Herbal*, p. 179.   [77] Majno, *The Healing Hand*, pp. 115–20.
[78] C. Singer, 'The Herbal in Antiquity, and its Transmission to Later Ages', *Jnl of Hellenic Studies* 47 (1927), 1–52.

include plantains as an ingredient in wound remedies and for skin afflictions. They are an ingredient in some half-dozen magical recipes, the most famous being the 'Nine Herbs Charm', where plantain is invoked: 'Swa þu wiðstonde attre 7 onflyge/ 7 þæm laþan þe geond lond fereð' ('So may you withstand venom and infection, and the loathsome one which roams through the land').[79]

The plantains have antibiotic activity, having the substance aucubin in all their parts (leaves, inflorescences, roots, seeds). Aucubin is especially plentiful in *Plantago major* (the broad-leaved plantain so common in lawns and paths), in *P. lancelota* (ribwort) and in *P. media* (the hoary plantain). It is a glucoside which is itself antibiotically inactive.[80] In the presence of a suitable enzyme such as emulsin (a β-glucosidase which is present in the plantains and is made available when they are crushed) it is hydrolized to an active aglycone form. Consequently, any part of a plantain ground up will show antibiotic activity against staphylococci, streptococci and clostrida (the bacteria responsible for skin infections, for throat and mouth infections and for tetanus respectively). In spite of this high antibiotic activity, the derivatives of aucubin are not likely ever to enter modern medical use, because the activated form is highly unstable and tends to form sticky inactive polymers, so that plantain medicines must be freshly prepared. Given the long-continued use of freshly prepared plantain in medicine one may infer that it did exert observably beneficial effects and that its activity against 'attre 7 onflyge' was appreciated.

The lichens are another group of plant types used in Anglo-Saxon medicine. Storms drew attention to six remedies having lichen as one ingredient, the source being specified in each recipe. These were a hazel tree, a sloe-thorn, a birch tree, a church, a crucifix and a hallowed crucifix.[81] One is tempted to assign magical properties to ingredients taken from churches and crucifixes. But it is not clear that in all remedies lichens had magical functions. It is worth our while to look at some of the recipes containing them: 'Dolh sealf hæsles ragu 7 holen rinde niþewearde 7 gyþrifen gecnua swiðe wel þa wyrta gemeng wið buteran seoð swiðe fleot of þæt fam aseoh þurh claò swiþe clæne' ('Wound salve: hazel lichen and the lower part of holly rind and githrife, pound the herbs very well, mix with butter, cook strongly, skim off the foam, strain through a cloth very clean').[82] Or again: 'Wiþ gongelwæfran bite nim æferþan niþowearde 7 slahþorn rage adrig to duste geþæn mid hunige lecna

[79] Grattan and Singer, *Anglo-Saxon Magic*, p. 152.
[80] O. Sticher, 'Plant Mono-, Di- and Sesquiterpenoids with Pharmacological or Therapeutic Activity', *New Natural Products and Plant Drugs with Pharmacological, Biological or Therapeutic Activity*, ed. H. Wagner and P. Wolff (Berlin, 1976), p. 149, where it is stated: 'Against a culture of *Staphylococcus aureus*, 1 ml of 2% aqueous solution of aucubin had in the presence of β-glucosidase the same effect as 600 I.U. pencillin.'
[81] Storms, *Anglo-Saxon Magic*, p. 79.   [82] *Leechdoms*, ed. Cockayne, II, 96.

þæt dolh mid' ('For spider bite: take aeferth the lower part and sloethorn lichen, dry to powder, moisten with honey, dress the wound with it').[83] And finally: 'Wiþ lungen adle wyrc sealfe on buteran 7 þige on meolcum nim brune wyrt meodowyrt berc rago nefte garclife' ('For lung disease make a salve in butter and eat in milk: take brown wort, meadow wort, birch lichen, catmint, garclife').[84]

Several common species of lichen or extracts from them are still used in folk and patent medicines, particularly in Scandinavia and Finland. These have constituents which possess antibiotic activities, particularly against bacteria such as the staphylococci and against tubercle bacilli. One common lichen, the dog lichen (*Peltigera canina*) was used in the eighteenth century to treat the bites of rabid dogs (unsuccessfully), which points to a history of its use in the treatment of animal bites. Most spider bites are more dangerous for the bacteria they introduce into the wound than for any venom injected, so that antibiotic agents should give good protection against most unpleasant sequelae of spider bites. *Lobaria pulmonaria*, taken as a tea, has been used in this century to treat pulmonary tuberculosis. Iceland moss (*Cetraria islandica*) and species of *Cladonia* have been boiled in milk and the lichen-milk taken to treat cough and pulmonary tuberculosis.[85] The similarities of these treatments to those of the *Leechbook* are striking, and are evidence that the ability of certain lichens to alleviate certain ailments for which they are now known to be effective was recognized by the Anglo-Saxon physician (or some predecessor) who devised the treatments.

Lichens are neither easy to describe clearly nor to identify accurately. It is possible that they were identified for medicinal purposes by the substrates on which they grew.

There are substances which traditionally have had strong magical associations and it is natural to assume that their use in medicine is always magical in intent. For example, iron has had a magical reputation since the earliest times of its use by man. The earliest sources of iron were iron-nickel meteorites, and ancient man seems to have been aware of this origin. The two hieroglyphs used by the Egyptians to designate iron both have meanings associated with the heavens.[86] In spite of any magical associations there were medical uses of iron which appear to be purely rational.

Among recipes which Storms quoted as showing the magical use of iron is the following: 'Læcedomas 7 swið drenc wiþ aswollenum milte acele ðu wealhat isen þonne hit furthum sie of fyre atogen on wine oððe on ecede sele

[83] *Ibid.* pp. 142–4.   [84] *Ibid.* p. 266.
[85] K. O. Bartia, 'Antibiotics in Lichens', *The Lichens*, ed. V. Ahmadjian and M. E. Hale (New York and London, 1973), pp. 547–61. See also Y. Asahina and S. Shibata, *Chemistry of Lichen Substances* (Amsterdam, 1971), pp. 216–24.   [86] Majno, *The Healing Hand*, pp. 87–8.

þæt drincan' ('Remedies and a strong drink for swollen spleen: cool very hot iron when it is just taken from the fire in wine or in vinegar, give it to drink').[87]

A function of the spleen is to remove from the blood damaged and worn-out red blood cells and to aid in the recovery and re-use of the iron in their haemoglobin. The malarial parasite multiplies in red blood cells causing extensive damage and loss. Consequently a malarial infection puts a heavy load on the spleen, which responds by becoming enlarged and hardened in its attempt to cope with the situation. Anything, such as the addition of iron to the diet in an assimilable form, that will relieve the load on the spleen, will be beneficial. Hot iron quenched in wine or in vinegar will form iron acetate, in which form it is relatively easily assimilated. This remedy provides a rational treatment for an enlarged spleen, and was commonly prescribed in medieval medicine.

The use of iron in medicine is very old; some remedies appearing to be rational, some highly irrational. Pliny discussed a number of both kinds which appear again and again in medieval recipe collections. Apropos to our discussion is this one: 'Calfit etiam ferro candente potus in multis vitiis, privatim vero dysentericis.'[88] With this may be compared a remedy in the *Leechbook*: 'Wiþ tobrocenum innoþum cellendres sæd wel gegniden 7 lytel sealtes gedo on searp win gedo on 7 gewyrme mid hate glowende isene sele drincan' ('For internal rupture [or, broken-out inwards]: coriander seed well ground up and a little salt, put in sharp wine; put in and heat with a glowing hot iron, give to drink').[89]

Iron rust was commonly used to treat wounds, a form of treatment which may have had a magical origin, on the principle of getting help from 'a hair of the dog that bit you', but seems in later times to have become a wholly rational procedure. For example, under the floor of the valetudinarium at Corbridge near Hadrian's Wall, archaeologists found a chest filled with scrap iron and brass. It has been suggested that this was the source for the iron and copper rusts used to treat wounds in that hospital.[90] No recent tests seem to have been made on the therapeutic value of iron salts in the treatment of wounds, although their value when ingested in restoring the iron balance of the body is well attested. At any rate, a remedy containing iron should not automatically be labelled as magical just because it has iron in it. The iron may have been added because it was known from experience to be effective.

---

[87] *Leechdoms*, ed. Cockayne, II, 256; Storms, *Anglo-Saxon Magic*, p. 78.

[88] *C. Plinii Secundi Naturalis Historiae Libri xxxvii*, ed. Mayhoff and Jan, V, 217.

[89] *Leechdoms*, ed. Cockayne, II, 236.

[90] R.W. Davies, 'A Note on the Hoard of Roman Equipment Buried at Corbridge', *Durham Univ. Jnl* 31 (1970), 177–80.

Many recipes forbid the use of iron in their preparation. This has usually been taken as a magical feature, and is sometimes obviously true as in this one: '[Gif mon on healf heafod ace . . .] adelf wegbradan butan isene ær sunnan upgang bind þa moran ymb þæt heafod mid wræte reade wræde sona him bið sel' ('[If one aches on half the head . . .] dig up plantain without iron before sunrise, bind the roots around the head with "crosswort" with a red fillet; he will soon be well').[91] So much of the procedure in this remedy smacks of magic that one may feel confident that the proscription of iron is also magical. But there are other recipes where one cannot be sure, such as the following one: 'Gif se vic weorðe on mannes setle geseten þonne nim þu clatan moran þa greatan III oððe IIII 7 berec hy on hate æmergean 7 ateoh þonne ða ane of ðan heorðe 7 cnuca 7 wyrc swylc an lytle cicel 7 lege to þæm setle swa ðu hatost forberan mæge þonne se cicel colige þonne wyrc þu ma 7 lege to 7 beo on stilnesse dæg oððe twegan þonne þu þis do hit is afandad læcecræft ne delfe hy nan man þa moran mid isene 7 mid wætere ne þwea ac stice hy mid claðe clæne 7 do swiþe þynne clað betweonan þæt setle 7 ðone cicel' ('If the fig [haemorrhoids] become established on a man's backside, then take the roots of clate (the big one(s)) three or four and smoke them in hot embers and then pull one out from the hearth and pound it and make a sort of little cake and lay on the backside as hot as it can be borne; when the cake cools then make more and lay on and let him be quiet for a day or two. When you do this (it is an approved remedy) let no one dig up the roots with iron, and do not wash with water, but wipe them clean with a cloth, and put a very thin cloth between the backside and the cake').[92]

The recipe proceeds so rationally that one is brought up short by the injunction to use neither iron in the digging nor water in the cleaning of the roots. This being so, one may legitimately ask if there is a rational reason for these restrictions. A problem in discussing the recipe is the identification of *clate*. It has usually been taken to mean burdock (*Arctium lappa*), the roots of which are very large, often penetrating more than a foot into the soil. The roots are still used in pharmacy, but only for their inulin, a storage polysaccharide which is taken into the human blood stream in undigested form from the gut tract and excreted by the kidney in proportion to the rate of uptake. Consequently it is useful in studies of urinary clearance rates. The cortex of the root is very bitter, but no analyses of its alkaloids and those of the pith of the root seem to have been made. The roots also contain tannins which, together with the heat of the cake made from them, could have had a drying and comforting effect on painful, itching haemorrhoids.

Iron reacts with many plant constituents, particularly with tannins and

---

[91] *Leechdoms*, ed. Cockayne, II, 306.   [92] Grattan and Singer, *Anglo-Saxon Magic*, p. 150.

other acidic substances, to produce coloured (often black) products which are unsightly and often relatively insoluble in water. Oak gall inks were made by having iron react with the tannins in the galls. It is also well known that fruit preserves and jellies should not be made in an iron pot, because of the undesirable colour and taste which may result from the interaction of the plant acids with the iron of the pot. One recalls that when the Bishop in Victor Hugo's *Les Misérables* gave his silver cutlery to Jean Valjean, Mme Magloire protested because, she said, tin spoons smelled and iron ones tasted.[93] We may suppose that these reactions to iron were familiar to medieval herb-gatherers and that they sought to avoid them by avoiding tools made of iron when gathering plants which were known to react with it. (I have dug up a burdock root and cut into it with an iron knife; the cut surface quickly blackened in an unsightly manner.) It does not seem proper, then, to assume that a prescription forbidding the use of iron is in consequence a magic one. The proscription may instead have resulted from intelligent inferences based on observation.

Why the roots should not have been washed remains a puzzle to me. The same proscription was applied in the *Herbarium* to the roots of betony.

It must not be thought that, by attempting to show that many recipes usually accepted as magical can equally easily be accepted as rational, I am suggesting that Anglo-Saxon medicine was entirely rational in its treatments. Indeed, much of the *materia medica* of the Anglo Saxons was magical in intent. Magic remedies were often used to treat intractable ailments that even today do not yield readily to rational procedures. It is pertinent to ask whether any of the treatments which used the rigmarole of charms and incantations could have been of any use.

Many illnesses which have very real physiopathic manifestations have also powerful psychopathic components which, if corrected, permit the physician to alleviate or even to remove the other symptoms. It is becoming clear in medical practice that the patient's (and the attending physician's) attitude to the illness is a critical factor in the success of treatment. This aspect of treatment must have been met in part by the rigmarole of the charms, which would have put the patient into a frame of mind to accept the idea that not only the physician but also the forces of Nature (the gods themselves) were on his side to help him overcome the malignancies of disease-bringing agents such as 'the loathsome one which roams through the land'. A confident patient in the hands of a confident physician has a good chance for recovery.

Lewis Thomas, a distinguished physician and humanist, has recently commented on certain treatments for warts.[94] Warts are caused by viral infections

---

[93] V. Hugo, *Les Misérables* (Paris, 1966), vol. I, 131.
[94] L. Thomas, *The Medusa and the Snail* (New York, 1979), pp. 76–81.

and are peculiarly difficult to eradicate. He has described two modern treatments. In one a harmless dye is painted on the wart and the patient is assured that the wart will disappear. In another the patient under hypnosis is given similar assurances but no other treatment of any kind. Either method of treatment often results in the disappearance of the warts, even those of long standing. Thomas adds: 'If it is true, as it seems to be, that the human central nervous system can figure out how . . . to instruct its blood vessels, lymphocytes and heaven knows what other participants in the tissue to eliminate a wart then it is clear that the human nervous system has already evolved a vast distance beyond biomedical science'.[95] This inference, that the body has resources to meet the challenge of infective and other insults to its integrity if the mind of the patient can be given assurance that healing is possible, should be kept in mind by anyone studying the medical records of the past. If modern medicine is willing to admit the possibility of such cures and even to participate in their use, surely the Old English medical charms deserve a sympathetic appraisal as medicine.

There was a broad spectrum of magical materials available to the Anglo-Saxon physician, drawn both from his ancestral pagan Teutonic background and from the Mediterranean culture introduced by Christian missionaries, and the two were blended into a more or less coherent whole by their Anglo-Saxon users. On a very broad classification medical magical remedies can be separated into two groups: those which are accompanied by a recipe for certain ingredients, and those which consist of a charm text alone. An outstanding example of the first kind is the attractive *Wið Færstice*, which consists of a quite rational salve for treating muscular cramps and similar pains combined with a metrical charm.[96] Because of its length, it will not be used here as an example of its kind. Instead, this shorter one will serve to show the same combination of rationality and magic: 'Wiþ utwærc brembel þe sien begen endas on eorþan genim þone neowran wyrttruman delf up þwit nigon sponas on þa winstran hand, and sing þriwa misere mei deus 7 nigon siþum pater noster genim þonne mucgwyrt 7 efelastan wyl þas þreo on meolcum oþ þæt hy reodian supe þonne on neaht nestig gode blede fulle hwile he oþerne mete þicge reste him softe 7 wreo hine wearme gif ma þearf sie do eft swa gif þu þonne got þurfe do þriddan siþe ne þearft þu oftor' ('For dysentery, a bramble of which both ends are in the ground; take the newer root, dig up, cut off nine slivers (shavings) into the left hand and sing three times *Miserere mei, deus*, and nine times *Pater Noster*, then take mugwort and everlasting; boil the three in milk until they become red;

---

[95] L. Thomas, *Late Night Thoughts on Listening to Mahler's Ninth Symphony* (New York, 1983), p. 80.
[96] Grattan and Singer, *Anglo-Saxon Magic*, pp. 172–6.

then sip after a night's fast a good dish full, a while before he eats other food; let him rest quietly and wrap him up warm. If more is needed, do the same again, then if you still need it, do it a third time; you will not need to more often').[97] There is no doubt of magical elements in this prescription: the use of the root from the rooted tip of a bent-down shoot and the singing of psalm LVI and the *Pater Noster* nine times. The rest is a perfectly sensible and effective remedy for loose bowels. Of the bramble Mrs Grieve writes: 'The bark of the root and the leaves contain much tannin, and have long been esteemed as a capital astringent and tonic, proving a valuable remedy for dysentery and diarrhoea, etc. . . . The root bark, used medicinally, should be peeled off the root . . . One ounce, boiled in 1½ pint water or milk down to a pint, makes a good decoction. Half a teacupful should be taken every hour or two for diarrhoea.'[98] Marcellus also recommended the bramble: 'Rubi spinae, radices et coliculi teneri cum vino amineo austero ad tertias decoquuntur, atque ex eo uino cyathus ad diem ieiuno uentris profluuio laboranti potui datus optime medebitur.'[99] There is no modern evidence for the efficacy of mugwort for loose bowels. If *efelasten* is the same plant as life everlasting or cudweed (*Antennaria dioica*) then it too was probably useful: it is 'said to be efficacious . . . for looseness of bowels.'[100] There is no doubt that the potion should have done some good on strictly pharmacological grounds. That dysentery is very difficult to cure probably accounts for the magical elements of the remedy.

We must try to put ourselves, however difficult it may be, in the place of the medieval patient. Today, the physician imparts confidence in his healing powers by his white coat, by his air of professional detachment, by the framed diplomas on his walls and by the atmosphere of his consulting room. They supply just as much a non-rational part of the treatment as the intoning of charms. One kind appeals in a society which boasts of its belief in a world governed by 'scientific' cause and effect; the other in a society where all things were believed to be at the whim of a god or gods, beneficent or malignant, who could be propitiated or threatened by means of the proper ritualistic approaches. The milieus are different and the rituals are different, but the effect is the same, a reassured patient; so presumably the results should be similar. This is a justification for magical treatments in a society which believes in magic as a ruling factor in the operation of the universe, and if it does not work in our society it is because we no longer believe in magic in that way.

Having cast doubt on the 'hundes headfod' remedy for headache as illustrating Nöth's type (1) charm, or indeed as being magical at all, it is only fair to

[97] *Leechdoms*, ed. Cockayne, II, 290–2.   [98] Grieve, *Herbal*, pp. 109–10.
[99] *Marcelli de medicamentis*, ed. Niedermann, p. 476.   [100] Grieve, *Herbal*, p. 175.

present a charm which is undoubtedly magical and which owes its supposed effectiveness to the principle of association discussed by Nöth. This interesting little charm of undoubted Christian origin is an obvious example.[101]

Wið blodrene of nosu wriht to his forheafod on xrs mel:

$$
\begin{array}{c}
S \\
t \\
o \\
m \\
e \\
n \\
S\ t\ o\ m\ e\ n \quad c\ a\ l\ c\ o\ s\ + \\
m \\
e \\
t \\
a \\
f \\
o \\
f \\
u \\
+
\end{array}
$$

('For nose bleed write on his forehead in the shape of a cross of Christ: Stomen calcos, stomen metafofu'). Singer, who published this charm, recognized its words as being part of the Greek mass of St John Chrysostom associated with the ritual of the eucharist: Στῶμεν καλῶς, στῶμεν μετὰ φόβου. ('Let us stand seemly, let us stand in awe').[102] The solemnity of the ritual and the injunction to stand both contribute to the magical association by which the blood is induced to stand in its flow from the nose. Although it is a perfect example of Nöth's type (1) remedy, it has been suggested to me that it might also have had a real physiological effect on a nosebleed. Both the awesomeness of the procedure and the physical rubbing of the finger tracing the words of the cross on the forehead could induce a flow of adrenalin into the blood stream of the patient which would cause constriction of peripheral blood vessels, thus restricting the flow of blood in the nose and permitting more rapid clotting to take place. Thus, although the remedy was wholly magical in intent, it may actually have worked.

With it we may compare a remedy of similar intention: 'Blod seten eft gehal beren ear bestinge on eare swa he nyte' ('Again, to stop blood: thrust a whole

---

[101] Oxford, St John's College 17 (Thorney, A.D. 1110–11), 175r.
[102] Grattan and Singer, *Anglo-Saxon Magic*, pp. 49–50.

ear of barley into the ear so that he is unaware of it').[103] Storms quite rightly suggests that this must be a charm of Anglo-Saxon origin, since only in Old English is there homonymy between 'ear' (of barley) and 'ear' (organ of hearing), and that its effectiveness might be expected to lie in the similarity of names.[104] But again, the sudden startle caused by the thrusting of the barley ear secretly into the patient's ear would almost certainly bring about the 'fight or flight' reaction of adrenalin with consequent constriction of peripheral blood vessels.

More examples are not needed to demonstrate that Anglo-Saxon medicine used purely magical treatments as well as rational ones and that some at least of these magical ones were probably sometimes successful for reasons beyond the knowledge of their users. That they did sometimes work must have encouraged their users to persist in the use of magical remedies for the treatment of illnesses.

Much has been made of the condemnation of pagan magic by the church, and its attitude to pagan magic can be assessed from a study of the laws promulgated to suppress it. But it was not magic *per se* which was being forbidden. For example, we read in the *Poenitentiale Ecgberti*: 'Nis na soðlice alyfed nanum cristenum men þæt he idele hwatung bega, swa hæðene men doð . . . ne wyrta gaderunge mid nanum galdre, butan mid Paternoster and mid Credan, oððe mid sumon gebede þe to Gode belimpe.'[105] That is, when herbs were gathered (as for medicine) it was not wrong to call on the Christian God to bless the gathering, but one must not invoke the blessing of a heathen deity. And in fact the *Lacnunga* gives two 'benedictiones herbarum' differing from pagan ones only in their invocation of the Christian God.[106]

Could such practices be called magic, given the cultural context in which they were used? Today, a believing Christian will call a Navaho rain dance a magical performance, but will on no account give the same attribution to his own prayers for rain as part of a church service. With this perspective in mind it is instructive to examine many 'magical' remedies in the Old English medical literature. To many of us, the use of holy water, consecrated wine and salt, and the oil of extreme unction may be a magical, or at least a superstitious, practice. But all these substances had been subjected to a Christian ceremony which dedicated them to a special use. Indeed, the bread and wine of the eucharist were believed to undergo a substantial transformation at the time they were eaten and drunk. If these substances were capable of being so

---

103 *Leechdoms*, ed. Cockayne, II, 54.   104 Storms, *Anglo-Saxon Magic*, p. 304.
105 This and other Anglo-Saxon laws against magic and witchcraft are conveniently gathered in Grendon, 'The Anglo-Saxon Charms', pp. 140–2; the one quoted above is on p. 140.
106 Grattan and Singer, *Anglo-Saxon Magic*, p. 202.

transsubstantiated in their ritual use, they must be, after their consecration, substantially different from what they had been before, no longer being simple water, bread, wine, salt or oil, and in their new guises might be expected to have medicinal properties different from their original ones. If we accept this view of medieval belief in the effects of consecration of substances, then we find that the amount of the truly magical (from the point of view of a medieval person) is much less than it appears to us.

We must also remember that the world, incomprehensible as it may appear to us today, was much more incomprehensible to the medieval mind. Given its world view, there was a legitimate place in medicine for what we call magic. In our own time, the knowledge of bacteria and viruses and the understanding of their role in contagion and infection have so vastly increased our comprehension of disease and its causes that we find it a most difficult task to put ourselves in the place of a physician who did not know that a dirty lancet and not the phase of the moon was the most frequent cause of infected wounds following blood letting. He was doing his best to understand what was happening when he postulated that the time of the day or the phase of the moon was important. He did not have our methods of experimental procedure to help him eliminate some factors and accept others. He had no knowledge of important food factors such as the essential amino acids and the vitamins, and so could not understand why some diets were healthful and others were not. He had no knowledge of immune reactions, and so could not diagnose allergic diseases or treat them intelligently. We could go on. It seems to me that, given the number of fields of medicine which were unknown to him, he was wise to call on his gods for help, being able to do so little himself. It is good to know that such calls for help must at times have benefited the patient, who was by them encouraged to bring to bear on his ailment those inner resources which seem to work best only when the patient and the doctor are convinced that they will work. We have seen earlier that even today some intractable ailments can be effectively dealt with in this way.

I will close by quoting Payne's kindly advice again:[107] 'The only way to understand these old writers is to try to put ourselves as far as possible in their place, and conceive how nature and science presented themselves to the eyes of the early teacher and learner in the tenth and eleventh centuries. . . . That they tried to understand them at all is a proof of their wisdom, not of their folly.'[108]

---

[107] See above, n. 13.

[108] I wish to thank Dalhousie University for the sabbatical leaves and grants in aid of research which made possible the initiation of the research on which this paper is based. I thank also the Hannah Institute for the History of Medicine for a travel grant to continue my researches. My best thanks go to my wife who has read and discussed endless drafts and ideas and whose encouragement and advice have been invaluable.

Evidence for knowledge of Greek
in Anglo-Saxon England

MARY CATHERINE BODDEN

More than half of the extant manuscripts from Anglo-Saxon England, both vernacular and Latin, contain Greek.[1] How much Greek did the early English know? M. L. W. Laistner accepted only a handful of early authors, Bede among them, as 'competent Hellenists'.[2] Bernhard Bischoff, too, noted that among the numerous witnesses to Greek writing in the medieval West, only a few show knowledge of the language itself, and the majority in their corrupt state suggest just the opposite; moreover, he points out, their function is very often liturgical.[3] By the same token, a recent survey of the rich Greek materials from Sankt Gallen makes the general observation that 'few medievals possessed an ability to read Greek prose, an ability based on, at least, an acquaintance with the elementary principles of grammar'.[4] For a number of years, I have been

---

[1] The number of manuscripts containing Greek would be, therefore, between six and seven hundred. For vernacular and Latin manuscript materials pertaining to England, *c.* 700–1100, the following works are standard: E. A. Lowe, *Codices Latini Antiquiores*, 11 vols. and supp. (Oxford, 1934–71); N. R. Ker, *Catalogue of Manuscripts Containing Anglo-Saxon* (Oxford, 1957), with his 'A Supplement to the *Catalogue of Manuscripts Containing Anglo-Saxon*', *ASE* 5 (1976), 121–31; *A Plan for the Dictionary of Old English*, ed. R. Frank and A. Cameron (Toronto, 1973); P. H. Sawyer, *Anglo-Saxon Charters, An Annotated List and Bibliography* (London, 1968); T. A. M. Bishop, *English Caroline Minuscule* (Oxford, 1971); and H. Gneuss, 'A Preliminary List of Manuscripts Written or Owned in England up to 1100', *ASE* 9 (1981), 1–60. For the origin and provenance of manuscripts cited in this article, I have adopted the abbreviations used by Gneuss, *ibid.*

[2] M. L. W. Laistner, *Thought and Letters in Western Europe* (London, 1931), pp. 191, 192n. and 201. A few more, Laistner thought, had 'an acquaintance with the Greek alphabet, with a few passages from the Greek liturgy, or with a certain number of isolated Greek words or phrases, generally from the Old and New Testament'. A long way behind those, he observed, was 'a little band of those whose Greek amounted not even to an elementary knowledge of the language, but only to familiarity with the alphabet and with a sprinkling of common words or phrases'.

[3] B. Bischoff, 'Das griechische Element in der abendländischen Bildung des Mittelalters', *Mittelalterliche Studien*, 3 vols. (Stuttgart, 1966–81) II, 246–75, at 256: 'Nur sehr wenige der so zahlreichen Denkmäler griechischer Schrift im Abendlande beweisen eine Kenntnis griechischer Sprache; die Mehrzahl in ihrer Mangelhaftigkeit zeugt vielmehr für das Gegenteil'; see also pp. 262–3, and nn. 86–95.

[4] B. Kaczynski, 'Greek Learning in the Medieval West: a Study of St. Gall, 816–1022' (unpubl. Ph.D. dissertation, Yale Univ., 1973); Kaczynski adds, however, that 'many literate persons [had] a simple familiarity with the alphabet, and with words or phrases culled from glossaries, Bibles, and liturgies' (pp. 10–11).

compiling a catalogue of Anglo-Saxon manuscripts containing Greek,[5] and on the basis of what I have seen,[6] these various assumptions – that much of the Greek was badly copied, that its vocabulary was largely ecclesiastical or liturgical, that such a vocabulary would necessarily repeat itself, yielding therefore perhaps no more than some 500 to 800 Greek words, and that knowledge of Greek grammar (declensions, inflexions, and so forth) was minimal – need major modification. In what follows, I shall examine these various assumptions in turn.

COPYING OF GREEK AND TRANSLITERATED GREEK

Greek was indeed badly copied by Anglo-Saxon scribes, especially when they attempted to preserve Greek characters affected by generations of successive copying. Such was not the case, however, in the late Anglo-Saxon period. The copying of both Greek characters and transliterated Greek, although occasionally unsteady, is fairly competent as, for example, in Cambridge, Trinity College O. 10. 28 (CaCC, s. xi/xii: Eutropius, *Historia*); London, British Library, Royal 5. E. xvi (Salisbury, s. xi[ex]: Isidore, *Differentiae*); and Cambridge, Corpus Christi College 130 (?CaA, s. xi/xii: papal decretals, and synods). Nevertheless, in the earlier period untutored attempts to preserve Greek characters often led to eccentric results.[7] The majuscule gamma, for example, was frequently construed as a tau; thus Γ became T. Majuscule eta was easily confused as a nu; thus H became N, and, *vice versa*, N became H; and alpha, delta and lambda (A, Δ, Λ) were generally either represented as an alpha

---

[5] The eventual Catalogue will (1) briefly identify Anglo-Saxon manuscripts containing Greek; (2) analyse the Greek, its orthography, syntax, declensions, etc.; (3) list the folios containing Greek; (4) provide reference to other manuscripts containing identical or similar Greek matter; (5) provide bibliography pertinent to the Greek matter in the text; (6) include an Index of relevant continental manuscripts; and (7) include a Glossary of Greek words found in the texts.

[6] These preliminary results are based upon an examination of about two-thirds of the thousand or so manuscripts of Anglo-Saxon origin or provenance. The corpus of Anglo-Saxon manuscripts which I consulted includes those in Ker and in Lowe which are not in Gneuss's list, e.g., manuscripts written by Anglo-Saxon scribes on the continent. For the latter, the best survey available is still Lowe's *Codices* (excluding vol. iv). See also F. A. Rella, 'Continental Manuscripts Acquired for English Centers in the Tenth and Eleventh Centuries: a Preliminary Checklist', *Anglia* 98 (1980), 107–16.

[7] For example, Oxford, Bodleian Library, Auctarium F. 1. 15 (CaA, CaCC and Exeter, s. x²: Boethius, *De consolatione Philosophiae*), 35r21, where the original once read ΔH $BPOTWN$ $OY\Delta EN$ $\Gamma E\Gamma WCI$ $BIOTON$, we have $\Lambda NBROTOWNON$ ΔEN $\Gamma EN\Gamma W$ $CHNKIW$. In two tenth-century copies of Bede's *De orthographia*, Cambridge, Corpus Christi College 221 (? CaA, s. x¹) and London, BL, Harley 3826 (? Abingdon, s. x²), the transmission of the Greek characters is relatively accurate in the first half of the text; in the second half, however, both precision and sense yield to surmise and wonder. In Harley 3826, forms such as $B\Lambda A\Pi TW$, $\Pi\Lambda AT\Upsilon$ and $\Pi APOIKOC$ become $BAA\Pi TW$, $\Pi AA\Pi N$, and $\Pi APWIKUC$ at 52r8, 54v14 and 46r17 respectively.

or as an elaborately obscure lambda, thus: *Λ*. Moreover, certain late Greek letter forms such as)─(for mu,)─ for nu, and *C* for sigma readily lent themselves to miscopying.[8] Mu when written as)─(frequently became either nu or sigma or eta; thus)─ or *C* or *H*.[9] Transliterated Greek fared much better. Cambridge, Corpus Christi College 356, pt. III (CaA, s. x^ex), a glossary containing over a hundred Greek terms, has only a handful of severe corruptions. BL Harley 3376 (s. x/xi), another glossary of Greek, Latin and Old English terms, contains a fairly accurate transcription of transliterated Greek terms, as do Brussels, Bibliothèque Royale, 1828–30 (185) (s. xi^in), fols. 36–109, and BL Royal 15. A. xvi, 74v–83v (the *Scholica graecarum glossarum*).[10] Among prose texts, both the ninth-century Welsh hand and the later, tenth-century English hand correcting a passage in Oxford, Bodleian Library, Auct. F. 4. 32 have produced a superior set of passages from the bilingual Easter Vigil Service. The transliterated Greek in London, BL Royal 15. A. xxxiii (Reims, s. x^in: Remigius, *In Martianum Capellam*), in Cambridge, Corpus Christi College 260 (CaCC, s. x: musical texts) and Oxford, Bodleian Library, Digby 146 (Abingdon, s. x^ex: Aldhelm, *De laude virginitatis*) is generally reliable and competent.

NATURE AND RANGE OF THE GREEK VOCABULARY

Far from being heavily ecclesiastical or liturgical, the vocabulary reflects a considerable interest in terms from various disciplines; even the very names of

---

8 As one of the features of the Greek hand of 'medieval Europe', Kaczynski ('Greek Learning', p. 92) includes C as a substitute for *Σ*. However, C is regularly substituted for *Σ* by the fourth century, and is found in purely Eastern as well as in Western texts. For numerous instances, see *Codices Graeci Bibliothecae Vaticanae Selecti*, IV, ed. H. Follieri (Vatican City, 1969).

9 For example, Harley 3376, 90r1, FRUNTIMOS was probably once *ΦΡΟ*)─ *I*)─(*OC* ('sensible'), and at 92r11, 'FEREMU grece uoce mea', was quite likely *ΦW*)─ *E MOU*. A more obvious example is found in London, Inner Temple 511.10: Macrobius, *In Somnium Scipionis*, 20v31–2, 'quae in ipsa diuina mente consistunt quam diximus *NOΥ*)─ uocari', which in Oxford, Bodleian Library, Auct. F. 2. 20, 30r9–11, reads '... quam diximus *NOΥH* uocari.'

10 Rella ('Continental Manuscripts', p. 112) regards Royal 15. A. xvi (*Scholica graecarum glossarum*) as a continental production of s. ix² whose folios received English Caroline additions at St Augustine's by s. x². Some qualification is necessary here. The material of the manuscript is indeed continental: the leaves are thin and yellowish, and the nap is poor. However, the script contains both English and continental features. The *Scholica*, therefore, were either copied from an Insular exemplar or were written by a hand trained in Insular practices. The latter is more likely: in addition to the slightly clubbed minims and the ascenders being more even and straighter than are usually found in continental manuscripts of this period, there is the unmistakably English feature of the *æ* ligature appearing in a number of Latin terms. Note, for example, 76r16 *cæna*, and *Antiæ*, 76v6 *Bulæ*, and 78r22 *poetriæ*, and cf. the similar letter-forms in contemporary English manuscripts such as Cambridge, Trinity College O. 4. 10 (s. x), BL Cotton Cleopatra A. iii (s. x^med), Vespasian D. vi (s. x^med), Vitellius A. xix (s. x^med), Harley 3376 and 3271 (s. xi¹).

disciplines or subjects of interest are recorded: for example, *AΠO TOU PHTOPIZEIN* (as in Cambridge, Trinity College B. 15. 33, 'apo tu retoresin, id est a copia locutionis') or *IΣTOPEIN* (as in 'Historia est narratio rei gestae, per quam ea quae in praeterito facta sunt dinoscuntur. Dicta grecae historia apo to historin, id est a uidere uel agnoscere', or 'Narrationum genera: Historia dicitur *AΠO TOY HISTORIN*, id est uidere'; interlinear gloss: '*YCTOPIN*').[11] Terms drawn from subjects such as grammar, dialectic, mathematics, liturgy and natural history can be found in nearly all the bilingual glossaries and among a high number of Latin texts glossed with Greek or Latin terms. Grammar and natural history, particularly the physical aspects of man, are the areas richest in the preservation of Greek terms in early English manuscripts. Greek grammatical terms include, for example, parts of speech: 'Ysocolon, ysos aequus, colon membrum' or '*APO* quidem greca prepositio est' or *YΠEP* as in 'Ponitur et pro praepositione in, ut dicimus pro uestris (*leg.* rostris) pro tribunali. Et pro eo quod est anti apud grecos, ut pro dulci ascanio ueniat, et pro eo quod est *YΠER*, ut unum illud tibi, nate dea, proque omnibus unum praedicam.'[12]

The much wider vocabulary of natural history includes such terms as *IOΣ* ('Aspis uocata quod morsu uenenum immittit et surgit. *IOS* grece uenenum dicunt et inde aspis quod morsu uenenato interimat'); *AEMA* ('*AEMA* sanguis, inde anima quasi anema, hoc est sine sanguine'); *AEGIDI* ('*AEGIDI* grece et pluuia et capra dicitur'); *CARDIAS* ('Cardo est locus in quo ostium uertitur et semper mouetur, dictus *APO TU CARDIAS* quod quasi cor hominem totum, ita ille cuneus ianuam regat ac moueat'); *DYNAMI* ('Uis duplicem habet significationem: et uirtutis uidelicet quae grece *DYNAMI* dicitur, et uiolentia, quae graece *BIA* uocatur'); *PALIN* ('Membra dicta quia in luctando eas premimus quae greci *PALIN* dicunt'); *CLEPTIN* ('Clypeum dicitur apo tu cleptin somata, id est a furando corpora'); *XEIPA* [i.e., *AI XEIPEΣ*] ('Scribendum uero cum h quia grece manus dicuntur *XEIPA*'); and *XHΛH* ('corpore scilicet suo *XHΛH* si per *H* longam scribatur brachium

---

[11] apo tu retoresin: Cambridge, Trinity College B. 15. 33, the opening line of bk II of Isidore's *Etymologiae*; apo to historin: Oxford, Bodleian Library, Digby 146, 37v, l. m. (Aldhelm, *De laude virginitatis*); and *AΠO TOY HISTORIN*: Royal 15. A. xxxiii, 123v8 (Remigius, *In Martianum Capellam*). Except where editions are cited, the Greek material quoted in this article represents the form(s) found in the manuscripts referred to, that is, with no accents and generally in capital letters. In the case of Isidore, *Etymologiae*, apart from a few citations from manuscripts, all other citations of Greek words from the *Etymologiae* are taken from *Isidori Hispalensis Episcopi Etymologiarum sive originum Libri XX*, ed. W. M. Lindsay (Oxford, 1911).

[12] Ysocolon: Royal 15. A. xxxiii, 121v19; APO: in BL Royal 15, A. xvi, 74v6–7; and *YΠEP*: Harley 3826, 54v17–55r5.

significat, si per e breuem labia; unde et achilles dictus est a tenuitate labiorum uel quasi sine labiis').[13]

In order to demonstrate clearly the range of Greek materials in Anglo-Saxon manuscripts I have compiled the accompanying Appendix (below, pp. 233–46). This Appendix indicates clearly the breadth of the Anglo-Saxons' Greek vocabulary, and also reveals a particular feature that emerges from their Greek vocabulary-lists and glosses, namely an increasing interest in Greek terms of a very mundane nature. Purely spiritual texts were sometimes glossed with (mundane) Greek terms, simply (I suspect) because those texts contained Greek terms available either in glossaries or in that universally known repository of Greek terms, Isidore's *Etymologiae*. A clear instance of this is Aldhelm's *De laude virginitatis*. Among the more than sixty Greek glosses on this text in Oxford, Bodleian Library, Digby 146, scarcely one concerns spiritual matters, much less virginity.[14] A considerable portion of the terms are, in fact, taken from bks XI, XIII, XIV and XX of the *Etymologiae* (namely, 'De homine et portentis', 'De mundo et partibus', 'De terra et partibus', and 'De mensis et escis et potibus et vasculis eorum', respectively).

Moreover, the Anglo-Saxons' interest in these words was not merely a matter of collecting and displaying arcane and recondite terms. Their sharp interest in the origin and composition of Latin words extended likewise to Greek. Etymology forms a respectable proportion of the words preserved in Anglo-Saxon texts: a gloss in London, BL Add. 34652 (Chrodegang, *Regula canonicorum*), 3r14–15, examines the components of 'cleronomia', a term whose etymology appears in a number of glossaries: 'nam cleros sors interpretatur grece cleronomia appellatur et heres'. In London, BL Cotton Otho E. i (glossary), 8r19–22, the word 'flebotomum' is analysed as follows: 'fleps uena, tomum uero incisio nominatur.' The word 'Sibylla' was a favourite subject of etymology. Note its treatment in three separate works: Isidore in the *Etymologiae* (VIII.viii.1) maintains that 'Sibyllae generaliter dicuntur omnes feminae vates lingua Graeca. Nam σιὸς Aeolico sermone deos, βουλὴν Graeci mentem nuncupant, quasi dei mentem', whereas in Remigius, *In Martianum Capellam*, we find 'Sybilla autem dicitur quasi *ZYOC BOYΛA*, id est iouis consilium' (Royal 15. A. xxxiii, 12v18–19). On the other hand, the entry in the

---

[13] IOS [*IOΣ*]: Oxford, Bodleian Library, Digby 146, 31v, r. m.; AEMA [AIMA]: BL, Royal 15. A. xvi, 76r29; AIGIDI [*AIΓIΔI*]: CCCC 356, pt III, 1r., col b., 20; CARDIAS [*KAPΔIAΣ*]: Digby 146, 46v, l. m.; DYNAMI [*ΔYNAMIC*]: BL Harley 3826, 68v12–15; PALIN [*ΠAΛΛEIN*]: Digby 146, 65v, l. m.; CLEPTIN [*AΠO TOY KΛEΠTEIN ΣOMATA* or *COMATA*] ('EI' often went to 'I' in later spellings): Royal 15. A. xxxiii, 127r22; *XEIPA*: Royal 15. A. xvi, 78r12–13, and *XHΛH*: Royal 15. A. xxxiii, 193v25–27.

[14] On the other hand, many of the Latin glosses are concerned with the spiritual content of the words.

Scholica graecarum glossarum (Royal 15. A. xvi, 83r21–2) reads: 'Sibilla dicta quasi syos bule, id est dei consilium uel dei os; nam sios Aeolice dicitur deus, bule consilium.'

An example of one of the more ingenious etymologies proposed for a word is found in London, BL Add. 24199 (Prudentius, *Psychomachia*), 4v, left margin: here the name of the second of the Furies, Tisiphone, is construed as 'altera tisiphone, quasi tuton phone (*ΤΟ ΥΤΩΝ ΦΩΝΗ*), id est istarum uox'. The true etymology of Tisiphone, however, is an excellent example of the Greek genius for making the condition the name, with the result that the myth or tale forever lurks in the name: in this case, τίσι (from *τίνω) 'payment made through penalty or punishment' + φονή (*from φένω) 'inclined to slay', 'murderous', thus Τισιφόνη, 'avenger of murder'.

Nor were these words preserved solely in glossaries. What was in the glossaries frequently made its way into texts, and *vice versa*. The several offspring of the word BROTOS (*ΒΡΩΤΟΣ*) provide a useful illustration. BL Harley 3376 (glossary), 10r6, contains only the simple interlinear gloss 'cibus' above 'brotos grece', whereas a rather inventive interpretation accompanies the word in many of the Anglo-Saxon manuscripts of Boethius's *De consolatione Philosophiae*.[15] The phrase *ΔΗ ΒΡΟΤΩΝ ΟΥΔΕΝ*[16] ('of mortals . . . none') has become AMBPOTONON, or a form thereof, producing in some manuscripts[17] the following gloss: 'Anbrotonos[18] dicitur homo quia brotos dicitur cibus.[19] Homo ergo anbrotonos dictus est quod solus inter omnes creaturas rationabili uescitur cibo. Aut antropon legendum est. Antropos dicitur quasi anatropos id est sursum uersus pronis enim omnibus animalibus terram spectantibus solus homo caelum suspicit rectus. Hinc Ouidius: cetera cum spectent pronas animalia terras, os hominum sublime dedit caelumque uidere, iussit et rectos ad sidera uultus.'[20] The text from which these glosses were adapted is that of *Etymologiae* xi.i.5 which, in BL Royal 6. C. 1, 86r28, reads: 'Greci autem anthropum appellauerunt eo quod sursum aspectet et subleuatus ab humo ad contemplationem artificis sui. Quod Ouidius poeta designat cum dicit: pronaque cum spectant animalia cetera terram, os hominis sublime dedit

---

15 One vernacular and thirteen Latin manuscripts (along with several fragments) have survived; see below n. 43.

16 Within the sentence L *W ΔΟΞΑ ΔΟΞΑ ΜΥΡΥΟUCI ΔΗ ΒΡΟΤWΝ ΟΥΔΕΝ ΓΕΓWCI ΒΙΟΤΟΝ ΟΓΚWCAC ΜΕΓΑΝ* (*De consolatione*, iii, pr.vi).

17 E.g., Antwerp, Plantin-Moretus Museum M. 16. 8 (190), 47v, l. m. and Paris, Bibliothèque Nationale, lat, 6401 A, 40r, r. m.

18 The Antwerp manuscript reads AMBROTONOS (I omit other minor orthographical variants).

19 'brotos dicitur cibus] brotos grecibus': BN lat. 6401 A, 40r, r. m. Perhaps 'grecibus' was misconstrued from 'dī cibus'.

20 'ad sidere uultus] ad sydere tollere uultus': Antwerp M. 16. 8, 47v, l. m.

caelumque uidere, iussit et erectos ad sidera tollere uultus. Qui ideo erectus caelum aspicit ut deum quaerat non ut terram intendat ueluti pecora quae natura prona et uentri obaedientia finxit.'

A more complex relationship characterizes the transmission of the Greek etymology assigned to the word '*FARUS*'. Preserving a snatch of information already well known in glossaries and in the *Etymologiae*,[21] the word is used by Aldhelm in his prose *De laude uirginitatis* (Digby 146, 30r8): 'farus seu quadrati rotundus obolisci globus.' Nearby is the following gloss: 'Farus turris est maxima quam greci ac latini in commune ex ipsius rei usu farum appellauerunt eo quod flammarum indicio longe uideatur a nauigantibus qualem Tholomeus iuxta Alexandriam construxisse octingentis talentis traditur.' This gloss has been copied verbatim from Isidore's *Etymologiae* (xv.ii.37). However, note how the glossaries in both Cotton Otho E. i and Cleopatra A. iii develop the etymology: 'Farus grecum est nomen, nam fos lux oros autem uisio apud eos nominatur. hinc compositum nomen est fari id est fyrtor.'[22]

EXTENT OF THE GREEK VOCABULARY

To take up the third point – that while the vocabulary does indeed repeat itself through constant mutual borrowings between glossaries and texts, the preponderance of evidence from the ninth century to the eleventh suggests that the Anglo-Saxons possessed a very considerable vocabulary of Greek words. From eight texts alone (out of, perhaps, some possible forty texts containing a substantial amount of Greek) we could construct a hypothetical core glossary of just over a thousand Greek words. The eight texts in question are: Isidore's *Etymologiae*, the *Scholica graecarum glossarum*, Remigius's *In Martianum Capellam*, the 'Harley Glossary', the Greek–Latin and Latin–Greek glossaries in both Brussels, Bibliothèque Royale, 1828–30 and CCCC 356, pt III, Bede's *De orthographia*, and Aldhelm's *De laude uirginitatis*.

The nature of such a core vocabulary is illustrated in the Appendix, which includes all the Greek glosses in Aldhelm's *De laude uirginitatis* from Digby 146 common to Isidore's *Etymologiae*. It includes, as well, certain terms from both the *Scholica graecarum glossarum* and Remigius's *In Martianum Capellam* which are also common or similar to Isidore's *Etymologiae*.

---

[21] PHARUS (-OS) (φάρος), an island near Alexandria, in Egypt, where King Ptolemy Philadelphus built a famous lighthouse, hence called Pharus, now Faro; transferred meaning: the lighthouse on the island of Pharos. The term already appears in Caesar, *Bellum ciuile* III.112: 'Pharus est in insula turris, magna altitudine, mirificis operibus extructa, quae nomen ab insula accepit'; cf. also Suetonius, *Claudius*, ch. 20 and Statius, *Siluae* iii.2, and, later, the *Etymologiae*, xv.ii.37, as well as at least two Latin–Old English glossaries: BL Cotton Otho E. i, 8v24–8 and Cleopatra A. iii, 43vb15–17 and 44ra1–4.

[22] OE *fyrtor*, 'fire tower'; in Cotton Cleopatra A. iii, a single folio earlier, is found the entry FARUS, *beacenstan* (42r).

A certain number of the terms in this core vocabuary seem to have circulated widely, appearing (sometimes as grecisms), in texts such as the *Psychomachia*, or in materials appended to grammatical texts, or in schoolbooks or glossaries. For example, the *Scholica graecarum glossarum* draws many of its glosses from Isidore's *Etymologiae*. Abbo of Saint-Germain-des-Prés borrowed indirectly from the *Scholica* (either from a version of it or from one of its chief sources) for his poem, *Bella Parisiacae Urbis*, especially bk III. Book III is the source of glosses in London, BL Cotton Domitian A. i, where they are combined with Greek terms from Priscian's *Institutio de nomine, pronomine et verbo*, the combination making up a list of 'Glosa diversa'. The list, written by a single hand (including the terms added from the Priscian text), is found at 37v–38v. For his commentary on Martianus Capella's *De nuptiis*, Remigius drew frequently upon the *Etymologiae* and perhaps occasionally upon a version of the *Scholica*,[23] and, finally, among the many sources of his *Enchiridion*, Byrhtferth cites the *Etymologiae* and is thought to have drawn upon Remigius as well.[24] If to the hypothetical glossary constructed from these eight texts one were to add the Greek words (excluding prepositions and articles) appearing in the remaining 500-odd manuscripts containing Greek, it becomes apparent that the cumulative Greek vocabulary of Anglo-Saxon educators, writers and students could have run to about 5,000 words.

KNOWLEDGE OF GREEK SYNTAX

In the present state of our knowledge little can be concluded about the Anglo-Saxons' knowledge of Greek syntax. One thing seems fairly certain: the

---

23 On the *Scholica graecarum glossarum*, see J. Contreni, 'Three Carolingian Texts Attributed to Laon: Reconsiderations', *SM* 3rd ser. 17 (1976), 797–813, at p. 806, for its use of Isidore; see also Kaczynski, 'Greek Learning', p. 281. The most recent study of bk III of the *Bella Parisiacae Urbis* and its use of the *Scholica graecarum glossarum* is P. Lendinara, 'The Third Book of the *Bella Parisiacae urbis* by Abbo of Saint-Germain-des-Prés and its Old English Gloss', *ASE* 15 (1986), 73–89. The study is most enlightening, with several splendid insights. Lendinara's point that 'Many discrepancies indicate that Abbo did not draw his material from any of the *known* manuscripts of the *Scholica*' (italics mine) is nicely complemented by a second observation that of the eighty lemmata (i.e., rare words, most of which are grecisms) 'only 14 of these do not recur in other glossaries' (p. 80 and n. 41). Elsewhere she questions the frequent criticism levelled against the pedantry of Abbo's bk III. She proposes, instead, that such 'pedantry' may well be the 'jocular component of the hermeneutic tradition'; Abbo, she suggests, 'composed a mockery, a very well constructed tour de force directed against the Greek vogue of the time, instead of complaining about it as Hincmar of Rheims had done to his nephew Hincmar of Laon' (p. 81). Lendinara's hypothesis is surely valid, but I think that Abbo's exercise was a *scherzo più grande* than we have assumed thus far, as I hope to show in a forthcoming article, 'The Influence of "Greek" Studies upon Anglo-Saxon Culture'.

24 M. L. W. Laistner, 'Notes on Greek from the Lectures of a Ninth Century Monastery Teacher', *Bull. of the John Rylands Lib.* 7 (1923), 421–56, at 421, and Contreni, 'Three Carolingian Texts', pp. 805 and 806.

elementary study of Greek grammar in England was doomed to a haphazard and brief existence. It faced the same fundamental deficiency which, according to Bischoff, affected such study on the continent, namely, the absence of a suitable textbook.[25] The *Ars grammatica* by Dositheus is not a Greek grammar, although it was used as though it were. It is, in fact, a Greek translation of a Latin grammar. Apart from the occasional bilingual paradigm, it offered no analyses of Greek verbs, much less of Greek syntax. Among extant copies of Dositheus's *Ars grammatica*, there is none certainly connected with Anglo-Saxon England.[26] On the continent, it seems that 'rather than learning Greek from a single text, students were obliged to piece together the rules of grammar for themselves from whatever works they could obtain'.[27] Moreover, neither on the continent nor in England were attempts to establish a tradition in Greek learning successful. The odds against doing so in England were much greater than those facing continental educators. The continent, at least, had sources[28] providing Greek grammatical information. However, of the four chief sources from which an elementary knowledge of Greek might have been pieced together, two are not attested at all in Anglo-Saxon England; the third has survived only in late eleventh-century copies, and the fourth in one late tenth-century copy. The first of the four sources, Dositheus's *Ars grammatica*, has already been discussed above. The second, Macrobius's *De differentiis et societatibus Graeci Latinique verbi epitome*, was a difficult but at least coherent work giving a comparison of the Greek and Latin verbs.[29] There is no evidence, however, of this text ever having been known in England. From the third source, Priscian's *Institutiones grammaticae*, whose Latin noun declensions and derivations often used Greek forms as models, 'one might, with a bit of effort, extract . . . most of the Greek rules for noun declensions, a notion of treatment of verb stems and a slight knowledge of syntax'.[30] Nevertheless, that bit of effort would suppose the availability of those sections which detailed the

---

[25] Bischoff, 'Das griechische Element', pp. 259 and 261.

[26] The manuscripts containing the *Ars grammatica* are London, BL Harley 5642 (St Gallen, s. ix/x), 9r–23v (*Ars grammatica*) and 24r–33r with 39v–47r (portions of *Hermeneumata*); Munich, Bayerische Staatsbibliothek, Clm. 601 (s. ix/x), 59v–66v (selections from *Hermeneumata*) and 67r–82v (*Ars grammatica*); and St Gallen, Stiftsbibliothek, 902 (St Gallen, s. ix^ex), pp. 8–43 (*Ars grammatica*) and pp. 43–59 (*Hermeneumata*). It will be noticed that the genuine *Ars grammatica* of Dositheus frequently travelled in manuscript with pseudo-Dositheus, *Hermeneumata*. Since one English manuscript now contains the *Hermeneumata* (Brussels 1828–30), there is a remote possibility that it (or its exemplar) once contained the genuine *Ars grammatica* as well. But this is mere speculation.

[27] Kaczynski, 'Greek Learning', p. 113.

[28] See Bischoff, 'Das griechische Element', *passim* and W. Berschin, *Griechisch-Lateinisches Mittelalter* (Bern, 1980).

[29] *Grammatici Latini*, ed. H. Keil, 8 vols. (Leipzig, 1857–80) v, 599–630.

[30] Kaczynski, 'Greek Learning', p. 120.

inflections of nouns and verbs, namely, bks IV–VIII of the *Institutiones*. Of the 527 manuscripts in Margaret Gibson's handlist of Priscian manuscripts,[31] sixty-one belong to the ninth and tenth centuries and 283 to the eleventh and twelfth centuries. No manuscript of 'Priscianus maior' (*Institutiones*, bks I–XVI) of English provenance dates earlier than the late eleventh century.[32] We cannot, therefore, know *absolutely* whether this limited source of information on Greek forms (i.e., bks IV–VIII) was available to the English before the late eleventh century. As for the fourth source, Donatus's *Ars maior*, only the incomplete copy in BL Cotton Cleopatra A. vi, 2r–31r, has survived among English manuscripts prior to the twelfth century.[33] No texts of Anglo-Saxon provenance are listed in Holtz's inventory of manuscripts of Donatus's *Ars*,[34] but he notes that the exemplar of the *Ars Donati* reflected in Boniface's grammar indicates the typically Insular redaction which lies behind the *Anonymus ad Cuimnanum*, an early Insular commentary on the *Ars*.[35] The nearly complete loss of Anglo-Saxon manuscripts of *Ars Donati* (and, thereby, of a source of Greek grammatical information) was due, apparently, to the Carolingian rediscovery of Priscian's *Institutiones*. Vivien Law remarks that although 'his [Priscian's] work still served as a basis of elementary instruction, pre-Carolingian grammars based on him – including almost all the Insular works – fell into disfavour from the middle of the ninth century and were rarely copied'.[36] Finally, it may be noted that a twelfth-century Canterbury booklist (Cambridge, University Library, Ii. 3. 12) lists a 'Donatus Grece' which is thought to have been a Greek grammar of some sort.[37]

There is accordingly a noteworthy absence of Greek grammatical materials from the Anglo-Saxon period; similarly there are very few surviving texts

---

31 M. Gibson, 'Priscian, *Institutiones Grammaticae*: A Handlist of Manuscripts', *Scriptorium* 26 (1972), 105–24.

32 See also the entry 'Priscianus maior' in a booklist on an end folio in Oxford, Bodleian Library, Tanner 3, ptd M. Lapidge, 'Surviving Booklists from Anglo-Saxon England', *Learning and Literature in Anglo-Saxon England*, ed. M. Lapidge and H. Gneuss (Cambridge, 1985), pp. 33–89, at 70 (no. 15).

33 Cotton Cleopatra A. vi is usually assigned to the second half of the tenth century, but features of the script (especially the open-headed *p*'s and the *st*-ligature) suggest to me, rather, the early tenth century.

34 L. Holtz, *Donat et la tradition de l'enseignement grammatical* (Paris, 1981), pp. 354–423.

35 *Ibid.* pp. 308 and 498.

36 V. Law, *The Insular Latin Grammarians* (Woodbridge, 1982), p. 16.

37 See M. Lapidge, 'The Hermeneutic Style in Tenth-Century Anglo-Latin Literature', *ASE* 4 (1975), 67–111, at 80, n. 1: 'In the earliest catalogue from Christ Church, Canterbury (*c.* 1170), there is an item "Donatus grece" (M. R. James, *The Ancient Libraries of Canterbury and Dover* (Cambridge, 1903), pp. lxxxv and 7). This was probably a copy of pseudo-Dositheus, not Dionysius Thrax as James suggests. If this Greek grammar was pre-Conquest, it indicates that Greek may have been studied at Canterbury.'

from that period which contain substantial excerpts of Greek prose. In the entire corpus of manuscripts of Latin texts containing Greek, only *one* such text, Boethius's *De consolatione Philosophiae*, survives in multiple copies. Quite obviously, this severely handicaps any study of transmission in which the successive copying of Greek might have contained clues about the Anglo-Saxons' comprehension of Greek grammar. Thirteen Latin copies and one vernacular version of the *De consolatione* survive from Anglo-Saxon England; yet only two manuscripts, Auct. F. I. 15 and Paris, Bibliothèque Nationale, lat. 6401 A,[38] keep fairly intact the initial words of the first of the text's several Greek sentences.[39] However, a number of the manuscripts accurately preserve the first half of the sentence, with interesting alternative Greek words, borrowed, apparently, from continental copies.[40] It would appear that, for a conclusive study of the Anglo-Saxons' knowledge of Greek grammar, our manuscript evidence is too little and too late.

REVIEW OF THE EVIDENCE

A review of the evidence is now in order. When compared to the Greek evident in the texts acquired, copied, and preserved by certain centres on the

---

[38] For a more detailed discussion of the transmission of Greek matter in these manuscripts, see M. C. Bodden, 'The Transmission and Preservation of Greek in Early England', in *Sources of Anglo-Saxon Culture*, ed. P. E. Szarmach, Stud. in Medieval Culture 20 (Kalamazoo, Michigan, 1986), 53–63. The Greek sentence of the original reads: ΄ΕΞΑΎΔΑ, ΜῊ ΚΕΥ̂ΘΕ ΝΟΩ̣, that is, 'Speak out, do not conceal your thoughts.'

[39] For convenience I cite the Gneuss numbers ('Preliminary List') for the thirteen Latin copies of the *De consolatione*: 12, 23, 68, 193, 534, 776, 823, 829, 886, 887, 899, 901 and 908. The vernacular version, Oxford, Bodleian Library, Bodley 180 (s. xii¹), does not retain the Greek matter.

[40] For example, of the thirteen Latin versions copied or used by the early English, ten retain the original *ΕΞΑΥΔΑ* ('Speak out!') in the first Greek sentence of the text. Two of these ten (BN lat. 14380 and Escorial E. II. I), also have the gloss *ΕξΟΜΟΛΟΓΟ* ('Confess!'). A third manuscript, BN lat. 6401, contains *ΕξΟΜΟΛΟΓΟ* as part of the text itself. Three other manuscripts, presumed to be Canterbury manuscripts, namely, Geneva, Bodmer C.B. 175, Cambridge, Trinity College O. 3. 7 and BN lat. 17814, show *ΕξΟΜΟΛΟΡѠ* (*–ΡΛ*), with 'confitere mihi' glossed above the word. Of these three, Bodmer and Trinity are closely related to each other while BN lat. 17814 appears to be more closely related to the continental versions. One manuscript bridges the English and continental groups: Paris, BN lat. 14380. Its text gives the complete *ΕξΑΥΔΑ* sentence, and in its margin is *ΕξΟΜΟΛΟΡѠ*. This same manuscript is also possibly from Canterbury, and postdates, slightly, Bodmer and Trinity. The fact that its marginal gloss is identical to that in the Bodmer and Trinity manuscripts suggests that ultimately its continental source was their source: *ΕξΟΜΟΛΟΡѠ* or variations of *ΕξΟΜΟΛΟΓΕѠ* is the reading substituted in half of the twelfth-century continental manuscripts which I have seen thus far (including Paris, BN lat. 1478, 6639, 12961, 15090 and 16093, Alençon, Bibliothèque municipale, 12, Orléans, Bibliothèque municipale, 271, Bern, Burgerbibliothek, 179, 181 and 421, St Gallen, Stiftsbibliothek, 844 and 845, Munich, Bayerische Staatsbibliothek, Clm. 14324, 15825, 18767 and 19452, and Vatican City, Biblioteca Apostolica Vaticana, lat. 3865).

continent in the ninth and tenth centuries,[41] Anglo-Saxon Greek matter seems almost boneless, as it were: nothing finely articulated or structured; little in the way of systematic inflections or paradigms, but much in the way of vocabulary. Certainly nothing both English and extant from the seventh to the twelfth centuries approaches the level of the scholarship of John Scottus Eriugena in the ninth century. Yet the testimony of both Bede (thought, himself, to have used the seventh-century Greek manuscript, Oxford, Bodleian Library, Laud Gr. 35, for his work on the Acts of the Apostles) and Aldhelm[42] suggests that, even if only briefly, knowledge of Greek seems to have flourished in England prior to the rise of the continent's most famed school of Greek studies, that of the cathedral school of Laon.[43]

Interestingly enough, only in the late eighth century and in the beginning of the ninth does Greek for its own sake begin to appear in English manuscripts, that is to say, Greek versions of texts commonly read and known in Latin. The most obvious examples are the doxology, creed, litanies and prayers. London, BL Harley 2965 and 7653, Royal 2. A. xx, and Cotton Galba A. xviii all contain Greek versions of Latin texts.[44] However, from the mid-ninth to the third quarter of the tenth century, Greek seems to have been copied for the sake of the text itself, that is, certain texts were valued (and therefore copied) as works preserved in their original language, or, as in the case of biblical texts, only once removed from the Hebrew version. For example, an English hand (of about the third quarter of the tenth century) has restored the final folio of the third gathering of Oxford, Bodleian Library, Auct. F. 4. 32 (Wales; prov-

---

41 For convenience a few relevant continental Greek manuscripts may be mentioned. BL Harley 5642 (see above, n. 26) a manuscript which also contains the bilingual 'Colloquium Harleianum' at 29r–33v (see also *Corpus Glossariorum Latinorum*, ed. G. Goetz, 7 vols. (Leipzig, 1888–1923) III, 108–16); Paris, BN lat. 528 (Saint-Denis, s. ix): only a fragment (134v–135r) remains of the Greek elementary lesson, 'Ti estin doctus' (see H. Omont, 'Grammaire grecque au ixᵉ siècle', *Bibliothèque de l'École des Chartes* 42 (1881), 126–7); BN lat. 6503 (Corbie, s. ix/x), 1r–4r, part of Aesop's Fables; BN lat. 7561 (s. ix), beginning at 111r, the Lord's Prayer with accents; St Gallen, Stiftsbibliothek, 17 (St Gallen, s. ix²), Greek–Latin Psalter and Canticles, Lord's Prayer; 902 (St Gallen, s. ix²), pp. 8–43 (Dositheus, *Ars grammatica*) and pp. 43–51 (selections from *Hermeneumata pseudo-Dositheana*) and 1395 (St Gallen, s. x), pp. 336–61, Greek–Latin Psalter; and most remarkable of all, Laon, Bibliothèque municipale, 444 (Laon, s. ix²), in particular the Greek–Latin glossary, (5r–255v) and the 'Graeca Prisciani de octo partibus et constructione' (276r–87v).

42 See Bede, *HE* IV.2, V.8, 20 and 23; on Aldhelm, see *Aldhelm: The Prose Works*, trans. M. Lapidge and M. Herren (Cambridge, 1979), pp. 8–9.

43 Martin Hiberniensis (818–75) was the first of Laon's three generations of masters of Greek learning; John Scottus, too, was associated with Laon in Martin's time: see J. J. Contreni, *The Cathedral School of Laon from 850 to 930: Its Manuscripts and Masters* (Munich, 1978), pp. 69–72 and 81–134.

44 Harley 2965 (WiNun, s. viii/ix); Harley 7653 (s. viii/ix); Royal 2. A. xx (Worcester, s. viii²) and Cotton Galba A. xviii (NE France, s. ix²; provenance Winchester, s. x¹).

enance Glastonbury, s. ix and x: 'Liber Commonei') by supplying a new half-leaf (36r) and carefully copying the bilingual liturgical readings from the former leaf.[45] Along with Auct. F. 4. 32, other Greek–Latin works preserved from this period include commentaries on both classical and ecclesiastical works, such as Cambridge, University Library, Ee. 2. 4 (Glastonbury, s. x[med]: Smaragdus, *Expositio in Regulam S. Benedicti*); BL Royal 15. A. xxxiii (Rheims, Worcester, s. x[in]: Remigius, *In Martianum Capellam*) and Cambridge, Trinity College O. 2. 30 (CaA, s. x[med]: *Regula S. Benedicti*), fols. 130–73; in each of these manuscripts transliterated Greek terms follow each section of the text.[46]

Texts of 'edited' Greek (that is, Greek compiled from various sources) such as glossaries or certain orthographies may be considered a sub-group of the category of manuscripts in which the Greek preserved seems to be for the sake of the text itself. To such a group belong, for example, the gloss on Martianus Capella's *De nuptiis* in CCCC 330, pt ii, and certain grammatical treatises containing brief examinations of Greek terms, for example, CCCC 221 or Harley 3826, both containing Alcuin, *De orthographia* and Bede, *De orthographia*.

IMPLICATIONS OF THE EVIDENCE

Two implications arise from such evidence. First, a real knowledge of *basic* Greek, limited, presumably, to but a handful of Anglo-Saxon clergy, flourished probably only in the seventh, eighth and early part of the ninth century. Second, the relative absence from the mid-ninth to the third quarter of the tenth century either of Greek versions of Latin texts or of 'edited' Greek[47] indicates the end of a rather heady culture which had begun so promisingly in the south-west, in Canterbury and in Northumbria. There are several ninth-century manuscripts containing a substantial amount of Greek which are listed among the manuscripts written or owned in England before

---

[45] Presumably from the former leaf: the forms of both languages appear to be consistent with the text of the preceding folios: see R. W. Hunt, *St Dunstan's Classbook from Glastonbury: Cod. Bibl. Bodl. Auct. F. 4. 32*, Umbrae Codicum Occidentalium 4 (Amsterdam, 1961).

[46] For example, note the following explanations in Trinity O. 2. 30: 134r8, 'Coenobite, commune uiuentes. Coenos, grece, latini commune dicunt'; 142v, end, 'Kalendae: calo greci dicunt uoco, latini conuocationes'; and 143r4–7, 'Analogium dicitum quod sermo inde praedicetur, nam logus grece, latine sermo dicitur.' On the other hand, in CUL Ee. 2. 4, the Greek etymologies occur within the text itself: 64v, col. 1: 'Analogium dictum ab eo quod sermo inde diuinus aut legatur aut praedicetur; logos enim apud graecos sermo dicitur.' Or at 65r, col. 1: 'Hortodoxi . . . horto enim apud graecos recte dicitur; doxa aut gloria uocatur; ergo hortodoxi uiri rectae gloriae dici possunt.'

[47] Two of the three glossaries from this period containing substantial amounts of Greek are from the continent: Leiden, Bibliotheek der Rijksuniversiteit, Voss. lat. F. 24 (W. France, s. ix/x) and CCCC 330, pt ii (s. ix[ex]: gloss on Martianus Capella's *De Nuptiis*).

1100. However, these are English solely by virtue of their interpolated corrections and additions, and were probably not in England before the tenth century; Auct. F. 4. 32, for example, is from Wales, and CCCC 330, pt II, the extended gloss on the *De nuptiis*, is from the continent. The nature of these materials supports Gneuss's thesis concerning both the decline of learning and the hiatus of book production in England, namely, that King Alfred's famous complaint in his preface to the *Pastoral Care* was an accurate assessment of the state of learning in England.[48]

In fact, from period to period, the various states of Greek learning in England very likely reflect Anglo-Saxon learning in general. In the earliest period we find an academic, so to speak, interest in Greek: that is to say, Greek for the sake of Greek – Greek versions of Latin texts, copied occasionally in Greek characters; more often, and more accurately, copied in transliterated Greek. The amount of such Greek is small and mainly liturgical. Then, during the century before the monastic revival, whatever Greek we have is both meagre and imported from the continent. It is significant that from this, the most active period of Greek studies on the continent, particularly in north-east France, there is not a single manuscript witness to similar activity in England. The fact that the only two Anglo-Saxon ninth-century manuscripts containing Greek are continental imports may be due not so much to the precariousness of manuscript survival, but, rather, to the possibilty that only on the continent was there any study (and therefore production) of Greek materials.

In the late tenth century, Greek re-appears, but mainly as 'edited' Greek, that is, Greek transmitted in the form of glossaries[49] or scholia drawn from texts (such as the scholia in Digby 146, mentioned earlier, drawn from Isidore's *Etymologiae*).[50] In this period, also, Greek matter is drawn from a variety of disciplines, coinciding, apparently, with the importation and production during the tenth century (and more so in the eleventh century) of classical texts such as Cicero's *Aratea*, the *Satirae* of Juvenal and Persius, the technical works of Vitruvius and Vegetius (the *De architectura* and the *Epitome rei militaris*, respectively) and the works of Macrobius and Martianus Capella. In the late eleventh century and in the twelfth, Greek begins to appear more frequently in Greek characters and increasingly with a greater accuracy in

---

[48] H. Gneuss, 'King Alfred and the History of Anglo-Saxon Libraries', *Modes of Interpretation in Old English Literature: Essays in Honour of Stanley B. Greenfield*, ed. P.R. Brown, G.R. Crampton and F.C. Robinson (Toronto, 1986), pp. 29–49, esp. pp. 40–1.

[49] For example, CCCC 356, pt III (s. x^ex), London, BL Cotton Otho E. i (s. x/xi), Harley 3376 (s. x/xi), Harley 3826 (s. x/xi), Royal 15. A. xvi (s. x^ex) and Oxford, Bodleian Library, Barlow 35 (s. x/xi).

[50] The Greek glosses in Digby 146 seem to be taken from a close descendant of Paris, BN lat. 7585 (France, s. ix¹: Isidore, *Etymologiae*).

transmission: in, for example, CCCC 330, pt I (Martianus Capella, *De nuptiis Philologiae et Mercurii*); CCCC 276 (Dudo of St Quentin, *Historia Normannorum*); Cambridge, Trinity College O. 2. 51, pt II (Priscian, *Institutiones grammaticae*); O. 4. 71 (Jerome, *De Hebraicis questionibus*, etc.); O. 7. 41 (Marianus Scottus, *Chronica*); B. 3. 5 (Jerome, *In prophetas*); BL Harley 3859 (Vitruvius, *De architectura* and Vegetius, *Epitome rei militaris*); and Royal 13. A. XI (Helpericus, *Computus*, and Bede, *De natura rerum* and *De temporum ratione*).

A closer examination of the materials of each century, particularly those of the eleventh and twelfth, remains to be undertaken. Several questions suggest themselves: is the interest in and the accumulation of an extensive Greek vocabulary related to the hermeneutic style witnessed in pre-Conquest Anglo-Latin poetry? Are Priscian and Isidore the major source of Greek vocabulary-lists and glosses? What was happening on the continent in the late eleventh and early twelfth centuries? Was there a similarly accelerated interest in Greek? How accurately was it copied, and what relationship existed between English copies and theirs? These questions await answers which, in the present state of our knowledge, are not yet possible.

Finally, it is worth asking at what scriptoria or monastic centres in England most of the texts containing Greek were copied. At first glance, Canterbury seems to be the chief source of many of the texts. However, sometimes manuscripts later owned by Canterbury were not in fact written there. For example, CCCC 221 (the texts of *De orthographia* by Alcuin and Bede) is listed as possibly St Augustine's, but the hand is apparently continental; Oxford, Bodleian Library, Douce 125 (labelled 'pseudo-Boethius, *De geometria*' but containing, in fact, agrommatic material and portions of a geometry text) is assigned to the Old Minster, Winchester, because of a fifteenth-century inscription now erased, but its script more closely resembles that of St Augustine's. The later provenance of a manuscript, therefore, is not always a pointer to its origin. Indeed, a scribe might have moved with an abbot promoted to a bishopric elsewhere and then have continued his scribal activity in the new quarters; in such a case, his earlier products could well be assigned – wrongly – to the new scriptorium. Such may well be the case with Glastonbury. Given that over a period of nearly a century, many of the archbishops of Canterbury had formerly been monks (and sometimes abbots) of Glastonbury,[51] it seems inconceivable that these primates did not sometimes take with them their most expert scribes and illustrators. This may explain, in part, the radically different concurrent scripts ascribed to St Augustine's

---

[51] See J. Scott, *The Early History of Glastonbury: An Edition and Translation of William of Malmesbury's De Antiquitate Glastonie Ecclesie* (Woodbridge, 1981), p. 137, and D. Knowles, *The Monastic Order in England*, 2nd edn (Cambridge, 1963), pp. 65, n. 3, and 697.

scriptorium (which enjoyed a close relationship with Christ Church), one of which must surely have descended from the Welsh round script, or, at the very least, must have been influenced by it. CCCC 356, pt III is a good example. More work on the Canterbury scriptoria needs to be done before manuscripts of various styles of script can be confidently assigned there.

CONCLUSIONS

This study has reviewed the four current assumptions concerning the knowledge of Greek in England. The following observations have emerged:

(1) Greek in Greek characters and Greek as a linguistic alternative to certain Latin texts, chiefly liturgical, form the main evidence for its 'knowledge' in the eighth and early ninth centuries. It reappears in the tenth century as both gloss and text in a number of classical texts, in most of the texts related to the trivium and quadrivium, and in commentaries. Interest in Greek increases, as does accuracy of transmission, in the late Anglo-Saxon period.

(2) Knowledge of Greek in England refers, essentially, to an extensive vocabulary which included words from every discipline.

(3) The chief vehicle of transmission for such vocabulary was glossaries, as distinct from grammars or colloquia. This is not unexpected, in as much as glossaries were used as aids to grammars. One other source (and one which I am beginning to think was more important than glossaries) for the transmission of Greek terms was Isidore's *Etymologiae*; however, more research is needed to verify that supposition.

(4) As for grammar, and in particular, syntax – apart from what we learn from Bede and conjecture about Aldhelm – there is no reliable evidence that the Anglo-Saxons had anything but an extremely limited and imperfect command of Greek.

Nevertheless, what deserves admiration is the Anglo-Saxons' respect for, if not their skill in, a language which led them to preserve in copy after copy of text upon text what they sensed to be linguistically and even theologically valuable. Their knowledge of Greek may not have been informed, but their attitude toward language was. The Anglo-Saxon, capable of exploiting his own vernacular to accommodate Latin theological abstractions as well as intricate riddles, understood through such modes of expression and inquiry that the history of man's relationship to the world and to God lay somehow in the history of language.[52]

---

[52] I am deeply grateful to Michael Lapidge, who has been kind enough to read closely the typescript of this article and who, at every stage of this project, has generously shared with me his expert knowledge of manuscripts and Greek materials. To two other scholars, Helmut Gneuss and Malcolm Wallace, I am also grateful for their long-term advice, encouragement and constructive criticism.

APPENDIX

ILLUSTRATIVE GREEK MATERIALS IN ANGLO-SAXON MANUSCRIPTS

The entries listed below have all been taken from Anglo-Saxon manuscripts; in sum, they give a clear impression of the range of Greek learning which was accessible to Anglo-Saxon commentators and glossators. As will be seen, the Greek explanations printed below are drawn principally from Isidore's *Etymologiae*. The Latin text which consistently attracted Greek explanations was Aldhelm's prose *De laude virginitatis*; substantial amounts of Greek etymology were also to be found in the *Commentarius in Martianum Capellam* by Remigius of Auxerre, and in the anonymous *Scholica graecarum glossarum*, both of which circulated in Anglo-Saxon manuscripts.

In selecting material for inclusion, two principles were followed: (1) if the term (however mangled) was a Greek term; and (2) if the Greek term (however corrupt) was said by the author/glossator to be 'Greek'. A statement to the effect that the term was Greek was not itself a criterion for inclusion: for example, phrases such as 'Grecum nomen' or 'a Graecis dictum', unaccompanied by a presentation of the term's component parts, or the word 'interpretatur' followed by Latin or Old English equivalents, were considered insufficient reasons for inclusion. On the other hand, where a Greek term was followed by a specific Latin or Old English equivalent (even without the verb 'interpretatur' as part of the entry), it is clear that the author-glossator considered those equivalents to be the Latin or vernacular 'interpretations' of the Greek word, and they are thus included. Note finally that in the case of citations from Isidore, I have recorded the Greek accents as they appear in Lindsay's edition.

The following manuscripts are cited:

DIG.146 = Oxford, Bodleian Library, Digby 146 (Aldhelm, prose *De laude virginitatis*)

ROY.15.A.xvi = London, BL, Royal 15. A. xvi (*Scholica graecarum glossarum*)

ROY.15.A.xxxiii = London, BL, Royal 15. A. xxxiii (Remigius, *Commentarius in Martianum Capellam*)

The following abbreviations are used:

ALDH.Virg. = Aldhelm, *De laude virginitatis* (prose)
ISID.Etym. = Isidore, *Etymologiae*
REM.IN MRT. = Remigius of Auxerre, *Commentarius in Martianum Capellam*
SCH.GR. = *Scholica graecarum glossarum*

r.m. = right margin
l.m. = left margin
t.m. = top margin
b.m. = bottom margin

[*'ΑΓΓΕΛΙΑ*] angelium ('announcement')
ALDH. Virg., DIG.146, 50r, r.m.
Euangelium interpretatur bona adnuntiatio. Grece enim eu bonum, ANGELIUM adnuntiatio dicitur. Unde et angelus nuntius interpretatur (ISID.Etym. vi.ii.43; 'eu'] εὖ; ANGELIUM] ἀγγελία).

[*'ΑΓΓΕΛΟΙ*] angeli ('messengers')
ALDH.Virg., DIG.146, 55r, b.m.
Apostoli missi interpretantur; hoc nomen eorum indicat. Nam sicut grece ANGELI latine nuntii interpretantur. Ita grece apostoli latine missi appelantur (ISID.ETYM. vii.ix.1; ANGELI] ἄγγελοι; 'nuntii interpretantur'] 'nuntii vocantur').

[*'ΑΖΥΜΟΣ*] azimus ('unleavened')
SCH.GR., ROY.15.A.xvi, 75r29
Acrizimus, panis, leuiter fermentatus quasi azimus (cf. ISID.Etym. xx.ii.15: 'Azymus non fermentatus; nam ἄζυμος est sine fermento, sincerus. Acroazimus leuiter fermentatus, quasi acroazymus').

[*'ΑΝΕΜΟΣ*] animos ('wind')
ALDH.Virg., DIG.146, 50r, l.m.
Anima a gentilibus nomen accepit, eo quod uentus sit. Unde et grece uentus ANIMOS dicitur quia ore trahentes aerem uiuere uideamur (ISID.Etym. xi.i.7; ANIMOS] ἄνεμος).

[*'ΑΡΕΤΗΣ*] aretis ('excellence, virtue')
REM. IN MRT., ROY.15.A.xxxiii, 19r9
Ars autem a uirtute dicta est, id est APO TIS ARETIS (cf. ISID.Etym. i.i.2: 'Ars vero dicta est, quod artis praeceptis regulisque consistat. Alii dicunt a Graecis hoc tractum esse vocabulum ἀπὸ τῆς ἀρετῆς, id est a virtute, quam scientiam vocaverunt').

[*'ΑΡΙΘΜΟΝ*] rithmon ('number')
ALDH.Virg., DIG.146, 51r, l.m.

Arithmetica est disciplina numerorum; grece numerum RITHMON dicunt (ISID. Etym. iii.i.1; RITHMON] ἀριθμόν).

[*'ΑΡΧΟΣ*] archos ('leader')
ALDH.Virg., DIG.146, 36v, t.m.
Patriarcha interpretatur patrum princeps. ARCHOS enim grece princeps est. Abraham primum uocatus est pater uidens populum (ISID.Etym. vii.vii.1; ARCHOS] 'Αρχός).

[*'ΑΡΧΟΣ*] archos ('leader')
ALDH.Virg., DIG.146, 55r, r.m.
Patriarcha interpretatur patrum princeps; ARCHOS grece princeps est (ISID.Etym. vii.vii.1; see above, ALDH.Virg., DIG.146, 'archos').

[*'ΑΦΡΟΣ*] afro ('foam, froth')
REM.IN MRT., ROY.15.A.xxxiii, 23r24
Venus autem afrodite uocatur, hoc est spuma, quia AFRO grece spuma dicitur (cf. ISID.Etym. viii.xi.77: 'Hanc Graeci 'Αφροδίτην vocant propter spuman sanguinis generantem. 'Αφρὸς enim Graece spuma vocatur. . . . et inde 'Αφροδίτην Venerem dici').

[*ΒΑΛΕ*] bali ('throw!')
ALDH.Virg., DIG.146, 56v, l.m.
Balista genus tormenti ab emittendo iacula dicta. BALI enim grece mitte dicitur. Torquentur enim uerbere neruorum et magna ui iacet, aut astas aut saxa (ISID.Etym. xviii.x.2; 'BALI enim grece mitte'] 'Βαλεῖν enim Graece mittere').

[*ΒΑΠΤΙΣΜΟΣ*] batismum ('a dipping in water')
ALDH.Virg., DIG.146, 51v, l.m.
BAPTISMUM grece latine tinctio interpretatur; quod idcirco tinctio dicitur, quia ibi homo spiritu gratiae in

melius immutatur, et longe aluid quam erat efficitur (ISID.Etym. vi.xix.43).

[*BAΣIΛÍKOΣ*] basilicus ('Basilisk') ALDH.Virg., DIG.146, 41r, t.m.

BASILICUS grece latine interpretatur regulus eo quod sit rex serpentium, adeo ut eum uidentes fugiant quia olfactus suo eos necat. Nam et hominem uel si aspicit interimit (ISID.Etym. xii.iv.6; 'olfactus'] 'olfactu'; 'aspicit'] 'aspiciat').

[*BÍBΛON*] biblum ('book') ALDH.Virg., DIG.146, 47r, r.m.

Liber enim greci BIBLUM uocant; et dicitur liber in quo scribimus quia ante usum carte uel membranarum de libris arborum uolumina fiebant (cf. ISID.Etym. vi.xiv.1 and xii.3; 'liber'] 'librum'; BIBLUM] βίβλον).

[*BOIΩTÍA*] boeti ('Boeotia, so called from its rich cattle-pastures') ALDH.Virg., DIG.146, 40v, t.m.

Bouem greci BOETI uocant (uel dicunt); hunc latini trionem uocant, eo quod terram terat, quasi terionem, Neuius, trionum hic moderator rusticus (cf. ISID.Etym. XII.i.30; BOETI] βοῦν; see also ISID.Etym. xiv.iv.11: 'sicque locum de nomine bovis Boeotiam nominavit').

[*BÓTPΥΣ*] botrio ('cluster of grapes') ALDH.Virg., DIG.146, 63r, intr.gls.

Racemus est botrioris pars et BOTRIO grecum est (ISID.Etym. xvii.v.15; 'botrioris'] 'botrionis').

[*ΓENEIÁΣ* or *ΓÉNEION*] genos ('beard') ALDH.Virg., DIG.146, 47v, r.m.

Gene sunt inferiores oculorum partes. Unde barbae inchoant. Nam grece GENOS barbae. Hinc et gene quia inde incipiant barbae gigni (ISID.Etym. xi.i.43; GENOS] γένειον).

[*ΔÓΞA*] doxa ('glory') ALDH.Virg., DIG.146, 43r, t.m.

Orthodoxus est recte credens et ut credit uiuens. Ortho enim grece recte dicitur. DOXA gloria autem uir recte glorie, quo nomine non potest uocari qui aliter uiuit quam credit (ISID.Etym. vii.xiv.5; 'Ortho'] *Ὀρθῶς*; DOXA] δόξα; 'gloria autem uir recte'] 'gloria est: hoc est vir rectae gloriae').

[*ΔÉOΣ*] theos ('fear; reverence') ALDH.Virg., DIG.146, 51v, l.m.

Nam deus grece THEOS phebos dicitur, id est timor. Unde tractum est deus quod eum colentibus sit timor (ISID.Etym. vii.i.5; THEOS] δέος; 'phebos'] *'φόβος'*).

[*ΔPÁKONTA*] draconta ('dragon, serpent') ALDH.Virg., DIG.146, 18r, r.m.

Draco maior cunctorum serpentium siue animantium omnium super terram; hinc uocant DRACONTA grece, unde deriuatum ut draco diceretur, qui sepe ab speluncis abstractus fertur (ISID.Etym. xii.iv.4; DRACONTA] δράκοντα; 'unde deriuatum ut'] 'unde et derivatum est in Latinum ut').

[*'EΘNIKOÍ*] ethnici ('foreign, gentiles') ALDH.Virg., DIG.146, 49v, l.m.

ETHNICI enim ex greco in latinum interpretantur gentiles. Ethnos grece gens dicitur (ISID.Etym. viii.x.3; 'Ethnos'] *Ἔθνος*).

[*'EΘNOΣ*] ethnos ('nation, people') ALDH.Virg., DIG.146, 49v, l.m.

Ethnici enim ex greco in latinum interpretantur gentiles. ETHNOS gens dicitur (ISID.Etym. viii.x.3; see above, ALDH.Virg., DIG.146, 'ethnici').

[*ΕΚΚΛΗΣΙΑ*] ecclesia ('assembly')
ALDH.Virg., DIG.146, 44r, r.m.

ECCLESIA grecum est quod in latinum uertitur conuocatio propter quod omnes ad se conuocet (ISID.Etym. VII.i.1; 'ad se conuocet'] 'ad se vocet').

[*ΕΠΤΑ*] epta ('seven')
ALDH.Virg., DIG.146, 55v, l.m.

Ebdomada dicta a numero uii dierum quorum repetitione et menses, et anni, et secula peraguntur. EPTA grece uii dicunt, hanc nos septimanam uocamus, quasi septem luces, nam mane lux est (ISID.Etym. v.xxxii.1; EPTA] ἑπτά).

[*ΕΡΓΑ*] erga ('works')
ALDH.Virg., DIG.146, 56r, r.m.

Ergasterium locus est ubi opus aliquod fit; greco sermone ERGA opera, sterio statio, id est, operarii statio (ISID.Etym. xv.vi.1; ERGA] ἔργα; 'sterio'] στήριον).

[*ΕΥ*] eu ('well')
ALDH.Virg., DIG.146, 50r, r.m.

Euangelium interpretatur bona adnuntiatio. Grece enim EU bonum, angelium adnuntiatio dicitur. Unde et angelus nuntius interpretatur (ISID.Etym. VI.ii.43; see above, ALDH.Virg., DIG.146, 'angelium').

[*ΘΕΟΣ*] theos ('God')
ALDH.Virg., DIG.146, 51v, l.m.

Nam deus grece THEOS phebos dicitur, id est timor. Unde tractum est deus quod eum colentibus sit timor (cf. ISID.Etym. VII.i.5; see above, ALDH.Virg., DIG.146, '*ΔΕΟΣ*/theos').

[*ΘΥΜΙΑΜΑ*] timiama ('incense, that which is burned as incense')
ALDH.Virg., DIG.146, 27v, l.m.

Timiama incensum. TIMIAMA grece uocatur quod sit odor exorabile (ISID.Etym. IV.xii: 'Thymiama lingua Graeca vocatur, quod sit odorabile').

[*ΙΟΣ*] ἰός ('poison, esp. of serpents')
ALDH.Virg., DIG.146, 31v, r.m.

Aspis uocata quod morsu uenenum immittit et spargit. IOS grece uenenum dicunt et inde aspis quod morsu uenenato interimat (ISID.Etym. XII.iv.12; IOS] ἰός).

[*ΙΣΤΟΡΕΙΝ*] historin ('to learn by inquiry, to narrate what one has learned')
ALDH.Virg., DIG.146, 37v, l.m.

Historia est narratio rei gestae, per quam ea quae in praeterito facta sunt dinoscuntur. Dicta grecae historia APOTO HISTORIN, id est a uidere uel agnoscere (ISID.Etym. I.xli; APOTO HISTORIN] ἀπὸ τοῦ ἱστορεῖν; 'agnoscere'] 'cognoscere').

[*ΙΣΤΟΡΕΙΝ*] historin ('to learn by inquiry, to narrate what one has learned')
REM.IN MRT., ROY.15.A.xxxiii, 123v8

Narrationum genera: Historia dicitur *ΑΠΟ ΤΟΥ HISTORIN*, id est uidere. (intrl. gls. YCTOPIN)

[*ΚΑΛΛΙ*-] calli (in compd. words: adds the idea of 'beautiful' to the simple word, or is like an adj. with its subst., as καλλίπαις = καλὴ παῖς)
SCH.GR., ROY.15.A.xvi, 80r10

Calliopea quasi CALLIphone, id est bona uox significatio tamen deriuatur a uerbo callio poio grece composito quod est bene facio uel compono.

[?*ΚΑΛΛΙΟΝ* for *ΚΑΛΛΙΩΝ*] callion ('more beautiful'; comp. of καλός, 'beautiful', but Lat. pulchra uox = καλὴ φωνή)
REM.IN MRT., ROY.15.A.xxxiii, 6v2

Interpretatur autem secundum fulgentium CALLION phone, id est pulchra uox; siue calliopea dicta pulchrifica uel pulchre faciens, quia callos grece pulcher, poio facio, hinc et poeta dicitur.

[*KAΛΏΣ*] callio ('beautifully, well')
SCH.GR., ROY.15.A.xvi, 80v11

Calliopea quasi calliphone, id est bona uox significatio tamen deriuatur uerbo CALLIO poio grece composito quod est bene facio uel compono.

[*KAΛΏΣ*] callos ('beautifully, well')
REM.IN MRT., ROY.15.A.xxxiii, 6v3

Interpretatur autem secundum fulgentium callion phone, id est pulchra uox; siue calliopea dicta pulchrifica uel pulchre faciens, quia CALLOS grece pulcher, poio facio, hinc et poeta dicitur.

[?*KAMOUP*] camur, prob. root of κάμπτω = 'to bend, curve'; cf. καμάρα = 'anything arched or vaulted'; cf. Lat. *camur*)
REM.IN MRT., ROY.15.A.xxxiii, 130v20

CAMIR grece, curuum latine, inde camera proprie dicitur punctus meridialis eo quod curuatur sol et inclinatur ab illo. Transfertur autem ad culmina aliarum rerum, Laqueata picta (cf. ISID.Etym. xv.viii.5: 'Camerae sunt volumina introrsum respicientia, appellatae, a curvo; καμουρ enim Graece curvum est. Lacquearia sunt quae cameram subtegunt et ornant, quae et lacunaria dicuntur').

[*KANῆ*] canon ('rule')
ALDH.Virg., DIG.146, 52v, l.m.

CANON grece latine regula nuncupatur. Canones generalium conciliorum a temporibus constantini ceperunt (cf. ISID.Etym. vi.xvi.1–2).

[*KAPΔÍAN*] cardian ('heart')
ALDH.Virg., DIG.146, 54r, t.m.

Cor a greca apellatione deriuatum quia illi CARDIAN dicunt siue a cura. In eo omnis sollicitudo et scientiae causa manet, quod ideo pulmoni uicinium est (ISID.Etym. xi.i.118; 'CARDIAN'] καρδίαν; 'quod'] 'Qui'; 'uicinium est']

'vicinus est ut, cum ira accenditur pulmonis humore temperetur').

[*KAPΔÍAΣ*] cardias ('heart')
ALDH.Virg., DIG.146, 46v. l.m.

Cardo est locus in quo ostium uertitur et semper mouetur, dictus APOTU CARDIAS quod quis cor hominem totum, ita ille cuneus ianuam regat ac moueat (ISID.Etym. xv.vii.7; APOTU CARDIAS] ἀπὸ τοῦ καρδίας; 'quis'] 'quasi').

[*KΛÉΠTEIN*] kleptin ('to steal; to conceal')
ALDH.Virg., DIG.146, 35r, t.m.

Clipeus est scutu maius dictus eoquod clipet, id est celet, corpus periculisque subducat APOTOΥ KΛEΠTIN (ISID.Etym. xviii.xii.1; APOTOΥ KΛEΠTIN] ἀπὸ τοῦ κλέπτειν).

[*KΛÉΠTEIN*] kleptin ('to steal; to conceal')
REM.IN MRT., ROY.15.A.xxxiii, 34r17–18.

Clypeum enim est maius scutum; dictum clypeum APO TU KLEPTIN somata, id est a furando corpora; siue ut quidam dicunt clypeum dicitur quasi clupeum a uerbo cluo, id est defendo.

[*KΛῆPOΣ*] cleros ('casting lots; a portion, inheritance')
ALDH.Virg., DIG.146, 35r, t.m.

Cleros uel clericos hinc apellatos quia mathias sorte electus est, quem primum per apostolos legimus ordinatum. CLEROS grece sors uel hereditas dicitur; propterea dicti clerici, quia de sorte sunt domini, uel quia domini partem habent (ISID.Etym. vii.xii.1; CLEROS] κλῆρος).

[*KΛÍNHN*] clinum ('that on which one lies, a couch, a bed')
ALDH.Virg., DIG.146, 52r, r.m.

Triclinium est cenaculum a tribus lectulis discumbentium dictum. Apud ueteres in loco, ubi conuiuii apparatus exponebatur, tres lectuli strati erant, in quibus discumbentes epulabantur. CLINUM grece lectum uel adcubitum dicitur ex quo confectum est ut triclinium (ISID.Etym. xv.iii.9; 'clinum grece lectum uel adcubitum'] '*κλίνη* enim Graece lectus vel adcubitus'; 'triclinium'] 'triclinium diceretur').

[?*KΛΩNÍA*] colodonia ('a young slip or shoot of a tree')
ALDH.Virg., DIG.146, 67r, r.m.

Pix grecum nomen est quam illi pissa uocant. Alii uolunt ex pino picem. Hec a grecis apellatur COLODONIA. Nos ramalem dicere possumus, cuius probabilis splendens, lenis, et munda (ISID.Etym. xvii.vii.72; 'pissa'] *πίσσαν*; 'picem'] 'picem vocari'; COLODONIA] *κλωνία*).

[*KÓKKON*] coccum (a kernel, a berry')
ALDH.Virg., DIG.146, 22r, t.m.

COCCUM greci nos rubrum seu uermiculum dicimus; est uermiculus ex siluestribus frondibus (ISID.Etym. xix.xxviii.1; COCCUM] *κόκκον*).

[*KYEÎN*] cine ('to contain, to carry in the womb')
ALDH.Virg., DIG.146, 51v, l.m.

Canabula sunt lectuli in quibus infantes iacere consuerunt, dicta quod partui adhibeantur, quasi cinabula; nam CINE est grece enixi (ISID.Etym. xx.xi.6; 'quasi cinabula; nam CINE est grece enixi'] 'quasi cynabula; nam *κυεῖν* est Graece eniti').

[*ΛAÓΣ*] lao ('the people')
ALDH.Virg., DIG.146, 66r, r.m.

Populus tota ciuitas est; populus uero COYXNA)─(OIC, id est *CΠOCYC*.

Unde et populus dictus est; grece autem populus LAO dicitur a lapidibus (cf. ISID.Etym. ix.iv.6: 'populus vero †*σουχναμοις*† dicitur, id est †*σιτοασις*†. Unde et populus dictus. Graece autem populus *λαός* dicitur, a lapidibus').

[*ΛAÓΣ*] laos ('the people')
SCH.GR., ROY. 15.A.xvi, 80v27

LAOS populus, inde laicus homo popularis dicitur (cf. ISID.Etym. vii.14.9: 'Laicus popularis. *Λαός* enim Graece populus dicitur').

[*ΛÉΩN*] leon ('lion')
ALDH.Virg., DIG.146, 54r, b.m.

Leonis uocabulum ex greca origine inflexum est in Latinum; grece LEON uocatur, et est nomen notum quia ex parte corruptum. Leo autem grece, latine rex interpretatur, rex eo quod princeps sit bestiarum omnium (cf. ISID.Etym. xii.ii.3: 'corruptum. Leaena vero totum Graecum est, sicut et dracaena. Ut autem leaena lea dicatur usurpatum est a poetis').

[*MANTEÍA*] mantia ('divination, prophecy')
ALDH.Virg., DIG.146, 47r, b.m.

Nicro enim grece mortuus. MANTIA diuinatio nuncupatur. Ad quos suscitandos cadaueri sanguis adicitur. Nam amare demones sanguinem dicunt. Ideoque quoties nicromantia fit cruor aquae miscetur ut colore sanguinis facilius prouocentur (ISID.Etym. viii.ix.11; 'Nicro'] *Nεκρός*; MANTIA] *μαντεία*; 'suscitandos'] 'sciscitandos'; 'dicunt'] 'dicitur'; 'colore'] 'cruore').

[*MAPΣÍΠION*] marsupia ('bag, pouch')
ALDH.Virg., DIG.146, 66v, l.m.

Marsupium sacculus nummorum quem greci MARSIPA apellant.

Quaedam greca nomina in latinum paululum inflectuntur propter romanum eloquium (ISID.Etym. xx.ix.5; MARSIPA] μαρσίπιον).

[*MÁPTYPEΣ*] martyres ('witnesses') ALDH.Virg., DIG.146, 5or, l.m.

MARTYRES grece lingua latine testes dicuntur. Unde et testimonia grece martyria nuncupantur. Testes ideo dicuntur quia propter testimonium christi passiones sustinuerunt, et usque ad mortem pro ueritate certauerunt (ISID.Etym. vii.xi.1; 'dicuntur'] 'vocati sunt').

[*MAPTYPÍA*] martyria ('testimony') ALDH.Virg., DIG.146, 5or, l.m.

Martyres grece lingua latine testes dicuntur. Unde et testimonia grece MAPTYPIA nuncupantur. Testes ideo dicuntur quia propter testimonium Christi passiones sustinuerunt, et usque ad mortem pro ueritate certauerunt (ISID.Etym. vii.xi.1; ἡ μαρτυρία, testimony; τὸ μαρτύριον, testimony; cf. E.A. Sophocles, *Greek Lexikon of the Roman and Byzantine Periods, From 146 B.C.–A.D. 1100* (New York, 1887)).

[*MÉΛAN*] melan ('black, dark') ALDH.Virg., DIG.146, 47v, b.m.

Melancolia dicta eo quod sit nigri sanguinis fecae admixta habundantia fellis. Greci enim MELAN nigrum uocant, fel autem colen apellant (ISID.Etym. iv.v.6; MELAN] μέλαν; 'colen'] χολήν).

[*MÉΛIΣΣA*] mellesse ('bee') ALDH.Virg., DIG.146, 52r, l.m.

Mel grece apellationis est quia ab apibus nomen habere probatur. Nam apis grece MELLESSE dicitur. Antea mella de rore erant, inueniebanturque in arundinum foliis (ISID.Etym. xx.ii.36; MELLESSE] μέλισσα).

[*MÉΣON*] meson ('middle, in the middle')
REM.IN MRT., ROY.15.A.xxxiii, 28v4

Valitudo autem TON MESON est. Nam et bonam et malam ualitudinem cum epyteto dicimus.

[*MÉΣON*] meson ('middle, in the middle')
SCH.GR., ROY.15.A.xvi, 83v1

TON MESON, medius sonus siue uerbum quod dupliciter potest intellegi, sicut seuus magnus et seuus crudelis. Ut seua iuno uirgilius pro magna.

[*METAΛΛÂN*] metallon ('to mine, quarry')
ALDH.Virg., DIG.146, 22r, r.m.

Metallum dictum grece *ΠAPA TO METAΛΛON* quod natura eius ea sit ut ubi una uena apparuerit, ibi sit alterius inquirini (ISID.Etym. xvi.xvii; *ΠAPATOMETAΛΛON*] παρὰ τοῦ μεταλλᾶν).

[*MÍHNH*] mene ('the moon')
ALDH.Virg., DIG.146, 63v, l.m.
Mensis nomen est grecum de lunae nomine tractatum; luna enim MENE greco sermone uocatur. Unde et apud hebreos menses legitimi non ex solis circulo sed ex lunae cursu enumerantur, quod est de noua ad nouam (ISID.Etym. v.xxxiii.1; 'tractatum'] 'tractum'; MENE] μήνη).

[*'OΛON*] olo ('whole, entire')
ALDH.Virg., DIG.146, 52r, r.m.
Oloserica tota serica; OLO enim totum (ISID.Etym. xix.xxii.14; OLO] ὅλον).

[*'OMΦÁKIAN*] onfacion ('oil from unripe olives or juice from unripe grapes')
ALDH.Virg., DIG.146, 45r., b.m.
Oleum autem ab olea nominatum. Nam ut diximus olea est arbor. Unde

Mary Catherine Bodden

deriuatio fit oleum, sed quod ex albis fuerit oliuis expressum uocatur spanum a grecis ONFACION apellatum (ISID. Etym. xvii.vii.68; 'spanum'] 'Hispanum'; ONFACION] ὀμφάκιον).

[*ΟΡΘΩΣ*] ortho ('rightly, justly') ALDH.Virg., DIG.146, 43r, t.m.

Orthodoxus est recte credens et ut credit uiuens. ORTHO enim grece recte dicitur. Doxa gloria autem uir recte glorie, quo nomine non potest uocari qui aliter uiuit quam credit (ISID.Etym. vii.xiv.5; ORTHO] *Ορθῶς*; Doxa] δόξα; 'gloria autem uir'] 'gloria est: hoc est vir').

[*ΠΑΙΔΑΓΩΓΟΣ*] pedagogus ('attending, training boys; hence, gen., teacher') ALDH.Virg., DIG.146, 22r, l.m.

PEDAGOGUS grecum Pedagogum eruditorem.

[*ΠΑΙΔΑΓΩΓΟΣ*] pedagogus ('attending, training boys; hence, gen., teacher') ALDH.Virg., DIG.146, 54v, b.m.

PEDAGOGUS est cui paruuli adsignantur; grecum nomen est et est compositum ab eo quod pueros agat, id est ductet et lasciuientem refrenet aetatem (cf. ISID.Etym. x.206).

[*ΠΑΛΗΝ*] palin ('wrestling') ALDH.Virg., DIG.146, 53v, r.m.

Membra dicta quod in luctando eas premimus quam greci PALIN dicuntur (cf. ISID.Etym. xi.i.94: 'Palae sunt dorsi dextra laevaque eminentia membra, dicta quod in luctando eas premimus; quod Graeci πάλην dicunt').

[*ΠΑΛΗΣ*] palesit ('wrestling') ALDH.Virg., DIG.146, 7v, l.m.

Locus luctationis palestra dicitur. Palestram uel APOTOS PALESIT, id est a luctatione, uel apoto palesin, id est a motu ruinae fortis nominatum dicunt.

(ISID.Etym. xviii.xxiv; APOTOS PALESIT] ἀπὸ τῆς πάλης; 'apoto palesin'] ἀπὸ τοῦ πάλλειν; 'nominatum'] 'nominatam').

[*ΠΑΛΗΣ*] palis ('wrestling') REM.IN MRT., ROY.15. A.xxxiii, 97v13–14

Palestra autem dicta APO TIS PALIS, id est a lucatione rustica, vel apo ton palon, id est a motu urnae, per sortem enim luctabantur.

[*ΠΑΛΛΕΙΝ*] palesin ('to wrestle, struggle') ALDH.Virg., DIG.146, 7v, l.m.

Locus luctationis palestra dicitur. Palestram uel apotos palesit, id est a luctatione, uel APOTO PALESIN, id est a motu ruinae fortis nominatum dicunt. (see above, ALDH.Virg., DIG.146, 'palesit').

[*ΠΑΛΩΝ*] palon ('wrestling, struggles') REM.IN MRT., ROY.15.A.xxxiii, 129v1

Palestra dicitur *ΑΠΟ ΤΟΝ ΠΑΛΟΝ*, id est a luctatione, hinc et palestrices luctator.

[*ΠΑΝ*] pan ('all, entire') ALDH.Virg., DIG.146, 63v, r.m.

Panis dictus quia cum omni cibo assumatur uel quia omne animal eum appetat; PAN grece omne dicitur (ISID.Etym. xx.ii.15: 'Panis dictus quod cum omni cibo adponatur, vel quod omne animal eum adpetat; πᾶν enim Graece omne dicitur').

[*ΠΑΣΧΕΙΝ*] pascin ('to suffer, to be affected') ALDH.Virg., DIG.146, 45r, t.m.

Pasche uocabulum non grecum sed hebreum est. Nec a passione quam PASCIN grece dicitur pati, sed a transitu hebreo uerbo pascha appellatum est,

240

eoquod tunc populus dei ex egipto transierit (ISID.Etym. vi.xvii.11; 'quam PASCIN'] 'quoniam πᾶσχειν').

[*ΠΕΛΛΑΓΟΣ*] pelagus ('sea, high, open sea')
ALDH.Virg., DIG.146, 26r, l.m.
PELAGUS gurges, uorago, mare greco. (cf. ISID.Etym. xiii.16.10: πλαγίου).

[*ΠΕΝΤΕ*] penta ('five')
ALDH.Virg., DIG.146, 63r, t.m.
Pentecosten sicut et pascha apud hebreos celebris dies erat quia post .v. decadas pasche celebratur. Unde et uocabulum sumpsit. PENTA grece .v. in quo die secundum legem panes propositiones de nouis frugibus offerebantur, cuius figuram anno iubileus in testamento uetere gessit (ISID.Etym. vi.xviii.4; 'celebratur'] 'colebatur'; PENTA] Πέντε).

[?*ΠΕΠΛΟΝ*] papaten ('any woven cloth, sheet, curtain; robe or shawl')
ALDH.Virg., DIG.146, 22r, r.m.
Bissum genus est quoddam lini nimium candidi et mollissimi quod grece PAPATEN uocant (ISID.Etym. xix.xxvii.4; cf. REM. IN MRT., ROY. 15.A.xxxiii 45r9–11: 'Uidebatur illud peplum ex netibus id est filis uel telis, candentis pro candidi, BYSSI. Apportat id est exigit. Byssus genus est lini candidissimi et mollissimi').

[*ΠΙΣΣΑΝ*] pissa ('pitch')
ALDH.Virg., DIG.146, 57v, l.m.
Pix, pice grecum nomen est, quam illi PISSA uocant (cf. ISID.Etym. xvii. vii. 72).

[*ΠΙΣΣΑΝ*] pissa ('pitch')
ALDH.Virg., DIG.146, 67r, r.m.
Pix grecum nomen est quam illi PISSA uocant. Alii uolunt ex pino picem; hec a

grecis apellatur colodonia. Nos ramalem dicere possumus, cuius probabilis splendens, lenis et munda (cf. ISID.Etym. xvii.vii.72).

[*ΠΛΑΓΙΟΥ*] plagia ('sides, sideways')
ALDH.Virg., DIG.146, 18v, l.m.
Pelagus est latitudo maris sine litore et portu, greco nomine APO TU PLAGIA, hoc est altitudine dictum (ISID.Etym. xiii.xvi.10; 'altitudine'] 'a latitudine'; cf. πελάγιος, α, ον, 'of or belonging to the sea').

[*ΠΛΑΓΙΟΥ*] plagia ('sides, sideways')
ALDH.Virg., DIG.146, 50v, r.m.
Pelagus est latitudo maris sine litore et portu greco nomine APOTU PLAGIA, hoc est altitudine dictum. Unde et plagia eo quod sint inportuosa (cf. ALDH.Virg. DIG.146, 18v, 'plagia').

[?*ΠΛΑΣΤΙΚΕΙΝ*, > *ΠΛΑΣΤΙΚΗ*] plasticen ('to form, mould, shape')
ALDH.Virg., DIG.146, 16v, l.m.
Protoplastus homo qui ex limo primis est conditus. PLASTICEN grece fingere terra similitudinem (cf. ISID.Etym. xix.xv.1: 'Unde et protoplastus est dictus homo qui ex limo primus est conditus'; cf. Lat. 'plastice').

[*ΠΟΔΑΣ*] podas ('feet')
ALDH.Virg., DIG.146, 58r, r.m.
Pedes ex greca ethimologia nomen sortiti sunt; hos greci PODAS dicunt qui alternis motibus solo fixi incedunt (ISID.Etym. xi.i.112; PODAS] πόδας).

[*ΠΟΙΕΩ*] poio ('make, produce')
REM.IN MRT., ROY.15.A.xxxiii, 6v3
Interpretatur autem secundum Fulgentium callion phone, id est pulchra uox; siue calliopea dicta pulchrifica uel pulchre faciens, quia callos grece pulcher, POIO facio, hinc at poeta dicitur.

[*ΠΟΙΕΩ*] poio ('make, produce')
SCH.GR., ROY.15.A.xvi,80v11

Calliopea quasi `calli phono, id est bona uox significatio tamen deriuatur a uerbo POIO grece composito quod est bene facio uel compono.

[*ΠΟΡΦΥΡΑ*] purphira ('the purple fish, transf., purple')
ALDH.Virg., DIG.146, 22r, t.m.

Purpura apud latinos a puritate lucis uocata. Apud grecos PURPHIRA dicitur (ISID.Etym. xix.xxviii.5; 'PURPHIRA dicitur'] *πόρφυρα* dicitur cum adspiratione, apud nos purpura sine adspiratione').

[*ΠΡΑΓΜΑ*] pragma ('a thing done, matter, affair')
SCH.GR., ROY.15.A.xvi, 82v14

PRAGMA, causa. Unde pragmatica negotia dicuntur. Auctor quoque causarum et negotiorum pragmaticus nuncupatur (ISID.Etym. v.xxii: '*Πρᾶγμα* Graecum est, quod Latine dicitur causa, unde et pragmatica negotia dicuntur, et actor causarum et negotiorum pragmaticus nuncupatur').

[*ΠΡΕΣΒΥΤΕΡΟΣ*] presbiter ('elder; gen. greater, higher')
ALDH.Virg., DIG.146, 45v, b.m.

PRESBITER grece latine senior interpretatur, non pro aetate uel decrepita senectute, sed propter honorem et dignitatem quam acceperunt presbiter nominantur (ISID.Etym. vii.xii.20).

[*ΠΥΡ*] pira ('fire')
ALDH.Virg., DIG.146, 57v, l.m.

Pira est quae in modum arce ex lignis construi sola ut ardeat. PIRA enim ignis est, sed pira est ipsa lignorum congeries cum nondum ardet (ISID.Etym. xx.x.9; 'arce'] 'arae'; 'sola'] 'solet'; PIRA] *πῦρ*).

[*ΠΕΙΝ*] rei ('to flow, gush')
ALDH.Virg., DIG.146, 67r, b.m.

Resinam greci retinam uocant. REI grece dicitur quicquid manat. Est enim lacrima sudore exalata lignorum ut cerasis. lentisci balsami uel reliquarum arborum sive uirgultarum quae sudare produntur; sicut et odorata orientis ligna, sicut gutta balsami ac ferularum uel sucinorum cuius lacrima durescit in gemma (ISID.Etym. xvii.vii.71; 'retinam'] *ῥητίνην*; REI] *ῥεῖν*; 'cerasis'] 'cerasi').

[*ΡΗΣΙΣ*] resis ('speaking; word, speech')
ALDH.Virg., DIG.146, 51r, r.m.

Dicta autem rethorica greca apellatione apoto rethoresin, id est a copia locutionis. RESIS apud grecos locutio dicitur (ISID.Etym. ii.i.1; 'apoto rethoresin'] *ἀπὸ τοῦ ῥητορίζειν*; 'RESIS'] *Ῥῆσις*).

[*ΡΗΤΙΝΗΝ*] retinam ('resin')
ALDH.Virg., DIG.146, 67r, b.m.

Resinam greci RETINAM uocant. Rei grece dicitur quicquid manat. Est enim lacrima sudore exalata lignorum ut cerasis lentisci balsami uel reliquarum arborum siue uirgultarum quae sudare produntur; sicut et odorata orientis ligna, sicut gutta balsami ac ferularum uel sucinorum cuius lacrima durescit in gemma (ISID.Etym. xvii.vii.71; see above, ALDH.Virg. DIG.146: *ΠΕΙΝ*).

[*ΡΗΤΟΡΙΖΕΙΝ*] rethoresin ('to practise oratory')
ALDH.Virg., DIG.146, 51r, r.m.

Dicta autem rethorica greca apellatione APOTO RETHORESIN, id est copia locutionis. Resis apud grecos locutio dicitur (see above, ALDH.Virg., DIG.146: *ΡΗΣΙΣ*).

[? 'ΡΎΓΧΟΣ] riahos ('of birds: a beak; of swine: a snout')
ALDH.Virg., DIG.146, 62v, l.m.
Rostrum os quod greci RIAHOS dicunt proprie tamen rostrum dicitur quod incuruum est in uultures accipieris.

[ΣΆΡΞ] sarca ('flesh')
ALDH.Virg., DIG.146, 47r, r.m.
Sarcofagum grecum est nomen eoquod ibi corpora adsumantur; SARCA enim grece caro latine, fagus comedere dicitur (ISID.Etym. xv.xi.2: 'Sarcophagus Graecum est nomen, eo quod ibi corpora absumantur; σάρξ enim Graece caro, φαγεῖν comedere dicitur').

[ΣΆΡΞ] sarca ('flesh')
ALDH.Virg., DIG.146, 57v, l.m.
Sarcofagum grecum nomen est eo quod ibi corpora assumantur; SARCA grece caro, fagus comedere dicitur. (cf. above, ALDH.Virg., DIG.146, 47r, 'sarca').

[ΣΆΡΞ] sarchia ('flesh')
ALDH.Virg., DIG.146, 32r, r.m.
Sarcophagum nomen grecum est eoquod ibi corpora assumantur. SARCHIA grece caro, phagus, comedere. (cf. above. ALDH.Virg., DIG.146, 47r, 57v, 'sarca').

[†ΣΙΤΟΑΣΙΣ†] sposus (unattested)
ALDH.Virg., DIG.146, 66r, r.m.
Populus tota ciuitas est; populus uero COYXNA)—(OIC, id est, CΠOCYC. Unde et populus dictus est, grece autem populus lao dicitur a lapidibus (ISID.Etym. ix.iv.6: 'Populus ergo tota civitas est; vulgus vero plebs est. Plebs autem dicta a pluralitate; maior est enim numerus minorum quam seniorum. Populus vero †σουχναμοις† dicitur, id est †σιτοασις†. Unde et populus dictus est. Graece autem populus λαὸς dicitur, a lapidibus.').

[†ΣΟΥΧΝΑΜΟΙΣ†]   souxnamis
(unattested; but, absol. συχνοί means 'many people together'; see also συχνὸν ποεῖν, 'make the small town populous'; cf. Plato, *Republic*, 370 d).
ALDH.Virg., DIG.146, 66r, r.m.
Populus tota ciuitas est; populus uero COYXNA)—(OIC, id est, CΠOCYC. Unde et populus dictus est, grece autem populus lao dicitur a lapidibus (cf. above, ALDH.Virg., DIG.146, ΣΙΤΟΑΣΙΣ/ CΠOCYC).

[ΣΤΉΡΙΟΝ] sterio ('place, station')
ALDH.Virg., DIG.146, 56r, r.m.
Ergasterium locus est ubi opus aliquod fit; greco sermone erga opera, STERIO statio, id est, operarii statio (ISID.Etym. xv.vi.1; 'erga'] ἔργα; STERIO] στήριον).

[ΣΤΟΙΧΕῖΟΝ] stochium ('in physics: primary matter, elements')
SCH.GR., ROY. 15.A.xvi, 80r5
Sed melius ab yle uenit quod est grecum et interpretatur materies, et mutatis litteris scribitur elementum quod grece dicitur STOCHIUM (cf. ISID.Etym. xiii.iii.2: 'Hanc ὕλην Latini materiam appellaverunt, ideo quia omne informe, unde aliquid faciendum est, semper materia nuncupatur. Proinde et eam poetae silvam nominaverunt, nec incongrue, quia materiae silvarum sunt. Graeci autem elementa στοιχεῖα nuncupant . . .')

[ΣΥΛΛΟΓΙΣΜΌΣ]   sillogismus
('syllogism')
ALDH.Virg., DIG.146, 52v, l.m.
Sillogismus est contorta et captiosa conclusionis significatio. SILLOGISMUS grece latine argumentatio interpretatur. Sillogismis, id est dialecticis. (ISID.Etym. ii.ix.1 and 16: 'Syllogismus Graece, Latine argumentatio appellatur; . . . latitudine

distans et productione sermonis a dialectis syllogismis, propter quod rhetoribus datur').

[*ΣΎΝΟΔΟΝ*] sinodum ('meeting, assembly')
ALDH.Virg., DIG.146, 47r, l.m.

SINODUM ex greco interpretari comitatum uel coetum. Concilii nomen tractum ex more Romano. Tempore quo cause agebantur conueniebant omnes in unum. (ISID.Etym. vi.xvi.11; 'in unum'] 'in unum communique intentione tractabant').

[*TÉKTONOΣ*] tectonos ('carpenter; any craftsman or workman')
ALDH.Virg., DIG.146, 45v, t.m.

Fabros autem siue artifices greci TECTONOS uocant. Id est instructores architecti autem cimentarii sunt qui disponunt in fundamentis, unde et apostolus de semetipso quasi sapiens inquit architectus fundamentum posui. (ISID.Etym. xix.viii.1–2; TEKTONOS] τέκτονας).

[*TPΑΓΟΣ*] tragos ('a he-goat')
ALDH.Virg., DIG.146, 57v, l.m.

Tragoedi dicti quia initium canentibus premium erat hyrcus quem greci TRAGOS uocant. Unde [H]oratius carmine qui tragico uilem certauit ob yrcum. (ISID.Etym. viii.vi.5; TRAGOS] τράγος).

[*TPINAKPÍA*] Trinacria ('three peaks')
ALDH.Virg., DIG.146, 66r, t.m.

Sicilia a sicano rege sicania cognominata est, deinde a siculo Itali fratre sicilia. Prius Trinacria dicta propter Trinacria, id est promontoria: pleorum, pachinum, et liberum. TRINACRIA grecum est quod latine triquadra dicitur. (ISID.Etym. xiv.vi.32; 'Trinacria'] 'tria ἄκρια'; 'liberum'] 'Lilybaeum'; 'triquadra

dicitur'] 'triquetra dicitur, quasi in tres quadras divisa').

[*TPINAKPÍA*] Trinacria ('three peaks')
REM.IN MRT., ROY.15.A.xxxiii, 131r27

TRINACRIA grece triquetra Latine. Trinacria dicitur sicilia a tribus acris, id est promunctoriis, nam acron greci dicunt summum et altum. Quae uidelicet tria promunctoria ita uocantur: pelorum, lilibeum, et pachinum.

[*ΎΔΩΡ*] idros ('water')
ALDH.Virg., DIG.146, 49v, b.m.

Ydropsis nomen sumpsit ab aquoso humore cutis; nam greci IDROS aquam uocauerunt. Est enim humor subcutaneus cum inflatione turgente et anhelitu foetido (ISID.Etym. iv.vii.23; IDROS] ὕδωρ).

[*ΎΛΗ*] yle ('wood; raw material of any kind; hence, metaph. the matter treated of')
SCH.GR., ROY.15.A.xvi, 80r3

Elimentum per i scribitur, ut quibusdam uidetur ueniens a uerbo quod est elimo, id est formo ipsumque a nomine trahitur, quod est lima instrumentum fabri. Sed melius ab YLE uenit quod est grecum et interpretatur materies; et mutatis litteris scribitur elementum quod grece dicitur stochium (cf. ISID.Etym. xiii.iii.1–2.: 'Hanc ὕλην Latini materiam appellaverunt, ideo quia omne informe, unde aliquid faciendum est, semper materia nuncupatur. Proinde et eam poetae silvam nominaverunt, nec incongrue, quia materiae silvarum sunt. Graeci autem elementa στοιχεῖα nuncupant. . .')

[*ΎMNOΣ*] ymnus ('a song of praise, hymn')

ALDH.Virg., DIG.146, 25v, r.m.

YMNUS est canticum laudantium quod greco in latinum laus interpretatur, pro eo quod sit carmen letitiae et laudis (ISID.Etym. vi.xix.17).

[*ΦΑΓΕῖΝ*] fage ('to eat')
ALDH.Virg., DIG.146, 62r, r.m.

Fauilla est cybus ignis, et dicitur a greco quod est FAGE, id est, comedere.

[*ΦΑΓΕῖΝ*] phagus ('to eat')
ALDH.Virg., DIG.146, 32r, r.m.

Sarcophagum nomen grecum est eoquod ibi corpora assumantur. Sarchia grece caro, PHAGUS comedere (see above, ALDH.Virg., Dig.146, 'sarca').

[*ΦΑΓΕῖΝ*] fagus ('to eat')
ALDH.Virg., DIG.146, 47r, r.m.

Sarcofagum grecum est nomen eoquod ibi corpora adsumantur; sarca enim grece caro latine, FAGUS comedere dicitur (see above, ALDH.Virg., DIG.146, 'sarca').

[*ΦΑΓΕῖΝ*] fagus ('to eat')
ALDH.Virg., DIG.146, 57v, l.m.

Sarcofagum grecum nomen est eo quod ibi corpora assumantur; sarca grece caro, FAGUS comedere dicitur (see above, ALDH.Virg., DIG.146, 'sarca').

[*ΦᾶΡΟΝ*] farum ('*Pharos*, an island in the bay of Alexandria, afterwards famous for its lighthouse')
ALDH.Virg., DIG.146, 30r, r.m.

Farus turris est maxima quam greci ac latini in commune ex ipsius rei usu FARUM apellauerunt eoquod flammarum indicio longe uideatur a nauigantibus; qualem Tholomeus iuxta Alexandriam construxisse octingentis talentis traditur (ISID.Etym. xv.ii.37).

[*ΦΙΛΌΣΟΦΟΙ*] philosophi ('loving wisdom or knowledge')

ALDH.Virg., DIG.146, 51r, r.m.

PHILOSOPHI greca apellatione uocantur, qui latine amatores sapientiae interpretantur. Est philosophus qui diuinarum et humanarum rerum scientiam habet (ISID.Etym. viii.vi.1).

[*ΦΌΒΟΣ*] phebos ('fear')
ALDH.Virg., DIG.146, 51v, l.m.

Nam deus grece theos PHEBOS dicitur, id est timor. Unde tractum est deus quod eum colentibus sit timor (ISID.Etym. vii.i.5; theos PHEBOS] δέος, φόβος).

[*ΦΩΝΉ*] phone ('sound, tone; voice')
REM.IN MRT., ROY.15.A.xxxii, 6v3

Interpretatur autem secundum Fulgentium callion PHONE, id est pulchra uox; siue calliopea dicta pulchrifica uel pulchre faciens, quia callos grece pulcher, poio facio, hinc et poeta dicitur.

[*ΦΩΝΉ*] phone ('sound, tone; voice')
SCH.GR., ROY.15.A.xvi, 80v10

Calliopea quasi calli PHONE, id est, bona uox significatio tamen deriuatur a uerbo callio poio grece composito quod est bene facio uel compono.

[*ΦῶΣ*] fos ('light')
ALDH.Virg., DIG.146, 61v, l.m.

Ab igni colendo et ligna antiqui apellauerunt focum; FOS grece latine ignis est. Unde et iuxta philosophos quosdam cuncta procreantur et reuera nihil sine calore nascitur. Adeo ut de septentrione dicat. Sterile non quicquam frigore gignit (ISID.Etym. xx.x.1; FOS] φῶς).

[*ΧΑΜΑΊ*] cami ('on the ground, generally, low')
ALDH.Virg., DIG.146, 60r, t.m.

Camelis causa nomen dedit, siue quia

quando honerantur, ut breuiores et humiles fiant, occubant, quia greci CAMI humile et breue dicunt; siue quia curuus est dorso camur uerbo greco curuum significat. Hos licet et aliae regiones mittant, sed arabia plurimos (ISID.Etym. XII.i.35; 'occubant'] 'accubant'; CAMI] χαμαί; 'camur'] καμουρ).

[*XOΛΉN*] colen ('gall, bile')
ALDH.Virg., DIG.146, 47v, b.m.

Melancolia dicta eo quod sit ex nigri sanguinis fecae admixta habundantia fellis. Greci enim melan nigrum uocant, fel autem COLEN apellant (ISID.Etym. IV.v.5; 'melan'] μέλαν; COLEN] χολήν).

[?*XPYΣÍON*] cyron ('gold, anything made of gold')
ALDH.Virg., DIG.146, 22r, r.m.

Obrizum aurum dictum eoquod obradiat splendore; est enim coloris optimi, quod hebrei ofaz greci CYRON uocant (ISID.Etym. XVI.xviii.2; 'obradiat'] 'obradiet'; 'ofaz greci CYRON uocant'] 'ophaz, Graeci κιρρὸν dicunt').

[*'ΩΛΈΝΑΣ*] ulenos ('lower arm; ell, cubit')
ALDH.Virg., DIG.146, 48r, l.m.

Ulna secundum quosdam utriusque manus extensio est, secundum alios cubitus; quem magis uerum est quia grece ULENOS cubitus dicitur (ISID.Etym. XI.i.64; 'quem'] 'quod'; 'ULENOS cubitus dicitur'] 'ὤλενος dicitur').

[*'ΩΛΈΝΑΣ*] olenos ('lower arm; ell, cubit')
REM.IN MRT., ROY.15.A.xxxIII, 130v19

Ulnas OLENOS grece, cubitus latine, inde ulna dicitur, id est, extensio manuum.

A handlist of Anglo-Saxon lawsuits

PATRICK WORMALD

There is no acknowledged corpus of Anglo-Saxon lawsuits. Scholars have had the benefit of Bigelow's *Placita Anglo-Normannica* for over a century, and this will soon be superseded by the definitive edition which has occupied Professor van Caenegem since 1952. But the nearest that Anglo-Saxonists have come to a counterpart is the set of thirty-five 'Select Cases in Anglo-Saxon Law' appended to the *Essays in Anglo-Saxon Law*, which four of Bigelow's fellow Bostonians published as a symbolic, if apparently unintended, celebration of America's origins in centennial 1876. The limitations of this admittedly useful exercise extend beyond the facts that three of its cases are not Anglo-Saxon at all, and that its editors were unable to distinguish between the Latin names for Dover and Canterbury. Since then, the selections of Harmer, Robertson and Whitelock have made many more texts generally available, but without isolating the procedural records from other 'historical documents'. Meanwhile, the English evidence was ignored in the impressive list which Hübner intended as the basis of *Placita* section in the *Monumenta Germaniae Historica*: that august institution has tracked Germanic footsteps across the Alps, the Rhine, the Pyrenees and even the Straits of Gibraltar, but it as seldom followed the Anglo-Saxons across the North Sea.[1]

The main purpose of this paper is to fill the gap. I aim simply to supply a calendar of the evidence for Anglo-Saxon law in action, together with some indication of the subject of each case, and a guide to where each record can most conveniently and/or reliably be consulted. The labours of such scholars as Birch, Stubbs, Robertson, Harmer, Whitelock, Blake, Winterbottom and Lapidge make a freshly edited collection of 'Placita Anglo-Saxonica' unnecessary, and the deficiencies of other editions should soon be remedied. Nor is this

---

[1] M. M. Bigelow, *Placita Anglo-Normannica: Law Cases from William I to Richard I* (London, 1879); Professor van Caenegem's replacement, which he has been kind enough to give me sight of, should be published by the Selden Society in 1989 or 1990. H. Adams, *et al.*, *Essays in Anglo-Saxon Law* (Boston, 1876), pp. 309–83. R. Hübner, 'Gerichtsurkunden der fränkischen Zeit', *Zeitschrift der Savigny-Stiftung für Rechtsgeschichte, germanistische Abteilung* 12 (1891), 'Nachtrag', 1–118, 14 (1893), 'Nachtrag', 1–258, and *separatim*. W. H. Stevenson offered a list of forfeitures for crime, *Cr.*, p. 113; it has been significantly expanded by S. D. Keynes, 'Crime and Punishment in the Reign of Æthelred the Unready' (forthcoming). See also A. Kennedy, 'Disputes about *bocland*: the Forum for their Adjudication', *ASE* 14 (1985), 175–95, esp. 181–9. For the abbreviations used in these notes, see pp. 258–9.

the place for detailed discussion of even a few cases, though I conclude with some comments on overall patterns. But there is a need for a catalogue which brings the case-law evidence together, as a *vade-mecum* for further research. The handlist is therefore meant to be comprehensive. I have tried to peruse all the sources for Anglo-Saxon history composed before about the year 1200 which seemed promising, including a number which remain unprinted. If, as is all too probable, I have missed any instance which appears to meet the criteria set out below, I would be grateful to be told.[2]

CRITERIA FOR INCLUSION IN THE LIST

It is necessary, first, to explain the criteria on which the handlist has been compiled. Actually, it is not easy to determine what constitutes evidence for Anglo-Saxon legal process and what does not. Of the ninety-five cases in the list's first category, those reflected by charters, only just over half are known from texts whose primary purpose is to describe the proceedings in question, like continental *placita* (nos. 1–8, 12–19, 21–6, 28, 32–5, 38–40, 43, 45–7, 49, 56–8 (vernacular passages), 62, 69, 74, 77, 80, 83–5, 93). Because, as will be seen (below, pp. 272–3), the formulaic prescriptions which enable one to identify a *placitum* on the continent barely exist in England, the specifically legal element in such descriptions can be elusive (nos. 16, 74, 83–5); and one can be left in doubt as to the personalities or issues involved (nos. 1, 2, 18, 33, 40, 43, 58). Another twenty cases in this category emerge more or less clearly from incidental references in diplomatic documents (nos. 27, 30, 37, 50, 52, 54, 56–8 (Latin sections), 60–1, 63, 65, 71–2, 75–6, 89–91). But for twenty-seven, there is deficient evidence on the parties (nos. 11, 20, 31, 53, 68, 78, 87, 92); on the matter (nos. 9–10, 36, 44, 51, 64, 70, 88); on the process (nos. 42, 59, 66–7, 95); on any two of these (nos. 41, 48, 55, 81); or on all three (nos. 73, 82). Finally, adequate knowledge of four suits in this class depends on information supplied from outwith the charter text itself (nos. 29, 79, 86, 94).

Such material merges almost imperceptibly with other charters which describe disputes, confiscations, bargains or restorations, but which lack explicitly judicial overtones. Many more documents may have had a concealed forensic context. For example, three listed cases are known only from royal

---

[2] I have already published a survey of the material, with special reference to nos. 11–12 and 45–6, 69: 'Charters, Law and the Settlement of Disputes in Anglo-Saxon England', *The Settlement of Disputes in Early Medieval Europe*, ed. W. Davies and P. Fouracre (Cambridge, 1986), pp. 149–68; and there will be much further discussion in my forthcoming book, *The Making of English law: King Alfred to King Henry I*. This paper was germinated by research for the latter, and fertilized by the discussions which gave rise to the former. I owe much to the advice and criticism of Peter Clarke, Robin Fleming, Jim Holt, Paul Hyams, Simon Keynes, Michael Lapidge, Patrick Sims-Williams, David Rollason and Chris Wickham; but even more to the 'Bucknell group', and most of all to its 'Scottish affairs correspondent'.

writs demanding or endorsing local judgements (nos. 87, 89, 92). The tone of most writs – as curt and challenging, if not as precise, as after the Conquest – is such as to suggest that court proceedings had occurred or were envisaged; and it is important that, in one instance, independent evidence establishes the existence of legal process which could not have been guessed from the related writ alone (no. 149). It must be stressed that this handlist is unlikely to be a fair reflection of the incidence of Anglo-Saxon litigation. Yet it would obviously be unhelpful to include transactions whose litigious dimensions can be no more than suspected.

Further, it is one of the objects of this exercise to show that there are nearly as many lawsuits in non-diplomatic sources as in charters. Domesday Book, together with the local histories of Abingdon, Ely, Evesham, Ramsey, Wells and Worcester, are rich quarries of Anglo-Norman pleas. But, like the vast spoil-heap of English judicial writs, this material also contains pre-Conquest ores which, except in the case of Ely and, to a lesser extent, Ramsey, have remained largely unsifted. They thus furnish the second and third categories of the handlist. Domesday Book and the cartulary-chronicles were themselves, in part, legal documents and the compilers of both exploited judicial records.[3] Inevitably, therefore, they suffer from the same limitations as the records which survive independently, with the additional drawbacks that they are evidence at one or more removes and have their own preoccupations. The Ely and Ramsey texts can supply vividly detailed accounts (nos. 108, 110, 113–14, 120–1, 124–8, 130, 140–3, 145–6, 150). But most of their cases, like all those from Domesday (nos. 96–102), Abingdon (nos. 133–4), Evesham (nos, 152–3), Wells (no. 151) and Worcester (nos. 103–6), are as blurred in their focus as many of the charters in the first class.

The fourth and final category in the handlist consists of lawsuits recorded incidentally in sources whose main concern was with the deeds of kings or the miracles of saints. The treason trials of the *Anglo-Saxon Chronicle* have been known as long as it has occupied its central position in early English studies, but they have had comparatively little attention in their own right (nos. 160–5, and cf. no. 175). The much more numerous English instances of saintly interference with the course of justice, now an acknowledged feature of continental hagiography, have, with two exceptions, received no attention at all; some of them certainly deserve it (nos. 154–9, 166–74, 176–8).[4] But it goes

---

[3] *LE*, pp. li–liii; Simon Keynes and Alan Kennedy are preparing an edition and translation of the *Libellus quorundam insignium operum beati Æthelwoldi episcopi*, which is the core of *LE* for these purposes. C. R. Hart, *The Earl Charters of Eastern England* (Leicester, 1966), e.g. pp. 30, 42.

[4] D. Whitelock, 'Wulfstan *Cantor* and Anglo-Saxon Law', *Nordica et Anglica: Studies in honour of Stefan Einarsson*, ed. A. H. Orrick (The Hague, 1968), pp. 83–92, with reference to nos. 154–5;

without saying that one can look neither to *gesta* nor to *miracula* for legal precision. The value of the latter, like that of the hagiographically tinted cartulary-chronicles, is compromised by the often evanescent line between natural and supernatural process.

Thus, in order to do justice to the range and variety of the sources for Anglo-Saxon legal practice, one has no choice but to confront the challenge of establishing a boundary between evidence which demonstrates, and that which merely hints. Relatively rigid criteria are all that can prevent an amoebic expansion of the material. The role followed here is that a case appears in the handlist if, but only if, it can be seen to have involved some degree of formal judicial procedure. Awards or punishments, wrangles or pacts, must at least have been based on ostensibly legal grounds, or have got as far as the constitution of a court, even the issue of a writ. The application of this rule is cruel necessity. No modern approach to legal history is going – or ought – to be satisfied only with the evidence of cases that 'came to court'. Precisely for that reason, formality cannot simply be assumed where explicit evidence is lacking. On the other hand, however real the role of informal proceedings, from *ad hoc* arbitration to bloody vendetta, in early English law, it needs to be demarcated with reference to the more solemn approaches which alone interested legal historians in the past. Either way, there is a place for a catalogue of pleas purporting to have been lawsuits in the traditional sense. Some borderline examples of matching inclusions and exclusions may show how the list's underlying principle has worked out; equally, and happily, they will give scholars the chance to make their own distinctions according to their own criteria.[5]

To start at the top. Controversy enveloped the accessions of many Anglo-Saxon kings. But King Alfred's will uniquely qualifies his own for inclusion in the handlist, because it says that, in response to the 'manegu yrfegeflitu' which this entailed, King Æthelwulf's 'yrfegewrit' was brought before 'eallum Westseaxena witum' (no. 20). Whatever was here meant by *yrfe*, the significant point for present purposes is the evidence that it was formally debated – evidence that is not so easily discounted as that of some famous, but perhaps rhetorical, Anglo-Saxon annals.[6] More prosaically, kings are found confiscating or restoring property almost as soon as there are extant charters.

but note that Wulfstan took the stories from Lantfred's *Translatio et miracula S. Swithuni* (see M. Lapidge, *The Cult of St Swithun*, Winchester Stud. 4.2 (Oxford, forthcoming)). F. Graus, 'Die Gewalt bei den Anfängen des Feudalisms und die "Gefangenbefreiungen" der merowingischen Hagiographie', *Jahrbuch für Wirtschaftsgeschichte* 1 (1961), 61–159.

5 This is also, by and large, the criterion applied by Professor van Caenegem in his forthcoming edition of post-Conquest pleas (see n. 1 above).

6 E.g. *ASC* 755 (= 757, for 786); '*Historia Regum*', *s.a.* 774, in *Symeonis Monachi Opera Omnia*, ed. T. Arnold, 2 vols., RS (London, 1882–5) II, 45.

A letter of Aldhelm shows this happening to Malmesbury, but the dispute seems to have been resolved informally.[7] However, similar treatment of Christ Church, Canterbury, in the second quarter of the ninth century is said to have been remedied at a *venerabile consilium* (no. 16). In a notorious charter, Offa was alleged to have removed lands from Christ Church on the grounds that their grantor had no dispositive rights, but neither the confiscation nor its subsequent reversal is ascribed to formal judgement (and Offa's pretexts could be glib).[8] King Berhtwulf may have been equally arbitrary in his transfer of Worcester property to *his* thegns, but this time the bishop is represented as having to state his case before the 'Merciorum optimates' in order to get it back (no. 17). King Eardwulf of Kent ended Rochester's problems with Walhhun the reeve, but there is no evidence that the church presented a plea.[9] On the other hand, there is no clue as to what the bishops of Leicester and Lichfield, of Sherborne and Winchester, were quarrelling about, but it can be seen that matters were settled at one of the great *Clofesho* councils typical of the period (nos. 9–10) – as was Æthelric's vindication of his inheritance against unidentified opposition (no. 11).

In the later Anglo-Saxon period, Selsey and the New Minster each secured the king's support against their opponents.[10] There is no sign, however, that they had to do more than win him over, whereas the claims of Malmesbury and Muchelney had to compete with those of rivals before the kingdom's great men (nos. 42, 55). King Æthelred repented of his youthful indiscretions as regards several churches.[11] But only when restoring Downton to Winchester was his change of heart associated with 'sapientum . . . ammonitionibus' (no. 59). When Eadric Streona demanded justice against the Kentish slayers of his (equally unpopular) brother, the king's cool response, according to Osbern, was that it served him right.[12] But when Christ Church sought to recover the revenues of Sandwich, the wrathful, if ailing, Harold Harefoot did manage (or

---

[7] S 1170 (688); *Aldhelmi Opera*, ed. R. Ehwald, MGH, Auct. antiq. 15 (Berlin, 1919), 502–3 (*Epistolae*, no. xiii). The two texts are associated and explained by Heather Edwards in 'The Charters of the Early West Saxon Kingdom' (unpubl. Ph.D. dissertation, Glasgow Univ., 1985), pp. 152–6.

[8] S 155 (799). Cf. S 149 (796), and this list's nos. 3, 6; P. Wormald, 'Bede, the *Bretwaldas* and the Origins of the *Gens Anglorum*', *Ideal and Reality in Frankish and Anglo-Saxon Society: Studies presented to J. M. Wallace-Hadrill*, ed. P. Wormald, D. Bullough and R. Collins (Oxford, 1983), pp. 99–129, at 115–17.

[9] S 30 (762, = 747).

[10] S 1291 (957); S 956 (1019). Cf. S 889 (996), or the famous (if obscure) *querela* in S 1368 (964?).

[11] S 876 (993); S 885 (995); S 893 (998). It must be admitted that S 876 comes very close to the terms of this list's no. 59, not least in that it too was issued at a great council concerned with the general affairs of the kingdom.

[12] *Osberni Precentoris Vita S. Elphegi*, in *Anglia Sacra*, ed. H. Wharton, 2 vols. (Oxford, 1691) II, 132.

so the text hints) to issue a writ (no. 83). There are several examples of bargains struck under royal auspices in the tenth and eleventh centuries.[13] Nos. 91 and 135 are hesitantly included in the list, because the language of the sources implies that the king was judge as well as witness.[14] Likewise, several Domesday entries describe disputes between Earl Harold and local churches, while a charter of William the Conqueror refers to one involving Tostig which King Edward sorted out.[15] Yet Shaftesbury alone could show the commissioners a royal writ in their favour (no. 96).

The same sort of distinction between disputes which achieved some sort of formal adjudication and those settled informally, if at all, can be applied at local level. The use of words like *placitando* and *adplacitavit* qualify nos. 105 and 153 for inclusion; stretching a point, *soken* is taken in the same sense for no. 82 (partly in order to register a rare victory for laity over clergy). The witness-lists of Sherborne's two agreements over Holcombe Rogus (nos. 74, 85) suggest that they involved the shire courts of Dorset and Devon, and the settlement of Abbot Ælfstan of St Augustine's claim to St Mildred's property seems to have had a similar context (no. 84); for no. 90 this is actually asserted. On the other hand, some of the arrangements made by Ely, Ramsey and Worcester apparently amounted to no more than tough talking.[16] Also to be excluded are the grievances of these and other churches which never reached the point of resolution.[17]

In cases of punishment, or the threat of it, the shibboleth is again the explicit presence of a formal element. The text describing the lawsuits of Queen Eadgifu features a forfeiture for which no reason is given, but her royal spouse is said to have 'accused' the victim, whereas Eadgifu's own loss of property under Eadwig is entirely unexplained (nos. 32–5). Similarly, the difference between Eadwig's treatment of Æthelstan of Sunbury and Edgar's was that the latter issued a *dom* (nos. 38–40). Even when there are no details of the criminal's name, of the nature of the offence, or of the property forfeited, the mere reference to an offence shows that legal principles had been invoked to

---

13 E.g. S 850 (983); S 1449 (964 × 975); *Ram.*, ch. 105.

14 Cf. S 1481 (1042 × 1055), where there is less explicit evidence of dispute before the king.

15 E.g. *DB* i.69a [*Wiltshire*, 23:7]; 121a [*Cornwall*, 4:21]; 174b [*Worcestershire*, 3:3]. *Regesta Regum Anglo-Normannorum 1066–1154: Vol. I, Regesta Willelmi Conquestoris et Willelmi Rufi 1066–1100*, ed. H. C. W. Davis (Oxford, 1913), no. 88.

16 E.g. *Lib.Æ*, ch. 36 [= *LE* ii.26]; *Ram.*, ch. 44; *Hem.*, pp. 259–60. Cf. S 1476 (*c.* 1053): the estate was evidently in dispute after the Conquest (*DB* i.43c [*Hampshire*, 10:11], but the triplicate recording of Wulfweard's agreement with the Old Minster does not prove that there was a law-case before 1066 (cf. S 1471 (*c.* 1045)).

17 E.g. *DB* i.136d–137a [*Hertfordshire*, 16–1]; 169a [*Gloucestershire*, 56:2]; 259b [*Shropshire*, 4,26:3]; 263a [*Cheshire*, B:13]; 264a [*Cheshire*, 2:1]; *Hem.*, pp. 276–7; *LibÆ*, ch. 60 [= LE ii.49–49b].Cf. such unresolved secular cases as *DB* i.57d [*Berkshire*, 1:38].

someone's cost (e.g. no. 48). So does the use of the word 'forfeiture' in its Latin or Old English versions (nos. 79, 88); while it is reasonable to think that land said once to have belonged to a thief had been forfeited by him (no. 41). The most ambitious entry in the entire list is perhaps no 73: it is a guess that the 'aforementioned matron' (anonymous) had been forfeited at all, let alone for what; but it is a good one, because her lands were 'michi iure decretario assignatas', and the previous mention actually omitted by the Burton cartularist might have been a vernacular statement of her crimes such as is found in two other Æthelred charters (nos. 56–8).[18] This instance can be contrasted with Harthacnut's well-documented attack on Worcestershire for refusing geld; he had ample legal justification, but there is no evidence that this interested him.[19]

Among narrative sources, some of the habitually bleak records of exile and forfeiture in the *Anglo-Saxon Chronicle* are given fuller procedural dimensions in the *Vita Ædwardi*, in the *Gesta Regum*, in Ramsey's *Chronicon* (perhaps), and even in Domesday Book (nos. 144–5, 162–3, 165). The others enrolled here are distinguished from such disgraces as Oslac's (975) and Osgot's (1046) by the fact that sentence is attributed to a great council (nos. 160–1, 164). The evidence presented in these cases may well, and perhaps rightly, persuade scholars that formal process should be 'read into' other instances of exile and outlawry too; but a list restricted to explicit evidence must leave this conclusion to them. To assume that *ira regis* necessarily adopted judicial form would entail the inclusion of an almost infinitely extendable number of casualties of Anglo-Saxon politics, from King Edwin and St Wilfrid onwards.[20] Similarly, the northern sources conventionally grouped under the name of Symeon of Durham can conjure up an atmosphere more often associated with Icelandic saga. But, while the (unsuccessful) attempt of *amici* to pacify the great feud between the house of Bamburgh and the Danish *holds* of York did not make use of state apparatus, Earl Tostig's arrest of Aldan-hamal for rapine, slaughter and fire-raising obviously did (no. 173).[21] And if it scarcely seems logical to incorporate the crime of possessing the king's wheat,

---

[18] On the other hand, one cannot be sure, in default of further evidence, that the reference to Ælfmær's land in S 988 is to forfeited or disputed property.

[19] *Florentii Wigorniensis Monachi Chronicon ex Chronicis*, ed. B. Thorpe, 2 vols. (London, 1848–9) I, 195–6. Cf. *The Chronicle of Hugh Candidus*, ed. W. T. Mellows (Oxford, 1949), p. 50, for Cnut's threat to annihilate the Ramsey *familia*.

[20] When Edgar seized lands from Æthelstan 'Half-King', the prelude to no. 108, nothing was said of a specific charge: *LibÆ*, ch. 5, *LE* ii.7. And Dr Fleming has pointed me to *DB* i.263a [*Cheshire*, B:7], the confiscation of land beyond the Dee from King Gruffydd, but this seems unlikely to have followed a formal hearing.

[21] *De Obsessione Dunelmi*, in *Symeonis Monachi Opera Omnia*, ed. Arnold, I, 219; the editor was reminded of the lifestyle of a 'Turkish Pacha'.

but not that of killing one's mother with a candlestick, the fact remains that the former led to arrest by the royal *dispensator*, the latter only to penance imposed by the pope (no. 156).[22]

Next, there is the problem of separating the judgements of divine, from those of earthly, authority. The critical point is that, whatever the miraculous *dénouement*, it must have been set up by normal legal procedure. This is clear enough when royal officers are supernaturally punished for infringement of sanctuary (nos. 169, 171), or when false witness is avenged from the same quarter (nos. 166, 177). Indeed, two stories in the *miracula* category are not really miracles at all (nos. 174, 178). However, other cases are nearer the stipulated borderline. Ely's experience with the estate at Brandon reads just like so many of its troubles after Edgar's death, except that there is no mention of the usual channels through which Bishop Æthelwold and Abbot Byrhtnoth operated, and it was divine chastisement that disposed of their opponents.[23] By contrast, the clash between Abingdon abbey and the men of Oxfordshire, which H. M. Chadwick made famous in connection with *Beowulf*, does seem to have led to a decision in the court of the shire, as well as in that of heaven (no. 133). Even if it was fear of the bishop of Sherborne's curse that induced Earl Godwine to patch up his obscure dispute with him, this was already 'die placito dicta' (no. 176). In considering these, and all the other marginal cases discussed above, it is of course important to remember that one is distinguishing at least as much between types of evidence as between methods of procedure. Most of the material for Anglo-Saxon law in action comes from sources that are trying to tell us about something else. To repeat: this handlist is necessarily restricted to what may well be the tips of icebergs, and scholars would be ill advised to neglect their possible submarine bulk.

The other criterion adopted here is more simply grasped, and has, on the whole, been more strictly applied. There must be a good reason for supposing a case to have been transacted before the Battle of Hastings if it is to appear in the handlist. The relevance of this principle is that Domesday Book is full of forfeitures by people with Anglo-Scandinavian names. Some of them may have been pre-Conquest; but the fate of the English landed classes under William the Conqueror makes it a fair bet that most were not. The seven Domesday cases included are all more or less explicitly ascribed to the *tempus regis Eadwardi*, except for one which probably dates from the reign of Harold (no. 99).[24] Enforcement of this criterion has unfortunately meant parting company with some fascinating stories in the works of Goscelin, which cannot

---

[22] *LE* ii.60. Cf. the similar penance imposed on the future Abbot Ealdwulf of Peterborough, who accidentally suffocated his son: *Hugh Candidus*, ed. Mellows, pp. 29–30.

[23] *LibÆ*, ch. 46 [= *LE* ii.35]. Such stories are of course generally commoner than accounts of restitution by orthodox means.

[24] Cf., e.g., *DB* ii.98r [*Essex*, 83:1].

be securely placed on either side of the Conquest.[25] On the other hand, three lawsuits have been included from other sources because the text strongly suggests a pre-Conquest date, in one case with surprising implications (nos. 94, 147, 153). It also seemed reasonable to think that Queen Edith is more likely to have been sending instructions to the hundred of Wedmore under her brother's rule than under his conqueror's (no. 95). Once again, the consequences of rigid adherence to criteria could be that almost as much which illuminates Anglo-Saxon justice is jettisoned as is salvaged. But a minimalist approach is really unavoidable in the initial establishment of a corpus. Meanwhile, 178 lawsuits are perhaps enough to be going on with. Such a number may indeed surprise many.

All the same, it must finally be admitted that some of the handlist's contents come from more or less suspect sources (nos. 29–31, 41–2, 79, 81, 91, 94, 133, 144(iv), 163(iii), 168, 170(iii), 175). The rescued prisoner and the penalized violator of sanctuary are hagiographical *topoi* (nos. 154–6, 158, 169, 171, 173). Yet in no case, except perhaps Abingdon's *démarche* with the local shire, and Dunstan's confrontation with the dispossessed *clerici*, are there real grounds for wondering whether the plea itself might be legendary (nos. 133, 168).[26] Even the fictionalization of Queen Emma's disgrace by the *Annales de Wintonia* (no. 170(iii)) might be re-assessed in the light of the notorious Ælfgifu episode in the Bayeux Tapestry, given the close connections both of Goscelin and of the Tapestry itself with St Augustine's, Canterbury.[27] Such cases surely deserve inclusion as evidence of 'atmosphere'. It could be significant that this sort of story was in circulation at all.

ARRANGEMENT OF THE LIST

Anglo-Saxon lawsuits are here divided into four categories, because different *genres* of evidence raise different problems. Of these categories, the second, Domesday cases, is self-explanatory: these alone owe their survival to a document composed and preserved, as a matter of certainty, by central

---

[25] E.g. Goscelin's *Vita S. Wulfsini episcopi et confessoris*, ed. C. H. Talbot, 'The Life of St Wulfsin of Sherborne by Goscelin', *RB* 69 (1959), 68–85, at 83–4; *Miracula S. Augustini*, in *Acta Sanctorum, Mai VI*, p. 402 (I would welcome enlightenment as to the industrial process that the three Kentishmen were engaged in).

[26] Cf. H. Vollrath, *Die Synoden Englands bis 1066*, Konziliegeschichte, ed. W. Brandmüller (Munich, 1985), pp. 251–8, 424–53; with all due respect to Dr Vollrath's erudition, it is difficult to accept her arguments that the 'Vigilantius, *De Basilica Sancti Petri*' which is cited as an authority for Dunstan's council in the *Liber de Hyda* represents a contemporary source, and without such authority, the historicity of the council itself is doubtful.

[27] N. P. Brooks and H. E. Walker, 'The Authority and Interpretation of the Bayeux Tapestry', *Proc. of the Battle Conference on Anglo-Norman Stud.* 1, ed. R. A. Brown (Ipswich, 1979), 1–34. D. W. Rollason, *The Mildrith Legend: a Study in Early Medieval Hagiography in England* (Leicester, 1982), pp. 60–7.

government. The other three are more problematic, not least because they overlap. The charters in category one merge into the charter-based chronicles of category three, which, inasmuch as they are impartially interested in human and divine justice, elide with the hagiographical texts of category four. The source edited in the Rolls Series as the *Chronicon Abbatiae de Evesham* is a good illustration of the possible complexities. It is actually a composite of at least two sources: the earlier-twelfth-century *Vita Ecgwini* of Dominic of Evesham, which exists separately, and which is itself based on Byrhtferth's work of the same title, has been incorporated into a chronicle which, in its extant form, is to be ascribed to Thomas of Marlborough in the early thirteenth-century, whose 'Liber Tertius' probably used an immediately post-Conquest biography of Abbot Æthelwig.[28] The *vitae* of Byrhtferth and Dominic belong in the fourth category (nos. 159, 172); but the hypothetical Æthelwig text appears to sustain its own claim to have used charter evidence, so its information is put in category three (nos. 152–3); and each component of the *Chronicon* casts some extra light on a case described by a very dubious document in category one (no. 94). In the circumstances, the pursuit of bibliographical consistency has seemed less important than the supply of instant guidance to the sort of evidence represented. Generally, where a case may be covered by records in more than one category, it is the most informative text that determines its class (nos. 63, 71–2, 79, 86, 94, 135, 144–5, 149, 162). Within each class, it is the earliest informative source that is cited (nos. 30, 154–6, 158); later sources are added only if they potentially contribute extra colour (nos. 144, 159, 163, 170).

Some texts contain more than one lawsuit, and some lawsuits extend over more than one text. The question to be decided here is whether there was more than one session of formal pleading. In the matter of Inkberrow (no. 4), the second document is dated fourteen years after the first, the third nearly twenty years later still, but we know of only one judicial hearing. The same applies to Selsey's Denton case (no. 7), while Bishop Æthelric of Sherborne's writ simply led to the Holcombe Rogus agreement (no. 74). (As a matter of interest, both Inkberrow and Holcombe Rogus came up again, the former very much later – nos. 77, 85.) However, it is reasonably clear that the documentation on Fonthill, Cooling and Sunbury reflects a series of suits, with different parties, issues or process (nos. 23–6, 32–5, 38–40). Wulfgeat and his wife were condemned on the same occasion (no. 72(a)); Leofsige and his sister were not (nos. 71, 75).[29] Another Leofsige's condemnation was obviously distinct from

---

28 For Dominic, see M. Lapidge, 'The Medieval Hagiography of St Ecgwine', *Vale of Evesham Hist. Soc. Research Papers* 6 (1977), 77–93, at 82–5; and 'Dominic of Evesham, "Vita S. Ecgwini Episcopi et Confessoris"', *AB* 96 (1978), 65–104. For the account of Æthelwig, see A. Gransden, *Historical Writing in England, c. 550–1307* (London, 1974), pp. 89–90 and 111–12.

29 Three cases in Æthelred II's time (nos. 63, 71–2) are covered by 'pairs' of charters, raising the possibility that they relate to different people and/or offences. For no. 63, the identity of the

his widow's (nos. 111–12). Although the complex litigation over St Ives and other places was eventually subsumed in a single judgement, the cases had originally been separate (nos. 140–2). So too, suggest the sources, were the suits over Upper Swell and St Ecgwine's shrine, though they had a common origin (nos. 94, 153). Nor is there any good reason to doubt that Earl Godwine was prosecuted by both Harthacnut and Edward for the death of their brother (nos. 175, 162).[30]

Each entry in the handlist is followed by citation of the edition to which reference was actually made when compiling it. For three sets of cases, those covered by charters and *notitiae*, by Domesday Book and by the *Liber Eliensis*, alternative reference systems are, or soon will be, available; these are placed at the start of the entry, so as to avoid an unsightly string of brackets at the end. The lawsuits in category one are arranged in order of the dates of the relevant charters, however approximate (the dates are usually those of Professor Sawyer's *List*, where available). This principle also applies to the date alleged in spurious documents (nos. 29–31, 41–2, 79, 81, 91, 94); no. 31 is ascribed to the reign of Æthelstan rather than Æthelheard, because both texts were very probably forged at the same time, and the details fit a tenth- rather than eighth-century context.[31] The position of cases spread over more than one document is determined by the date of the first. When there is internal or independent evidence of a case's actual date, it is supplied, with the reasons given, but its place in the list remains that of the cited text. The resulting chronological sequence is distorted only in order to keep the various Helmstan suits together (nos. 23–6 – the probability is that the document itself is to be dated very early in the reign of Edward the Elder anyway). The Domesday cases likewise follow the survey's own order: only two can be dated more closely than to the *tempus regis Eadwardi* as a whole (nos. 98–9).

In categories three and four, the primary order is decided by the dating of the sources themselves. It must be remembered here that all but the last of the suits in the *Liber Eliensis* (nos. 107–32, 135) in fact come from the indepen-

---

two Ælfrics is almost certain: each text refers to the same predecessor as tenant, and to the sentence of a Council of Cirencester. In no. 71, the equation of the two Leofsiges seems highly likely: only one 'Leofsige *dux*' appears in witness-lists of Æthelred's charters. In no. 72, however, though it remains probable that the same Wulfgeat features in each, it does happen that a 'Wulfgeat *minister*' subscribes S 922 (1009), so that S 934 (1015) could be referring to his disgrace, rather than that of the Wulfgeat forfeited in 1006; for this reason, I have, exceptionally, listed the two references as 72(a) and 72(b). But I implicitly accept Dr Keynes's arguments (*The Diplomas of King Æthelred 'the Unready' 978–1016* (Cambridge, 1980), pp. 184–5) that the Æthelsiges of nos. 56, 60 are (probably) not the same person.

30 Compare Barlow's comment, *VÆR*, p. 13, n. 4.

31 See below, p. 279. I discuss the circumstances of these forgeries further in 'Æthelwold and his Continental Counterparts: Contact, Comparison, Contrast', *Bishop Æthelwold: His Career and Influence*, ed. B. Yorke (Woodbridge, 1988), pp. 13–41, at 39–40.

dently extant *Libellus quorundam insignium operum beati Æthelwoldi episcopi*, which is sixty years earlier; that the parts of the Evesham *Chronicon* to be ascribed to Dominic have a different date from those now surviving only from the pen of Thomas of Marlborough, as already indicated (nos. 152–3, 172, cf. also no. 159); and that the precise chronology of the sources cited for nos, 168–75 is open to question. Within each source, the order is that of the text itself, again modified only to serve the interests of clarity by keeping linked cases together, and in their temporal sequence where this is not itself confusing (nos. 107–8, 113–14, 124–7, 140–2). Once more, evidence is given, where available, for the real date of each dispute; but because the chronological determinants are usually the same throughout the Ely and Ramsey material, it will avoid repetition to tabulate here the relevant *termini ante* and *post quem*:

957 Accession of Edgar
969 Foundation of Ramsey
970 Refoundation of Ely
975 Death of Edgar
984 Death of Bishop Æthelwold
991 Death of Ealdorman Byrhtnoth
992 Death of Ealdorman Æthelwine
996 ? Death of Abbot Byrhtnoth (and effective *terminus* for the original underlying the *Libellus . . . beati Æthelwoldi*).

The party given first for each case was the actual or probable winner, where this is an appropriate consideration. Place-names are those registered by Sawyer and/or the relevant volume in the Leicester series, except that I have ventured my own suggestion in no. 166.

Abbreviations

Ab.	*Chronicon Monasterii de Abingdon* i, ed. J. Stevenson, RS (London, 1958).
ASC	*The Anglo-Saxon Chronicle*. Text, *Two of the Saxon Chronicles Parallel* i, ed. C. Plummer (Oxford, 1892); translation, *English Historical Documents c. 500–1042*, ed. D. Whitelock, 2nd edn (London, 1979). Manuscripts of the *Chronicle* are cited by Whitelock's *sigla* where this seems necessary.
BCS	*Cartularium Saxonicum*, ed. W. de Gray Birch, 3 vols. (London, 1885–93).
Ca	*Charters of Rochester*, ed. A. Campbell, AS Charters 1 (London, 1973).
Cr.	*The Crawford Collection of Early Charters and Documents*, ed. A. S. Napier and W. H. Stevenson (Oxford, 1895).
DB	*Domesday Book seu Liber Censualis Wilhelmi Primi Regis Angliae*, ed. A. Farley, 2 vols. (London, 1783) [*county volumes*, ed. J. Morris (Chichester, 1975–86)].
Eve.	*Chronicon Abbatiae de Evesham*, ed. W. D. Macray, RS (London, 1863).
Gaim.	*L'Estoire des Engleis by Geffrei Gaimar*, ed. A. Bell, Anglo-Norman Texts 14–16 (Oxford, 1960).

GR   *Willelmi Malmesbiriensis Monachi, De Gestis Regum Anglorum Libri Quinque* I, ed. W. Stubbs, RS (London, 1887).

H   *Select English Historical Documents of the Ninth and Tenth Centuries*, ed. F. E. Harmer (Cambridge, 1914).

Ha   F. E. Harmer, *Anglo-Saxon Writs* (Manchester, 1952).

Hem.   *Hemingi Chartularium Ecclesiae Wigorniensis*, ed. T. Hearne, 2 vols. (Oxford, 1723).

Hyd.   *Liber Monasterii de Hyda*, ed. E. Edwards, RS (London, 1866).

KCD   J. M. Kemble, *Codex Diplomaticus Aevi Saxonici*, 6 vols. (London, 1839–48).

Lant.   Lantfred of Winchester, *Translatio et miracula S. Swithuni*, in M. Lapidge, *The Cult of St Swithun*, Winchester Stud. 4.2 (Oxford, forthcoming) – cited by chapter number.

LE   *Liber Eliensis*, ed. E. O. Blake, Camden Soc. 3rd ser. 92 (London, 1962).

LibÆ   *Libellus quorundam insignium operum beati Æthelwoldi episcopi*, in S. D. Keynes and A. Kennedy, *Anglo-Saxon Ely* (forthcoming); text also incorporated in *LE*.

Memorials   *Memorials of St Dunstan*, ed. W. Stubbs, RS (London, 1874).

Os.   Osbern, *Vita S. Dunstani*, in *Memorials*.

PSE   Abbo, *Passio Sancti Eadmundi*, in *Three Lives*.

R   *Anglo-Saxon Charters*, ed. A. J. Robertson, 2nd edn (Cambridge, 1956).

Ram.   *Chronicon Abbatiae Rameseiensis*, ed. W. D. Macray, RS (London, 1886).

S   P. H. Sawyer, *Anglo-Saxon Charters: an Annotated List and Bibliography*, R. Hist. Soc. Guides and Handbooks 8 (London, 1968).

Three Lives   *Three Lives of English Saints*, ed. M. Winterbottom (Toronto, 1972).

VÆR   *Vita Aedwardi Regis*, ed. F. Barlow (London, 1962).

Vit. Ken.   *Vita Sancti Kenelmi*, ed. R. von Antropoff (unpubl. PhD dissertation, Bonn Univ., 1965).

W   *Anglo-Saxon Wills*, ed. D. Whitelock (Cambridge, 1930).

HANDLIST OF LAWSUITS

A. Charters and notitiae

1. S 1429 (736 × 737). Dispute between Abbess Hrothwaru and her unnamed mother over the minster at Withington, Gloucs. (BCS 156)

2. S 1256 (759). Dispute between Abbot Ecgwold of Tisbury, Wilts., and an unnamed minster over land by Fontmell Brook, Dorset. (BCS 186)

3. S 1257 (781). Dispute between Bishop Heathored of Worcester and King Offa of the Mercians over the minster at Bath and other properties in Warwicks. and Worcs. (BCS 241)

4. S 1430 (789) + S 1260 (803) + S 1432 (822 × 823). Dispute between Bishops

Heathored, Deneberht and Heahberht of Worcester and Wulfheard, son of Cussa, over property at Inkberrow and Bradley, Worcs. (BCS 256 + BCS 308 + R 4)

5. S 137 (794). Dispute between Bishop Heathored of Worcester and Bynna, *comes regis*, over land at Aust, Gloucs. (BCS 269)

6. S 1258 (798). Dispute between Archbishop Æthelheard of Canterbury and Abbess Cynethryth (? of *Bedeford* = ? Bedford) over the minster at Cookham, Berks. (BCS 291)

7. S 158 (801) + S 1435 (825). Dispute between Bishops Wihthun and Coenred of Selsey and King Coenwulf of the Mercians over land at Denton, Sussex. (BCS 302 + BCS 387)

8. S 1431 (803). Dispute between Bishop Deneberht of Worcester and Bishop Wulfheard of Hereford over the minster at Cheltenham and Beckford, Gloucs. (BCS 309)

9. S1431 (803). Dispute between Bishop Werenberht of Leicester and Bishop Aldwulf of Lichfield. (BCS 309)

10. S 1431 (803). Dispute between Bishop Wigberht of Sherborne and Bishop Ealhmund of Winchester. (BCS 309)

11. S 1187 (804). Dispute between Æthelric, son of Æthelmund, and an unnamed party over the disposition of the minster at Westbury, Gloucs. (BCS 313)

12. S1433 (824). Dispute between Bishop Heahberht of Worcester and the *familia* of Berkeley, Gloucs., over the minster at Westbury. (BCS 379)

13. S 1434 (824). Dispute between Archbishop Wulfred of Canterbury and Abbess Cwoenthryth of Minster-in-Thanet, Kent, over land at Easole, Kent. (BCS 378)

14. S 1436 (825). Dispute between Archbishop Wulfred of Canterbury and King Coenwulf of the Mercians, with his daughter, Abbess Cwoenthryth, over the minsters at Reculver and Minster-in-Thanet, Kent. (BCS 384)

15. 1437 (825). Dispute between Bishop Heahberht of Worcester and Hama, with other *swangerefan*, over wood-pasture at Sinton in Leigh, Worcs. (R 5).

16. S 1438 (838–9). Dispute between Archbishop Ceolnoth of Canterbury and Kings Ecghberht and Æthelwulf of the West Saxons over land at South Malling, Sussex [or East Malling, Kent: cf. N.P. Brooks, *The Early History of the Church of Canterbury* (Leicester, 1984), pp. 136–7)]. (BCS 421)

17. S 192 (840). Dispute between Bishop Heahberht of Worcester and King Berhtwulf of the Mercians over land at Stoulton, Worcs., and elsewhere in Gloucs. and Worcs. (BCS 430)

18. S 1439 (844). Dispute between Beornthryth and unnamed parties over the *hereditas* of her husband, Oswulf, *dux atque princeps*. 810: said in no. 19 to have happened thirty-four years before. (BCS 445)

19. S 1439 (844). Dispute between Archbishop Ceolnoth of Canterbury, with the *familiae* at Folkestone, Dover and Lyminge, Kent, and Æthelwulf, son of Æthelheah, over the *hereditas* of Oswulf. (BCS 445)

20. S 1507 (879 × 888). Disputes between King Alfred of the West Saxons and unnamed parties over the terms of the will of his father, King Æthelwulf. (H 11)

21. S 1441 (896). Dispute between Bishop Wærferth of Worcester and Æthelwald over woodland at Woodchester and elsewhere in Gloucs. (H 14)

22. S 1442 (897). Dispute between Wullaf, with Bishop Wærferth and the *familia* of Worcester, and Æthelwulf, *dux*, with the *familia* of Winchcombe, over land at Upton in Blockley, Worcs. (BCS 575)

23. S 1445 (900 × 924). Conviction of Helmstan for theft of a belt, 897 × 899: said to have happened immediately before no. 24. (H 18)

24. S 1445 (900 × 924). Dispute between Helmstan and Æthelhelm Higa over land at Fonthill, Wilts. 897 × 899: King Alfred was involved in the case, which was 'one and a half or two years' before no. 25. (H 18)

25. S 1445 (900 × 924). Conviction, forfeiture, outlawry and pardon of Helmstan for theft of oxen. 899 × 900: Edward the Elder was involved in the case, 'one and a half or two years' after no. 24, and it was followed by the transaction independently recorded in S 1284 (900). (H 18)

26. S 1445 (900 × 924). Dispute between Ordlaf, with Bishop Denewulf of Winchester, and Æthelhelm Higa over land at Fonthill, Wilts. (H 18)

27. S 362 (901). Forfeiture of Wulfhere, *dux*, and of his wife, for desertion and breach of oath sworn 'regi et suis omnibus optimatibus'. 871 × 899?: the implication is that punishment as well as crime happened under King Alfred. (BCS 595)

28. S 1446 (*c.* 903). Dispute between Bishop Wærferth of Worcester and Eadnoth over property at Sodbury, Gloucs. (H 15)

29. S 375 (909). Forfeiture of Ælfred, *miles*, for adultery. Party identified in S 814. (BCS 623). Cf. no. 30?

30. S 414–15 (931). Forfeiture of Ælfred for conspiracy against King Æthelstan after his accession. (BCS 670–1). Cf. no. 29?

31. S 443 (938). Forfeiture and condemnation to death for theft of unnamed possessors of Withiel Florey, Somerset, and *Cearn*, Dorset. Allegedly in the reign of King Æthelheard (726 × 740). (BCS 727 – cf. S 254)

32. S 1211 (*c.* 959). Dispute between the future Queen Eadgifu and Goda over land at Cooling, Kent. 908 × 909: property said to have been withheld from her for six years after the death in battle of her father, Sigehelm, dated by *ASC* A to 904 and by BCD to 905 (= 902/903). (H 23)

33. S 1211 (*c.* 959). Forfeiture of Goda under King Edward the Elder's unexplained accusation. 909 × 924: 'on fyrste' after no. 32. (H 23)

34. S 1211 (*c.* 959). Settlement of dispute between Queen Eadgifu and Goda. 924 × 939: in the reign of Æthelstan. (H 23)

35. S 1211 (*c.* 959). Leofstan and Leofric, sons of Goda, judged to have committed 'manfull reaflac' against Queen Eadgifu, whose property is restored. *c.* 959: this occurred after King Eadgar 'astiþude', which is likely to mean 'came to full power' (i.e. over all the English), in that the dispute relates to properties S. of the Thames, which should have been under Eadwig's rule 957–9. (H 23)

36. S 687 (960). Forfeiture of Wulfric, *minister, cuiusdam offensaculi causa.* (BCS 1055)

37. S 753 (967). Forfeiture of Eadwold, *laicus*, for *publicum latrocinium.* (BCS 1198)

38. S 1447 (968). Forfeiture of Æthelstan of Sunbury, Middx, for theft of a *wimman*, and failure to pay his wergeld. 951 × 955: occurred in the reign of King Eadred and when Ealdorman Byrhtferth was in office. (R 44)

39. S 1447 (968). Judgement of no. 38 upheld by King Edgar and the Mercian *witan*,

with Æthelstan again unable to pay his wergeld. 957 × 959: in reign of Edgar as king north of the Thames. (R 44)

40. S 1447 (968). Forfeiture of Ecgferth for 'þa swyrd þa him on hype hangode þa he adranc'. 957 × 962: the property was re-granted by Edgar, after Ecgferth's forfeiture, in S 702 (962). (R 44)

41. S 792 (973). Probable forfeiture by *fur quidam* of land at Titchmarsh, Northants. (BCS 1297)

42. S 796 (974). Dispute between Malmesbury abbey and Æthelnoth over land at Eastcourt in Crudwell, Wilts. (BCS 1301)

43. S 1377 (963 × 975). Forfeiture of unnamed widow and son for witchcraft (widow executed, son outlawed). (R 37)

44. S 842 (982). Forfeiture of Lufa, one-time *fidelis* of King Eadred, for 'cuiusdam culpae'. (*Hyd.*, pp. 217–27 – cf. S 1498)

45. S 1457 (975 × 987). Forfeiture of Brihtwaru as accessory after the fact of the theft of charters, sold by the thieves to her deceased husband, Ælfric. 963 × 975: occurred at a council of Edgar's which was attended by Bishop Æthelwold; widow identified in S 1511. (R 59)

46. S 1457 (975 × 987). Dispute between Brihtwaru, with her kinsman, Brihtric, and the unnamed bishop of Rochester, over lands at Snodland, Bromley and Fawkham, Kent. 975 × 982: the suit was heard by Ealdorman Eadwine. (R 59). Cf. no. 69

47. S 1458 (961 × 988). Dispute between Archbishop Dunstan, with St Andrew's, Rochester, and Leofsunu, over lands at Wouldham and elsewhere in Kent. (R 41)

48. S 869 (988). Forfeiture of land at *Lamburna* by an unnamed party, 'pro quodam facinore'. (*Hyd.*, pp. 238–42)

49. S 1454 (990). Dispute between Wynflæd and Leofwine over land at Hagbourne and Bradfield, Berks. (R 66)

50. Redemption of outlawry incurred by Osgot, for slaying. 966 × 992: dates are those of Ealdwulf's abbacy of Peterborough. (R 40)

51. Redemption of outlawry incurred by Wulfnoth. 966 × 992: see no. 50. (R 40)

52. Dispute between Abbot Ealdwulf of Peterborough and Ælfweard of Denton, Northants., over land at Warmington, Northants. 966 × 992: see no. 50. (R 40)

53. S 1453 (972 × 992). Forfeiture to Archbishop Osketel of York by two brothers who had one wife. 957 × 971: the dates of Osketel's episcopate. (R 54)

54. S 883 (995). Pardon of Æthelwig, reeve of Buckingham, accused of allowing Christian burial to Ælfnoth and Ælfric, whose *homo*, Leofric, had stolen a bridle, and who were killed in *bellum* with the bridle's owners. (KCD 1289)

55. S 884 (995). Dispute between Muchelney Abbey and unnamed tenants over property at Ilminster, Somerset. (*Two Cartularies of the Benedictine abbeys of Muchelney and Athelney*, ed. E. H. Bates, Somerset Record Soc. 14 (1899), 43–5).

56. S 886 (995). Forfeiture and outlawry of Æthelsige for theft of swine. (KCD 692). Cf. no. 60?

57. S 877 (996). Forfeiture of Wulfbald's property and person for seizure of land and fourfold defiance of royal orders to desist and pay his wergeld. 978 × 990: during the reign of Æthelred II, and before no. 58. (*Hyd.*, pp. 242–3, R 63)

58. S 877 (996). Judgement of no. 57 enforced on Wulfbald's unnamed widow and son, both for his crimes and for their slaying of their kinsman, Eadmær, the king's thegn, with his fifteen companions. 989 × 990: the date of the council that pronounced sentence. (Text as no. 57)

59. S 891 (997). Restitution by King Æthelred of the English to the Old Minster, Winchester, of land at Downton and Ebbesborne, Wilts., which he had previously 'usurped'. (KCD 698)

60. S 893 (998). Forfeiture and loss of *dignitas* by Æthelsige, declared a 'publicus hostis' for killing the king's reeve, who was trying to protect royal property, 'inter cetera quae saepe comisit furti et rapinae flagitia', and as well as other indiscriminate annexations. (Ca 32). Cf. no. 56?

61. S 892 (998). Forfeiture of Wistan for *unrihtum monslihte*. (*Cr.* 8)

62. S 939 (995 × 999). Charge against Æthelric of Bocking, Essex, that he was involved in the *unræd* to receive Swein in Essex, withdrawn on the plea of his widow. (W 16(ii))

63. S 896 (999) + S 937 (999?). Forfeiture and exile of Ælfric, *comes*, 'cognomento puer', for 'multa et inaudita . . . piacula', and 'reum maiestatis'. 985: dated by *ASC*. (KCD 703 + KCD 1312)

64. S 937 (999?). Enmity of King Æthelred of the English incurred by Æthelweard, son of Ceolflæd, with his unnamed brother, 'exigentibus suis reatibus'. (KCD 1312)

65. S 1497 (985 × 1002). Dispute between Æthelgifu and her unnamed husband's kinsmen, including Eadhelm, over the terms of his or her will. Before 956? (D. Whitelock, *et al.*, *The Will of Æthelgifu*, (Oxford, 1968))

66. S 1242 (995 × 1002). Dispute between Bishop Æthelwold of Winchester and Leofric, with his sister, Wulfgyth, over land at Ruishton, Somerset. 965 × 975: text implies settlement in the reign of Edgar, and presumably after his marriage to Ælfthryth. (Ha 108)

67. S 1242 (995 × 1002). Queen Ælfthryth challenged that she had used excessive force in settling no. 66. (Ha 108)

68. S 901 (1002). Forfeiture 'cuiusdam foeminae fornicaria praevaricatione'. (KCD 1295)

69. S 1456 (995 × 1005). Dispute between Bishop Godwine of Rochester and Leofwine, son of Ælfheah, over land at Snodland, Kent. (R 69). Cf. nos. 45–6

70. S 911 (1005). Forfeiture of Leoftæt, *suis ineptiis*. (KCD 714)

71. S 916 (1007) + S 926 (1012). Exile and outlawry of Leofsige, *dux*, for killing Æfic, a royal reeve, in his own home. 1002: dated by *ASC*. (Cr. 11 + Ca 33). Cf. no. 75.

72. (a) S 918 (1008). Forfeiture of Wulfgeat, with his wife, Ælfgifu, 'causa suae machinationis propriae'. 1006: dated by *ASC?* (KCD 1305)
     (b) S 934 (1015). Forfeiture of Wulfgeat, *minister*, for association with the king's enemies, and 'quia . . . in facinore inficiendi etiam legis satisfactio ei defecit'. 1006: dated by *ASC?* (KCD 1310)

73. S 923 (1011). Presumed forfeiture of an unnamed *matrona*. (*Charters of Burton Abbey*, ed. P. H. Sawyer, AS Charters 2 (London, 1979), no. 33)

74. S 1383 (1001 × 1012) + S 1422 (1012). Dispute between Bishop Æthelric of

Sherborne and Edmund the Ætheling over land at Holcombe Rogus, Devon. (Ha 63 + R 74). Cf. no. 85

75. S 926 (1012). Forfeiture of Æthelflæd, sister of Leofsige, for ignoring his outlawry and doing everything to assist him. (Ca 33). Cf. no. 71

76. S 927 (1012). Forfeiture of Leofric's property and person, 'rebellando meis militibus in mea expeditione, ac rapinis insuetis, et adulteriis, multisque aliis nefariis sceleribus'. (KCD 1307)

77. S 1460 (1023). Dispute between Bishop Æthelstan of Hereford, with Leofric of Blackwell, Warwicks., and Wulfstan, with his son, Wulfric, over land at Inkberrow, Worcs. (R 83)

78. Godwine, son of Earwig, cleared of Bishop Leofgar's accusation, 'æt ðan unrihtwife'. 1017 × 1027: dates are the outside limits of Leofgar's episcopate. (KCD 803).

79. S 991 (1017 × 1030). Forfeiture of Bengeworth, Worcs.; by Northman? 1017?: identification is perhaps implied by *Eve.*, p. 84, and date is then supplied by *ASC*. (Ha 48)

80. S 1462 (1016 × 1035). Dispute between Edwin, son of Enniaun, and his unnamed mother, over lands at Wellington and Cradley, Herefords. (R 78)

81. S 1223 (1033 × 1038). Forfeiture of Hampton, Worcs., 'ex praevaricatione'. 978 × 1016: said to have occurred in the reign of Æthelred. (KCD 938)

82. S 1527 (s. xi × 1038). Dispute between Thurketel of Palgrave and 'þo munekes' (of Bury St Edmunds?) over a moor. (W 24)

83. S 1467 (1038 × 1040). Dispute between Archbishop Eadsige, with the *hired* of Christ Church, Canterbury, and Abbot Ælfstan of St Augustine's, Canterbury, with King Harold Harefoot, over the port of Sandwich and its revenues. (R 91)

84. S 1472 (1044 × 1045). Dispute between Abbot Ælfstan, with the *hired* of St Augustine's, Canterbury, and Leofwine, *preoste*, over property of St Mildred's, Thanet. (R 102)

85. S 1474 (1045 × 1046). Dispute between Bishop Ælfwold of Sherborne and Care son of Toki over land at Holcombe Rogus, Devon. (R 105). Cf. no. 74

86. S 1404 (1045 × 1048). Dispute between Bishop Siward, co-adjutor of Canterbury and ex-abbot of Abingdon, followed by Abbot Ordric of Abingdon, and Brihtwine, son of Brihtmund, over land at Leckhampstead, Berks. (Ha 3 + *Ab.*, pp. 457–9, 475–7, which passages extend the dispute into the period 1053 × 1065)

87. S 1123 (1049). Dispute between Westminster Abbey and an unnamed party over land at Datchworth and Watton, Herts. (Ha 79)

88. S 1229 (1042 × 1052). Forfeiture of Ælfric, *se þegen*. 1016 × 1035: said to have occurred in the reign of Cnut. (R 96)

89. S 1077 (1052). Dispute between Bury St Edmunds and Semer over land at Kirby Cane, Norfolk. (Ha 17)

90. S 1408 (1052 × 1056). Dispute between Bishop Ealdred of Worcester and Aki, son of Toki, *minister regis*, over lands at Teddington and Alstone, Gloucs., and in Worcester. (KCD 805)

91. S 1029 (1060). Dispute between Abbot Leofric of Peterborough and Queen Edith over land at Fiskerton, Lincs. (KCD 808)

92. S 1090 (1053 × 1061). Dispute between Christ Church, Canterbury, and an unnamed party over land at Mersham, Kent (Ha 35)

93. S 1110 (1055 × 1065). Dispute between Abbot Ælfwine of Ramsey and Provost Siward of Thorney, with Abbot Leofric of Peterborough, over the boundary along King's Delph, Northants. 1055: the writ is addressed to Earl Tostig, but Abbot Leofsige of Ely is present among the arbitrators in both writ and memorandum. (Ha 62 + *Cartularium Monasterii de Rameseia*, ed. W. H. Hart and P. A. Lyons, 3 vols., RS (London, 1884–93), I, 188 (no. cxv), + Cambridge, University Library, Add. 3021, p. 372)

94. S 1026 ('1055' = 1062 × 1065?). Forfeiture of – or judgement against – Earnsige, son of Oki, and Ealdgyth, in dispute with Abbots Mannig and Æthelwig of Evesham, over land at Upper Swell, Gloucs. (KCD 801 + *Eve.*, pp. 45–6, 93–4). Cf. no. 153

95. S 1241 (1066 × 1075). Dispute between Queen Edith and Wudumann over her rent. (Ha 72)

B. *Domesday Book*

96. *DB* i.78d. Dispute between Shaftesbury Abbey and Earl Harold over lands at Long Cheselbourne, Stour and Melcombe Horsey, Dorset. 1053 × 1065: presumably when Harold was earl of Wessex. (*Dorset*, 19:14)

97. *DB* i.252d. Exile and forfeiture of Spirites, *canonicus* of St Mary's Bromfield. 1042 × 1065: before no. 98. (*Shropshire*, 3d:7)

98. *DB* i.252d. Dispute between the *canonici* of St Mary's Bromfield and Robert fitz Wymarc, over the land at Bromfield, Shropshire, forfeited in no. 97. 1065: case deferred 'ad curiam instantis natalis', i.e. the Christmas when King Edward died. (*Shropshire*, 3d:7)

99. *DB* i.376b. Forfeiture by Grimketill to Mærlsveinn, sheriff of Lincolnshire. 1066: the Domesday formula, 'anno quo mortuus est isdem rex [i.e. Edward]', seems likely to be an attempt at *damnatio memoriae* of the reign of Harold. (*Lincolnshire*, CW:12)

100. *DB* ii.2v. Execution and forfeiture of a smith, 'proper latrocinium'. (*Essex* 1:3)

101. *DB* ii.310v–311r. Outlawry and forfeiture of Eadric of Laxfield. 1044/1045 × 1053?: the second reference perhaps implies that Harold was earl of East Anglia at the time. (*Suffolk*, 6:79; cf. ii.313r (6:92), 342v (7:114))

102. *DB* ii.401v–402r. Dispute between Bury St Edmunds and Robert fitz Wymarc, about jurisdiction over the theft of the horses found in the house of Brungar, *liber homo*. (*Suffolk*, 27:7)

C. *Cartulary-Chronicles*

103. Dispute between Prior Wulfstan of Worcester and Earngeat, son of Grim, over land ? at Hampton Lovett, Worcs. *c.* 1057: Wulfstan is described as 'bishop', but Earl Leofric was also involved. For the property disputed here and in nos. 104–5, see the *Worcestershire* volume in the Morris series, App. v, Worcs. G, nos. 15, 20, 25. (*Hem.*, pp. 260–1)

104. Dispute between Prior Æthelwine of Worcester and Sigemund, *miles* of Earl Leofric, over land at Crowle, Worcs. 1044 × 1057: dates are the outside limits of Æthelwine's priorate, though the text dates the episode to the 'time when the Danes were possessors of this country'. (*Hem.*, pp. 264–5)

105. Recovery by Bishop Lyfing of Worcester, *placitando*, of land at Elmley Castle, Worcs., alienated by Bishop Brihtheah 'cuidam ministro suo'. 1038 × 1042: Lyfing became bishop in 1038, and the land at issue was leased by him in S 1396 (1042). (*Hem.*, pp. 267–8)

106. Dispute between Earl Sweyn and his mother over the identity of his father. 1046 or before: the episode is placed before Sweyn's seizure of the abbess of Leominster. (*Hem.*, p. 275)

107. *LibÆ*, ch. 5. Forfeiture of Wulfwine *Cocus*, with his wife, Ælfswyth, *per transgressionem*. Before no. 108 (*LE* ii.7)

108. *LibÆ*, ch. 5. Dispute between Bishop Æthelwold of Winchester, with the *fratres* of Ely, and Ealdorman Æthelwine, with his unnamed brothers, over land at Hatfield, Herts. 975 × 983: the dispute was settled before Ealdorman Ælfhere. (*LE* ii.7, and cf. *Ram.*, ch. 28)

109. *LibÆ*, ch. 6. Dispute between Ely Abbey and Leofric of Brandon, Suffolk, over land at Linden End, Cambs. 975 × 996. (*LE* ii.8)

110. *LibÆ*, ch. 8. Dispute between Abbot Byrhtnoth of Ely and Ælfwold of Mardleybury, Herts., over land at Stretham, Cambs. 975 × 996. (*LE* ii.10)

111. *LibÆ*, ch. 10. Dispute between Bishop Æthelwold of Winchester and Leofsige over land at Peterborough, Oundle and Kettering. 975 × 984. (*LE* ii.11)

112. *LibÆ*, ch. 11. Judgement against Leofsige reissued against his widow, Sigeflæd, followed by settlement of dispute between them and Ely Abbey over land at Downham,Cambs. 975 × 984. (*LE* ii.11)

113. *LibÆ*, ch. 14. Dispute between Ulf and the unnamed wife of Ælfwold *Grossus*, over land at Chippenham, Cambs. Six months before no. 114. (*LE* ii.11a)

114. *LibÆ*, ch. 14. Dispute between Abbot Byrhtnoth of Ely and the unnamed wife of Ælfwold *Grossus*, over land at Chippenham, Cambs. 970 × 984: the case was followed by a transaction involving Bishop Æthelwold. (*LE* ii.11a)

115. *LibÆ*, ch. 15. Dispute between Abbot Byrhtnoth of Ely and Somerled over land at Witchford, Cambs. 975 × 992. (*LE* ii.12)

116. *LibÆ*, ch. 27. Dispute between the Church of Ely and Uvi, kinsmen of Ogga of Mildenhall, Suffolk, over land in Cambridge. *c.* 960 × 975: *multos annos* after it had been granted, which was *c.* fifteen years before Æthelwold took possession of Ely (*LE* ii.18). Cf. no. 120

117. *LibÆ*, ch. 28. Dispute between Abbot Byrhtnoth of Ely and Uvi over land in Cambridge. 975 × 996. (*LE* ii.18)

118. *LibÆ*, ch. 29. Forfeiture, then amercement, of Oslac. 970 × 975. (*LE* ii.19)

119. *LibÆ*, ch. 29. Dispute between Abbot Byrhtnoth of Ely and Oslac over land at Cambridge and Dullingham, Cambs. 975 × 996. (*LE* ii.19)

120. *LibÆ*, ch. 34. Dispute between Abbot Byrhtnoth of Ely and Begmund of Holland, Essex, with his kin, over land at Stonea, Cambs. 975 × 992. (*LE* ii.24). Cf. no. 116

121. *LibÆ*, ch. 35. Dispute between Wulfnoth, with Abbot Byrhtnoth of Ely, and the unnamed sons of Boga of Hemmingford, Hunts., over land at Bluntisham, Hunts. 975 × 984. (*LE* ii.25)

122. *LibÆ*, ch. 38. Dispute between Bishop Æthelwold of Winchester, with Abbot Byrhtnoth of Ely, and Ælfwold, brother of Eadric the Tall, with his kin, over land at Hauxton with Newton, Cambs. 975 × 984. (*LE* ii.27)

123. *LibÆ*, ch. 39. Dispute between Ealdorman Æthelwine and Æthelnoth, brother of Leofric, over land at Wangford, Suffolk, 975 × 992. (*LE* ii.30, and cf. *Ram.*, ch. 28). Cf. no. 139

124. *LibÆ*, ch. 42. Arraignment of Æthelstan, *presbyter*, for custody of stolen dagger and precious clothes. 957 × 971: dates are those of Osketel's episcopate. (*LE* ii.32)

125. *LibÆ*, ch. 42. Disputes between Bishop Æthelwold of Winchester and Æthelstan, *presbyter*, over land at Eye, Cambs., and over the treasures of the church at Horningsea, Cambs. 970 × 975; after no. 124. (*LE* ii.32)

126. *LibÆ*, ch. 43. Dispute between Abbot Byrhtnoth of Ely and Æthelstan, *presbyter*, with his brothers, Bonda and Ælfstan, over land at Eye, Cambs. 975 × 991. (*LE* ii.33)

127. *LibÆ*, ch. 42. Arraignment of Leofstan, *presbyter*, nephew of Wulfric, *praepositus*, for theft of a cloak. Four years before no. 125. (*LE* ii.32)

128. *LibÆ*, ch. 44. Dispute between Ealdorman Byrhtnoth and Leofsige, *presbyter*, over unspecified land. 975 × 991. (*LE* ii.33)

129. *LibÆ*, ch. 45. Forfeiture of land at *Berelea* for theft. 957 × 975. (*LE* ii.34)

130. *LibÆ*, ch. 45. Dispute between Bishop Æthelwold, with Abbot Byrhtnoth of Ely, and Wynsige, with his kin, over land at Swaffham, Cambs. 975 × 984. (*LE* ii.34)

131. *LibÆ*, ch. 54. Forfeiture of Waldgist, 'per transgressionem'. 939 × 946: in the reign of King Edmund. (*LE* ii.43)

132. *LibÆ*, ch. 60. Loss to Ely Abbey of land at Armingford, Cambs., 'quae per pugnam et per furtum facta erat transgressioni obnoxia'. Probably before 970. (*LE* ii.49b)

133. Dispute between the monks of Abingdon and the 'comprovinciales Oxenefordensis pagi' over the meadow between the Thames and Iffley. 939 × 946: allegedly in the reign of King Edmund. (*Ab.*, pp. 88–90)

134. Dispute between Eadwine Rainere, with other tenants, and on behalf of Queen Edith, and an unnamed reeve over land at Lewknor, Oxon. 1045 × 1047: text seems to date the episode in Æthelstan's abbacy. (*Ab.*, pp. 459–60)

135. Dispute between Abbot Wulfric, with the *fratres* of Ely, and Esgar the Staller over land at Pleshey, Essex. 1055 × 1065: in the reign of Edward, and also the abbacy of Wulfric, which may not have begun before 1055 (cf. no. 93). (*LE* ii.96, and cf. *DB* ii.60v [*Essex* 30:27])

136. Dispute between Ramsey Abbey and Æthelstan, *presbyter*, over land at Burwell, Cambs. 969 × 975. (*Ram.*, ch. 25)

137. Dispute between Ramsey Abbey and Wynsige over land at Burwell, Cambs. 975 × 992. (*Ram.*, ch. 25)

138. Dispute between Æthelflæd, wife of Ealdorman Æthelwine, and unnamed party over land at Sawtry, Hunts. 970 × 992: the land had been exchanged by Æthelflæd's father with an Ealdorman Æthelstan, presumably the one known as 'Rota' whose last subscription was in 970 (S 1268); cf. C. Hart, 'Athelstan "Half-King" and his family', *ASE* 2 (1973), 115–44, at 126–7. (*Ram.*, ch. 28)

139. Dispute between the *fratres* of Ramsey Abbey and unnamed parties over land at Wangford, Suffolk. (*Ram.*, ch. 28). Cf. no. 123

140. Dispute between King Edward the Martyr and the *fratres* of Ramsey Abbey over land at Barnwell, Northants. 975 × 978. (Ram., ch. 47)

141. Dispute between Leofwine, son of Ealdorman Æthelwine, and the unnamed son of Osweard, *presbyter*, over land at Weekley and Oakley, Northants. Before no. 142. (*Ram.*, ch. 47)

142. Dispute between the *fratres* of Ramsey Abbey and Osweard, *presbyter*, over land at St Ives, Hunts. 987 × 992: the case followed the commemoration of the donor, Æthelstan Mannessune, (*Ram.*, ch. 47, and cf. ch. 33)

143. Dispute between Prior Eadnoth, with some Ramsey *fratres*, and Ælfnoth, son of Goding, over land at Swaffham, Cambs. 990 × 992: see C.R. Hart, *The Early Charters of Eastern England* (Leicester, 1966), p. 42. (*Ram.*, ch. 49)

144. Forfeiture of English noblemen, 'proscripti et exterminati' by judgement of King Cnut, as 'antecessorum suorum regum proditores', 1016 × 1035 – 1017?: is this a reference to Eadric Streona among others? (*Ram.* ch. 74, and cf. *ASC* 1017 + *GR*, ii.181 + *Gaim.* 4447–70)

145. Trial of Thorkel, with his unnamed wife, for the murder of his son, and forfeiture of land at Elsworth, Cambs. 1017 × 1034 – 1021?: *if* this is Thorkel the Tall, *ASC* 1021 supplies the date; the outside limits are the dates of Æthelric's episcopate; the case appears to follow the forfeiture of no. 144. (*Ram.*, ch. 74)

146. Dispute between Bishop Æthelric of Dorchester and an unnamed Danish couple over land at Elton, Hunts. 1017 × 1034: see no. 145. (*Ram.*, ch. 75)

147. Dispute between Morkere, *monachus*, with St Benedict's, Ramsey, and an unnamed party over land at Langton by Horncastle and elsewhere in Lincs. Before 1066?: text certainly implies a pre-Conquest date, but one would not expect to find Edward of Salisbury in office at this date. (*Ram.*, ch. 90)

148. Punishment of an unnamed Irishman for murder of Abbot Æthelstan of Ramsey, 'iuxta forensium santionem legum graviter'. 1043. (*Ram.*, ch. 92)

149. Dispute between Abbot Ælfwine of Ramsey and unnamed parties over the soke of *Bichamdic*, Norfolk. 1053 × 1057: dating limits are those of the related writ, S 1108. (*Ram.*, chs. 96–8)

150. Dispute between Abbot Ælfwine of Ramsey and Ælfric, son of Wihtgar, kinsman of Æthelwine the Black, over land at Clapham and elsewhere in Beds. 1049 × 1065: in Edward's reign, and soon after the Council of Rheims. (*Ram.*, ch. 103)

151. Dispute between Bishop Giso of Wells and Ælfsige over land at Winsham, Somerset. 1061 × 1065: evidently after Giso's election, and before Harold's accession. (J. Hunter, 'Historiola de primordiis episcopatus Somersetensis',

Ecclesiastical Documents: viz. I. A brief history of the bishoprick of Somerset, Camden Society (London, 1840), p. 17)

152. Dispute between Abbot Brihtmær of Evesham and Godwine of Towcester, Northants., over the property of Evesham Abbey. 1002 × 1013: dates are the outside limits for the abbacy of Brihtmær. (*Eve.*, pp. 79–82)

153. Dispute between Abbot Æthelwig of Evesham and an unnamed *potens homo* over the shrine of St Ecgwine. 1058 × 1066: text implies a pre-Conquest date for Æthelwig's initiative. (*Eve.*, pp. 93–4, and cf. *ibid.*, pp. 45–6). Cf. no. 94

D. Gesta and Miracula

154. Trial of a servant of Flodoald, *negotiator*, 'pro quodam facinore'. 971 × 972: dates are those furnished in *Lant.* (*Lant.*, ch. 25)

155. Mutilation of a man for *crimen latrocinii*. 971 × 972: see no. 154. (*Lant.*, ch. 26)

156. Arraignment of a man for appropriation of the king's corn. 971 × 972: see no. 154. (*Lant.*, ch. 27)

157. Execution of eight thieves for attempted burglary of St Edmund's church. 924 × 953: between the translation of St Edmund in the reign of King Æthelstan and the death of Bishop Theodred of London. (*PSE*, ch. 15)

158. Flogging and imprisonment of a thief by Bishop Ælfheah of Winchester. 984 × 1006: limits of Ælfheah's Winchester episcopate. (*Vita S. Æthelwoldi*, ch. 46; *Three Lives*, p. 63)

159. Dispute between Wigræd, *senior* of the church at Evesham, and a *rusticus* over unspecified land of the abbey. Before 970?: Wigræd is unrecorded elsewhere, and the episode could not be dated by later Evesham writers. (Byrhtferth, *Vita S. Ecgwini*, iv.10, *Byrhtferth of Ramsey; the lives of Oswald and Ecgwine*, ed. M. Lapidge, Oxford, forthcoming + *Eve.*, pp. 42–4)

160. Outlawry of Ealdorman Æthelweard. 1020. (*ASC* 1020; C also includes Eadwig, *ceorla cyngc*, who is listed by DE with those proscribed in 1017 – cf. no. 144)

161. Earl Sweyn declared *niðing* for murder of Earl Beorn. 1049. (*ASC* 1049 C)

162. Exile and forfeiture of Earl Godwine and his sons for defiance of royal orders (? and on suspicion of complicity in the death of the Ætheling Ælfred). 1051. (*ASC* 1052 D, 1048 E (= 1051) + *VÆR*, ch. 3 + *DB* i.186a [*Herefordshire* 19:2–3])

163. Acquittal of Earl Godwine and his children, and outlawry of Archbishop Robert of Canterbury, with 'ealle þa Frenciscean þe ær unlage rærdon 7 undom demdon, 7 unræd ræddon into ðissum earde'. 1052. (*ASC* 1052 CD, cf. E + V ÆR, ch. 4, cf. *Gaim.* 4895–5034)

164. Outlawry of Earl Ælfgar as 'þas cynges swica 7 ealra land leoda'. 1055. (*ASC* 1055 E, cf. CD)

165. Outlawry of Earl Tostig, 'for þam þe he rypte God ærost 7 ealle þa bestrypte þe he ofer mihte æt life 7 æt lande', and acquittal of Earl Harold for conspiracy against him. 1065. (*ASC* 1065 C, cf. DE + *VÆR*, ch. 7)

166. Dispute between Abbot Godwine of Winchcombe and Osgot the Dane, *cognomine digera*, over land at Naunton in Toddington, Gloucs. 1016 × 1035: *sub*

rege Cnuto. For identification of the disputed land cf. *DB* i.165d [*Gloucesershire* 11:6]. (*Vit. Ken.*, pp. xv–xvi)

167. Godric, 'notissimus', accused 'de collectu censu plebis'. (*Vit. Ken.*, p. xvi)

168. Dispute between Archbishop Dunstan and *complurium ecclesiarum clerici* over their expulsion from their prebends. 973 × 975/7: text seems to date the confrontation after Edgar's coronation and, if not before his death, then before the Council of Calne, *ASC* 978 DE (= 977). (*Os.*, i.36)

169. Asylum and pardon of a *latro*. 984 × 1000: under Abbess Wulfthryth, but after St Edith's death. (*Vita S. Edithae Virginis*, ii.5, ed. A.Wilmart, 'La légende de Sainte Edith en prose et vers par le moine Goscelin', *AB* 56 (1938), 5–101, 265–307, at 272–3)

170. Forfeiture of Queen Emma (? and of Bishop Stigand of Elmham) for encouraging King Magnus of Norway to invade England. 1043: date from *ASC* 1043. (*Translatio S. Mildrethae*, ch. 18, ed. D.W. Rollason, 'Goscelin of Canterbury's Account of the Translation and Miracles of St Mildrith (*BHL* 5961/4): An Edition with Notes', *MS* 48 (1986), 139–210, at 176–8; cf. also *ASC* 1043 C + *Annales de Wintonia*, in *Annales Monastici*, ed. H.R. Luard, 3 vols., RS (London, 1864–9) II, 20–4)

171. Asylum of a woman accused by Sheriff Leofstan of unspecified crime. In the lifetime of two of the original guardians of the shrine which was constituted in or soon after the reign of Æthelstan (924 × 939). (Hermann, *De Miraculis S. Edmundi*, ch. 2, in *Memorials of St Edmund's Abbey*, ed. T. Arnold, 3 vols., RS (London, 1890–6) I, 30–2; but cf. *PSE*, ch. 16)

172. Dispute between Abbot Osweard of Evesham and a *rusticus* over unspecified land of the abbey. *c.* 978: in abbacy of Osweard but also in the reign of Æthelred II. (*Eve.*, pp. 41–2)

173. Arraignment of Aldan-Hamal by Earl Tostig, 'furtis atque rapinis, homicidiis atque incendiis'. 1055 × 1065: during Tostig's Northumbrian rule. (*De Miraculis et Translationibus S. Cuthberti*, ch. 5, in *Symeonis Monachi Opera Omnia*, ed. T. Arnold, 2 vols., RS (London, 1882–5) I, 243–5)

174. Three moneyers sentenced to lose their hands, 'cum falsa moneta capti'. 959 × 988: in archiepiscopate of Dunstan. (Eadmer, *Vita S. Dunstani*, i.27, *Memorials*, pp. 202–3; cf. *Os.*, i.31)

175. Earl Godwine acquitted (? or amerced) on the count of complicity in the death of the Ætheling Ælfred. 1040. (*Florentii Wigorniensis Monachi Chronicon ex Chronicis*, ed. B. Thorpe, 2 vols. (London, 1848–9) I, 194–5; cf. *VÆR*, ch. 1, and *GR*, ii.188)

176. Dispute between Bishop Ælfwold of Sherborne and Earl Godwine for unspecified reason. 1045 × 1053: after accession of Ælfwold and before death of Godwine. (William of Malmesbury, *De Gestis Pontificum Anglorum Libri Quinque*, ed. N.E.S.A. Hamilton, RS (London, 1870), ii.82, pp. 179–80)

177. Dispute between Abbot Leofstan of St Alban's and a *clericus* close to Archbishop Stigand over unspecified land. 1052 × 1064: after accession of Stigand and before death of Leofstan. (*Miracula S. Albani*, in London, BL Cotton Faustina B. iv, 22v–23v)

178. Execution of three men, and branding of a *clericus*, for robbery of Holy Cross Abbey, Waltham. 1042 × 1062: the stolen ornaments had been made for Gytha, who married Tofi, founder of the abbey, in 1042, and the episode pre-dated the major endowment of the abbey which is dubiously documented in S 1036 (1062). (*De Inventione Sanctae Crucis*, ch. 24, in *The Foundation of Waltham Abbey*, ed. W. Stubbs (Oxford, 1861), pp. 33–4)

DISCUSSION

Authorship

Of the immediate questions raised by the corpus of Anglo-Saxon lawsuits, the first concerns the agencies responsible for the existence of the evidence. To say that its survival is due, in all instances except the seven from Domesday Book, to the Church merely states the obvious. Most of the narratives in categories three and four were of course written and preserved in particular churches, to secure their property or glorify their saints. The charters in category one were bequeathed to posterity by churches; of the cases where an ecclesiastical interest is least apparent, no. 49 was kept at Christ Church, Canterbury, as is shown by the pithy (and noteworthy) twelfth-century endorsement, *inutile*, while no. 80 was incorporated in a Hereford cathedral gospel-book, prompting suspicion of some link with Hereford's tenure of one of the two estates at stake within half a century.[32] In terms of the *provenance* of the individual sources, and omitting cases from Domesday Book, the *Anglo-Saxon Chronicle*, the *Vita Ædwardi* and Gaimar (nos. 96–102, 135(ii), 144(ii), (iv), 160–5, 170(ii), 175(ii)), the breakdown is as follows:

Ely	107–32, 135(i)	27
Worcester	1, 3–4(i–iii), 5, 8–12, 15, 17, 21–2, 28, 77, 90, 103–6, 175(i)	23
Christ Church	6, 13–14, 16, 18–19, 23–6, 32–5, 49, 62, 83–4, 88, 92, 168, 174	22
Ramsey	93(i–ii), 136–43, 144(i), 145–8, 149(i–ii), 150	18
Abingdon	36, 54, 56, 63(i–ii), 64, 68, 72(a)–(b), 76, 86(i–ii), 133–4	14
Winchester (OM)	27, 29, 31, 59, 66–7, 154–6, 158, 170(iii)	11
Evesham	79, 81, 94(i–ii), 152–3, 159, 172	8
Rochester	45–7, 60, 69, 71(ii), 75	7
Malmesbury	30(ii), 42, 144(iii), 175(iii), 176	5
Peterborough	43, 50–2, 91	5
Westminster	37–40, 87	5
Winchester (NM)	20, 44, 48, 57–8	5
St Edmunds	82, 89, 157, 171	4
St Albans	65, 71(i), 177	3
Sherborne	74(i–ii), 85	3

---

[32] *DB* i.182a [*Herefordshire*, 2:30].

Selsey 7(i–ii); Thorney 41, 93(iii); Wells 95, 151; Winchcombe 166–7   *each* 2
Bath 30(i); Burton 73; ? Coventry 61; Durham 173; Eynsham 70;
   Hereford 80; Lichfield 78; Muchelney 55; St Augustine's 170(i);
   Shaftesbury 2; Waltham 178; Wilton 169; York 53   *each* 1

The spread of the evidence is such as to inspire some confidence that it is representative; its distribution, at any rate, is roughly that of post-Bedan Anglo-Saxon records as a whole.[33]

If the provenance of the evidence is ecclesiastical, what of its *authorship*? Is there any reason to think that it had official status, or was the composition as well as the preservation of case-law the work of directly or indirectly interested parties? For the purposes of this discussion, it is appropriate to discount the cases in category two, which were obviously the government's responsibility, and those in categories three and four which, equally obviously, were not. Also excluded from category one, for the same sort of reason, are probably spurious texts (nos. 29–31, 41–2, 79, 81, 91, 93(i), 94), wills (nos. 11, 20, 65, 82), personal writs (nos. 66–7, 74(i), 86(i), 95), private memoranda (nos. 50–3), and two brief *notitiae* in liturgical books (nos. 78, 88). What is then left are, on the one hand, the records primarily designed to report legal proceedings (nos. 1–8, 12–19, 21–6, 28, 32–5, 38–40, 43, 45–7, 49, 56–8 (vernacular passages), 62, 69, 74(ii), 77, 80, 83–5, 93(ii)); and, on the other, the documents with more or less incidentally revealing contents (nos. 27, 36–7, 44, 48, 54–5, 56–8 (Latin sections), 59–61, 63–4, 68, 70–3, 75–6, 87, 89, 90, 92).

The first set of records are Anglo-Saxon England's nearest equivalent to continental *placita*, and comparison between them and their continental counterparts is illuminating. It is no longer so easy to be sure about the official status even of Frankish texts which bear a 'chancery' stamp; yet, whoever produced these reports, there was an established, if not always rigid, tradition of notarial practice and formulaic habit to keep prejudice within bounds.[34] Against this background, Anglo-Saxon texts are notable not so much for their regular profile as for their infinite variety. In the indispensable 'Sawyer', they appear as 'royal charters' (nos. 5, 7(i), 17, 56–8, 62); as 'grants by the laity' (nos. 32–5); as 'grants by bishops' (nos. 2–3, 4(ii), 6, 43); as 'grants by other ecclesiastics' (no. 74(ii)); and, of course, as 'miscellaneous texts' (nos. 1, 4(i), (iii), 7(ii), 8–10, 12–16, 18–19, 21–6, 28, 38–40, 45–7, 49, 69, 77, 80, 83–5). Indeed, they defeat the list's normally flawless logic: there is no obvious difference between the 'royal' and 'miscellaneous' texts for no. 7; the records

---

33   The only obvious absentee among well-documented houses is Glastonbury – presumably because such documents did not interest its cartularists. See S 1705 (922), S 1777 (979 × 1016), with H. P. R. Finberg, *The Early Charters of Wessex* (Leicester, 1964), nos. 447, 506.

34   See 'Conclusion', *The Settlement of Disputes*, ed. Davies and Fouracre, pp. 207–14, with cross-references.

for nos. 5 and 17 ('royal') have king and parties in the third person, like those classified as 'miscellaneous', but king and bishop share the first person in the document for no. 3, which is grouped with episcopal grants; as for no. 93, a spurious writ appears as a 'royal charter', while its authentic source escapes notice altogether. The heterogeneity of the material is itself a pointer to its diverse origins.

That said, the specifically legal records themselves fall roughly into two groups. Those dating before 900 (nos. 1–8, 12–19, 21–2) are all in Latin, except for three from Worcester (nos. 4(iii), 15, 21 – the second perhaps an early translation). The rest are all vernacular texts. In some of the first group, a tendency towards a pattern is just discernible. These are records of great councils of most or all the southern English prelates, together with the Mercian ruler and aristocracy, which met in the reigns of Offa, Cenwulf and Beornwulf (nos. 4(i–ii), 5, 7(i–ii), 8–10, 12–15); there are also isolated parallels involving the West Saxon kings, Ecgberht and Æthelwulf (no. 16), and Ealdorman Æthelred of the Mercians (no. 21). Such councils are said to have discussed a variety of business, ecclesiastical and secular, but the document is in each case concerned with a single item: judgement in favour of the archbishop of Canterbury (nos. 13–14, 16), the bishop of Worcester (nos. 4(i–ii), 5, 8, 12, 15, 21), or the bishop of Selsey (nos. 7(i–ii)). Some sets of reports bear the same date, and nos. 4(ii) and 8 seem certain to be proceedings of the same assembly, dated as they are to 6 and 12 October 803 respectively.[35] This is probably also the case with the texts dated 824 (nos. 12–13) and 825 (nos. 7(ii), 14–15). Nos. 12–13 take roughly the same form, but relate respectively to Worcester and Canterbury, and tabular comparison of their opening formulae, set alongside equivalent passages from other documents of this type for the same churches, yields significant results (see table, p. 274).

Although Anglo-Saxon diplomatic is tiresomely stubborn about giving answers to the sort of questions posed here, the implications of the table are relatively clear. The texts of nos. 12–13 have enough in common to argue a common formulaic origin, perhaps a now lost set of conciliar decrees. Yet each text has its own quirks, and these usually recur in other judgements for the same beneficiary. For Worcester records, a place 'is said' (*dicitur*), but for those of Canterbury, it 'is named' (*nominatur*) or 'called' (*appellatur*) – even though documents of other types from these sees use the opposite alternatives.[36]

---

[35] BCS 312 has the most detailed ecclesiastical witness-list of the whole Anglo-Saxon period; it too is dated 12 October 803, and it is thus an eloquent comment on the shortcomings of the lists in S 1260, S 1431 and BCS 310 – or, by extension, any other list of the period – as evidence for attendance at a synod.

[36] E.g. S 164 (809); S 177 (814); S 186 (822); S 187 (823); S 296 (845) – Canterbury. S 1273 (855); S 210 (864) – Worcester. But note also the characteristic Canterbury formulation of S 168 (811).

Patrick Wormald

Handlist no. 12	Handlist no. 13
(a) Factum est pontificale et sinodale conciliabulum (4(i)) Factum est pontificale conciliabulum (8) Factum est sinodali conciliabulum (15) ða wæs sinodlic gemot	Congregatum est synodus (14) Congregatum est venerabile concilium (16A) Congregatum est venerabile concilium (16B) Factum est venerabile concilium
(b) in loco qui dicitur Clofeshoas (4(i)) in loco famosa qui dicitur Celchyð (4(ii)) in loco qui dicitur Clofeshoas (5) in loco qui dicitur Clofeshoas (15) on ðære meran stowe ðe mon hateþ Clofeshoes	in loco celebri ubi nominatur æt Clofeshoum (14) in loco praeclaro quae nominatur æt Clofeshoum (16A) in illa famoso loco quae appellatur Cyninges tun (16B) in loco quae dicitur æt Astran
(c) praesidente ... ac ... Wulfredo archiepiscopo (4(i)) praesidentibus duobus archiepiscopis (8) praesidente Æthelheardo archiepiscopo	praesidenti ... atque ... Wulfredo archiepiscopo anno xviiii⁰ episcopatus sui (14) praesidente ... Wulfredo archiepiscopo anno xx⁰ episcopatus eius
(d) Ibi in alia plura colloquia aliqua contentio allata est (4(i)) Ibi inter alia plura aliqua contentio facta est (8) de necessariis et pluribus universae ecclesiae statutis ... ibi etiam inter plura facta est contentio	querentes ... et scrutantes non solum de necessitatibus saecularium dignitatum sed etiam monasteriales disciplinas et ecclesiasticas regularesque mores ... Interea (14) ecclesiarum Dei utilitatem et necessitatem tractantes et scrutantes monasterialisque vitae regulam et observantiam seu etiam generositatem stabilitatemque regni terrestris consiliantes et querentes. Interea (15) intentione spiritalium saeculariumque rerum necessitatibus ... Interea

Canterbury sources give the regnal year of the archbishop as well as of the king, and are more verbose about the range of ecclesiastical problems under review. Even allowing that Worcester parallels came from before, Canterbury parallels from after, the 824 council, there can be little doubt that these are the scribal habits of different *scriptoria*. In Canterbury's case, the argument is strengthened inasmuch as the records of nos. 13–14 are contemporary texts, the second from the hand of a probable Canterbury scribe; moreover, the formulation of these documents is closely echoed by two splendid forgeries now known to have been composed by Archbishop Wulfred at this time.[37] It must also be significant that the traits of no. 16 cease to be those characteristics of Canterbury judgements when it is palaeographically apparent that a West Saxon scribe takes over.[38] If decisions taken by great synods of the southern English establishment, where one might have expected to have an official record, were nevertheless committed to writing by those respectively favoured, one can hardly postulate any other arrangement for judgements made in less solemn circumstances.[39]

Almost all the other indications point in the same direction. Four early records are explicitly episcopal charters (nos. 2–3, 4(ii), 6). Another has a telltale lapse into the first person (no. 17). Several are visibly biassed, one spectacularly so (no. 19). Judgements for Worcester refer to their city as ['the'] *ceastre* (nos. 12, 21). The text of no. 8, in Worcester's interest, is strikingly unconcerned with the Leicester–Lichfield and Sherborne–Winchester pleas *eodem die*, which it also mentions (nos. 9–10). In short, the evidence for the early phase of Anglo-Saxon litigation accords with the presently accepted view that English diplomatic before the tenth century was local and episcopal rather than royal or central. Indeed, it is among the strongest evidence that this was so.[40]

In the later, vernacular, group of texts, there is no pattern at all, and its very absence is, again, suggestive. The script of just one apparently contemporary record appears elsewhere, and this only shows that it is in fact a later copy.[41] All texts are almost entirely lacking in formulaic structure, let alone distinctive varieties of one. Their common forms are confined to the opening phrase: 'Her swutelaþ/cyð on þissum gewrite hu/ðæt . . .'. This admittedly serves to isolate two documents from Rochester beginning *þus*, but its formulaic significance is

---

[37] N.P. Brooks, *The Early History of the Church of Canterbury* (Leicester, 1984), pp. 191–7.

[38] Brooks, *Canterbury*, pp. 323–4.

[39] Vollrath, *Synoden Englands*, pp. 124–32. I am indebted to C.R.E. Coutts for kindly drawing my attention to canon IX of the Council of Chelsea (816), in *Councils and Ecclesiastical Documents relating to Great Britain and Ireland*, ed. A.W. Haddan and W. Stubbs, 3 vols. (Oxford, 1869–78) III, 583, whose relevance I and others had inexplicably missed: it effectively *instructs* bishops to make and keep records of *iudicia* concerning their own dioceses. Her Cambridge Univ. Ph.D. research into 'English Church Councils to *c*. 850' will add much to knowledge of these matters.

[40] In general, see Brooks, *Canterbury*, pp. 168–70 and 327–30; also P. Wormald, *Bede and the Conversion of England: the Charter Evidence* (Jarrow, 1985), pp. 9–11.

[41] *Facsimiles of English Royal Writs to A.D. 1100, presented to V.H. Galbraith*, ed. T.A.M. Bishop and P. Chaplais (Oxford, 1957), no. 4. N.P. Brooks, 'The Early Charters of Christ Church Canterbury' (unpubl. D.Phil. dissertation, Oxford Univ., 1969), p. 90. The other work of this scribe indicates a *floruit* in the 1070s.

of course nugatory. There is no trace of the vernacular collection of legal prescriptions known as *Swerian*.[42] Some reports are *ex parte* to the extent that they look like ammunition for further dispute, actual or anticipated: the famous account of the Helmstan cases is couched as a letter to Edward the Elder by Ealdorman Ordlaf in defence of his own rights, and just *might* have been penned by him (nos. 23–6; cf. nos. 32–5, 38–40, 43, 45–7, 83). But only one record says anything about the circumstances of its composition; and here it was the winner's formidable husband, Thurkill the White, who had it written into the Hereford gospel-book where it may still be found (no. 80).

The general impression, of even less central control over the reporting of lawsuits than was evident in the earlier period, is sustained, as before, by one particular example (no. 62). Æthelric of Bocking was lucky to die in his bed. He may have been one of the survivors of Maldon; he certainly stood accused of treasonable dealings with King Swein of Denmark. He contrived to escape sentence on his person, but his testamentary bequests were challenged by King Æthelred after his death. The case was heard at the royal court, and its record made and read before the king. The text took the form of a triple chirograph, and one of the three copies was to be kept 'æt þæs cinges haligdome': this is the only Anglo-Saxon instance of a judgement recorded in the way that, from the later twelfth century, would produce the central government archive of 'Feet of Fines'.[43] The elements of the situation could almost be said to have conspired to favour the 'centralized production' of a legal record. Yet it is not the king's side to which the author of the text inclines. The king is indeed blessed, but only because he relented and allowed Æthelric's dispositions to stand. The main beneficiary, as a result, was Christ Church, Canterbury. The king's change of heart was for the sake, among others, of 'ealra þæra haligra ðe æt xpes circean restaþ', a formulation that recurs in the highly coloured Christ Church account of its Sandwich suit before Harold Harefoot. The signs are, therefore, that Christ Church produced the Æthelric record, as well as preserving the extant medieval copies. For this to have happened at all, the tradition that judgements were written up by favoured parties must have remained well established in the later Anglo-Saxon period.

The remaining evidence, such as it is, supports this view. In the later Inkberrow case (no. 77), the king had ordered Archbishop Wulfstan (then Bishop of Worcester also) to draw up a charter of the original sale; and the capitalization of 'Saint Mary' in the extant chirograph on the subsequent

42 *Die Gesetze der Angelsachsen*, ed. F. Liebermann, 3 vols. (Halle, 1903–16) I, 396–9. Cf. 'Hit Becwæð', *ibid.*, p. 400.
43 Other extant chirographs among documents in the list are nos. 49, 77, 84; to judge from the existence of identical copies in the Ramsey and Thorney cartularies, the narrative record of no. 93 was also produced in this way. For deposit of other documents with the king, see S 1520 (1017 × 35), S 1521 (1035 × 1044) and S 1478 (1053 × 1055); also the spurious S 981.

dispute may suggest that St Mary's Worcester drafted it too (Worcester had an interest in the property, as the text seems to say). Likewise, Sherborne's two Holcombe Rogus pleas (nos. 74(ii), 85), though perhaps heard in different shire courts, share a formula that does not occur elsewhere in recorded lawsuits: the estate was to revert to the 'holy minster', 'mid mete 7 mid mannum'. If none of these arguments is conclusive in itself, they have some cumulative force. It cannot be said that official (and to that extent impartial) reports of early English legal proceedings were *never* made. But it must be said that almost all surviving accounts of Anglo-Saxon case-law in any sort of detail seem to have been written by or on behalf of the eventually successful disputant.

The diplomas which throw incidental light on legal process (above, p. 248) are of course another matter. These *are*, on the whole, stereotyped and formal documents; and whatever might be thought about the generally laconic references in texts from the first three quarters of the tenth century (nos. 27, 36–7), the sometimes vivid accounts of crime and punishment that appear in charters of King Æthelred for a number of different beneficiaries have long been among the strongest arguments for a royal writing office (nos. 44, 48, 54, 56–8, 60–1, 63–4, 68, 70–3, 75–6).[44] The view one holds of the status of these records, as well of the less informative reflections of property disputes in royal charters or writs (nos. 55, 59, 87, 89, 92), depends on the position one takes in the ongoing controversy between Drs Chaplais and Keynes.[45] As it happens, the formulation of the discursive passages themselves does not much help either side. Two are in the vernacular as well as Latin, and these vernacular sections, unlike the Latin charters in which they feature, have been classed above with documents of *placita* type, because they may once have had an independent existence; but, if so, little can be said about how or why they were made (nos. 56–8). There is evidence for local as well as central inspiration in some of the relevant texts (nos. 48, 54, 57–8, 60, 63–4, 71(i), 76).[46] Perhaps the main point to make here is that this material is important wherever the king's

---

[44] F. M. Stenton, *The Latin Charters of the Anglo-Saxon Period* (Oxford, 1955), pp. 74–82; *English Historical Documents, c. 500–1042*, ed. D. Whitelock, 2nd edn (London, 1979), p. 379; Keynes, *Diplomas*, pp. 95–126.

[45] See now Dr Chaplais' *riposte* to Keynes, *Diplomas*: 'The Royal Anglo-Saxon "Chancery" of the Tenth Century Revisited', *Studies in Medieval History presented to R. H. C. Davis*, ed. H. Mayr-Harting and R. I. Moore (London, 1985), pp. 41–51; and S. D. Keynes 'Regenbald the Chancellor (*sic*)', *Anglo-Norman Studies X*, ed. R. A. Brown (Woodbridge, 1988), pp. 185–222. I have attempted to find a measure of common ground in a review of Keynes, *Diplomas*: *History* 67 (1982), 309–10.

[46] Keynes, *Diplomas*, pp. 92–4, 96, 102–4, 113, 122–3 and 201. The links noted by Dr Keynes between S 842 (no. 44) and S 869 (no. 48) extend to the wording of the forfeiture clause; it is interesting (if scarcely explicable) that the same wording reappears in S 877 (nos. 57–8), which was also preserved at the New Minster.

scribes spent their off-duty hours. Nearly always, and for the first time in Anglo-Saxon diplomatic, the king expresses himself vigorously and in the first person about offence and forfeiture, with reference to the security of the realm and its integrity under God. It is at least as significant if these were the sentiments of major English churches as if they were espoused at court; perhaps more so.

The value of the evidence for pre-Conquest justice in action should not, however, be dismissed as vitiated by its apparent lack of official standing. Texts may tell only one side of the story, so that one is left ignorant not only of the opposing case but also of any concessions made to it in the outcome. But the imposingly bureaucratic monuments of English justice in the high Middle Ages are now notorious for concealing as much as they reveal.[47] Formulae may be some guarantee against the wilder flights of prejudice, but they are also tourniquets, cutting off the flow of colourful information. We should not learn much about the crimes of a Helmstan or the moods of a Harold Harefoot from early Frankish or later Italian *placita*.

Statistics

It may be interesting to conclude with some preliminary statistical impressions from the handlist – not that pre-Domesday statistics are ever very useful. The first point to note is that, while 178 lawsuits are probably more than most scholars have reckoned with, the number is relatively small by comparison with contemporary continental, or post-Conquest English, material. The Anglo-Saxon evidence covers 330 years. For a rather longer span of Frankish history (early seventh to early eleventh centuries), Hübner lists over 600 cases (though a significant proportion of these are Formulae). For the period 740–1066, co-terminous with the English sequence, he gives over 800 Italian suits. And Professor van Caenegem's comprehensive *English Secular Law Cases from William I to Richard I* will contain 664 items.

Apart from its size, a further limitation of the English evidence is that it is concentrated into a number of fairly short, and not necessarily representative, periods. Of the thirty cases before 909, fourteen fall between 781 and 825 (nos. 3–15, 18), and up to ten between 896 and 909 (nos. 21–9, 32). The reign of Edgar has twenty-two suits securely assigned to it, and another fifteen that might well be (nos. 35, 36?, 37, 39–43, 44?, 45, 47–8?, 50–2?, 53, 66, 107?, 113–14?, 116, 118, 124–5, 127, 129, 132, 136, 138, 139?, 154–6, 159?, 168?, 171?, 174?). The admittedly long and troubled period of his sons' reigns saw forty-eight or forty-nine 'certainties' and a possible total of sixty-one (nos. 44?, 46,

---

47 See M. T. Clanchy, 'A Medieval Realist: Interpreting the Rules at Barnwell Priory, Cambridge', *Perspectives in Jurisprudence*, ed. E. Attwooll (Glasgow, 1977), pp. 176–94; and 'Law and Love in the Middle Ages', *Disputes and Settlements: Law and Human Relations in the West*, ed. J. Bossy (Cambridge, 1983), pp. 47–67.

47–8?, 49, 50–2?, 54–64, 67–71, 72(a)–(b), 73–6, 81, 107?, 108–12, 113–14?, 115, 117, 119–23, 126, 128, 130, 137, 139?, 140–3, 152, 158, 168?, 169, 172, 174? – it will be noted that all these queries represent possible overlaps with Edgar rather than Cnut). By contrast, the half-century between Æthelred II's death and the Conquest is less well represented, that between 909 and Edgar's establishment much less so, and that between Ecgberht's triumph and his grandson's accession hardly at all.

The second immediate impression made by the handlist is that here, as so often, the reign of Alfred seems to mark a watershed. It is not just that there is a lot more evidence after 895, or that the directly informative texts are now vernacular. Reports of criminal as opposed to civil justice (inasmuch as the distinction exists under early medieval conditions) begin then with the graphic story of Helmstan (nos. 23, 25). This can hardly be because there were no criminal prosecutions before late in Alfred's reign, but it may very well be connected with the fact that there is no authentic earlier reference to the legal forfeiture of property.[48] The Helmstan record exists because his property was in dispute, and the case turned on whether or not leased land was liable to forfeiture. Precisely the same eventality at exactly this time is foreshadowed in no. 21. Within a year or two begins the series of royal grants of property forfeit for crime, with specific reference to the oath and pledge enforced by King Alfred (no. 27).[49] The significance of all this cannot be pursued further here, but the concurrence seems unlikely to be fortuitous.

Another contrast between earlier and later periods is nicely pointed up by the two Inkberrow disputes (nos. 4, 77). Both were suits between a local landowner and a bishop. But Bishop Heathored and Wulfheard, son of Cussa, took their difference before a general council of southern English authorities, whereas Bishop Æthelstan and Wulfstan, with his son, Wulfric, were heard by the *scirgemot* at Worcester. The case-law strongly suggests that, whatever earlier laws meant by *scir*, the shire as it is (or rather, alas, was) familiar to Englishmen was not a legal forum before the tenth century. Even the most local-looking of previous cases (no. 2) was settled by the bishop of Winchester, though the land at issue lay in the diocese of Sherborne. The first possible reference to shire justice is, again, the Helmstan report (no. 25). There is, however, no unmistakable instance before the mid-tenth century, and the best examples come from Æthelred's or Cnut's reigns (in roughly chronological order, nos. 133, 65, 159, 154, 172, 114, 112, 121, 130, 49, 126, 120, 137, 143, 110, 69, 74, 77, 80, 166, 84–7, 89–90, 92, 177, 93, 151, 147). Here, then, the date of

---

[48] See p. 247, n. 1, and p. 257 above: S 138 (795 = 792), cited by Stevenson as another early reference to forfeiture, is, like S 254, spurious.

[49] Laws of Alfred, ch. 1 (*Gesetze*, ed. Liebermann, 1, 46–7). Forfeiture for serious crime *was* already envisaged in the laws of Ine, ch. 6 (*ibid.*, pp. 90–1); the fact remains that there is no good pre-Alfredian evidence for its enforcement.

change is less clear than with forfeiture, but the fact of change seems sure; though this did not mean that 'national' hearings were unknown in the later period, any more than in the earlier (nos. 27, 30, 39, 42–3, 45, 54–5, 57–9, 62–3, 71, 72(a), 91, 108, 111, 134, 140, 146, 150, 152, 160–5, 168, 174).

Crime is the third area where the handlist is *prima facie* revealing. Considering that most of the evidence for it exists only because of its bearing on the destiny of property, the ratio of 'criminal' to 'civil' pleas is extremely high at 4:5 (there is some overlap, in that losers of 'civil' pleas could be punished as 'criminals' – 111, 116, 120, 134, 143, and cf. nos. 35, 46, 49). In itself, this may say something significant about Anglo-Saxon justice. The implication is that forfeiture had made *iustitia* into *magnum emolumentum* well before the days of the *Dialogue of the Exchequer*. Equally revealing is a rough break-down of 'crimes' reported according to the reigns in which they apparently occurred:

Alfred to Eadwig: 23, 25, 27, 29–31, 33, 38, 131, 157	10
Before or under Edgar: 36–37, 171	3
Under Edgar: 40–1, 43, 45, 53, 118, 124, 127, 129, 132, 154–6	13
Under Edgar or after 975: 44, 48, 50–1, 107, 174	6
Under Edward or Æthelred: 54, 56–8, 60–4, 68, 70–1, 72(a)–(b), 73, 75–6, 81, 144, 158, 169	20/21
Under Cnut: 78–9, 88, 145, 160	5
Cnut to 1066: 94, 97, 99–102, 148, 161–5, 170, 173, 175, 178	16

[It is assumed here that, in the absence of other evidence, 'crimes' may have been committed up to fifteen years before the record of the forfeiture to which they gave rise – cf., e.g., no. 63.]

The table gives a minimum of ten and maximum of thirteen cases for the sixty years up to the accession of Edgar; between fourteen and twenty-two for Edgar's reign; from twenty to twenty-seven for his sons; and twenty-one for the half-century before 1066. Historians should nowadays be criminologically sophisticated enough to beware talk of crime-waves, even if journalists are not. Nevertheless, the statistics invite some modification of the reputation of Æthelred II's reign for a 'law and order' problem. Edgar's government launched more prosecutions *per annum* than Æthelred's, even on the minimum figures for the first and the maximum for the second; the period from the death of Cnut to the battle of Hastings saw not many less. Æthelred's record does seem to be disfigured by more cases where the king's own honour was at stake (nos. 57–8, 60, 62–3, 71, 72(a)–(b), 75–6, 144). Only one suit under Edgar was of this type (no. 40), and most offences were straightforward or unspecified. On the other hand, the proportion of such prosecutions between 1035 and the Conquest was much the same (nos. 161–5, 170, 173). What has really damaged Æthelred is the memorably rhetorical detail of his charters, which meant, as Dr Keynes has shown, that the victims of high politics departed the scene with the maximum of mud sticking to their memory. This permits historians to enrol those whose disgrace is reported by the *Chronicle* among the crime figures.[50] Similar episodes are even commoner in the *Chronicle* for the last three decades of Anglo-Saxon history, but they are not so luridly illustrated by other sources; as a result, some, as has been seen, have to be excluded from the list altogether (above, pp. 253–4). It is instructive that only four 'criminal' cases from 1016 to 1066 are known from charters at all. For Edgar's reign, there is little *Chronicle* information, and generally vague charters, but these deficiencies are more than compensated by the cartulary-chronicle from Æthelwold's Ely and *miracula* from his Winchester – houses where Edgar of course loomed very large. If the criminal statistics do qualify one of the nostrums of Anglo-Saxon history, they are also a final warning that what lies hidden beyond the necessary boundaries of the handlist may be just as interesting as what it reveals.

Ultimately, perhaps the *most* interesting question raised by this paper is, why was it necessary to write it at all? It is in the nature of the evidence to tell only part of the story, and it hardly needs saying that the parties who recorded Anglo-Saxon litigation were almost always – the winners invariably – members of the elite (if not God). Yet students of most legal systems nowadays regard case-law as the most important part of their evidence. That no one has followed up the 1876 initiative for over a century is astonishing (the relevant material has nearly all been in print for most of this period). The reason must be that, since Pollock and Maitland, Anglo-Saxon law has been thought 'irrelevant' for the eventual emergence of the Englishman's legal birthright. Scholars from Liebermann downwards have directed their gaze on whatever it was in Anglo-Saxon custom that seemed to throw light on the 'archaic', 'Germanic' 'system'. They have (they thought) found enough of what they sought in the law-codes which Liebermann himself superbly edited. Whether Anglo-Saxon law was really either 'archaic' or 'irrelevant' is, in my view, a very open question indeed. But whatever the answer, it can only be found if 'Placita Anglo-Saxonica' at least receive their due share of attention.

---

[50] See Keynes, 'Crime and Punishment', forthcoming; also his 'A Tale of Two Kings: Alfred the Great and Æthelred the Unready', *TRHS* 5th ser. 36 (1986), 195–217, at 211–13.

Bibliography for 1987

CARL T. BERKHOUT, MARTIN BIDDLE,
MARK BLACKBURN, C. R. E. COUTTS,
DAVID DUMVILLE, SARAH FOOT and SIMON KEYNES

This bibliography is meant to include all books, articles and significant reviews published in any branch of Anglo-Saxon studies during 1987. It excludes reprints unless they contain new material. It will be continued annually. The year of publication of a book or article is 1987 unless otherwise stated. The arrangement and the pages on which the sections begin are as follows:

Carl Berkhout has been mainly responsible for sections 2, 3 and 4, David Dumville for section 5, Sarah Foot for section 6, Mark Blackburn for section 7, C. R. E. Coutts for section 8 and Martin Biddle for section 9. Section 9 has been compiled with help from Birthe Kjølbye-Biddle. References to publications in Japan have been supplied by Professor Yoshio Terasawa. Simon Keynes has been responsible for co-ordination.

The following abbreviations occur where relevant (not only in the bibliography but also throughout the volume):

A Ae   *Archaeologia Aeliana*
AB   *Analecta Bollandiana*
AC   *Archæologia Cantiana*

AHR	*American Historical Review*
AIUON	*Annali, Istituto Universitario Orientale di Napoli: sezione germanica*
AntJ	*Antiquaries Journal*
ArchJ	*Archaeological Journal*
ASE	*Anglo-Saxon England*
ASNSL	*Archiv für das Studium der neueren Sprachen und Literaturen*
ASSAH	*Anglo-Saxon Studies in Archaeology and History*
BAR	British Archaeological Reports
BBCS	*Bulletin of the Board of Celtic Studies*
BGDSL	*Beiträge zur Geschichte der deutschen Sprache und Literatur*
BIAL	*Bulletin of the Institute of Archaeology* (London)
BN	*Beiträge zur Namenforschung*
BNJ	*British Numismatic Journal*
CA	*Current Archaeology*
CBA	Council for British Archaeology
CCM	*Cahiers de civilisation médiévale*
CMCS	*Cambridge Medieval Celtic Studies*
DAEM	*Deutsches Archiv für Erforschung des Mittelalters*
EA	*Études anglaises*
EconHR	*Economic History Review*
EEMF	Early English Manuscripts in Facsimile
EETS	Early English Text Society
EHR	*English Historical Review*
ELN	*English Language Notes*
EPNS	English Place-Name Society
ES	*English Studies*
FS	*Frühmittelalterliche Studien*
HZ	*Historische Zeitschrift*
IF	*Indogermanische Forschungen*
JBAA	*Journal of the British Archaeological Association*
JEGP	*Journal of English and Germanic Philology*
JEH	*Journal of Ecclesiastical History*
JMH	*Journal of Medieval History*
JTS	*Journal of Theological Studies*
LH	*The Local Historian*
MA	*Medieval Archaeology*
MÆ	*Medium Ævum*
MLR	*Modern Language Review*
MP	*Modern Philology*
MS	*Mediaeval Studies*
MScand	*Mediaeval Scandinavia*
N&Q	*Notes and Queries*
NChron	*Numismatic Chronicle*

NCirc	*Numismatic Circular*
NH	*Northern History*
NM	*Neuphilologische Mitteilungen*
OEN	*Old English Newsletter*
PA	*Popular Archaeology*
PBA	*Proceedings of the British Academy*
PMLA	*Publications of the Modern Language Association of America*
PQ	*Philological Quarterly*
RB	*Revue bénédictine*
RES	*Review of English Studies*
SBVS	*Saga-Book of the Viking Society for Northern Research*
SCBI	Sylloge of Coins of the British Isles
SCMB	*Seaby's Coin and Medal Bulletin*
SettSpol	*Settimane di studio del Centro italiano di studi sull'alto medioevo* (Spoleto)
SM	*Studi Medievali*
SN	*Studia Neophilologica*
SP	*Studies in Philology*
TLS	*Times Literary Supplement*
TPS	*Transactions of the Philological Society*
TRHS	*Transactions of the Royal Historical Society*
YES	*Yearbook of English Studies*
ZAA	*Zeitschrift für Anglistik und Amerikanistik*
ZDA	*Zeitschrift für deutsches Altertum und deutsche Literatur*
ZVS	*Zeitschrift für vergleichende Sprachforschung*

1. GENERAL AND MISCELLANEOUS

[Anon.] 'Maldon as It Really Was', *Scandinavian Stud.* 59, 367–9

Bately, Janet, and Jane Roberts, 'In Memoriam: Julian Brown (1923–87)', *OEN* 20.2, 14

Berkhout, Carl T., 'Old English Bibliography 1986', *OEN* 20.2, 53–79

Berkhout, Carl T., Martin Biddle, Mark Blackburn, C. R. E. Coutts, David Dumville, Sarah Foot and Simon Keynes, 'Bibliography for 1986', *ASE* 16, 309–55

Brown, George H., 'In Memoriam: Morton Wilfred Bloomfield (1913–87)', *OEN* 20.2, 15

'In Memoriam: Stanley B. Greenfield (1922–87)', *OEN* 21.1, 14

Clemoes, Peter, *et al.*, 'Second Progress Report: *Fontes Anglo-Saxonici*', *OEN* 20.2, 22–3

Conner, Patrick W., 'ANSAXNET: Telecommunications for Anglo-Saxonists', *OEN* 20.2, 25

Desai, B. T., 'A Note on the Linguistic Sources of G. M. Hopkins' *Windhover*', *Dibrugarh Univ. Jnl of Eng. Stud.* 4 (1985), 115–19

Domínguez, Pablo, 'Anglo-Saxon Studies Today: an Interview with Peter Clemoes', *Revista Canaria de Estudios Ingleses* 13–14, 289–97

Evans, Deanna Delmar, 'Basing the Freshman Research Paper Class on Anglo-Saxon Materials', *Minnesota Eng. Jnl* 17.1 (1986), 5–12

Griffin, Henry William, 'Beer, Beowulf, and the English Literature Syllabus, 1936', *CSL: Bull. of the New York C.S. Lewis Soc.* 17.4 (1986), 1–3

Hieatt, Constance B., 'A Further Note on the IBM Quietwriter', *OEN* 21.1, 32

Hieatt, Constance B., and O.D. Macrae-Gibson, 'Progress in Computer-Assisted Learning: Beginning Old English/Learning Old English', *OEN* 20.2, 26–7

Kossick, Shirley, Brian S. Lee and Jean Freed, [reminiscences of Morton W. Bloomfield], *Med. Soc. of Southern Africa Newsletter* 14, 31–5

Lester, Geoffrey, *Handbook of Teachers of Medieval English Language and Literature in Great Britain and Ireland* (Sheffield)

Löfstedt, Leena, 'L'*Exchequer* anglais', *Actes du 9ᵉ Congrès des Romanistes Scandinaves*, ed. Elina Suomela-Härmä and Olli Välikangas, Mémoires de la Société Néophilologique de Helsinki 44 (Helsinki, 1986), 221–31

McKee, George D., 'A Note on Bibliographic Utilities', *OEN* 20.2, 31–3

Matonis, Ann, ed., *A Celtic Studies Bibliography for 1983–1985* (Philadelphia)

O'Keeffe, Katherine O'Brien, and Sheryl E. Perkins, 'Printing Strategies for Old English Characters Using WordPerfect', *OEN* 20.2, 28–30

Owen-Crocker, Gale R., 'Early Anglo-Saxon Dress – the Grave-goods and the Guesswork', *Textile Hist.* 18, 147–57

Palumbo, Linda J., 'The Later Wordsworth and the Romantic Ego: Bede and the Recreant Soul', *Wordsworth Circle* 17 (1986), 181–4

Robinson, Fred C., 'Stanley B. Greenfield, 1922–1987', *Med. Eng. Stud. Newsletter* (Tokyo) 17, 4–5

Rubin, Stanley, 'The Anglo-Saxon Physician', *Medicine in Early Medieval England*, ed. Marilyn Deegan and D.G. Scragg (Manchester), pp. 7–15

Sandred, Karl Inge, 'Erik Tengstrand (1898–1984)', *Onoma* 28 (1985–6), 1–3

Scheler, Manfred, 'Mediaeval English Studies in Berlin 1810–1985', *Med. Eng. Stud. Newsletter* (Tokyo) 17, 1–3

Simon-Vandenbergen, A.M., ed., *Studies in Honour of René Derolez* (Gent) [includes biographical note and bibliography]

Sonderegger, Stefan, 'Rasmus Kristian Rask und die Brüder Jacob und Wilhelm Grimm', *Festschrift für Oskar Bandle*, ed. Hans-Peter Naumann, Beiträge zur nordischen Philologie 15 (Basel and Frankfurt am Main, 1986), 115–30

Stanley, Eric Gerald, *A Collection of Papers with Emphasis on Old English Literature*, Publ. of the Dictionary of Old English 3 (Toronto)

Szarmach, Paul E., ed., *Old English Newsletter* 20.1–2 (Binghamton, 1986–7)

Trahern, Joseph B., Jr, ed., 'Year's Work in Old English Studies 1986', *OEN* 21.1, 39–201

2. OLD ENGLISH LANGUAGE

Aitken, A.J., 'The Period Dictionaries', *Studies in Lexicography*, ed. Robert Burchfield (Oxford), pp. 94–116

Bibliography for 1987

Amodio, Mark C., 'Some Notes on Laȝamon's Use of the Synthetic Genitive', *SN* 59, 187–94

Anderson, John M., 'Old English Morphology and the Structure of Noun Phrases', *Folia Linguistica Historica* 7 (1986), 219–24

Arngart, O., 'Middle English *wumme*', *SN* 59, 195–9

Bammesberger, Alfred, *Der Aufbau des germanischen Verbalsystems*, Indogermanische Bibliothek, ser. 1: Lehr- und Handbücher (Heidelberg, 1986)
    'Altenglisch *gewif*', *Anglia* 105, 115–20
    'Zu ae. *-uurbul/-huurful* in Epinal 1047/Corpus 2008', *Studies in Honour of René Derolez*, ed. Simon-Vandenbergen, pp. 26–9

Benediktsson, Hreinn, 'The 1st Singular Preterite Subjunctive in Germanic', *In Honor of Ilse Lehiste*, ed. Robert Channon and Linda Shockey, Netherlands Phonetic Archives 6 (Dordrecht and Providence, RI), 307–21

Bodden, Mary Catherine, see sect. *3a*

Bridges, Margaret, 'The Economics of Salvation: the Beginnings of an English Vocabulary of Reckoning', *Studies in Honour of René Derolez*, ed. Simon-Vandenbergen, pp. 44–62

Brinton, Laurel J., see sect. *3bi*

Clark, Cecily, 'Spelling and Grammaticality in the *Vespasian Homilies*: A Reassessment', *Manuscripta* 31, 7–10

Collier, L. W., 'The Chronology of *i*-Umlaut and Breaking in Pre-Old English', *North-Western European Lang. Evolution* 9, 33–45

Cooke, W. G., 'Notes on the Development of the English Pronouns', *ELN* 24.3, 1–6

Cronan, Dennis, see sect. *3bi* [*gelad*]

Crozier, Alan, 'Old English *drēogan*', *ES* 68, 297–304
    '*Ørlygis draugr* and *ørlǫg drýgja*', *Arkiv för Nordisk Filologi* 102, 1–12 [related OE terms]

D'Aronco, Maria Amalia, 'Inglese antico *galluc*', *AIUON* 28–9, Filologia germanica (1985–6), 83–100

Dekeyser, Xavier, 'English Contact Clauses Revisited: a Diachronic Approach', *Folia Linguistica Historica* 7 (1986), 107–20
    'Relative Clause Formation in the Anglo-Saxon Chronicle', *Studies in Honour of René Derolez*, ed. Simon-Vandenbergen, pp. 111–21
    'Relative Markers in the Peterborough Chronicle: 1070–1154, or Linguistic Change Exemplified', *Folia Linguistica Historica* 7 (1986), 93–105

Denison, David, 'On Word Order in Old English', *Dutch Quarterly Rev. of Anglo-American Letters* 16 (1986), 277–95
    'The Origins of Periphrastic *do*: Ellegård and Visser Reconsidered', *Papers from the 4th International Conference on English Historical Linguistics*, ed. Eaton *et al.*, pp. 45–60

De Smet, Gilbert A. R., 'Scandalum und Scandalizare in einigen altenglischen Übersetzungsdenkmälern', *Studies in Honour of René Derolez*, ed. Simon-Vandenbergen, pp. 122–31

Diller, Hans-Jürgen, see sect. *3a* [*wlanc*]

Donoghue, Daniel, see sect. *3bi*

Eaton, Roger, *et al.*, ed., *Papers from the 4th International Conference on English Historical Linguistics, Amsterdam, 10–13 April, 1985*, Amsterdam Stud. in the Theory and Hist. of Ling. Science 4: Current Issues in Ling. Theory 41 (Amsterdam and Philadelphia, 1986)

Fell, Christine, see sect. 8

Fischer, Andreas, *Engagement, Wedding, and Marriage in Old English*, Anglistische Forschungen 176 (Heidelberg, 1986)

Fischer, Olga, and Frederike van der Leek, 'A "Case" for the Old English Impersonal', *Explanation and Linguistic Change*, ed. Willem Koopman *et al.*, Current Issues in Ling. Theory 45 (Amsterdam and Philadelphia), 79–120

Frank, Roberta, 'A Note on Old English *swigdagas* "silent days"', *Studies in Honour of René Derolez*, ed. Simon-Vandenbergen, pp. 180–9

Fujiwara, Yasuaki, 'On Identifying Old English Adverbs', *Hirose Festschrift*, ed. T. Nakao (Tokyo), pp. 3–20

Fulk, R.D., 'Reduplicating Verbs and Their Development in Northwest Germanic', *BGDSL* (Tübingen) 109, 159–78

Giese, L.L., 'An Emendation of the *OED* Definition of *hie*, v., 1', *N&Q* 34, 146–7 [*higian*]

Goossens, Louis, 'Modal Tracks: the Case of *magan* and *motan*', *Studies in Honour of René Derolez*, ed. Simon-Vandenbergen, pp. 216–36

Grinda, Klaus R., 'Altenglisch *hefeld* "licium, liciatorium" und seine nordisch/niederdeutschen Verwandten. Versuch einer semantischen Zuordnung', *Althochdeutsch, II: Wörter und Namen. Forschungsgeschichte*, ed. Rolf Bergmann *et al.* (Heidelberg), pp. 1113–44 [also *websceaft*]

Gysseling, Maurits, 'Substratwörter in den germanischen Sprachen', *North-Western European Lang. Evolution* 10, 47–62

Hanson, Kristin, 'On Subjectivity and the History of Epistemic Expressions in English', *Papers from the 23rd Annual Regional Meeting of the Chicago Linguistic Society* (Chicago) 1, 133–47

Healey, Antonette di Paolo, 'The Dictionary of Old English and the Final Design of Its Computer System', *Computers and the Humanities* 19 (1985), 245–9

'Old English Language Studies: Present State and Future Prospects', *OEN* 20.2, 34–45

Hickey, R., 'Remarks on Syllable Quantity in Late Old English and Early Middle English', *NM* 88, 1–7

Hoad, T.F., 'Developing and Using Lexicographical Resources in Old and Middle English', *Dictionaries of English: Prospects for the Record of Our Language*, ed. Richard W. Bailey (Ann Arbor, MI), pp. 49–65

ed., *The Concise Oxford Dictionary of English Etymology* (Oxford, 1986)

Hofstetter, Walter, *Winchester und der spätaltenglische Sprachgebrauch: Untersuchungen zur geographischen und zeitlichen Verbreitung altenglischer Synonyme*, Münchener Universitäts-Schriften, Philosophische Fakultät, 14 (Munich)

Holland, Joan, 'Dictionary of Old English: 1986 Progress Report', *OEN*20.2, 19–21

Hubmayer, Karl, 'Phonetische Aspekte der Dehnung altenglischer Kurzvokale vor "homorganer" Doppelkonsonanz', *Philologie und Sprachwissenschaft: Akten der 10. Österreichischen Linguisten-Tagung*, ed. Wolfgang Meid and Hans Schmeja (Innsbruck, 1983), pp. 93–105

Hug, Sibylle, *Scandinavian Loanwords and their Equivalents in Middle English*, European Univ. Stud., ser. 21: Ling. 62 (Bern)

Iartseva, Viktoriia Nikolaevna, *Istoriia angliĭskogo literaturnogo iazyka IX–XV vv.* (Moscow, 1985)

Ide, Mitsu, *'beon/ wesan/ weorþan forþforen and forþferde'*, *Bull. of Kanto Gakuin Univ.* 50, 167–78 [in Japanese]

Ikegashira, Atsuko Kadota, 'OE Breaking and OE Retraction', *Hirose Festschrift*, ed. T. Nakao, (Tokyo), pp. 142–55

Kahlas-Tarkka, Leena, *The Uses and Shades of Meaning of Words for 'every' and 'each' in Old English, with an Addendum on Early Middle English Developments*, Mémoires de la Société Néophilologique de Helsinki 46 (Helsinki)

Kaminashi, Keiko, 'WGmc Gemination and Other Gemination Processes: a Nonlinear Approach', *Descriptive and Applied Ling.* 20, 95–104

'On Gemination and Vocalization: A Non-Linear Approach', *Hirose Festschrift*, ed. T. Nakao (Tokyo), pp. 156–78

Kemenade, Ans van, 'Old English Infinitival Complements and West-Germanic V-Raising', *Papers from the 4th International Conference on English Historical Linguistics*, ed. Eaton *et al.*, pp. 73–84

Keyser [S. J.], and [Wayne] O'Neill, *Rule Generalization and Optionality in Language Change*, Stud. in Generative Grammar 23 (Dordrecht and Cinnaminson, NJ, 1985)

Keyser, Samuel Jay, and Wayne O'Neill, 'The Simplification of the Old English Strong Nominal Paradigms', *Papers from the 4th International Conference on English Historical Linguistics*, ed. Eaton *et al.*, pp. 85–107

King, Anne, 'The Ruthwell Cross – a Linguistic Monument (Runes as Evidence for Old English)', *Folia Linguistica Historica* 7 (1986), 43–78

Kobayashi, Miki, 'Impersonal Non-Passive and Impersonal Passive Constructions in OE', *Hirose Festschrift*, ed. T. Nakao (Tokyo), pp. 24–40

'On the Development of Impersonal Constructions', *Descriptive and Applied Ling.* 20, 105–16

Köbler, Gerhard, *Altenglisch-neuhochdeutsches und neuhochdeutsch-altenglisches Wörterbuch*, Arbeiten zur Rechts- und Sprachwissenschaft 19 (Giessen, 1985)

Koopman, Willem F., 'Verb and Particle Combinations in Old and Middle English', *Papers from the 4th International Conference on English Historical Linguistics*, ed. Eaton *et al.*, pp. 109–21

Kristensson, Gillis, 'English Dialectal *toll* "clump of trees" and Cognates', *Studier i modern språkvetenskap* n.s. 8, 53–5

'The English West Midland *mon*-Area', *North-Western European Lang. Evolution* 10, 41–6

Kryger Kabell, Inge, 'The Old English *rēodmūþa* and the Bird Today Called the Pheasant', *SN* 59, 3–6

Krzyszpień, Jerzy, 'A Semantic Interpretation of Verbs in the OE and ME Impersonal Construction with Experiencer', *Kwartalnik Neofilologiczy* 34, 23–40

Kyto, Merja, '*Can (could)* vs. *may (might)* in Old and Middle English: Testing a Diachronic Corpus', *Neophilologica Fennica*, ed. Leena Kahlas-Tarkka, Mémoires de la Société Néophilologique de Helsinki 45 (Helsinki), 205–40

Lagerquist, Linnea M., 'The Impersonal Verb in Context: Old English', *Papers from the 4th International Conference on English Historical Linguistics*, ed. Eaton *et al.*, pp. 123–36

Lass, Roger, *The Shape of English: Structure and History* (London and Melbourne)

Lehmann, Winfred P., *A Gothic Etymological Dictionary* (Leiden, 1986)

'Agreement with the Available Material', *Studies in Honour of René Derolez*, ed. Simon-Vandenbergen, pp. 299–304 [Germanic ghost words]

Lendinara, Patrizia, 'Due glosse di origine germanica nel ms. Paris, Bibliothèque Nationale lat. 13833', *AIUON* 28–9, Filologia germanica (1985–6), 313–49

Lucas, Peter J., see sect. *3bi*

Machin, Roger, 'Gender and Linguistic Borrowings: the Case of Old English Loanwords in Welsh', *Bull. of the Faculty of Liberal Arts* (Chukyo Univ.), 21.2, 2

Markey, T. L., 'The English Progressive and the Origins of *-ing*', *Studies in Honour of René Derolez*, ed. Simon-Vandenbergen, pp. 317–33

Matzel, Klaus, 'Zu den verba pura des Germanischen', *ZVS* 100, 146–203

Mertens-Fonck, Paule, 'Spelling Variation in the *Vespasian Psalter* Gloss', *Studies in Honour of René Derolez*, ed. Simon-Vandenbergen, pp. 351–61

Milani, Celestina, see sect. 4

Minkova, Donka, 'Of Rhyme and Reason: Some Foot-Governed Quantity Changes in English', *Papers from the 4th International Conference on English Historical Linguistics*, ed. Eaton *et al.*, pp. 163–78

Mochizuki, Hiroshi, 'A Diachronic Approach to English Modals and Modality', *Descriptive and Applied Ling.* 20, 117–25

Moffat, Douglas, 'The Occurrences of *āc* "oak" in Old English: a List', *MS* 49, 534–40

Molencki, Rafał, 'The Accusative and Infinitive Construction in Old English: a Transformational Approach', *Kwartalnik Neofilologiczy* 34, 41–56

Morris, Katherine, 'Witch Words: the Origin and Background of German *Hexe*', *General Ling.* 27, 82–95

Morrison, Stephen, 'On Some Noticed and Unnoticed Old English Scratched Glosses', *ES* 68, 209–13

Nagucka, Ruta, 'Remarks on Complementation in Old English', *Papers from the 4th International Conference on English Historical Linguistics*, ed. Eaton *et al.*, pp. 195–204

Nakamura, Yuji, 'Agentive Prepositions in Ælfric's *Lives of Saints*', *Descriptive and Applied Ling.* 20, 127–34

Nevanlinna, Saara, 'Variation in the Syntactic Structure of Simile in OE Prose', *Papers from the Third Scandinavian Symposium on Syntactic Variation*, ed. Sven Jacobson, Stockholm Stud. in Eng. 65 (Stockholm, 1986), 89–98

see also sect. *3biii* [language of *Paris Psalter*]

Nishinarita, Michio, 'OE Equivalents of *Salvum Facere*', *Rikkyo Rev. of Eng. Lang. and Lit.* 16, 122–33

Niwa, Yoshinobu, 'A Classification of the Prefixed and Phrasal Constructions in Old English', *Stud. in Lang. and Culture* (Nagoya Univ.) 8:2, 1–10 [in Japanese]

Norri, Juhani, 'Notes on the Study of English Medical Vocabulary from the Historical Point of View', *Neophilologica Fennica*, ed. Leena Kahlas-Tarkka, Mémoires de la Société Néophilologique de Helsinki 45 (Helsinki), 335–50

Ogawa, Hiroshi, '"Modal Auxiliaries" in the Prose of Alfred's Reign: a Study of Syntax and Style in Old English', *Jnl of Social Sciences and Humanities* (Tokyo Metropolitan Univ.) 191 (*Stud. in Eng. Lang. and Lit.*), 49–85

Ogura, Michiko, 'Latinisms? – Constructions Chiefly Found in the Gospel, the Psalter, and the Hexateuch', *Tsuru Univ. Rev.* 27, 53–67

Ono, Shigeru, 'Old English *agan* + Infinitive Revisited', *Jnl of Social Sciences and Humanities* (Tokyo Metropolitan Univ.) 191 (*Stud. in Eng. Lang. and Lit.*), 33–48 [in Japanese]

Page, R.I., 'Yet Another Note on Alfred's *æstel*', *Leeds Stud. in Eng.* n.s. 18, 9–18 see also sects. 5, 9*i* [runes]

Peeters, Christian, 'Germanic Comparative Notes', *General Ling.* 27, 80–1 [eight words with OE cognates]

Pheifer, J.D., see sect. 4

Plank, Frans, 'Number Neutralization in Old English: Failure of Functionalism?' *Explanation and Linguistic Change*, ed. Willem Koopman *et al.*, Current Issues in Ling. Theory 45 (Amsterdam and Philadelphia), 177–238

Polomé, Edgar C., 'Some Comments on Germano-Hellenic Lexical Correspondences', *Aspects of Language: Studies in Honour of Mario Alinei*, ed. Nils Århammar *et al.* (Amsterdam, 1986) 1, 171–98

Poussa, Patricia, 'Historical Implications of the Distribution of the Zero-Pronoun Relative Clause in Modern English Dialects: Looking Backwards towards OE from Map S5 of *The Linguistic Atlas of England*', *Papers from the Third Scandinavian Symposium on Syntactic Variation*, ed. Sven Jacobson, Stockholm Stud. in Eng. 65 (Stockholm, 1986), 99–117

'A Note on the Voicing of Initial Fricatives in Middle English', *Papers from the 4th International Conference on English Historical Linguistics*, ed. Eaton *et al.*, pp. 235–52

Rissanen, Matti, 'Expression of Exclusiveness in Old English and the Development of the Adverb *only*', *Papers from the 4th International Conference on English Historical Linguistics*, ed. Eaton *et al.*, pp. 253–67

'Old English Indefinite Pronouns Meaning "some" and "any", with Special Reference to *hw*-Forms', *Neophilologica Fennica*, ed. Leena Kahlas-Tarkka, Mémoires de la Société Néophilologique de Helsinki 45 (Helsinki), 411–28

'Variation and the Study of English Historical Syntax', *Diversity and Diachrony*, ed. David Sankoff, Current Issues in Ling. Theory 53 (Amsterdam and Philadelphia, 1986), 97–109

Russom, Geoffrey, see sect. 3*bi*

Rydén, Mats, 'English Names for *Convallaria Majalis L.*', *Studier i modern språkvetenskap* n.s. 8, 61–70 [*glofwyrt*]

Samuels, M. L., 'The Great Scandinavian Belt', *Papers from the 4th International Conference on English Historical Linguistics*, ed. Eaton *et al.*, pp. 269–81

'The status of the Functional Approach', *Explanation and Linguistic Change*, ed. Willem Koopman *et al.*, Current Issues in Ling. Theory 45 (Amsterdam and Philadelphia), 239–50

Sasagawa, Junko, 'The Stress Doublets in Middle English', *Descriptive and Applied Ling.* 20, 171–8

Schabram, Hans, 'Altenglisch *sāp*: ein altes germanisches Wort für "Bernstein"?' *Althochdeutsch, II: Wörter und Namen*, ed. Rolf Bergmann *et al.* (Heidelberg), pp. 1210–15

Schipper, William, 'A Worksheet of the Worcester "Tremulous" Glossator', *Anglia* 105, 28–49

Schlerath, Bernfried, '"Gabe und Lohn" in den altgermanischen Bibelübersetzungen', *Sprachwissenschaftliche Forschungen: Festschrift für Johann Knobloch*, ed. Hermann M. Ölberg *et al.*, Innsbrucker Beiträge zur Kulturwissenschaft 23 (Innsbruck, 1985), 361–78

Schneider, Karl, 'Zur Etymologie von ae. *eolhsand* "Bernstein" und *elehtre* "Lupine" im Lichte bronzezeitlichen Handels', *Collectanea Philologica: Festschrift für Helmut Gipper zum 65. Geburtstag*, ed. Günther Heintz and Peter Schmitter (Baden-Baden, 1985) II, 669–81

Scott, Charles T., 'English Front Round Vowels: a Synchronic and Diachronic Interpretation', *SAP* 18 (1986), 3–14

Scragg, D. J. [for D. G.], 'Old English *forcile*', *KM 80: a Birthday Album for Kenneth Muir, Tuesday, 5 May, 1987*, ed. Philip Edwards, Vincent Newey and Ann Thompson (Liverpool), p. 128

Serdiuk, E. I., 'Ob odnom istochnike terminov drevneangliĭskogo prava', *Vestnik Moskovskogo Universiteta, seriia 9: Filologiia* 1987, no. 4, 81-[9] [law terms]

Seynnaeve, Johan, 'On the Morpheme Structure Function of the Consonant Gemination in West Germanic', *Leuvense Bijdragen* 76, 433–46

Sgarbi, Romano, see sect. 3*c*

Smith, Roger, see sect. 3*bi* [*garsecg*]

Stanley, E. G., 'Old English in *The Oxford English Dictionary*', *Studies in Lexicography*, ed. Robert Burchfield (Oxford), pp. 19–35

Stockwell, Robert P., 'Assessment of Alternative Explanations of the Middle English Phenomenon of High Vowel Lowering when Lengthened in the Open Syllable', *Papers from the 4th International Conference on English Historical Linguistics*, ed. Eaton *et al.*, pp. 303–18

Tajima, Matsuji, *The Syntactic Development of the Gerund in Middle English* (Tokyo, 1985)

Takeuchi, Shinichi, 'On *sellan* and *giefan* in *The Peterborough Chronicle*', *Descriptive and Applied Ling.* 20, 191–201

Taylor, Paul Beekman, 'Logaþore and Loðurr: the Literary Contexts', *Studies in Honour of René Derolez*, ed. Simon-Vandenbergen, pp. 603–11 [*logðor*, etc.]

Thornburg, Linda, 'The Development of the Indirect Passive in English', *Proceedings of the Twelfth Annual Meeting of the Berkeley Linguistics Society*, ed. Vassiliki Nikiforidou *et al.* (Berkeley, 1986), pp. 261–70

Toon, Thomas E., 'Old English Dialects: What's to Explain; What's an Explanation?' *Explanation and Linguistic Change*, ed. Willem Koopman *et al.*, Current Issues in Ling. Theory 45 (Amsterdam and Philadelphia), 275–93

Toporova, T. V., 'Semantika "kontsa" v drevnegermanskoĭ modeli mira i problema rekonstruktsii germanskogo eskhatologicheskogo mitha', *Izvestiia Akademii Nauk SSSR, seriia literatury i iazika* 46, 132–40 [terms for death, doomsday, etc.]

Vargina, N. V., and V. N. Sinel'nikova, 'Kommunikatinaia rol' glagola-zamestitelia *don* v drevneangliĭskom iazyke', *Vestnik Leningradskogo Universiteta* 1987, ser. 2.1, 87–8 [function of the verb-substitute *don* in OE]

Vigil, Julián Josué, *Equivalents in Anglo-Saxon and Gothic* (Guadalupita, NM)

Voyles, Joseph, 'The Cardinal Numbers in Pre- and Proto-Germanic', *JEGP* 86, 487–95

Wakelin, Martyn, 'On the Etymology of English *prawn*: a Note', *Aspects of Language: Studies in Honour of Mario Alinei*, ed. Nils Århammar *et al.* (Amsterdam, 1986) I, 239–42

Weidmann, B. G., 'On the Semantic Development of English *ghost* and German *Geist*', *Orbis* (Louvain) 32 (1987 for 1983), 223–40

Zabulene, Laĭma, 'K voprosu o statuse diftongov prelomleniia', *Lietuvos TSR Aukštųjų Mokyklų Darbai: Kalbotyra* 36.3 (1986), 130–4 [on the status of OE breaking diphthongs]

3. OLD ENGLISH LITERATURE

a. General

Bodden, Mary Catherine, 'Anglo-Saxon Self-Consciousness in Language', *ES* 68, 24–39

Bolton, W. F., 'The Conditions of Literary Composition in Medieval England', *The Middle Ages*, ed. W. F. Bolton, Sphere Hist. of Lit. 1 (London, 1986), 1–27 and 401–2 [revised republications of 1970 edn]

Brown, George Hardin, see sect. 1

Burrow, J. A., *The Ages of Man: a Study in Medieval Writing and Thought* (Oxford, 1986)

Busse, Wilhelm, *Altenglische Literatur und ihre Geschichte: zur Kritik des gegenwärtigen Deutungssystems*, Studia Humaniora 7 (Düsseldorf)

Crabtree, Rachel, see sect. 5

Cross, J. E., 'The Old English Period', *The Middle Ages*, ed. W. F. Bolton, Sphere Hist. of Lit. 1 (London, 1986), 29–80 and 403–4 [revised republication of 1970 edn]

Diller, Hans-Jürgen, 'Wortbedeutung und literarische Gattung. Ein Versuch am Beispiel von ae. *wlanc*', *Gattungsprobleme in der anglo-amerikanischen Literatur: Beiträge für Ulrich Suerbaum zu seinem 60. Geburtstag*, ed. Raimund Borgmeier (Tübingen, 1986), pp. 1–11

Hill, Joyce, 'Old English Literature [1984]', *Year's Work in Eng. Stud.* 64 (1986), 74–118

'Old English Literature [1985]', *Year's Work in Eng. Stud.* 65, 67–104

Lindow, John, 'Norse Mythology's English Connection: Methodological Notes', *The Sixth International Saga Conference, 28.7.–2.8.1985: Workshop Papers* (Copenhagen, 1986) II, 673–99

Palmer, Elizabeth, 'Old English Literature [1980]', *Year's Work in Eng. Stud.* 61 (1982), 61–76

'Old English Literature [1982]', *Year's Work in Eng. Stud.* 63 (1985), 44–73

Swanton, Michael, *English Literature before Chaucer* (London and New York)

Ternes, Charles-Marie, 'Influences de l'épopée antique sur la littérature anglo-saxonne, de la fin de l'antiquité à l'époque de Geoffrey Chaucer', *Colloque L'Epopée gréco-latine et ses prolongements européens, Calliope II*, ed. R. Chevallier (Paris, 1981), 187–98

b. Poetry

i. General

Amodio, Mark C., see sect. 2

Brinton, Laurel J., 'A Linguistic Approach to Certain Old English Stylistic Devices', *SN* 59, 177–85

Cronan, Dennis, 'Old English *gelad*: "a passage across water"', *Neophilologus* 71, 316–19

Donoghue, Daniel, *Style in Old English Poetry: the Test of the Auxiliary*, Yale Stud. in Eng. 196 (New Haven and London)

Earl, James W., 'Transformation of Chaos: Immanence and Transcendence in *Beowulf* and Other Old English Poetry', *Ultimate Reality and Meaning* 10, 164–85 [*Christ I, Maxims I, Seafarer*]

Evans, Dafydd, 'Old English and Old French Epics: Some Analogues', *Guillaume d'Orange and the 'Chanson de geste'*, ed. Wolfgang van Emden and Philip E. Bennett (Reading, 1984), pp. 23–31

Ford, Patrick K., and Karen G. Borst, ed., *Connections between Old English and Medieval Celtic Literature*, [Berkeley] OE Colloquium Ser. 2 (Lanham, MD, 1983) [includes introduction by Ford and select bibliography by Borst]

Frank, Roberta, 'Did Anglo-Saxon Audiences Have a Skaldic Tooth?' *Scandinavian Stud.* 59, 338–55

Higley, Sarah L., 'Lamentable Relationships? "Non-Sequitur" in Old English and Middle Welsh Elegy', *Connections between Old English and Medieval Celtic Literature*, ed. Ford and Borst, pp. 45–66

Kitson, Peter, 'Some Unrecognized Old English and Anglo-Latin Verse', *N&Q* 34, 147–51

Lucas, Peter J., 'Some Aspects of the Interaction between Verse Grammar and Metre in Old English Poetry', *SN* 59, 145–75

Meier, Hans H., 'Old English Style in Action: the Battle Scene (with a Hint on *Hildebrand*)', *Studies in Honour of René Derolez*, ed. Simon-Vandenbergen, pp. 334–50

Melia, Daniel F., 'An Odd but Celtic Way of Looking at Old English Elegy',

Connections between Old English and Medieval Celtic Literature, ed. Ford and Borst, pp. 8–30

Ono, Eri, 'The Syntax and Semantics of *Gast* in Old English Poetry', *Annual Collection of Essays and Stud.* (Faculty of Letters, Gakushuin Univ.) 33, 103–37 [in Japanese]

Overing, Gillian R., 'Some Aspects of Metonymy in Old English Poetry', *Concerning Poetry* 19 (1986), 1–19

Parks, Ward, 'The Flyting Speech in Traditional Heroic Narrative', *Neophilologus* 71, 285–95

'The Traditional Narrator and the "I heard" Formulas in Old English Poetry', *ASE* 16, 45–66

Renoir, Alain, 'Oral-Formulaic Rhetoric: an Approach to Image and Message in Medieval Poetry', *Medieval Texts and Contemporary Readers*, ed. Laurie A. Finke and Martin B. Schichtman (Ithaca, NY, and London), pp. 234–53

Richardson, John, 'The Critic on the Beach', *Neophilologus* 71, 114–19 [critique of oral-formulaic theory]

Russom, Geoffrey, *Old English Meter and Linguistic Theory* (Cambridge)

Smith, Roger, '*Garsecg* in Old English Poetry', *ELN* 24.3, 14–19

Yamanouchi, Kazuyoshi, 'Traditional Theories of Old English Prosody', *Stud. in Humanities: Annual Reports of Departments of Sociology and Humanities* (Shizuoka Univ.) 37, 41–80 [in Japanese]

ii. *'Beowulf'*

Barquist, Claudia Russell, 'Phonological Patterning in *Beowulf*', *Lit. and Ling. Computing* 2, 19–23

Berlin, Gail Ivy, 'Grendel's Advance on Heorot: the Functions of Anticipation', *Proc. of the Patristic, Med. and Renaissance Conference* 11 (1986), 19–26

Boenig, Robert, 'Time Markers and Treachery: the Crux at *Beowulf* 1130', *ELN* 24.4, 1–9

Bosse, Roberta Bux, and Jennifer Lee Wyatt, 'Hrothgar and Nebuchadnezzar: Conversion in Old English Verse', *Papers on Lang. and Lit.* 23, 257–71

Butts, Richard, 'The Analogical Mere: Landscape and Terror in *Beowulf*', *ES* 68, 113–21

Canitz, A. E. C., 'Kingship in *Beowulf* and the *Nibelungenlied*', *Mankind Quarterly* 27 (1986), 97–119

Collins, Rowland L., 'Blickling Homily XVI and the Dating of *Beowulf*', *Medieval Studies Conference, Aachen 1983*, ed. Wolf-Dietrich Bald and Horst Weinstock, Bamberger Beiträge zur englischen Sprachwissenschaft 15 (Frankfurt am Main, 1984), 61–9

Crossley-Holland, Kevin, trans., *Beowulf* (Woodbridge)

Daldorph, Brian, '"Mar-Peace," Ally: Hunferð in *Beowulf*', *Massachusetts Stud. in Eng.* 10 (1986), 143–60

Damico, Helen, '*Þrymskviða* and Beowulf's Second Fight: the Dressing of the Hero in Parody', *Scandinavian Stud.* 58 (1986), 407–28

D'Aronco, Maria Amalia, 'Per una rilettura del *Beowulf* fra rito e fiaba', *Rivista di cultura classica e medioevale* 28 (1986), 139–59

Diller, Hans-Jurgen, 'Contiguity and Similarity in the *Beowulf* Digressions', *Medieval Studies Conference, Aachen 1983*, ed. Wolf-Dietrich Bald and Horst Weinstock, Bamberger Beiträge zur englischen Sprachwissenschaft 15 (Frankfurt am Main, 1984), 71–83

Donoghue, Daniel, 'On the Classification of B-Verses with Anacrusis in *Beowulf* and *Andreas*', *N&Q* 34, 1–5

Edwards, Paul, 'Alcohol into Art: Drink and Poetry in Old Icelandic and Anglo-Saxon', *Sagnaskemmtun: Studies in Honour of Hermann Pálsson*, ed. Rudolf Simek *et al.* (Vienna, Cologne and Graz, 1986), pp. 85–97

Feldman, Thalia Phillies, 'A Comparative Study of *feond, deofl, syn* and *hel* in *Beowulf*', *NM* 88, 159–74

Frank, Roberta, see sect. 3*bi*

Frey, Leonard, '*Comitatus* as a Rhetorical-Structural Norm for Two Germanic Epics', *Recovering Lit.* 14 (1986), 51–70

Fulk, R.D., 'Unferth and His Name', *MP* 85, 113–27

Gahrn, Lars, 'The Geatas of Beowulf', *Scandinavian Jnl of Hist.* 11 (1986), 95–113

Georgianna, Linda, 'King Hrethel's Sorrow and the Limits of Heroic Action in *Beowulf*', *Speculum* 62, 829–50

Glosecki, Stephen O., '*Beowulf* 769: Grendel's Ale-Share', *ELN* 25.1, 1–9
  'Men among Monsters: Germanic Animal Art as Evidence of Oral Literature', *Mankind Quarterly* 27 (1986), 207–14

Green, Eugene, 'Power, Commitment, and the Right to a Name in *Beowulf*', *Persons in Groups*, ed. Richard C. Trexler, Med. and Renaissance Texts and Stud. 36 (Binghamton, 1985), 133–40

Haarder, Andreas, trans., *Sangen om Bjovulf* (Copenhagen)

Heinrichs, Heinrich Matthias, '*Beowulf* und andere altenglische Heldendichtung', *Epische Stoffe des Mittelalters*, ed. Volker Mertens and Ulrich Müller, Kröners Taschenausgabe 483 (Stuttgart, 1984), 156–64

Helder, William, 'The Song of Creation in *Beowulf* and the Interpretation of Heorot', *Eng. Stud. in Canada* 13, 243–55

Huppé, Bernard F., *Beowulf: a New Translation* (Binghamton)

Jorgensen, Peter A., 'Additional Icelandic Analogues to *Beowulf*', *Sagnaskemmtun: Studies in Honour of Hermann Pálsson*, ed. Rudolf Simek *et al.* (Vienna, Cologne and Graz, 1986), pp. 201–8

Köberl, Johann, 'The Magic Sword in *Beowulf*', *Neophilologus* 71, 120–8

Kumazawa, Sukeo, 'Verb-Positions of Finite Verbs in Adverb Clauses in *Beowulf*', *Research Report of Ikutoku Technical Univ.: Pt A Humanities and Social Science* A–11, 31–49 [in Japanese]

Liberman, Anatoly, 'Beowulf-Grettir', *Germanic Dialects: Linguistic and Philological Investigations*, ed. Bela Brogyanyi and Thomas Krömmelbein (Amsterdam and Philadelphia, 1986), pp. 353–401

Magnusson, Magnus, Sheila Mackie and Julian Glover, *Beowulf: an Adaptation by Julian Glover of the Verse Translations of Michael Alexander and Edwin Morgan* (Gloucester)

Nagy, Joseph F., 'Beowulf and Fergus: Heroes of Their Tribes?' *Connections between Old English and Medieval Celtic Literature.* ed. Ford and Borst, pp. 31–44

Nicholson, Lewis E., '*Beowulf* and the Pagan Cult of the Stag', *SM* 3rd ser. 27 (1986), 637–69

Obst, Wolfgang, *Der Rhythmus des Beowulf: eine Akzent- und Takttheorie*, Anglistische Forschungen 187 (Heidelberg)

Overing, Gillian R., 'Swords and Signs: a Semeiotic Perspective on *Beowulf*', *Amer. Jnl of Semiotics* 5.1, 35–57

Parker, Mary A., '*Beowulf*' and *Christianity*, Amer. Univ. Stud., ser. 4: Eng. Lang. and Lit. 51 (New York)

Pàroli, Teresa, 'The Elusive "Death of Beowulf"', *Res Publica Litterarum* 10, 263–6

Russom, Geoffrey, 'Word and Foot in *Beowulf*', *Style* 21, 387–99

Schichler, Robert Lawrence, 'Heorot and Dragon-Slaying in *Beowulf*', *Proc. of the Patristic, Med. and Renaissance Conference* 11 (1986), 159–75

Schneider, Karl, *Sophia Lectures on 'Beowulf'*, ed. Shoichi Watanabe and Norio Tsuchiya (Tokyo, 1986)

Tripp, Raymond P., Jr, 'Beowulf 1834, *gārholt*: "spear-wood", Wordplay and Plowshares', *In Geardagum* 8, 19–34

Vidal Tibbits, Mercedes, 'El Cid, hombre heróico, y Beowulf, héroe sobrehumano', *Josep Maria Solà-Solé: homage, homenaje, homenatge*, ed. Antonio Torres-Alcalá (Barcelona, 1984) 1, 267–73

Weise, Judith, 'The Meaning of the Name "Hygd": Onomastic Constrast in *Beowulf*', *Names* 34 (1986), 1–10

iii. *Other poems*

Amano, Koichi, 'A Japanese Translation of an Old English Poem *The Dream of the Rood*', *Treatises and Stud. by the Faculty of Kinjo Gakuin Univ.* 119, 1–20

Anderson, Earl R., 'Style and Theme in the Old English *Daniel*', *ES* 68, 1–23

Atsushi, Ajiro, 'The Compressed Expression in *Exodus* – hapax legomena', *Daito Bunka Rev.* (Soc. of Eng. and Amer. Lit.) 18, 55–68 [in Japanese]
'The Old English Poem "*Exodus*" – A Japanese Translation and its Commentary', *Bull. of Daito Bunka Univ. Humanities* 25, 47–65 [in Japanese]

Baird, Joseph L., '*Natura plangens*, the Ruthwell Cross and *The Dream of the Rood*', *Stud. in Iconography* 10 (1984–6), 37–51

Biggs, Frederick M., *The Sources of 'Christ III': a Revision of Cook's Notes*, OEN Subsidia 12 (Binghamton, 1986)

Bosse, Roberta Bux, and Jennifer Lee Wyatt, see sect. 3*bii* [*Daniel, Elene*]

Brown, George Hardin, 'Solving the "Solve" Riddle in B. L. MS Harley 585', *Viator* 18, 45–51

Chappell, Virginia A., '*Reordberendra gesyhthe* and Christian Mystery: Narrative Frames in *The Dream of the Rood*', *Comitatus* 18, 1–20

Chase, Dennis, 'Existential Attitudes in the Old English "Wanderer"', *Univ. of South Florida Lang. Quarterly* 26.1–2, 17–19

'"The Wife's Lament": an Eighth-Century Existential Cry', *Univ. of South Florida Lang. Quarterly* 24.3–4 (1986), 18–20

Couch, Christopher L., 'From Under Mountains to Beyond Stars: the Process of Riddling in Leofric's *The Exeter Book* and *The Hobbit*', *Mythlore* 14.1, 9–13 and 55

Dempsey, G. T., see sect. 4 [Paris Psalter]

Doane, A. N., 'Three Old English Implement Riddles: Reconsiderations of Numbers 4, 49, and 73', *MP* 84, 243–57

Donoghue, Daniel, see sect. 3*bii* [*Andreas*]

Earl, James W., 'Hisperic Style in the Old English "Rhyming Poem"', *PMLA* 102, 187–96

Elsakkers, Marianne, 'The Beekeeper's Magic: Taking a Closer Look at the Old Germanic Bee Charms', *Mankind Quarterly* 27, 447–61

Evans, D. A. H., '*Maldon* 215', *N&Q* 34, 5–7

Frank, Roberta, see sect. 3*bi*

Gerritsen, Johan, 'Leiden Revisited: Further Thoughts on the Text of the Leiden Riddle', *Medieval Studies Conference, Aachen 1983*, ed. Wolf-Dietrich Bald and Horst Weinstock, Bamberger Beiträge zur englischen Sprachwissenschaft 15 (Frankfurt am Main, 1984), 51–9

Gillam, Doreen M. E., 'Love Triangle at Commedia: Some Sidelights on Cynewulf's Handling of Personal Relationships in *Juliana*', *Studies in Honour of René Derolez*, ed. Simon-Vandenbergen, pp. 190–215

Greenfield, Stanley B., trans., '*Exodus*', *OEN* 21.1, 15–20 [lines 1–275]

'The Petitions of the *Advent Lyrics* and the Question of Unity', *Studies in Honour of René Derolez*, ed. Simon-Vandenbergen, pp. 237–47

Hall, J. R., '*Daniel*, Line 610b', *Explicator* 45.2, 3–4

'Old English *Exodus* and the Sea of Contradiction', *Mediaevalia* 9 (1986 [1987] for 1983), 25–44

'Two Dark Old English Compounds: *ælmyrcan* (*Andreas* 432a) and *guðmyrce* (*Exodus* 59a)', *Jnl of Eng. Ling.* 20, 38–47

Horgan, A. D., '*The Wanderer* – a Boethian Poem?' *RES* 38, 40–6

Ikegami, Keiko, 'On Syndetic Parataxis: its Tentative Analysis and their Application to *The Life of St Guthlac*', *Research Reports of Seijo Junior College* 18, 1–51

Jember, Gregory K., 'Prolegomena to a Study of the Old English Riddles', *Jnl of the Faculty of Liberal Arts, Saga Univ.* 19, 155–78

'Some Hints on Ambiguity and Meaning in *Riddle 39*', *Hiroshima Stud. in Eng. Lang. and Lit.* 31, 26–37

Kilpiö, Matti, 'Hrabanus' *De laudibus sanctae crucis* and *The Dream of the Rood*', *Neophilologica Fennica*, ed. Leena Kahlas-Tarkka, Mémoires de la Société Néophilologique de Helsinki 45 (Helsinki), 177–91

King, Anne, see sect. 2 [Ruthwell Cross]

Klinck, Anne L., 'Animal Imagery in *Wulf and Eadwacer* and the Possibilities of Interpretation', *Papers on Lang. and Lit.* 23, 3–13

'*Resignation*: Exile's Lament or Penitent's Prayer?' *Neophilologus* 71, 423–30

Le Saux, Françoise, 'Didacticism in the *Dream of the Rood*', *Etudes de Lettres* (Université de Lausanne) 1987, nos. 2–3, pp. 167–77 [and *Physiologus*]

Lewis, David J.G., 'The Metre of *Genesis B*', *ASE* 16, 67–125

Lupi, Sergio, 'I problemi esterni del *Heliand*', *Atti dell' Accademia Peloritana dei Pericolanti, Classe di lettere, filosofia e belle arti* 61 (1987 for 1985), 84–110 [posthumous reprint, revised, of 1965 article; see Schwab below]

Machan, Tim William, and Robyn G. Peterson, 'The Crux of Riddle 53', *ELN* 24.3, 7–14

McKill, L. N., 'The Artistry of the Noah Episode in *Genesis A*', *Eng. Stud. in Canada* 13, 121–35

McPherson, Clair, 'The Sea a Desert: Early English Spirituality and *The Seafarer*', *Amer. Benedictine Rev.* 38, 115–26

Mandel, Jerome, *Alternative Readings in Old English Poetry*, Amer. Univ. Stud., ser. 4: Eng. Lang. and Lit. 43 (New York) [*Wanderer, Seafarer, Deor, Wife's Lament*]

Miletich, John S., 'Old English "Formulaic" Studies and *Caedmon's Hymn* in a Comparative Context', *Festschrift für Nikola R. Pribić*, ed. Josip Matešić *et al.* (Neuried, BRD, 1983), pp. 183–94

Moffat, Douglas, 'A Case of Scribal Revision in the Old English *Soul and Body*', *JEGP* 86, 1–8

  ed., *The Soul's Address to the Body: the Worcester Fragments*, Med. Texts and Stud. 1 (East Lansing, MI) [*Soul and Body I* and *II*, *The Grave*]

Neuman de Vegvar, Carol L., see sect. 5 [Franks Casket, Ruthwell Cross]

Nevanlinna, Saara, 'Simile in the Old English *Paris Psalter*: Syntax and Variation', *Neophilologica Fennica*, ed. Leena Kahlas-Tarkka, Mémoires de la Société Néophilologique de Helsinki 45 (Helsinki), 317–34

Niles, John D., 'Skaldic Technique in *Brunanburh*', *Scandinavian Stud.* 59, 356–66

Ó Carragáin, Éamonn, see sect. 9*i* [Bewcastle Cross, Ruthwell Cross]

O'Keeffe, Katherine O'Brien, 'Orality and the Developing Text of Caedmon's *Hymn*', *Speculum* 62, 1–20

Orton, P. R., '"The Battle of Brunanburh", 40B–44A: Constantine's Bereavement', *Peritia* 4 (1985), 243–50

Pilch, Herbert, 'The Intonation of Old English Verse', *Studies in Honour of René Derolez*, ed. Simon-Vandenbergen, pp. 427–52 [*Elene*]

Price, Jocelyn G., 'The *Liflade of Seinte Iuliene* and Hagiographic Convention', *Medievalia et Humanistica* n.s. 14 (1987 for 1986), 37–58 [*Juliana*]

Pulsiano, Phillip, 'Bees and Backbiters in the Old English *Homiletic Fragment I*', *ELN* 25.2, 1–6

Rapetti, Alessandra, 'Three Images of Judith', *Etudes de Lettres* (Université de Lausanne) 1987, nos. 2–3, pp. 155–65

Sandred, Karl Inge, 'An Old English Poetic Word in the Light of Some Place-Names', *Namn och Bygd* 75, 23–9 [originally published in *Nordiska Namnstudier* (Uppsala, 1985), pp. 372–8; *beorhstede*, in *Phoenix*]

Savage, Anne, 'Mystical and Evangelical in *The Dream of the Rood*: the Private and the Public', *Mysticism: Medieval and Modern*, ed. Valerie M. Lagorio (Salzburg, 1986), pp. 4–11

Schaefer, Ursula, 'Two Women in Need of a Friend: a Comparison of *The Wife's Lament* and Eangyth's Letter to Boniface', *Germanic Dialects: Linguistic and*

Philological Investigations, ed. Bela Brogyanyi and Thomas Krömmelbein (Amsterdam and Philadelphia, 1986), pp. 491–524

Schwab, Ute, 'Un problema affine: il "testo critico" della *Genesi* as./ags.', *Atti dell' Accademia Peloritana dei Pericolanti, Classe di lettere, filosofia e belle arti* 61 (1987 for 1985), 111–26 [*Genesis B*; reflections on article by Lupi, above]

Speirs, Nancy, 'The Two Armies of the Old English *Exodus*: *twa pusendo*, line 184b, and *cista*, lines 229b and 230a', *N&Q* 34, 145–6

Suzuki, Seiichi, '*Wulf and Eadwacer*: a Reinterpretation and Some Conjectures', *NM* 88, 175–85

Swanton, Michael, ed., *The Dream of the Rood* (Exeter) [revised reprint of 1970 edn]

Szarmach, Paul E., see sect. 3*c* [*Dream of the Rood*]

Toporova, T.V., see sect. 2 [*Christ III*]

Tristram, Hildegarde L.C., 'In Support of Tupper's Solution of the Exeter Book Riddle (Krapp-Dobbie) 55', *Germanic Dialects: Linguistic and Philological Investigations*, ed. Bela Brogyanyi and Thomas Krommelbein (Amsterdam and Philadelphia, 1986), pp. 585–98

Wheeler, Ron, 'A Note on *æðele spald*: *Elene* 297b–300 and John 9:1–7', *ELN* 25.2, 7–8

c. Prose

Bately, Janet M., ed., *The Anglo-Saxon Chronicle: MS A*, The Anglo-Saxon Chronicle: a Collaborative Edition 3 (Cambridge, 1986)

Bodden, Mary Catherine, ed. and trans., *The Old English Finding of the True Cross* (Cambridge)

Clayton, Mary, 'Homiliaries and Preaching in Anglo-Saxon England', *Peritia* 4 (1985), 207–42

Collins, Rowland L., see sect. 3*bii*

Cross, James E., see sect. 4

Davey, William, see sect. 4

Deegan, Marilyn, 'Pregnancy and Childbirth in the Anglo-Saxon Medical Texts: a Preliminary Survey', *Medicine in Early Medieval England*, ed. Marilyn Deegan and D.G. Scragg (Manchester), pp. 17–26

Dekeyser, Xavier, see sect. 2

Donaghey, B.S., 'Nicholas Trevet's Use of King Alfred's Translation of Boethius, and the Dating of His Commentary', *The Medieval Boethius*, ed. A.J. Minnis (Cambridge), pp. 1–31

Eaton, R.D., 'Anglo-Saxon Secrets: *run* and the Runes of the Lindisfarne Gospels', *Amsterdamer Beiträge zur älteren Germanistik* 24 (1986), 11–27

Endo, Sachiko, 'A Study of *Sculan* in King Alfred's *Old English Version of Boethius De Consolatione Philosophiae*', *Jnl of Eng. Lang and Lit.* (Nihon Univ.) 35, 137–60

Godden, M.R., 'Ælfric and Anglo-Saxon Kingship', *EHR* 102, 911–15

Koike, Kazuo, 'Some Linguistic Characteristics of Ælfric's *Colloquy*', *Obirin Stud. in Eng. Lang. and Lit.* 25:8, 71–85

Kretzschmar, William A., Jr, 'Adaptation and *anweald* in the Old English Orosius', *ASE* 16, 127–45

Law, Vivien, 'Anglo-Saxon England: Aelfric's *Excerptiones de arte grammatica anglice*', *Histoire Epistémologie Langage* 9.1, 47–71

Mertens-Fonck, Paule, see sect. 2 [*Vespasian Psalter*]

Nakamura, Yuji, see sect. 2

Ogawa, Hiroshi, see sect. 2

Ogura, Michiko, see sect. 2

Ohba, Keizo, 'Homiletic Literature of Ælfric', *Medieval English Literature and Preaching*, ed. I. Saito (Tokyo), pp. 32–51 [in Japanese]

'Homiletic Literature of Ælfric', *Asphodel* (Doshisha Women's College of Liberal Arts) 21, 1–20 [in Japanese]

Page, R.I., see sect. 2 [Alfred's *æstel*]

Reinsma, Luke M., *Ælfric: an Annotated Bibliography*, Garland Reference Lib. of the Humanities 617 (New York and London)

Serdiuk, E.I., see sect. 2 [laws]

Sgarbi, Romano, 'Per una "synkrisis" lessematica alemanno-anglosassone in interpretazioni di fondamentali nozioni boeziane', *Aevum* 61, 313–26

Sjöberg, Anders, 'Old Church Slavonic and Old English Translation Techniques: on the Lexical Variants in the OCS Translation of the Gospels', *Studier i modern språkvetenskap* n.s. 8, 146–50 [*Pastoral Care*]

Stoneman, William P., see sect. 5 [Ælfric]

Szarmach, Paul E., 'Ælfric, the Prose Vision, and the *Dream of the Rood*', *Studies in Honour of René Derolez*, ed. Simon-Vandenbergen, pp. 592–602

Takeuchi, Shinichi, 'On *Sellan* and *Geifan* in the *Peterborough Chronicle*', *Descriptive and Applied Ling.* (International Christian Univ., Tokyo) 20, 191–201

Waterhouse, Ruth, see sect. 4

Weinstock, Horst, 'Laut und Name mittelalterlicher Buchstaben', *Linguistik in Deutschland*, ed. Werner Abraham and Ritva Arhammar (Tübingen), pp. 405–21 [Ælfric's *Grammar*]

'"Nomen" and "Potestas" of Medieval Letters', *Studies in Honour of René Derolez*, ed. Simon-Vandenbergen, pp. 684–708

Wright, Charles D., '*Docet Deus, docet diabolus*: a Hiberno-Latin Theme in an Old English Body-and-Soul Homily', *N&Q* 34, 451–3

Yerkes, David, see section 5

4. ANGLO-LATIN, LITURGY AND OTHER LATIN ECCLESIASTICAL TEXTS

Bestul, Thomas H., ed., *A Durham Book of Devotions*, Toronto Med. Latin Texts 18 (Toronto)

Bieler, Ludwig, *Ireland and the Culture of Early Medieval Europe*, ed. Richard Sharpe, Variorum Collected Studies 263 (London)

Blair, John, 'Saint Frideswide Reconsidered', *Oxoniensia* 52, 71–127 [editions of two *uitae*]

Bonner, Gerald, 'The Saints of Durham', *Sobornost* n.s. 8.1 (1986), 34–46

Brown, George Hardin, *Bede the Venerable*, Twayne's Eng. Authors Ser. 443 (Boston)

Burnett, Charles, ed. and trans., *Pseudo-Bede, De mundi celestis terrestrisque constitutione*, Warburg Inst. Surveys and Texts 10 (London, 1985)

Cameron, M. L., 'Aldhelm as Naturalist: a Re-examination of Some of His *Enigmata*', *Peritia* 4 (1985), 117–33

Clayton, Mary, see sect. 3*c*

Crick, Julia, see sect. 5

Cross, James E., *Cambridge Pembroke College MS 25: a Carolingian Sermonary Used by Anglo-Saxon Preachers*, King's College London Med. Stud. 1 (London)

'The Insular Connections of a Sermon for Holy Innocents', *Medieval Literature and Antiquities: Studies in Honour of Basil Cottle*, ed. Myra Stokes and T. L. Burton (Cambridge), pp. 57–70

Davey, William, 'The Commentary of the Regius Psalter: its Main Source and Influence on the Old English Gloss', *MS* 49, 335–51

Dempsey, G. T., 'Aldhelm of Malmesbury and the Paris Psalter: a Note on the Survival of Antiochene Exegesis', *JTS* 38, 368–86

Frank, Roberta, see sect. 2

Fransen, Paul-Irénée, 'D'Eugippius à Bède le Vénérable: à propos de leurs florilèges augustiniens', *RB* 97, 187–94

Fros, Henri, ed., *Bibliotheca Hagiographica Latina Antiquae et Mediae Aetatis. Novum Supplementum*, Subsidia Hagiographica 70 (Brussels, 1986)

Gatch, Milton McC., 'The Anglo-Saxon Tradition', *The Study of Spirituality*, ed. Cheslyn Jones *et al.* (London, 1986), pp. 225–34

Haendler, Gert, 'Bonifatius', *Gestalten der Kirchengeschichte, 3: Mittelalter I*, ed. Martin Greschat (Stuttgart, 1983), 69–86

Herren, Michael W., *The Hisperica Famina, II: Related Poems. A Critical Edition with English Translation and Philological Commentary*, Stud. and Texts 85 (Toronto)

Hiley, David, 'Thurstan of Caen and Plainchant at Glastonbury: Musicological Reflections on the Norman Conquest', *PBA* 72 (1986), 57–90

I Deug-Su, *Cultura e ideologia nella prima età carolingia* (Rome, 1984)

Jeudy, Colette, 'Le Florilège grammatical inédit du manuscrit 8° 8 de la bibliothèque d'Erfurt', *Bulletin Du Cange* 44–5 (1985), 91–128 [Bede]

Kelly, Joseph F., 'The Venerable Bede's Sense of Scripture', *Studies in Honour of René Derolez*, ed. Simon-Vandenbergen, pp. 276–82

Kerlouégan, François, *Le De Excidio Britanniae de Gildas. Les destinées de la culture latine dans l'île de Bretagne au VIe siècle* (Paris)

Kitson, Peter, see sect. 3*bi*

Kottje, Raymund, 'Beda Venerabilis', *Gestalten der Kirchengeschichte, 3: Mittelalter I*, ed. Martin Greschat (Stuttgart, 1983), 58–68

'Busspraxis und Bussritus', *SettSpol* 33 (1985), 369–403 [includes discussion]

Latham, R. E., and D. R. Howlett, ed., *Dictionary of Medieval Latin from British Sources: Fascicule III, D–E* (London, 1986)

Law, Vivien, see sect. 3*c*

Löfstedt, Bengt, 'Zu Bedas Evangelienkommentaren', *Arctos* 21, 61–72

Martin, Lawrence T., 'Bede's Structural Use of Wordplay as a Way to Truth', *From Cloister to Classroom*, ed. E. Rozanne Elder, Cistercian Stud. 90 (Kalamazoo, MI, 1986), pp. 27–46

    trans., 'Homily on the Feast of St Benedict Biscop by the Venerable Bede', *Vox Benedictina* 4, 81–92

McEnerney, John I., '*Alcuini Carmen* 59', *Res Publica Litterarum* 10, 215–19

Milani, Celestina, 'Note sul *Corpus Glossary*', *Quaderni di lingue e letterature* (Università di Verona) 9 (1984), 285–319

Mostert, Marco, *The Political Theology of Abbo of Fleury: a Study of the Ideas about Society and Law of the Tenth-Century Monastic Reform Movement*, Med. Stud. and Sources 2 (Hilversum)

Munier, Charles, *Vie conciliaire et collections canoniques en Occident, IVe–XIIe siècles*, Variorum Collected Studies 265 (London)

O'Keeffe, Katherine O'Brien, see sects. 3*biii*, 5

Pheifer, J. D., 'Early Anglo-Saxon Glossaries and the School of Canterbury', *ASE* 16, 17–44

Prescott, Andrew, see sect. 5

Prill, Paul E., 'Rhetoric and Poetics in the Early Middle Ages', *Rhetorica* 5, 129–47

Ray, Roger, 'Bede and Cicero', *ASE* 16, 1–15

Thomson, Rodney, *William of Malmesbury* (Woodbridge and Wolfeboro, NH)

Vogüé, Adalbert de, 'Les plus anciens exégètes du Premier Livre des Rois: Origène, Augustin et leurs épigones', *Sacris Erudiri* 29 (1986), 5–12 [Bede]

Warren, F. E., *The Liturgy and Ritual of the Celtic Church*, 2nd edn with new introduction and bibliography by Jane Stevenson, Stud. in Celtic Hist. 9 (Woodbridge and Wolfeboro, NH)

Waterhouse, Ruth, '"Wæter æddre asprang": How Cuthbert's Miracle Pours Cold Water on Source Study', *Parergon* n.s. 5, 1–27

Weinstock, Horst, see sect. 3*c* [Bede *et al.*]

Whitman, F. H., 'Aenigmata Tatwini', *NM* 88, 8–17

Winterbottom, M., 'Notes on the Life of Edward the Confessor', *MÆ* 56, 82–4

Wright, Neil, 'Imitation of the Poems of Paulinus of Nola in Early Anglo-Latin Verse', *Peritia* 4 (1985), 134–51

5. PALAEOGRAPHY, DIPLOMATIC AND ILLUMINATION

Avril, François and Patricia Danz Stirnemann, *Manuscrits enluminés d'origine insulaire VIIe–XXe siècle*, Manuscrits enluminés de la Bibliothèque Nationale (Paris)

Bain, Iain, *Celtic Knotwork* (London, 1986)

Bascombe, K. N., 'Two Charters of King Suebred of Essex', *An Essex Tribute*, ed. Neale, pp. 85–96

Belkin, Ahuva, 'The Antichrist Legend of the Utrecht Psalter', *Rivista di storia e letteratura religiosa* 23, 279–88

Bevan, Michael, 'A Saxon Boundary in Warminghurst', *Sussex Archaeol. Collections*, 124 (1986), 260

Carley, James P., 'Two Pre-Conquest Manuscripts from Glastonbury Abbey', *ASE* 16, 197–212

Chaplais, Pierre, 'The Spelling of Christ's Name in Medieval Anglo-Latin: "Christus" or "Cristus"?', *Jnl of the Soc. of Archivists* 8, 261–80

'William of Saint-Calais and the Domesday Survey', *Domesday Studies*, ed. Holt, pp. 65–77

Clement, Richard W., 'Thomas James's *Ecloga Oxonio-Cantabrigiensis*: an Early Printed Union Catalogue', *Jnl of Lib. Hist.* 22, 1–22

Corsano, Karen, 'The First Quire of the Codex Amiatinus and the *Institutiones* of Cassiodorus', *Scriptorium* 41, 3–34

Crabtree, Rachel, 'Ladders and Lines of Connection in Anglo-Saxon Religious Art and Literature', *Medieval Literature and Antiquities: Studies in Honour of Basil Cottle*, ed. Myra Stokes and T.L. Burton (Cambridge), pp. 43–53

Crick, Julia, 'An Anglo-Saxon Fragment of Justinus's *Epitome*', *ASE* 16, 181–96

Dempsey, G.T., see sect. 4

Dumville, David N., 'English Square Minuscule Script: the Background and Earliest Phases', *ASE* 16, 147–79

Fischer, Bonifatius, *Lateinische Bibelhandschriften im frühen Mittelalter*, Vetus Latina 11 (Freiburg im Breisgau, 1985)

Forsberg, Rune, see sect. 8

Fritze, Ronald Harold, '"Truth hath lacked witnesse, tyme wanted light": the Dispersal of the English Monastic Libraries and Protestant Efforts at Preservation, ca. 1535–1625', *Jnl of Lib. Hist.* 18 (1983), 274–91

Ganz, David, 'The Preconditions for Caroline Minuscule', *Viator* 18, 23–44

Gray, Nicolette, *A History of Lettering, Creative Experiment and Letter Identity* (Oxford, 1986)

Gubbins, Donald, 'Domesday Rebound 1986', *Bookbinder* 1, 9–17

Guilmain, Jacques, 'The Geometry of the Cross-Carpet Pages in the Lindisfarne Gospels', *Speculum* 62, 21–52

Gullick, Michael, 'The Great and Little Domesday Manuscripts', *Domesday Book: Studies*, ed. Williams and Erskine, pp. 93–112

Hart, Cyril, 'A Charter of King Edgar for Brafield on the Green', *Northamptonshire Past and Present* 7, 301–4 [Sawyer no. 750]

Hart, Cyril, and Anthony Syme, 'The Earliest Suffolk Charter', *Proc. of the Suffolk Inst. of Archaeol. and Hist.* 36, 165–81 [Sawyer no. 703]

Haseloff, Günther, 'Insular Animal Styles with Special Reference to Irish Art in the Early Medieval Period', *Ireland and Insular Art*, ed. Ryan, pp. 44–55

Henderson, George, *From Durrow to Kells: the Insular Gospel-books 650–800* (London)

Henderson, Isabel, 'The Book of Kells and the Snake-Boss Motif on Pictish Cross-Slabs and the Iona Crosses', *Ireland and Insular Art*, ed. Ryan, pp. 56–65

Ker, N. R., ed., *Medieval Libraries of Great Britain: a List of Surviving Books. Supplement to the Second Edition*, ed. Andrew G. Watson, R. Hist. Soc. Guides and Handbooks 15 (London)

Kitson, Peter, see sect. *3bi*

McGurk, Patrick, 'The Gospel Book in Celtic Lands before AD 850: Contents and Arrangement', *Irland und die Christenheit*, ed. Ní Chatháin and Richter, pp. 165–89

Neuman de Vegvar, Carol L., *The Northumbrian Renaissance: a Study in the Transmission of Style* (Selinsgrove, PA, Toronto and London)

Nordenfalk, Carl, 'One Hundred and Fifty Years of Varying Views on the Early Insular Gospel Books', *Ireland and Insular Art*, ed. Ryan, pp. 1–6

Ó Cróinín, Dáibhí, 'Merovingian Politics and Insular Calligraphy: the Historical Background to the Book of Durrow and Related Manuscripts', *Ireland and Insular Art*, ed. Ryan, pp. 40–3

O'Keeffe, Katherine O'Brien, 'Graphic Cues for Presentation of Verse in the Earliest Manuscripts of the *Historia Ecclesiastica*', *Manuscripta* 31, 139–46

O'Reilly, Jennifer, 'The Rough-Hewn Cross in Anglo-Saxon Art', *Ireland and Insular Art*, ed. Ryan, pp. 153–8

O'Sullivan, William, 'Insular Calligraphy: Current State and Problems', *Peritia* 4 (1985), 346–59

Page, R. I., 'A Sixteenth-Century Runic Manuscript', *Studies in Honour of René Derolez*, ed. Simon-Vandenbergen, pp. 384–90

Prescott, Andrew, 'The Structure of English Pre-Conquest Benedictionals', *Brit. Lib. Jnl* 13, 118–58

Richter, Lukas, 'Die beiden ältesten Liederbücher des lateinischen Mittelalters', *Beiträge zur Musikwissenschaft* 29, 1–12 [C.U.L. MS Gg. 5. 35]

Roth, Uta, 'Early Insular Manuscripts: Ornament and Archaeology, with Special Reference to the Dating of the Book of Durrow', *Ireland and Insular Art*, ed. Ryan, pp. 23–9

Rumble, Alexander R., 'The Domesday Manuscripts: Scribes and Scriptoria', *Domesday Studies*, ed. Holt, pp. 79–99

'Methods of Textual Abbreviation in Great Domesday Book', *Domesday Book: Studies*, ed. Williams and Erskine, pp. 162–3

Ryan, K., 'Parchment as Faunal Record', *MASCA Jnl* 4 (1986–7), 124–38

Ryan, Michael, ed., *Ireland and Insular Art A.D. 500–1200: Proceedings of a Conference at University College Cork, 31 October–3 November 1985* (Dublin)

Schick, Eduard, 'Il Codice di Fulda: storia e significato di un manoscritto della Volgata del secolo VI', *La Biblia 'Vulgata' dalle origini ai nostri giorni*, ed. Tarcisio Stramare, Collectanea biblica latina 16 (Rome and Vatican City), 21–9

Schipper, William, see sect. 2

Sperk, Klaus, 'The Laws of Ine and Alfred: Textual History as a Mirror to Legal History', *Studies in Honour of René Derolez*, ed. Simon-Vandenbergen, pp. 583–91

Stevick, Robert D., 'The St Cuthbert Gospel Binding and Insular Design', *Artibus et Historiae* 15, 9–19

Stoneman, William P., 'Another Old English Note Signed "Coleman"', *MÆ* 56, 78–82

Thomson, R. M., 'The Norman Conquest and English Libraries', *The Role of the Book in Medieval Culture* II, ed. Peter Ganz, Bibliologia 4 (Turnhout 1986), 27–40

Thorn, Caroline, 'Marginal Notes and Signs in Domesday Book', *Domesday Book: Studies*, ed. Williams and Erskine, pp. 113–35

'The Marginalia of Great Domesday Book', *Domesday Book: Studies*, ed. Williams and Erskine, pp. 160–2

Watson, Andrew G., 'The Manuscript Collection of Sir Walter Cope (d. 1614)', *Bodleian Lib. Record* 12, 262–97

Wieland, Gernot R., 'The Anglo-Saxon Manuscripts of Prudentius's *Psychomachia*', *ASE* 16, 213–31

Yapp, W. Brunsdon, 'Animals in Medieval Art: the Bayeux Tapestry as an Example', *JMH* 13, 15–73

Yerkes, David, 'The Foliation of the Old English Life of Machutus', *Florilegium Columbianum: Essays in Honor of Paul Oskar Kristeller*, ed. Karl-Ludwig Selig and Robert Somerville (New York), pp. 89–93

6. HISTORY

Addison, William, 'The Making of the Essex Landscape', *An Essex Tribute*, ed. Neale, pp. 47–55

Alcock, Leslie, *Economy, Society and Warfare among the Britons and Saxons* (Cardiff)

Amos, Thomas L., 'Monks and Pastoral Care in the Early Middle Ages', *Religion, Culture, and Society in the Early Middle Ages: Studies in Honor of Richard E. Sullivan*, ed. Thomas F. X. Noble and John J. Contreni, Stud. in Med. Culture 23 (Kalamazoo, MI), 165–80

Andersson, Theodore M., 'The Viking Policy of Ethelred the Unready', *Scandinavian Stud.* 59, 284–95

Ayton, Andrew, and Virginia Davis, 'Ecclesiastical Wealth in England in 1086', *The Church and Wealth*, ed. W. J. Sheils and Diana Wood, Stud. in Church Hist. 24 (Oxford), 47–60

Bachrach, Bernard S., 'Some Observations on the Bayeux Tapestry', *Cithara* 27.1, 5–28

Beech, George, 'The Participation of Aquitanians in the Conquest of England 1066–1100', *Anglo-Norman Studies IX*, ed. Brown, pp. 1–24

Blair, John, 'Local Churches in Domesday Book and Before', *Domesday Studies*, ed. Holt, pp. 265–78

'Parish Churches in the Eleventh Century', *Domesday Book: Studies*, ed. Williams and Erskine, pp. 65–8

Bonner, Gerald, see sect. 4

Brown, Phyllis R., 'The Viking Policy of Ethelred: a Response', *Scandinavian Stud.* 59, 296–8 [response to Andersson, this sect.]

Brown, R. Allen, ed., *Anglo-Norman Studies IX: Proceedings of the Battle Conference 1986* (Woodbridge)

Burton, Janet E., 'Monasteries and Parish Churches in Eleventh- and Twelfth-Century Yorkshire', *NH* 23, 39–50

Butler, Lawrence, 'Two Twelfth-century Lists of Saints' Resting Places', *AB* 105, 87–103

Cain, T.C., 'An Introduction to the Rutland Domesday', *The Northamptonshire and Rutland Domesday*, ed. Williams and Erskine, pp. 18–34

Campbell, James, 'The Debt of the Early English Church to Ireland', *Irland und die Christenheit*, ed. Ní Chatháin and Richter, pp. 332–46

 'Some Agents and Agencies of the Late Anglo-Saxon State', *Domesday Studies*, ed. Holt, pp. 201–18

Ciggaar, Krijnie, 'Byzantine Marginalia to the Norman Conquest', *Anglo-Norman Studies IX*, ed. Brown, pp. 43–63

Clarke, Helen, 'Agriculture in Late Anglo-Saxon England', *Domesday Book: Studies*, ed. Williams and Erskine, pp. 43–7

 'West Sweden and England: the Evidence for Viking Age Trade', *Sachsen Symposion 1983* (Skaraborg, 1984), 82–3

Crawford, Barbara E., *Scotland in the Early Middle Ages 2: Scandinavian Scotland*, Studies in the Early History of Britain (Leicester)

Darby, H.C., 'Domesday Book and the Geographer', *Domesday Studies*, ed. Holt, pp. 101–19

 'The Geography of Domesday England', *Domesday Book: Studies*, ed. Williams and Erskine, pp. 25–36

Davies, R.R., *Conquest, Coexistence, and Change: Wales 1063–1415*, History of Wales 2 (Oxford and Cardiff)

Davis, R.H.C., 'Domesday Book: Continental Parallels', *Domesday Studies*, ed. Holt, pp. 15–39

Derry, Thomas Kingston, 'The Martyrdom of St Edmund, A.D. 869', *Historisk Tidsskrift* (Oslo) 66, 157–63

Devroey, Jean-Pierre, 'Units of Measurement in the Early Medieval Economy: the Example of Carolingian Food Rations', *French Hist.* 1, 68–92

Down, J., 'The Problem of the Location of the Battle of Assandun', *Essex Jnl* 22, 7–9

Drew, Katherine Fischer, 'Another Look at the Origins of the Middle Ages: a Reassessment of the Role of the Germanic Kingdoms', *Speculum* 62, 803–12 [includes discussion of Anglo-Saxon laws]

Dumville, D.N., see sect. 7

Einarsson, Bjarni, 'De Normannorum Atrocitate, or On the Execution of Royalty by the Aquiline Method', *SBVS* 22 (1986), 79–82

Evans, Margaret Carey, 'The Contribution of Hoxne to the Cult of St Edmund King and Martyr in the Middle Ages and Later', *Proc. of the Suffolk Inst. of Archaeol. and Hist.* 36, 182–95

Fernie, Eric, 'The Effect of the Conquest on Norman Architectural Patronage', *Anglo-Norman Studies IX*, ed. Brown, pp. 71–85

Fleming, Robin, 'Domesday Book and the Tenurial Revolution', *Anglo-Norman Studies IX*, ed. Brown, pp. 87–102

Godden, M. R., see section 3*c*

Gould, Jim, 'Saint Edith of Polesworth and Tamworth', *Trans. of the South Staffordshire Archaeol. and Hist. Soc.* 27 (1987 for 1985–6), 35–8

Grierson, Philip, 'Weights and Measures', *Domesday Book: Studies*, ed. Williams and Erskine, pp. 80–5

Haendler, Gert, see sect. 4

Hall, D. N., 'An Introduction to the Northamptonshire Domesday', *The Northamptonshire and Rutland Domesday*, ed. Williams and Erskine, pp. 1–17

Hamshere, J. D., 'Domesday Book, Cliometric Analysis and Taxation Assessments', *EconHR* 2nd ser. 40, 262–6

'Domesday Book: Estate Structures in the West Midlands', *Domesday Studies*, ed. Holt, pp. 155–82

'Regressing Domesday Book: Tax Assessments of Domesday England', *EconHR* 2nd ser. 40, 247–51

Hart, Cyril, 'The Ealdordom of Essex', *An Essex Tribute*, ed. Neale, pp. 57–84

Harvey, Barbara F., 'The Life of the Manor', *Domesday Book: Studies*, ed. Williams and Erskine, pp. 39–42

Harvey, Sally P. J., 'Taxation and the Economy', *Domesday Studies*, ed. Holt, pp. 249–64

Haubrichs, Wolfgang, 'Die Angelsachsen und die germanischen Stämme des Kontinents im frühen Mittelalter: sprachliche und literarische Beziehungen', *Irland und die Christenheit*, ed. Ní Chatháin and Richter, pp. 387–412

Hill, Thomas D., 'The Myth of the Ark-Born Son of Noe and the West-Saxon Royal Genealogical Tables', *Harvard Theol. Rev.* 80, 379–83

Hillgarth, J. N., 'Modes of Evangelization of Western Europe in the Seventh Century', *Irland und die Christenheit*, ed. Ní Chatháin and Richter, pp. 311–31

Hødnebø, Finn, 'Hvem var de første vikinger?' *Maal og Minne* 1987, 1–16

'Who were the First Vikings?', *Tenth Viking Congress*, ed. Knirk, pp. 43, 54

Hollister, C. Warren, 'The Greater Domesday Tenants-in-Chief', *Domesday Studies*, ed. Holt, pp. 219–48

Holt, J. C., '1086', *Domesday Studies*, ed. Holt, pp. 41–64

ed., *Domesday Studies: Papers read at the Novocentenary Conference of the Royal Historical Society and the Institute of British Geographers, Winchester 1986* (Woodbridge)

Hooke, Della, *et al.*, 'Anglo-Saxon Estates in the Vale of the White Horse', *Oxoniensia* 52, 129–43

Hughes, Kathleen, *Church and Society in Ireland A.D. 400–1200*, ed. David Dumville, Variorum Collected Studies 258 (London)

Hyams, Paul, '"No Register of Title": the Domesday Inquest and Land Adjudication', *Anglo-Norman Studies IX*, ed. Brown, pp. 127–41

Jones, Glanville R. J., 'The Portrayal of Land Settlement in Domesday Book', *Domesday Studies*, ed. Holt, pp. 183–200

Jones, Graham, 'Holy Wells and the Cult of St Helen', *Landscape Hist.* 8 (1986), 59–75

Keynes, Simon, *Anglo-Saxon History: a Select Bibliography*, OEN Subsidia 13 (Binghamton, NY)

Kirby, D. P., see section 7

Knirk, James E., ed., *Proceedings of the Tenth Viking Congress, Larkollen, Norway, 1985*, Universitetets Oldsaksamlings Skrifter, n.s. 9 (Oslo)

Lang, Jim, 'The Year of St Cuthbert', *Tyne and Tweed: Jnl of the Assoc. of Northumberland Local Hist. Soc.* 42, 14–17

Legge, M.D. 'Bishop Odo in the Bayeux Tapestry', *MÆ* 56, 84–5

Lewis, Terry, *The Battle of Hastings*, Stud. in Evidence 2 (Edinburgh)

Lindow, John, 'Norse Mythology and Northumbria: Methodological Notes', *Scandinavian Stud.* 59, 308–24

Löwe, Heinz, 'Pirmin, Willibrord und Bonifatius. Ihre Bedeutung für die Missionsgeschichte ihrer Zeit', *Kirchengeschichte als Missionsgeschichte, II: Die Kirche des frühen Mittelalters, 1*, ed. Knut Schäferdiek (Munich, 1978), 192–226 [reprint, with added bibliography, of article in *SettSpol* 14 (1965), 217–61]

Loud, G.A., 'Domesday Book after Nine Hundred Years', *NH* 23, 231–5

Loyn, H.R., 'The Beyond of Domesday Book', *Domesday Studies*, ed. Holt, pp. 1–13
  'A General Introduction to Domesday Book', *Domesday Book: Studies*, ed. Williams and Erskine, pp. 1–21

Lund, Niels, 'Peace and Non-Peace in the Viking Age – Ottar in Biarmaland, the Rus in Byzantium, and Danes and Norwegians in England', *Tenth Viking Congress*, ed. Knirk, pp. 255–69

McDonald, John, and G.D. Snooks, 'The Economics of Domesday England', *Domesday Book: Studies*, ed. Williams and Erskine, pp. 86–9
  'The Suitability of Domesday Book for Cliometric Analysis', *EconHR* 2nd ser. 40, 252–61

McKinnell, John, 'Norse Mythology and Northumbria: a Response', *Scandinavian Stud.* 59, 325–37 [response to Lindow, this sect.]

McLaughlin, Mary Martin, 'Looking for Medieval Women: an Interim Report on the Project "Womens' Religious Life and Communities, A.D. 500–1500"', *Medieval Prosopography* 8, 61–91

Magnusson, Magnus, *Lindisfarne: the Cradle Island* (Stocksfield, Northumberland, 1984)

Martin, G.H. 'The Domesday Boroughs', *Domesday Book: Studies*, ed. Williams and Erskine, pp. 56–60
  'Eleventh-Century Communications', *Domesday Book: Studies*, ed. Williams and Erskine, pp. 61–4

Morland, Stephen C., 'The Glastonbury Manors and their Saxon Charters', *Proc. of the Somerset Archaeol. and Nat. Hist. Soc.* 130 (1986), 61–105

Neale, Kenneth, ed., *An Essex Tribute: Essays presented to Frederick G. Emmison* (London)

Ní Chatháin, Próinséas, and Michael Richter, ed., *Irland und die Christenheit* (Stuttgart)

Ní Chatháin, Próinséas, 'Early Ireland and Western Christendom: the Bible and the Missions', *Irland und die Christenheit*, ed. Ní Chatháin and Richter, pp. 473–504

Nightingale, Pamela, 'The Origin of the Court of Husting and Danish Influence on London's Development into a Capital City', *EHR* 102, 559–78

Niles, John D., and Mark Amodio, 'Introduction: the Vikings and England', *Scandinavian Stud.* 59, 279–83 [special issue on 'Anglo-Scandinavian England']

Page, R.I., '*A Most Vile People*': *Early English Historians on the Vikings*, Dorothea Coke Memorial Lecture 1986 (London)

Palmer, J.J.N., 'The Domesday Manor', *Domesday Studies*, ed. Holt, pp. 139–53

Parker, M.S., 'Some Notes on the Pre-Norman History of Doncaster', *Yorkshire Archaeol. Jnl* 59, 29–43

Picken, W.M.M., 'Bishop Wulfsige Comoere: an Unrecognised Tenth-century Gloss in the Bodmin Gospels', *Cornish Stud.* 14 (1986), 34–8

Poole, Russell, 'Skaldic Verse and Anglo-Saxon History: Some Aspects of the Period 1009–1016', *Speculum* 62, 265–98

Postles, David, 'The Bordars of Domesday Derbyshire', *Derbyshire Archaeol. Jnl* 106 (1986), 123–6

Reynolds, Susan, 'Towns in Domesday Book', *Domesday Studies*, ed. Holt, pp. 295–309

Richter, Michael, 'Practical Aspects of the Conversion of the Anglo-Saxons', *Irland und die Christenheit*, ed. Ní Chatháin and Richter, pp. 362–76

Ridyard, S.J. '*Condigna veneratio*: Post-Conquest Attitudes to the Saints of the Anglo-Saxons', *Anglo-Norman Studies IX*, ed. Brown, pp. 179–206

Roffe, David, 'The Origins of Derbyshire', *Derbyshire Archaeol. Jnl* 106 (1986), 102–22

'The Seventh-Century Monastery of Stow Green, Lincolnshire', *Lincolnshire Hist. and Archaeol.* 21 (1986), 31–3

Roffe, David, and Christine Mahany, 'Stamford and the Norman Conquest', *Lincolnshire Hist. and Archaeol.* 21 (1986), 5–9

Rowlands, Marie B., *The West Midlands from A.D. 1000*, A Regional Hist. of England 4.2 (London)

Sawyer, Birgit, Peter Sawyer and Ian Wood, ed., *The Christianization of Scandinavia: Report of a Symposium held at Kungälv, Sweden, 4–9 August 1985* (Alingsås)

Sawyer, Peter, 'The Bloodfeud in Fact and Fiction', *Tradition og Historie-Skrivning*, ed. Kirsten Hastrup and Preben Meulengracht Sørensen (= *Acta Jutlandica* 63.2, Humanistisk ser. 61) (Aarhus), 27–38

'Ethelred II, Olaf Tryggvason, and the Conversion of Norway', *Scandinavian Stud.* 59, 299–307

Scarfe, Norman, *Suffolk in the Middle Ages* (Woodbridge and Dover, NH, 1986)

Schäferdiek, Knut, 'Die Grundlegung der angelsächsischen Kirche im Spannungsfeld insular-keltischen und kontinental-römischen Christentums', *Kirchengeschichte als Missionsgeschichte, II: Die Kirche des frühen Mittelalters, 1*, ed. Knut Schäferdiek (Munich, 1978), 149–91

Short, David, 'Braughing. A Possible Saxon Estate', *Hertfordshire's Past* 23 (Autumn), 8–15

Sinclair Williams, C.L., 'Who was Bretel of Trevellion, Tempore Edward the Confessor?', *Devon and Cornwall N & Q* 39 (1986), 394–7

'*Pertica* as Quarter of a Hide in Pre-Conquest Dorset', *Proc. of the Dorset Nat. Hist. and Archaeol. Soc.* 108 (1986), 197–8

Smith, William, 'The Winchester Saints in the Calendar of the Wilton Psalter', *Wiltshire Archaeol. and Nat. Hist. Mag.* 81, 57–62

Sperk, Klaus, see sect. 5

Tanaka, Masayoshi, *The Evolution of Medieval English Boroughs* (Tokyo) [in Japanese]

Thomas, Hugh M., 'A Yorkshire Thegn and His Descendants after the Conquest', *Med. Prosopography* 8.2, 1–22

Thorn, F.R., 'Hundreds and Wapentakes', *The Northamptonshire and Rutland Domesday*, ed. Williams and Erskine, pp. 35–9

Todd, Malcolm and Andrew Fleming, *The South West to A.D. 1000*, A Regional Hist. of England 8.1 (London)

Vollrath, Hanna, 'Taufliturgie und Diözesaneinteilung in der frühen angelsächsischen Kirche', *Irland und die Christenheit*, ed. Ní Chatháin and Richter, pp. 377–86

Warner, Peter, *Greens, Commons and Clayland Colonization: the Origins and Development of Green-side Settlement in East Suffolk*, Occasional Papers in English Local Hist. 4th ser. 2 (Leicester)

'Shared Churchyards, Freeman Church Builders and the Development of Parishes in Eleventh-century East Anglia', *Landscape Hist.* 8 (1986), 39–52

Warren, W.L., *The Governance of Norman and Angevin England 1086–1272*, The Governance of England 2 (London)

Wilkinson, Donald, and John Cantrell, *The Normans in Britain* (London)

Williams, Ann, 'Apparent Repetitions in Domesday Book', *Domesday Book: Studies*, ed. Williams and Erskine, pp. 90–2

'How Land was Held Before and After the Norman Conquest', *Domesday Book: Studies*, ed. Williams and Erskine, pp. 37–8

Williams, Ann, and R.W.H. Erskine, ed., *Domesday Book: Studies* (London)

ed., *The Northamptonshire and Rutland Domesday*, 2 vols. (London)

Wood, I.N., 'Anglo-Saxon Otley: an Archiepiscopal Estate and its Crosses in a Northumbrian Context', *NH* 23, 20–38

'The Merovingian North Sea', *Sachsen Symposion 1983* (Skaraborg, 1984), 84–95

'Pagans and Holy Men, 600–800', *Irland und die Christenheit*, ed. Ní Chatháin and Richter, pp. 347–61

Yapp, W. Brunsdon, see sect. 5 [Bayeux Tapestry]

7. NUMISMATICS

Axe, D.C., 'Dating the So-called King Hoaud Stycas', *Coinage in Ninth-Century Northumbria*, ed. Metcalf, pp. 235–43 (with discussion by D.M. Metcalf and E.J.E. Pirie)

Biddle, Martin and John Blair, 'The Hook Norton Hoard of 1848: a Viking Burial from Oxfordshire', *Oxoniensia* 52, 186–95

Biddle, Martin, *et al.*, 'Coins of the Anglo-Saxon Period from Repton, Derbyshire: II', *BNJ* 56 (1986), 16–34

Bispham, J., 'Recent Metal Detector Finds from Essex and Lincolnshire', *BNJ* 56 (1986), 183–5

Blackburn, M.A.S., and M.J. Bonser, 'Single Finds of Anglo-Saxon and Norman Coins – 3', *BNJ* 56 (1986), 64–101

Blunt, C. E., 'Two Curious Coins of Alfred', *Coinage in Ninth-Century Northumbria*, ed. Metcalf, pp. 355–9 (with discussion by D. M. Metcalf)

Booth, James, 'Coinage and Northumbrian History: *c.* 790–*c.* 810', *Coinage in Ninth-Century Northumbria*, ed. Metcalf, pp. 57–89 (with comments by D. M. Metcalf) 'History *vs.* Numismatics: "Sceattas" and "Stycas"', *NCirc* 1987, 6

Brooks, Nicholas, 'Epilogue', *Coinage in Ninth-Century Northumbria*, ed. Metcalf, pp. 397–401

Burnett, A. M., 'A Provençal Solidus from Hawkwell, Essex', *NChron* 147, 182–3 (late sixth-century)

Chown, John, 'Some Continental Imitations of Late Saxon and Early Norman Coins', *NCirc* 1987, 220–1

Dumville, David N., 'Textual Archaeology and Northumbrian History Subsequent to Bede', *Coinage in Ninth-Century Northumbria*, ed. Metcalf, pp. 43–55

Freeman, Anthony, 'Reading: its Status and Standing as a Minor Late Anglo-Saxon Mint', *Berkshire Archaeol. Jnl* 72 (1983–5), 53–8

Gilmore, G. R., 'Metal Analysis of the Northumbrian Stycas: Review and Suggestions', *Coinage in Ninth-Century Northumbria*, ed. Metcalf, pp. 159–73

Gilmore, G. R., and E. J. E. Pirie, 'Consistency in the Alloy of the Northumbrian Stycas: Evidence from Redwulf's Short Reign', *Coinage in Ninth-Century Northumbria*, ed. Metcalf, pp. 175–85 (with discussion by D. M. Metcalf and E. J. E. Pirie)

Graham-Campbell, James, 'The Re-provenancing of a Viking-Age Hoard to the Thames, near the Deptford (S. E. London)', *BNJ* 56 (1986), 186–7 'Some Archaeological Reflections on the Cuerdale Hoard', *Coinage in Ninth-Century Northumbria*, ed. Metcalf, pp. 329–44

Grierson, Philip, 'The Monetary System under William I', *Domesday Book: Studies*, ed. Williams and Erskine, pp. 75–9

Jonsson, Kenneth, *The New Era: the Reformation of the Late Anglo-Saxon Coinage*, Commentationes de nummis saeculorum IX–XI in Suecia repertis, Nova series 1 (Stockholm)

Keen, Laurence, 'A Hoard of 9th-Century Coins from Winterborne Whitechurch', *Proc. of the Dorset Nat. Hist. and Archaeol. Soc.* 108 (1986), 85

Kenny, Michael, 'The Geographical Distribution of Irish Viking-Age Coin Hoards', *Proc. of the R. Irish Acad.* 87C, 507–25

Kent, J. P. C., 'The Coins', in Vera I. Evison, *Dover: the Buckland Anglo-Saxon Cemetery*, Hist. Buildings and Monuments Commission for England Archaeol. Report 3 (London), 180–1 and 399 [includes Roman coins re-used as Anglo-Saxon weights, two sixth-century tremisses, and two Pada sceattas]

Kirby, D. P., 'Northumbria in the Ninth Century', *Coinage in Ninth-Century Northumbria*, ed. Metcalf, pp. 11–25

Klotz, Eva, 'Myntskatten från Fyrunga i Västergötland', *Svensk Numismatisk Tidskrift* 1987, 220–1 [deposited after 1084; includes four Anglo-Saxon coins]

Kluge, Bernd, *State Museum Berlin, Coin Cabinet: Anglo-Saxon, Anglo-Norman, and Hiberno-Norse Coins*, SCBI 36 (Oxford)

Lyon, Stewart, 'Ninth-Century Northumbrian Chronology', *Coinage in Ninth-Century Northumbria*, ed. Metcalf, pp. 27–41 [with comments by H. E. Pagan and V. J. Smart]

Malmer, Brita, 'Hamwic och Wodan/Monster-sceattas', *Nordisk Numismatisk Unions Medlemsblad* 1987, 7

ed., *Corpus Nummorum Saeculorum IX–XI qui in Suecia reperti sunt* 3.1, *Skåne: Århus-Grönby* (Stockholm, 1985)

Malmer, Brita, and Lars O. Lagerqvist, ed., *Corpus Nummorum Saeculorum IX–XI qui in Suecia reperti sunt* 3.4, *Skåne: Maglarp-Ystad* (Stockholm)

Marshall, Chris, 'My Saxon Coin Hoard', *Treasure Hunting* January 1987, 40–2 [Walmgate, Lincs., hoard deposited *c.* 873]

Metcalf, D. M., 'Some Finds of Thrymsas and Sceattas in England', *BNJ* 56 (1986), 1–15

'Hexham and Cuerdale: Two Notes on Metrology', *Coinage in Ninth-Century Northumbria*, ed. Metcalf, pp. 383–96

'"A Peney Life will give you all the Facts"', *NChron* 147, 184–8 [review article on Anthony Freeman, *The Moneyer and the Mint in the Reign of Edward the Confessor, 1042–1066* (Oxford, 1985)]

'The Taxation of Moneyers under Edward the Confessor and in 1086', *Domesday Studies*, ed. Holt, pp. 279–93

'A Topographical Commentary on the Coin Finds from Ninth-Century Northumbria (*c.* 780–*c.* 870)', *Coinage in Ninth-Century Northumbria*, ed. Metcalf, pp. 361–82

ed., *Coinage in Ninth-Century Northumbria. The Tenth Oxford Symposium on Coinage and Monetary History*, BAR Brit. ser. 180 (Oxford)

Metcalf, D. M., and J. P. Northover, 'Herreth', *Coinage in Ninth-Century Northumbria*, ed. Metcalf, pp. 91–101 (with comments by E. J. E. Pirie)

'Interpreting the Alloy of the Later Anglo-Saxon Coinage', *BNJ* 56 (1986), 35–63

'The Northumbrian Royal Coinage in the Time of Æthelred II and Osberht', *Coinage in Ninth-Century Northumbria*, ed. Metcalf, pp. 187–233 (with discussion by E. J. E. Pirie)

Mikołajczyk, Andrzej, *Polish Museums: Anglo-Saxon and Later Medieval British Coins*, SCBI 37 (Oxford)

Molvôgin, Arkadi, 'Grundzüge der Zirkulation des Münzsilbers im östlichen Bereich der Ostsee am Ende des 11. Jahrhunderts und in der ersten Hälfte des 12. Jahrhunderts', *Visby-Colloquium des Hansischen Geschichtsvereins 15.–18. Juni 1984*, ed. Klaus Friedland, Quellen und Darstellungen zur Hansischen Geschichte 32 (Cologne and Vienna), 83–98

Op den Velde, W., 'Escharen 1980', *Jaarboek voor Munt- en Penningkunde* 72 (1987 for 1985), 5–12 [hoard of nine sceattas (Series D), deposited *c.* 710]

'Sceatta's in Friese schatvondsten', *De Beeldenaar* 11, 61–6

Pagan, H. E., 'A Cnut Hoard from Cornwall', *NCirc* 1987, 39 [Constantine hoard]

'Some Thoughts on the Hoard Evidence for the Northumbrian Styca Coinage',

Coinage in Ninth-Century Northumbria, ed. Metcalf, pp. 147–58 (with discussion by E. J. E. Pirie)

Pirie, E. J. E., 'Adamson's Hexham Plates', *Coinage in Ninth-Century Northumbria*, ed. Metcalf, pp. 257–327

'Phases and Groups within the Styca Coinage of Northumbria', *Coinage in Ninth-Century Northumbria*, ed. Metcalf, pp. 103–45 (with discussion by D. M. Metcalf and J. Booth)

Sellwood, Lyn, and D. M. Metcalf, 'A Celtic Silver Coin of Previously Unpublished Type from St Nicholas at Wade, Thanet: the Prototype for Anglo-Saxon Sceattas of *BMC* type 37?', *BNJ* 56 (1986), 181–2

Smart, Veronica J., 'Moneyers of the Late Anglo-Saxon Coinage: the Danish Dynasty 1017–42', *ASE* 16, 233–308

'The Personal Names on the Pre-Viking Northumbrian Coinages', *Coinage in Ninth-Century Northumbria*, ed. Metcalf, pp. 245–55

see also sect. 8

Spufford, Peter, 'Coinage and Currency', *Cambridge Economic History of Europe*, II: *Trade and Industry in the Middle Ages*, 2nd edn, ed. M. M. Postan and Edward Miller (Cambridge), 788–873 and 945–56

Stewart, Ian, 'CVNNETTI Reconsidered', *Coinage in Ninth-Century Northumbria*, ed. Metcalf, pp. 345–54 (with discussion by D. M. Metcalf and C. S. S. Lyon)

'A Solidus from Yorkshire', *BNJ* 56 (1986), 182–3 [ninth-century, imitating Louis the Pious]

Talvio, Tuukka, 'Anglo-Saxon Coins from Finnish Finds in the Royal Coin Cabinet in Stockholm', *Studia Præhistorica Fennica C. F. Meinander Septuagenario Dedicata* (Helsinki), pp. 199–206

Togami, Hajime, 'Coinage in the Reign of King Athelstan', *Jnl of Economics and Business Administration* 138.6 (1978), 58–79 [in Japanese]

'Development of the Anglo-Saxon Coinage', *Jnl of Economics and Business Administration* 135.6 (1977), 75–94 [in Japanese]

'History and Numismatics', *History and Geography* 251 (1979), 1–12 [in Japanese]

'King Eadgar's Reform of the English Coinage: Facts and Hypotheses', *Jnl of Economics and Business Administration* 133.2 (1976), 50–70; 133.5 (1976), 34–51 [in Japanese]

'King Offa of Mercia: His Penny and Supremacy', *Jnl of Economics and Business Administration* 125.3 (1972), 40–59 [in Japanese]

'The Monetary System in Later Anglo-Saxon England: Facts and Hypotheses Reconsidered', *Jnl of Economics and Business Administration* 155.2 (1981), 31–47 [in Japanese]

'Numismatics and Monetary History', *Jnl of Economics and Business Administration* 137.5 (1978), 93–103 [in Japanese]

'Silver Coinage of the Seventh and Eighth Centuries in England', *Jnl of Economics and Business Administration* 142.3 (1980), 1–20 [in Japanese]

'The Silver "pening" in the Tenth Century: some Perspectives on the Unification of

England', *Jnl of Economics and Business Administration* 147.5 (1983), 53–69 [in Japanese]

Zedelius, Volker, 'Eighth-Century Archaeology in the Meuse and Rhine Valleys: a Context for the Sceatta Finds', *Coinage in Ninth-Century Northumbria*, ed. Metcalf, pp. 405–13

8. ONOMASTICS

[Anon.] 'Onomastic Bibliography', *Onoma* 28 (1985–1986), 1–3

Bleach, J., 'Watercote, a British Settlement in an Anglo-Saxon Estate', *Ringmer Hist.* 7 (1986), 35–41

Clark, Cecily, 'English Personal Names ca. 650–1300: Some Prosopographical Bearings', *Med. Prosopography* 8, 31–60

'A Witness to Post-Conquest English Cultural Patterns: the *Liber Vitae* of Thorney Abbey', *Studies in Honour of René Derolez*, ed. Simon-Vandenbergen, pp. 73–85

Dodgson, J. McN., 'Domesday Book: Place-Names and Personal Names', *Domesday Studies*, ed. Holt, pp. 121–37

'The *-er-* in Hattersley Cheshire and Hothersall Lancashire', *Leeds Stud. in Eng.* n.s. 18, 135–9

Evans, G. G., 'Stream Names of Montgomeryshire', *Montgomeryshire Collections* 75, 29–49

Fell, Christine E., 'Modern English *Viking*', *Leeds Stud. in Eng.* n.s. 18, 111–23

'Old English *wicing*: a Question of Semantics', *PBA* 72, 295–316

Fellows-Jensen, Gillian, 'The Vikings' Relationship with Christianity in the British Isles: the Evidence of Place-Names Containing the Element *kirkja*', *Tenth Viking Congress*, ed. Knirk, pp. 295–308

'York', *Leeds Stud. in Eng.* n.s. 18, 141–55

Field, John, 'Crops for Man and Beast', *Leeds Stud. in Eng.* n.s. 18, 157–71

'What to Read on Place-Names in Britain', *LH* 17, 396–404

Forsberg, Rune, 'The Boundaries of BCS 987 Once Again', *Namn och Bygd* 75, 90–5 [Sawyer no. 574]

Fulk, R. D., see sect. *3bii*

Gardiner, Mark, and Richard Coates, 'Ellingsdean, a Viking Battlefield Identified', *Sussex Archaeol. Collections* 125, 251–2

Gelling, Margaret, 'Anglo-Saxon Eagles', with appendix by David Miles, *Leeds Stud. in Eng.* n.s. 18, 173–81

'Kenneth Cameron's Work on English Place-Names: an Appreciation' and 'The Published Writings of Kenneth Cameron 1956–1985', *Leeds Stud. in Eng.* n.s. 18, 265–9

Gould, Jim, 'Old English *ād* and the Bounds of Barr', *Namn och Bygd* 75, 82–9 [Sawyer no. 574]

Hjertstedt, Ingrid, *Middle English Nicknames in the Lay Subsidy Rolls for Warwickshire*, Acta Universitatis Upsaliensis, Studia Anglistica Upsaliensia 63 (Uppsala)

Insley, John, 'Some Aspects of Regional Variation in Early Middle English Personal Nomenclature', *Leeds Stud. in Eng.* n.s. 18, 183–99

Kenyon, D., 'Danish Settlement in Greater Manchester: the Place-Name Evidence', *Greater Manchester Archaeol. Jnl* 2 (1986), 63–9

Mills, A.D., *Dorset Place-Names: their Origins and Meaning* (Wimborne, 1986)

'Some Alternative Analyses of Medieval Field-Names', *Leeds Stud. in Eng.* n.s. 18, 201–7

Padel, O.J., 'Some South-Western Problems', *Leeds Stud. in Eng.* n.s. 18, 209–17

Parker, Michael, 'Dirnesherth: a Place-Name and Institution from Anglo-Saxon South Yorkshire', *Trans. of the Hunter Archaeol. Soc.* 14, 56–63

Rumble, Alexander R., 'Old English *Bōc-land* as an Anglo-Saxon Estate-Name', *Leeds Stud. in Eng.* n.s. 18, 219–29

Sandred, Karl Inge, 'Domesday Book 1086–1986', *Ortsnamnssällskapets i Uppsala Årsskrift* 1986, 86–96

'Ingham in East Anglia: a New Interpretation', *Leeds Stud. in Eng.* n.s. 18, 231–40

'The Vikings in Norfolk: Some Observations on the Place-Names in *-by*', *Tenth Viking Congress*, ed. Knirk, pp. 309–24

see also sect. 3*biii*

Smart, Veronica, 'Goldcyta – a Hawk from a Hybrid?' *Leeds Stud. in Eng.* n.s. 18, 241–6

Svensson, Örjan, *Saxon Place-Names in East Cornwall*, Lund Stud. in Eng. 77 (Lund)

Turville-Petre, Thorlac, and Margaret Gelling, ed., *Studies in Honour of Kenneth Cameron* = *Leeds Stud. in Eng.* n.s. 18 (Leeds)

Watts, Victor, 'Place-Name Evidence for the Allocation of Land by Lot', *Leeds Stud. in Eng.* n.s. 18, 247–63

Weise, Judith, see sect. 3*bii*

9. ARCHAEOLOGY

a. General

Abramson, P., ed., 'The Yorkshire Archaeological Register: 1986, Anglo-Scandinavian', *Yorkshire Archaeol. Jnl* 59, 196–7

[Anon.] 'The Lost Kingdom', *PA* 8.10 (November), 37 [review of exhibition of 'The Search for Anglo-Saxon Lindsey']

[Anon.] 'Notes', *Berkshire Archaeol. Jnl* 72 (1983–5), 60–90

[Anon.] 'Wiltshire Archaeological Register for 1985', *Wiltshire Archaeol. and Nat. Hist. Mag.* 81, 140–3

Baker, E., 'Bedfordshire County Planning Department 1985', *South Midlands Archaeol.* 16 (1986), 15–28 [see Grove Priory, p. 24]

Bradley, Richard, 'Time Regained: the Creation of Continuity', *JBAA* 140, 1–17 [Yeavering and other Northumbrian places, and their juxtaposition with prehistoric sites]

Bruce-Mitford, Rupert, 'Ireland and the Hanging-Bowls – a Review', *Ireland and Insular Art*, ed. Ryan, pp. 30–9

Bibliography for 1987

Butler, Lawrence, 'Symbols on Medieval Memorials', *ArchJ* 144, 246–55

CBA, *Archaeological Bibliography for Great Britain and Ireland 1980*

CBA, *Archaeology in Britain* 1986 [short reports on work of official, national, regional and local bodies relating to all periods]

CBA, *Brit. Archaeol. Abstracts* 20.2 [articles on all periods published between 1 January 1987 and 30 June 1987]

CBA, *British Archaeol. News* 2, 2–8 [short reports and comments on current work and legislation relating to archaeology]

CBA, Group 1 (Scottish Regional Group), *Discovery and Excavation in Scotland 1987* [annual summary of archaeological discoveries, excavations, surveys and publications]

CBA, Group 3, *News Bulletin* [reviews work on all periods in Cleveland, Cumbria, Durham, Northumberland, Tyne and Wear]

CBA, Group 9, *South Midlands Archaeol.* 16 (1986), and 17 [review work on all periods in Bedfordshire, Buckinghamshire, Northamptonshire and Oxfordshire]

CBA, Group 12, *Newsletter* [reviews work on all periods in Wessex and Channel Islands]

CBA, Group 14, *East Midlands Archaeol.* 2 (1986) [reviews work on all periods in Derbyshire, Leicestershire, Lincolnshire and Nottinghamshire]

Crosby, D. D. B., and J. G. Mitchell, 'A Survey of British Metamorphic Hone Stones of the 9th to 15th Centuries A.D. in the Light of Potassium–Argon and Natural Remanent Magnetization Studies', *Jnl of Archaeol. Science* 14, 483–506

Dennison, E., ed., 'Somerset Archaeology, 1984–5', *Proc. of the Somerset Archaeol. and Nat. Hist. Soc.* 130 (1986), 1–36

ed., 'Somerset Archaeology 1986', *Proc. of the Somerset Archaeol. and Nat. Hist. Soc.* 130 (1986), 141–7

Dix, Brian, ed., 'Archaeology in Northamptonshire 1983–4', *Northamptonshire Archaeol.* 20 (1985), 147–56 [Anglo-Saxon, pp. 152–3]

Farrell, Robert T., 'News and Notes in Archaeology', *OEN* 20.2, 46–9

Graham-Campbell, James, 'From Scandinavia to the Irish Sea: Viking Art Reviewed', *Ireland and Insular Art*, ed. Ryan, pp. 144–52

Grinsell, Leslie, 'The Christianisation of Prehistoric and Other Pagan Sites', *Landscape Hist.* 8 (1986), 27–37

Heighway, Carolyn, *Anglo-Saxon Gloucestershire* (Gloucester)

Hughes, Mike, ed., *Archaeology and Historic Buildings in Hampshire. Annual Report for 1986* [Anglo-Saxon, pp. 16–22, 45, 56]

Laing, Lloyd, 'The Romanization of Ireland in the Fifth Century', *Peritia* 4 (1985), 261–78

Martin, Edward, *et al.*, 'Archaeology in Suffolk, 1986', *Proc. of the Suffolk Inst. of Archaeol. and Hist.* 36.3, 225–40

Millett, Martin, 'The Question of Continuity: Rivenhall Reviewed', *ArchJ* 144, 434–44

Neuman de Vegvar, Carol L., see sect. 5

Newman, J., 'Recent Archaeological Survey Work in South East Suffolk', *Colchester Archaeol. Group, Annual Bull.* 29 (1986), 58–9

Nordic Archaeological Abstracts 1985 [pp. 118–65 abstract many items of Anglo-Saxon importance, incl. finds in both Scandinavia and the British Isles]

O'Meadhra, Uaininn, 'Irish, Insular, Saxon and Scandinavian Elements in the Motif-Pieces from Ireland', *Ireland and Insular Art*, ed. Ryan, pp. 159–65

Preston-Jones, A., and P. Rose, 'Medieval Cornwall', *Cornish Archaeol.* 25 (1986), 135–85

Priddy, D., 'Excavations in Essex 1985', *Essex Archaeol. and Hist.* 17, 156–65

Thomas, Charles, 'The Earliest Christian Art in Ireland and Britain', *Ireland and Insular Art*, ed. Ryan, pp. 7–11

Wamers, Egon, 'Egg-and-Dart Derivatives in Insular Art', *Ireland and Insular Art*, ed. Ryan, pp. 96–104

Youngs, Susan M., John Clark and Terry Barry, 'Medieval Britain and Ireland in 1986', *MA* 31, 110–91

b. Towns and other major settlements

Addyman, P. V., 'The Work of the York Archaeological Trust in 1986', *Yorkshire Philosophical Soc. Annual Report for the Year 1986*, 41–8 [esp. for the discovery of *Eoforwic*]

Anderson, Ian, and Paul Blockley, 'Christ Church College', *Canterbury's Archaeology 1986–7. 11th Annual Report*, 11 [Anglo-Saxon occupation]

[Anon.] *The Maldon Burh Jigsaw*, Maldon Archaeol. Group (1986)

[Anon.] 'Viking Waterfront Rescued at York', *PA* 8.11 (December), 36

Barton, K. J., 'Excavations at Cuthman's Field, Church Street, Steyning, 1962', *Sussex Archaeol. Collections* 124 (1986), 97–108 [Late Saxon occupation]

Biddle, Martin, 'Early Norman Winchester', *Domesday Studies*, ed. Holt, pp. 311–31

Blockley, Paul, '7 Adelaide Place', *Canterbury's Archaeology 1986–7. 11th Annual Report*, 12 [Anglo-Saxon sunken building]

Bond, C. J., 'Anglo-Saxon and Medieval Defences', *Urban Archaeology in Britain*, ed. Schofield and Leech, pp. 92–116

Bradley, John, 'The Medieval Borough of Louth: an Archaeological Study', *Jnl of the County Louth Archaeol. and Hist. Soc.* 21, 8–22

Burch, Mark, 'Roman and Medieval Occupation in Queen Street', *PA* 8.11 (December), 9–12 [11th-cent. sunken timber building in London]

Cane, J., 'Stafford Town', *Birmingham Univ. Field Archaeol. Unit Report 1984*, 12–13 [Anglo-Saxon defences]

Carver, Martin, *Underneath English Towns: Interpreting Urban Archaeology* (London) 'The Nature of Urban Deposits', *Urban Archaeology in Britain*, ed. Schofield and Leech, pp. 9–26

Chitwood, Prince, and Julian Hill, 'Excavations at St. Alban's House, Wood Street', *PA* 8.11 (December), 13–16 [Late Saxon occupation in London]

Cowie, Robert, 'Lundenwic. "Unravelling the Strand"', *PA* 8.5 (June), 30–4

Drage, C., 'Urban Castles', *Urban Archaeology in Britain*, ed. Schofield and Leech, pp. 117–32 [important for relationship of castles to pre-conquest towns]

Durham, B., 'Oxford: 7–8 Queen Street', *South Midlands Archaeol.* 26 (1986), 103–4

'Oxford: 89 St Aldates (Trill Mill Stream)', *South Midlands Archaeol.* 26 (1986), 104

'Oxford: 240 St Michael's Street, Saxon Defences', *South Midlands Archaeol.* 26 (1986), 105–6

'Oxford: St Michael at the Northgate Tower', *South Midlands Archaeol.* 26 (1986), 104–5

Ellis, Peter, 'Excavations in Winchcombe, Gloucestershire, 1962–1972: a Report on Excavation and Fieldwork by B. K. Davidson and J. Hinchliffe at Cowl Lane and Back Lane', *Trans. of the Bristol and Gloucestershire Archaeol. Soc.* 104 (1986), 95–138 [Late Saxon occupation]

Evans, Jane, 'Excavations in Fletcher's Croft, Steyning, 1967–8', *Sussex Archaeol. Collections* 124 (1986), 79–95 [Late Saxon occupation]

Farley, M., 'Excavations at the Prebendal Court, Aylesbury, 1985', *South Midlands Archaeol.* 16 (1986), 37–8

Finlayson, Rhona, 'Oh! What a Lovely Waterfront', *Interim: Archaeology in York* 12.3 (Autumn), 3–8 [Anglian and Viking-Age finds from ABC Cinema site]

Guy, C. J., 'Excavations at Back Lane, Winchcombe, 1985', *Trans. of the Bristol and Gloucestershire Archaeol. Soc.* 104 (1986), 214–20 [Anglo-Saxon occupation]

Hill, D., 'The Saxon Period', *Urban Archaeology in Britain*, ed. Schofield and Leech, pp. 46–53

Haslam, J., 'Market and Fortress in the Reign of Offa', *World Archaeol.* 19, 76–93

Hassall, Tom, *Oxford: the Buried City* (Oxford)

Jones, Andrew K. G., 'Some Fishy Business at the University', *Interim: Archaeology in York* 12.1 (Spring), 29–36 [Viking-age fish remains]

Keeley, H. C. M., ed., *Environmental Archaeology: a Regional Review*, Directorate of Ancient Mon. and Hist. Buildings, Occasional Paper 6 (London, 1986) [includes Anglian and Anglo-Scandinavian York]

Kemp, Richard, 'Anglian York – The Missing Link', *CA* 104, 259–63

Manley, John, *et al.*, '*Cledemutha*: a Late Saxon Burh in North Wales', *MA* 31, 13–46

Mundy, Charles, 'Worcester Archaeology Project 1985/86', *West Midlands Archaeol.* 28 (1985), 7–14 [includes Anglo-Saxon oven]

Ottaway, Patrick, 'Olé! Romans and Vikings at Granada', *Rescue News* 43, 2 [Anglo-Scandinavian deposits against south-east wall of legionary fortress]

'Testing, Testing . . . Excavations at Leedham's Garage', *Interim: Archaeology in York* 12.4 (Winter, 1987–8), 15–21 [Anglo-Scandinavian occupation; ?Anglian metal fitting]

Parker, M. S., see sect. 6

Rady, Jonathan, '8 St Radigund's Street', *Canterbury's Archaeology 1986–7. 11th Annual Report* 12–15 [Anglo-Saxon occupation and road]

'Nos. 36–37 Stour Street', *Canterbury's Archaeology 1986–7. 11th Annual Report* 10 [Anglo-Saxon occupation and sunken buildings]

Roffe, David, and Christine Mahaney, 'Stamford and the Norman Conquest', *Lincoln-shire Hist. and Archaeol.* 21 (1986), 5–10

Schofield, John, 'Archaeology in the City of London: Archive and Publication', *ArchJ* 144, 424–33 [guide to records of archaeology in London, esp. since 1973]
  'Recent Approaches in Urban Archaeology', *Urban Archaeology in Britain*, ed. Schofield and Leech, pp. 1–8

Schofield, John, and Roger Leech, ed., *Urban Archaeology in Britain*, CBA Research Report 61 (London)

Scull, C., and B. Durham, 'Christ Church, Cathedral Cloister', *South Midlands Archaeol.* 16 (1986) 102

c. Rural settlements, agriculture and the countryside

Alcock, Leslie, *et al.*, 'Reconnaissance Excavations on Early Historic Fortifications and Other Royal Sites in Scotland, 1974–84: 1, Excavations Near St Abb's Head, Berwickshire, 1980', *Proc. of the Soc. of Antiquaries of Scotland* 116 (1986), 255–79

[Anon.] 'West Cotton', *CA* 106, 337–9 [Anglo-Saxon occupation]

Austin, David, 'The Archaeology of the Domesday Vill', *Domesday Book: Studies*, ed. Williams and Erskine, pp. 48–55
  'The Medieval Settlement and Landscape of Castle Eden, Peterlee, Co. Durham: Excavations 1974', *Durham Archaeol. Jnl* 3, 57–78 [Anglo-Saxon occupation and burial]

Barford, P.M., 'The Excavations and Fieldwork of R.H. Farrands 1950–1985', *Colchester Archaeol. Group, Annual Bulletin* 29 (1986), 3–15

Barker, Katherine, 'Pen, Ilchester and Yeovil: a Study in the Landscape History and Archaeology of South-East Somerset', *Somerset Archaeol. and Nat. Hist.* 130 (1987 for 1986), 11–45

Bedwin, O., 'The Excavation of 3 Ring Ditches at Broomfield Plantation Quarry, Alresford, Essex, 1984', *Essex Archaeol. and Hist.* 17, 69–81

Beresford, Guy, *Goltho. The Development of an Early Medieval Manor c. 850–1150*, Historic Buildings and Monuments Commission for England, Archaeol. Report 4 (London)

Blackburn, M.A.S., and M.J. Bonser, see sect. 7 [Middle Anglian site near Royston, Herts.]

Boddington, A., 'The Bywell Project', *Univ. of Durham. Univ. of Newcastle upon Tyne. Archaeol. Reports for 1986* 10, 52–8

Buckley, D.G., and S. Tyler, 'Springfield Lyons Excavation: the Anglo-Saxon Periods', *Essex Jnl* 22.1, 3–6

Carr, Jane, 'Excavations on the Mound, Glastonbury, Somerset, 1971', *Proc. of the Somerset Archaeol. and Nat. Hist. Soc.* 129 (1985), 37–62 [includes 10th- to 12th-cent. occupation]

Carter, G.A., 'The End of the Road for Britain's First Street?', *Essex Jnl* 21.1 (1986), 3–8

Chambers, R. A., and C. Halpin, 'Radley: Barrow Hills', *South Midlands Archaeol.* 26 (1986), 106–11

Davis, Susan M., 'The Poundbury Pipe-Line: Archaeological Observations and Excavations', *Proc. of the Dorset Nat. Hist. and Archaeol. Soc.* 108 (1986), 80 [5th- to 8th-cent. settlement]

Drewett, Peter, *et al.*, 'The Excavation of a Saxon Sunken Building at North Marden, West Sussex, 1982', *Sussex Archaeol. Collections* 124 (1986), 109–18

Foard, Glenn, and Terry Pearson, 'The Raunds Area Project: First Interim Report', *Northamptonshire Archaeol.* 20 (1985), 3–21

Gee, M., 'Broomfield Borrow Pit, TL 714095 (TL 70–3)', *Essex Archaeol. and Hist.* 17, 144–7

Goodburn, D. M., 'Medmerry: a Reassessment of a Migration Period Site on the South Coast of England, and Some of its Finds', *Int. Jnl of Nautical Archaeol.* 16, 213–24

Hall, D., *The Fenland Project, Number 2: Fenland Landscapes and Settlement between Peterborough and March*, East Anglian Archaeol. 35

Hannan, Alan, *et al.*, 'Raunds', *CA* 106, 323–7

Hayfield, Colin, *An Archaeological Survey of the Parish of Wharram Percy, East Yorkshire 1. The Evolution of the Roman Landscape*, BAR Brit. ser. 172 (Oxford)

Hinchliffe, J., 'An Early Medieval Settlement at Cowage Farm, Foxley, Near Malmesbury', *ArchJ* 143, 240–59

Hope, J. H., 'The Knights Templar and the Excavations at the Cressing Temple, 1978–1981', *Essex Jnl* 22.3, 67–71 [for Period VI, p. 68]

Hurst, J. G., *Wharram Research Project Interim Report on 38th season*, Medieval Village Research Group

Leech, Roger H., 'Excavations at Lower Court Farm, Long Ashton', *Bristol and Avon Archaeol.* 5 (1986), 12–35 [Late Saxon settlement]

McAvoy, F., 'Excavations at Daw's Castle, Watchet, 1982', *Somerset Archaeol. and Nat. Hist.* 130 (1986), 47–60

Medieval Settlement Research Group Annual Report 1 (1986) [national survey of year's work, including Anglo-Saxon sites]

Poulton, Rob, 'Excavations on the Site of the Old Vicarage, Church Street, Reigate, 1977–82. Part 1, Saxo-Norman and Earlier Discoveries', *Surrey Archaeol. Collections* 77 (1986), 17–94

'The Former Goblin Works, Leatherhead: Saxons and Sinners', *London Archaeologist* 5, 311–17

Powlesland, D., C. Haughton, and J. Hanson, 'Excavations at Heslerton, North Yorkshire 1978–82', *ArchJ* 143, 53–173

Ryan, K., see sect. 5

Shaw, Michael, 'Excavations on a Saxon and Medieval Site at Black Lion Hill, Northampton', *Northamptonshire Archaeol.* 20 (1985), 113

Taylor, Alison, 'Prehistoric, Roman, Saxon and Medieval Artefacts from the Southern Fen Edge, Cambridgeshire', *Proc. of the Cambridge Antiquarian Soc.* 74 (1985), 1–52

Turnbull, Percival, 'Gayle Lane Earthwork, Wensleydale', in *Archaeology in the Pennines*, ed. T. G. Munby and P. Turnbull, BAR Brit. ser. 158 (Oxford), 205–11

Bibliography for 1987

Watson, J., 'Domesday Greenwich', *Trans. of the Greenwich and Lewisham Ant. Soc.* 10.3, 108–18

Wickenden, N. P., 'Prehistoric Settlement and the Romano-British "small town" at Heybridge, Essex', *Essex Archaeol. and Hist.* 17, 7–68

Williams, R. J., 'Bancroft Mausoleum', *South Midlands Archaeol.* 16 (1986), 43–9

Williamson, T., 'The Development of Settlement in North West Essex: the Results of a Recent Field Survey', *Essex Archaeol. and Hist.* 17, 120–32

d. Pagan cemeteries and Sutton Hoo

Alexander, M. L., 'A "Viking-Age" Grave from Cambois, Bedlington, Northumberland', *MA* 31, 101–5

Carver, M. O. H., 'Sutton Hoo', *Birmingham Univ. Field Archaeol. Unit Report* 7 (1984), 1–4

'Sutton Hoo', *Birmingham Univ. Field Archaeol. Unit Report* 8 (1985–6), 1–3

Chambers, R. A., 'An Inhumation Cemetery at Castle Hill, Little Wittenham, Oxon., 1984–5', *Oxoniensia* 51 (1986), 45–8 [possibly Anglo-Saxon]

Crawford, Gilles, 'Wasperton', *Birmingham Univ. Field Archaeol. Unit Report* 6 (1983), 9–10 [Anglo-Saxon grave]

Down, A., 'Excavations at the Saxon Cemetery Site at Appledown [Sussex]', *ArchJ* 144, 439–40

Evison, Vera I., *Dover: the Buckland·Anglo-Saxon Cemetery*, Historic Buildings and Monuments Commission for England, Archaeol. Report 3 (London)

Freke, David, 'Pagan Lady of Peel', *PA* 8.1 (Feb.), 40–5 [Viking period woman's grave]

Gallagher, D. B., 'The Anglo-Saxon Cemetery of Hob Hill, Saltburn', *Yorkshire Archaeol. Jnl* 59, 9–27

Hills, Catherine, 'The Anglo-Saxon Cemetery at Spong Hill, Norfolk', *Colchester Archaeol. Group, Annual Bull.* 29 (1986), 49

Hills, Catherine, Kenneth Penn and Robert Rickett, *The Anglo-Saxon Cemetery at Spong Hill, North Elmham, Part IV: Catalogue of Cremations*, East Anglian Archaeol. Report 34 (Norfolk)

Kennet, D. H., 'Recent Work on the Anglo-Saxon Cemetery found at Kempston', *South Midlands Archaeol.* 16 (1986), 3–14

Martin, Max, 'Redwalds Börse: Gewicht und Gewichtskategorien völkerwanderungszeitlicher Objekte aus Edelmetall', *FS* 21, 206–38

Miles, David, and Simon Palmer, 'Lechlade', *Trans. of the Bristol and Gloucestershire Archaeol. Soc.* 104 (1986), 241–2 [6th- and 7th-cent. Anglo-Saxon cemetery]

Preston-Jones, A., 'Road Widening at St Buryan and Pelynt Churchyards', *Cornish Archaeol.* 26, 153–60

Robinson, Paul, 'Saxon Burials at Elston, Orcheston', *Wiltshire Archaeol. and Nat. Hist. Mag.* 81, 132

Roth, Uta, see sect. 5

Stanes, R., 'Blackdown Barrows', *Devon and Cornwall N&Q* 39 (1986), 384–6

Trudgian, P., 'Excavation of a Burial Ground at Saint Endellion, Cornwall', *Cornish Archaeol.* 26, 144–52

e. Churches, monastic sites and Christian cemeteries

Bassett, Steven, *The Wootton Wawen Project: Interim Report No. 5* (Birmingham)

Bennett, Paul, *et al.*, 'Rescue Excavations in the Outer Court of St Augustine's Abbey, 1983–84', *AC* 103, 79–117

Bettey, J. H., 'The Impact of Historic and Religious Changes on the Parish Churches of Avon', *Avon Past* 12, 10–16

Biddle, Martin, *et al.*, see sect. 7 [coins in graves]

Boddington, Andy, 'Raunds, Northamptonshire: Analysis of a Country Churchyard', *World Archaeol.* 18.3, 411–25

Boddington, A., A. N. Garland, and R. C. Janaway, ed., *Death, Decay and Reconstruction* (Manchester) [includes consideration of Anglo-Saxon cemetery practices, esp. in relation to Raunds]

Boore, Eric J., 'The Church of St. Augustine the Less, Bristol: An Interim Statement', *Trans. of the Bristol and Gloucestershire Archaeol. Soc.* 104 (1986), 211–14 [Saxo-Norman]

'Excavations at St Augustine the Less, Bristol, 1983–84', *Bristol and Avon Archaeol.* 4 (1985), 21–33 [Saxo-Norman graves]

Coppack, Glyn, 'St Lawrence Church, Burnham, South Humberside. The Excavation of a Parochial Chapel', *Lincolnshire Hist. and Archaeol.* 21 (1986), 39–60 [Anglo-Saxon origins]

Cox, D. C., and M. D. Watson, 'Holy Trinity Church, Much Wenlock: a Reassessment', *JBAA* 140, 76–87

Cramp, R. J., and R. Daniels, 'New Finds from the Anglo-Saxon Monastery at Hartlepool, Cleveland', *Antiquity* 233, 424–32

Daniels, Robin, 'Hartlepool', *CA* 104, 273–7

Doggett, Nicholas, 'The Anglo-Saxon See and Cathedral of Dorchester-on-Thames: the Evidence Reconsidered', *Oxoniensia* 51 (1986), 49–61

Fernie, Eric, 'The Effect of the Conquest on Norman Architectural Patronage', *Anglo-Norman Studies IX*, ed. Brown, pp. 71–85

Hall, Richard, 'Ripon Yarns 2: Return to the Hill', *Interim: Archaeology in York* 12.3 (Autumn), 15–22 [7th- to 10th-cent. cemetery at Ailcy Hill]

Hooke, Della, 'Two Documented Pre-Conquest Christian Sites Located upon Parish Boundaries: "Cada's Minster", Willersey, Gloucs., and "The Holy Place", Fawler in Kingston Lisle, Oxon.', *MA* 31, 96–101

James, T., 'Excavations at the Augustinian Priory of St John and St Teulyddog, Carmarthen, 1979', *Archaeol. Cambrensis* 134 (1986), 120–61

MacGowan, K., 'Saxon Timber Structures from the Barking Abbey Excavations 1985–1986', *Essex Jnl* 22.2, 35–8

Morris, Richard, 'Parish Churches', *Urban Archaeology in Britain*, ed. Schofield and Leech, pp. 177–91

Radford, C. A. R., 'The Early Medieval Church: its Appearance and Setting', *Avon Past* 12, 3–9

Roffe, David, 'The Seventh-Century Monastery of Stow Green, Lincolnshire', *Lincolnshire Hist. and Archaeol.* 21 (1986), 31–4

Royal Commission on the Historical Monuments of England, *Churches of South-East Wiltshire* (London)

Russell, A. D., 'Little Somborne', *Archaeology and Hist. Buildings in Hampshire. Annual Report for 1986*, ed. M. Hughes, p. 17

Shepherd, Liz, 'The Saxon Church at St Margaret's Rectory [Ironmonger Lane, City of London]', *PA* 8.11 (December), 23–5

Spurrell, Mark, ed., *Stow Church Restored, 1846–1866*, Lincoln Record Soc. Publication 75 (Woodbridge, 1984) [19th-cent. restoration of important Anglo-Saxon church]

Taylor, H. M., 'St Wystan's Church, Repton, Derbyshire: a Reconstruction Essay', *ArchJ* 144, 205–45

Wenham, L. P., R. A. Hall, C. M. Briden, and D. A. Stocker, *St Mary Bishophill Junior and St Mary Castlegate*, Archaeol. of York 8.2 (London) [with separate folder of unbound illustrations]

Westman, Andrew, 'The Church of St. Alphege', *PA* 8.11 (December), 17–22 [late Saxon church]

Wilmott, Tony, 'Pontefract', *CA* 106, 340–4 [Anglo-Saxon church and cemetery]

Woods, Humphrey, 'Excavations at Wenlock Priory, 1981–6', *JBAA* 140, 36–75

f. Ships and seafaring

Crumlin-Pedersen, O., and Max Vinner, eds., *Sailing into the Past* (Roskilde, 1986) [papers of 1984 International Ship Replica Seminar at Roskilde: includes Viking-age replicas]

Jones-Barker, Doris, 'Graffito of a Danish or Viking Ship, Church of St Mary, Stow-in-Lindsey, Lincolnshire', *AntJ* 66 (1986), 394–6 and 402–3

McGrail, Sean, 'Early Boatbuilding Techniques in Britain and Ireland – Dating Technological Change', *Int. Jnl of Nautical Archaeol.* 16, 343–6

g. Sculpture on bone, stone, and wood

Baird, Joseph L., see section 3*b* iii

Heslop, T. A., 'A Walrus Ivory Seal Matrix from Lincoln', *AntJ* 66 (1986), 371–2 [possibly post-conquest, but of English manufacture]

Ohlgren, Thomas H., 'The Crucifixion Panel on the Gosforth Cross: a Janusian Image?' *OEN* 20.2, 50–1

Tweddle, Dominic, 'Handle – with care!', *Interim: Archaeol. in York* 12.2 (Summer), 39–42 [Salin Style II carved bone knife handle]

  'Ringerike', *Interim: Archaeology in York* 12.4 (Winter), 27–30 [carved boxwood knife handle]

Wood, I. N., see section 6

h. Metal-work and other minor objects

Biddle, Martin, *et al.*, see sect. 7 [gold finger-ring]

Boland, Peter, and Roger Brownsword, 'A Note on a "Pewter" Anglo-Saxon Brooch from Dudley Castle', *West Midlands Archaeol.* 28 (1985), 31

Brownsword, Roger, and David A. Hinton, 'An Anglo-Saxon Copper-Alloy Disc', *AntJ* 66 (1986), 384–6 and 399–400

Cameron, Esther, 'Viking Sword at Repton', *Rescue News* 41 (Winter, 1986), 7

Going, Chris, 'A Middle Saxon Buckle from Lincoln Road, Enfield', *London Archaeologist* 5, 301–2

Graham-Campbell, James, 'The Re-provenancing of a Viking-Age Hoard to the Thames, near Deptford (S.E. London)', *BNJ* 56 (1986), 186–7

Hines, John, 'What is the Source of the Anglian English Wrist-Clasps?', *Sachsen Symposion 1983* (Skaraborg, 1984), 96–8

Hood, Nancy, and George Speake, 'An Anglo-Saxon Gilt-bronze Lozenge-shaped Mount from Culham, now in Abingdon Museum', *Oxoniensia* 52, 184–5

Keen, Lawrence, 'Late Anglo-Saxon Strap-ends of Dorset', *Proc. of the Dorset Nat. Hist. and Archaeol. Soc.* 108 (1986), 195–6

Laing, Lloyd R., *et al.*, 'The Early Christian Period Settlement at Ronaldsway, Isle of Man: Reappraisal', *Jnl of the Manx Museum* 9 (1984–7), 389–415 [discusses influences on Anglo-Saxon metalwork]

Lester, Geoff, 'The Anglo-Saxon Helmet from Benty Grange, Derbyshire', *OEN* 21.1, 34–5

Margeson, Sue, 'A Ringerike-style Mount from Stoke Holy Cross', *Norfolk Archaeol.* 40.1, 126–7

Ottaway, Patrick, see sect. *9b*

Ryan, Michael, 'Some Aspects of Sequence and Style in the Metalwork of Eighth- and Ninth-Century Ireland', *Ireland and Insular Art*, ed. Ryan, pp. 66–74

  ed., see sect. 5

Rynne, Etienne, 'The Date of the Ardagh Chalice', *Ireland and Insular Art*, ed. Ryan, pp. 85–9

Stevenson, Robert B.K., 'Brooches and Pins: Some Seventh- to Ninth-Century Problems', *Ireland and Insular Art*, ed. Ryan, pp. 90–5

Tweddle, Dominic, *Finds from Parliament Street and Other Sites in the City Centre*, Archaeol. of York 17.4 (London, 1986)

Tylecote, R.F., ed., *The Metallurgy of Early Ferrous Tools and Edged Weapons*, BAR Brit. ser. 155 (Oxford, 1986)

Tyler, S., 'Three Anglo-Saxon Bone Combs from Great Wakering', *Essex Archaeol. and Hist.* 17, 170–2

Wamers, Egon, 'A 10th-Century Metal Ornament from Mainz, West Germany', *MA* 31, 105–9

Whitfield, Niamh, 'Motifs and Techniques of Celtic Filigree: are They Original?' *Ireland and Insular Art*, ed. Ryan, pp. 75–84

Willson, John, 'A Saxon Button-Brooch from Dover', *Kent Archaeol. Rev.* 87 (Spring), 154 and cover

i. Inscriptions

Carletti, Carlo, 'I graffiti sull'affresco di S. Luca nel cimitero di Commodilla: addenda et corrigenda', *Rendiconti della Pontificia Accademia Romana di Archeologia* 57 (1984–5), 129–43

Derolez, René, 'Anglo-Saxons in Rome', *OEN* 21.1, 36–7

King, Anne, see sect. 2 [Ruthwell Cross]

Ó Carragáin, Éamonn, 'A Liturgical Interpretation of the Bewcastle Cross', *Medieval Literature and Antiquities: Studies in Honour of Basil Cottle*, ed. Myra Stokes and T. L. Burton (Cambridge), pp. 15–42

'The Ruthwell Cross and Irish High Crosses: Some Points of Comparison and Contrast', *Ireland and Insular Art*, ed. Ryan, pp. 118–28

Page, R. I., *Runes* (London)

'Scandinavian Runes in the British Isles', *PA* 8.6 (July), 35–9

j. Pottery and glass

[Anon.] 'Medieval Pottery Research Group Annual Bibliography 1986', *Med. Ceramics* 10 (1986), 131–44 [national coverage of Anglo-Saxon and later periods]

Betts, Ian M., 'Analytical Analysis and Manufacturing Techniques of Anglo-Saxon Tiles', *Med. Ceramics* 10 (1986), 37–42

Capelle, Torsten, 'Animal Stamps and Animal Figures on Anglo-Saxon and Anglian Pottery', *MA* 31, 94–6

Elder, Jane, and Pam Garrard, 'Small Finds and Conservation', *Canterbury's Archaeol. 1986–7. 11th Annual Report*, 33 [Anglo-Saxon relief-decorated polychrome tile from the archbishop's palace]

Esmonde Cleary, A. S., 'Rocester', *West Midlands Archaeol.* 28 (1985), 50–1 [10th-cent. pottery – 'Stafford-type ware']

Fasham, P. J., 'The Medieval Settlement at Popham, Excavations 1975 and 1983', *Proc. of the Hampshire Field Club and Archaeol. Soc.* 43, 83–124 [for grass-tempered pottery, see p. 117]

Le Patourel, Jean, 'Potters and Pots', *Med. Ceramics* 10 (1986), 3–16 [reviews late Saxon potting]

Macpherson-Grant, Nigel, 'Prehistoric and Post-Roman Pottery', *Canterbury's Archaeol. 1986–7. 11th Annual Report*, 28–30

Mainman, Ailsa, 'Pot Spot', *Interim: Archaeology in York* 12.1 (Spring), 25–8 [Ipswich-type ware in York]

'Pot Spot', *Interim: Archaeology in York* 12.2 (Summer), 36–8 [Viking-age crucibles]

Näsman, Ulf, 'Vendel Period Glass from Eketorp-II, Öland, Sweden', *Acta Archaeologica* 55 (1984), 55–116 [with many references to England and the Continent]

Pearson, Terry, 'Saxon and Medieval Pottery: an Outline of the Evidence from Raunds, Furnells', *Northamptonshire Archaeol.* 20 (1985), 9–21

Richards, J.D., *The Significance of Form and Decoration of Anglo-Saxon Cremation Urns*, BAR Brit. ser 166 (Oxford)

Riddler, Ian David, 'Pottery Stamps – a Middle Saxon Faunal Viewpoint', *Med. Ceramics* 10 (1986), 17–22

Stokes, Michael A., 'Late Saxon Tiles from Coventry', *Med. Ceramics* 10 (1986), 29–35

Turner-Rugg, Alison, 'St Albans Pottery: the Saxon and Medieval Sequence', *Hertfordshire's Past* 23 (Autumn), 20–5

Tweddle, Dominic, 'A Note on the Design of the Interlace Tile from Coventry', *Med. Ceramics* 10 (1986), 35–6

Tyler, S., 'Goldhanger: Note on Loomweights from Site 1, Chigborough Farm, TL 880083 (TL 80–44)', *Essex Archaeol. and Hist.* 17, 147–8

Vince, Alan, 'The Study of Pottery from Urban Excavations', *Urban Archaeology in Britain*, ed. Schofield and Leech, pp. 201–13

k. Musical instruments

Remnant, Mary, *English Bowed Instruments from Anglo-Saxon to Tudor Times* (Oxford, 1986)

10. REVIEWS

Acobian, Richild, ed., *Festgabe für Hans Pinsker zum 70. Geburtstag* (Vienna, 1979): H. Weinstock, *Anglia* 105, 414–18

Alexander, Michael, *Old English Literature* (London, 1983): J. Roberts, *MLR* 82, 434–5

Anderson, Earl R., *Cynewulf: Structure, Style and Theme in His Poetry* (Rutherford, Madison and Teaneck, NJ; London and Toronto, 1983): G. Whatley, *Speculum* 62, 102–4

Anderson, James E., *Two Literary Riddles in the Exeter Book* (Norman, OK, and London, 1986): E.G. Stanley, *N&Q* 34, 520

Angenendt, A., *Kaiserherrschaft und Königstaufe, Kaiser, Könige und Päpste als geistliche Patrone in der abendländischen Missionsgeschichte* (Berlin and New York, 1984): M. Reydellet, *Francia* 14, 693–4

Archibald, M. M., and C. E. Blunt, *British Museum, Anglo-Saxon Coins*, v: *Athelstan to the Reform of Edgar, 924–c. 973*, SCBI 34 (London, 1986): F. Dumas, *Revue numismatique* 6th ser. 29, 261; D. A. Hinton, *MA* 31, 211; S. Keynes, *AntJ* 66 (1986), 451–2; H. E. Pagan, *BNJ* 56, 192–3

Arnold, C. J., *Roman Britain to Saxon England: an Archaeological Study* (London, 1984): L. Abrams, *Classical World* 80, 324; N. P. Brooks, *EHR* 102, 460

Ayers, Brian, *Excavations Within the North-East Bailey of Norwich Castle, 1979*, East Anglian Archaeol. Report 28 (Dereham, 1985): D. Parsons, *ArchJ* 144, 479–80

Backhouse, J., D. H. Turner, and L. Webster, ed., *The Golden Age of Anglo-Saxon Art* (London, 1984): J. Graham-Campbell, *Antiquity* 231, 141–2

Bammesberger, Alfred, *English Etymology* (Heidelberg, 1984): H. Käsmann, *BN* 22, 209–10; P. Swiggers, *Leuvense Bijdragen* 76, 270–3

A Sketch of Diachronic English Morphology (Regensburg, 1984): P. Swiggers, *Leuvense Bijdragen* 76, 267–9

ed., *Problems of Old English Lexicography* (Regensburg, 1985): M. Görlach, *Lexicographica* 3, 253–5; T. H. Leinbaugh, *N&Q* 34, 355–8; P. Lendinara, *Schede Medievali* 11, 456–7; N. E. Osselton, *ES* 68, 193–6; M. Stokes, *RES* 38, 64–5; C.-D. Wetzel, *Kratylos* 32, 130–40

Barney, Stephen A., *Word-Hoard: an Introduction to Old English Vocabulary*, 2nd edn (New Haven and London, 1985): A. Ward, *RES* 38, 125

Bately, Janet M., ed., *The Anglo-Saxon Chronicle: MS A* (Cambridge, 1986): J. Campbell, *N&Q* 34, 517–19; F. H[ockey], *Revue d'Histoire Ecclésiastique* 82, 431.

Bendixen, K., *Sceattas and Other Coin Finds. Ribe Excavations* 1, ed. M. Bencard (Esbjerg, 1981): B. Malmer, *Fornvännen* 81, 197–200

Berkhout, Carl T., and M. McC. Gatch, ed., *Anglo-Saxon Scholarship: the First Three Centuries* (Boston, 1982): D. G. Calder, *YES* 17, 241–2

Berndt, Rolf, *A History of the English Language* (Leipzig, 1982): H. Sauer, *ASNSL* 224, 143–8

Biddick, Kathleen, ed., *Archaeological Approaches to Medieval Europe*, Studies in Medieval Culture 18 (Kalamazoo, 1984): S. Bonde, *Speculum* 62, 197–201

Blackburn, M. A. S., ed., *Anglo-Saxon Monetary History* (Leicester, 1986): C. J. Becker, *Nordisk Numismatisk Unions Medlemsblad* 1987, 19–20; R. Hodges, *Antiquity* 61, 156–7; K. Jonsson, *BNJ* 56, 193–4

Blackburn, Mark, Christina Colyer and Michael Dolley, *Early Medieval Coins from Lincoln and its Shire* c. *770–1100* (London, 1983): L. Butler, *Lincolnshire Hist. and Archaeol.* 21, 66; B. Malmer, *Fornvännen* 81, 197–200

Blake, N. F., and Charles Jones, ed., *English Historical Linguistics: Studies in Development* (Sheffield, 1984): M. Rissanen, *Jnl of Eng. Ling.* 20, 150–6

Boon, George C., *Welsh Hoards 1979–1981* (Cardiff, 1986): N. Mayhew, *BNJ* 56, 194–5

Bourcier, Georges, *An Introduction to the History of the English Language* [adapted from the French (1978) by Cecily Clark] (Cheltenham, 1981): H. Sauer, *ASNSL* 224, 143–8

Brewer, D., and E. Frankl, *Arthur's Britain: the Land and the Legend* (Cambridge, 1985): L. Alcock, *Antiquity* 61, 157–8

Bridges, Magaret, *Generic Contrast in Old English Hagiographical Poetry* (Copenhagen, 1984): A. Crépin, *EA* 40, 463–4; J. Roberts, *N&Q* 34, 249–51

Briggs, Grace, Jean Cook, and Trevor Rowley, ed., *The Archaeology of the Oxford Region* (Oxford, 1986): D. A. Hinton, *Oxoniensia* 51, 205–6

Brooks, Nicholas, *The Early History of the Church of Canterbury* (Leicester, 1984): M. McC. Gatch, *Albion* 19, 211–13; M. Gibson, *JTS* 38, 227–9; T. Reuter, *DAEM* 43, 698–9

Brown, Phyllis Rugg, *et al.*, ed., *Modes of Interpretation in Old English Literature* (Toronto, Buffalo and London, 1986): K. Schoening, *Comitatus* 18, 103–5; P. A. Thompson, *Univ. of Toronto Quarterly* 57, 100–1

Bryan, George B., *Ethelwold and Medieval Music-Drama at Winchester: the Easter Play, its Author and its Milieu* (Bern, Frankfurt am Main, and Las Vegas, 1981): J. F. Vickrey, *Speculum* 62, 765

Butler, L. A. S., and R. K. Morris, ed., *The Anglo-Saxon Church* (London, 1986): E. Fernie, *AntJ* 67, 177–8; E. N. Gorsuch, *Albion* 19, 210–11; R. Hill, *MA* 31, 192–3

Calder, Daniel G., *et al.*, trans., *Sources and Analogues of Old English Poetry, 2* (Cambridge and Totowa, NJ, 1983): E. G. Stanley, *MLR* 82, 432–4

Callmer, Johann, *Sceatta Problems in the Light of the Finds from Åhus* (Lund, 1984): K. Jonsson, *Fornvännen* 82, 47–8; V. Zedelius, *Zeitschrift für Archaeol. des Mittelalters* 12, 221–3

Cameron, Angus, Allison Kingsmill and Ashley Crandell Amos, *Old English Word Studies* (Toronto, Buffalo and London, 1983): J. Roberts, *N&Q* 34, 515–16

Chance, Jane, *Woman as Hero in Old English Literature* (Syracuse, NY, 1986): L. S. Robinson, *Women's Rev. of Books* (June), p. 14

Clemoes, Peter, *et al.*, ed., *Anglo-Saxon England* 14 (Cambridge, 1985): C. Gauvin, *EA* 40, 464–5; H. R. Loyn, *JEH* 38, 452–3; E. G. Stanley, *N&Q* 34, 516–17

Colgrave, Bertram, ed. and trans. [four Anglo-Latin biographies reprinted by Cambridge Univ. Press, 1985]: M. Budny, *Hist. Today* (October), p. 60; R. W. Pfaff, *Church Hist.* 56, 239–40

Cook, Alison M., and Maxwell W. Dacre, *Executions at Portway, Andover, 1973–1975* (Oxford, 1985): A. Boddington, *ArchJ* 144, 472–4; C. Hills, *AntJ* 67, 178–9; S. M. Hirst, *MA* 31, 195–6

Cronyn, J. M., and C. V. Horie, *St Cuthbert's Coffin* (Durham, 1985): R. N. Bailey, *AntJ* 66, 446–7; C. Hicks, *MA* 31, 213–14; R. C. Janaway, *ArchJ* 144, 474

Deshman, R., *Anglo-Saxon and Anglo-Scandinavian Art: an Annotated Bibliography* (Boston, 1984): R. J. Cramp, *ArchJ* 143, 390–1

Dobson, R. B., and S. Donaghey, *The History of Clementhorpe Nunnery*, Archaeol. of York 2.1 (London, 1984): T. Dyson, *ArchJ* 143, 399–400

Dumville, David N., ed., *The Historia Brittonum 3: the 'Vatican' Recension* (Cambridge, 1985): M. Jones, *Folklore* 98, 111; J. F. Kelly, *Church Hist.* 56, 110–11; K. Simms, *Celtica* 19, 199–201; I. N. Wood, *Britannia* 18, 385–6

Dumville, David, and Michael Lapidge, ed., *The Annals of St Neots, with Vita Prima Sancti Neoti* (Cambridge, 1985): J. Campbell, *N&Q* 34, 517–19; R. W. Pfaff, *Church Hist.* 56, 111–12

Elmer, Willy, *Diachronic Grammar: the History of Old and Middle English Subjectless Constructions* (Tübingen, 1981): H. Kirsten, *ZAA* 35, 81

Everitt, Alan, *Continuity and Colonization: the Evolution of Kentish Settlement* (Leicester, 1986): [Anon.] *Mankind Quarterly* 27, 493–4; D. Hooke, *Jnl of Hist. Geography* 13, 423–4

Fausbøll, Else, ed., *Fifty-six Ælfric Fragments* (Copenhagen, 1986): E. G. Stanley, *N&Q* 34, 449

Fell, Christine, Cecily Clark and Elizabeth Williams, *Women in Anglo-Saxon England and the Impact of 1066* (London and Bloomington, IN, 1984): G. Ferrari, *Schede Medievali* 11, 437–8; A. M. Hutchison, *Canadian Women Stud.* 7, 109–10

Fellows-Jensen, Gillian, *Scandinavian Settlement Names in the North-West* (Copenhagen, 1985): R. Farrell, *Speculum* 62, 935–6; J. Insley, *Ortsnamnsallskapets i Uppsala Årsskrift*, 45–53; V. E. Watts, *NH* 23, 229–30

Fischer, Andreas, *Engagement, Wedding, and Marriage in Old English* (Heidelberg, 1986): R. L. Thomson, *General Ling.* 27, 264–9

Frantzen, Allen J., *King Alfred* (Boston, 1986): S. Keynes, *Hist. Today* (July), pp. 60–1

Freeman, A., *The Moneyer and the Mint in the Reign of Edward the Confessor, 1042–1066* (Oxford, 1985): K. Jonsson, *Fornvännen* 82, 47

Gelling, Margaret, *Place-Names in the Landscape* (London, 1984): E. Christiansen, *EHR* 102, 460–1; M. Welch, *BIAL* 23: Review Suppl., 12–13

Gleissner, Reinhard, *Die 'zweideutigen' altenglischen Rätsel des 'Exeter Book' in ihrem zeitgenössischen Kontext* (Frankfurt am Main, 1984): P. S. Baker, *Anglia* 105, 468–71

Green, Martin, ed., *The Old English Elegies: New Essays in Criticism and Research* (Rutherford, Madison and Teaneck, NJ; London and Toronto, 1983): S. A. J. Bradley, *MLR* 82, 697–8

Greenfield, Stanley B., and D. G. Calder, *A New Critical History of Old English Literature* (New York and London, 1986): M.-M. Dubois, *EA* 40, 345–6

Greenfield, Stanley B., and Fred C. Robinson, *A Bibliography of Publications on Old English Literature from the Beginnings to the End of 1972* (Toronto, Buffalo and London, 1980): K. Bitterling, *Mittellateinisches Jahrbuch* 21, 257–8

Grierson, Philip, and Mark Blackburn, *Medieval European Coinage* 1. *The Early Middle Ages (5th–10th centuries)* (Cambridge, 1986): A. M. Balaguer, *Acta Numismatica* 16, 234–5; J.-M. Doyen, *Cercle d'Etudes Numismatiques* 25, 16–22; H. Frère, *Revue Belge de Numismatique* 133, 226–8; C. Martin, *Schweizer Münzblatter* 37, 51–2; D. M. Metcalf, *BNJ* 56, 190; C. Morrisson, *Antiquity* 61, 477–8; D. M., *Numismatisches Nachrichtesblatt* 36, 130–1; I, S[tewart], *NCirc* 1987, 78; R. E. Zupko, *Jnl of Geog. Hist.* 1988, 782–4

Haarder, Andreas, trans., *Sangen om Bjovulf* (Copenhagen): B. Morris, *TLS* 6 February, p. 140

Haslam, Jeremy, ed., *Anglo-Saxon Towns in Southern England* (Chichester, 1984): J. Campbell, *JBAA* 140, 211–13; M. J. Jones, *MA* 31, 201–2; S. Reynolds, *EHR* 102, 462

Hayfield, Colin, *Humberside Medieval Pottery* (Oxford, 1985): P. Armstrong, *ArchJ* 144, 477–8; H. Healey, *Lincolnshire Hist. and Archaeol.* 21, 81–2

Heighway, Carolyn, *The East and North Gates of Gloucester and Associated Sites. Excavations 1974–81* (Gloucester, 1983): J. Wood, *ArchJ* 144, 460–2

Hey, David, *Yorkshire from A.D. 1000* (London, 1986): D.M. Palliser, *NH* 23, 247–8

Higham, Nick, *The Northern Counties to A.D. 1000* (London and New York, 1986): M. Anderson, *London Archaeologist* 5, 307; A.F. Harding, *Durham Archaeol. Jnl* 3, 108–9; J.B. Klein, *Albion* 19, 213–14; D.C.A. Shotter, *Britannia* 18, 395

Hiltunen, Risto, *The Decline of the Prefixes and the Beginnings of the English Phrasal Verb* (Turku, 1983): Y. Niwa, *Stud. in Eng. Lit.* (Tokyo) 63, 389–93

Hinton, David A., ed., *Twenty-Five Years of Medieval Archaeology* (Sheffield, 1983): S. Bonde, *Speculum* 62, 197–201

Hirst, Susan M., *An Anglo-Saxon Inhumation Cemetery at Sewerby, East Yorkshire* (York, 1985): A. Boddington, *ArchJ* 144, 472–4; C. Hills, *AntJ* 67, 178–9; M.G. Welch, *MA* 31, 193–5

Hooke, Della, *The Anglo-Saxon Landscape: the Kingdom of the Hwicce* (Manchester, 1985): K. Biddick, *Speculum* 62, 692–4; P. Dixon, *Jnl of Hist. Geography* 13, 424–5; C.H. Knowles, *Albion* 19, 47–9; N.J.G. Pounds, *ArchJ* 143, 389–90; D. Wilson, *Landscape Hist.* 8, 111–13; B. Yorke, *Midland Hist.* 12, 122–3

The Landscape of Anglo-Saxon Staffordshire: the Charter Evidence (Keele, 1983): B. Yorke, *Midland Hist.* 12, 122–3

ed., *Medieval Villages: a Review of Current Work* (Oxford, 1985): G. Foard, *ArchJ* 144, 480–1

Hoover, David L., *A New Theory of Old English Meter* (New York, Bern and Frankfurt am Main, 1985): P.S. Baker, *Speculum* 62, 950–2; T. Hahn, *ES* 68, 196–7; J. Longo, *Rocky Mountain Rev. of Lang. and Lit.* 41, 102–3; W. Obst, *Anglia* 105, 461–4

Howe, Nicholas, *The Old English Catalogue Poems* (Copenhagen, 1985): R.D. Fulk, *PQ* 66, 149–51; J. Harris, *Speculum* 62, 953–6; E.G. Stanley, *N&Q* 34, 519–20

Huppé, Bernard F., *The Hero in the Earthly City: a Reading of 'Beowulf'* (Binghamton, 1984): J. Hill, *Anglia* 105, 465–8

Hurst, David, trans., *Bede the Venerable: the Commentary on the Seven Catholic Epistles* (Kalamazoo. MI, 1985): W.W. Dickerson III, *Fides et Historia* 19, 93–4; M.McC. Gatch, *Church Hist.* 56, 240–1

Hurst, H.R., *Gloucester, the Roman and Later Defences. Excavations on the East Defences and Reassessment of the Defensive Sequence* (Oxford, 1986): J. Wood, *ArchJ* 144, 460–2

Kingsholm (Cambridge, 1985): T.C. Darvell, *Trans. of the Bristol and Gloucestershire Archaeol. Soc.* 104, 250–2

Iartseva, Viktoriia Nikolaevna, *Istoriia angliĭskogo literaturnogo iazyka IX–XV vv.* (Moscow, 1985): I.A. Sizova, R[eferativnyĭ] Zh[urnal]: obshchestvennye nauki v SSSR 1986, ser. 6.6, 36–41

I Deug-Su, *Cultura e ideologia nella prima età carolingia* (Rome, 1984): M. Cortesi, *Quellen und Forschungen aus italienischen Archiven und Bibliotheken* 65, 481–2; R. Leotta, *Giornale italiano di filologia* 16, 295–7

L'Opera agiografica di Alcuino (Spoleto, 1983): M. Cortesi, *Quellen und Forschungen aus italienischen Archiven und Bibliotheken* 65, 482–3; R. Leotta, *Giornale italiano di filologia* 16 297–9

Jones, Martin, *England Before Domesday* (London, 1986): A. Selkirk, *CA* 106, 328; P. Stafford, *Agric. Hist. Rev.* 35, 199

Jonsson, Kenneth, *Viking-Age Hoards and Late Anglo-Saxon Coins* (Cambridge, 1986): M. Blackburn, *NCirc* 1987, 152; J. S[teen] J[ensen], *Nordisk Numismatisk Unions Medlemsblad* 1987, 146–7

Ker, N.R., *Books, Collectors and Libraries*, ed. Andrew G. Watson (London and Ronceverte, WV, 1985): A.B. Cobban, *History* 72, 88–9; M.-C. Garand, *Scriptorium* 41, 162–6; S.J. Ogilvie-Thomson, *RES* 38, 235–6

Kluge, Bernd, *State Museum, Berlin, Anglo-Saxon, Anglo-Norman, and Hiberno-Norse Coins*, SCBI 36 (London): D.M. M[etcalf], *NCirc* 1987, 298

Lapidge, Michael, and David Dumville, ed., *Gildas: New Approaches* (Woodbridge, 1984): F. Kerlouégan, *Peritia* 4 (1985), 380–3; T. Reuter, *DAEM* 43, 619–20

Lapidge, Michael, and Helmut Gneuss, ed., *Learning and Literature in Anglo-Saxon England* (Cambridge, 1985): M. Budny, *Hist. Today* (February), 57–8; R. Frank, *Univ. of Toronto Quarterly* 56, 461–3; H. Mayr-Harting, *JTS* 38, 548–9

Lapidge, Michael, and James L. Rosier, trans., *Aldhelm: the Poetic Works* (Cambridge, 1985): G.H. Brown, *Speculum* 62, 494–5; J.D. Pheifer, *N&Q* 34, 247–8

Latham, R.E., and D.R. Howlett, ed., *Dictionary of Medieval Latin from British Sources, Fascicule III, D-E* (London, 1986): V. Law, *TLS* 23 January, 94

Law, Vivien, *The Insular Latin Grammarians* (Woodbridge and Totowa, NJ, 1982): M. Dubuisson, *Le Moyen Age* 93, 101–2

Loyn, H.R., *The Governance of Anglo-Saxon England 500–1087* (London, 1984): N. Brooks, *History* 72, 159–60; M. Budny, *Hist. Today* (October), 60

Lyth, Philip, *The Southwell Charter of 965 A.D.: an Exploration of its Boundaries* (Southwell, 1984): D. Hooke, *Landscape Hist.* 8, 113

MacGregor, A., *Bone, Antler, Ivory and Horn. The Technology of Skeletal Materials since the Roman Period* (Beckenham, 1984): S. Margeson, *MA* 31, 205–7; A. Selkirk, *CA* 107, 378

McLaughlin, John, *Old English Syntax: a Handbook* (Tübingen, 1983): J. Dor, *Le Moyen Age* 93, 304–5

Macrae-Gibson, O.D., ed., *The Old English 'Riming Poem'* (Cambridge, 1983): J. Roberts, *MLR* 82, 434–5

Mitchell, Bruce, *Old English Syntax* (Oxford and New York, 1985): R.D. Fulk, *PQ* 66, 279–83; S.B. Greenfield, *JEGP* 86, 392–9; W. Koopman, *Neophilologus* 71, 460–6; P. Lendinara, *Schede Medievali* 11, 396–8

Moffat, Douglas, ed., *The Soul's Address to the Body: the Worcester Fragments* (East Lansing, MI): E.G. Stanley, *Yearbook of Langland Stud.* 1, 150–2

Morris, John, ed., *Domesday Book, 30: Yorkshire*, ed. M.L. Faull and M. Stinson (Chichester, 1986): G. Jones, *Yorkshire Archaeol. Jnl* 59, 206–8

Moulden, Jean, and D. Tweddle, *Anglo-Scandinavian Settlement South-West of the Ouse* (London, 1986): L. Butler, *Yorkshire Archaeol. Jnl* 59, 213–14

Myres, J.N.L., *The English Settlements* (Oxford, 1986): C.J. Arnold, *History* 72, 155–6; R.A. Butlin, *Geographical Jnl* 153, 104; T.M. Charles-Edwards, *Hist. Today* (March), 56–8; E. Christiansen, *EHR* 102, 107–8; H.R. Loyn, *MA* 31, 210, and *N&Q* 34, 246–7; David A.E. Pelteret, *Albion* 19, 46–7

Niles, John D., *'Beowulf': the Poem and its Tradition* (Cambridge, MA, and London, 1983): S. A. J. Bradley, *MLR* 82, 697–8; B. Schik, *Anglia* 105, 178–81

Ohlgren, Thomas H., comp., *Insular and Anglo-Saxon Illuminated Manuscripts* (New York and London, 1986): J. Backhouse, *The Library* 6th ser. 9, 58–9; E.G. Stanley, *N&Q* 34, 62–3; P. Stirnemann, *Bulletin Monumental* 145, 158–9

Owen-Crocker, Gale R., *Dress in Anglo-Saxon England* (Manchester, 1986): B. Griffiths, *Durham Univ. Jnl* 79, 377–8; J. Harris, *Textile Hist.* 18, 220–1; A. MacGregor, *JBAA* 140, 213–14; C. Walkley, *TLS* 16 January, 67

Padel, O. J., *Cornish Place-Name Elements* (Nottingham, 1985): W.F.H. Nicolaisen, *Names* 34, 314–15

Phillips, D., *Excavations at York Minster, ii. The Cathedral of Archbishop Thomas of Bayeux* (London, 1985): H.M. Taylor, *ArchJ* 143, 396–7

Pinsker, Hans, with U. Fries and P. Bierbaumer, *Altenglisches Studienbuch* (Düsseldorf, Bern and Munich, 1976): C.-D. Wetzel, *IF* 92, 312–17

Pirie, E. J. E., *Post-Roman Coins from York Excavations 1971–81* (London, 1986): S. B[endall], *NCirc* 1987, 153; M. A. S. Blackburn, *BNJ* 56, 191–2; L. Butler, *Yorkshire Archaeol. Jnl* 59, 213–14; H. Pagan, *AntJ* 67, 179–80; P. Rahtz, *MA* 31, 197–9; P. Seaby, *SCMB* 1987, 12–13

Robinson, Fred C., *'Beowulf' and the Appositive Style* (Knoxville, 1985): A. Bammesberger, *Literaturwissenschaftliches Jahrbuch* 28, 346–8; M. Rissanen, *NM* 88, 359–63

Rodwell, W. J., and K. A. Rodwell, *Rivenhall: Investigations of a Villa, Church and Village 1950–1977* (London, 1985): M. Millett, *ArchJ* 144, 434–44; R. Reece, *Essex Archaeol. and Hist.* 17, 180; C.C. Taylor, *AntJ* 87, 176–7

Royal Commission on the Historical Monuments of England, *Inventory of the Historical Monuments in the County of Northampton 5: Archaeological Sites and Churches in Northampton* (London, 1985): D. Parsons, *ArchJ* 143, 391–3

Sawyer, Peter, ed., *Domesday Book: a Reassessment* (London, 1985): R.P. Abels, *AHR* 92, 395–6; D. Renn, *AntJ* 66, 452–3

Seltén, Bo, *The Anglo-Saxon Heritage in Middle English Personal Names: East Anglia 1100–1399* II (Lund, 1979): H. Voitl, *Anglia* 105, 426–9

Shoesmith, R., *Hereford City Excavations, 3. The Finds* (London, 1985): D. A. Hinton, *ArchJ* 144, 485–6

Smith, Andrea B., ed., *The Anonymous Parts of the Old English Hexateuch* (Cambridge, 1985): P. Lendinara, *Schede Medievali* 11, 478–9; E.G. Stanley, *N&Q* 34, 248–9

Smyth, Alfred P., *Warlords and Holy Men: Scotland A.D. 80–1000* (London, 1984): I. Henderson, *EHR* 102, 173–5

Spurrell, Mark, ed., *Stow Church Restored, 1846–1866* (Woodbridge, 1984): R. Gem, *AntJ* 66, 490–1

Stafford, Pauline, *The East Midlands in the Early Middle Ages* (Leicester, 1985): M. Budny, *Hist.Today* (October), 60; S. Keynes, *Hist. & Arch. Rev.* 2, 85–6; C.H. Knowles, *Albion* 19, 47–9

Stanley, E.G., 'Unideal Principles of Editing Old English Verse', *PBA* 70 (1984), 231–73: K. Grinda, *Anglia* 105, 457–61

Steane, J., *The Archaeology of Medieval England and Wales* (Beckenham, 1985): A. Boddington, *ArchJ* 143, 395–6; S. Bonde, *Speculum* 62, 197–201

Svensson, Orjan, *Saxon Place-Names in East Cornwall* (Lund): M. J. Swanton, *Devon & Cornwall N&Q* 36, 75–8

Swanton, Michael, *English Literature before Chaucer* (London and New York): D. K. Fry, *Albion* 19, 595–7

trans., *Three Lives of the Last Englishmen* (New York and London, 1984): K. Urwin, *CCM* 30, 194

Szarmach, Paul E., ed., *Studies in Earlier Old English Prose* (Albany, NY, 1985): F. Hockey, *Revue d'Histoire Ecclésiastique* 82, 384; B. Mitchell, *RES* 38, 290; S. Ono, *Stud. in Eng. Lit.* (Tokyo) 64, 152–7

Taylor, H. M., *Anglo-Saxon Architecture* III (Cambridge and New York, 1978): M. Budny, *Hist. Today* October, p. 60; W. T. Foley, *Church Hist.* 56, 269

Taylor, Simon, ed., *The Anglo-Saxon Chronicle: MS B* (Cambridge and Totowa, NJ, 1983): T. H. Leinbaugh, *Speculum* 62, 206–9

Thompson, E. A., *Saint Germanus of Auxerre and the End of Roman Britain* (Woodbridge, 1984): R. P. C. Hanson, *Peritia* 4, 377–9

Who was Saint Patrick? (New York, 1985): M. Chibnall, *AHR* 92, 641; M. E. Jones, *Albion* 19, 209–10; D. Ó Cróinín, *Britannnia* 18, 379–81

Todd, M., *The South-West to AD 1000* (London): A. Fox, *Cornish Archaeol.* 26, 143–4

Tripp, Raymond P., Jr, *More about the Fight with the Dragon: 'Beowulf' 2208b–3182* (Lanham, MD, 1983): H. Ushigaki, *Poetica* (Tokyo) 25–6, 193–200

Vollrath, Hanna, *Die Synoden Englands bis 1066* (Paderborn, 1985): R. W. Pfaff, *Church Hist.* 56, 388–9; P. Wormald, *Catholic Hist. Rev.* 73, 431–2

Welch, Martin, *Early Anglo-Saxon Sussex* (Oxford, 1983): M. J. Allen, *BIAL* 23: Review Suppl., 11–12

Werner, M., *Insular Art: an Annotated Bibliography* (Boston, 1984): R. J. Cramp, *ArchJ* 143, 390–1

Whittock, Martyn J., *The Origins of England 410–600* (London and Sydney, 1986): B. S. Bachrach, *Albion* 19, 393–4; K. F. Drew, *History: Reviews of New Books* 16, 14; S. Keynes, *Hist. Today* July, pp. 60–1; M. G. Welch, *MA* 31, 211

Wieland, Gernot Rudolf, *The Latin Glosses on Arator and Prudentius in Cambridge University Library, MS Gg. 5. 35* (Toronto, 1983): B. M. Marti, *CCM* 30, 100–2

Williams, J. H., M. Shaw, and V. Denham, *Middle Saxon Palaces at Northampton* (Northampton, 1985): D. Parsons, *ArchJ* 143, 391–3; P. Rahtz, *AntJ* 66, 450–1

Williams, P. W., *An Anglo-Saxon Cemetery at Thurmaston, Leicestershire* (Leicester, 1983): B. N. Eagles, *ArchJ* 143, 388–9

Wilson, D. M., *Anglo-Saxon Art from the Seventh Century to the Norman Conquest* (London, 1984): R. Deshman, *Speculum* 62, 225–6; S. H. Fuglesang, *Fornvännen* 82, 153–4; J. Graham-Campbell, *Antiquity* 61, 141–2

The Bayeux Tapestry (London, 1985): J. J. G. Alexander, *Jnl of Hist. Geography* 13, 73–5; G. Haseloff, *Germania* 65, 308–16; R. A. Higham, *MA* 31, 207–8

Witney, K. P., *The Kingdom of Kent* (Chichester, 1982): G. J. Dawson, *BIAL* 23: Review Suppl., 12

Woods, J. Douglas, and David A. E. Pelteret, ed., *The Anglo-Saxons: Synthesis and Achievement* (Waterloo, Ont., 1985): R. H. C. Davis, *Albion* 19, 45–6; J. F. Futhey, *Eng. Stud. in Canada* 13, 323–5

Wormald, Patrick, ed., *Ideal and Reality in Frankish and Anglo-Saxon Society* (Oxford, 1983): J.-P. Genet, *Annales* 42, 718–19

Yerkes, David, ed., *The Old English Life of Machutus* (Toronto, Buffalo and London, 1984): J. Roberts, *Univ. of Toronto Quarterly* 56, 588–90

Zanni, Roland, *Heliand, Genesis und das Altenglische* (Berlin and New York, 1980): U. Schwab, *SM* 3rd ser. 28, 263–82

DATE DUE

AUG 15 '88			
	261-2500		Printed in USA